The American Critical Archives is a series of reference books that provide representative selections of contemporary reviews of the main works of major American authors. Specifically, each volume contains both full reviews and excerpts from reviews that appeared in newspapers and weekly and monthly periodicals, generally within a few months of the publication of the work concerned. There is an introductory historical overview by the volume editor, as well as checklists of additional reviews located but not quoted.

This volume is the first to collect the critical responses of Steinbeck's generation to his many fiction and nonfiction works as they appeared from the late 1920s on. The articles trace the record of his progress through the 1930s, a decade capped by the publication of his two masterworks, *Of Mice and Men* and *The Grapes of Wrath*. They go on to reflect Steinbeck's achievements through the 1960s, including his attainment of the Nobel Prize in 1962. These articles offer at last a means of seeing Steinbeck's writings as they were perceived by his contemporaries, whose task it was to be first to evaluate and interpret them for an ever growing readership.

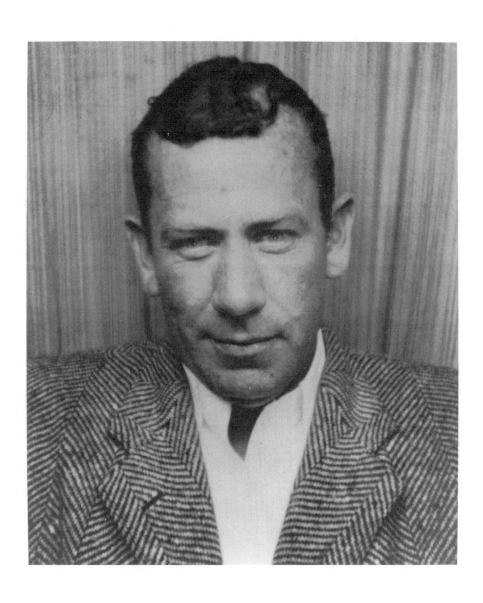

AMERICAN CRITICAL ARCHIVES 8
John Steinbeck: The Contemporary Reviews

The American Critical Archives

GENERAL EDITOR: M. Thomas Inge, Randolph-Macon College

John Steinbeck

The Contemporary Reviews

Edited by

Joseph R. McElrath, Jr.
Florida State University

Jesse S. Crisler
Brigham Young University

Susan Shillinglaw
San Jose State University

CAMBRIDGE
UNIVERSITY PRESS

Published by the Press Syndicate of the University of Cambridge
The Pitt Building, Trumpington Street, Cambridge CB2 1RP
40 West 20th Street, New York, NY 10011–4211, USA
10 Stamford Road, Oakleigh, Melbourne 3166, Australia

First published 1996

Printed in the United States of America

Library of Congress Cataloging-in-Publication Data
John Steinbeck: the contemporary reviews / edited by Joseph R.
McElrath, Jr., Jesse S. Crisler, and Susan Shillinglaw.
p. cm.—(American critical archives; 8)
Includes index.
ISBN 0–521–41038–X (hc)
1. Steinbeck, John, 1902–1968—Criticism and interpretation.
2. American fiction—20th century—Book reviews. I. McElrath,
Joseph R. II. Crisler, Jesse S. III. Shillinglaw, Susan.
IV. Series.
PS3537.T3234Z7155   1996
823'.912—dc20   95–13434
                                            CIP

A catalog record for this book is available from the British Library.

ISBN 0–521–41038-X hardback

Frontispiece portrait courtesy of The Steinbeck Research Center, San Jose State University.

Contents

Series Editor's Preface

The American Critical Archives series documents a part of a writer's career that is usually difficult to examine, that is, the immediate response to each work as it was made public on the part of reviewers in contemporary newspapers and journals. Although it would not be feasible to reprint every review, each volume in the series reprints a selection of reviews designed to provide the reader with a proportionate sense of the critical response, whether it was positive, negative, or mixed. Checklists of other known reviews are also included to complete the documentary record and allow access for those who wish to do further reading and research.

The editor of each volume has provided an introduction that surveys the career of the author in the context of the contemporary critical response. Ideally, the introduction will inform the reader in brief of what is to be learned by a reading of the full volume. The reader then can go as deeply as necessary in terms of the kind of information desired—be it about a single work, a period in the author's life, or the author's entire career. The intent is to provide quick and easy access to the material for students, scholars, librarians, and general readers.

When completed, the American Critical Archives should constitute a comprehensive history of critical practice in America, and in some cases Great Britain, as the writers' careers were in progress. The volumes open a window on the patterns and forces that have shaped the history of American writing and the reputations of the writers. These are primary documents in the literary and cultural life of the nation.

M. THOMAS INGE

Introduction

John Steinbeck did not particularly like book critics, "these curious sucker fish who live with joyous vicariousness on other men's work and discipline with dreary words the thing which feeds them."[1] It is hardly surprising. Each book published in his lifetime was attacked by prestigious reviewers, and for a highly sensitive man the criticism bit deeply. "Once I read and wept over reviews," he wrote in 1954; "then one time I put the criticisms all together and I found that they canceled each other out and left me nonexistent."[2] That complaint points to the central feature of this collection of reviews. With the publication of each book, Steinbeck was both roundly attacked and as widely lauded. Reading the reviews in American, English, and Canadian magazines and newspapers, one is struck by the consistency of dissent; even books considered his weakest—*Burning Bright* and *The Wayward Bus*—received plaudits from important reviewers. There was never a consensus on a Steinbeck text.

Still, a common and persistent misconception about Steinbeck's work is that critics panned the post-*Grapes* fiction. That assumption became commonplace in the 1960s. Writing in the *Saturday Review* in 1969 about the posthumously published *Journal of a Novel*, Lawrence William Jones posited this view of Steinbeck's career: "Steinbeck's post-war reception was one of nearly unrelieved and often misdirected hostility. Of the eight fictional works published during this period, only *The Pearl* was even fleetingly praised, and it has inevitably suffered from constant comparison with Hemingway's *The Old Man and the Sea*." The only specific truth articulated in that statement is that Steinbeck was with some regularity compared to Hemingway, as when, in 1952, they published within weeks of one another *The Old Man and the Sea* and *East of Eden*—both late and, to some minds, stunning novels. It is also true that many felt critical disdain toward Steinbeck for supposedly compromising his talent. For them, his later work was frivolous, artificial, ponderous, or trite, whereas the work of the 1930s resonated with a clarity and force absent in the later books. But false and misleading is the suggestion that Steinbeck's postwar reception was one of nearly unrelieved hostility. What the reviews in this volume teach us, first, is that the "great" social novels of the 1930s produced no such positive consensus during that decade, and, second, that each subsequent text was met with broadly divergent opinions. Some, in fact, called *East of Eden, Cannery Row,* and even *Travels with*

ix

Charley the writer's greatest. The word "delightful" repeatedly described *The Short Reign of Pippin IV*. For Norman Cousins, *Burning Bright* was Steinbeck's "most mature" book because it "tries to emancipate men from the tyranny of the personal self. It tries to develop an aspect of man's nature, too often hidden, which hungers truly for larger understanding and mutuality in life." Hemingway, in contrast, seemed "too close to the ego and not close enough to the human heart." In short, John Steinbeck, who resolutely resisted pigeonholes and declared each new work an experiment, as frequently puzzled as amazed his critics with his virtuosity.

The consistently mixed reviews can be explained, in part, by the Steinbeck legend. By 1940, his stature was unassailable and each new book an event. Certainly he lacked Hemingway's charisma and Faulkner's celebrated obfuscation, but Steinbeck was, like them, a writer with whom one had to contend. This said, however, he never quite seemed to make the mark. Expectations were high; disappointments, inevitable. Critics were dealing with an enormously popular and salable author, one whose public reception seemed to some unwarranted. The demand for *The Moon Is Down* in 1942, for example, was exceptional: A week before its formal publication, Viking had sold 70,000 copies; one month afterward, approximately 500,000 copies had been purchased, according to the *Life* reviewer. Beginning with *Of Mice and Men*, five books were Book-of-the-Month Club selections. *The Winter of Our Discontent* was a Literary Guild choice as well; it was the first time that both clubs had offered the same book as a selection for their members. A 1962 review of *Travels with Charley* by Van Allen Bradley noted, "A few years ago a United Nations survey placed John Steinbeck in third place, as I recall it, among those living writers whose books are most widely translated and distributed through the world." Perhaps critics felt an unconscious need to prick the balloon, to note the ways in which Steinbeck was not quite of the first rank. It appears that this tendency, exacerbated by acknowledged discomfort on the part of the eastern literary establishment with this unpredictable westerner, played a major role in shaping Steinbeck's complex reception as it developed through roughly four phases.

I. Apprenticeship: 1929–1935

Reactions to *Cup of Gold* (1929), *The Pastures of Heaven* (1932), *To a God Unknown* (1933), and *Tortilla Flat* (1935) constitute the first phase, and in the distinctively different natures of these works lies one reason for the wide variety of reactions to Steinbeck thereafter: Was one dealing with a writer of adventure romances, a symbolic realist, a mythic and perhaps mystic fabulist, or a devil-may-care humorist? By what standard should one evaluate him? Like a Californian of the previous generation, Frank Norris, Steinbeck initiated his career with an extraordinarily diverse series of fictions, although the first commercially successful one, *Tortilla Flat*, established the popular image of an offbeat, comic author defying the values associated with the Protestant work ethic as he reveled in the amoral antics of the Mexican-American underclass in Monterey.

Although the first three books received scant attention, their reviews show a surprising consistency with subsequent assessments: They were mixed. *Cup of Gold* is, in fact, a better book than William Faulkner's first, and the smattering of notices given the novel acknowledged its drama, its "thoroughly masculine" appeal, and its facility with characterization. Perceptive critics identified protagonist Morgan as "always the child reaching for a dream," a thematically significant image that long held the writer's interest. It was, according to longtime friend and New York *Herald Tribune* critic Lewis Gannett, who wrote a preface to the 1936 edition of *Cup*, the key to understanding Steinbeck's work. Also apparent was resistance to Steinbeck's troublesome tendency to write "brutal" fiction—"decidedly not for juvenile perusal," as the St. Louis *Star* reviewer noted. Three strains of Steinbeck criticism were already noticeable: Critics repeatedly focused on his restless dreamers, measured his relative success in casting believable characters, and debated his frank language and bold choices of subject matter. Throughout a publishing career of nearly four decades, the "coarseness" of several books would both offend and be defended: His language became a focus of debate. While most praised Steinbeck's fine ear, to some his prose seemed stark, his language uncultivated—or downright crude—and his themes dark. "Mr. Steinbeck knows how to write about and handle the gloomy substance of his thoughts," wrote J. E. S. Arrowsmith of *The Pastures of Heaven*. Steinbeck's reputed "fascination with the abnormal" became a frequent lament. But that book, with *To a God Unknown*, received a majority of positive reviews acknowledging the young writer's promise. This author, declared a discerning Gerry Fitzgerald when reviewing *Pastures*, is a "romantic realist."

Until the publication of *Tortilla Flat*, the romantic realist's gloom may have been warranted. A promising career as a novelist seemed well out of reach. Determined to be a writer since age fourteen, Steinbeck had practiced his craft doggedly in the intervening years, publishing three books and a handful of short stories for an indifferent world. The stories he wrote from 1932 to 1934, however, gave clear evidence of his mature powers. These are the years in which he composed "The Promise," "Chrysanthemums," and "Flight"—later collected in *The Long Valley*—as well as *Tortilla Flat*, a book seven times rejected by New York publishers. But the world caught up with Steinbeck in 1935. *Tortilla Flat* was a stunning success. "The trouble with a book like this," wrote one of Steinbeck's most loyal supporters throughout the 1930s—friend, novelist, and San Francisco *Chronicle* reviewer Joseph Henry Jackson—"is that you can't describe it. The best you can do is to indicate it—faintly, in the sketch book manner. . . . I can't reflect the charm, the humor, the pathos, the wit and wisdom and warm humanity which illuminate every one of Mr. Steinbeck's pages. . . . Simple as it is, it has in it all the elements that go to make the best stories." Jackson here uses words that would become leitmotifs in Steinbeck criticism. Many subsequent reviewers relished these qualities in the author, compared him to both Dickens and Twain, and embraced the "lovable characters" in the "lighthearted" books: *Tortilla Flat*, *Cannery Row*, *Sweet Thursday*, and *The Short Reign of Pippin IV*. Edmund Wilson, four years after his much quoted discussion of Steinbeck's "subhuman" characters in *The Boys in the Back Room* (1941), would claim that he'd never enjoyed Steinbeck more than when he read *Cannery Row*.

There were in 1935—and would be with the publication of each comic novel—dissenting voices claiming that Steinbeck had romanticized drunken bums, exploited his subjects, and celebrated "amoral" characters. The sensitive author heeded those words, perhaps unfortunately, for he added a disclaimer to a subsequent edition of *Tortilla Flat*: In a foreword to the 1937 Modern Library edition, he wrote that he would "never again subject to the vulgar touch of the *decent* these good people of laughter and kindness, of honest lusts and direct eyes, of courtesy beyond politeness."[3] It was the first of several public responses to his critics and reviewers who, he felt, did not always comprehend his work. He had a point. Few knew quite what to say about the dark ending of *Tortilla Flat*, and fewer still could get a handle on the Arthurian parallels. Several wanted the book to include a moral; indeed, in his own review Joseph Henry Jackson would take to task the *Nation*'s reviewer, Helen Neville, for demanding that Steinbeck write more socially conscious fiction. But Steinbeck, like Wallace Stegner after him, was fundamentally a westerner. His easy way with language and people, his feel for the land and sea, his nonteleological acceptance of "what is," and his fierce independence as an artist left some uncomfortable. His *paisanos*, like his *Cannery Row* bums, are in essence westerners—untrammeled and virtuous, raw and loyal. "The West . . . could use a little more confidence in itself," wrote Stegner, "and one way to generate that is to breed up some critics capable, by experience or intuition, of evaluating western literature in the terms of western life. So far, I can't think of a nationally influential critic who reads western writing in the spirit of those who wrote it, and judges them according to their intentions."[4] Both western writers felt abused by the eastern critical establishment, which seemed to demand they publish to its tastes. Throughout his career, whether writing about California or about Russia, Steinbeck voiced in letters doubts that his intentions were clear, as often they seemingly were not for critics stubbornly expecting what Steinbeck as resolutely refused to deliver on order: socially conscious fiction. But West Coast critics, particularly Joseph Henry Jackson, fell into the practice of defending Steinbeck against eastern misunderstanding; Wilbur Needham of the Los Angeles *Times* consistently lauded the independent-minded author who "always has his feet on the ground—rooted in the earth and the things of earth," as he wrote in his review of *Of Mice and Men*.

II. Steinbeck and the Working Man: 1936–1939

The smile of the *Tortilla Flat* humorist disappeared from Steinbeck's public visage in the late 1930s as he mordantly exposed, with the somberness of a New England conscience, how the "other half" is preyed upon in a capitalistic economy within the larger framework of Darwin's nature. Steinbeck's new course was determined in large part by his politically conscious wife, Carol. The unsigned *Nation* review of *The Pastures of Heaven* noted that if Steinbeck "could add social insight to his present equipment he would be a first-rate novelist," a remark that makes successful writing look surprisingly like a cookie recipe. But, in fact, that is more or less the approach Steinbeck adopted. Goaded by his loyal and liberal wife, he attended meetings of the John Reed Club in Carmel, and the staunchly apolitical Steinbeck awoke to the socioeconomic turmoil that was California in the 1930s. His labor trilogy became his life's most significant work; it became a body of prose fiction that critics, however divided on its value during the 1930s, would look back to with great frequency as Steinbeck's main contribution to twentieth-century literature.

When *In Dubious Battle* was published in 1936, Wilbur Needham declared in the Los Angeles *Times*: "The man is unpredictable; he never writes in the same way in any two novels, and he never uses the same emotional or intellectual points of view." That unpredictability became, in fact, the source of an opening line for reviewers for the next thirty years. After the raucous *Tortilla Flat*, the weighty, "brutal" proletarian novel was unexpected—but Steinbeck was again lauded by a majority of reviewers. What impressed them was that Steinbeck's text transcended the generic "strike novel." He did not take sides. "He keeps himself out of the book," wrote Fred T. Marsh for the *New York Times Book Review*. Marsh was pleased to find "no editorializing or direct propaganda." It may have been the evenhandedness of Steinbeck's treatment of common people that won him readers for decades; that essential trait certainly ensured the popularity of his work of the late 1930s. Steinbeck, proclaimed Joseph Henry Jackson in his 1936 evaluation of *Cup of Gold*, is a writer with "integrity."

But to reiterate what became commonplace: One dissenting voice in particular touched a nerve in the author. Mary McCarthy's "Minority Report" was just that. In a letter to Louis Paul, Steinbeck responded to her article on *In Dubious Battle*:

> The pain occasioned by this review is to some extent mitigated by the obvious fact that she understood Caesar's Commentaries as little as my poor screed, that she doesn't know her Plato very well, and that she hasn't the least idea of what a Greek drama is. Seriously what happened is

this—Mary Ann reviewed *Tortilla Flat*, saying that I had overlooked the fact that these paisanos were proletariats. Joseph Henry Jackson, critic on the S.F. Chronicle took her review and played horse with it. So Mary Ann lay in ambush for me to give me my come-uppance. And boy, did she give it to me. Wurra! Wurra![5]

What this letter tells us about McCarthy may well be inaccurate, but her attack was unwarranted from an artistic standpoint. Her critique, like many published during the next few years, was more ideological than aesthetic. What stung the author was that she belittled his art because she disagreed with his ideas. Hers was a repeated stance of reviewers not with Marxist leanings per se but with a liberal gaze that scrutinized Steinbeck's politics. For the next few years, Steinbeck as frequently would be judged for his ideology—or seeming lack of it—as he would be appraised on his merits as an artist.

Of Mice and Men (1937) and, in particular, *The Grapes of Wrath* (1939) also touched off heated sociological debates, while both were being lavishly praised by a growing readership. Advance orders for Steinbeck's "big book" nearly trebled those for all previous Steinbeck titles put together, reported Burton Rascoe in his *Newsweek* review of *Grapes*. In part, his popularity was the result of a series of astonishingly well-publicized creative endeavors. Written as a "playable novel," in Steinbeck's words, *Of Mice and Men* was the novelist's first Book-of-the-Month Club selection. The Broadway-play version opened in November of that same year and was awarded the New York Drama Critics Circle Award as the year's best play. The Lewis Milestone *Mice* film premiered in December 1939, eight months after publication of *The Grapes of Wrath*. John Ford's film about the Joads' trek was released on 24 January 1940. *Grapes* received both the National Book Award and the Pulitzer Prize. *The Grapes of Wrath*, noted Louis Kronenberger, "makes one feel that Steinbeck is, in some way all his own, a force." Undoubtedly, some of his success can be attributed to the fact that he published three books on labor at the precise moment when the country was ready to read them. If movies and art of the decade were often escapist, if writers of the "hard-boiled school" were increasingly grim, Steinbeck seems to have struck a needed balance between sentiment and uncompromising realism. "What gives [*Of Mice and Men*] an almost irresistible fascination," wrote Walter Sidney of the Brooklyn *Eagle*, "is the contrast between the horror of the theme and the poetic tenderness with which it is told." The most consistently supportive of Steinbeck's critics, Lewis Gannett of the New York *Herald Tribune*, concurred: "And it is, perhaps, that compassion, even more than the perfect sense of form, which marks off John Steinbeck, artist, so sharply from all the little verbal photographers who record tough talk and snarl in books which have power without pity." Reviewer after reviewer noted the "quality of mercy in the depiction of the small man" (Theodore Smith) in a novel of "gripping" power and "immemorial theme" (Fred T. Marsh). This compassion was to remain a benchmark for those measuring his talent. In *Of Mice and Men*, George and Lennie articulated the dreams and frustrations of a nation. And the Joads of *Grapes* lived the dream for a restless population. In his assessment of "American Novels: 1939," Bernard DeVoto put *Grapes* at the top of the list because "one is so engaged with the lives of its people that their experience becomes one's own."

If Steinbeck's empathy won him devoted readers—loyal for the next three decades—dissenting voices on both texts were characteristically shrill. If the artificiality of *Mice* rankled some, by far the most persistent objections were directed, first, to Steinbeck's language (a complaint that resulted in *Of Mice and Men*'s top ranking on lists of banned books) and, second, to his treatment of Lennie as "sentimental wallowing." Joseph Wood Krutch asked whether the dramatized version was "really a tale of eerie power and tenderness, or whether, as it seems to me, everything from beginning to end is completely 'literary' in the bad sense, and as shamelessly cooked up as the death of Little Nell." (Joseph Henry Jackson responded to that charge as well in "A Bookman's Notebook," 18 December 1937.) Steinbeck would long face similar charges of sentimentalism, one of the most persistent and damning of the objections made to his characters. "Steinbeck's sentimentalism is good in bringing him close to the lives of his people," asserted Louis Kronenberger, "but bad when it blurs his insight." In short, he seemed to walk unsteadily the line between emotive power and emotionalism, drama and melodrama, the tragic and the sensationally pathetic. The terms were repeatedly used when Steinbeck was weighed. In fact, what both novels touched off was a lively and often incendiary debate on the nature of realistic writing. Is sentimentality realistic? Must language be unexpurgated to be authentic? Must the author of *Mice* portray life in its meanest guise, "serving his strong meat fresh and still warm from life's slaughter house" (Maxine Garrard) and focusing on "subhuman" types (Mark Van Doren's epithet)? Is Steinbeck insistently didactic? With the 1939 publication of *The Grapes of Wrath*, the question became especially highly charged for many Californians and Oklahomans: Does this "termite," "liar," and "communist" tell the truth about our state and our citizens?

Grapes, in fact, polarized the country in a debate over the province of realism. Long anticipated, this book was as long praised and vilified, spawning a controversy matched only by the literary and political frenzy that had greeted *Uncle Tom's Cabin*. On one side, reviewers used rapturous prose: "Here at last," wrote Michael March of the Brooklyn *Citizen*, "is the great proletarian novel, a bitter, anguished, brutal saga, alive with human aspiration and struggle and defeat, peopled with human beings vividly portrayed and deeply understood." Precisely those qualities that he and like-minded reviewers across the nation praised, others lambasted. The book was too brutal, the characters idealized with "too little of the fine-point etching" (Art Kuhl), and the subject matter unsavory. The novel's didacticism was called heavyhanded. But two charges, offensive language and inaccuracy, became central. The "vile" language made some foam with disdain, for example, Randolph Bartlett: "The canine imprecation is strewn upon the pages with a pepperbox, and becomes so meaningless that when it drops casually from the lips of a twelve-year-old girl in the later episodes it is barely shocking. The various appellations of deity roll lazily from every tongue." As to the subject, Bartlett on Steinbeck recalled Thackeray castigating Jonathan Swift: "Sexual aberrations abound. Filth and slime, references to sanitary matters, entrails of animals, dirt, dirt, and still more dirt—these are the decorations with which Mr. Steinbeck has adorned his tale. And all without purpose." In Buffalo, New York, *Grapes* was publicly burned for its "vulgar words," and in Kansas City, Missouri, the "obscene" book was banned from public libraries.

What kept *Grapes* to the fore in the public's mind, however, was charges made against its accuracy. Representative Lyle H. Boren of Oklahoma, for one, practiced book reviewing on the floor of the House of Representatives: "I cannot find it possible to let this dirty, lying, filthy manuscript go heralded before the public without a word of challenge or protest." The Associated Farmers of California wooed Los Gatos author Ruth Comfort Mitchell to give "California's Answer to *The Grapes of Wrath*," which she did in *Grapes*'s longest "review," her novel *Of Human Kindness*, published in 1940. Harold E. Pomeroy, executive secretary of the Associated Farmers, delivered a speech on 14 August 1939 to the Bakersfield, California, Kiwanis Club, in which he attacked both *Grapes* and Carey McWilliams's *Factories in the Field*. Steinbeck had "built his story on a few shreds of truth and distorted his presentation of the migrant situation in California." Pomeroy further declared, "Now is the opportunity for true Americans to use initiative in combating the evil forces of radical labor leaders and communistic minority groups who are pounding against the principles of democracy."[6] Newspapers across the country covered this story as it developed. Kern County, California, banned *Grapes* from schools and libraries that August, and the proscription was not rescinded until January 1941.

III. The Novelist as Virtuoso: 1940–1952

Steinbeck's retreat from the fray is hardly surprising. He decided to become a serious student of marine biology and, to the puzzlement of some critics who scarcely knew what to say about a scientific narrative, in 1941 published a book with friend and marine biologist Edward F. Ricketts about their 1940 voyage cataloguing marine life along the Baja peninsula. Critics found *Sea of Cortez*—part narrative account of the voyage and part scientific study, part comical and part philosophical—either puzzling or brilliant, but impossible to classify, seemingly a new type of book. John Steinbeck "abhors the conventional," wrote Harry Hansen, a widely syndicated reviewer, "and he did not write a conventional scientific monograph." Indeed, Steinbeck would never choose a conventional course, never repeat himself. Nonfiction such as *Bombs Away* (1942) and *A Russian Journal* (1948) seemed to belie his talent, whereas the propagandistic *The Moon Is Down*, the 1942 novel and play, provoked doubts about the writer's patriotism. Remarkably dissimilar novels—*Cannery Row* (1945), *The Wayward Bus* (1947), *The Pearl* (1947), and *Burning Bright* (1950)—even more clearly marked a break from the fiction of the late 1930s, challenging reviewers to see the Steinbeck of eclectic propensities as either a successful or failed virtuoso. They found it especially difficult to draw a bead on the protean author who would try who-knows-what next. It was almost a mercy to the reviewers that Steinbeck allowed them to recall the point of reference that was *Grapes* when he published another "big book," *East of Eden*. The major novel he was long expected to write finally came before them in 1952.

There is little need to reiterate those qualities that readers liked and disliked in Steinbeck's work, a relative constant after the mid-1930s. What intrigues in the third phase of reviewer response is, first, the incisive attempts by his critics to give shape to his career. "*Sea of Cortez*," noted the Boston *Herald* reviewer, is "not another *Grapes of Wrath*, and yet a certain common denomination can be found for both books in the intense interest Mr. Steinbeck has in man as a species." The best reviewers of Steinbeck's work traced such parallels between earlier and new works; others simply noted a decline in his talent after the "great" period of Depression Era fiction. "Don't forget," Steinbeck wrote to his literary agents, McIntosh and Otis, in 1937, "that criticism of my work now is not aimed at the thing in itself, but is conditioned by the others,"[7] that is, his other books. How much more true after 1939, when many waited for him to return to socially conscious fiction. During the next two decades, few books published in America received weightier notices than *The Moon Is Down*, *The Wayward Bus*, *East of Eden*, and—in the next phase—*The Winter of Our Discontent* (1961). Finally, reviewers across the nation gave Steinbeck, for the most part, evenhanded commentary. Far from lashing into him, most seemed more inclined to forgive his lapses and appreciate each experiment for what it was.

It is revealing to follow the changes in a single newspaper's stance or one reviewer's attitude. Two critics who regularly reviewed the books and also produced critical overviews and biographical sketches assessed Steinbeck's 1940s work quite differently. Heretofore staunchly supportive, Joseph Henry Jackson gave a lukewarm notice to *The Forgotten Village* (1941), an illustrated book accompanying a film about a cholera epidemic in a Mexican village. Jackson disliked the "mystico-poetical text [that] succeeds only in talking down to the reader. Some day," he continued, "a critic will take time to analyze the curious, fatherly-godlike love that Steinbeck manifests for his characters, to examine the chastiseth-whom-he-loveth attitude implicit in so much of Steinbeck's work, the insistent diminishment of his human characters (no not his turtles) by which the author-creator unconsciously magnifies himself in relation to them." He pinpoints better than any the quality that sharply divided readers on Steinbeck's treatment of *paisanos*, bums, Okies, and misfits, and his primitivism that both attracted and repelled. (See, for example, the Edmund Wilson essay closing the *Grapes* section.) Jackson also disliked *Cannery Row* and found the characters in *The Wayward Bus* "dehumanized. . . . Add to this something which has always been something of an obsession with Steinbeck—his interest in the non-wholeness of people—and you have a tendency which is growing, I think, to the point where it is damaging to his work." Lewis Gannett, on the other hand, was undaunted. He was one of the few to understand that *Sea of Cortez* discloses aspects of Steinbeck's personality that are essential to one's understanding of both the novels and the man. And in a sympathetic review of *Bombs Away*, the 1942 propaganda piece on bomber crews that Steinbeck wrote on assignment for the War Department, he offered a character sketch that goes a long way in explaining Steinbeck's gradual mid-career shift from treatment of the group, aggregate humanity, to assessment of individual character in his writings:

> John Steinbeck is half-Irish, and he has a conscience, perhaps inherited from the New England missionary who was his grandmother on the other side. When an Irishman gets mad he wants to fight, and when a New Englander gets mad he begins by preaching. Steinbeck, moreover, started out to be a biologist before he took to writing stories: in a way he is still a biologist. And he is forty years old. Put that all together and you may understand how John Steinbeck came to write *Bombs Away*.

Much later, shortly after Steinbeck's Nobel Prize was announced in 1962, he wrote that Steinbeck "retain[s] the primitive's or the child's capacity to move from joy to rage in seconds [and] is one of the modern world's consummate story tellers."[8] Both Gannett and Jackson, friends of the author's, understood the man and his work.

When, in 1942, Steinbeck published his first novel after *Grapes*, a play-novelette about an occupied European town, *The Moon Is Down*, it was a thin, "message"-driven one, a Book-of-the-Month Club selection and, surprising to modern readers, as widely reviewed and as hotly debated as *Grapes* had been. Observed the *New Republic* reviewer: "A few weeks ago we predicted the controversy over John Steinbeck's new novel would be prolonged and bitter, but we didn't realize at the time that it was going to develop into all-out warfare on the literary front." Steinbeck's timing seemed unerring (as it had been with the publication of *Grapes*). "Here, without doubt is the book the world has been waiting for," declared the Youngstown (Ohio) *Vindicator*; "Since the fall of France, a bewildered public has expected some artist, some dramatist, some poet to distill out of the chaos of fears and hopelessness an elixir of new faith and new confidence in the basic principle of human freedom." Repeatedly *The Moon Is Down* inspired critics with patriotic fervor like that expressed by Cara Green Russell in the Greensboro (N.C.) *News*: "He projects and brilliantly dramatizes the idea, wonderfully consoling to us just now, that the totalitarian use of naked force to conquer a people accustomed to freedom is sure to fail." Once more, Steinbeck ministered to the public heart—with two prominent and well-spoken exceptions: Clifton Fadiman, writing for the *New Yorker* twice; and James Thurber, whose acerbic critique appeared in the *New Republic*. Both claimed that what the moment called for was not such flaccid idealism but "raw reality." "The Nazis believe in evil and make no attempt to disguise the fact," Fadiman asserted. Steinbeck's Nazis were, they charged, too humane. To Fadiman, Steinbeck appeared deluded, and "comfortable agreement with Mr. Steinbeck's reasoning will lead to dangerous inaction." Once again, then, Steinbeck was subjected to ideological mud slinging—not too strong a descriptive phrase—and the controversy went on for months, because it was renewed by the Broadway dramatic production and—as was the case with *Grapes*—the film version released in 1943. Some novelists would revel in the attention, perhaps, but Steinbeck was stung by attacks on his motives, his patriotism, and his supposed lack of sophistication. From this and the *Grapes* reception he never recovered respect for critics, if ever he had possessed it. Too often, in Steinbeck's eyes, they wrote from their own insularity.

For many reviewers, no novel of the 1940s seemed big enough or serious enough to satisfy. *Cannery Row* is a "miniature gem" wrote A. C. Spectorsky in the Chicago *Sun*, but to others it seemed merely "charming," sadly "transparent," and objectionably escapist. Still others complained of the writer's continual fascination with low life, and a few asserted that the great documentarian of the 1930s was coasting. Malcolm Cowley coined an epithet that stuck: The novel was a "cream puff"—though a "very poisoned" one. Steinbeck is reported by Toni Jackson Ricketts to have retorted that "if Cowley had read it yet again . . . he would have found how very poisoned it was."[9] In the author's mind, reputable critics repeatedly failed to comprehend all that he was up to. Certainly publication of *The Wayward Bus* in 1947, another Book-of-the Month Club selection, did not improve his status. Viking touted the work as his first full-length novel in eight years, and reviewers applauded his return to "serious" themes; they also debated the worth of his allegorical intentions, and *Bus* was termed by Daphne Alloway McVicker a "dreary" story about "horrible little people." But a constant throughout his career—unexpected with minor books—was the fact that serious, incisive, and famous critics were engaged by Steinbeck's texts: Bernard

DeVoto praised the "craftsmanship" of *Bus*, and Carlos Baker suggested that the book "might even be good for one's soul." Norman Cousins marked the occasion with an incisive little essay on realism, regretting the writer's tendency to "extraneous realism," mere details recorded without moral force. Orville Prescott was more severe: He noted that Steinbeck had not even measured up as a literary naturalist. It may well be that Steinbeck is our best measure of the inadequacy of mid-twentieth-century critical categories: a writer with one foot in the realism/naturalism camp, one dug into an ecological perspective few then noted, and another tripping over the modernists' experimental approaches to the novel (a genre he declared "dead" as early as the 1930s). That makes him a three-legged creature, which he seemed to those critics who attempted to type him conventionally.

So-called slight books both preceded and followed publication of the epical *East of Eden* in 1952. Far less controversial than *The Wayward Bus, The Pearl* was, the same year, either labeled "fake primitive" or lauded as a luminous parable, a rarefied "cultured" pearl. "It returns to the style of Genesis," stated a sympathetic Bill Bedell of the Houston *Post. A Russian Journal*, an account of a 1947 tour of Russia with photographer Robert Capa, was regarded as thin. It was described in the New York *Times* as "pleasant reading but it doesn't add up to much"—an assessment later given to the pieces in *Once There Was a War*, written while on overseas assignment in 1943 and collected in 1958. Insubstantiality was a charge often brought against Steinbeck's journalism, which he wrote with greater frequency in the 1940s and 1950s. He could be good on seemingly insignificant topics—or he could be just inconsequential. Yet the absence of the ponderous, or the lightness of touch, in Steinbeck's nonfiction was seen by others as the very source of his appeal: *A Russian Journal* was written by an author described as approachable, eminently readable, and one who, noted William McFee, possessed an "observant eye, a deadpan humor, and a command of the English language unsurpassed by any American of our time." The book's outstanding quality, wrote Richard Watts in the *New Republic*, "is its friendliness and its refusal to take itself too seriously." *Travels with Charley* (1962) would be embraced for precisely the same warmth. As the reviewer of the Newark (N.J.) *News* related, *Travels* "gives us a chance to meet a man, which is what most of us want to do with every book. This one is worth knowing—unaffected, simpatico, with the tolerance of approaching age." Unlike Faulkner and Hemingway, Steinbeck was reviewed and read appreciatively by people who, quite simply, liked him. Slouchy dresser, champion of the small man, novelist of compassion, he appeared a regular guy and wrote accessible prose. You might find fault with such a writer, but you stuck with him, even through a "high art" experiment such as *Burning Bright*, although Lewis Gannett found its prose "fatal on the printed page."

Burning Bright, however, was seen as obviously signaling an important change in Steinbeck. Famous for his social vision in the late 1930s, he was increasingly recognized for his sensitivity to the individual and his moral condition. "John Steinbeck has enrolled . . . on the side of individual worth and human dignity," wrote Orville Prescott when reflecting on the focus of *Burning Bright*. In 1952, Robert R. Brunn unwittingly disagreed with Prescott but made a like observation concerning *East of Eden* in the *Christian Science Monitor*. He proclaimed that Steinbeck "wrestles with a moral theme for the first time." It was *Eden* that won Joseph Henry Jackson back to Steinbeck's camp, largely for the same reason: "The whole novel turns upon the qualities in men which make them more than animals, not less." This large and "ambitious" novel that he published only a few weeks after Hemingway's *Old Man and the Sea* also indicated, in the eyes of many critics, that both writers were again working up to par. Steinbeck's book was exhaustively reviewed with, however, the usual mixed results. Its best qualities were those of an eighteenth-century novel—expansive, ambitious, vital. Joseph Wood Krutch liked it because it held "the attention to an extraordinary degree throughout the six hundred long pages." On the front page of the *New York Times Book Review*, Mark Schorer declared it "probably the best of John Steinbeck's novels." Orville Prescott, also writing for the *Times*, said that "he has achieved a considered philosophy and it is a fine and generous one." But *Newsweek* hated the "shambling, stuttering Sherwood Anderson prose." Granville Hicks disliked its "helter skelter" form. Anthony West and Leo Gurko regretted the melodrama. And nearly everyone felt uncomfortable with the heroine, Cathy. If Steinbeck's name was still associated with conflict, the discussion was, happily, carried out on new ground, not sociological but artistic, aesthetic, or formal, as can be seen especially in Mark Schorer's review. To a significant degree, Steinbeck was at last being liberated from the ideological matrix in place since the 1930s.

IV. The Final Phase: 1953–1968

The many who stuck with Steinbeck through thick and thin were rewarded in 1954 with the sequel to *Cannery Row*, *Sweet Thursday*—a book that delighted those whom Carlos Baker termed the "unregenerate thousands whose intellectual bridgework still permits them to relish salt-water taffy." As Edward Weeks explained in the *Atlantic*, those readers would appreciate its "comedy—bawdy, sentimental, and in places implausible"; when "read in the spirit with which it is written, [*Sweet Thursday*] is good fun." But the last phase in the long-developing author-reviewer relationship was once more characterized by controversy as Steinbeck again proved to be Steinbeck. From the high seriousness of *East of Eden*, he had "descended" to the comical nether realm of *Tortilla Flat*. He set his new book in Monterey among the wacky, often cartoonlike characters familiar to readers of *Cannery Row*, and his return to that landscape was disconcerting to many reviewers ready for another *Eden*. Further, *Sweet Thursday* did not at all prepare them for his next jaunt in 1957, to France, for his *Candide*-inspired satire in *The Short Reign of Pippin IV*. And in 1961 Steinbeck performed another about-face: Before he amiably returned to nonfiction in *Travels with Charley*, the Voltairelike "smile of reason" seen in *Pippin* vanished as he brooded over modern morality in his last "big book," *The Winter of Our Discontent*. Whereas *Newsweek* celebrated the return of "The Old Steinbeck," discontent with *Winter* and a good many of Steinbeck's other works was uttered in a remarkable way by Arthur Mizener. In 1962, one day after Steinbeck was recognized for his achievements by the Swedish Academy, Mizener's "Does a Moral Vision of the Thirties Deserve a Nobel Prize?" appeared in the *New York Times Book Review*.[10] That headline encapsulates Steinbeck's treatment by many critics: It's a question; it's mean-spirited; it looks backward; and it grudgingly acknowledges that he's won. The issues of a career, then, greeted his last novel, another Book-of-the-Month Club selection, which won praise for its trenchant criticism of modern life but was as often dismissed as a dud. Extolled for its compelling moral vision, *Winter* was, paradoxically, also cited for lacking moral conviction: Whereas some saw Robert Poole's "Resurgent Steinbeck" reemerging "as one of America's most subtle and human writers, one whose work gathers enormous power from the calm restraint of the writing," *Time* found his style "overworked." John K. Hutchins noted "implausibility at the heart of" *Winter*. "In it," concluded Fanny Butcher, "are to be found Steinbeck at both his best and his worst. It is almost two different books," one amusing and one profound.

That split would remain a Steinbeck legacy. "We have come to think of John Steinbeck as a writer with two literary faces, the one gleeful, the other outraged, but both startlingly and memorably alive," noted Virgilia Peterson in a positive review of *Winter* for the New York *Herald Tribune*. The last two of his books published during his lifetime, neither fictional, embody those two faces: that of the genial novelist who traveled with Charley and that of the moralist whom Walter Havighurst of the Chicago *Tribune* found appraising America with "curiosity, impatience, love and anger" in his final book of essays on issues facing his country, *America and Americans* (1966). In short, Steinbeck was a man of multiple interests and tastes, and, despite the many consistencies in his writings, his works are properly, and fairly, described only when their multiple discrete forms and the intentions giving rise to them are recognized. Each work begs for consideration as, if not wholly original, a unique attempt by Steinbeck to move in a new direction and through new experiences, both personal and literary. Reviewers who did not approach his books thus were at odds with others who did—hence many of the radical disagreements recorded in these reviews. Indeed, it may prove impossible to determine any consensus regarding individual titles, and, if one finally does, many qualifications would typically be necessary. A primary value of this volume, then, is that it puts a present-day student of the history of American literary taste in touch with the complex, often contradictory critical reception of an evolving literary canon, positioning him or her in light of the reviewers' valid insights, as well as their faux pas, to determine what are now the most appropriate approaches to understanding and appreciating Steinbeck.

As one contextualizes the books vis-à-vis the reviews for the sake of developing a historically informed perspective on the canon, one other factor should be kept in mind: Steinbeck's own view of what each new work meant to him as an opportunity for continued development as an artist. "I don't care about the critics," Steinbeck told Art Buchwald in 1955. "The only joy for the writer should be the doing, not the end. Reception of a work should not be a part of the pleasure of writing. There is no creative satisfaction when a thing is finished. The thing I want to learn to do is write as freshly as when I first started. A writer should never learn to write. He must continually experiment or his technique will take over and he'll never write anything good again."[11] Here was a man who never quit writing and whose prose shaped each day of his professional life. This is the Steinbeck seen in full in two posthumous publications, journals recording what it meant to be ever striving for a better "doing" of his craft: *Journal of a Novel: The* East of Eden *Letters* (1969) and *Working Days: The Journals of* The Grapes of Wrath (1989). The reviews of these books, like those of the others, aid us in our critical discriminations. However, their contents, like other reflections by Steinbeck on his craft, are just as significant as the reviews if one believes, as we do, that an understanding of authorial intention is as important as reviewers' judgments to anyone seeking to come to terms with what John Steinbeck wrought.

This volume was initially conceived as a means of providing an overview of Steinbeck's critical reception, as comprehensively as possible within the standard space limitations of the series of which it is a part. This meant, we soon discovered, that a writer reviewed so widely had to be treated selectively: We had to identify representative and especially noteworthy reviews of his works for reprinting and relegate the remainder to the lists of "Additional Reviews" at the ends of most of the sections devoted to individual titles. Also, for so productive a writer, even already modified ambition had to be further curbed. We had to draw the line for the number of works to be treated at 32. Omitted are items in the following categories: films for which Steinbeck wrote the script (published or unpublished); anthologies such as the 1943 *Steinbeck* in the Viking Portable Library series; books including the first publications of letters by Steinbeck, such as *Steinbeck: A Life in Letters* (1975); and limited editions such as *Their Blood Is Strong* (1938; published again as *The Harvest Gypsies* in 1988). Two publications, however, are given special treatment: the 1936 edition of *Cup of Gold*, a novel that received relatively little attention when first published in 1929, and the small-circulation, deluxe 1937 edition of *The Red Pony*, because of the immediate attention it received from reviewers and 1938 reviewer reaction to the inclusion and expansion of its story-sequence in *The Long Valley*.

The reviews were condensed editorially when plot summaries proved essentially repetitive of those given earlier in the chronologically arranged reviews; when reviewers turned to other authors and works, and their commentaries were not directly related to Steinbeck's writings; and when reviewers indulged themselves, normally at the beginnings of reviews, in general reflection deemed not immediately pertinent to the evaluation of the work by Steinbeck at hand.

It is assumed that the reviews that are reprinted provide the "main story" regarding how Steinbeck fared with his critics; but the reader is encouraged to trust his or her own judgment finally, by both consulting the reviews only listed at the ends of sections and continuing the search for as yet unrecovered reviews of Steinbeck's works.

Notes

1 *Journal of a Novel: The* East of Eden *Letters* (New York: Viking, 1969), 141. Quotations from, and references to, writings about Steinbeck in this introduction are identified in notes only when those writings are not reprinted in this volume and are not listed at the ends of the sections on individual works. The Index directs one to the pages on which commentators' pieces are reprinted or listed; unsigned reviews can be located via indexed periodical titles.
2 Quoted in Bernard Kalb, "Trade Winds," *Saturday Review*, 36 (27 February 1954), 8.
3 New York: Modern Library, 1937, pp. ii–iii.
4 *Where the Bluebird Sings to the Lemonade Springs* (New York: Viking, 1993), 141.
5 Elaine Steinbeck and Robert Wallsten, eds., *Steinbeck: A Life in Letters* (New York: Viking, 1975), 121.
6 "Pomeroy Flays Two New Books," Bakersfield *Californian*, 14 August 1939, pp. 9, 13.
7 Quoted by Lewis Gannett in "Introduction," *Steinbeck*, enlarged edition in the Viking Portable Library series, ed. Pascal Covici (New York: Viking, 1946), 23.
8 "John Steinbeck," New York *Herald Tribune*, 28 October 1962, Section 6, p. 1.
9 See Tony Seixas, "John Steinbeck and the Non-teleological Bus," in E. W. Tedlock and C. V. Wicker, eds., *Steinbeck and His Critics* (Albuquerque: University of New Mexico Press, 1957), 275–80.
10 112 (9 December 1962), 43–5.
11 Art Buchwald, "PS from New York," New York *Herald Tribune*, 29 March 1955, p. 21.

CUP OF GOLD

CUP OF GOLD

A LIFE OF HENRY MORGAN,
BUCCANEER

*With Occasional
Reference to
History*

by
JOHN STEINBECK

ROBERT M. McBRIDE & COMPANY
NEW YORK   1929

Will Cuppy.
"*Cup of Gold.*"
New York *Herald Tribune*, 18 August 1929, "Books" section, p. 12.

Being a life of Henry Morgan, buccaneer, with occasional references to history, and a promising stab at a novel of adventure. Strangely enough, the tale lacks the color and spirit traditional to its genre, perhaps because the author has preferred to tinker with a realistic method—or maybe it was an oversight. Mr. Steinbeck lapses into pedestrian narrative at times, but even so, enough brave names and places are bandied about to hold the interest of most fans; and Mr. Steinbeck's graceful manner lifts the yarn above the adventure groceries of this degenerate age. The tale tells of Henry's boyhood in the Welsh glens, his sailing for the Indies at the age of fifteen, his slavery in Barbados and later triumphs on the Spanish Main, including the sack of Panama, the Cup of Gold, for love of the mysterious Ysobel, alias the Red Saint, and his respectable death years later as lieutenant governor of Jamaica.

"*Cup of Gold.*"
St. Louis *Star*, 1 September 1929, p. 11.

Henry Morgan, pirate, freebooter and lieutenant governor, whose greatest ambition was to sack "The Cup of Gold" in Panama, has, through the pen of John Steinbeck, presented his life story for the readers of good fiction in one of the latest books from the Robert McBride Publishing Company. While most previous stories, whether historical or fictional of Morgan's life, were written for the consumption of school boys, here is one that is decidedly not for juvenile perusal. For here is presented Morgan's complete life (including his loves) dealing with every phase, whether real or legendary, of England's most noted buccaneer. Here is seen Morgan in all his brutalness, his ambition and his passion. One cannot help but thrill at the downright courage of the man, nor fail to sympathize with him at his disappointments. Morgan, for one of the few times in a life which has appeared many times on paper, is actually seen as a man. He was really human at times, loving all earthly pleasures and, according to the worthy Mr. Steinbeck, actually possessed ideals. He had a natural tendency for exaggeration which, one suspects, has been handed down to his most recent biographer, which is altogether excusable in as much as no claim is made to the historical accuracy of the book. *Cup of Gold* is thoroughly masculine and should find much favor with those male readers who used to delight in those bloody tales of piracy and rebellion.

"Morgan, the Pirate, Sails Raging Main."
Columbus *Ohio State Journal*, 15 September 1929, "Magazine Section," p. 3.

This is a romanticized story of Morgan, pirate, pillager, killer, lieutenant-governor of Jamaica and sacker of Panama, known to the world of that day as "the Cup of Gold." From the time when Morgan was a lad on his father's country acres until the day he died in his bed at Jamaica, the story takes him, through his slavery, his years as a buccaneer, his knighting by King Charles, and finally his death. He started with nothing save a love for far places; he took a brown-skinned slave for a mistress, and was defeated when he attempted a similar conquest of the Red Saint of Panama; finally, he married his orphan first cousin, then died like a gentleman.

There is little of fact or history here, although, as the author says, there is an occasional historical reference. The story is fiction, purely, and Morgan is perhaps a more romantic figure here than he was in real life. Some of his cruelties are softened, and under Mr. Steinbeck's pen the buccaneer is at times a strange, abstract creature who knows neither love nor sorrow; who, dying, could not recall that he had any sins to confess or to repent.

There is enough of the biographical novel here to take away the shimmer of imagination, so that the net result is a meaty, pleasing yarn wherein action sets the pace and clever writing plays the tune.

F.H.M.
"Morgan, Buccaneer."
New York *Evening Post*,
28 September 1929,
Section M, p. 7.

This novelized "Life of Henry Morgan, Buccaneer," written "with occasional reference to history," somehow does not "come off." It seems to fall between two stools

of style in considering the historical subject, the modern naturalistic and the period manner, and they do not harmonize. Yet there is much swing and movement to the narrative at times, and Henry's many undesirable qualities are not camouflaged. Morgan was a cruel, orgiastic brute. And when the author makes him philosophize in his "don't call it love" affairs with his women, Henry does not ring true. The actual record of his life shows he was no introspect. He looked into the wine when it was red, and into women's eyes when he was ready for them. It is a question whether he ever looked into his own soul. Yet Mr. Steinbeck's fantasy is enjoyable reading, with its highlighting of the sack of Panama, the West Indian "Cup of Gold," even though we find it hard to believe that Morgan died thinking he "always had some rather good end in view," in all his deviltries.

A.M.
"The Reviewer."
Stanford [Calif.] *Daily*,
30 October 1929, p. 2.

There were once two Steinbecks, cousins. One of them came to Stanford and became President of the student body. The other came to Stanford and became a novelist.

Cup of Gold, by John Steinbeck, is a fanciful, rather weird, and sometimes historical novel concerning the life of one Henry Morgan, buccaneer, pirate, and member of the "Brotherhood" that caused so much trouble to Spain's power on the seas during the sixteenth century. And Henry is the whole show. We see him first as a boy of fifteen, dreaming of life beyond the seas and eternally yearning for the wild adventurous life of men who did things. We leave him just as death is coming, and all the terrible deeds of his past life are passing by in bewildering confusion.

Cup of Gold is the picture of a dreamer—of a dreamer who eternally searched for some ephemeral happiness. Cities and countries richer than man ever dreamed of, fell before his armies. He had women, gold, ships, and power. But peace was not there and Henry Morgan was a lost soul looking for something he could never find. And thus he died.

All novelists have some sort of a philosophy and John Steinbeck is no exception. Says he, "All the world's great have been little boys who wanted the moon; running and climbing, they sometimes caught a firefly. But if one grow to a man's mind, that mind must see that it cannot have the moon and would not want it if it could—and so it catches no fireflies."

It is not the plot in *Cup of Gold* that makes the book interesting, for there have been many such plots. And it is not the characters, for there have been many such in the minds of all writers. It is the vivid, complete, and truly introspective picture of Henry Morgan's life and character that make the book a thing to be remembered. As one reads the book he feels as though he had experienced the same things in his own life. If you ever left the place in which you grew up, then you know how Henry felt that wintry morning he bid goodbye to the valleys of Cambria.

John Steinbeck is a Stanford man, a member of the class of '24. Since leaving school he has spent his time traveling abroad and in this country, writing things when time allowed. *Cup of Gold* is his first attempt in the field of novel-writing.

Paul G. Teal. *"Cup of Gold."* San Jose [Calif.] *Mercury-Herald*, 1 December 1929, p. 7.

Henry Morgan, pirate of note and ruler of the Spanish main who was never defeated, as far as men knew, humiliated and repulsed by a woman, who used only a pin for a weapon.

Henry Morgan, a swashbuckler of power and might, envied by half the world, the most lonesome man that sailed the seven seas—

Henry Morgan, who chose a friend from his crew of adventurers and then killed the friend because he was afraid of his pity—

And lastly, Henry Morgan, "respected" citizen and overlord of Port Royal, who put former members of his crew to death on charges of piracy, with the excuse: "I do not hang you because you are pirates but because I am expected to hang pirates. I am sorry for you. I would like to send you to your cells with saws in your pockets, but I cannot. As long as I do what is expected of me I shall remain the Judge. When I change for whatever motive, I may myself be hanged."

Cup of Gold seems everything that a novel, a history and a book of travel should be. It impresses the reader as containing all elements of literature clamped between two cloth-bound covers. There is pathos and horror in it and nobleness and smallness. There are descriptions of cities and islands and swamps. Its people are broad and narrow, strong and weak, clever and dull and all of these virtues and vices are bound up in Henry Morgan as portrayed by John Steinbeck, who, by the way, is a Palo Alto man.

The tale follows the history of this famous pirate accurately. Not an action of his that is known or sufficiently rumored has been left out. And into this bit of history, which is far from dull even when recounted by the most drab of historians, Steinbeck has woven bits of scintillating beauty, incidents of stark horror, and has peopled all incidents with genuine human beings.

He begins with Morgan as a small boy in Scotland, merely an adventurous small boy who leaves home. Henry is indentured as a slave in Barbados, an island of the British West Indies. His master took an interest in the boy, taught him history and English and gave him access to a large library. Here the future buccaneer studied war. Everything he could find out about fights at sea he consumed—for young Henry had long determined to become a pirate. By way of assuring his future he soon became manager of his master's plantation and stole and laid aside enough money to set him up in the pirate business.

Because of his actual knowledge of sea warfare, his ability to handle men and his sagacity, Henry Morgan soon became the most successful pirate in the trade. Thousands of men flocked to his standard when he called.

The sack of Panama, the Spanish city known as the "Cup of Gold," was the high point in Morgan's career. The reason for this venture was the high point in his affairs of the heart—if he could be said to have a heart.

For Henry Morgan sacked Panama so that he might find a woman there. Her name was La Santa Roja—The Red Saint—and she was known the world over for her charm. And when Henry Morgan found The Red Saint she scorned him and jeered at him and defended herself with a pin until he left the city like a whipped cur.

Desire of The Red Saint put Henry Morgan on his way to Panama. He called for volunteers and an army of pirates responded. They knew that Morgan never failed. The destination was not announced until the pirates had landed on the beach that mouthed the swampy sloughs that led to Panama. The crew nearly revolted with dread at the thought of attacking the impregnable city. But they thought too of The Red Saint.

"There is a woman in Panama and she is lovely as the sun. They call her the Red Saint in Panama. All men kneel to her. She has stolen worship from the Blessed saints." This was the rumor of the Red Saint.

Barges were built and the army and supplies began their watery march toward Panama. Disease and fatigue harassed them but under the lash of Morgan's will they continued.

The city was taken easily and sacked. Morgan failed to find the Red Saint at first. She heard he was searching for her and came to his headquarters. He offered her marriage and she scorned him. He asked for her hand in the sweetest words he could remember.

"You forget only one thing, sir," she said. "I do not burn. You do not carry a torch for me and I hoped you did. I came this morning to see if you did. And I have heard your words so often and so often in Paris and Cordova. I am tired of these words that never change. Is there some book with which aspiring lovers instruct themselves? The Spanish men say the same things, but their gestures are a little more practiced, and so a little more convincing. You have much to learn. I wanted force—blind, unreasoning force—and love not for my soul or for some imagined beauty of my mind, but for the white fetish of my body," she told the pirate.

Her husband was soft and delicate, she said. She was tired of such men.

Morgan, thinking this his cue, tried force. But The Red Saint was not interested. She repulsed his advances by stabbing a small pin in his face. She dared him to kill her. He hadn't the nerve. He was cowed. A woman had defeated the world's greatest pirate.

Infuriated Henry Morgan killed the first man that crossed his path—an epileptic whom he despised. Half crazed he returned to the palace of the Governor and sat amidst the gold that had been looted. His only friend entered. Morgan thought of the pity and comfort his friend would have for him when he explained his failure. Morgan couldn't stand the thought of that. He shot his friend through the heart.

But, nevertheless, Morgan finished things in a business-like way in Panama. He sold The Red Saint back to her husband for a great sum. He took the treasures back to the coast, piled them aboard his ship, made all but a few men drunk, then scuttled all ships but his and sailed away with the swag. His army wakened next day to face starvation. A few escaped but most of them died.

Morgan bribed British officials with some of his fortune and was knighted instead of being jailed. The government sent him to Port Royal where he judged and hung wrong-doers until he died.

W[ilbur] N[eedham]. "Steinbeck's First." Los Angeles *Times*, 26 July 1936, Part 3, p. 8.

Here is a new edition of John Steinbeck's first book—practically a new book, since it is doubtful if more than a handful of people ever read its miscroscopically small first edition. By now, those who like Steinbeck are aware of the fact [that], as Lewis Gannett puts it [in] his preface, "no two of his books have ever fitted in the same valise." *Tortilla Flat* made him famous; but, stubbornly, he went on to write, not another amusing tale of the Monterey *paisanos*, but a dramatic labor novel, *In Dubious Battle*. His astounded readers are now treated to the spectacle of Steinbeck wallowing in gore and action, color and hard, brilliant romance.

Cup of Gold is a novelization of Sir Henry Morgan's life, from his birth in the Welsh glens to his Carib exploits and the capture of Panama and his death in Jamaica, written "with occasional reference to history." It is a gorgeous story; but you may be sure Steinbeck has not handled it in any orthodox fashion. I hope its publication may lead many to discover, with further surprise, his two really great books: *The Pastures of Heaven* and *To a God Unknown*.

Joseph Henry Jackson. "A Bookman's Notebook." San Francisco *Chronicle*, 31 July 1936, p. 15.

This, first of all, is not a new book. It has been taken over by the present publisher from the firm that originally brought it out in 1929. On record (as they very well might be) as believing completely and thoroughly in Steinbeck's work, Covici-Friede wanted to be the publisher of all his books, and added this one to his others which they already have. His first novel, it never had a very wide public, and a great many who discovered him with *Tortilla Flat*, and have since read his *In Dubious Battle*, and perhaps his *To a God Unknown* and *Pastures of Heaven*, will be glad of this chance to get hold of it.

In the sentence immediately preceding this I spoke of *Cup of Gold* as a novel. The publisher calls it that, in his jacket-note, and perhaps it is. Mr. Steinbeck himself must have considered it more or less in that light when he wrote it, although it is subtitled *A Life of Sir Henry Morgan, Buccaneer, with Occasional References to History*. As a matter of fact, the book partakes a little of the nature of a biography and quite a good deal of the nature of fiction. Which is far from being a black mark against it.

As to the content of the book, it is just what it is called. There is no point in reciting an outline of it here. Morgan was a young man who knew very well what he wanted and went out and got it. Like most adventures he had a strong romantic streak in him, and perhaps just a dash of the mystic about his thought processes. At least, Steinbeck shows him that way, and it is as likely an interpretation as another. Whatever the reason, he was a curious and in many ways a significant figure. And as you follow his progress in this tale you find yourself admiring the man more than you should admire a gentleman of the ruthlessness and piratical makeup of Morgan. It is, at any rate, a story very well worth reading; one in which you will find all the adventure you could ask for, and all the color a book of its kind could possibly contain. On that ground alone it is a book you should read.

But the most interesting thing about it is that it was Steinbeck's first book.

In a preface to this new edition Lewis Gannett sketches Steinbeck's career briefly, but takes time to note how the characteristics that were later to be so notable in the author's work may be traced here at their beginnings. It is a youthful book, as Mr. Gannett says. But it shows very plainly where the youth who wrote it was headed. And I should like to quote for you something that Gannett says in this connection, something which indicates how well he has understood this point, and how well he understands Steinbeck and his writing altogether. This is how he concludes his preface: "Perhaps one may find, in this glowingly youthful book, in this story of young Henry Morgan—particularly in the boy's conversation, on the mountain-top with old Merlin—a sort of key to Steinbeck himself: 'Merlin searched the boy's face closely. "I think I understand," he said softly. "You are a little boy. You want the moon to drink from, as a golden cup; and so it is very likely that you will become a great man if only you remain a little child. All the world's great have been little boys who wanted the moon; running and climbing, they sometimes caught a firefly. But if one grow to a man's mind, that mind must see that it cannot have the moon and would not want it if it could—and so, it catches no fireflies."'"

And Mr. Gannett concludes: "Steinbeck still catches fireflies, as lovely and as various fireflies as any man writing in America today. By some rare magic he has united a child's heart, a child's seeing eyes, with a man's mind. I believe his fireflies to be among the most beautiful and most significant specimens in American literature today. The scientists have never solved the miracle of the firefly's 'cold light'; they can only assure us of its existence and perfection. Nor can critics do more than assure the reader that

Steinbeck's magic, which anyone who reads must feel, is authentic magic."

It was no part of my intention to make Mr. Gannett, willy-nilly, write this review for me, but I see that he has done it.

Those are precisely the things that needed to be said about Steinbeck—or at least some of them. I shall add only that if you have discovered the charm in *Tortilla Flat*, if you have read *In Dubious Battle*, and appreciated the integrity which led its author to refuse to take sides in the extremely controversial matters about which he wrote in that book, if you have perhaps read either or both of his other two novels and realized—as you could hardly fail to do—that what Gannett says about Steinbeck's "authentic magic" is true, then you must get hold of this *Cup of Gold*. It is a story, yes; as rousing and adventurous a yarn as you will find anywhere. But in addition to that it is a perfect literary preview of the work of a man who has since become widely known for books so different that you would hardly believe the same stamp could be on all of them. Yet, as Mr. Gannett points out, it is. And since Steinbeck is without question the one most worth watching of any of the younger writers of the Pacific Coast—and certainly one of those anywhere in America of whom it may be said that they are going places—I am sure that no one who cares about this work will want to let pass this chance to see how he began.

Charles Marriott. "Satire and Sentiment." Manchester *Guardian*, 29 January 1937, p. 7.

... It is by no means unlikely that Sir Henry Morgan, the seventeenth-century buccaneer, had a streak of mysticism, and Mr. Steinbeck has done well to exploit it in his "life," with "occasional references to history," to quote the sub-title. One feels, however, that either the references to history should have been more precise or else the general treatment should have been more free. As it is, the novel tends to fall between two stools, and the story "sags" rather badly in Morgan's sudden change from youth to maturity at Barbados, with an effect of a missing text which would not have occurred with more freedom in the treatment of the whole. Mr. Steinbeck's writing, too, is not quite the best for the purpose: he is too fond of phrases like "the sensuous sureness of her were tonic things"; all right for the author observing directly, but not so right for the boy's impression of the ship; any more than is "a pleasant hypnosis in the brain" for his experience at sea. But the story shows constructive imagination, it has moments of excitement, and the episode of Morgan's emotional defeat by La Santa Roja at Panama is very well managed.

"Cup of Gold." Times Literary Supplement [London], 20 March 1937, p. 214.

Unfortunately, *The Cup of Gold* must be classified as fiction rather than biography, although Mr. Steinbeck makes more reference to history than his sub-title suggests. For he follows the known and traditional events of Morgan's life, inventing incidents, motives and somewhat unconvincing dialogue when he sees fit. He tells of his youth in Wales (without

9

committing himself to name Llanrhymny, the Glamorganshire village in which the Morgans lived), his kidnapping in Cardiff (ascribed by Esquemeling to Bristol and denied by Morgan), his slavery in Barbados (also denied), and his subsequent career as a buccaneer.

The expedition to Panama, the "Cup of Gold," is the climax of the book; but Mr. Steinbeck makes Morgan's inducement not the gold of Panama but an attractive young woman named La Santa Roja. His luck did not hold with the Red Saint, and Mr. Steinbeck makes him meekly accept her refusal. He offers neither criticism nor explanation of Morgan's conduct when he played his men the shabbiest trick in the annals of piracy by sailing off with the loot and leaving his companions in the lurch; but since he accompanies his hero to his death-bed he might, in one of his occasional references to history, have mentioned that nine years after being knighted and appointed Lieutenant-General of Jamaica Morgan was deprived of his office for outrageous conduct.

Such efforts, of course, seem unusually odd at a moment when the complaints over the censoring of European news will no doubt make Americans extremely sensitive to any sort of censorship, whether native or foreign.

Two earlier books by Mr. Steinbeck have just appeared in new, inexpensive editions. One is *In Dubious Battle*, first published in 1936, and far more like the Steinbeck who wrote *The Grapes of Wrath* than the Steinbeck who wrote *Of Mice and Men*. The other is *Cup of Gold*, first published ten years ago, and perhaps sufficiently described in its subtitle as "The Amazing Career of Sir Henry Morgan, Buccaneer, With Occasional Reference to History."

Checklist of Additional Reviews

Charles Poore.
"New Editions of the Week."
New York *Times*,
15 September 1939, p. 27.

The astounding popularity of John Steinbeck's magnificent novel, *The Grapes of Wrath*, must by now have surpassed just about every one's expectations. It continues to be the most popular book in America—even in States that have seen an effort or two to censor it.

P.D.M. "News and Views of Happenings in Book World." Raleigh [N.C.] *Times*, 28 August 1929, p. 11.

Louise V. Wiegand. "Adventure Story of Stirring Days in Indies Related." Salt Lake [City] *Telegram*, 8 September 1929, "Magazine" section, p. 1.

"Weekly Book Review and Book Gossip and Chat." Quincy [Ill.] *Herald-Whig*, 22 September 1929, Part 1, p. 9.

First Reader. "The Reading Lamp." South Bend [Ind.] *Tribune*, 6 October 1929, "Women's Section," p. 12.

Edwin Francis Edgett. "A Buccaneer on His Swaggerings through Fiction." Boston *Evening Transcript*, 21 July 1936, p. 13.

"*Cup of Gold*." Washington [D.C.] *News*, 25 July 1936, p. 12.

THE PASTURES OF HEAVEN

THE PASTURES OF HEAVEN

by

JOHN STEINBECK

NEW YORK, 1932
BREWER, WARREN & PUTNAM

R[obert] M. Coates. "Books." *New Yorker*, 8 (22 October 1932), 54–5.

The best of the novels I looked into this week is, oddly enough, hardly a novel at all, at least in the sense of having a settled cast of characters and a continuous story about them. This is *The Pastures of Heaven*, by John Steinbeck, published by Brewer, Warren & Putnam, and it has to do with the communal life of the inhabitants of a valley in California so charming and so fertile that the Spanish settlers called it by the name which now serves as the title of Mr. Steinbeck's book.

Such a story, dealing with a variety of characters and the intricacies of their relations, must almost necessarily be episodic in treatment, and the danger is that, unless some mood or central theme can be found to bind it all together, it may fall in too loose a pattern, becoming merely a sequence of short stories rather than parts of a connected whole.

It may, indeed, be said that at times Mr. Steinbeck fails to recognize this danger, and gives away occasionally to a leaning for a sort of O. Henry twist at the end of some of his episodes which, while surprising the reader, also has the effect of leaving him a little up in the air. And again, perhaps because this is a first novel, his debt to some of his predecessors in this field of writing—Sherwood Anderson, George Milburn, etc.—is sometimes a little too plainly evident.

But in the main his grasp of the whole sweep of the valley, and the people in it and their lives, is comprehensive and sure; and his characters—the penniless Shark Wicks, who made himself, by sheer power of imagination, a miser; T. B. Allen, the garrulous storekeeper; Miss Morgan, the school-teacher; the shiftless Bert Monroe; Tularecito, the daft little Mexican boy; and all the others—weave in and out of each other's lives casually, ironically or tragically, but always with an effect as of real life. I think you'd enjoy it.

Margaret Cheney Dawson. "In a Peaceful Valley." New York *Herald Tribune*, 23 October 1932, "Books" section, p. 2.

The Pastures of Heaven—*Las Pasturas del Cielo*—was the felicitous name given to a little California valley which, "by some regal accident," had escaped being ravaged both by Spanish adventurers in the old days and American adventurers in the new. As Mr. Steinbeck pictures it, still before the "development" which he suggests will one day be its fate—it holds in its gentle grip something almost unique in California, indeed in America, today: peace. It offers a very normal, friendly kind of atmosphere in which the accents of disaster and sorrow are not lacking, but which nevertheless seems dominated by a kind of magic. Whether the spell is cast by nature's beauty or the author's charming serenity of style the reader will probably neither know nor care, but he will feel it and believe in it.

The inhabitants of the Valley farmed the easy-yielding soil, attended school board meetings and barbecues, talked about stock prices and cake recipes. The

13

framework was solidly conventional, but the picture itself often arrestingly vivid. Take Shark Wicks, for instance. Shark had two treasures, his incredibly beautiful and equally stupid daughter Alice and his reputation for shrewdness. The first he guarded with suspicious vigilance and the second he enhanced by manipulating imaginary investments in a ledger until the profit column showed six-figure entries. "Shark ain't nobody's fool," the villagers would say, and Shark, throwing out a hint now and then about real estate or utility values, let the impression of his riches grow until he came to think of them as real himself. Then, in a fatal hour, one treasure canceled the other. For Shark, enraged by a whisper of gossip about Alice, rushed off with a gun and fell straightway into the hands of the law. And when the judge tried to put him under bond to keep the peace the awful truth was out: he had no money. Then the fleshly daughter absconded, in effect, with the imaginary ducats. Shark, in chagrin, left the valley.

Tularecito, also, was cast for a tragic role. Nobody knew where he came from, this "frog-child" with thick, short arms and long, dangling legs. He had been found crying in the sage bush one night by a Mexican Indian, who swore that the baby winked at him and said: "Look! I have very sharp teeth!" Whatever the truth of this report, the little "frog," far from being an intellectual prodigy, grew to have the strength of a giant but only the brain of a five-year-old child. Under one circumstance he was vicious: when any one destroyed his handiwork. It must have seemed reasonable to him that if the teacher made him draw animals on the board then no one should be allowed to erase them, and that no one should dare fill in the hole he had dug deep into the earth to find his brothers, the gnomes. But his murderous defense of these logi-

cal conclusions landed poor Tularecito in the asylum for the criminal insane.

Thus each of the chapters presents an individual or group enacting some small drama against the backdrop of Heaven's Pastures. Short stories they are really— these tales of the giggling, pious Lopez sisters who became "bad women" with the air of two little girls pretending to "get lost," and the New England patriarch who tried to found a dynasty in defiance of California's genius for restlessness, and all the others. Yet there is at least, besides the little intermingling of events and names, a binding unity of feeling that perhaps justifies the author in calling this a novel. And there is a clarity, good humor and delicacy in Mr. Steinbeck's writing that makes the book fine reading, regardless of its category.

M.D.
"A Rich Stream Marks Steinbeck's Tale."
Chicago *Daily Tribune*, 19 November 1932, p. 14.

John Steinbeck has had a varied career. Besides being the author of one other novel, he has been a newspaper man, a ranch hand, a carpenter's helper, a painter's apprentice, a chemist, and a laborer. Finally he spent two years as a caretaker of an estate, during which time he was for eight months completely snowed in, with no means of communication with the rest of the world. It was in this period that he wrote the novel *The Pastures of Heaven*, which, he says, is a book purged of all hate.

Las Pasturas del Cielo is a valley in

California in which many families of widely diverse interests live. Somehow or other, sometimes in a significant way and other times simply trivially, they cross one another's paths, make entrances into and exits from one another's lives. There is the family of the Munroes, who decide to take a house that is considered haunted and that brings bad luck to all its occupants. The Munroes, however, succeed in all their enterprises.

The Wickses have an only daughter who is the most perfectly beautiful and stupid girl in the valley. The father's two passions in life are his protection of his daughter's purity and the creation of an illusion that he is wealthy. Another man has in his charge a boy whose mind had stopped growing when he was five. He has a superb talent for drawing and making things with his hands. Harmless and good, he is finally confined to an asylum for an act that seemed vicious to the authorities.

One family after another enters the story to give up its secrets, its family skeletons, its foibles and finenesses. Thus a rich stream of life flows through the book.

The novel is well plotted, though, perhaps the conclusion is of a somewhat obvious type. The characters are as vitally real as your next door neighbor, and the style and presentation of the novel are restrained, compassionate, as well as compelling.

Anita Moffett. "A Sheltered Valley." *New York Times Book Review*, 82 (20 November 1932), 15–16.

"*Las Pasturas del Cielo*"—"The Pastures of Heaven"—was the name given by the Spanish corporal to the sheltered valley "floored with green pasturage, on which a herd of deer browsed," when he caught sight of it from the top of a neighboring ridge. Unimaginative and violent though he was, he was so impressed by the beauty of the place that he planned to return to it in his old age; but this, like so many human wishes, was not destined to fulfillment.

A hundred years later the valley was settled by a community of some twenty families, farmers and fruit growers; it had a schoolhouse, a postoffice and a general store. John Steinbeck gives the reader a brief but penetrating glimpse into the life of each family and the drama which is being enacted under each of the roofs that seem so peaceful from a distance.

The Battle farm had been abandoned, and the place had the reputation of being haunted. About it lay that intangibly disquieting atmosphere peculiar to deserted houses. George Battle, its original builder, had come to California in '63 to escape the draft; the wife whom he had married for her money had the taint of insanity in her blood. After her removal to an asylum George found an outlet for his disappointed life and inarticulate aspirations in the care of his beautifully kept farm and orchard. His son, who with his mother's religious fanaticism inherited her insanity, became a traveling evangelist; the farm in his time became a place haunted by imaginary devils.

Oversensitive, obscurely troubled and disappointed, Bert Monroe, into whose hands the place eventually came, took refuge there from an increasing sense of failure. In some strange way he came to feel that his own ill luck and that of the place had neutralized each other; he prospered and regained an outlook of hope.

Junius Maltby, who had come to the valley for his health's sake, was unfitted for farming; his place was allowed to run to waste while he and the hired man, Jakob Stutz, sat on a sycamore limb by the stream in endless philosophical discussion. At 5 his son Robbie took part as an equal in these talks, his opinions courteously listened to and considered. Neither the boy nor his father thought of himself as poor until, on Robbie's going to school, well-meaning neighbors attempted to make him a charitable present of new clothes.

Mr. Steinbeck tells of Molly Morgan, the young school teacher, who dreamed of the absent father who had been a romantic childhood memory, but could not face the disillusioning reality of his return; of Tularecito, who could draw or carve every animal that lived, but whose mind had ceased growing at 5; and of Richard Whiteside, disappointed in the hope of the children for whom he had built the white house that dominated the valley.

Briefly, but with no effect of oversimplification or undue condensation, Mr. Steinbeck tells the story of these and other inhabitants of the valley, penetrating in each case to the hidden springs of action, the secret weakness or unfulfilled desire. He writes with deep feeling for the tragedy implicit in each situation, yet undeceived by the self-delusion or self-dramatization of the persons involved. Racy, realistically direct and caustically humorous, his writing is noteworthy for originality of phrase and image and a strongly poetic feeling.

"The New Books."
Saturday Review, 9
(26 November 1932),
275–6.

Though advertised as a novel, Mr. Steinbeck's book is rather a collection of short stories

unrelated except by the unity of place and the occasional appearance of one or another character in an episode in which he is not primarily featured.

The place: a paradisiacal valley in California—*Las Pasturas del Cielo*, originally settled by Spanish military. The characters: farmers, merchants, and well-to-do settlers and their families. The stories possess a fairly wide scope, ranging over the various field of human emotion without plowing it too deeply—loneliness; insanity; poverty; well-being. There is much humor of a tenderly ironic tinge, the book as a whole makes for excellent entertainment and will be extravagantly praised for its apparently objective attitude. Nevertheless, there is an air about it of the case-book—as though its author had made a careful selection of variant human types, jotted down interesting stories of people with whom he was more or less familiar, and dished them up. Many of these tales are slick, many are pat and run smoothly to foregone conclusions. Notable among these are the tales of the Banks poultry farm, the Lopez sisters, Pat Humbert's loneliness, and the frustrated dynastic ambitions of the Whiteside family—narratives which in themselves bear the seeds of richly human fiction, but which in their present form are somehow suspect as the fruit of a journalistic talent rather than of a creative imagination.

Cyrilly Abels.
"Keeping Up with the Novelists."
Bookman, 75
(December 1932), 877–8.

Mr. Steinbeck postulates "a long valley floored with green pasturage" where "perfect live oaks grew in the meadow of the lovely place, and the hills hugged it jealously against the fog and wind" as contrast for the gray fortunes of his decentralized characters. Those watchful for new talent may have noticed that in England another young man, Mr. Hilton, has just written a novel, *Ill Wind*, which also blows various characters varied disappointments or misfortunes, although Nature is not apotheosized. What is particularly interesting is that both books share not only the same mood—disillusionment, with faint overtones of a faith not quite talked away—but the same form, short stories loosely linked together. The craftsmanship of the Englishman is more finished, but Mr. Steinbeck seems to give more promise—perhaps because of his very immaturity.

A Spanish Corporal, rounding up a group of twenty converted Indians who had abandoned religion while the Carmelo Mission of Alto California was being built, discovered *Las Pastures del Cielo* in 1776. After the World War Bert Munroe brings his family to the valley to rehabilitate his finances. He acquires a farm which has passed through the hands of an owner eventually committed to an asylum and of the Mustrovics, who appeared one day, worked the farm industriously, and, two years later, disappeared. Bert's confidence in himself is renewed: he comes to feel that he has rid himself and the farm of their respective curses. Shark Wicks, who fanatically guards his beautiful-but-dumb daughter from the supposed snares of Bert's young son, carefully spreads the rumour that he is wealthy; when he is found out he deserts the valley for new soil with his punctured ego reinflated by his loyal wife. Nearby, Tularecito, a foundling who resembles a giant-gnome, is over-stimulated by the country school-teacher, who fosters the sub-normal boy's talent for drawing and who sees no harm in

suggesting a belief in fairy-tale people; digging a pit on the Munroe farm in quest of his brother-gnomes Tularecito almost murders Bert because he interferes. The teacher leaves the valley because a happy memory of her father is threatened when she hears of a drunken farmhand in the neighbourhood who resembles the parent whose faults she tries to hide from herself. A mother aggravates the psychopathic tendencies in her own child, cultivates day-dreams of her dead husband, and eventually shoots her daughter. Junius, a man of culture, comes to the valley because of his lungs; he stays to marry and live a lazy contemplative life, despised by his neighbours; he leaves, after his wife's death, when a gift of clothes from the School Board brings home the fact that his boy is growing up as a little animal. A son of a New Englander, like his father before him, pictures his house passing from generation to generation, but finds himself with a son who cares neither for Thucydides, his father's house, or the Pastures of Heaven, but for modern commerce in town. And so on.

As we read we are almost persuaded to believe in this community by the author's talent for character sketching, while his gentle irony forces forgetfulness of the fact that he is picturing pathetic, sometimes tragic, lives. His style itself—suggesting now Erskine Caldwell, now James Stephens, and again Anatole France—makes good reading, although its simplicity is often ostentatious. We can put two constructions on his book: that civilization shows a pathetic gray against the delightful green of Nature, or that even the Garden of the Hesperides brings disillusion. To point a quite different irony, Mr. Steinbeck incorporates on the last page of his narrative a warning he himself needs: an old man looking down into the Pastures of Heaven "beat his hands helplessly against his hips. 'I've never had time to think anything out. If I could go down there and live down there for a little—why, I'd think over all the things that ever happened to me, and maybe I could make something out of them, something all in one piece, that had a meaning, instead of all these trailing ends, these raw and dragging tails.' "

"*The Pastures of Heaven.*" *Booklist*, 29 (December 1932), 116.

A secluded mountain valley in California, named by early settlers Pastures of Heaven, provides the setting for these short stories and links the fortunes of a dozen families through a common environment. Sensitivity, a very human pity, and humor preserve the book from an unwholesome impression that the themes of horror and abnormality might have conveyed in less skilful writing.

"Shorter Notices." *Nation*, 135 (7 December 1932), 574.

Not really a novel, nor yet a book of short stories, this series of connected sketches presents a group of out-of-the-ordinary characters who live in the California valley called the Pastures of Heaven. It is the first flight of a fine writing talent which, while kindlier than that of Faulkner, is yet related to it in its preoccupation with the abnormal. Mr. Stein-

beck presents an idiot, two moronic sisters, several chronic failures, and an unfeeling and essentially stupid son who, coming at the end of a line of distinguished men, destroys his father's will to carry on. There is no heartlessness or cruelty in Mr. Steinbeck's view of them; he rather forgives them all their trespasses in excellent analytical narratives, written in a supple prose. His future work should lead to his recognition as an excellent psychological analyst. If he could add social insight to his present equipment he would be a first-rate novelist.

H[arold] B[righouse]. "Rural Depression." Manchester *Guardian*, 9 June 1933, p. 7.

"One of those whom God has not quite finished" is a good phrase, and the way of a patient man with a nagging wife is neatly expressed by "It would be impolite, he considered, to notice her when she was not being a lady. It would be like staring at a cripple." Mr. Steinbeck has the short-story writer's happy tensity, and in effect his novel is a collection of short stories about people in a Californian valley, which he names in irony "The Pastures of Heaven." Occasional characters recur, but the book is a series of episodes, and the writing is distinguished. Perhaps it needs to be. The suggestion is that the valley is more of hell than of heaven in its influence: it gathers failures, idiots, and simple-minded impracticables, and though some gleams of humour are permitted to play upon them the intention is, clearly, to "debunk" California. The valley lies near Carmel, and Carmel, we admit, is provoking—a beauty spot as self-conscious as Clovelly and twice as arty. An American author distressed by Carmel is justified in selecting its neighbourhood for the scene of an attack upon the Californian legend; but to others, to those who must read this book unbiased by local circumstance, it may seem little better than well-written morbidity. The publisher, it is fair to add, is able to quote high praise from American reviews. We can agree that Mr. Steinbeck stylishly associates himself with the American novel's contemporary mood of pessimism.

E. B. C. Jones. "New Novels." *New Statesman and Nation* [England], 5 (10 June 1933), 764–5.

. . . Unlike Miss McPherson [in *Few Things Are Needful*], Mr. Steinbeck has a sense of humour. He has taken a small beautiful valley in California, after which his book is called, and has loosely strung together stories of its inhabitants. Some of the stories are grim, for when the local supply of epileptics, congenital idiots and lunatics runs low, the author imports one from San Francisco; he is determined that his valley shall belie its name. He has been much influenced by French authors— Rosa and Maria Lopez, for instance, have an obvious origin in Maupassant—and for this reason, and because of a surface-culture, *The Pastures of Heaven* recall that overrated book *The Bridge of San Luis Rey*, although it is not irritatingly precious. Like Mr. Forester, Mr. Steinbeck deals straightforwardly with lives which are active; he is at his best when least literary. . . .

"The Pastures of Heaven." *Times Literary Supplement* [London], 15 June 1933, p. 413.

This book comes from America with a considerable advance reputation. The author's central idea is that Eden is not a garden but an inner condition, and that any attempt to recover the Golden Age merely by creating the appropriate external circumstances is doomed to failure. The Pastures of Heaven is a fertile rock-bound valley in California and as perfect a setting for a new Eden as one could hope to find. But the people who settle there bring with them not only friendship and love but also the crime, disease, insanity and injustices of the world without. A queer misshapen outcast with artistic genius is removed to a lunatic asylum because he is different from other people. A dreamer, who goes ragged for the sake of his dreams, loses his heaven when his neighbours force him to become industrious and respectable. The dominating figures are Richard Whiteside and his son. Their ambition is to be the patriarchs and law-givers of the valley, to build for permanence and found a dynasty; but the son lives to see their great house destroyed by fire. The book is well conceived and pleasantly written; and the characters, although, with one or two exceptions, they do not live as individuals, effectively symbolize humanity and abstract human types.

J. E. S. Arrowsmith. "Fiction—I." London *Mercury*, 28 (July 1933), 268–9.

... In the short story vein, though not actually a collection of separate short stories, is *Pastures of Heaven*, by John Steinbeck. Each episode in the book relates the story of a different family arriving in the loveliest valley, to settle. The publishers of this volume have put themselves to great pains trying to evolve a theory, or moral, from the stories therein. And express their anxiety to see if the reviewers will decide whether it is the sinister effects of this deceptive valley upon the souls that enter it that makes them so tormented, or if it is merely that in the most pleasant "pastures" man's troubled spirit is always spoiling the going for him. Personally I see no necessity to take either view. This is a sort of *Spoon River Anthology*, and the fact of the valley having been christened "The Pastures of Heaven" by the first invader who viewed it—a Spanish conquistador who discovers a valley in California, so lovely that he whispers "Holy Mother! Mother! here are the Green Pastures of Heaven to which our Lord leadeth us"—this fact adds, simply, a touch of irony to the morbid tale that follows of the lives of the subsequent settlers. This irony is sufficient art; and a very good touch. The stories themselves are boldly told and march with a swing. Mr. Steinbeck knows how to write about and handle the gloomy substance of his thoughts. The publishers, besides what they have already said, claim for him "consummate artistry" and a "masterly" skill. Again I see no reason to be led by them. "Artistry" and "skill" are here; but the adjectives are superfluous, as well as very hackneyed. It is a strong, holding book and eminently readable; the writing is both effective and fluent. . . .

Helen MacAfee. "Outstanding Novels." *Yale Review*, 22 (Winter 1933), xxii.

... *The Pastures of Heaven* is in structure much like a loose-leaf sketchbook. Without serious damage, the order in which various sketches stand could be changed, which may be equivalent to saying that the author has not quite mastered his chosen form. There is, however, no question of the excellence of some of the individual portraits, the young teacher, for example, or of the binding unity given to the series by the description of the remote valley in the California mountains, *Las Pasturas del Cielo*, as a place of refuge, not so happy as its name, for a community of restless souls. . . .

Checklist of Additional Reviews

Gerry Fitzgerald. "Carmel Valley Inspires Story." Los Angeles *Times*, 23 October 1932, Part 3, p. 16.

TO A GOD UNKNOWN

TO A GOD UNKNOWN

by
JOHN STEINBECK

NEW YORK
ROBERT O. BALLOU

"To a God Unknown." Christian Century, 50 (20 September 1933), 1179.

Already a comparison between Steinbeck and D. H. Lawrence has been suggested. To most readers it will be a misleading comparison, but there is a fierce beauty here which gives it point. *To a God Unknown* is the story of a young farmer's passion for the soil—a love passing the love of woman—and the growing sense of his own identification with it. The novelist has dealt imaginatively with the mystery of man's relation to the earth and the animals, and with those instinctive and irrational practices by which man has tried to give expression to his consciousness of that relation and to influence his earth-bound destiny. The story might be considered a modern appendix to *The Golden Bough*.

Margaret Cheney Dawson. "Some Autumn Fiction." New York *Herald Tribune*, 24 September 1933, "Books" section, pp. 17, 19.

This strange and mightily obsessed book is for those who are capable of yielding themselves completely to the huge embrace of earth-mysticism. Of all the brands of mysticism, religious or poetic, there is none so vast and awesome as that which arises from the earth and is a pas-

sion simply for the miracle of a body that yields, puts forth, grows and dies; which is unconcerned with good or evil, solace or punishment, error or reason. And of all the books written out of such passion, this is the purest expression of it that I have ever encountered.

The chief characters are a man, a tree and an enormous stone. The man is Joseph Wayne, who set out from his Vermont home to take up land in California with his father's blessing ("Maybe I can find you later," the old man had said, meaning that he would soon be dead and hence free to travel also). The tree is the oak on Joseph's new homestead in the Valley of Nuestra Senora which became to him the reincarnation of his father's spirit. And the stone? Symbol of ancient pagan religion, repository of earth lore and haunt of both good and evil forces, stern avenger of insult, last green fortress of the earth against drought, altar for the sacrifice of human blood—these are some of the roles it plays.

What it actually stood for in Joseph's life and worship is not easily hobbled by words. One can only say that he came closer and closer to it in feeling until, when his crops and animals were dead from the dryness of two years and all his family gone in search of a less treacherous land, he chose to remain behind, living in the shadow of the rock, husbanding the little water that ran from its side to pour over its still-green moss, finally dying with cut wrists on its back, offering his blood to bring back the rain.

All that happened to Joseph between the time of his coming to the lush California valley and his final martyrdom for the land was influenced by the tree-spirit of his father and the stone-spirit of the earth. After he had established himself there, built a house and started to work, he sent for his three brothers.

Thomas was the one who could handle

the animals, treating them without sentiment, but with "a consistency that beasts
could understand." Burton was meager,
pious and afraid. Benjy was sweet and
wayward, lying and getting drunk and
winning from bewildered women the gifts
of their pity and virtue. With these men
came their wives and children, and later
Joseph was to have a wife and child also.
Over them presided the oak tree, and
Joseph (to Burton's horror) hung offerings in its branches and poured wine at
its root. The tribe flourished, and Joseph
was wild with joy at its increase and at
the growing size of the herd. Then Burton decided to leave, go to some small
town and set up a little shop. It would
suit him better, and he was ill with fear
over Joseph's practices. Before he left he
girdled the tree, so that it shortly died.

After that, the tide of disaster rose around
them, until the Wayne ranch became only
a cluster of deserted houses and a huge
empty barn. All but Joseph had left, and
he lay in communion with his stone.

It would be futile to urge this book
upon any one who draws back from
strong expression of a strong emotion. Its
lust and furious power will repel some
readers, and others who were charmed
by the lucidity of *The Pastures of Heaven*,
may be dismayed to find Mr. Steinbeck
on so different a tack.

Virginia Barney.
"Symbols of Earth."
New York Times Book Review, 83
(1 October 1933), 18.

The unknown god of the hero of Mr.
Steinbeck's second novel is an earth god
whose sole commandment is "increase
and multiply." It is a heathen god, manifest wherever life is reproductive, disdain-
ful of sterility. Joseph Wayne meets and is
moved by false gods but he never yields
to them. His brother Benjy seeks the god
of the pleasures of the senses. Brother
Burton worships the god of his Calvinist
ancestors. Brother Thomas identifies himself with the pure animalism of creature
feeling. Rama, wife to Thomas, symbolizes the mother of all living. The Catholic
priest worships a god he can respect but
cannot follow. Joseph is even drawn to
the strange mortal who, living on a California cliff, has figured it out that he is
the last man of the Western world to see
the evening sun go down and who, therefore, at each sunset, sacrifices some live
thing to the sun god.

In his wife, Elizabeth, Joseph discovers a woman who is both of earth and of
aspiration. Rama is earth itself; but Elizabeth is the spirit of earth. And so when
Elizabeth dies in the solitary place by the
big rock; when the tree which, to Joseph,
embodies the spirit of his father is killed
by Burton who disapproves of it as a pagan symbol; when the lean years come
and the land and the beasts that feed
upon it become unproductive; when arid-
ity, sterility and death, disease and famine come, Joseph is defeated. Taking
a leaf from the eccentric cliff dweller, Joseph
sacrifices a calf to the rain god. Then the
truth comes to him and in the solitary
place by the big rock he sacrifices himself. And even before consciousness departs the rain comes and fertility is assured.

The bare narrative, reduced from its
wrappings, is very brief. Joseph Wayne
leaves his revered father in Vermont to
seek land of his own in California. The
father dies shortly afterward, but Joseph
communes with him through a tree. His
brothers come to California and take up
homesteads adjacent to him. Joseph woos

and wins the school teacher Elizabeth, who bears him a child. Life moves on rhythmically at the ranch. A great fiesta is given. All is well. Then Benjy is killed in the arms of a jealous Mexican's wife and a whole chain of disaster follows.

This is a symbolical novel conceived in mysticism and dedicated to the soil. To this reviewer it is little more than a curious hodgepodge of vague moods and irrelevant meanings. It cannot be said to be successful even of its kind. It treads dangerous ground without a touch of that sureness and strength which characterize the very few good works of its order in modern times. The elements of realism and symbolism fail to cohere and it oversteps all the bounds of convincingness even on the mystic plane. *To a God Unknown* is a novel which attempts too much; and by any standard it achieves too little.

"Shorter Notices."
Nation, 137
(18 October 1933), 456.

This book reads like a novelized version of a Robinson Jeffers poem, and its setting is what may be known to tourists of the future as the "Robinson Jeffers country." It is the story of a Yankee Abraham who has emigrated to California and who, in obedience to the voice of his God which is the earth and the fulness thereof, sacrifices his wife and ultimately himself on the altar of fertility. In the bas-relief of a poem, where much is taken for granted, the characterization of the story might have been adequate, but in a novel, which demands treatment in the round, it is pitifully thin and shadowy and invalidates the most ambitious effects of the book.

C.S.
"To a God Unknown."
Saturday Review, 10
(28 October 1933), 224.

A novel such as this one prompts us to speculate as to how much there is really left in the pantheistic view of the world for writers in twentieth-century America. Steinbeck's is not the only novel dedicated "to a god unknown." His is unusual, and curious, because it serves to evoke, not one god, but a great many—almost every mysterious power, one is tempted to say, from Pan to the Freudian Unconscious.

To a God Unknown is a mystical and symbolical tale. Its characters worship nature, fear certain stones, offer sacrifices to trees, talk to the spirits of their fathers, suffer defeat and death at the hands of mysterious powers, and in general show their dependence upon an unseen Will. The fact that the characters are given American names and a New England ancestry (the story is laid in California a hundred years ago) does not alter its essential nature. The difficulty is that the particular gods the author is striving to evoke are not given names or their images even approximate outlines.

Joseph Wayne migrated to California from a New England farm, settled on a piece of land in the valley of "Nuestra Sonora," and brought his family to form a colony. Soon after Joseph's arrival, his father's spirit—so Joseph believes—enters a large tree under which his house is built. Joseph turns to the tree for inspiration and guidance, talks to it and offers sacrifices to it.

A stone in a nearby grove he also feels to have a mysterious power. From it rushes a stream—the last to dry up when drought strikes and the homestead is deserted. On this rock Joseph's wife falls and is killed, and here he ends his own life. "I am the land, and I am the rain." He has always felt himself to be the source of all life on the farm. And, sure enough, the rain pelts down just as he expires, to make the land fertile again.

The book is full of worship—worship of the sun, the land, nature, the sexual act. And yet, curiously enough, it is almost entirely without religious feeling. It does paint a fairly interesting and (apparently) accurate picture of the region and the life of the times. Steinbeck can do the genre novel if he tries. We hope he can find a more stable and definite principle upon which to build his next novel.

"To a God Unknown." New Republic, 77 (20 December 1933), 178.

It is a surprise to find Mr. Steinbeck leaping from the sharp characterization of his first book to mystic symbols of nature worship. He writes of his principal character with the fervor of a faithful apostle. Joseph had no creed, no desire to be remembered; above such human emotional indulgences as pain and sorrow, he lived like a man who, having Nature for a mistress, was willing to go through any straits to satisfy and please her. Nothing disturbed his passion except sterility, and, when that came to him in the form of a drought that ruined his lands, Joseph stretched himself on the rock which symbolized his worship and cut open his veins, exchanging his life for the life of the soil.

"To a God Unknown." Forum, 90 (November 1933), viii.

. . . If Mr. Steinbeck were not an unusually powerful and poetic writer this novel would seem as grossly implausible as by rights it should. The story of an earth-mystic from Vermont who went a-pioneering in old California, it has an uncanny, half-mad atmosphere which somehow binds the reader with its spell. Those who like the book at all will probably like it a lot. . . .

H[arold] B[righouse]. "Pan in California." Manchester *Guardian*, 27 March 1935, p. 7.

California's lonely valleys and giant redwoods of all but fabulous age are plausibly a haunt of Pan. Neither that nor the Indian name is given to the pastoral god who darkly moves the people of the Wayne ranch, but behind these passionate pages there is the ancient and mystical spirit of fecundity. It is two years since Mr. Steinbeck published *The Pastures of Heaven*, and there is internal besides the external evidence of deliberation in his second book. We do not deny that the Wayne brothers reach elemental bigness, but Mr. Steinbeck's earnest seeking for the terse and telling phrase has some disconcerting results. "The red wine sang," "the tyres cried on the rocks," and when Elizabeth thought "If only he had the body of a horse I might love him more" we remembered Gilbert, who almost wrote that the meaning doesn't matter if it's only idle chatter of a D. H. Lawrence kind. This is, however, a novel built to a climax. At that climax, dealing with drought, Joseph Wayne sacrifices his own blood to the rain god, and we are unconscious of absurdity. It is action for which Mr. Steinbeck's character-drawing of Joseph has prepared us; it is a poet-novelist's victory over common sense.

V. S. Pritchett. "Fiction." *Spectator* [England], 154 (5 April 1935), 580.

. . . Mr. Steinbeck . . . is a good descriptive writer. He can describe the California land, its richness and fertility, its torrential rains, its scaly droughts with a warm, vivid and simple poetic gravity. He can suggest the pagan past immanent in the hidden forests. His Vermont farmers who go west to open up this splendid land are plain men and women well drawn, and he has the right touch of realistic humour in dealing with the Mexican hangers-on. He is so clearly a far better novelist than most, and for this reason, will stand much more serious criticism, while one picks out a few conventional words of praise for his more saleable made-to-measure contemporaries. This is one of the injustices of reviewing, and if I were a reader I should always put down on my library list the book on which the reviewer has spent time, space and spleen in pulling to pieces. Now for Mr. Steinbeck's crime. Fundamentally, it arises from a failure to understand that there is a difference between truth expressible in poetry and truth expressible in the novel. His chief character, Joseph, loves the land. He feels a deep, mystical kinship with it. He worships its increase, he *feels* it as part of himself and as part of his patriarchal father whose momentous nature he inherits; he loves with the land and suffers with it. Thus, he performs all kinds of primitive acts. He talks to the tree, calling it "sir," and because he sees in it his Abraham-like father; he does odd things with bits of calfskin; he visits a forgotten pagan altar-stone on which—at the end of the book—he makes a literal blood-sacrifice of himself in order to break the drought which has skinned the land clean. The story of Joseph is one of a man with a mysterious intuition, who is gradually absorbed into a cult which Christianity had silenced. It is not an impossible theme for a novel, but the trouble is that we are painfully aware of Mr. Steinbeck, text-book in hand, telling Joseph what to do next. The cult is not truly ancient: it is a revival. And when Joseph marries a schoolmistress and drives home with her across the mountains, there ensues a dialogue which is D. H. Lawrence at his symbolic worst:

"'. . . and there are times when the people and the hills and the earth, all, everything except the stars, are ones, and the love of them all is strong like a sadness.'

"'. . . Not the stars, then?'

"'. . . No, never the stars. The stars are always strangers—sometimes evil, but always strangers. Smell the sage, Elizabeth. It's good to be getting home.'"

Joseph has walked out of the Old Testament *via* Vermont to become a gigantic piece of half baked mysticism. The hiatus between idea and living man becomes more and more distressing. The result is poetry gone flat. It is a pity because Mr. Steinbeck's grasp of the scene is masterly.

"Fiction."
Times Literary Supplement [London], 11 April 1935, p. 236.

"*To a God Unknown* will remind the reader inevitably of D. H. Lawrence"— so runs the wrapper. The novel is unlikely to do anything of the kind, though it may well depress and perhaps annoy the person whose respect for Lawrence's work is a matter of genuine literary taste. Here the tale is of a farmer in California at the beginning of the century who had thoughts about the mating of man and the earth. Joseph Wayne would observe his animals from time to time, whisper to trees, bend down and kiss the ground, and so on. Sometimes he would express poetic ideas about lust and fertility and God and creation. When after a time he began to think about marriage a young schoolmistress named Elizabeth, who had some knowledge of algebra, chose to tremble in his presence. Eventually he married her, after which she inconsiderably slipped on a rock in a forest glade and broke her neck, whereupon Joseph severed the veins in his wrists, hoping that his death would somehow put an end to the drought.

The author could make better use of his abilities. There is no harm in borrowing a habit of mind from somebody else, but the unfortunate thing here is that what is borrowed is not merely unbecoming to the author but presents an appearance of marked artistic falsity. The "literary" conversation of these farming people about imponderable things is, in fact, like the invocation of mystery in the description of bulls and trees and hills and rocks, of the kind best described as shy-making. However, there are occasional passages of straightforward narrative that may be read with interest.

"New Books."
London *Mercury*, 32 (June 1935), 196.

Drought in California gives an American writer the motive for an earthy novel. Its hero is an ancestor-worshipper and has an over-developed sense of fecundity; also, after converse with an old man who kills something at every sunset, a belief in blood-sacrifice; when the drought comes he sends his cattle to distant pastures and himself remains to barter his blood for rain. Mr. Steinbeck has talent but not the genius required to make his paganism acceptable. But his descriptions of the drought are impressive.

TORTILLA FLAT

TORTILLA FLAT

By John Steinbeck

Illustrated by Ruth Gannett

Covici · Friede · PUBLISHERS · New York

Harry Hansen.
"The First Reader."
New York *World-Telegram*, 28 May 1935, p. 23.

I was having a perfectly grand time leaning back in my chair and laughing at the devices of Pablo and Pilon to get wine for themselves in *Tortilla Flat* when Miss Marx said, casually, "You know the *Russian Revolution*, by Chamberlin, is ready Tuesday, don't you?"

"Listen," I said, "Pablo and Pilon are two good-for-nothing wine guzzlers, mixed breeds, in a part of Monterey, Cal., that you don't care a rap about, but they are drinking to each other's health, and John Steinbeck, who writes the book, says this is what follows:—

"Two gallons is a great deal of wine, even for two paisanos—Spiritually the jugs may be graduated thus:—Just below the shoulder of the first bottle, serious and concentrated conversation. Two inches farther down, sweetly sad memory. Three inches more, thoughts of old and satisfactory loves. An inch, thoughts of old and bitter loves. Bottom of the first jug, general and undirected sadness.

"Shoulder of the second jug, black, unholy despondency. Two fingers down, a song of death or longing. A thumb, every other song each one knows. The graduations stop here, for the trail splits and there is no certainty. From this point on anything can happen."

I looked at Miss Marx, and she said, "You do know that the Ru*ssian Revolution*, by William Henry Chamberlin, is published tomorrow?"

"What, again?" I said.

"In two volumes," she said, with what I take to be a look of malicious mischief.

"It will have to wait," I said. "You know what life was like last week. Four volumes of Pareto, and even if I didn't read them through I did that other unpardonable thing for reviewers—I continued reading in them after writing my review. Two volumes of the life of William Booth—a grand book, by the way, but two volumes. Don't you think I should be allowed to review a few thin pamphlets for a change?"

So I went back to Tortilla Flat, which happens to be the name of the place where the backwash of Monterey, Cal., lives. Danny, the chief character, is a *paisano*, a "mixture of Spanish, Indian, Mexican and assorted Caucasian bloods." A *paisano* has lived in California for a hundred or two years. He speaks English with a *paisano* accent and Spanish with a *paisano* accent. We shall have to get Professor Louise Pound to make some talking machine records of *paisano* accents.

Since the behavior of Danny and his friends is rather low-life, the things they do are not for a conference of clergymen. Danny served in the war; so did the others, and Big Joe Portagee was six months late getting his discharge because he had been sentenced to the hoosegow for striking the sergeant with a kerosene can and stealing two gallons of cooked beans. Theft was a familiar way of getting what they wanted; when Pablo and Pilon couldn't lift a few articles they adopted deceit, and Tortilla, the Italian, and various women were victims of their devices.

Big Joe Portagee had done entirely too much shoveling while in the army to be interested in Pilon's desire to look for buried treasure—he "abhorred the whole principle of shoveling." But Pilon had the naive belief, shared with other residents of Tortilla Flat, that you are apt to come upon buried treasure on St. Andrew's

Eve. After a night of wandering among the pines, cautiously avoiding other forms that moved in and out among the trees on the same errand—some of whom might be the shades of the folk who had buried the treasure—Pilon and Big Joe dug up a square block of concrete with a metal plate on top of it. It was a marker sunk by the United States Geodetic Survey.

"Maybe we can take this good piece of metal and sell it," said the Portagee.

"Johnny Pom-pom found one," said Pilon sadly. "Johnny took the metal piece and tried to sell it. It is a year in jail to dig one of these up and two thousand dollar fine."

The characters of *Tortilla Flat* belong to the immortal band of vagabonds who romp through the books of all nations, combining a childlike belief with cunning and never profiting very much by their knavery. These are twilight stories, that never get into good company, that repeat anecdotes one has heard told about other louts in other localities.

In the end the author gets Danny roaring drunk and lands him at the bottom of the gulch, with injuries from which he never recovers, so that Danny becomes a legendary hero of Tortilla Flat, a fellow with enormous vinous capacity. He has realized Danny only partially, for the story skips back and forth between Danny and his cronies, and the tragic end of Danny seems a trifle too casual to be moving.

John Steinbeck, the author, is a native of Salinas, Cal., and 32 years old. He lives at Pacific Grove, between Monterey and Carmel, Cal. After he attended Stanford University he worked as rancher, painter and carpenter's helper, then came east and worked as a day laborer on the Madison Square Garden, then building. This is similar to the career of William Saroyan, who worked his way east a number of years

ago and became a teletype operator for a telegraph company near the Washington Market. Steinbeck has written some effective short stories, and one of them we republished in the "O. Henry Prize Stories for 1934." It was called "The Murder" and had a singularly effective ending. *Tortilla Flat* has been illustrated with drawings by Ruth Gannett. . . .

Joseph Henry Jackson. "A Bookman's Notebook." San Francisco *Chronicle*, 28 May 1935, p. 16.

This is a story of California's own Monterey, but not the kind of story you think it is.

It is no tale of the fading glories of old Spain, nor yet a tale of pioneer days in California; it is a story of today, and of a handful of *paisanos* who have, all in all, a pretty good time. What is a *paisano*? Let Mr. Steinbeck answer that himself: "He is a mixture of Spanish, Indian, Mexican and assorted Caucasian bloods. His ancestors have lived in California for a hundred or two years. He speaks English with a *paisano* accent and Spanish with a *paisano* accent. He is a *paisano*, and he lives in that uphill district in the town of Monterey known as Tortilla Flat, although it isn't a flat at all."

These, then, are the people about whom Mr. Steinbeck has written this completely charming little book. Specifically, he has written about four of them—Danny, Pilon, Pablo and Big Joe Portagee, who together form the Athos-Porthos-Aramis-and-D'Artagnan combination of Tortilla Flat.

Danny had grown up in Tortilla Flat, but he hadn't been much of a figure in the little community's life until after he came back from driving mules in Texas for the duration of the war.

When he returned, he found that he was an heir and an owner of property, no less. The *viejo*—that is, his grandfather—had died and left him two small houses on Tortilla Flat. Danny bought a gallon of red wine and went to look at the property. It wasn't long before his three friends had rallied round him. One house Danny took for himself as was his right. The other he rented to Pablo, Pilon and Big Joe. That they paid no rent was a minor detail. They were his friends, and they shared what they had with him, which was chiefly wine. Even when they burned down the house and moved in with Danny, it was all right. There was too much responsibility about owning two houses anyway.

After their move, the Tortilla Flat Musketeers grew even closer friends.

Whatever one did was a matter for all. There was the adventure of The Pirate, for instance; they were together on that, even to the extent of lending The Pirate their best clothes when it came time for him to go to the church and see with his own eyes the golden candlestick that was his vow dedicated by Father Ramon to the service of San Francisco. There was the time, too, that Danny gave the vacuum cleaner to Dolores Ramirez as a present. Dona Ramirez's house had no electric wires, but the cleaner was a present nevertheless, and a fine one, and it got Danny the lady's favors. But, though it was well enough to have Danny fooling with the ladies, too much was too much. The remaining three friends got Danny out of that by their wisdom and shrewdness, and afterward Danny was glad.

They stuck together, also, on another memorable occasion—when Teresina Cortez and his steps-and-stairs family were in danger of starving. It must never be said that Danny and Pilon and Pablo and Big Joe couldn't remedy so simple a situation as that. And there was a minor crime wave in Monterey; but nobody ever discovered who was to blame for the sacks of beans that vanished from the warehouse. Nobody ever discovered, either, which of the four had fathered Teresina's new baby. But that was not, after all, important.

Such a fine life, with a real house to live in and wine almost all the time, cannot go on forever; such things do not happen.

And that was true in this case. The four had had their day when Fate took a hand and removed Danny. That was the end of it, and it is the end of Mr. Steinbeck's book. But the day had been a good one, and it had lasted long enough to furnish the materials of this saga, for which the reader may be thankful.

The trouble with a book like this is that you can't describe it. The best you can do is to indicate it—faintly, in the sketch book manner, at best leaving out all the intangibles that really give it its quality. I can't reflect the charm, the humor, the pathos, the wit and wisdom and warm humanity which illuminate every one of Mr. Steinbeck's pages. If I could, I should be writing just the same kind of book. But I can at least urge you to read *Tortilla Flat*. Don't, please, miss it. Simple as it is, it has in it all the elements that go to make the best stories. And unless you are a very dour person indeed you will relish it as you have very few books in your experience.

Lewis Gannett.
"Books and Things."
New York *Herald
Tribune*, 29 May 1935,
p. 17.

Danny of Tortilla Flat behind Monterey was undoubtedly what settlement workers would call an anti-social character; and so were his friends, Pilon and Pablo, and Big Joe Portagee and Jesus Maria Corcoran. But they were among the most lovable men whom I have met for many a day; and in his book about them, *Tortilla Flat* . . ., John Steinbeck has fulfilled that promise which some of us so enthusiastically discerned three years ago in his *Pastures of Heaven*. . . .

Tortilla Flat is full of such engaging and moral legends. It includes also the stories of the Pirate who, with his five dogs, gathered pitchwood in the forest and hid his earnings in the sand; and of a little Mexican corporal who, also, for a time, lived in Danny's house, where the windows were never washed because, as Pilon pointed out, if the windows were clear the light would be better and then they would be tempted to stay indoors instead of going out into the fresh air; and of that final party for Danny which the entire Flat still remembers with reverence. But I shall not spoil the Danny saga by repeating more of it.

Mr. Steinbeck is an artist; and he tells the stories of these lovable thieves and adulterers with a gentle and poetic purity of heart and of prose that reminds one of Robert Nathan's lovely *One More Spring*. I like *Tortilla Flat*, and I do not think that I am prejudiced in its favor merely because I lived with Danny for two months before I read the book, while Ruth Gannett was drawing pictures to illustrate it. John Steinbeck is a born writing man, and *Tortilla Flat* a book to cherish. . . .

William Rose Benét.
"Affectionate Bravos."
Saturday Review, 12
(1 June 1935), 12.

This is young Mr. Steinbeck's fourth novel, but I believe he is prouder of the fact that when he left after helping build the New Madison Square Garden, Red Mike Flaherty, his foreman, told him he "had the makin's of a dom fine laborer." He is another of those writers who have held all sorts of jobs and roamed about. And he's been writing since the age of twelve. Hence it wasn't hard for him to get to know the real Monterey, California; the Monterey the tourists never guess. I've been there myself and seen a little of it, including—years ago—the late Jules Simoneau, who used to be a friend of Robert Louis Stevenson. But I never got to know the *paisanos*, whose "ancestors have lived in California for a hundred or two years." Their speech either in English or Spanish, Mr. Steinbeck tells us, has a peculiar *paisano* accent. Tortilla Flat is their stamping ground, and is in the "uphill district above the town of Monterey."

There lived Danny, and there gathered Danny's Round Table, like the knights of old—with a few differences. This tale of Danny and his *paisano* friends is full of gusto and humor. It is a short novel into which is packed a lot, and incidentally it is perfectly illustrated by Ruth Gannett.

The innocent guile of these *amigos* is all too touching. They are utterly without morals or scruples and yet they are pious and of an almost overwhelming kindliness of spirit. It takes so little to disperse their sense of obligation, and how they can dispose of gallons of wine! They are a Robin Hood's band without any organization save that dictated by their slyness. They live off the country and each other and never by any chance pay the rent. After three of the friends returned from the Great War it all began by Danny finding himself an heir, actually with two whole houses on his hands. Unto himself he added his friend, Pilon, and soon Pilon and Pablo and Jesus Maria were living in Danny's other house. Finally came catastrophe. Then Danny and Pablo and Pilon and Jesus Maria were all living in Danny's own house. And so it goes with wistful abandon, with deliciously demure comment upon these pleasant scoundrels.

The flavor of this book is something new; the setting and the people carry thorough conviction; and the extraordinary humors of these curiously childlike natives are presented with a masterly touch. These silly bravos are always about to do something nice for each other, their hearts are soft and easily touched; and yet almost absentmindedly they live with atrocious disregard for scruple. To have so presented them and made their story sometimes almost hysterically funny is no slight achievement.

Fanny Butcher.
"Is This a Best Seller?"
Chicago *Daily Tribune*,
1 June 1935, p. 14.

Tortilla Flat is a novel which . . . may well find itself on the best seller lists. It is rather a series of episodes than a novel in the strict sense of a novel's being a record of the development of character in adverse or propitious circumstances.

The heroes of *Tortilla Flat* are all like Pilon and Pablo, who "sat under a pink rose of Castile in Torrelli's yard, and quietly drank wine and let the afternoon grow on them as gradually as hair grows." They have a great many adventures of the flesh, but they are as unchanged as the California sunshine when the last page is ended.

The chief character is Danny, who finds himself the heir of two tumbledown houses on a hillside in Monterey. His "friends" gather about him in the same carefree fashion that he and they gather their sustenance. They take what is needful from whatever source offers itself. They beg or steal food, achieve wine with amazing and amusing frequency, and have a blood brotherliness that is as simple—and as complicated—as Robert's *Rules of Order*.

Their rules of friendship are as stern as a senator's rules, but their actions would give even a senator a laugh. Their economics are as simple as the law of supply and demand: the supply is there, they provide the demand and take what they need.

They are all sons of nature, and their complete lack of accepted morality, their childlike acceptance of the sunshine and the joys of wine and women is an emulsion of the vinegar of reality and the oil of romance, a luscious dressing for a fantastic tale. There are parts of it that sound like Robert Nathan, other parts that sound like Jim Tully, and it's not like anything else.

Harriet Colby.
"The Allies of Tortilla Flat."
New York *Herald Tribune*, 2 June 1935, "Books" section, p. 4.

"It is good to have friends," said Danny. "How lonely it is in the world if there are no friends to sit with one and to share one's grappa." Thus Danny sums up the philosophy acquired during a lifetime of doing nothing and doing it thoroughly and extensively.

Danny and his friends are *paisanos* of the seaside town of Monterey, California. And *paisanos*, Mr. Steinbeck explains, are a blend of Spanish, Indian, Mexican and assorted Caucasian bloods. It is perhaps this mixture which makes them at once so nebulous and so alive; they are beings from another and more benign world who still maintain the best qualities of this one. Robust and loving ghosts, they wind themselves round you and disarm you, and the more firmly you are entrenched in order and respectability the more difficult you will find it to resist them.

When the *viejo* died, Danny, returning from Texas where he had been breaking mules for America for the duration of the war, found that he had inherited the two small houses on Tortilla Flat—an ideal community where, without benefit of economic planning, nobody works and everybody has a superb time simply by being irresponsible. But Danny was somewhat floored by being a landowner—until one night he met Pilon, coming along the road with a bottle of brandy. Now Pilon was a realist and he solved Danny's problem by renting the smaller of the two houses for $15 a month—a sum which existed only in Pilon's mind and had a very fragile existence even there.

For a while it looked as if this vulgar business arrangement was going to interfere with Pilon's friendship for Danny. Once or twice Pilon earned a dollar or two cleaning fish, but somehow on his way to give it to Danny his higher nature always conquered and he bought wine instead. "It is better so," he thought. "If I give him hard money, it does not express how warmly I feel toward my friend. But a present, now. And I will tell him the two gallons cost $5." But even so Pilon worried a good deal about the rent, so it was a relief to him to come upon Pablo lying in a ditch. He brought Pablo back to the house on Tortilla Flat and charged him $15 a month rent, and everybody was happy, because now Pilon could say that he couldn't pay till Pablo paid.

And so the curious little brotherhood grew, with Danny always its soul and its center. Pablo and Pilon were joined by Jesus Maria Corcoran, that "pathway for the humanities," and when Pilon's house caught fire and burned down entirely, they moved in with Danny. Then Pilon began to worry about the Pirate, because God had not given the Pirate all the brain he should have and because the Pirate lived all alone in a henhouse with his five dogs—Enrique, Pajarito the curly, Rudolph the American dog, Fluff the pug, and Señor Alec Thompson, who "seemed to be a kind of an Airedale." Pilon had also observed that the Pirate was very skillful at getting food from the backdoors of restaurants and that he earned 25 cents a day selling pitchwood. Since he never spent any money Pilon's active business sense leaped to the conclusion that [the] Pirate must have a secret hoard. And this made Pilon and his friends wan with anxiety, because they felt that some black-hearted knave might rob the Pirate of his treasure. So the Pirate also came to live at Danny's house where he could be protected, and where a corner of the living room was marked off with a piece of blue chalk for him and the five dogs. And Big Joe Portagee came too, and peace and sweetness reigned at Danny's house—except that Big Joe caused a good deal of trouble by having no more sense at all.

Gradually Danny's house became a kind of symbol, a stronghold, a last outpost of charity and compassion. Together the friends drank wine and told stories. The amorous irresponsibilities of the lively Cornelia Ruiz—to whom only two things ever happened: "Love and fighting"—were an endless fount of philosophical conversation. Mrs. Torrelli, wife of the bootlegger, could always be betrayed into parting with a gallon or two of wine in exchange for a worthless object; and Mrs. Morales' chickens had the fortunate habit of straying into Danny's yard through a gap in the hedge which the kindly Pilon had provided because he felt sorry for them scratching all the time in the bare dirt of their own chicken yard.

But suddenly the friends began to perceive that something was wrong with Danny. He began to brood and to grow restless; a great lethargy descended upon him. For awhile he disappeared entirely and the only inkling his friends had of his whereabouts were the ravages he committed and the mischief he got into. Then one day he came back, but he wasn't the same Danny As a last resort the friends decided to give a party—a real party, with "music and wine and chicken." It was a party to end all parties and to this day it is remembered and talked about in Tortilla Flat. For Danny it was both an end and a beginning, for it was on this night that Danny entered into godhead.

How, and with what alarums and excursions, the miracle, if it was a miracle, was accomplished, must not be mocked with words.

It is perhaps fitting that Danny should be the vaguest, the most difficult to define, of Mr. Steinbeck's company of loyal waifs. Little John is more memorable than Robin Hood, Lancelot than King Arthur; a god lives in the devotion of his followers. Pilon, that moralist, that St. Paul among Danny's disciples, runs away with the story. An adept at flushing a whole covey of birds with one stone, he is never so satisfied as when cooking up extravagantly good motives for some outrage, and drawing a profound and useless moral lesson into the bargain.

But to attempt to pin down Danny's friends and analyze them is by their very nature impossible. There is no generalization into which they can be made to fit without losing the very qualities which make them beguiling. Lionhearted and yet mild as milk, devious as quicksilver yet innocent as babes, they defy description. It takes the wondering gentleness, the wide-eyed and extremely skillful naïveté, the clear precision of Mr. Steinbeck's writing—as well as the blend of tender formality and sudden billingsgate which is their language—to give them their special life and sharpness. They will make you laugh very hard—but as Jesus Maria says, "there is another kind of laughing . . . when you open your mouth to laugh, something like a hand squeezes your heart."

Fred T. Marsh.
"Life in a California
Shantytown."
*New York Times Book
Review*, 84
(2 June 1935), 5.

Tortilla Flat is the tumbledown section of the town of Monterey in California. Here live the *paisanos*, a mixed race of Spanish, Indian, Mexican and assorted Caucasian bloods. In Mr. Steinbeck's humorous and whimsical tale they appear as a gentle race of sun-loving, heavy wine-drinking, anti-social loafers and hoodlums who work only when necessity demands and generally live by a succession of devious stratagems more or less outside the law. *Tortilla Flat* is not as sad and gentle a story as *Mrs. Wiggs of the Cabbage Patch*. It is not as raucous in its humor nor as grim in its realism as *Tobacco Road* or *God's Little Acre*. It is not as whimsical and pathetic as *One More Spring*. It comes closer, perhaps, to the novels that deal in a spirit of charm and amused sympathy with the manners and vagaries of Southern Negroes.

Mr. Steinbeck writes with affection about the group that gradually accumulates in Danny's house, the little wooden shack set in a weedy yard and half hidden by straggling pines. "The paisanos," he says, "are clean of commercialism, free of the complicated system of American business, and, having nothing that can be stolen, exploited or mortgaged, that system has not attacked them very vigorously."

Danny and his friends, most of them, did not have even a house in the early days. But Danny came back from the war to learn that his grandfather had died and left him two houses up in Tortilla Flat. The news is too much for Danny, who gets gloriously drunk, smashes a few windows and winds up in jail. Jail is a pleasant place to rest in for a few days, especially since Tito Ralph, the keeper, is an old friend. But it becomes boring after a while. So one night when he goes out with Tito to drink wine at the Torrellis he decides not to return but to go up and inspect his new property, already becoming a burden and a responsibility on his hitherto carefree soul.

On the way he runs into his old friend Pilon, Pilon the realist and the contriver. Taking possession of the first house is a thrill and Pilon decides that he, too, should become a man of property. After some dickering he strikes a bargain with Danny to rent the second house for fifteen dollars a month. The fact that Pilon has never had fifteen dollars in cash at one time in his life is forgotten in the excitement of the moment. But once Pilon is established the burden rests on his spirit. So he takes in Pablo, who is to pay him fifteen dollars a month, thus passing on the weight of his responsibility and easing his conscience.

But Pablo has no money either. And Danny, who is taking an interest in Mrs. Morales, the widow lady of substance next door, begins to hint for some money. So Pablo and Pilon rescue Jesus Maria Corcoran, a good man, from his bed in a ditch by the roadside and pass the burden on to him. All three are relieved when the little shack burns down. They have done their best. Now they can all go to live in Danny's house free of responsibility.

The further adventures of the friends in their daily search for free food and a dollar or two with which to buy wine continues through the story, interrupted by occasional flashes of drama and love making. But the policy of taking new members into their community in the hope of solving the financial problem is for the most part a mistake. In desperation they lure The Pirate, a poor half-wit of the town, from his chicken house where he had lived happily many years with his five dogs. They know The Pirate earns twenty-five cents a day collecting and selling pitch and never spends any of it, since he begs from the back doors of restaurants enough food for himself and his dogs. But when the innocent Pirate brings out his hoard, over a thousand quarters, and tells them how he is saving to buy a candlestick for St. Francis, who had spared one of his dogs from death, the brotherhood mournfully resign themselves to protecting The Pirate's money as their own.

Mr. Steinbeck tells a number of first-rate stories in his history of Danny's house. He has a gift for drollery and for turning Spanish talk and phrases into a gently mocking English. The book is as consistently amusing, we think, as *February Hill*. But we doubt if life in Tortilla Flat is as insouciant and pleasant and amusing as Mr. Steinbeck has made it seem.

Ella Winter.
"Sketching the Author of *Tortilla Flat*."
San Francisco *Chronicle*, 2 June 1935, Section D, p. 4.

John Steinbeck, whose charming story, *Tortilla Flat*, was published last week, does not like publicity. He likes it so little that his publisher knows practically noth-

ing about him. The following story about him is the first appearance in print of any details of his life. . . .

Down out of the hills he came, he said; he felt as if he had somehow always lived in them. And John Steinbeck looks as if he might have; of giant height, sun-burned, with fair hair and fair moustache, and eyes the blue of the Pacific on a sunny day, and a deep, quiet, slow voice. He belongs to this Coast, the Monterey bay, the ranges and cliffs of the Big Sur country. His father was born and lived most of his life in Salinas where he remained a public official—County Treasurer—for many years. He has just died. His mother taught in the tiny red school house of the Big Sur 60 years ago.

He reminds one of Robinson Jeffers immediately; his height, his blue eyes, his slow talk, his entwinement with the hills and stones, canyons and people of this strange coast. He has never met Jeffers; he hardly dares to because "his poetry is perfect to me, and I don't think one should get the man mixed up with his work. I have tried hard to get myself out of my own books, and I think I have just about succeeded now."

His first books, *The Pastures of Heaven* and *To a God Unknown*, are about ranch people and the almost mystic love of land they nurse; *Tortilla Flat*, just published, is a charmingly roguish story of the *paisanos*—native Californians whose ancestry includes native and American strains who live in the wooden-shacked "slums" above the old sea town and drink and laze and philosophize and do good and evil joyously as the days pass by. It is humorous, as his first books are not; but humour with a wise, light, almost wistful touch. One can't imagine Steinbeck either coarse, or clumsy any more than one can imagine him hard, sophisticated or smart in the modern manner.

Steinbeck was born in Florida and lived there till his seventh or eighth year and then came West. Two of his sisters are much older than John; one was brought up with him. He went to Stanford off and on for eight years, but was only happy there when they accepted that he wasn't anxious for a degree and wanted to study only what interested him. Then they let him be.

He has been about a good bit; twice to New York, where he worked on a newspaper and got fired because he couldn't report facts, but only the poetry or philosophy he saw in the facts; where he helped carry bricks for the building of Madison Square Garden; where he worked as chemist, painter's apprentice, laborer. He has lived at Lake Tahoe, where he took care of an estate in the silent, snow-bound winter. His father, who wanted him to have all the chances he didn't have, gave his son a tiny pittance.

For some years now he has done nothing but write. John lives with his wife in a tiny dark brown frame house surrounded by many other brown and white and yellow frame houses, in a little dirt lane in Pacific Grove; the house is mostly hidden by honeysuckle and other creeping vines. Steinbeck's tall, black-haired and soft-voiced wife, Carol, who is from San Jose, comes out on the little porch to talk enthusiastically of John's work and their funny runaway marriage five years ago in Los Angeles and her historical research in the SERA [State Emergency Relief Association] in Monterey, and their boating on the bay. They have just bought Neil Weston's self-made launch—Edward Weston's son—for Neil is going to Japan on an old windjammer. Whenever they can, the Steinbecks go out in it and fish and sail. The fish are a valuable addition—or rather subtraction—from their budget, for they have been living for a long while on $25 a month.

Steinbeck reads little fiction although he likes the writers who had leisure to think about what they really thought. He likes Thackeray, for instance, but he doesn't like Proust "because Proust was sick, he wrote his sickness and I don't like sick writing."

He doesn't seem to think you can explain much in words. "Everything is nonsense," he says. "We are on the verge of a new age, but how can anyone tell what it will be till it's here? And so everything anyone talks or writes or says is just nonsense." (This is very much Robinson Jeffers' attitude.) Steinbeck loves to read physics and philosophy and biology, however. "The biologists are on the verge of new discoveries that make a new world outlook." His blue eyes with their black pin-point pupils look far out, through you and the walls of the room and the eucalyptus and cypress hedge, way out over Point Lobos and those "possessed" hills and the ocean. Much of the time you feel he is divining something outside and beyond the mere earthly creatures sitting there and talking plain practical words.

He doesn't like publicity and he doesn't like photographs and he doesn't like personal fuss, not as a pose, but because they do you damage; get you in the way of your work; and because they seem so unimportant compared to the life in the hills out of which he came.

Gladys Hoover.
"In Monterey."
San Jose [Calif.] *Mercury-Herald*, 7 June 1935,
p. 12.

A novel whose scene could be laid only in an old Spanish-California town is *Tortilla Flat*, an amusing story about the tumble-down colony of people of mixed races inhabiting a certain region on the fringe of Monterey.

The happy-go-lucky folk who dwell in this California shanty-town are of mixed blood, Latin strains with Mexican, Spanish and Portuguese predominating, with here and there strains of American Indian intermingling with the others. Life is greatly enjoyed by these *paisanos* as long as they do not have to work for a living, and with a skill that approaches the miraculous they manage to eat, love, and drink with seldom an hour's labor to their discredit! For when one of the colony is seen working the news is quickly spread abroad—something portentous in the air, for only dire necessity can reduce them to such a plight!

The story centers around Danny, who had aided his country in the World War by breaking army mules in Texas, and then returned to Monterey to find to his amazement that he had inherited two shanties from his grandfather. Such wealth was too much to contemplate, but aided by his friends he found a way to ease the burden somewhat.

The incredible and frankly-described adventures attributed to these dark-skinned men and women are described by Mr. Steinbeck in a highly amusing way that relieves a shocked reader at times when he needs some sort of mental protection. There is no effort to make the reader feel that these people should be reformed or the community "cleaned up," physically or morally, but it is merely a well-written and entertaining narrative about those who might live in another world so untouched are they by American principles and ideals. The story is skillfully written. . . .

"Wine: Steinbeck Outlines the Spiritual Graduations of a Jug."
Newsweek, 6
(8 June 1935), 40.

"Two gallons is a great deal of wine, even for two paisanos. . . .

"Spiritually the jugs may be graduated thus: Just below the shoulder of the first bottle, serious and concentrated conversation. Two inches farther down, sweetly sad memory. . . . Shoulder of the second jug, black, unholy despondency. Two fingers down, a song of death or longing. A thumb, every other song each one knows.

"The graduations stop here, for the trail splits and there is no certainty."

Most of *Tortilla Flat* takes off where the wine trail splits. The *paisano* protagonists—part Spanish, part Indian, part Mexican, part Caucasian hoboes in Monterey, Calif.—see to that.

Each "claims pure Spanish blood and rolls up his sleeve to show that the soft inside of his arm is nearly white." Each does nothing—except as it may become necessary to steal food and wine, woo corpulent country housekeepers, or hunt, on St. Andrew's Eve, for fabulous buried treasure. This quest results in discovery of a United States Geodetic Survey marker. But it can't be sold; its removal would mean one year in jail and a $2,000 fine.

Danny, the chief character, inherits two shacks. He occupies one and rents the other to his buddy, Pilon, for $15. Where can Pilon find $15? He takes in a boarder at that figure. Neither has, or pays, a cent. Their consciences rest more easily after the shack burns down. Then comes along Jesus Maria Corcoran with a genial smile and $3. He, Pilon, and the ex-boarder get drunk and move in with Danny.

In this volume, earnest readers will find no new light on race problems, the younger generation, or class struggle. But those seeking leisurely entertainment will enjoy a good tale spiced with wine-song and scandalous chatter.

At various times the 32-year-old Californian author has turned his hand to chemistry, carpentry, ranching, house painting, and newspaper reporting. Once he took the job of overseeing an estate on Lake Tahoe, high up in the Sierras. He passed one Winter there, alone and snowbound. From that experience, he says, he emerged a "compassionate writer."

Helen Neville. "Aristocrats without Money." Nation, 140 (19 June 1935), 720.

The subject matter of *Tortilla Flat*—five men living by their wits on the thin edge of society—is surely grim enough, but Mr. Steinbeck's approach to it is wholly in the light-hearted, fantastic tradition; it suggests such novels as *Vile Bodies* and *South Wind*. Yet it is an approach somewhat justified by the temperament of the characters who manage to preserve, in the midst of their various vicissitudes, an equanimity comparable to the author's own.

Economically, these five *paisanos* living in a squalid section of Monterey, in Southern California, may occupy one of the most desperate positions in the social scheme, but in their aristocratic immunity to the problems of such a position they deserve to rank with those gay and moneyed bohemians whom we encounter in the novels of Evelyn Waugh. Such necessities as rent and food scarcely seem to trouble them; as long as they can "lift" an occasional jug of wine, or enough money to pay for one, they are completely happy. The rent problem is permanently solved when Danny, the hero, falls heir to two houses, in one of which he installs his friend Pilon. Pilon agrees to pay him fifteen dollars a month—an agreement which neither party takes very seriously, since both know that whatever money flows in Pilon's direction is sure to be spent on wine. After a night of revelry Pilon's house burns down; and he and the two friends whom he has invited to join him go to live in Danny's house, where the question of rent has not even a nominal significance. The question of food is permanently settled when they annex to their clan a genial half-wit, practiced in the art of procuring hand-outs from back kitchens. All these situations are handled in the spirit of farce—a spirit with which the men themselves would seem to be in perfect agreement. Only Danny succumbs, somewhat unconvincingly, to a fit of despair, but neither this nor his suicide, to which it ultimately leads, supplies a tragic note; they are merely occasions for getting drunk in his honor and singing bawdy songs.

Mr. Steinbeck's attempt to impose a

mood of urbane and charming gaiety upon a subject which is perpetually at variance with it is graceful enough, but the odds are against him. The traditional "smart" novel—such as *Tortilla Flat* aims to be—generally deals with a stratum of society with which such a mood is wholly consistent; in doing so, it avoids a certain confusion. The theme of such a novel as *Vile Bodies* was, of course, that of utter futility; but it was the kind of futility which lent itself inevitably to satire or farce, and each of its situations, no matter how absurd or impossible it might be, was entirely convincing, since it never seemed to yield implications other than those which the author had found in it. The futility in *Tortilla Flat* is of quite a different order; its situations are rife with possibilities which, despite the amount of indifference to them manifested by Mr. Steinbeck and his characters, it is not always easy to ignore.

Joseph Henry Jackson. "A Bookman's Notebook." San Francisco *Chronicle*, 22 June 1935, p. 8.

San Francisco: John Steinbeck's *Tortilla Flat* is meeting with an extraordinary fine reception here and elsewhere. Something about his carefree, wine-bibbing, lazy *paisanos*, comfortable and happy in their ramshackle house in Monterey, has caught the fancy of the public and people are going around asking their friends if they've read *Tortilla Flat* yet. Which, of course, is the very best of all kinds of advertising for a book or anything else.

Speaking of that book, *The Nation*, in

its current issue, has a most interesting review of it—interesting because it reflects so plainly the weakness of that too, too earnest little periodical's attitude toward all fiction.

The reviewer makes the error of placing Monterey in "Southern California"; that, of course, is excusable enough in a New Yorker who hasn't been out here. But that isn't the point I want to make. What amused me was the evident irritation of the reviewer at Mr. Steinbeck's failure to draw a moral from his story. Here are five men, "living by their wits on the thin edge of society," as the reviewer puts it (never mind the fact that they prefer to live that way, as Mr. Steinbeck makes plain). And here is Mr. Steinbeck; totally ignoring the social implications of this sad state of things. Such a situation, *The Nation*'s reviewer believes, "is surely grim enough." Yet Mr. Steinbeck thinks it is funny. And he has been and gone and written a book whose "situations are rife with possibilities which, despite the amount of indifference to them manifested by Mr. Steinbeck, and his characters, it is not always easy to ignore."

Apparently the characters of the story are just as bad as the author, too. Poor fellows, they also are indifferent. Living "on the thin edge of society" (by implication because of our present faulty social and economic setup), they just don't seem to care. Instead of raising the dickens about the capitalistic regime or something, they just go on drinking another gallon of wine and having a fine time. And they utterly refuse—as does their creator—to realize that they are rife as rife can be with "possibilities."

It is too bad of them, of course. And it's too bad of Mr. Steinbeck not to have made his book a tract on the weaknesses of our present social order. Here was his chance and he muffed it. He might have written a fine sermon, and all he did was to write a funny story.

There, in a nutshell, is the precise weakness of which I spoke a moment ago. Why is it impossible for the reviewer whose major interest in life is the class struggle (which is his or her own affair, naturally) to consider a book, written around some totally different theme, excepting from the class-struggle viewpoint? Why must King Charles' head keep popping into the discussion?—if that reference isn't too old-fashioned for the moderns. Why must a review of so simple an affair as Mr. Steinbeck's *Tortilla Flat*, for instance, exercise itself about the author's "failure" to do something he never wanted to do in the first place? Why, in short, bother?

There is no use laboring the point, of course. But I have made it here because this particular review is so good an example of a critical viewpoint that has been widespread in the past few years. From this view Keats was simply wasting his time and the reader's when he wrote "On Looking Into Chapman's Homer." Think of *Huckleberry Finn*, too; there was a book "rife with possibilities," if you like, what with Huck's "grim situation on the thin edge of society" and all. How could Mark Twain have let pass such a chance to drive home a lesson?

You see the absurdities into which such a view leads you. Yet it is precisely the view deliberately chosen by a large group of critics who would have the ordinary reader believe that no book or play or any work of art at all can be considered a work of art unless it (a) concerns itself with the class struggle, and (b) puts forward the particular opinions regarding that struggle with which these critics are in sympathy. No; it doesn't make good sense. But that's the way they'd have it.

There are, of course, plenty other tests by which to determine a novel's worth. You will have no trouble finding them. But the most important is the single question: "Has the author done well the things he set out to do?" If you can answer that question satisfactorily then you have the best yardstick of all for the measuring of fiction.

In *Tortilla Flat* Mr. Steinbeck has done just what he tried to do, and done it delightfully. Moreover (since Mr. Steinbeck, by all accounts, is a bright enough young man), it is altogether likely that he was quite aware of the "possibilities" in his subject, but had the good sense to see that this was the place of all places to ignore them. In which case he deserves, not a patronizing sneer from a reviewer afflicted with the class itch, but the congratulations of readers who also realize that there are times and places for everything.

Jerre Mangione. "Under the Round Table." *New Republic*, 83 (17 July 1935), 285.

Not since the days of W. W. Jacobs, making his charming characters out of scoundrels, has there been a book quite like this one. Both Jacobs and Steinbeck must have worked on the assumption that most of us, having a slice or two of Caspar Milquetoast in our systems or a streak that calls for out and out anarchy, are likely to revel in the antics of anyone getting away with what he shouldn't. The *paisanos* of Tortilla Flat get away with a great deal in their tireless efforts to supply their gullets with red wine. They are a mixture of Spanish, Indian, Mexican and assorted Caucasian bloods. A sunny-eyed, unmoral lot, with invisible means of support, their paganism is chiefly expressed in their disreputable ways and means of acquiring wine.

The incidents that make up the book are based on this driving force and revolve around Danny and friends, who live in Danny's house, drinking enough wine to tell their stories, chase their women, and beat the daylights out of each other when the spirit moves them. Despite their free and easy lives these knights from under the round table have a sense of philanthropy and will steal any day to help a friend in need. Mr. Steinbeck knows the humorous side of his *paisanos*, and if he has emphasized their eccentricities to the point of burlesquing them, he can be excused on the grounds that he rarely fails to be amusing. When he isn't amusing it is either because he is trying too hard to eulogize a philosophy of life that is as dust-laden as your copy of the *Rubaiyat*, or because he lets his nature worship display itself too much. Mr. Steinbeck's pantheism, much more prominent in his other books than in this one, often confuses the effect of his otherwise fine narrative manner.

"Latest Fiction."
Saturday Review [England], 160 (23 November 1935), 501.

... A novel of unusual type, but distinguished for its delightfully facile style and the whimsical humour underlying its sharp and clear-cut presentation of char-

acter, is John Steinbeck's *Tortilla Flat....* It deals with a company of lovable, unmoral people belonging to a race of Californian cross-breeds and is one of the most entertaining books I have recently read....

William Plomer.
"Fiction."
Spectator [England], 155 (6 December 1935), 960.

... It is time ... Heinemann granted a long, long holiday to their gushing blurb-writer, whose fond lucubrations are calculated to put any intelligent reader off even opening the novels of Mr. Steinbeck.... *Tortilla Flat* suggests that the brutal and laconic tone of so much contemporary American fiction may be only an inversion of an inordinate sentimentality. Writing of a pack of vagabond *paisanos*, people of mixed blood inhabiting a suburb of Monterey, idle, drunken, dishonest and promiscuous, Mr. Steinbeck lays himself out to make them appear wholly humorous and lovable. He exploits with ingenuity and talent the sentimental appeal of vagabondage, companionship in drink, simple-mindedness, crime altruistically committed, dogs, and funerals. His brand of humour, surprisingly broad in one small instance, is mostly that of the comic strip—wriggling one's toes to keep the flies off them, stealing from people who are asleep, hunting for non-existent treasure, snoring, and so on—and has resulted in a fairy-tale for grown-ups. The book may make a wet afternoon wetter for its readers, as their "droppings of warm tears" alternate with sly chuckles at the winsome knaveries of

45

these gangsters or groupsters, Danny, Pilon, Pablo, the Pirate, and Big Joe, to say nothing of the ladies. . . .

"On Monkey Hill."
Times Literary Supplement [London], 21 December 1935, p. 877.

Tortilla Flat is the district in Monterey where the *paisano* has his being. The *paisano* claims to be pure Spaniard, and but for the numerous other elements in his blood he would be. He and his kind appear to be in the community of Monterey but not of it. We come to think of the Flat as Monkey Hill at the Zoo in its zenith, and of Mr. John Steinbeck as a broadcaster describing it with genial irony and now and then dropping a hint that care-free poverty is a desirable state.

Peering over the rails, Mr. Steinbeck announces to his public what the denizens are at and discloses their affinities with it. Their appetites are much the same though less complicated, but with no secret made about them. They help themselves to whatever they can lay hands on, including members of the opposite sex, and it is these raids which are the subject of the broadcast. Wine flows in gallons through the Flat, and it is that rather than money which is its currency. So far we might be having yet another modern satire. But that is not what we are given. The meanest of Mr. Steinbeck's creatures "boasts two soul sides" and the *paisano* boasts a moral side with tears in his cups. He does not, we infer, recognize obligations to people outside the railings of Monkey Hill, but he proclaims himself incapable of doing an injury to a friend. If he surreptitiously removes a friend's blanket and sells it for wine, that is because he knows that what the friend really needs is cheering up, and he gives him—or at any rate proposes to give him—some of the wine.

The central figure is Danny. On the death of his grandfather Danny found himself possessed of a house in Tortilla Flat—a house with a bed in it. By degrees there come to lodge with Danny some half-dozen friends, and it is of these friends and their contributions to the housekeeping that Mr. Steinbeck discourses. They are all individualized, and if we give "the Pirate" precedence it is for the soul-side reserved for his friends. The charitable gave him scraps for his five adored dogs, and on these he lived himself. But he worked at wood-cutting an hour a day. Why? The friends reckoned he must have a buried hoard; and they tried every dodge to find it—not for themselves, of course, but to lay out the idle money in the Pirate's interest. At last the simple Pirate brought the undiscoverable hoard to them himself, because, knowing that he had been followed, he thought it would be safer among the friends. That made things difficult; what made them impossible was that when one of the dogs was ill the Pirate, who had no use for money himself, had vowed a gold candlestick to St. Francis if the dog recovered. And it had recovered. Hence the hour's work and the hoard. St. Francis got his candlestick.

Checklist of Additional Reviews

Wilbur Needham. "Quietly Uproarious Novel Reveals Humble Lives." Los Angeles *Times*, 19 May 1935, Part 2, p. 6.

John Chamberlain. "Books of the Times." New York *Times*, 28 May 1935, p. 23.

Joseph Henry Jackson. "A Bookman's Notebook." San Francisco *Chronicle*, 1 June 1935, p. 8.

Theodore Smith. "John Steinbeck Scores Hit in Creating *Tortilla Flat*." San Francisco *News*, 28 June 1935, p. 7.

Charles Raymond Krank. "They Were Valiants All." Brooklyn *Citizen*, 5 August 1935, p. 16.

IN DUBIOUS BATTLE

IN
DUBIOUS
BATTLE

BY JOHN STEINBECK

New York

COVICI · FRIEDE

Publishers

Joseph Henry Jackson. "*Tortilla Flat* Author Produces Proletarian Novel of Sound Worth." San Francisco *Chronicle*, 1 January 1936, Section D, p. 4.

One of the pleasant successes of last year's fiction crop was a very amusing yarn called *Tortilla Flat*, a story of a handful of carefree ragged edgers living in California's Monterey and getting along however they might, provided only that they had enough money or could develop enough schemes to get hold of a jug of wine sufficiently often. It was a gay, tenderly written little tale and it found thousands of admirers. People, indeed, went around telling other people they simply must read it, which in the end is the way best sellers are made.

Now, in this new novel, John Steinbeck has done something totally different; something as startling in its way (at least to those whose acquaintance with the author is limited to *Tortilla Flat*) as though, say, P. G. Wodehouse should have written *Germinal*. This *In Dubious Battle* is just as little like its immediate predecessor as you could very well imagine. It is a story of men on the thin edge of society, to be sure, but men who are workers rather than charming loafers, men who have to labor but want a fair return for the work they do. It is, in fact, a "proletarian novel," and a better one than most that advertise themselves as such.

Mr. Steinbeck has chosen as his central figure not so much an individual as a working principle. The hero of his book is really The Strike. Naturally he needs an individual on whom he may hang his story; his character, Jim Nolan, serves that purpose.

You meet Jim at an important moment in his life. He has made up his mind that the system has kicked him around long enough. His father was killed by a riot gun. His mother had died because she just didn't want to live any more; life had dealt too harshly with her. Jim himself had been a shipping clerk until one night he had stopped to hear a speaker in The Square. The speech had wound up in a riot and Jim, an innocent bystander, had been slugged and dumped into jail. He had tried to explain about it after he woke up. The police called his boss on the telephone. When they said he had been picked up at a "radical meeting" the boss said he had never heard of him. That was the last straw. Jim was through with the system. He would join the Party; that is, he would if they would have him. They took him and decided to train him for "field work."

His first experience in the field, as helper to a man trained in up-to-date Party methods is what makes this story. For Jim was put to work immediately with McLeod who knew the game.

Down in the apple country 2000 fruit tramps had gathered to handle the crop. The Grower's Association had waited until the pickers arrived; then they announced a pay cut. Their attitude was that since most of the pickers had to have some kind of work at any price at all, in order to keep alive, much less move on to the next crop, they would have to take the cut. There was nothing they could do about it.

That was what Mac and Jim were working to stop. It was a tremendously difficult task. Fired by Party principles, they knew what they had to do—or at least Mac did. But they had to do it blindly. They ran the chance, almost a certainty it was, that they would be hated as cordially by the pickers as by the growers. A few pickers, maybe, would be for a strike, would be glad to have the man among them who knew how to organize. But when the shoe began to pinch, they would turn tail. They would forget principles and tomorrow and hate the man who had persuaded them to demand fair play. Nine out [of] 10 of them would take any pay they could get, in order to get away and move on. It wouldn't occur to them that if the Grower's Association succeeded in the pay cut, the growers in the next valley or in control of the next crop would follow suit.

Mac knew that he and Jim were up against this situation. But he was able to think about tomorrow, next year, the next 20 years. Not all the time; sometimes he got mad. But mostly he could bring his mind back to the principle of the thing. That was why he was such a good organizer and why Jim was sent out with him to train.

And Mr. Steinbeck's novel is the story, seen from inside, of how the strike was promoted, how it flared up, almost died, was stimulated again by the skill and strength of the man called Mac, of the methods the growers used to combat it—the whole story as it has happened again and again, not only in California but almost anywhere you like to mention.

It isn't an argument, this book; at any rate, it isn't consciously an argument. Mr. Steinbeck sits aloof as far as he can; tells the story from the mountain top looking down—though with a very powerful pair of field glasses, I should say. Just the same, it is the kind of book that should do much to make the ordinary, decently liberal citizen see two sides of the labor question.

Steinbeck is just as willing to show his reader the brutalities of the strikers as he is to show them the brutalities of the so-called "Citizens' Vigilante Committee," made up, as he very shrewdly points out, of "a bunch of fool shoe clerks and the American Legion boys trying to pretend they aren't middle aged." Certainly Legionaires may not like that description of themselves; but some of them have earned it, whether it applies to all or not. He is out to show both sides, and only a stupidly reactionary reader will be unwilling to admit that the "vigilance" idea has almost as much blood on its head—and hands—as the strike idea.

A great many people will not like what he is saying here, of course. The reader who belongs to the let-'em-eat-cake school will consider Mr. Steinbeck's eminently just presentation nothing less than subversive, wicked and revolutionary; I can see such readers—the vigilante boys who went out and broke windows and heads on no more evidence than an anonymous letter dropped into the lion's mouth—positively sweating in their haste to get Steinbeck nominated for inclusion in Mrs. Dilling's "Red Network."

But those readers may as well calm themselves. Because a good many out-and-out communists aren't going to like the book any better than they will. Plenty of extreme leftists are going to go into nice little rages at Steinbeck's failure to make his book a fine hot argument for their cause. They are going to feel very badly because Jim Nolan's first effort to serve the Party ends in his death, and because the strike he helped foment doesn't in the book prove a great success, set the growers back on their heels, and prove the match that touches off the blaze of better days for labor. They're not going to like this, either: Says Dr. Burton to Mac, "You people have an idea that if you can once establish a thing, the job'll be done. Nothing stops, Mac. If you were able to put an idea into effect tomorrow, it would start changing right away. Establish a commune and the same gradual flux will continue." Especially they won't care about this paragraph, in which Dr. Burton, on-the-fencer, expresses very much what Mr. Steinbeck himself seems to feel: "I just want to see it, Mac. I[t] might be like this: When group-man wants to move he makes a standard, 'God wills we recapture the Holy Land'; or he says, 'We fight to make the world safe for democracy'; or he says, 'We will wipe out social injustice with communism.' But the group doesn't care about the Holy Land or democracy or communism. Maybe the group simply wants to move, to fight, and uses those words simply to reassure the brains of individual men. I say, it might be like that, Mac." No; the enthusiast battling for a new social order under communism or any other banner, won't care for anything as mild as that. And he'll be disappointed in Mr. Steinbeck because he doesn't shout and wave his arms and emit war cries.

However, the reader who absorbs *In Dubious Battle* intelligently will find out these things for himself. It remains only to say that it is a splendidly written, excellently conceived and executed novel. Mr. Steinbeck writes, as always, with strength and beauty. If you find that, after 200 pages or so of magnificently realistic writing (poetically realistic writing, if you'll allow the description) he goes a trifle mystical; well, if he sees the thing that way, then that's the way he sees it. His conception, for example, of the mob, the crowd, as "not men, but a different kind of animal" is thoroughly sound. His observation, put into Mac's mouth, that "Guy after guy gets knocked into our side by a cop's nightstick" makes such good sense that it's a wonder the men who line up against labor don't see it, for

their own sakes. But in the latter half of the book, Jim Nolan gets beyond me in precisely the degree that Mr. Steinbeck makes him get beyond himself. I can't follow him quite to that exalted level to which the author raises him. I can't feel him as all genuine, for instance, when he talks about pulling the bandage off his wounded head in order to stir up the men with the sight of blood. But it may be my fault.

However, there is no question about the quality of the book as a whole. Mr Steinbeck, as I've already said, has written a better proletarian novel than most of those that claim that distinction. He has also written a far better novel.

John Chamberlain. "Books of the Times." New York *Times*, 28 January 1936, p. 17.

Last year John Steinbeck wrote *Tortilla Flat*, a sunny book about some amoral, wine-guzzling vagabonds who lived, philandered and roistered without benefit of money or clergy in the more poverty-stricken section of Monterey, California. Reviewers promptly compared Mr. Steinbeck with Victoria Lincoln and Robert Nathan, and the best-seller lists each week have continued to testify to Mr. Steinbeck's hold on the capacious American heart. But if readers expect to get a succession of warmly whimsical and humorous stories from Mr. Steinbeck, they are in for a rude surprise. For Mr. Steinbeck's *In Dubious Battle* is a grim thing, wildly exciting at times, but with no trace of the sweet gentleness of *Tortilla Flat*. Certainly the publication of *In*

Dubious Battle marks Mr. Steinbeck as the most versatile master of narrative now writing in the United States.

In Dubious Battle is another strike novel. But it is not just another strike novel. Every one has read about vigilantes and broken heads and "Reds" in the fruit-growing districts of California, and most liberal Americans have bewailed the situation as evidence that fascism can come delivered to us with a sunkist label. Mr. Steinbeck's novel is about a strike in the California apple country. It is somewhat disconcerting to me, as an ex-fruit tramp who once packed oranges in Claremont and Lindsay, to be told that California raises apples in a valley that is next door to cotton country, but we can let that pass. The situation which Mr. Steinbeck describes would have been essentially the same if he had chosen a more specifically Californian product. It is the strike and how the fruit-tramps and the top dogs of the Torgas Valley respond to it, that is the important thing here.

Most strike novels tell about the growing political consciousness of the workers. They show us typical groups being roused by the education of events to drastic decisions, and many of these books have ended on the note of solidarity forever. Mr. Steinbeck's book concentrates more on the problems that face labor leadership, and it differs from more orthodox Left novels in showing us how a strike disintegrates in a spot that has been previously organized to the hilt by the owning class. Two men dominate *In Dubious Battle*. They are Mac, an experienced Communist organizer, and Jim Nolan, an apprentice. When Nolan, the disciple, has just had the elements of leadership ground into him, he is ambushed and killed by vigilantes. There is no "Red dawn" on the final page of *In Dubious Battle*, for the fight is like the one which raged on the plains of Heaven in Milton's *Paradise Lost*, with Satan ultimately relinquishing the field and retaining only his "unconquerable will . . . and the courage never to submit or yield."

Last Spring I read *In Dubious Battle* in manuscript for Pat Covici. He had had a Communist read the manuscript, and the Communist had reported that Mr. Steinbeck had the "party line" all wrong. Mac, Mr. Steinbeck's Red organizer, is a cool proposition who works toward one end alone: that of increasing working class intransigence in the United States. He doesn't like to see individuals hurt, but he is willing to sacrifice individuals for the end involved, just as a general is willing to sacrifice soldiers to capture a salient. To Mac, the working stiffs of the Torgas Valley are just so much revolutionary clay. If he can help things along by a good deed, such as is depicted in the marvelously dramatic scene where he pretends to be a doctor and successfully delivers Lisa, London's daughter, of a child, then Mac will gladly do a good deed. But Mac is even willing to lose the apple strike if the fight will only serve to prevent the cotton growers from cutting their wages over in the next valley. He is willing to let one man be busted over the head if the blow will only serve to make the onlookers into radicals.

Mr. Covici's Communist reader objected that Mac was Mr. Heart's idea of a Red, one who is always fishing in troubled waters. And Mr. Covici's Communist reader may be right. For all I know, Mac may be a complete caricature of a Red. Maybe a real Communist leader in the California fruit country would stress immediate demands; maybe he would be unwilling to use individuals in the way Mac used Al, the lunch-wagon proprietor, or Al's father, who owned a small apple orchard. (Vigilantes smash Al's wagon and Al's face, and Al's father loses his picked crop when vigilantes fire his barn.) But, as a lay reader, all I could report to Mr. Covici was that Mr. Steinbeck had written a dramatic and stirring book.

Call it fantasy if you like. Call it Communist propaganda, or call it subtle anti-Communist propaganda. The point is that *In Dubious Battle* is a wildly stirring story. It is stirring in the way Liam O'Flaherty's *The Informer* is stirring, as a "melodrama of the conscience." Jim Nolan joins the Communist party because "he wants to feel good" again. He has seen his father beaten by life; he has seen the apathy grow on his mother's face. His sister has disappeared, probably to wind up as a prostitute. And Jim decides that he doesn't want to be "gnawed to death" by life. He wants to sink himself into a movement that is larger than himself. And Mac's movement seems to him to offer a way out of his psychological impasse.

As the publishers say, John Steinbeck is only "secondarily an observer of the class struggle." His interest is in the dramatic confrontations which the Torgas Valley presents. As an acute master of characterization, Mr. Steinbeck is at home in showing how different individuals respond to a given situation. Dick, the good-looking Red who collects money from the "sympathizers"; Al, the little lunch-wagon man; London, the natural leader of the fruit tramps; Lisa, the young mother; Dakin, who loved his shiny green Chevrolet truck; Sam, who burns Hunter's house; Doc Burton, who loves mankind, but who doesn't think the "class war" will ever be settled; Bolter, who wanted to compromise the strike— these, and scores more, live vividly in the pages of *In Dubious Battle*.

They may, quite possibly, live vividly in relation to inconceivable polarizers in the persons of Mac and Jim Nolan. Earl Browder and William Z. Forster will

have to say the final word on that. But, whatever the truth about the "line" in *In Dubious Battle*, it is undeniable that Mr. Steinbeck has written a novel that is as exciting as *Tortilla Flat* was genuinely warming. As a thinker, Mr. Steinbeck may be crazy; as a dramatic artist, he is as brilliant as he is versatile.

R.W.S.
"Hard Punching Labor Trouble."
Boston *Evening Transcript*,
29 January 1936,
Section 3, p. 2.

Proletariat novels are, as a general rule, rather cagily written opuses tactfully designed to interest, but not shock, possible converts in the capitalistic fold and, at the same time, appropriately hearten the "comrades." This technique has culminated in nauseating extremists on both sides, showing only the very dubious profit of throwing the borderline pink groups into a pretty dither of class-consciousness. Since the pinks are not particularly admired by anybody but themselves, a stigma looms over this type of literature.

John Steinbeck definitely ends all this shilly-shallying. *In Dubious Battle* merits many adjectives, but "frightening" would be all inclusive. It will cause the solid bourgeois to gulp and roll his eyes. Teacups in pink parlors all over the land will quiver in terror. The rampant radicals alone will exult for at last a writer has arisen whose ability commands the services of reputable publishers, despite an uncompromising "don't give a damn" attitude. Steinbeck is a literary power to reckon with regardless of his affiliations—his writing is breathless, raw, and, if not superb, it is at least hypnotic.

In Dubious Battle is laid among the transient working class of California as was *Tortilla Flat*, Steinbeck's earlier success, but there the comparison ends for the latter was a picaresque whimsy that left all class-consciousness to the reader's deduction.

The apple pickers come to the California orchards in their usual shoe-string style. The owners, knowing their necessity, drop their hourly wage rate at the last minute. Disgruntled and unimaginatively sullen, they prepare to pick in order to eat.

The stage is perfectly set for Mac and Jim, the two party organizers who are, if the phrase is possible, the incredibly believable combination of brute and idealist. They reach the apple-pickers' camp just as Boss London's daughter is going through the unattended throes of childbirth. Seeing this priceless opportunity to gain their confidence, Mac takes charge and delivers the child with a common sense technique that works out happily. He is thenceforth called "Doc" by the grateful pickers even though he confesses to Jim that he had worked in abysmal ignorance of his next move, "but the chance was too good to miss." Their work must be furthered at any cost.

After this auspicious beginning, the workers are easily organized and the strike is called. A small farmer, who does not belong to the organized growers, is persuaded to give them a pasture to camp in. An authentic doctor, Burton, is imported by Mac to keep the camp on the legal side of the sanitary regulations. He is the book's most human character. In sympathy with no cause in particular, the gyrations of mankind fascinate him, and

their hurts touch him. He is one of a growing type—the courageous intellectual brave enough to sit on the fence and ask questions of both sides and quite aware of the futility of a cause such as Mac's.

There are a series of brutal clashes between the workers and the usual capitalistic weapons of scabs and police. This looks like failure to Jim, but Mac is quite content. "If they will only call out the militia," he prays, "and shoot a few men," then the strike will be a success because workers all over the country will hear of it, and be stirred regardless of the outcome of this piddling little affair. The powerful growers finally climax their persecution by burning the innocent farmer's barn with his entire crop. All Mac can find to say is "That's tough," but he does relax his disciplinary control just long enough to permit a like retaliation on the principal grower. He regrets this immediately because of the bad publicity. Jim, who has played the role of disciple, has an hour of genius in which he turns the tide of the strike towards success when Mac's iron nerve weakens. *In Dubious Battle* ends in an unsatisfactory manner— the strike is not settled, nor does it indicate a trend, and the lovable Doc Burton's mysterious disappearance remains entirely unexplained. The catastrophe of Jim's death is a climax of grimness that leaves the reader with a feeling of shock as real as the sight of the horrible accident.

William Rose Benét. "Apple Pickers' Strike." *Saturday Review*, 13 (1 February 1936), 10.

If anyone anticipates in this novel such characters as the rogue Mexicans of *Tor-*

tilla Flat, he will not find them. This is a proletarian novel, and, as it seems to me, one that handles its material with accuracy. Jim Nolan joins the Communist party and is set to work. "Mac" Mcleod takes him down into the apple country of California to organize the apple-pickers, where they are going to work for a drastically cut wage. Before long the occasion for a strike is found. How it is got going, the work of organizing it, the progress of it, and the interaction of the chief characters make a vivid and exciting story. I shall not retail the episodes of that story, as the novel is well worth reading.

For one thing the locale is excellently described, the characterization strong, the communist point of view and methods authentically presented, and the workers in mass or separately, both in their speech and their actions, are extremely real. The character of the doctor who is called in to see to the sanitation of the strikers' camp on Anderson's property is outstanding. Though a sympathizer, he is not a party member, and his depth of philosophy is not for men who are fighting for their bare existence as migratory workers.

The battle between those in authority and the strikers has plenty of bloody moments. The book ends with the fight still going on. The situation is given in all its aspects, and one feels that what did happen is just about what would have happened. Back of this immediate war looms the whole economic struggle of the day, but what we witness in the foreground is a single battle for one definite objective. In that desperate fight there is cruelty on both sides, there is the terrible side of the roused mass-animal. Though this book is on a smaller scale one is somewhat reminded of Frank Norris's *The Octopus* (not at all in style) by the vigorous realism of this presentation.

There is no place for humor in this book. The issue is too serious to those involved. The author's attempt has been to bring out heroic motive and action in those whom the newspapers denounce as "Reds," and at the same time to state events as they would naturally happen as logically and fairly as possible. This is a book one respects. Mr. Steinbeck writes most graphic prose and conveys the thought and speech of ordinary laborers with great ability. The idealism of Jim Nolan, both noble and tragic, pervades the story. The wavering of the men as a group, the tactics of their opponents, particularly the interview between Bolter, the new president of the Fruit Growers' Association of the valley, and London, the boss of the strikers,—these developments carry conviction. The language of the story is never handled with gloves. But here are no puppets of propaganda. Here are real men of flesh and blood.

"*In Dubious Battle*." *Literary Digest*, 121 (1 February 1936), 28.

The author of *Tortilla Flat* in this volume goes enthusiastically proletarian. His hero is a Communist; his big scene is the outbreak of violence among the striking apple-pickers in California. Propaganda fairly spouts from every chapter, but despite the author's fascination with the class struggle, at no time does he permit the theme to render his story dull.

As an experiment, *In Dubious Battle* is an interesting literary event in its own right. The author's loyalty to the tradition of story-telling should assure him a wider public than the run-of-the-mine labor novel which only too often goes astray in the mazes of political economy.

With a fine head for yarning, Mr. Steinbeck starts his young Communist off at organizing. The strike hits the district; the strikers set up a camp. The town at first is tolerant.

Day by day, however, the men become more determined and it can only be a question of time before an active clash between strikers and the authorities is bound to come. The manner in which it breaks out; how distrust enters camp along with failure of the food supply; how even men fighting for a living can be as mean and base as those in other stations, and how London and Mac got the bloodshed needed to stiffen the dwindling spirit of the men are best left to the author's telling.

As a tale of how the other half gets along—in the tramps' jungles, following the harvests, inarticulate, and its members not always sure in their own minds just what they desire—Mr. Steinbeck's novel reeks with power.

Joseph Henry Jackson. "A Bookman's Notebook." San Francisco *Chronicle*, 1 February 1936, p. 9.

San Francisco—A last minute notice from the publisher, Covici, Friede & Co., explains that John Steinbeck's new novel, *In Dubious Battle*, is delayed one week. Publication date is now February 3—next Monday.

While we're on the matter of Mr. Steinbeck, and particularly his new book, I should like to reprint here an editorial from the San Francisco *News*, which should make some conservatives think twice.

Here it is:

VIGILANTES

"John Steinbeck", the Salinas-Stanford-Pacific Grove lad who rang the bell with his *Tortilla Flat*, now publishes a novel of blood and iron taking one of California's orchard strikes for its theme and agitators for its chief characters.

"Neither conservatives nor radicals will be pleased with Steinbeck's *In Dubious Battle* because he stays above the conflict, calls the turn on both sides, and doubts the finality of the Utopian society on which radicals are intent. Some of his fruit pickers behave as outrageously as their oppressors. But how the boy can write! And he has one of his characters say something about vigilantes that is worth repeating:

"'Why, they're the dirtiest guys in any town. They're the same ones that burned the houses of old German people during the war. They're the same ones that lynch Negroes. They like to be cruel. They like to hurt people, and they always give it a nice name, patriotism or protecting the Constitution. The owners use 'em, tell 'em we have to protect the people against reds. You see, that lets them burn houses and torture and beat people with no danger. And that's all they want to do, anyway. They've got no guts; they'll only shoot from cover, or gang a man when they're 10 to 1. I guess they're about the worst scum in the world.'

"Said by the off-side Steinbeck, who is as far from being a red as a vigilante, that bites!"

No further comment should be necessary. Mr. Steinbeck said something that ached to be said, the *News* did its part in helping to spread it, and it is reprinted here for the same reason.

"Little Reviews."
Newsweek, 7
(1 February 1936), 44.

Last year John Steinbeck wrote *Tortilla Flat*, a novel of charm and humor. *In Dubious Battle* leaves charm far behind and plunges into a bloodthirsty strike.

Communist field workers, professional agitators, engineer a strike among the itinerant apple pickers in the Torgas Valley of California. A wage-cut has given a real grievance. But even without it, Jim and Mac want strikes to spread the class war, deepen the workers' sense of solidarity and hasten the revolution. Mr. Steinbeck tells his grim tale with brutal directness, sparing no gruesome details.

W[ilbur] N[eedham].
"California's Radicals."
Los Angeles *Times*,
2 February 1936, Part 3,
p. 4.

Readers who discovered John Steinbeck when *To a God Unknown* and *The Pastures of Heaven* appeared are due for a shock here; and those who knew him only when *Tortilla Flat* came amusingly forward to give him his deserved and long-delayed success, are not going to recognize him, either. The man is unpredictable; he never writes in the same way in any two novels, and he never uses the same emotional or intellectual points of view.

When Jim Nolan, tired of a life that offers him nothing and angry at being jailed for vagrancy, comes to Communist headquarters and joins the party, he does not know what lies before him. But he finds out, soon enough, when he and a labor organizer, McLeod, are ordered to the battle front in California apple orchards, where the migratory workers are enraged over wages being cut.

Writing brutally and frankly, shorn of the warmth and style he showed in two aspects in *Tortilla Flat* and *To a God Unknown*, Steinbeck has created a novel whose timeliness is only exceeded by the controversies it will arouse. Jim and Mac organize the workers and enter into a life of violence and bloodshed that leads only to failure of the strike. Steinbeck remains on the side lines and watches these men as they talk over theories and courses of action, as they rise to acts of appalling brutality.

Neither radicals nor reactionaries will like the book, for they will never be sure just where Steinbeck stands. And it will arouse a storm of protest because of the delicacy of the situation he has treated; because of the indelicacy he often displays in treating it.

Fred T. Marsh.
"*In Dubious Battle* and Other Recent Works of Fiction."
New York Times Book Review, 85
(2 February 1936), 7.

You may remember *Tortilla Flat*, Mr. Steinbeck's last novel, which described with genial gusto and gentle irony the picaresque adventures of a small group of Latin-American vagabonds in a California suburban slum. That was a gay, melancholy and charming book. It did for the lotus eaters of a bum's paradise what *Penrod* did for the small boys of the middle-class suburbs of pre-war days—described them accurately, wittily, ironically, engagingly, as they would appear to bustling outsiders nostalgic for the simple amoral life. You would never know that *In Dubious Battle* was by the same John Steinbeck if the publishers did not tell you so.

It seems to me one of the most courageous and desperately honest books that has appeared in a long time. It is also, both dramatically and realistically, the best labor and strike novel to come out of our contemporary economic and social unrest. It will alienate many of Steinbeck's readers, particularly in California, where *Tortilla Flat* headed the best-seller lists for weeks and where the new story is laid. But it is not cut to any orthodox, Communist or other pattern. It is such a novel as Sinclair Lewis at his best might have done had he gone on with his projected labor novel instead of turning to the far easier, although possibly no less valuable job of striking a blow against fascism.

Steinbeck keeps himself out of the book. There is no editorializing or direct propaganda. His purpose is to describe accurately and dramatize powerfully a small strike of migratory workers, guided by a veteran Communist organizer, in a California fruit valley. It is true the book is focused on strike headquarters—on the two Communist field workers, the little doctor who gives his services to the strikers but remains philosophically and ironically but sympathetically detached from the spirit of fervor, and the strikers' natural leaders, some of whom have no use for "Reds," but decide to strike in personal and group rebellion against what seems to them a double-cross on the part of the owners. But the arguments on the other side are also given, though not without the caustic commentaries and violent reactions of the workers and the ideological counter-arguments of their Communist mentors.

All the elements of such a strike are here. The concealed discontent and hostility emerged into the open. The party workers succeed in winning over the leaders to a program of united and effective action. A small fruit-grower, at odds with the powerful interests in the valley, is induced to give the men a camping-ground on his place. A doctor is imported to enforce sanitation and prevent the authorities from using the health laws as an excuse to oust the strikers. Bribes and promises are offered. Overtures are made and rejected. Scabs are imported and the strike enters the stage of violence.

First blood is drawn by "vigilantes," irresponsibles of the kind which short-sighted capitalists—knowing they cannot depend 100 per cent on the law, which, after all, is dependent on popular support—foster and encourage, sometimes getting more than they bargain for. Thousands of peaceful citizens in the valley, resentful against the domination of a "big three" owning group, sympathize with the strikers and supply them with food. The law wavers and tries to get rid of them peaceably before it turns against them. Violence results in counter-violence. The strikers are doomed. But to the irreconcilables they have won a moral victory, a minor victory on a broad front.

But his is a story of individuals as well as one of mass action and of mental and spiritual attitudes translated into action. Mac, the hard-boiled organizer; Jim, the new convert, intense and brooding and passionate; London, the born leader whom Mac and Jim succeed in winning over and putting at the head of the little army— these three principals are real men, who, like men in other fields of endeavor, lead both public and private lives; are plain human beings off guard and off duty, but something else again as leaders in a cause or a fight. Just so, the thousand or more men under them integrate and disintegrate, now an amorphous tangle of individuals and small groups, now an army, now a fanatic mob moving as one, fused into a single will, with double the strength of their numbers, only to dissolve again into helpless disorder. It is his extraordinarily effective and moving handling of these elements which makes Steinbeck's book not only a powerful labor novel of our times but a profound psychological novel of men and leadership and masses.

In Dubious Battle will not change the opinions of those already seated firmly in the saddle of their various faiths, opinions and prejudices. These strikers and their leaders and their arguments and actions will, however, win the admiration and sympathy of many middle-grounders. They will repel many others—just as do their prototypes in real life. It's an honest book, and it is also a swift-moving and exciting story.

Bernard Smith.
"John Steinbeck Comes of Age."
New York *Herald Tribune*,
2 February 1936,
"Books" section, p. 6.

John Steinbeck has written a proletarian novel: he tells here the story of a strike and of the making of a revolutionary, and he tells it from the standpoint of a radical sympathizer. That fact must be stated immediately and baldly in order to warn the readers of Mr. Steinbeck's previous book, *Tortilla Flat*, who thought it merely "another *February Hill*" and were "charmed" and "amused" by it and looked forward to another titillating novel by the same author. This book has neither humor, gayety nor gentleness; what it has are such painful emotional qualities as hatred and bitterness. And what it deals with are such painful physical entities as hunger, torture and death.

From the first page of cold, brief, yet strangely tense description of a lower-class rooming house to the last agonizing line of oratory, Mr. Steinbeck's narrative builds and mounts and at last soars. The dramatic movement has a cumulative power, the characters are vividly portrayed, and the dialogue is compact, natural, and in manner and flavor invariably true to type. All of this amounts to saying that Mr. Steinbeck is an artist, which he is. With material as inherently rich in sheer human interest as this, he could not help but produce a book capable of holding any but the most antagonistic reader.

But this is a story which is interesting for more reasons than that which arises out of the experiences of its characters. To begin with, it announces the enlistment of one of the most gifted writers of our younger generation into the ranks of the proletarian novelists. Mr. Steinbeck is no raw youngster coming to the radical movement to learn the elements of his craft. He comes as a mature, technically proficient writer, with a valid emotion and a remarkable intuitive understanding of people.

Another reason is what it indicates about the development of the author considered purely from the point of view of aesthetic achievement. It indicates that he has found himself, that he has integrated his sentiments with his observations and both with his art, and that there is now nothing to prevent him from doing something very big, perhaps even great. I can explain what I mean by referring to the faults of his two preceding novels, in one case a fault of conception, in the other a fault of structure. *To a God Unknown* (published in 1933) was architecturally sound, but weak and soppy inside. Invested with a beautiful feeling about the land—the soil and the things that come of it—and expressed sensitively and poetically, it petered out finally in a murky symbolism which suggested that the author was uneasy and unsure about his feelings concerning the relation of mankind to the terrible forces of nature. His search within himself led to a mystical paganism, which helped him not at all. But his next work, *Tortilla Flat*, proved that he was coming out of the clouds of introspection and landing on his feet. He was looking at men with his eyes wide open. Unfortunately, it proved also that he was seeing them in fragments, so to speak, for the book was not really a novel but a collection of character sketches and anecdotes. It lacked causality, growth and completion. In *In Dubious Battle*, however, it is clear that he has discovered a unifying idea, a vision, that enables him to see his characters whole and consistently in the light of reality. Here the drama never falters, the development and conclusion are logical and forceful, and there is no final surrender to symbolism.

Only one thing is still lacking: He has yet to make his vision so much a part of himself that his understanding of it is as near being instinctive as such things can be. If that sounds too literary, I can make it matter-of-fact by saying that he is not yet expert in his knowledge of the issues and processes which stir him so deeply. This reveals a curious situation. It was not very long ago that proletarian novels were usually written by men who were excellent students of economics and labor tactics, but indifferent writers. Now we are beginning to get proletarian novels by men who are excellent writers, but indifferent students of political theory. For example, there is the central character of Mr. Steinbeck's book. He is a labor organizer, member of a revolutionary party; he is brave and wise and magnetic, and he is consumed by a flaming devotion to his party and his ideals. But Mr. Steinbeck makes that man say things for which he could be expelled in disgrace from his party twenty times over. Specifically, this man displays a recklessness and a cold-blooded manipulation of violence which are romantic fictions of the author's imagination.

The truth is that Mr. Steinbeck is outside the movement about which he writes. His natural sympathies with the underdog together with the dramatic and heroic aspects of the revolutionary's life have aroused him to an artistic understanding of his subject, but they cannot give him a factual and intellectual understanding. It is to be hoped that further study of the grubbier everyday side of his material will subdue a little his Hemingwayish adoration of physical conflict.

We need not fear that such study will reduce the passion or impair the sensitiveness of his writing. Mr. Steinbeck is too much an artist to be sapped by his political and social investigations. He can absorb the latter and be the better for it; he is not likely to become simply a politician. The reader of this story cannot doubt that. Embodying innumerable complexities of emotion and thought, yet simple in method, courageously direct in appeal, and combining lucidity with strength in style, it could only have come from a man who possesses a completely disciplined craft, and that means more than the ability to put the right words together in the right sequence. Focusing the reader's attention upon the broad social drama—the welding together of a mob of migratory workers in the California apple region, into a communal fighting army—he is actually giving the reader an insight into the minds of rebels: the diverse but significantly related characters that emerge from the class struggle and the motives that make such men elect a cruel and dangerous life. The impersonal epic is there—the battles with the deputies and the vigilantes, the tumult of the picket-line, the last desperate stand against destruction—but with it goes the personal epic. And when it is all done you realize that the latter has permitted you to penetrate into the psychological sources of types of personality that are too little known in American literature. And you realize, too, that Mr. Steinbeck has achieved this with a minimum of effort, with a phrase here and a line of dialogue there, and that is why you must have faith in his future.

Harry Thornton Moore. "Though the Field Be Lost." *New Republic*, 86 (19 February 1936), 54.

Despite his preoccupation with localized atmosphere, John Steinbeck has always written of the common people as one of them, with an intense love of their simplicity and heartiness and what might in the best sense be called their vulgarity. His leading characters have been good earthy men who have lived life in the full. But they have gone down in some form of defeat. Now Steinbeck has identified his characters with the class struggle, and

although in the present novel they fight a battle whose outcome is dubious, they taste a promise of victory such as their predecessors have not known. It is a victory of integration for them and for their author as well; and the proletarian novelists have been reinforced by one of the ablest young writers in the country.

The foreground heroes of this story are two young agitators, an old hand and a greenhorn, who are controlling a strike of fruit-pickers. They are likable and always real. Besides the struggle of keeping the strike going against crushing odds, they have fierce internal conflicts between their momentary feelings and their devotion to the long view. And through them and beyond them runs the story of the background heroes, the migratory workers who have been practically dehumanized before the start of the story. You sense the strike awaking them, restoring their humanity: another thousand men have been aroused to resistance by the wholesale sadism of hired bullies, and even though this strike is lost, with some of the strikers brutally murdered, you know the others will carry on the fight on other fronts.

Steinbeck creates a marvelously living world here, very full and vivid. You get the feel of the whole place, the zombie-men coming to life, then all the tension of resentment and opposition—you sympathize strongly and want hard to participate. Many of the surrounding characters are done in the flat—all the strikers and all the opposition—but Jim and Mac are very good people and they take you with them. Their development (that of Jim especially) is interesting to watch, and the cool way they go after things. Steinbeck sees them, he sees all of his people, sympathetically; he has a great tenderness; and he goes whole-hog, pulling none of his punches.

In Dubious Battle cannot be dismissed

as a "propaganda" novel—it is another version of the eternal human fight against injustice. It is an especially good version, dramatically intense, beautifully written without being too literary for the subject matter, and its climaxes have a sweeping power. It is the real thing; it has a vigor of sheer story-telling that may sweep away many prejudices and win it the wide audience it deserves.

Mary McCarthy.
"Minority Report."
Nation, 142
(11 March 1936), 326–7.

The surface action of John Steinbeck's new book, which has already been acclaimed as a topnotch proletarian novel, moves about a strike in the California apple-picking country. A group of itinerant workers, dispirited and disorganized, are bullied, cajoled, and harangued by two Communist organizers into a sort of solidarity which enables them to fight a bitter battle for better wages and better conditions. The incidents of the strike are, of course, dramatic: murder, kidnapping, and arson scar its progress. Nevertheless, the novel which Mr. Steinbeck has woven about the events in Torgas Valley is, in an odd way, academic, wooden, inert. Mr. Steinbeck's novel is no strike drama but a kind of interior monologue on the part of the author about the technique of strikes in general. This interior monologue is not presented brazenly as such; rather, it is couched in the form of a Socratic dialogue between the two organizers—Mac, the elder, seasoned in party work, and Jim, the green recruit to the Communist Party, who is

being initiated into its methods. Other characters join the conversation with occasional observations of their own; of these, London, the itinerant worker, the natural leader of men, and Dr. Burton, the philosophic, disillusioned observer of men, have the most to say. Almost the whole novel is in dialogue form. The dramatic events, the small, separate climaxes of the strike, take place for the most part off stage, and are reported to the conversationalists, as in the Greek drama, by a breathless observer.

It is quite possible that a successful proletarian novel could be written according to this classic scheme; but I submit, in this minority report, that Mr. Steinbeck was not the man to write it. If a revolutionary general with a talent for prose—say Trotsky—had cast his reflections upon the technique of class warfare into the form of a novel, though they would fall more naturally, as did Caesar's, into the form of a memoir, the results might have been exciting. Caesar—and doubtless Trotsky—had something to say about the curious and wonderful behavior of embattled human beings; Mr. Steinbeck, for all his long and frequently pompous verbal exchanges, offers only a few, rather childish, often reiterated generalizations.

Mr. Steinbeck may be a natural story-teller; but he is certainly no philosopher, sociologist, or strike-tactician. Mr. Steinbeck, for instance, is interested in crowds. Men in a crowd, he declares over and over again, behave differently from men by themselves. How a crowd is different, why a crowd is different, he cannot say; he is content to assert at great length that a crowd likes the sight of a little blood, that a crowd is certainly different, and no more. That the legitimately dramatic incidents to the strike should be subordinated to such infantile verbalizations is unfortunate. The reader who is not allowed to see the vigilantes burning a barn or the kidnapping of Doc Burton, and who is not given adequate, intellectual compensation for the loss, has every right to be annoyed. In several unpretentious scenes Mr. Steinbeck shows how well he can report the behavior of men dealing with simple, material things. His picture of two men eating hamburgers, for example, gives a suggestion of what this strike novel might have been like had he confined himself to the facts and restrained himself from ponderous comment upon them. For the most part, however, the author and his characters remind one of those tedious persons who in the theater indefatigably chat through the climaxes of the play, and whose vocal efforts have nothing to recommend them but their loudness.

Peter Quennell.
"New Novels."
New Statesman and Nation [England], 11 (2 May 1936), 670.

. . . *In Dubious Battle* is the story of a strike. I did not enjoy Mr. Steinbeck's previous novel, *Tortilla Flat*; but his new book is one of the best novels of social conflict I have yet read. American proletarian literature is seldom digestible; but *In Dubious Battle* is a well-written and unpretentious story, all the more interesting because it lacks the usual touch of violent *parti pris*. This is an account of how two professional Communist agents go down to foment a strike among the Californian apple-pickers. They succeed; but the strike collapses for want of adequate financial backing; and Jim comes

to a violent and bloody end. Mr. Steinbeck gives us a convincing account of the two enthusiasts and of the feeling, half-romantic, that grows up between them.

William Plomer.
"Fiction."
Spectator [England], 156 (8 May 1936), 850.

. . . In *In Dubious Battle* is another book about revolutionary strife, in California this time. Mr. Steinbeck was the author of *Tortilla Flat*, an effort in the sentimental picaresque. His new novel is much better, and, although it is pretty plain where his sympathies lie, he cannot be accused of being too tendentious. After a large number of casual labourers have arrived in the apple-growing country to pick the crop, a cut in their wages is proposed. Two agitators, idealists both, make this the excuse for fomenting a strike. Are they successful? Yes and no, but as usual the cause is the thing.

> ". . . What though the field be lost?
> All is not lost—the unconquerable will,
> And study of revenge, immortal hate,
> And courage never to submit or yield:
> And what is else not to be overcome?"

The two agitators, Mac and Jim, are too single-minded, and the relationship between them somewhat sentimentalised, but this is a small defect in what might almost be called a story of adventure, exciting, well put together, full of pleasant

65

American dialogue, and vividly told—sometimes a little too vividly, as in the stress laid upon the physical signs of emotion, the tears of fury, the chest that shudders, the shoulders that "gradually widen," the necks that "take on a dangerous gleam," the flushes that "steal up the neck and out on the cheeks," so that these emotional creatures seem to be chameleons and contortionists. "Sometimes," says a non-red character, "I think you realists are the most sentimental people in the world." He is not altogether wrong, and we are not surprised to hear of a victim of the law that "there was a kind of ecstasy in him all the time, even when they beat him." Mr. Steinbeck is an inventive story-teller, and he knows something about mob psychology, whether among strikers or vigilantes, who "like to be cruel. They always give it a nice name—patriotism or protecting the constitution—that lets 'em burn houses and torture and beat people with no danger. . . ."

"Strike in California." *Times Literary Supplement* [London], 16 May 1936, pp. 417–18.

Mr. Steinbeck's work, we fancy, has not found particular mention as a contribution to America's new "proletarian literature," and it is probably better in fact that such labels should be avoided—better that *In Dubious Battle* should be recognized simply as one of the best "strike" novels (and there have been some good ones) published in recent years, and problems of specific sympathies and political alignments left wholly out of account. That its two leading, and most sympa-

thetic, characters are members of a "red" organization definitely setting out to engineer and direct a local strike among Californian apple-pickers has its implications not entirely to be ignored, but its real virtue lies in its clarity, one might almost say its cleanness, of presentation of personality and event. The vigour and directness common to so many American novels is here sharpened and refined by a definite purpose, but with a minimum of romanticization.

When Jim Nolan joins "the Party" he finds comradeship; there are, however, no other luxuries. He and the more experienced Mac are sent to the apple-orchards to see what profit they can make among the pickers from the announcement of a pay-cut. Perhaps they can spread the strike, perhaps it will remain local; in either event it is deemed to have its propaganda value in disciplining the workers and teaching them their inevitable enemy. Mac especially is shown in no gentle colours. He is an expert at turning every event to his own ends. He will play with a woman's life, smash a boy's face, have a corpse out of its coffin, if any of these things will forward his cause. With all this, he is shown as an honest and in many ways likeable human being, but the author clearly does not regard his wisdom as ultimate. When the strike begins, to meet ruthless opposition, something is wakened which even Mac, with all his skill, cannot completely control, the mass- or mob-spirit so much easier to turn to destructive violence than creative cooperation.

It is partly his sense of the interplay between individual and mass feeling, partly his knowledge of his background, and partly his sheer literary efficiency which give Mr. Steinbeck's book its distinction. It moves quickly and economically throughout, adventure following on adventure, the talk hard, sinewy, colloquial. If it is less pretty than exciting, so is American life lived on this particular level.

Carlos Baker.
"*In Dubious Battle* Revalued."
New York Times Book Review, 92
(25 July 1943), 4, 16.

Among Steinbeck's best novels, the least known is probably *In Dubious Battle*, the start-to-finish, play-by-play story of a fictional strike among the itinerant apple-pickers in a fictional valley in California. In any period the novel would repay a serious reader. In a time harassed by war, strikes and race riots, *In Dubious Battle* takes on the proportions of a parable for our day. It also furnishes a handle by which one can grasp the larger intentions of Steinbeck's work. For these two reasons, as well as for its intrinsic merit as a work of art, Steinbeck's strike novel, now seven years old, is distinctly worth a review and revaluation.

Steinbeck came of writing age in the depression of the Thirties, and, like *Of Mice and Men* and *The Grapes of Wrath*, *In Dubious Battle* bears on its face the grooves and scars of a decade of social agony. The devil (whose names and preoccupations are legion) was much abroad in those years. His carbonaceous footprints are almost as visible between the lines of *In Dubious Battle* as they are in the pages of Milton's *Paradise Lost*, from which Steinbeck drew the title, and perhaps the basic parable, of his novel.

Before one can get at this basic parable and its significance, for our time,

one must measure the driving force, the mind-set, the ruling emphasis, which has fixed the direction of Steinbeck's writing in the past seven years. One way of describing this force is to call it an interest in the phenomena of group action. Steinbeck is supremely interested in what happens to men's minds and hearts when they function, not as responsible, self-governing individuals, but as members of a group. What happens to separate identities when they merge into corporate identities? In what way does the single organism change its characteristics when it mutually interacts with other organisms in its environment?

Biologists have a word for this very important problem; they call it bionomics, or ecology. Bionomics comes from two Greek words meaning the management of modes of life. Steinbeck's bionomic interest is visible in all that he has done, from *Tortilla Flat*, in the middle Thirties, through his semi-biological *Sea of Cortez*, to his latest communiqués as a war correspondent in England. This interest is especially clear in the novel under consideration.

In Dubious Battle is an attempt to study a typical mid-depression strike in bionomical terms. It is the story of two Communist organizers, Mac and Jim, who seek to function as the directive, disciplinary force, the brain, for 900 striking men, an extremely complex super-organism in which all those lesser individualities are merged. As an experienced organizer, Mac initiates Jim into the practical mysteries of the science.

The problem resembles that of an army colonel who, surrounded by the foe, must provide tents, food, sanitary facilities and some manner of discipline. It differs from a military problem in that the task is to win the strike, not to assault the enemy physically. The organizers must perform the particularly difficult feat of keeping strikers' morale at high pitch, yet never allowing the enthusiasm to overflow into violent action. For violence would adversely prejudice public opinion and invite reprisal. Upon the working out of these problems the novel is built; out of these problems its inner tensions arise. They are enough to keep the reader on the edge of his chair.

Mac is a practical-minded graduate of the school of mob experience. His method is opportunistic: to seize and capitalize on any event which can fuse his 900 individual charges into a compact, unanimous entity. He knows, for example, that men like to work together. When he first appears among the apple-pickers he finds a young wife in labor and doctorless. If he can safely usher in the baby, and convince scores of pickers that they have had a share in the undertaking, he will have promoted a single-minded *esprit de corps* which will be helpful to him when the time comes for the strike to begin. He sets up huge cans of boiling water and urges the pickers to contribute articles of clothing to be sterilized for use at the child-bearing.

It does not matter that he will be able to use only a fraction of the shirts, undershirts and handkerchiefs that are contributed. "Every man who gave part of his clothes felt that the work was his own. They all feel responsible for that baby. . . . To give back the cloth would cut them out. There's no better way to make men part of a movement than to have them give something to it." Thus far, in creating the psychological environment which will best serve his immediate ends, Mac is a practicing ecologist.

Mac's adroit resourcefulness stands him in good stead until the strike is well started. Then begins a series of events which show that his control is by no means complete. Dr. Burton, the genu-inely scientific and detached observer (whom Steinbeck introduces as a rough equivalent of the chorus in a Greek tragedy) pronounces judgment on Mac's methods. "You practical men always lead practical men with stomachs. And something always gets out of hand. Your men get out of hand, they don't follow the rules of common sense, and you practical men either deny that it is so, or refuse to think about it."

Mac protests that the organizers have a job to do and no time to fool around with high-falutin' ideas. "Yes," says Burton, "and so you start to work not knowing your medium. And your ignorance trips you up every time."

Ignorance of what? Well, ignorance of both means and ends. Ignorance of the bionomic mysteries which result when one has joined nearly a thousand men into a crowd. Like Mrs. Shelley's Frankenstein, Mac has assembled, and is trying to handle effectively, a monster which works under a new and different set of rules. A force of this sort is perhaps useless unless it is unleashed, and (being unleashed) is too often a force destructive of the ends for which it was created.

Not only is Mac ignorant of the uses of the implement he has forged, he is ignorant also of the ends toward which he is moving. This practical man's vision of the future, when justice, fairness and freedom from want and fear may be realized actualities, is constantly befogged by immediate emotional drives which he does not know how to control. He takes sentimental refuge in the notion that he is working for a long-term cause. Actually he may be doing the cause more harm than good. He can't see the forest because he has stuck his head inside one rotten tree. "Mac," says Dr. Burton, "you're the craziest mess of cruelty and hausfrau sentimentality, of clear vision and rose-colored glasses, I ever saw."

Steinbeck's sympathies are with the strikers here, just as surely as they are with the Joads in *The Grapes of Wrath* or the beleaguered townspeople in *The Moon Is Down* or the ne'er-do-wells of *Tortilla Flat*. But he does not allow his sympathies to betray him into "hausfrau sentimentality," for he retains that necessary objectivity which is his inheritance from the naturalistic writers of this and the last century. This is part of the strength of *In Dubious Battle*. One notices with admiration, too, Steinbeck's ability to shear away the extrinsic, so that the movements of the novel take on an appearance of tragic inevitability. Shearing clean to the bone, as he does in *The Moon Is Down*, involves a certain sacrifice of textural richness. He contrives to leave more warmth and flesh in the strike novel.

Yet the real strength of *In Dubious Battle* lies deeper than texture, and beyond the niceties of structure. For the book exists on a double level. There is the explicit social level, the description of the strike, the probing of a festered wound in the body politic. If this were all, the novel might be mere strike propaganda, either pro or con, depending on the reader's political position.

But the explicit social level is not the only one. At the psychological level the novel takes on parabolical significance. Where reason and the more violent emotions struggle for mastery, the best-laid strategical plans are often circumvented by bionomic unknowns. In psychology and sociology there are few absolutes. Mac and Jim, trying to function as the directive brain for the unwieldy body of strikers, are themselves the prey of the very emotions they must stifle among their men if their plans are to succeed.

Moreover, their control over their charges is no more absolute than the control of any reasonable mind over any potentially wayward body. This battle, like a struggle in the mind, is of dubious outcome. That his emotions override his reason is the flaw in Othello's mentality, which leaves the opening through which Iago can reach a corrupting finger, like Satan in a medieval sermon. This is the flaw on which Milton expatiates in his great epic of the fall of man. And this is the flaw that brings to tragic issue not a dubious battle on the plains of heaven, but the equally dubious struggle among the fruitful apple orchards of California.

Checklist of Additional Reviews

George Currie. "Passed in Review." Brooklyn *Eagle*, 29 January 1936, p. 18.

Herschel Brickell. "John Steinbeck Swaps Whimsy of *Tortilla Flat* for a Dramatic Novel of California Fruit Strike." New York *Post*, 30 January 1936, p. 19.

Theodore Smith. "John Steinbeck Deserts Role of Gay Troubadour to Depict Strike Scenes in *In Dubious Battle*." San Francisco *News*, 8 February 1936, p. 7.

Sibyl Hayes. "*In Dubious Battle*." San Jose [Calif.] *Mercury-Herald*, 23 February 1936, p. 12.

D.A.N. "In the Margin." Brooklyn *Eagle*, 28 February 1936, Section C, p. 17.

John Chamberlain. "The World in Books." *Current History*, 43 (March 1936), iv.

OF MICE AND MEN (THE NOVEL)

OF MICE AND MEN

John Steinbeck

NEW YORK · COVICI · FRIEDE · PUBLISHERS

Charles A. Wagner. "Books." New York *Mirror*, 24 February 1937, p. 25.

Of the two selections for March made by the Book-of-the-Month Club, and just published, we like best the young American Steinbeck's novel, though the veteran Britisher Wells, who shares the selection, has returned to the grand manner.

John Steinbeck's *Of Mice and Men* . . . is just about the closest thing to a little prose masterpiece in the social stir we have seen in years.

It is the story of two barley bucker pals who migrate from job to job along the grain belt. One is a towering giant with the strength of ten men but the brain of a child. The other hasn't the heart to get rid of him, for fear he will come to harm; to which, of course, he does.

But the cycle of friendship, even in tragedy, remains unbroken. And in the course of his swift-moving tale, Mr. Steinbeck gives us a holiday pageantry of portraits in toil, in men's passions and repressions, in workers' dreams and devilments, told with a poet's eye to sounds and silences which makes his book a memorable thing indeed, and something at last to cheer about.

Lewis Gannett. "Books and Things." New York *Herald Tribune*, 25 February 1937, p. 17.

"Guys like us, that work on ranches," George told Lennie, "are the loneliest guys in the world. They got no family. They don't belong no place. They make a little stake and then they go into town and blow it in, and the first thing you know they're poundin' their tail on some other ranch."

"But not us," Lennie interrupted. (This is in John Steinbeck's story *Of Mice and Men* . . . which the Book-of-the-Month Club sends its members this month.) "We got a future. Some day gonna have a little house and a couple of acres an' a cow an' some pigs, an' live off the fatta the lan'— an' have rabbits! An' I get to tend the rabbits."

It was a sort of incantation with which George, a small, quick, bony-nosed man, soothed Lennie when that huge, shapeless halfwit grew restless. They had a dream, and Lennie lived for it, and George, who loved him, knew it could never come true.

"Funny how you and him string along together," said Slim, the jerkline skinner, prince of the ranch, who could drive twenty miles with a single line to the leaders. "It seems kinda funny, a cuckoo like him and a smart little guy like you travelin' together."

"It ain't so funny," George said. "Him and me was both born in Auburn. When his Aunt Clara died Lennie just come along with me out working. Got kinda used to each other after a little while. He ain't no cuckoo. He's dumb as hell, but he ain't crazy."

"He's a nice fella," said Slim. "Guy don't need no sense to be a nice fella. Seems to me sometimes it jus' works the other way around. Take a real smart guy and he ain't hardly ever a nice fella."

Danny and Big Joe Portagee and Jesus Maria Corcoran, citizens of *Tortilla Flat*, didn't have much sense either; nor did the farmers of *The Pastures of Heaven*. They talked tough, and they had no morals, but you ended the books loving them; and you will close this strange, tragic little idyll with a vast sense of compassion for big, dumb Lennie and for George, who knew Lennie would never get to tend those rabbits, and that if he did stroke their fur with his too strong hands he would kill them. And it is, perhaps, that compassion, even more than the perfect sense of form, which marks off John Steinbeck, artist, so sharply from all the little verbal photographers who record tough talk and snarl in books which have power without pity. The most significant things John Steinbeck has to say about his characters are never put into words; they are the overtones of which the reader is never wholly conscious—and that is art.

John Steinbeck said once that when he was six an aunt—one of his string of fabulous aunts, down in the Big Sur country, south of Salinas and Carmel—gave him a copy of Malory's *Morte d'Arthur*, and that he read it through again and again. He said, too, that though his name was German his heritage was rather Irish. I think that Celtic background lives in all his sagas of the California behind the concrete roads, as well as in that first *Cup of Gold*, where Malory shone like a star behind a mountain peak. The Celts have never lost the sense of wonder; nor has Steinbeck, though to the real smart guys who are hardly ever nice fellas it vanished long ago. It gives a richness to Celtic lives and to Steinbeck's writing.

James Ross Oliver. "Book News and Views." Monterey [Calif.] *Peninsula Herald*, 25 February 1937, p. 5.

Book reviewing can be a joy at times, and it so happens that this is one of them. The cause for the good feeling at the moment is that we have just finished reading the one book we have encountered in some months which has impressed us with the extreme artistry of its composition. It happens less frequently than one might suppose.

As usual, this kind of a book can, and does stir up all manner of argument, intellectual and violent. And John Steinbeck's *Of Mice and Men* ... will be no exception. Of course publishers and authors are quite willing to let the storm rage. Sales never suffer from it.

Of Mice and Men is a small book of only 186 pages, but it is big in its accomplishment. Again Steinbeck convinces us that his is the mission to bring to the reader the lives and minds of the lower class. It is that purpose that has brought upon him the condemnation of many; expressed doubts in no uncertain terms concerning the immorality of his writing. But considering the characters the author brings us, and considering again his thoroughness in doing this, no condemnation is just. If one will only glance through Steinbeck's pages, one will see that these things which they decry are not the author's—rather those of whom he writes. Pressing still further, and as a last plunge to get this thing off our chest, anyone who knows these people will agree that he is right in his work.

But enough of that.

Of Mice and Men is what it is because of its inherent simplicity. The plot is not great, nor are its characters great, but they are both real and carried through to completion. It is a plot upon which the characterizations and story are laid as effectively as flesh upon bone.

Lennie is a huge hulk of a man whose brain stopped functioning somewhere in his early childhood. But he is a kindly soul, harmless. But being stupid he makes blunders. George, the small faithful companion, is destined to keep Lennie out of trouble. Yet Lennie and George are forced to flee from Weed, and through an agency in San Francisco they get work on a ranch south of Soledad. George purposely postpones their arrival so that he may coach Lennie to silence. For, as George says, "Lennie doesn't think very well, but he can do the work of five men."

And though Lennie's future is wholly made of rabbits to care for, or live mice to pet, he blunders into trouble again. We might say the trouble was waiting for him. Curley, the boss's son, had married a young woman of questionable character from Salinas. At any rate, she had eyes for all the men. Most of them saw her for what she was, but that realization was beyond Lennie.

Dramatically, skillfully, Steinbeck takes us on to as simple yet magnetic a climax as one could wish for. And the accomplishment which impressed us the most is that the author, in his faultless plot, has pegged, or forewarned us of each development: some trifling event, some symbol, some twist of character, goes before like a perfect prologue. The artistry of it is that we do not object to it in the least.

Once more John Steinbeck has presented us with a simple, realistic portrayal of simple, earthy men and women. They are the hardest characters to delineate.

Tortilla Flat made Steinbeck a prominent writer. *In Dubious Battle* increased his prestige. Then comes *Of Mice and Men*, and his reputation is further made. But we mustn't forget that he wrote novels before these. There are many critics who feel that one of those is among his best. To test that theory for yourself, we would suggest that you read his book about a hidden valley, *Pastures of Heaven*.

Of Mice and Men will be released through your favorite book store on Saturday, the 27th.

F[anny] B[utcher].
"Books."
Chicago *Daily Tribune*,
27 February 1937, p. 11.

The author of *Tortilla Flat* has written *Of Mice and Men* so simply, so movingly, so factually that only when its last page is finished does the reader realize what a remarkable literary feat John Steinbeck has performed.

The book tells the story of Lennie, a huge moron who has a passion to touch anything soft and goes into a panic if it is taken from him, and of George, who watches over Lennie with touching care. George, a little man with a quick mind, is the only person in the world (since Lennie's Aunt Clara's death) who can do anything with the giant moron. He can do everything with him, and does everything for him, including thinking.

When the book opens Lennie and

George are about to start on a new job, after having had to flee for their lives from their last one. All they ask of life is to lay aside a little money and buy a farm and "live on the fatta the lan'" where they can raise rabbits. They think they can. But the reader knows they can't—knows that fate is piling up something for them as one after another sinister shadow is cast.

Brutality and tenderness mingle in these strangely moving pages. Language that gentle ears would never hear seems as inevitable as Lennie's clumsy devotion to the puppy which he kills with his petting.

The reader is fascinated by a certainty of approaching doom. It comes swiftly, inevitably, and the final moments of George's service to Lennie are high tragedy. One false word, and *Of Mice and Men* would have been melodrama, and bad melodrama at that. But the author never, after the first few pages, writes that one false word.

Henry Seidel Canby. "Casuals of the Road." *Saturday Review*, 15 (27 February 1937), 7.

Mr. Steinbeck has given us *In Dubious Battle*, a proletarian novel about the rights of laboring men, which did not please the party workers because there was as much sentiment as ideology in it. He has given us *Tortilla Flat*, a loose-hung story of California Mexicans as irresponsible as children, which did not please the serious-minded because the characters found liquorous wastefulness so perfectly delightful. Now he has written a long short story which should please everybody.

It should please everybody because it has every element of good story-telling, and it must be remembered that most of our successful novels of recent years, with any substance of art to them, have succeeded by violating most of the canons of the storyteller's art in order to emphasize ideology, the stream of consciousness, or behaviorism.

Of Mice and Men is the story of a defective. His weakness is soft things, strokable things. Upon them his great fingers sooner or later close. He does "a bad thing," he kills them. But the principle in Lennie is nevertheless the principle of good. And defective though he may be, it is his longing for living things that are lovable and to be taken care of—like rabbits—that makes articulate the longing of all the rough hands at the ranch for something of their own, land, a house, animals, perhaps a wife—something different from their wandering from lousy bunks to gilt saloons, getting nowhere, owning nothing. George, Lennie's friend, who has got him out of danger before, and Crooks, the nigger hostler, and Candy, the broken-down swamper, and even Slim, who is the just and capable man in the story, all feel it. And slowly the plan develops. "Everybody wants a little bit of land, not much. Jus' som'thin' that was his."

This is the principle of good, even in the moron, Lennie. The principle of evil is, obscurely, in the conditions of life that keep these men bummers and vagabonds. But it focuses in the boss's vicious son Curley, the ex-prizefighter, and in Curley's wife, a poor little prostitute infected by egoism because some one once told her she could go into the pictures, and held here among these men by Curley, where all she can do is to wander about like some venereal germ looking salaciously for a victim. And she finds Lennie, trying not to do a bad thing.

The story is as simple as that, but superb in its understatements, its realisms which are used, not to illustrate behavior, but for character and situation. Indeed, there has been nothing quite so good of the kind in American writing since Sherwood Anderson's early stories. It is a limited kind, but close to the heart of the whole fiction business. If you can create a character—a fresh character, belonging to his soil and shaped by a fresh set of experiences; and if (choosing sentiment rather than the other offgivings of human nature—and sentiment is quite as real as its opposite), and if you can make that character make its own story, you are closer to the job of fiction than most writers come in our time.

I question the extravagant claims for style in the jacket blurbs of this book. The excellence of Mr. Steinbeck's book is precisely that it does not make you think of style or of "soaring beauty." Its style is right for its subject matter, and that subject matter is deeply felt, richly conceived, and perfectly ordered. That is praise enough for a book.

"Steinbeck Touches the Sublime."
San Francisco *Call*,
27 February 1937, p. 6.

Through California's fertile valleys trudge "the loneliest guys in the world."

They are cattle-ranch hands, drifting from job to job.

"They got no fam'ly. They don't belong no place. . . . They ain't got nothing to look ahead to."

But George and Lennie HAVE something to look ahead to. They dream of saving a stake, of buying a few cheap acres in the hills, of having their own rooftree, of raising their own fruit and chickens and pigs and rabbits. Lennie is a simple-minded Hercules. George, wiser, watches over him, snatches Lennie from the disasters into which he blunders, keeps his dear dream alive.

The dream seems ready to come true when simple Lennie runs afoul of shrewd, bullying Curley, the boss's son, and Curley's man-chasing, painted, voluptuous, tantalizing wife. Then comes tragedy, stark, utter, smashing.

It IS tragedy, pure classic, profoundly concerned with human weakness and suffering, hurtling from heights of pity to depths of agony. And all simple, direct, mincing no word, wasting not a single magnificent brush-stroke. Call it the finest published work of one of America's most gifted writers.

Ralph Thompson.
"*Of Mice and Men.*"
New York *Times*,
27 February 1937, p. 15.

The boys have whooped it up for John Steinbeck's new book, *Of Mice and Men*, . . . so enthusiastically that there isn't much else left to say in the way of praise. It *is* a grand little book, for all its ultimate melodrama; and although this reader can't begin to string along with Harry Hansen, who calls it "the finest bit of prose fiction of this decade," he must admit that it is a long time since he laid eyes on anything as completely disarming.

Mr. Steinbeck's story is of two wandering farmhands, George and Lennie. George and Lennie are friends, sticking to each other in desperation and dreaming of the day when they won't have to bum around the country looking for work—of the remote day when they will have enough money to buy some sort of place of their own.

This probably sounds like sentimental truck, and in a way it is. But under Mr. Steinbeck's magic touch it is also strong, moving and very funny. Lennie is a grown-up baby, physically powerful and mentally weak, with a passion for soft, furry things. George is a tough and irritable codger, but he bears patiently with Lennie....

... What happens when the two reach a ranch where they are to work is the story. Read it and see how aptly John Steinbeck turns a tale.

Joseph Henry Jackson. "Steinbeck's Art Finds Powerful Expression in *Of Mice and Men*." San Francisco *Chronicle*, 28 February 1937, Section D, p. 7.

About two years ago the public became conscious for the first time of a young Western writer who had produced a great yarn—or rather a bookful of loosely connected yarns—called *Tortilla Flat*. That book had charm, humor, what the reviewers used to call "local color," and a pleasant delicacy of style which did not hide the robustness beneath it. It was widely read, too, and for most readers it was their introduction to the author, John Steinbeck. He had already done three books but the public at large didn't know them. *Tortilla Flat* was, to all intents and purposes, his bow to his audience.

Steinbeck followed that book with a novel, *In Dubious Battle*. I have an idea that it hadn't occurred to him that it would make so many different kinds of people so angry. Especially I don't think he realized ahead of time that the proletarian critics would be quite so irritated because he had (in their view) missed his chance to point a moral. But the realization didn't throw him off stride. If that was the way people felt, very well, they felt that way. As for him, his business was to go on writing what he wanted to write in the best way he knew how to write it. He may or may not have based that conviction on the knowledge that all good writing comes at length out of just such a determination; my own idea is that he knew instinctively what his job was. At any rate, that's what he did. He listened to none of the argufiers, but simply went on writing his stuff his way. Out of that undisturbed pursuit of his own private purpose has come *Of Mice and Men*, one of two books chosen by the Book-of-the-Month Club as its March selection for its members.

Of Mice and Men, first of all, is not a "proletarian novel" in the sense in which the arm-wavers currently use the term.

It does concern working men, yes. Its setting is the road, the field and the bunkhouse. Its central figures—there are two of them—are workers who take what jobs they can get where they can get them, in the fruit, wrestling grain bags, running cultivators, skinning mules. But the author's first preoccupation is not with these men as symbols or even as units in the mass of beaten-down labor. As always, Steinbeck is interested in his characters as men, as human beings who think and do and desire the many and various things that men have always thought and done and longed for. Indeed it is the very commonplace desire of George and Lennie for their own little heaven-on-earth that gives Steinbeck his story. These two, like other men, had plans. And how their plans went astray. (All right, "agley" if you insist. There will be a fine, grand misquoting of Burns before all the reviewers are done with this book.) How their plans, in fact, could never have come to fruition anyhow is Steinbeck's theme. It is a simple story, one that combines a curious dream-like quality with the swift streamlining of a good play. It is a story that will sweep you irresistibly with it, too. Even though you may shudder more than once you will not put it down.

You meet George and Lennie as they have made their way to a camping spot by a stream near the ranch where they have a job promised them for the next day.

George, small and shrewd, is the brains of the pair in much more than the usual sense. For Lennie, huge and strong and willing, hasn't good sense. He can't remember things. He will do anything George tells him but by himself he is lost. Sometimes George grows furious with Lennie for his stupidity, long as he has known him. Lennie repeats things he shouldn't because though he remembers what he has heard now and then he can never remember that he shouldn't blurt them out. Sometimes, too, Lennie gets into trouble. He never means to do anything bad, but he can't resist anything that feels soft to his enormous but sensitive fingers. When he pets a mouse he pets it hard and kills it. Up in the north George and Lennie had to clear out in a hurry because Lennie couldn't help himself—he had to feel the soft silk of a little girl's dress. Lennie had meant no more but the girl

screamed and they had to hide in a ditch all night. Sometimes George wished he could put Lennie in a cage with about a million mice and leave him there. But he couldn't. And he couldn't stay angry at Lennie. He had to take care of him anyway; somebody had to, that was sure. And besides, he and Lennie shared a dream.

That dream was a little ranch somewhere. Lennie liked to hear George tell about it, over and over again—"a big vegetable patch and chickens and a rabbit hutch [rabbits were soft and smooth and Lennie loved them]. And when it rains in the winter we'll just say the hell with goin' to work, and we'll build up a fire in the stove and set around it an' listen to the rain on the roof...." There was nothing strange about their dream as you see. Men everywhere have had it. But so far George and Lennie had never been able to fulfill it.

As the story opens, however, they are still dreaming it. And when they come to the ranch and go to work there develops out of nowhere, by sheer luck, a chance that their dream may be realized. Another man has had that dream too, and he has the one thing George and Lennie have never been able to scrape together— a stake. A little more money, no more than George and Lennie can earn and save in a month or two, and they can buy the place they want. They even know the one, and how much it will take.

How that dream, so near fulfillment, was snatched away is the story *Of Mice and Men*. You know what's coming; you can't help knowing. Steinbeck has done such a masterly job of story-telling that you feel the horror that is ahead even before it begins to grow. You see the fate that is going to overtake these men and their dream. You realize what's going to happen, what can't help happening. But—well, let me see you stop reading, that's all. And in spite of the grimness of the tale, let me hear you deny, after you have finished it, that Steinbeck has written it beautifully as well as powerfully.

There is no question, of course, that there will be the usual chorus of recriminations. Here (so it will go) Steinbeck had the materials for a fine propaganda novel, a tale of the class struggle that might show how the working man is exploited, etc., etc., etc., and he didn't make use of his chance to strike a blow for freedom. He didn't Unite with the Front. He didn't do this and he didn't do that. He might have done such-and-such and he should have done it thus-and-so. They've said it about Steinbeck before and they'll say it all again. And they'll make it sound plausible, too.

But I'm pretty sure that he won't care. I hope he won't. I hope he will go right on, sharpening his talent as he is doing, changing his subjects, his interests whenever he feels like it, writing about whatever is close to his heart at the moment he writes, doing books that are sensitive, beautifully written, imaginative works of art. That's plenty to expect of any writing man who cares as much for what he is doing as Steinbeck does. As for the books written to prove this or to demonstrate that, to put forward a thesis or to help the acceptance of an idea—let the ones who want to write them do so. Sometimes such books will be literature. Sometimes, if the writers of them happen to be artists, they will also be beautiful books. But more often you will find beauty in books that were written because their authors wanted to write them, just for their own sakes. So far, Steinbeck has stuck to that plan. And *Of Mice and Men* is the best evidence that it is the right way for him to write.

Fred T. Marsh.
"John Steinbeck's Tale of Drifting Men."
New York Times Book Review, 86
(28 February 1937), 7.

John Steinbeck is no mere virtuoso in the art of story-telling; but he is one. Whether he writes about the amiable outcasts of *Tortilla Flat* or about the grim strikers of *In Dubious Battle*, he tells a story. *Of Mice and Men* is a thriller, a gripping tale running to novelette length that you will not set down until it is finished. It is more than that; but it is that.

George and Lennie belong to the floating army of drifting ranch hands. "Guys like us," George says, "are the loneliest guys in the world. They got no family. They don't belong no place. They come to a ranch and work up a stake and then they go inta town and blow their stake, and the first thing you know they're poundin' their tail on some other ranch. They ain't got nothing to look ahead to."

The relationship between these two buddies of roads and ranches is a strange one and causes comment at the new ranch. George is small, dark, wiry, restless, keen-witted. Lennie is a huge, hulking man with an expressionless face, pale blue eyes and wide, sloping shoulders, walking heavily, "dragging his feet a little, the way a bear drags his paws." He is stupid, but well-meaning.

George and Lennie came from the same Southern town, and George has taken it on himself to take care of the big fellow. Sometimes he wishes he were free of him. He'd get ahead much faster.

Lennie is always getting them into trouble—like the time he wanted to stroke the pretty red skirt of the girl on the last ranch and in his dumb strength tore it off her. They had to run away again to keep Lennie out of jail. The baby boy in the big man's body has baby urges—to stroke, pet and fondle animals, all soft or pretty things, and he kills or destroys them unaware of his strength. But when George is around he is all right, for he obeys George implicitly.

George is a keen thinking man. There is nothing in this knocking about. If only he and Lennie could get together $600 he knows of a little place with a few acres they could buy and settle down to work for themselves. If only Lennie can be kept out of trouble. And so he keeps drumming it into Lennie's head that he must be good and not do bad things. Then they can get a stake together and live on the fat of the land in a place of their own. They'll grow their own stuff, keep a few pigs and chickens and raise rabbits; Lennie can take charge of the rabbits and have all the pets he wants. The big fellow never grows tired of hearing this story just as a child likes to hear a tale told over and over again. And at the new ranch, the way things are shaping up, the dream seems to be on the point of coming true.

The tension increases and the apparently casual acts and conversation nevertheless fit together to create suspense in an atmosphere of impending doom. There are trouble makers in the bunkhouse. Curley, the boss's son, a little fellow handy with his fists, likes to take on big clumsy fellows, pick fights with them. He wins no matter how the fight comes out, because if he licks the big fellow every one says how game he is; and if he gets the worst of it every one turns on the big fellow for not taking [on] some one his own size. Then Curley's wife, a lush beauty, is always coming around where the men are on the pretense of looking for Curley, giving all the men the eye and, because, being a town girl, she is bored on the ranch, bent on stirring up excitement. The other boys know how to keep out of trouble. But Lennie only knows what George tells him when George is right there on the spot. The girl spots Lennie as the only soft guy in the bunch. The climax comes, not as a shock, but as a dreaded inevitability.

The theme is not, as the title would suggest, that the best laid plans of mice and men gang aft agley. They do in this story as in others. But it is a play on the immemorial theme of what men live by besides bread alone. In sure, raucous, vulgar Americanism, Steinbeck has touched the quick in his little story.

Wilbur Needham.
"John Steinbeck Does Dramatic Novel."
Los Angeles *Times*,
28 February 1937, Part 3,
p. 8.

Once more, John Steinbeck refuses to be neatly pigeonholed. He has qualities lamentably rare in modern novelists: imagination and a restless, inquiring mind. He will not sit down, like Thomas Wolfe, and contemplate his navel. He refuses to exploit one locality or any single idea or set of characters. That is the way novelists achieve fame and shelves of books all stamped with their trademarks; and Steinbeck cannot be accused of courting fame, for he chooses queer balconies.

Beyond that, the man is something

more than original in creation. Those who seek originality are almost always experimenters; and the results they offer are—experiments, usually unsuccessful. Steinbeck, obviously, does experiment; but he has a discernment in approach, an uncanny touch in creation, that lift everything he writes out of ephemeral brackets of experimental work. That is because he always has his feet on the ground—rooted in the earth and the things of earth—no matter what mountain peaks his level eyes look on.

Cup of Gold was a novel of Sir Henry Morgan. *Pastures of Heaven* contained short stories, held together by feeling and locale. *To a God Unknown* was filled with a hunger for the land and a mysticism that baffled many readers. *Tortilla Flat* and its Monterey *paisanos* everyone knows. *In Dubious Battle* seized the most difficult of proletarians to handle—migratory workers—and made them live, where other novelists for the most part failed with easier material, workers who remain in one environment. No two of these books had anything in common—except John Steinbeck, who was outwardly different in each, inwardly no one but himself.

Now, *Of Mice and Men*. A little book, half the size of an ordinary novel (the gods be praised for that!) but containing more. In everything but its superficial form, the novel is a play. I was not surprised to learn that a second script is being rehearsed at a San Francisco theater now. It does not creak: and it will not, on the boards. There is fluid movement, here, and inevitability; never spoiled by theatrical mechanics—and yet, it is theater, as theater ought to be. With inner rhythms that move out into a prose that is Steinbeck's own.

George Milton and Lennie Small wander from one job to another on California ranches. They don't want to drift; but

Lennie, a hulking fellow, is not quite bright, and he gets them both in trouble. Lennie likes to pet soft things, mice and rabbits and dresses and shining women's hair. The mice die, surprisingly, for Lennie is very gentle; or, he thinks he is. But his great paws have an unconscious power; and the mice die and the women scream. So they drift on to other parts, sometimes none too quickly.

Always before them is a dream of a little place of their own, where they can live on the "fatta the lan'" and Lennie can "get to tend them rabbits." Always before them; and now, it seems about to turn real. Here the drama, ever close beside Steinbeck's strange inventiveness and native humor, begins to outpace it and to draw away.

Of the book's inner meaning, never obvious but never entirely obscured by unexpected laughter and the movement of the story, I will not speak. If you do not like inner meanings, you will certainly not find one here; and, if you do, you'll see more than one for yourself.

Louis Paul. "Prose Made of Wind and Soil and Weather." New York *Herald Tribune*, 28 February 1937, "Books" section, p. 5.

The weeds and the willows and the tall waving grain of California's sweet valleys, rabbits and mice and a woman's soft hair, the hot slanting sun and the hungry desire of a pair of floaters to own a handful of dirt are the materials out of which this lovely new novel by John Steinbeck is evoked. Purling water is purling water here, without overtones; a gracious sky is as beautiful as in any lyric poetry. The men are lads sent down to the ranch from Murray and Ready's in San Francisco: Lennie, like Nature itself, whose powerful fingers killed little animals before he knew it, and George, struggling to become human. *Of Mice and Men* is another of John Steinbeck's parables of earth, and no writer I know shapes the soil into truer patterns for us to understand.

In *Pastures of Heaven* this dream had its first fruition. A tapestry whose threads were woven from the design the lives of the men and women of a fertile valley created in the author's imagination, these stories are unforgettable. A prose that seemed made of wind and weather and growing acres came alive in them. *To a God Unknown* continued Steinbeck's inner examination of earth, when a tree and a mossy rock and the silent fury of a drought murdered the fragile human figures. And then, because Nature is anything but monotonous, this versatile novelist went down into Monterey, bought himself a "balloon" of claret, made the acquaintance of Danny and his *paisano* pals, and decided to recount the adventures and achievements of Pilon, Pablo, Big Joe and Company in *Tortilla Flat*. Again when the fun of living with the childlike was done, the writer presented for our information, in *In Dubious Battle*, what is unquestionably the most important study of strike technique to find its way on paper in this nation.

These works have been called dissimilar. Versatile, perhaps; in a day when success has the tendency to standardize, versatility in a novelist or any one else is thought of with some astonishment. The threads that run continuously through these stories by John Steinbeck are, under examination, more than perceptible. Not especially rare are those authors who think in terms of panaceas, whose lack of courage and vitality draws back from the monumental task of understanding; they are all for short cuts, for adopting some ready-made philosophy and rushing on from there, and what we get from these authors are drab second-hand discoveries, valueless, intrinsically dull. Here, however, is an intelligence as explicit as any research scientist's, an intelligence directed toward the understanding of the relationship between men and earth. In each successive book this desire to explore the complex affinity is more apparent, until, with the publication of *Of Mice and Men*, it achieves such cumulative impact as to be undeniable.

Of Mice and Men is made of a theme which some lesser novelist might have called too insignificant to expound—two indigent members of the strange tribe of casual workers destroyed by the simple mystery of loyalty. But before they are destroyed there burns brilliantly between the covers of this little book the image of the fire inside the flesh of two human beings, whom fate has crushed before birth, human beings whose lives mean no more to Nature than robins caught up by hawks.

The story seems simple when accomplished by a superb craftsman: the desire and struggle of those who till the soil for others to own a tiny plot of the earth for themselves; against this primitive hunger, like the rising tide of a destructive river, is played the forces which make a naive aspiration impossible of attainment. "Sure, we'd have a little house an' a room to ourself. Little fat iron stove, an' in the winter we'd keep a fire goin' in it. It ain't enough land so we'd have to work too hard. Maybe six, seven hours a day. We wouldn't have to buck no barley eleven hours a day. An' when we put in a crop, why, we'd be there to take the crop up.

We'd know what come of our planting." And while George dreams in the crummy ranch bunk-house, he knows that his words are lies; and the reader knows his words are the lies we use to escape our destinies. And the author knows. They are not ugly lies, you understand; merely the imagination evoking for the moment its little dream, an escape into a fairyland where there is no barley to buck.

In the cities men go to "movies." There are little dumps on the Bowery where for 10 cents the disinherited may observe life aboard a yacht or in a penthouse, or cowboys riding the beautiful ranges of Arizona. In Arizona the cowboys ride fence, one leg propped over against the saddle horn, absorbed in a magazine of hair-raising adventure stories. Men in factories tiredly dream of grubbing for gold "out West," and office workers dance themselves all night into insensibility. Men take whisky into them and, with its drug, bump their heads against the stars in their rosy fancy. And serious observers, infuriated by a world which impels us frantically toward escape, babble in an impotent fashion of cures. Those who speak of books hunt down such observations and interpret them in terms of social significance.

But the poet who immortalizes the fleeting tragedy of two such men as George and Lennie is his own social force. That Lennie was an idiot, no less, and victim of a pathological disease, is entirely beyond the point. John Steinbeck does not know what makes men idiots and victims of disease; such knowledge comes slowly and painfully, as does the cure for cancer. We sting the flesh of our economic body with patent medicines, wondering, let us say, if Lennie's tragedy might not be avoided if the government in Washington gave every crop floater and bindle stiff and lettuce picker and wheat sacker a little farm in Salinas Val-

ley. Such nonsense invalidates the very spirit in which the author of such a work as Of Mice and Men is creating.

The verities we can live with are those thoughts born out of dreams which, in the end, distinguish us from the robins and the waving grain. Of such verities does John Steinbeck write, out of a warm and a rich knowledge. With the genuine artist's respect for his materials and love of his craft he puts away cheap prejudice, the distortion which comes from anger; his thought is to tell the little truths he had discovered with his eyes and callused hands and intelligence, and if these truths do not touch your social conscience nothing can. In Of Mice and Men the truth is made into a moving and profoundly beautiful book full of singing prose and enchantment. If, standing upon some pinnacle of dry logic, we suspect that his creations of these ignorant American laborers are idealizations, that without the magic of his poetry they must remain sweat-soaked beasts of the fields, we but doubly assure ourselves of his essential humanity and pay his artistry the highest compliment we know.

Maxine Garrard. "*Of Mice and Men* by Steinbeck: Powerful and Absorbing Novel." Columbus [Ga.] *Enquirer-Sun*, 1 March 1937, p. 2.

Of Mice and Men by John Steinbeck is a book so powerful it will make the reader's hair stand on end and curl a little in the bargain. Mr. Steinbeck is a contributor to *Esquire* and has been startling its readers since that magazine exploded upon the public a few years ago. His *Tortilla Flat* caused comment and *Of Mice and Men* will bring on even more talk. Weak-hearted readers and lovers of moonlight and romance should take a word of warning—this is not of the pleasant school of thought wherein things turn out fine in the end; they don't.

Serving his strong meat fresh and still warm from life's slaughter house, John Steinbeck shades nothing in presenting his terrifying tale; however beneath the superficial horror of the story the reader senses a dream of breathless beauty shimmering through the lives of the two main characters. These vagabonds are men predestined to a stark, empty existence but between them flickers some unexplained devotion and future vision of the time when they will "live on the fatta the lan'." . . .

From the sordid lives of a cocky tramp and a balmy moron, John Steinbeck has written a drama of indescribable magic and heart-breaking futility. Even if you think you are tough and can "take it," this book will cause an emotional upheaval. It is strong, it is powerful and it is wonderful, but unless you can swallow raw stuff—lay off.

"Young Man's Dream." *Time*, 28 (1 March 1937), 69.

George and Lennie were ranch hands. George was small, wiry, tough, shrewd; Lennie was enormous, floppy-looking but Herculean, and a half-wit. George and Lennie were pals. Lennie was always getting them into trouble, losing them jobs, getting them run out of town because he liked to pet things—mice, little girls, rab-

bits. Not conscious of his blundering strength, Lennie was apt to kill what he petted. George kept him in line as well as he could by bawling him out, threatening to leave him, telling him a beautiful fairy story about how they would save enough money to buy a little farm, settle down in comfort, let Lennie take care of rabbits.

They had just had to leave one job in a hurry because Lennie's passion for petting things had been misunderstood by a frightened little girl. On the new ranch everything went all right at first. Lennie was a terrific worker, did beautifully as long as George was at hand to tell him what to do. It looked for a while as if they could really make their stake, buy their little farm, settle down to make their dream come true. But then things began to go wrong. The boss's son was an ugly customer, and he had just married a floozy who kept him at a white heat of suspicion. When he picked on Lennie, the big half-wit got so panicky that he seized his little tormentor's hand, crushed it nearly to bits. George managed to get them out of that scrape, but when Lennie accidentally broke the floozy's neck, there was only one thing George could do to remedy that. Knowing where Lennie was hiding, George got to him ahead of the posse, got trusting Lennie to turn his head while he shot him behind the ear.

To Americans whose eyes are still smarting from the unhappy ending of the Wall Street fairy tale of 1929, John Steinbeck's little dream story will not seem out of line with reality: they may even overlook the fact that it too is a fairy tale. An oxymoronic combination of the tough and tender, *Of Mice and Men* will appeal to sentimental cynics, cynical sentimentalists. Critic Christopher Morley found himself "purified" by this "masterpiece . . . written in purest compassion and truth." Readers less easily thrown off their trolley will still prefer Hans Andersen.

Ralph Thompson.
"Books of the Times."
New York *Times*,
2 March 1937, p. 19.

... John Steinbeck's *Of Mice and Men* ... is the most recently published of books mentioned here, and in bulk one of the smallest, yet it should not be overlooked by any one interested in American fiction. In retrospect, the lovable half-wit Lennie seems even more improbable a character than at first reading he appeared to be. But improbable or not, he is memorable—a blend, if such a thing can be imagined, of Paul Bunyan, Tiny Tim and Browning's sprawling Caliban. . . .

Harry Thornton Moore.
"Of Mice and Men."
New Republic, 90
(3 March 1937), 118–19.

George and Lennie are two drifting ranch hands who dream, as rootless men do, of a piece of land of their own, where they will "belong." They have never been able to work up a stake because big, blundering, simple-witted Lennie keeps getting them into trouble. He can never remember things. He tenderly loves puppies and mice but always forgets about not squeezing them too hard, and kills them. Fabulously strong but very timid, he is quite docile in the hands of George, the pilot-fish of the pair. George feels that Lennie has been given into his keeping. He controls him by talking about the rabbit farm they will have one day, where Lennie may look after the rabbits if he is good—for George too is webbed in the dream. They come to work in the Salinas Valley and it is there, among the people they meet at the ranch, that their story is worked out.

This story has that common denominator of most good imaginative writing, a shadow of the action that means something beyond the action. But the underlying theme (of the danger of dreaming) never clogs the primary story. The book is well contrived and effectively compressed, driving ahead with straight and rapid movement, as magnificently written as Steinbeck's other four California novels. He again shows a deep understanding of both place and people, and his presentation of the ranch and its daily life has the gleam of actuality. The people, human beings reduced to bareness of thought and speech and action, are on the side-tracks of the main line of western culture. They exist in a hard reality but most of them are susceptible to dreams. Some of them are lost in compensatory dream-images of themselves, others are set afire by the wish-dream of George and Lennie. But in one way or another all the dreams and some of the people (both good and bad) are smashed: a spirit of doom prevails as strong as in Steinbeck's fellow Californian, Jeffers.

A writer deep in the ways of his own people feels (in many cases unconsciously) a racial compulsive: the actual and mythical experience of his people helps generate his material. But the final shaping of it depends upon the artist's own vision. In the present story Lennie is cast up from the midst of us and we all know him. Baffled, unknowingly power-ful, utterly will-less, he cannot move without a leader. And we also know many Georges, good-heartedly trying to help the Lennies of life muddle through; but all the while, despite their courage and good intentions, none too certain of themselves. John Steinbeck sees them as unable to prevent their charges (or often themselves) from steering into ca-tastrophe. In book after book his pro-tagonists, tragic or comic, are shattered; and it goes hardest with those who had the brightest dreams. It is disturbing to find these men of good will so consis-tently going down in spiritual defeat or meeting with a brutal death.

Heywood Broun.
"It Seems to Me."
St. Paul [Minn.] *Daily News*, 4 March 1937,
p. 8.

I'd like to come along with the large group of critics who have already re-corded their enthusiasm for John Steinbeck's new novel, *Of Mice and Men.*

This is a book written with compas-sion, celerity and an admirable sense of structure. It is that rare and much to be desired thing—a short novel. The telling takes no more than 31,000 words, and yet the narrative is fully rounded out and complete. For instance, in my opinion, *Of Mice and Men* is infinitely more im-portant in the literary scheme of things than *Gone With the Wind.*

I am moved to great excitement about the emergence of Steinbeck because he so neatly splits the bracket between the old

romanticists and the stern-faced boys and girls who have recently been treating the novel as if it were nothing more than a candid camera. Steinbeck knows his farm workers as well as anybody else. Lennie and George talk straight. No spurious lit-erary phrase creeps into the mouth of ei-ther. Nevertheless many long stretches of their conversation are animated by true poetic content.

I think life is like that and that mod-ern authors are beginning to find it out. Transcripts of talk may be as faithful as you please and still take on the cadence and color which make for beauty. Per-haps somewhat after the manner of Molière's hero who discovered that he had been talking prose all his life the common run-of-the-mine American may wake up to the fact that he uses a good deal of poetry in dealing with his daily concerns. That may be a shock to some, since along certain levels poetry means Eddie Guest and a rhyme scheme fit to break the ear with its persistent beat, like that of night club drums.

I do not know which native author should be selected as the spiritual ances-tor of Steinbeck. Every writer has to have an ancestor forced upon him, whether or not he recognizes the old gentleman. Off-hand it would seem to me that Ring Lardner might have suggested in part the manner and mode of John Steinbeck. To be sure, there is little similarity in subject matter and none at all in point of view save the quality of compassion for those who get pushed around.

I assume that at some period of his life Steinbeck read Upton Sinclair. Mr. Sin-clair is a good model for young authors, since he can serve both as an inspiration and at the same time as a horrible ex-ample. I think that writers will be lucky if they can catch from Upton something of his terrific zeal about present problems in the workaday world, and yet if the younger men are exposed to his influence too long they may become infected with the flatness and bleakness of the Sinclair prose.

I'm aware that Upton Sinclair is a poet as well as a novelist. And his is a style which doesn't get in the way when he has a fast moving and deeply biting story to tell. It is smoother, of course, than the English of Dreiser, and yet never ornate. Fine writing and bad writing may be equally destructive in the matter of getting into the reader's eye when he is in close pursuit of the theme itself. Of course, I'm using "fine writing" in the worst sense of the phrase.

The proper time to admire the style of a man is when you have finished the last sentence on the last page of his story. So it was with *Of Mice and Men* as far as I was concerned. I had put the book down all stirred by the logical poignance of its conclusion. And it was only then that I suddenly realized that this man Steinbeck could write like a magician.

Until then I had been too much interested in what he had to say to pay very much attention to the manner in which he said it. Like a conjurer, a novelist should be able to take the rabbit out of the hat without letting his audience in on the way in which he did it. John Steinbeck seems to me right now to be the wonder man of current American letters.

Mark Van Doren. "Wrong Number." *Nation*, 144 (6 March 1937), 275.

All but one of the persons in Mr. Steinbeck's extremely brief novel are sub-human if the range of the word human is understood to coincide with the range thus far established by fiction. Two of them are evil, one of them is dangerous without meaning to be, and all of them are ignorant—all of them, that is, except the one who shall be named hereafter. Far from knowing the grammar of conduct, they do not even know its orthography. No two of their thoughts are consecutive, nor for that matter do they think; it is rather that each of them follows some instinct as a bull follows the chain which runs through a hole in his nose, or as a crab moves toward its prey. The scene is a ranch in California, and the bunkhouse talk is terrific—God damn, Jesus Christ, what the hell, you crazy bastard, I gotta gut ache, and things like that. The dialect never varies, just as the story never runs uphill.

George and Lennie, the itinerant workers who come to the ranch one day with a dream of the little farm they will own as soon as they get the jack together, seem to think their new job will last at least that long; but the reader knows from the beginning that it will not last, for Lennie is a half-witted giant with a passion for petting mice—or rabbits, or pups, or girls—and for killing them when they don't like it. He is doomed in this book to kill Curley's wife; that is obvious; and then—. Lennie, you see, cannot help shaking small helpless creatures until their necks are broken, just as George cannot relinquish his dream, and just as Curley cannot ever stop being a beast of jealousy. They are wound up to act that way, and the best they can do is run down; which is what happens when Mr. Steinbeck comes to his last mechanical page.

What, however, of the one exception? Ah, he is Slim the jerkline skinner, the tall man with the "God-like eyes" that get fastened on you so that you can't think of anything else for a while. "There was a gravity in his manner and a quiet so profound that all talk stopped when he spoke. . . . His hatchet face was ageless. He might have been thirty-five or fifty. His ear heard more than was said to him, and his slow speech had overtones not of thought, but of understanding beyond thought. His hands, large and lean, were as delicate in their action as those of a temple dancer." He looks through people and beyond them—a feat never accomplished save in mechanical novels. And he understands—why, he understands everything that Mr. Steinbeck understands. It is the merest accident of education that he talks like the rest; "Jesus, he's jes' like a kid, ain't he," he says. If he had his creator's refinement of tongue he could write such sentences as this one which introduces Lennie: "His arms did not swing at his sides, but hung loosely and only moved because the heavy hands were pendula." It wouldn't have done to write pendulums. That would have given the real sound and look of Lennie, and besides it is a real word.

Mr. Steinbeck, I take it, has not been interested in reality of any kind. His jerkline skinner (mule driver) is as hopelessly above the human range as Lennie or Candy or Curley's painted wife is below it. All is extreme here; everybody is a doll; and if there is a kick in the story it is given us from some source which we cannot see, as when a goose walks over our grave, or as when in the middle of the night the telephone rings sharply and it is the wrong number. We shall remember it about that long.

S.W.
"Current Literature."
Philadelphia *Inquirer*,
6 March 1937, p. 14.

. . . Most stories of those President Roosevelt calls the "underprivileged" sound a protestant note. It is as if the author had a graphophone record of remarks by Norman Thomas or Mr. John L. Lewis at his elbow. So fiction suffers; and argument is confused. Such things may not be said of the novels of John Steinbeck. On his record of six books he takes rank as the best interpreter of the semi-submerged in this country. Whether good or bad, unfortunate or self-stricken, he goes to the core of character with the precision of a surgeon whose diagnosis is given in terms of art. Tricky rhetoric he eschews. The manner of his expression is fine and true. In his newly published short novel, *Of Mice and Men*, [what] might seem vulgar is dignified, and at times transfigured, by a soul shining through. This is the story of George and Lennie, strange partners in grain-bucking on a California ranch. The story of George, small and active, and Lennie, the hulking giant with a child's mind and a passion for petting a mouse, a rabbit, a piece of velvet, anything soft. With affectionate strategy George stands between Lennie and disaster until Curley's wife, the foolish jade, invites him to stroke her hair. So there is one thing more for George to do in the most affecting passage of recent American fiction.

Eleanor Roosevelt. "My Day." New York *World-Telegram*, 16 March 1937, p. 21.

. . . I have just finished a little book called *Of Mice and Men* by John Steinbeck, which a fellow columnist, Mr. Heywood Broun, reviewed in his column not long ago. My admiration for Mr. Broun leads me to want to look into anything he praises, and so I sent for the book to bring it away with me. It is beautifully written and a marvelous picture of the tragedy of loneliness.

I could see the two men, one comes across their likes in many places, not only in the West described in the book but in every part of the country. When I closed *Of Mice and Men* I could not help but think how fortunate we are when we have real friends, people we can count on and turn to and who we know are always glad to see us when we are lonely.

Dorothea Brande Collins. "Reading at Random." *American Review*, 9 (April 1937), 100–13.

. . . As for *Of Mice and Men*—surely no more sentimental wallowing ever passed for a novel, or had such a welcome, as this sad tale of a huge half-wit and his cowboy protector! Mr. Steinbeck this time wrings the Tears of Things from a ten-gallon hat, and reviewers who cannot bear the mawkishness of a Milne, the crudity of a Coward, or the mysticism of a Morgan were able to take the sorrowful symmetries of a Steinbeck to their hearts and write their reviews with tears running down their cheeks.

Who does not know by this time of Lennie, who loved to stroke soft furry things, but didn't know his own strength? Of Slim, with the "God-like eyes," knight *sans peur et sans reproche* of the bunkhouse? Of George, who loved Lennie well enough to shoot him? Of "Curley's wife," that wax-dummy girl who might have come straight out of the window of a chain dress-shop, so glossy, so hard, so brightly painted—and so far from ever having drawn a breath?

Mr. Steinbeck is "economical." He is, indeed. That is perhaps the secret of his charm. I feel sure that all those reviewers who cheered so hard for *Of Mice and Men* would, if they could have been caught while still sobbing over George and Lennie, have admitted that even critics are only boys at heart, for that is just the mood that Mr. Steinbeck's work induces. So perhaps again, they would admit that the secret of his success is that a certain simple type of reader feels, when he discovers that he has foreseen correctly any movement of a story, a kind of participation in the creative act of the author. Almost any critic would admit this if the book under consideration were one of the Tarzan books, or a book by Lloyd Douglas, or any one of a dozen "popular novelists" of the sort they affect to despise, but perhaps they have not noticed that the symmetry and expectedness (or, if you prefer, read "economy") of Mr. Steinbeck's work put the average pulp-writer to shame.

If Lennie kills a mouse by stroking it, you may be sure he will unintentionally kill something larger in the same way; when you hear of Curley's wife's soft hair, "like fur," you can begin to co-operate with the author by expectation of her end. When George learns that a poor old worthless smelly dog can be dispatched easily by a shot in the back of his head, you are unwarrantably guileless if you do not suspect the manner in which Lennie will meet his death. If an old man dreams of a home, peace, and security, you may be sure that a home, peace, and security are what he will most agonizingly just miss. And so forth. You can call this sort of foreshadowing "economy" if it pleases you; but if "economy" is the word you choose you should abandon the word "obvious" hereafter and forever.

It may be some time before the current vogue for Steinbeck passes. Masculine sentimentality, particularly when it masquerades as toughness, is a little longer in being seen through than the feminine or the inclusively human variety. Undoubtedly there are plenty who would deny, even today, that *The Sun Also Rises* and *What Price Glory?* are (although far more distinguished) prototypes of *Of Mice and Men*. Surely it should not be too hard to find the soft spots where the decay shows: the romantic overestimation of the rôle of friendship, the wax-figure women, bright, hard, treacherous, unreal—whether a Lady Brett, the French girl behind the lines, or "Curley's wife," these are all essentially hateful women, women from whom it is a virtue to flee to masculine companionship. There was certainly a sort of stag-party hysteria and uproar about the approval we have been hearing for this padded short story about underdogs and animals, bunkhouses and bathos, which has seldom risen so high since "Wait for baby!" soared over the footlights. . . . Ah, I was forgetting Mr. Chips.

Edward Weeks. "The Bookshelf." *Atlantic*, 159 (April 1937), [pp. 14, 16 at back of issue].

Since the death of Ring Lardner, an element once characteristic of American fiction has been conspicuous by its absence: laughter. The short stories and the novels of our younger writers are so often pervaded by a humorless intensity or by an irony and didacticism that leave the reader cold. Now from California comes a novelist with a better balance, a shrewder skill, a more native sense of reality. His name is John Steinbeck: he has five novels to his credit. Farsighted reviewers began to spot him three years ago; the reading public, slower with its recognition, will now hurry to make amends.

John Steinbeck must have footed his way through that California which is neither movies nor real estate. He knows the wanderers—the fruit pickers, the ranch hands, the hoboes; he knows this migratory race—its pride, its humor, its gullibility and futility. New Steinbeck readers might follow this programme: first, *Tortilla Flat*, light-hearted, wholly delightful; next, *In Dubious Battle*, which, partisan though it be, is quite our most vital story of an American strike; and so coming down to his *Of Mice and Men . . .*, a short tale of two harvest hands, the one a slow-witted elephant, the other a ferret. You feel the affection that binds Lennie and George together. You hear talk as natural as grass. You recognize in them a hunger which moves all men. There are moments when the tension and brevity of the story make it read like a theatrical script: I mean that Slim's authority and Candy's dog mean more to me than the drama in the barn or at the pool. But, whatever be your favorite passages, here is indisputable proof of a vital and experienced story-teller. . . .

"Dorothea Brande Doesn't Enjoy Steinbeck." Charlotte [N.C.] *News*, 6 June 1937, p. 9A.

In the same measure that John Steinbeck's *Of Mice and Men* gave pleasure to many readers, so it outraged the critical sensibilities of two reviewers—Mark van Doren and Dorothea Brande Collins. Professor van Doren was dreadfully put out by its profanity, which suggests that he is the Rip Van Winkle of our times. Mrs. Collins (the author of *Becoming a Writer*, which tells how to make your unconscious do the work) decided that the story was so obvious that it bowled over only critics who were boys at heart.

Commenting in the *American Review*, she says the secret of Steinbeck's success is "that a certain simple type of reader feels, when he has foreseen correctly any movement of a story, a kind of participation in the creative act of the author. . . . If Lennie kills a mouse by stroking it, you may be sure he will unintentionally kill something larger in the same way; when you hear Curley's wife's soft hair 'like fur,' you can begin to cooperate with the author by expectation of her end."

Mrs. Collins evidently feels that in saying that the author meets the expectations of the readers she has dealt his story a body blow. As a matter of fact, she has merely expressed her dislike for a technique that is one of many employed by writers; her interests are intellectual, and her concern with the novel is chiefly as an exercise for the mind. This is a high form of artistic appreciation and expression, but by no means the only one. What counts in *Of Mice and Men* is that the author meets the expectations of his readers (women as well as the stag line) a bit more successfully than many other workers in his medium.

Harold Brighouse. "New Novels: Archers of the Long Bow." Manchester *Guardian*, 14 September 1937, p. 5.

. . . In [Wallace Stegner's] *Remembering Laughter* the farm and the landscape are realised without sentimentality. Mr. Steinbeck, in *Of Mice and Men*, is both melodramatic and sentimental. Assume that there is love between a performing bear and its keeper; the bear hugs a woman to death and the keeper has to shoot it. For "bear" read Lennie, a giant of a man mentally defective, and for "keeper" read George. They came, partners, through the Californian woods to a farming ranch, and George's dream was to save wages till they could own land of their own. There is an incident, made significant, of the shooting of a sheepdog, stinking in useless old age, and insistence upon Lennie's passion for stroking mice and rabbits till his brutish affection killed them. So it was that he stroked the red hair, and she not unwilling, of the raffish wife of the rancher's son, and, stroking, killed her. It is a pitiful tragedy amongst people the brightest of whom is hardly more than half-witted, and the publisher is rhapsodical about it. Personally, I think Mr. Steinbeck has done better work than this.

V. S. Pritchett.
"New Novels."
New Statesman and Nation [England], 14 (25 September 1937), 448–9.

... *Of Mice and Men* is decidedly surprising and queer. It is the story of two casuals who run out of one job into the next. One is a huge half-wit with a grip like a vice and a brain like a pea. He has a sinister mania for touching things—mice, puppies, velvet, girls' hair and sometimes he strokes too hard; the other is a dogged little chap who "travels around" with him and tries in vain to keep the soft-headed, hard-handed fellow out of trouble. The feeble talk of cowboys, their pathetic hopes and affections, their childish preoccupations, are perfectly recorded. The American underdog has provided Mr. Steinbeck with some macabre material. The reader must not be put off the book by its awful jacket and its pointless illustrations. . . .

"*Of Mice and Men*."
London *Mercury*, 36 (October 1937), 595.

Mr. Steinbeck's tale of two cattle-ranch hands, Lennie, the "natural," and George,

his devoted protector, is an extremely skilful variant of the tough tabloid. The companions have an escape-story of a place of their own with cows and rabbits where they will live "on the fatta of the lan'," which George tells Lennie on their long tramps from job to job. Lennie's daftness takes the form of killing small, soft things, including women. The final scene, in which George, preparing to shoot his friend to save him from being lynched, tells the little story for the last time, is a triumph of the sentimental macabre.

"*Of Mice and Men*."
Times Literary Supplement [London], 2 October 1937, p. 714.

This is a moving story of two drifting cattle-ranch hands in California. George and Lennie are friends, owning nothing but what they pack from one job to the next. But they are optimists. The dream that buoys and binds them is of the bit of land they are going to buy—some day. The vision comes excitingly near, then vanishes.

The disaster is inherent in Lennie's nature. A phenomenal worker but a want-wit, he is pathetically incapable of looking after himself, or even of controlling his huge body. George, small, active, querulous, is incessantly watchful over his infantile friend and liability. They have been chased from their last job because Lennie innocently touched a girl's red dress. Now a promising fresh start offers on another ranch. But when the wanton wife of the owner's unpleasant son makes up to Lennie, he shakes her, not in anger but in fear of George's wrath, and finds he has killed her. He acts on George's standing instruction that in event of trouble he is to hide by the river. The lynchers go in pursuit. But George, with a stolen pistol, reaches Lennie first and deals quick death, the best that could come to his friend.

It is a tremendous climax to a short tale of much power and beauty. Mr. Steinbeck has contributed a small masterpiece to the modern tough-tender school of American fiction.

Checklist of Additional Reviews

Joseph Henry Jackson. "A Bookman's Notebook." San Francisco *Chronicle*, 6 February 1937, p. 13.

Theodore Smith. "John Steinbeck Adds New Book to List on Transient Workers." San Francisco *News*, 20 February 1937, p. 15.

Herschel Brickell. "H. G. Wells and John Steinbeck Prove that Books Do Not Have to Be Long to Be Important." New York *Post*, 25 February 1937, p. 19.

"Friendship." *Newsweek*, 9 (27 February 1937), 38–9.

"A Tender, Touching Tale Admirably Told." Chicago *Tribune*, 27 February 1937, p. 11.

Charlotte Becker. "John Steinbeck Writes Miniature Epic in *Of Mice and Men*, a Story of the Human Vagabonds and Flotsam He Depicts So Well." Buffalo *Times*, 28 February 1937, p. 8C.

Walter Sidney. "Treacle from a Talent."

Brooklyn *Eagle*, 28 February 1937, Section C, p. 17.

"Steinbeck Tells Story of Harvest." Knoxville *Journal*, 28 February 1937, Section 4, p. 3.

Sterling North. "Blessed Are the Meek Portrayed by John Steinbeck." Chicago *Daily News*, 3 March 1937, p. 31.

"Somerset Maugham, H. G. Wells and John Steinbeck." Philadelphia *Inquirer*, 6 March 1937, p. 14.

Harry Hansen. "Critic Hails John Steinbeck Story as Finest Bit of Fiction in Decade." Pittsburgh *Press*, 7 March 1937, "Society" section, p. 14.

Russell Smith. "Steinbeck Humanizes Statistics." Washington *Post*, 7 March 1937, p. 8.

Emma Wilson. "*Of Mice and Men*." Chico [Calif.] *Record*, 9 March 1937, p. 5.

Hume Dow. "*Of Mice and Men*." *Harvard Advocate*, 1 April 1937, p. 32.

Gilbert E. Govan. "Roamin' the Book World." Chattanooga *Times*, 29 May 1937, p. 10.

Helen MacAfee. "Outstanding Novels." *Yale Review*, 26 (June 1937), vi.

"Book Review." Corona [Calif.] *Independent*, 1 September 1937, p. 3.

Joseph Henry Jackson. "John Steinbeck: A Portrait." *Saturday Review*, 16 (25 September 1937), 11–12, 18.

Helen E. Haines. "Novels of Last Year." Pasadena *Star-News*, 1 January 1938, p. 24.

T. C. Worsley. "General Release." *New Statesman and Nation* [England], 20 (19 October 1940), 396.

James Newcomer. "Reappraisals IV: Steinbeck's *Mice and Men*." Dallas *News*, 14 August 1949, p. 32.

THE RED PONY

◈ THE RED PONY ◈

BY

JOHN STEINBECK

NEW YORK ◈ MCM XXX VII

COVICI · FRIEDE · PUBLISHERS

Christopher Morley.
"Boy against Death."
Saturday Review, 16
(25 September 1937), 18.

Tortilla Flat and *Of Mice and Men* were not accidents. It is unlikely that anything Mr. Steinbeck publishes will be casual; he is a controlled, deliberate and ascertained workman. In this little book he again shows himself equal in power and in sensitiveness, and purposeful in both. It would not be fair to suppose that because *The Red Pony* appears in a deluxe limitation that he (or his publisher) regards it as hors d'œuvre. It may be a sketch of some shape of things to come; it may be a mood (of memory or fancy) that the author prefers to keep within restricted bounds. It has on it his own mark of beauty and pain.

It would be possible (as it always is possible) to read into these three episodes in the life of a ten-year-old boy some larger meanings and suggestions. Is it the first glimmering in the boy's mind of the collapse of faith or certainty? For first the death of the pony, and then the death of the mare in bearing another foal, are attributable (in the boy's mind) to Billy Buck who knew all about horses. So Billy (a notable character portrait) proves fallible after all. That is one suggestion of fable that the reader may find; and there are others. Mr. Steinbeck is a writer of such gauge that we enjoy speculating what he may have intended between the lines. It is an impertinence: but he has earned the right to be subjected to it. As in the book before us, we know by the sound of his tread on the floor that he is wearing riding boots; but the boy always looks under the table to make sure.

These three episodes are told with illuminated simplicity. Steinbeck knows what effect he desires, and he gets it without fumbling. In the first we have the gift of the Red Pony, its training, its tragic death. The second chapter is a charming interlude—ostensibly quite apart from the theme—of the old *paisano* who comes to the ranch (because he was born there) and, finding himself *de trop*, rides off into the mountains to die, on the old horse that is also ready for death. And the third chapter (or fable) is of the breeding and birthing of new promise—the colt to come. So we have the boy Jody, in his ranch-childhood, encountering Death on three planes: the last time in all the blood and disgust of an equine cæsarian. And the buzzards, and the gold-hilted rapier, and the emphasized thematic opposition of the mossy spring uphill in line with the frightening black cauldron where the pigs are slaughtered: all these elements are thought, focussed, and intended.

So, I repeat, Mr. Steinbeck knows what he is doing; he does it thrillingly; in theme as well as in its deliberately restricted publication (although the three sections have appeared as short stories in *The North American Review* and *Harper's*) this is a book for comparatively few. But the few are important, and sometimes they eventually prevail.

Randolph Bartlett.
"Tang of Sage."
New York *Sun*,
27 September 1937, p. 6.

John Steinbeck, scrawling rowdy caricatures in charcoal on butcher's paper, has laid aside his familiar tools to prove his artistry with—of all things—the etcher's needle. There was never any doubt of his mastery of the other medium. He proved it in the boisterous and bawdy *Tortilla Flat* and the sinister and fleshly *Of Mice and Men*. It was not to be expected that he would be equally at home in a medium which requires finesse in place of brutality, and yet here is *The Red Pony*.

This latest work consists of three novelettes, each self-contained and yet threaded in sequence, depicting the life of a boy on a ranch in that part of California Mr. Steinbeck knows so thoroughly, between the naive south and the sophisticated north, the Monterey region. Delicately, and affectionately, he reveals the very soul of the lad, his love for animals, his appreciation of generosity, his faith in his elders, his great need to do some violent thing when tragedy has shattered his hopes and dreams.

The first story tells of a gift from his father of a pony of his own, a pony he must teach to love and respect him, a pony to train and one day to ride. Lest it might be inferred that this is a mere tale for boys it must be added that Mr. Steinbeck is equally effective in picturing the family background of his little hero, Jody. There is his father, a man of keen understanding and with all the wisdom of the ranges; his mother, stern but gentle, and quick to sense her son's needs; Billy Buck, the ranch hand, who knew all about horses that there was to know. It is a kindly atmosphere.

The second story, "The Great Mountains," deals with the return to the ranch of a man who had been born there, a Mexican, now grown old and asking only a place to sleep and a little food. This is an interlude between the other two novelettes, in which the boy fills in a void in his life by dreaming and inquiring about the mountains in the distance, what is to be found there, and what lies beyond.

The third story, "The Promise," carries the boy to the fulfillment of his wish, through doubts and apprehension which have crept into his consciousness because of the experiences through which he has gone in the two previous episodes. This time, a horse is to be bred for him, and at the end of the long period of waiting there occurs a denouement that is the one touch of the ruthless Steinbeck in the series.

An interesting characteristic of this work is that in the transition from charcoal to stylus, Mr. Steinbeck has lost nothing of his force and vitality. He merely seems to have realized that in dealing with this essentially human narrative, it was necessary to adopt a different technic than was useful in picturing the denizens of Tortilla Flat or the men of violence in *Of Mice and Men*.

The effectiveness of his work is due in a very large measure to the fact that he obviously knows intimately the region of which he writes. The reader cannot fail to sense the tang of sage in the dusty air, nor to see the nodding bunches of wild oats on the hillside. Horses too he knows, inside and out, and what is going on in their minds, and boys he knows and must love, or he could not have written of Jody as he did.

It must be assumed that there will be subsequent editions of this charming work. The present format is exquisite, a large paper edition with a flexible linen cover, and limited to 699 copies, as if Covici-Friede were anxious to accentuate the difference between the old Steinbeck and the new. The picture is entirely worthy of its luxurious frame.

Ralph Thompson.
"Death and Jody."
New York *Times*,
29 September 1937, p. 21.

... As for Mr. Steinbeck's latest, ... any one who can afford a handsome sum for handsome presswork and design (this is a Pynson Printers job, each copy signed by the author) will be well rewarded. Mr. Steinbeck had three stories to tell, each one relating to a 10-year-old boy named Jody, who lives on a ranch in the West and is much concerned with the life about him.

The first story is about a red pony. Like young Lincoln Steffens, Jody went down to the barn one day and found a pony of his very own, which he had now to manage and, in time, to ride. But Mr. Steinbeck, unable to abide for long a sentimental situation, does not let it go at that. Before many weeks have passed the red pony sickens and dies, horribly.

The second story also ends in death, though this time Jody does not see it with his own eyes. The third story, a little masterpiece dealing with the breeding of a mare and the subsequent birth of a colt, again comes to tragedy—tragedy quite as melodramatic and deliberate as that in *Of Mice and Men*. Yes, yes, of course, it is true that in real life everything does die sooner or later. But it is hardly necessary for Mr. Steinbeck to make that point time and time again, particularly if in so doing he cramps his talent into the confines of a formula.

Eda Lou Walton.
"The Simple Life."
Nation, 147
(1 October 1937), 331–2.

A romantic ardor for the simple life is the bridge between John Steinbeck's earlier work and his later. What has always seemed to him the cure for modern neuroses is man's identification with nature. His scene has been California and particularly the Salinas Valley. His first books had to do with the psychologically sick intellectual brought to health by a return to nature; his later books have had to do with the sick farm laborer cured, again, largely by nature.

Once he stopped treating of characters like himself, Steinbeck pruned his style, swept away most of his lushness and emotionalism, and became a realist. But he continued to rely for his symbols essentially on the Freudian psychology that marked his earlier books. He merely turned to a large circle of characters, to a new class, to exemplify his thesis that man and his natural environment should not be separated. In turning from self-examination to the applications of his thesis in simple characters, he lost something of his personal passion but became a more competent writer relying on a realistic technique and dramatic shock to make his points.

I am not asserting that Steinbeck's first books were his best. They were overwritten and sentimental, but Steinbeck himself appeared in a different light. In his latest books his Freudianism remains, but he has turned from working out a personal solution—in its nature somewhat reactionary—to the application rather than the evolution of the psychology of frustration. That society alters personal psychology he knows, but he reveals little feeling for social evolution in itself.

How does all this affect his work? Every short story in this book springs from a preconceived symbol, not from a rich knowledge of character (although the outlines of these character drawings are clear) or a social situation. In every narrative, therefore, character and action, as by a formula, exemplify a symbol. The most significant symbols to Steinbeck are always life, death, nature. This fact causes him to place his emphasis on the bravery and pathos of the simple poor of the farm laboring class. But because his symbols do not necessarily evolve out of the situations presented, nor out of his impassioned vision of his characters' significance, they seem obvious. The alert reader will know in a paragraph or two of each story just how the author proposes to prove his point.

These stories are clever, but they move toward nothing. Nor do Steinbeck's novels move toward any consistent vision of life or toward any set of values. He has written one study of labor struggle which reads like a detective story (*In Dubious Battle*), inconclusive in its social philosophy but effective in dramatic plot. *Of Mice and Men* is far more certainly a study of neuroses than it is a picture of the proletarian. The best short story in this new collection, *The Red Pony*, is forced, by the interjection of an act of violence, to prove that through violence life springs from death. This story of a boy's loss of his first pony, of his learning about life in watching the entire process of his second pony's conception, prenatal growth, and emergence into the world, would have been right had the author not insisted that the second pony's mother, too, meet death in order to show that life is born of death. The killing of the mare in order to save the colt is a totally forced

situation, and forced, as always, to emphasize Steinbeck's symbolism.

In general, Steinbeck's Salinas Valley farmers never indicate more than their own characters, manipulated to some extent by the author. Toward what ideology, if any, do they move? Toward what ideology does the author himself move? Nothing in his work seems resolved or progressing toward resolution. His stories are competent, but reading them one goes through no authentic experience.

J.H.C.
"Dreams and Tragedies in Salinas Hills."
Los Angeles *Times*, 10 October 1937, Part 3, p. 8.

If American collectors know one-tenth as much as we believe they do the entire edition of Steinbeck's *Red Pony* is exhausted. The publisher has sold out his stock, and it is to be hoped that Los Angeles admirers of this powerful California writer have not failed to secure their copies.

There are three stories printed between the elegant covers of this volume: "The Gift," "The Mountains," "The Promise." They are episodes in the life of Jody, a 10-year-old farm boy from up Salinas way. Jody had dreams and they quivered into life over far horizons. Then Jody got a red pony, and Billy Buck, who knew all about horses, taught him how to take care of it. But Jody's faith in Billy was shaken when, in spite of everything, the pony died; all because Billy was not a rain prophet. That tale is followed by a touching interlude concerning the fate of old men and horses. The last story shows how Jody got another pony—at a price.

Once upon a time Mr. Aristotle laid down the rules for writing masterpieces. Whether he got it out of Aristotle or not, Steinbeck knows the rules. He knows what he intends to do and does it in the simplest and most effective fashion. He knows life at both ends and the middle. He grips your heart and satisfies your mind if you have one. If you have not, it makes no difference, he takes hold of you anyway.

Edith H. Walton.
"Three Short Stories by John Steinbeck."
New York Times Book Review, 87
(10 October 1937), 4.

In a very short time—just, indeed, since the success of *Tortilla Flat*—it has become bromidic to say of John Steinbeck that no two of his books ever resemble one another. They do, however, have many traits in common. Power, for one thing, and a lovely gift of words, and an astonishing way of making the simple seem important. As for the latter trait, nothing could be more starkly simple than this new book, *The Red Pony*, which consists merely of three episodes in the life of a 10-year-old boy. In other hands, these slight, delicate stories, quite unremarkable in theme, might have struck one as somewhat jejune and certainly not exciting. As it is, they are pure gold and furnish the most exacting proof he has given of Mr. Steinbeck's artistry.

Jody is a polite, shy little boy whose home is that mountainous California country near Salinas and Monterey. His parents own a small ranch and with them lives a brusque, kind ranch-hand, Billy Buck, who knows an inordinate amount about horses. In the first and best story, "The Gift," his father presents Jody with a wild red pony which the boy cares for and trains and loves almost raptly. Then, cruelly, the red pony dies, not only bringing to Jody his first real sorrow but filling him with doubts of Billy Buck's omniscience. Unreasonably, he blames Billy—who redeems himself with difficulty in the third story, "The Promise," which concerns the breeding and birthing of a colt that is to be Jody's. Jody gets his colt, as Billy has grimly promised, but to compass this fulfillment the mare has to die.

Between these two stories, which are closely related and both richly poignant, there is a curious, legend-like interlude which affects the boy more intangibly. An old *paisano*, born in the neighborhood of the ranch, returns there with the stubborn desire to die where he belongs. When, however, he finds himself unwanted, he rides off to the great mountains which have always tantalized Jody, taking with him an ancient horse which has likewise outlived its usefulness. This story has charm and a kind of eerie beauty, but it seems a shade more artificial than either "The Gift" or "The Promise." Because of its very singularity, it does not move one to the same half-painful extent.

If one speaks of the tenderness and sense of compassion which run through these stories, there is danger that *The Red Pony* may sound like a sentimental book. Actually it is nothing of the kind. Mr. Steinbeck has avoided this note with the most rigorous care and skill. As well, the tone of his three episodes varies subtly and often. Both "The Gift" and "The Promise" build up to a climax which is bloodily brutal in its harshness; there is the shrewdest kind of humor in Mr. Steinbeck's character drawing of the likable Billy Buck. Slight as they seem, tenuous as are their plots, all three of these stories have more depth, intensity and variety than one could possibly anticipate.

The Red Pony has been published in a limited, de luxe edition, exquisite in format and, of course, very expensive. Presumably, John Steinbeck and his publishers quite honestly believed that this is a book for the few and not for the public in general. If so, they could hardly be more wrong. The stories in *The Red Pony* have such a fine, candid simplicity, are so moving and so real, that only the wholly philistine could possibly fail to respond to them. They are not tidbits for the connoisseur, however fastidious their workmanship, but warmly human tales which a larger public should know about. To restrict their circulation is to do that public an injustice.

"Steinbeck Inflation."
Time, 29
(11 October 1937), 79.

For a parallel to the inflation that has skyrocketed the value of John Steinbeck first editions, bibliophiles must turn to the classic rise in the price of calves' liver, once given away in most butcher shops, currently selling at 85¢ a lb. Distributed free to Publisher Covici-Friede's friends last Christmas, Author Steinbeck's *St. Katy the Virgin*, a short story, is now quoted at $10. Published last fortnight in an edition limited to 699 autographed, de luxe copies, Novelist Steinbeck's latest work, *The Red Pony*, was quoted at $10 a copy, and no man knew where it would go from there.

Some readers, baffled by the famine-price set on this slim, 81-page volume (all the more remarkable in view of Steinbeck's proletarian themes), may jump to the wrong conclusion that *The Red Pony* contains erotic or esoteric matter too caviarish for the general. On the contrary, *The Red Pony* is neither scandalous nor abstruse but of an innocence that almost qualifies it for juvenile readers. It consists of three episodes based on Author Steinbeck's youth. Central character is a healthy, shy, tow-headed, 10-year-old farm boy named Jody Tiflin. Given a red pony colt by his father, coached in its training by the hired hand, Jody is in perpetual seventh heaven except when he is in school. A few days before the pony is ready to ride, it catches pneumonia, sneaks away to die in the woods, where Jody is found beside the corpse, hammering insanely on the long-since smashed head of a buzzard that was too slow to escape his wild grief.

Most tenuous, but also the most interesting in showing how the early Steinbeck twig of romanticism was bent is the second episode: Jody who feels deeply the mystery of the distant California Sierras, thinks he has the answer when he watches an old Mexican going off into the mountains to die.

Last episode relates how Jody got his second pony. In return for Jody's putting in a summer's hard work, Farmer Tiflin lays out $5 to breed their own mare Nellie. Jody dedicates himself completely to Nellie's prenatal care, to giving his father more than his five-dollars' worth. When complications develop at the delivery, the hired hand kills Nellie with a hammer, and in a gory Cesarean delivers Jody his promised colt.

California-born (1900), big, blond, blue-eyed, slow-spoken John Ernest Steinbeck has been a farm hand, hod carrier, caretaker, chemist and painter's apprentice, itinerant newspaper-man. At Stanford University off and on for six years, he treated it as a sort of public library where he read only what took his fancy: physics, biology, philosophy, history. Indifferent to most fiction, he thinks Thackeray passable, cannot stomach Proust because he "wrote his sickness, and I don't like sick writing." He is dead set against publicity, photographs, speeches, believes "they do you damage." Now living in Los Gatos, Calif., since publication of his best-selling *Of Mice and Men* (167,000 copies), Mr. Steinbeck can well afford to abandon an erstwhile $25-a-month budget which he and his tall, brunette wife Carol supplemented by fishing, not for fun, from their own launch in Monterey Bay.

Joseph Henry Jackson. "A Bookman's Notebook." San Francisco *Chronicle*, 12 October 1937, p. 11.

One of the things that the ordinary reader is going to wonder about is the price of this latest Steinbeck book. To be sure, it's printed in a small limited edition—600-odd copies—and very beautifully designed and printed, with a slip cover and all that sort of thing. Moreover, each and every copy is signed by the author and bears its number in the edition all carefully written in the back. Obviously, just as a limited edition of the work of a man who has suddenly become very well known indeed to the public at large, the product is worth the price asked—at any rate, on the supply-and-demand basis.

But why? The average reader is going to ask, "Why the limited edition in the first place?"

Well, there's a good enough reason. First consider the story itself.

The Red Pony is not a novel, nor even strictly a novelette—"novella," as the word is coming to be, borrowed from the Italian. It's a group of three related short stories, all having to do with the same small boy, Jody, and with his acquisition of a red pony—two ponies, as a matter of fact. That's on the face of it.

Beneath this, the book is a presentation of a small boy's first encounters with death—death that is unavoidable, natural, yet frightful and violent as death always must be to the human being when he first comes into contact with it. Twice in the form of death to animal life, once in the form of death as an old *paisano* meets it, Jody sees what dying is like. And even though once it means birth, too, nevertheless it is death, bloody and horrible. Steinbeck could have called the book, "Jody Looks at Death and Life"—though it wouldn't have been a very good title.

That Steinbeck writes these stories with extraordinary delicacy of touch almost goes without saying. Even in the most violent, most frightful scenes, the delicacy is there: Don't mistake this for "delicacy" in the sense our mothers and maiden aunts used the word in the nineties; that's not what I mean at all. They would have called *The Red Pony* anything but that; "excessively indelicate" is what they would have said, if, indeed, they had been able to read it at all without fainting. The delicacy is in the precise, beautiful handling of words, in the equally precise and exact placing of scenes, in the even more exact and lovely balance of the whole. It bears the Steinbeck mark; you can't help but recognize it.

Outside the nature of the story, though, why the limited edition, to come back to that?

The reason is simply publisher's figuring.

Steinbeck's last book, *Of Mice and Men*, is still on the best-seller lists. Moreover, it is a short book. It was very nicely printed and bound and designed, and in order for the publisher to get anywhere at all with it, he had to charge $2 for it. The public, odd animal that it is, doesn't like books at say, $1.50; no one knows why, but it doesn't. It just doesn't buy them.

But even though that's the case, the public at large, which gets heavy tomes such as *Gone With the Wind* and *Anthony Adverse* for $2.50 and $3, did regard *Of Mice and Men* as just a bit on the slim side. People are like that. They still think of books by length and breadth, even though they know, abstractly, that it's content that counts.

Steinbeck, then, is nearly finished with his next full-length book. It's coming next year; the publisher doesn't know exactly when, but probably late in the spring. In the meantime, here's *The Red Pony*, slimmer than *Of Mice and Men*, a story involving horror, yet the author's next work and by all means worth printing. What to do? Present it in a regular "Trade Edition" at a dollar or a dollar and a half? By no means. (You can almost see the publisher working it out in his head.) What then? Well, in order to bridge the gap in Steinbeckiana, and to cultivate interest in an important field, which is the collector of Steinbeck. Ah! A limited edition, of course! And there you are.

Naturally none of these steps in figuring it out occurred to Steinbeck. He doesn't bother his head about such matters. He bothers his head about writing. At the moment, he's working like a slave on the next book, and that's all that concerns him. The play made from *Of Mice and Men* is in rehearsal in New York. Jack Kirkland is said to be working on a dramatization of *Tortilla Flat*. The book printing of the play *Of Mice and Men* will be out any minute. The *Modern Library* edition of *Tortilla Flat* is just on the market, and so is a regular-size dollar reprint of it. In the meantime, John Steinbeck is doing what he wants to do, which is to pay attention strictly to the book he has in hand, and stay as far as possible from New York. Which is very good sense indeed.

Joseph Henry Jackson. "Bookman's Notebook." San Francisco *Chronicle*, 6 September 1945, p. 12.

As you probably know, John Steinbeck has become a collectors' item; his books in their first editions and in mint condition, or even fair condition, command premium prices, and while fads in collecting change it's pretty safe to say that Steinbeck firsts and special editions will stand up well.

This note is prefatory to the notice that there is published today a new edition of one of Steinbeck's great favorites, *The Red Pony*....

Another point here, in addition to the fact that the book is beautifully illustrated, makes this a Steinbeck item.

The first edition of *The Red Pony* appeared in a slim de luxe printing of 1000 copies at $10. It contained three connected stories about the boy, Jody, his father and his pony. They'd appeared in magazines, but never before as a book.

This first printing was soon gone and that was that. Then "The Red Pony" appeared in a larger volume, *The Long Valley*, which was a collection of Steinbeck's short stories. In that collection, too, was a story, also involving Jody, called "The Leader of the People"; it had been written later than "The Red Pony," wherefore it was not included in the original first edition.

That fourth part, which really belongs with the whole story, is now included in the new, illustrated edition, which is what makes it, in a sense wholly apart from other printings, a Steinbeck "first."

The pictures, however, constitute a reason in themselves, and the publisher has found precisely the right man to do them—Wesley Dennis, who has long been well known as a painter of horses. Working in water color, Dennis has done a beautifully imaginative job of it, his 13 full color pictures and end-papers interpreting the story vigorously and yet with just the mystical touch that the narrative needs. Of the 13 illustrations, there is only one which seems to me at all out of key, and that's a good enough illustration in itself. It's the heading for Part II, "The Great Mountains," and it's a rather too comic painting of Jody's dog catching its nose in a mousetrap. *The Red Pony*, after all, is neither a funny story nor a child's story, and this one picture suggests that it might be either or both. Quite possibly Steinbeck himself—who's in Mexico at the moment, living in the old Marik Hotel, from whose windows you get such a magnificent view of Popo—wouldn't agree with me, and obviously the publisher and the artist don't feel that way. Anyhow, it isn't an important enough point to damage the total effect of Mr.

Dennis' work, which is splendidly suited to the next.

As for typography, the whole book has been redesigned and set, and somewhere the publisher has managed to get hold of thoroughly good paper and buckram cloth for binding. Just as book, it seems to me worth more than the original $10 edition, and at half the price. Doubtless the fact that the Book-of-the-Month Club is to make it a dividend book had something to do with it; a large printing would naturally bring down the unit cost.

You'll note, by the way, that I've said nothing about the story. The assumption is that readers will already know about it. Just in case some don't know it, better let me repeat that it isn't a children's story. For my money, however, it and the novel, *In Dubious Battle* are the two best things Steinbeck has ever done.

A. C. S[pectorsky].
"A Postwar Publisher
Luxuriates."
Chicago Sun Book Week,
3 (10 September 1945), 2.

The first bite of a point-free steak, the first easing of a tired body into a soft bed, the soldier's first civilian suit are all in the running but not on a par with the publishing thrill the people at Viking Press treated themselves to when they reissued, last week, Steinbeck's *The Red Pony*.

Since the early days of wartime paper rationing, new books have pretty much gobbled up the available paper, and thin paper plus small margins and run-in chapters were the rule.

Imagine the pleasure, then, of relaxing the reins and bringing out a handsomely printed, fine-quality, new edition of a fine older book, illustrated beautifully with 13 full-color pictures done by Wesley Dennis, known for his painting of horses.

We hope it presages equally good things to come and feel optimistically that it does. Meanwhile, if you own no copy of *The Red Pony* or if you want to have or to give a truly handsome and lasting one, this volume is what you've been waiting for. It is the complete story, too, in a volume by itself, for the first time—the original edition of 1,000 copies (at $10) did not contain one part of the story, which first appeared in *The Long Valley*.

May Lamberton Becker. "Books for Young People." *New York Herald Tribune Weekly Book Review*, 22 (4 November 1945), 6.

As a rule only the first appearance of a book is chronicled in this department, but two new editions are of such importance that attention must be called to them. John Steinbeck's *The Red Pony* stands out among the year's books because a fine story for grown-ups, already adopted by boys who love horses, has now received its perfect pictures—scenes and portraits in color by Wesley Dennis, making it a book of the class truly described as "a handsome present." [It] will be welcomed by public libraries as standard literature in handsome form, one that will bring them new readers. . . .

OF MICE AND MEN (THE PLAY)

Of Mice and Men

A PLAY IN THREE ACTS

by John Steinbeck

New York · COVICI · FRIEDE · *Publishers*

Margaret Shedd.
"Of Mice and Men."
Theatre Arts, 21
(October 1937),
774–80.

San Francisco had two world premieres this summer. That both plays will be headlined fall openings in New York is not the point to be recorded here, which is, instead, the almost extravagant difference between Jean Giraudoux's *Amphitryon 38* ... and the production with which this review is concerned: John Steinbeck's *Of Mice and Men* presented by the San Francisco Theatre Union.

Whatever the cause—ingenuousness, curiosity, lust for contemporaneousness of scene,—one expects a great deal from a play about the living, wandering men who plant crops they never see harvested, and harvest where they have not seen the planting, in a soil which refuses them roots, men who are lonely beyond our natural heritage of loneliness. All the exciting dramatic realities are in the theme, and when the curtain goes up on *Of Mice and Men* the play seems authentic: characters who demand we learn all about them, situations which we feel impelled to follow through to a consummation or an intensity of non-consummation which is the same thing. A simple background of Santa Clara hills and a non-existent river in the orchestra pit, beside which Lennie and George lie down to sleep, give promise of evoking what is inherent in the tragic saga of the itinerant agricultural worker.

But *Of Mice and Men*, in its present form, does not tell that saga; it does no more than block in the tantalizing outlines, with too much sentimental detail of rabbits and murders and with gaping omissions. Why? Maybe the answer to that question would also answer the "why" of the whole socially-minded theatre.

The San Francisco Theatre Union's production is good! It is forthright, giving off a clear integrity not easy to overrate. The group draws its personnel from workers; rehearsal must come in their spare time. This means that several months are spent on every play, and so the actor has, perforce, a chance for slow identifications with his part. Combined with this impression of growth is a striking directness of attack which may be explained partly by the fact that bindlestiffs are familiar people to the garage repairman, milkman, store salesperson, who make up the cast; no doubt many of these actors themselves originated in agricultural communities.

The Theatre Union was justly appreciative of the opportunity to predate the rest of the world with *Of Mice and Men*. Long before the book was out the Union knew that Steinbeck was living and working in one of the agricultural areas. All intelligent Californians realize that history is being made in those centres. The Theatre Union, whose administration has been consistently clear and direct, believed it should have plays about local current history. Wellman Farley, the president, said this to John Steinbeck and forthwith Steinbeck handed him an as yet unpublished manuscript, *Of Mice and Men*.

There is something nice about that transaction; one dislikes to be querulous about the result of it. Steinbeck, I believe, made no pretense that this was a critic-proof, completed play: the six scenes are taken verbatim from the novel. So it would be unjust to criticize the play, as given in San Francisco, from a structural technical angle. Let that be done when New York sees its version. But a non-technical analysis is integral to the western production because here is an excellent left-wing group with competent actors and direction, situated in what is probably the best theatre town in America, which opens its new playhouse with a production written by a young man whose novel on the same theme holds for months the top spot on best-selling lists and who, at the same time, is admittedly social minded. And the play is a success, favorably received by good audiences. It sounds like the dream come true of a real people's theatre. But what?

Of Mice and Men could have been a character study of eight or ten persons in relation to each other, a slow digestive process for the audience, at the end of which Lennie and Candy and Slim and all would have been absorbed, understood, pitied, loved, hated. Or it could have been essentially a study of Lennie, the pathetic, destructive village idiot, all too common and all too misunderstood. Or it could have been a high-powered tragedy on almost classical lines. That does not exhaust the list of possibilities for the play, but in any one of these forms it would have been a social document with a punch far greater than it now carries. As it stands it looks like a social document (a highly personalized one), for the negative reason that it doesn't look like anything else. And the violences, which are probably what have sold the book to a majority of its readers, appear to have been thrown in for high seasoning. The result is, to say the least, confusing.

For instance, at what appears to be the climax of the play—that is if you consider that the theme is the stiff's right to be a man—a point in Scene 3 where George, Candy and Lennie are pyramiding up their hope for a little ranch of their own, a point which has been built to a fine natural tight excitement by the audience's intense desire that these men shall be different from the other fifty thousand and really get their ranch, abruptly the tension is ruined by an extraneous remark of Candy's, apropos of his dog, that he hopes when he gets old somebody will take him out and shoot him too. The remark is not in character. Candy on the whole is excellently developed and he is well played by Carl Anderson. But no actor can compete with the author if he decides to walk into a play and interrupt him. The timing and movement of this particular scene have been meticulously rehearsed; but eternal rehearsal could never have given rhythm to it because the rhythm is not there. And that in turn is because there is no basic dramatic pattern there.

If this sounds like harsh criticism of small detail I must answer that there is no criticism too severe for an author who, through confusion of purpose, destroys epic material. Precisely this happens over and over in *Of Mice and Men*.

The question "why" repeats itself often to the audience mind, because adequate motivation is not furnished. The very core of the play, Lennie's obsession for stroking mice, is an example of the confusion and of the lack of motivation. It is widely known that many itinerants carry small animals with them on their travels—rats, dogs, rabbits: this has in it the raw element of human interest. It is also a matter of common knowledge that a great many bindlestiffs are feeble-minded; there is certainly the raw element of human tragedy in that. But for an author merely to throw together these two facts to make a curiosity is not enough. Steinbeck at no point establishes whether Lennie's destruction of the animals he strokes is a matter of abnormality or of accident. He implies it is accident, which, happening so often, is not convincing. The audience assumes it is sadism and gets a little excitement out of that. Actually there is no excuse for this confusion. If Lennie is to be any sort of universal symbol, anything more than an isolated monstrosity, and if the play is to be more than a reporter's notebook, then all questions of behavior psychology must be settled before they arise. "Strange as it seems" is no longer satisfactory predication for serious writing.

And always the "why" comes up. Why doesn't George leave Lennie to his fate? For the clumsy, pitiful fool to be pursued and killed by such a bully as Curley is the way the cards might really fall. When George shoots Lennie it needs explaining, and to watch that scene is to witness something shocking, not conclusive. One doubts that George could have done it, because his author has been to some pains to show how beaten and frustrated he is: George who abandons the plan for a home although the money for it is still available; George who, after numerous allusions to his certainty that they will get into trouble at this ranch, has still stayed on there; George who goes off of a Saturday evening and leaves Lennie alone with Curley's wife (that the murder does not happen that night is merely another of Steinbeck's vagaries). In fact most of the events seem vagrant. This should be tragedy, but it has no stature. Its authenticity lies in its small talk, not in the consistent development of a theme.

The best projected character is George, the little man, played by Sal Pizzo, who successfully suggests the unwilling wanderer's galling helplessness and at the same time his essential manliness. Wellman Farley, as Lennie, keeps the simpleton hero too much on the one note of pitiful, clumsy childishness; but that, as well as the limitations of the character of Curley's wife (which has in it the makings of a great acting part) are dictated by the author. Perhaps Farley in the one case and Alice Hult in the other do well to keep the motivation in simple channels.

The direction by Florence Hagee shows a consistent effort to organize the play into bounds of some sort, with the curious result of creating time and again an unfulfilled prediction that just around the next corner the play will solidify, take form. Mrs. Hagee's direction is, in effect, of the play as it might have been rather than as it is.

Perhaps what the proletarian theatre wants is not literature but photographic reality of scene, a factual presentation of working class life. T. K. Whipple's recent analysis, *Literature in the Doldrums*, would indicate exactly that. And yet the Theatre Union's production of *Of Mice and Men* indicates something else. I think the Union hoped it had the makings of a great play, not just another tract.

Their painstaking effort to suggest a Chekhovian texture, would show that: the magnificent weaving in of incidental background events, references to past detail which seem insignificant but which are never accidental nor wasteful.

The fifth scene of *Of Mice and Men* should have been—but is not—such a delight. Here we have Lennie, who has just fondled his puppy to death (and whom by now we know quite well) and the girl, Curley's wife, about whom we have accidentally learned a good deal. Up to this point the story of the girl has been nicely suggested: there is much tragic humor in the character of this little trollop who thinks her husband isn't a nice man, who was a natural for the movies but didn't get in them because her old lady must have stole the letter from the guy in Hollywood.

These two—both dull as to wits and with a desperate need for communication; and the only communication there can seem to be between them results in the destruction of both. The scene climaxes in the girl's murder, of course, and in its way it is an absorbing scene. It is at the same time a denunciation of its author. It becomes at once apparent that the background, as essential as the seen happenings, is only an accident. The impression given is that Steinbeck had to have a girl for Lennie to kill, and in a workmanlike desire for verisimilitude he knew the girl had to have a background, just as she had to have soft hair; so he looked in his notebook and pulled out a girl, probably an actual girl he had talked to.

But this real girl leaps out of the notebook, and the fugitive but moving events of her background completely dwarf the events we see. That she is choked to death seems beside the point.

Let the girl live and speak her real piece! Let Lennie live! Why does their author hurry to put them under the ground? Or if he must kill them let him at least not do it wantonly! He does not know what dynamite he has in those characters. Nor does the so-called left-wing theatre know what it has. And exactly because, in the case of the left-wing theatre, it does not know what it wants.

... The one thing the left theatre knows it wants, and gets, is "agit prop" plays. It does them well, witness *Waiting for Lefty*. But if it chooses to be anything more than a high-powered propaganda device for class consciousness it must go farther than that. It must want great plays. When they appear it may not be able to produce them adequately but it must recognize them. If it does not, no one will, because the modern great play, when it does appear, is going to break molds, be searching to express a new human consciousness.

Of Mice and Men is certainly not a great play, although, just as certainly, it has in it the raw material of one. The very fact that the San Francisco Theatre Union produced the play is an occasion for good cheer. And yet, even with clarification of its dramatic cloudiness, *Of Mice and Men* would still be only a study of men, not of classes. Is it possible that the left wing theatre really wants a play like that?

Brooks Atkinson. "John Steinbeck's *Of Mice and Men* in a Production Staged by George S. Kaufman." New York *Times*, 24 November 1937, p. 20.

Having a story to tell in *Of Mice and Men*, John Steinbeck has told it with reticence and integrity, and the theatre has had the genius to look at it from his point of view. Although the performance which opened at the Music Box last evening makes no artistic pretensions, it is art in the keenness of its expression. Mr. Steinbeck has caught on paper two odd and lovable farm vagrants whose fate is implicit in their characters. As the director, George S. Kaufman has put it on the stage with consummate adroitness. Although many people may shy away from the starkness of the fable, every one will admire the honesty of the author's mind and the clarity of its statement in the theatre. There is considerable magnificence in the tight-lipped telling of this singular tragedy in the comradeship of two footloose men.

Mr. Steinbeck first told it in a compact novel that startled the bookshops about a year ago. The comrades are George, a likable farm laborer in the West, and Lennie, a huge, powerful, feeble-minded youth with a sweet humility in his nature. Out of George's loyalty and manly forbearance and Lennie's pathetic helplessness an interdependence has grown up that is fine and rudely affectionate. George keeps Lennie straight by vigilant understanding. But it is a lost cause from the beginning, for Lennie's poor, dumb impulses of love result in death. He kills the mice he loves. He kills the puppy he loves. Finally, he kills the woman who lets him stroke her hair. A lynching posse sets out after him with firearms. Recognizing the hopelessness of defending Lennie any further, George kills him as mercifully as he can.

If the story were callously told the conclusion might be unbearable. But Mr. Steinbeck has told it with both compassion and dexterity. The patient comradeship is developed in a series of homely episodes, conveyed in the vernacular of two lonely men blundering around their small world. In the bunkhouse of a ranch in California the story ensnares some other rootless lives and expands into dreams of a glorious deliverance. Although Mr. Steinbeck's talent is for spareness in expression, he is a virtuoso in the free-hand sketching of a narrative. Under the comedy and the gusto of ranch life the note of doom is constantly echoing, and the tragic conclusion is foreshadowed in the first scene of the play. *Of Mice and Men* is the dark side of an idyll. Out of some tatterdemalion simplicities comes a rushing of the fates.

If Mr. Steinbeck's talent is for pithy statement, he has met his match in the laconical Mr. Kaufman, who also works best in that way. He has cast the play with assurance of choice, and, excepting the off-stage sounds of wild life and husbandry in the barns, he has brilliantly staged it. Wallace Ford's George is a marvel of patience, courage and grief—casual and sincere. Broderick Crawford's lumbering Lennie is the perfect counterpart in uncomprehending earnestness and good-will. John F. Hamilton brings a third figure into the compact with his portrait of a defeated field laborer who grasps at straws for deliverance. Claire Luce acts vividly the part of a restless wife who cannot abide her husband. As the best mule-skinner on the place, Will Geer plays with a wholesomeness that gives further scope to the tragedy. Sam Byrd, Walter Baldwin, Charles Slattery, Thomas Findlay and Leigh Whipper complete the tale with able acting in the other parts.

In designing the outdoor and ranch building sets, Donald Oenslager has captured the natural beauty against which this rueful fable is told. By the completeness of their sympathy, all the workmen associated with this production have turned *Of Mice and Men* into a masterpiece of the New York stage.

Russell Rhodes.
"The Stage at Eve."
Where to Go [New York],
1 December 1937, p. 7.

Intelligent playgoing was resumed last week when George S. Kaufman, the theatre's miracle man at reticent homespun dialogue, etched John Steinbeck's tragic tale of loneliness among the barley hustlers of Central California across an artist's parchment at the Music Box under the banner of Sam H. Harris. Steinbeck's novel is packed to the hilt with stark, repressed emotion—a gaunt story that Steinbeck himself has translated in dramatic dialogue with a shrewd sense of theatre unusual in a novelist. For its staging, no better talent could have been found than Kaufman, who has an understanding genius for phrases that cut like a knife. He has cast his characters flawlessly.

Of Mice and Men bristles with profanity and the vulgar speech of drifting vagabonds. The Catholic White List censor would shear it to ribbons after hearing the opening speeches and turn a professionally deaf ear to the rest. But its honesty pierces, for this is vastly more than a shocker from the garbage heap of lost men. George, the strong, is a dreamer who wants a little place of his own, where there'll be no more toil. Lennie, a great hulking giant with an idiot's brain, depends for his very existence upon George. There is a genuine link of affection between these two. Lennie wants something to love, but whatever he touches dies. His unwitting strength kills a mouse, a puppy and the brazen hussy whose hair he fondles. When the posse attempts to track him down George kills him in a bush, like a lion despatching a cub.

Were this all to *Of Mice and Men*, it would be nothing less than cheap melodrama. But Steinbeck has crammed it with a homely philosophy and the fragile, half-articulate dreams of men lost in the flotsam and jetsam of life. Wallace Ford as George is a marvel of forbearance; Broderick Crawford displays hitherto unexpected gifts in his portrayal of the fumbling Lennie; Claire Luce is a shrill siren-tramp; John F. Hamilton, as the crippled Candy, turns in another one of his unforgettably crisp characterizations.

Donald Oenslager's sets for the Salinas River bank, the bunkhouse and the barn fit the picture and mood admirably. The only discordant notes are the ridiculous forest and barnyard noises. *Of Mice and Men* must go into the record as a high spot of the current Broadway season. . . .

Grenville Vernon. "Of Mice and Men." Commonweal, 27 (10 December 1937), 191–2.

Those who have read John Steinbeck's novel realize that a new and original talent has risen in the literary world. *Of Mice and Men* is not a pleasant story. It deals with a group of men and one woman who are not in the genteel tradition, and the chief protagonist, Lennie, is a half-wit. To tell the story of these people, most of whom belong to the flotsam and jetsam of the world, is a difficult thing to do without offense against the basic decencies of art, yet Mr. Steinbeck by his sense of pathos and his poetic feeling robbed some of the story of its unpleasantness, informing the tale with tragedy and pity. In short, Mr. Steinbeck is not just another hard-boiled realist, but a poet sensitive to the plight of the unfortunate and underprivileged, of those inarticulate men and women, without roots or basic intelligence, who are one of the chief problems of American civilization. Out of this novel Mr. Steinbeck has fashioned a play holding the essential spirit of the book, a drama of suspense and brooding tragedy. Moreover, George S. Kaufman has cast and directed it superbly. It throbs with life and is permeated with an implicit poetry. . . .

So far *Of Mice and Men* deserves praise and only praise. But then comes the matter of the dialogue. It is true to life, at times poetic, utterly dramatic, but is none the less appalling. It is unquestioned that the people of Mr. Steinbeck's creation would use the language allotted them, but are such people fitted for dramatic representation unexpurgated in their speech? Mr. Steinbeck has made their language less brutal than it would be in real life, but it is to be wished that the dramatist had gone farther, and employed suggestion rather than bald statement. To say everything violates the canons not only of good taste but of art itself. *Of Mice and Men* is an unusual play, but it would have been an even better one had it allowed less license to its language. . . .

Joseph Wood Krutch. "Oh, Hell, Said the Duchess." *Nation*, 145 (11 December 1937), 663–4.

John Steinbeck's *Of Mice and Men* has been lifted from between the covers of his book and set down upon the stage of the Music Box Theater. Very little change in even the order of events proved necessary, and what one gets in the theatre is almost the total effect of the short novel plus the additional vividness of fine, imaginative sets, expert direction, and highly accomplished performances. No wonder, then, that the play is already established as the solidest dramatic success of the season, for the novel itself was something of a sensation and the dramatic version now contributes additional elements of obvious appeal. Little re-

mains for any critic to say upon this level of criticism, and it is hardly worth discussing either novel or dramatization any farther unless one is willing to go on to ask how genuine either the one or the other really is. Many critics have already found in both a combination of high imagination, stunning reality, and a most ineffable tenderness. I found, I must confess, only great adroitness and a sense, so acute as to constitute genius of one particular kind, of what a particular public wants at a particular moment. *Of Mice and Men* puts its author in the topmost class of popular writers. It does not, I think, lift him out of that class.

Unfortunately, so far as the effective presentation of my own case goes, it is difficult to tell the story without seeming to be doing it a deliberate injustice. It is, as doubtless most of the reading public already knows, concerned with a strange friendship between two migratory harvest workers, one of whom is a witless but amiable giant given to fondling all soft and helpless things with a hand so unintentionally heavy that, sooner or later, he infallibly breaks their necks. The theme is tenderness taking strange forms in a brutal environment, and the dramatic tension arises out of our foreknowledge of the fact that at some time and for some reason the heavy hand will be laid with fatal results upon the camp's only member of the female sex—a pathetic little nymphomaniac married to the boss's cruel son. All the grotesqueness inherent in the tale is emphasized rather than concealed (we first meet the strange pair when the giant is being unwillingly deprived of a dead mouse he has been keeping too long in his pocket), but the skill of the writing is such that the whole is carried off far better than one could well imagine and that success is absolute in so far as it consists merely in forcing the spectator to take the whole with perfect seriousness. The only question is the question whether he is right so to take it, whether what we are presented with is really a tale of eerie power and tenderness, or whether, as it seems to me, everything from beginning to end is completely "literary" in the bad sense and as shamelessly cooked up as, let us say, the death of Little Nell.

After all, Dickens, as well as thousands of his readers, sincerely believed that Little Nell was the real thing, and there lies a fascinating but largely unexplored field ready for any psychologist-critic who wishes to examine the reasons behind the demand of every age that sentiment be served up according to some formula the peculiar charm of which no previous age would have recognized and which every succeeding age finds patently ridiculous. Your Victorian was ready to weep over the fate of any sentimental monster if that monster could be described in sufficiently convincing terms as "innocent." Today nothing arouses the suspicions of any audience more infallibly than either that word or that thing, but a tough Little Nell, thoroughly familiar with four-letter words, would be a sensation on any stage, and the moronic giant of Mr. Steinbeck seems real because all the accidents of his character and surroundings are violent and brutal. Mr. Steinbeck, as I have already suggested, writes with great technical adroitness. But neither that adroitness nor all the equal expertness of staging and acting exhibited in the performance of his play would avail if the whole were not concocted according to a formula quite as definite as that proposed in the story current a decade ago and recalled in the title of this review. It is not exactly aristocracy, profanity, and sex which is called for at the present moment, but it is toughness, violence, and just the soupçon of social criticism which Mr. Steinbeck

supplies. Flavor your sentiment with those and the public is sure that it has got the real thing at last. . . .

Brooks Atkinson. "Episode in the Lower Depths." New York *Times*, 12 December 1937, Section 11, p. 3.

After speaking contemptuously of the commercial theatre on many occasions, this column is prepared to eat its words this morning. *Of Mice and Men* is the quintessence of commercial theatre and it is also a masterpiece. John Steinbeck, who first wrote it as a novel, offers it as his first play without artistic bravado. George S. Kaufman, who has staged it, never looks at a box office with disdain. Sam H. Harris, the producer, is in the theatre to make money with the most expert plays he can find. The actors have been hired off the auction block of Broadway or Hollywood. Donald Oenslager, the scene designer, takes the jobs that are offered him without fastidious quibbling. Although this grim bucolic of Central California is not sure-fire box office, like *I'd Rather Be Right* and *You Can't Take It with You*, it appears under the same hard-headed auspices, and the honesty and perfection of the workmanship put it in the front rank of the new plays produced this year.

When the theatre falls on lean days it retreats to Shakespeare and adaptations of novels. The recrudescence of Shakespeare, the staging of new versions of old plays and of plays based on novels are signs of the theatre's loss of spontaneity. *Of Mice and Men*, however, is no product of weariness. As nearly every one knows by now, Mr. Steinbeck first wrote it as a novel with the stage in mind. The economy of the story, the unity of the mood, the simple force of the characters, the tang of the dialogue are compactly dramatic, and *Of Mice and Men* is not theatre at second hand. Since I did not read the novel until after seeing the play, it was all fresh to me and infinitely moving—an isolated chapter in life, but one that is somberly beautiful. Although the novel contains a few descriptions of a nature which the theatre cannot use, they are merely crisp evocations of tone which the theatre captures without speaking a word. What was in the book is now to be seen and heard on the stage, admirably vitalized in the patient and subdued acting of Broderick Crawford, Wallace Ford and John F. Hamilton and in the selfless direction of Mr. Kaufman.

In less scrupulous hands *Of Mice and Men* might have degenerated into a chilling shocker. The dialogue could be scandalous if it were a less honest expression of male life in a ranch bunkhouse. The "mercy killing" that concludes the play might be sadistic or cheaply sensational. If Lennie were played with less compassion by Mr. Crawford, he might be the sort of lumbering monster the meretricious theatre likes to truckle with to draw gasps out of the gaping public. But the supreme virtue of the story, on the stage as well as in print, is the lyric perfection of all these rude materials—the violence springing naturally out of the situation and the bawdy dialogue tumbling without self-consciousness out of the mouths and minds of "bindle-stiffs." Although you may resent the tragedy and the harrowing of your feelings, you cannot retort that it is false or gratuitous. Given these materials, this is what happens; Mr. Steinbeck, once started, has no choice. To be technical about it, *Of Mice and Men* is a perfect work of art.

The shattered playgoer may soothe himself a little by remembering that, after all, the story Mr. Steinbeck is chronicling is no more than an episode in the stupendous pattern of life. Not all dogs have to be shot as deliberately as Candy's blind and moldy cur who stinks up the bunkhouse unbearably. Not all feeble-minded boys have to be shot by their most loyal comrades. Although *Of Mice and Men* is written as skillfully as *Madame Bovary* and *Ethan Frome*, it is lacking in scope and universal meaning and it has no general significance. We may be terrified by the swiftness with which Mr. Steinbeck's furies ride, but we are not purged by it or rebuked. Compare it with O'Neill's dour and gnarled *Desire Under the Elms*, in which the characters are larger than life and the morbid passions are expressions of man in conflict with nature. *Of Mice and Men* is tragedy without that much compass. But the charge that the characters are ignoble shows obtuseness to the effort George, Candy and Slim make to live as honorably as they can according to their poor enlightenment. They do as well as they know how, which is an improvement on the behavior of many of their superiors. Although George, Lennie and Candy are a shiftless, drifting lot, they are driven onward, like most human beings, by pathetically imagined dreams of peace and comfort and a life of their own. Out of their loneliness rises anguished talk of a better day. Mr. Steinbeck's characters have more stature than the chaotic situation into which they fall.

Although Mr. Kaufman is celebrated for his wit and his craftsmanlike facility in stage direction, admit *Of Mice and Men* as evidence of the fact that he can also enter into the spirit of a fine play and give it the most humble sort of expression. Apart from the casting, the performance is meticulously and affectionately modulated; the silences are as eloquent as anything Mr. Steinbeck has said in the play. Mr. Crawford's meek and bewildered Lennie, Mr. Ford's belligerent George, with his warm heart and forbearing nature, Mr. Hamilton's broken bunkhouse swamper and Leigh Whipper's acrimonious Negro stableman are remarkable portraits of character. It is seldom that distinctive acting and individual voices merge so quietly into a whole. Although the commercial theatre is seldom inspired, it has produced *Of Mice and Men* as though it were grateful for a chance to serve a distinguished piece of work. A theatre-goer may find the story heartbreaking, but in all honesty he cannot suggest a kinder way of telling it.

Stark Young. "Two from the Novel." *New Republic*, 93 (15 December 1937), 170–1.

... *Of Mice and Men*, rewritten for the stage by the author himself, follows its novel more closely than is commonly the case. There are the two men, one a defective, the other cherishing and guarding him, and their story retains its character and its leading importance. The compact impression of the work as a whole is carried over from book into theatre. The single love motif is still secondary: that of the restless wife, shut off in the loneliness of the ranch, eyeing the other men while her husband is on a rampage about his husband-honor, planning at length to run away, and ironically killed by the crazy man, or freak, whatever you want to call him. There is the same projection into a kind of lurid unreality, expressed in terms of a violent realism in detail and circumstances.

How one might describe *Of Mice and Men* as we get it at the Music Box I do not know; I have never seen a play quite like it, have no previous acquaintance with the nature of its suspenses, or with the curious artistic satisfaction that its development affords. But from that last point its quality derives, I am sure of that. That is to say you never quite recognize or believe the characters or the active moments; the speech is not compelling as an actual, sharp recording out of life; the locale is not borne in on you as exactly literal, as inevitable realism, an indisputable entity. But the whole of it seems to come off right in its own kind. It remains artifice, theatre, a work of art; but it loses nothing by it. It loses nothing in compulsion, projection, mood. Good or only pretty good, it turns out to be one of the few plays these several seasons that know their own mind, though you may or may not like that mind, which is another issue entirely. The repetition of motifs is bold and insistent, as in the first scene, for instance, where three or four things are said over and over with startling assertion of sheer pattern in theme and style. The total mood of the play dominates all else; all actuality, forward movement, detailed record, character analysis, are superseded by the design that establishes this play's inner and outer force.

Of Mice and Men would appear by report to be drawing what is known as carriage trade, which on Times Square might mean society people and otherwise might imply a certain sophistication. There was a suggestion of this kind of audience the night I saw the play; and a part of them when things got hot seemed to be getting out of it something of the kick of the Grand Guignol; others took it as a shocker, while others took it as a picture from life, and others yet as, whatever else, vivid theatre. But the attention was remarkable. The whole play turned out to be an absorbing work of theatre art. Meanwhile it must be said that the evening might much more likely have been regarded as preposterous, to say the least, had not the way been prepared for it by such a piece as *Tobacco Road*. Compared to *Tobacco Road*, *Of Mice and Men* has a much less vivid, basic and promising speech—rooted English idiom, shall we say, tang of the soil, heat and authenticity of blood. It has a less genuine and far less vivid locale, and less living color and variety; and it has less of an immediate social application. It has far less bounce, gusty relish, scope and trenchant humor; and less of the outline of significant fable. Nevertheless it survives the comparison, and holds its own, in its own kind. A comparison arises also with *Little Ol' Boy*, a play three or four seasons back that quickly failed but that left with those who saw it an impression of directing by Mr. Joe Losey and acting by Mr. Burgess Meredith that was unforgettable. *Of Mice and Men* is more secure, single, and as to mood more successfully calculated and stamped.

Joseph Henry Jackson. "A Bookman's Notebook."
San Francisco *Chronicle*, 18 December 1937, p. 8.

San Francisco—The play version of John Steinbeck's *Of Mice and Men* is finally out and on sale at the bookstores. The play, as you doubtless know, opened in New York on November 23, and was almost unanimously voted a fine thing by the critics.

I write "almost unanimously" because I have just read in *The Nation* the remarks of Joseph Wood Krutch who doesn't seem quite sure about it all. He writes, "I found (in the play), I must confess, only great adroitness and a sense, so acute as to constitute genius of one particular kind, of what a particular public wants at a particular moment. *Of Mice and Men* puts its author in the topmost class of popular writers. It does not, I think, lift him out of that class." Later, Mr. Krutch adds: "The question is whether what we are presented with is really a tale of eerie power and tenderness, or whether, as it seems to me, everything from beginning to end is completely 'literary' in the bad sense, and as shamelessly cooked up as the death of Little Nell."

As for Little Nell, anyone will agree, I suppose, that her death was "cooked up." Dickens was, if you like, a cooker-upper. (That there is anything "shameless" about "cooking up"—in the case of Dickens or anyone else—is another matter. Mr. Krutch is disingenuous in his use of the term here; he employs it with much the same effect as that of the first syllable of damyankee. "Cooking up" may or may not be "shameless." It depends, one would think, on the end to which the cooked up mess was concocted.)

But the point is not the use-for-effect of the term "shamelessly." The point is that Mr. Krutch is confused. Steinbeck, he writes, has at least one quality "so as acute as to constitute genius." But Steinbeck is also not "out of the class of popular writers." Still further, Mr. Krutch feels that he . . . isn't sure. There is a question in his mind. Is the play "really" powerful or is it—I suppose "really"—bad?

Without doubt it is sometimes a difficult thing to make up one's mind. I am not blaming Mr. Krutch for his confusion; rather I feel he deserves full marks for admitting it. But in his review he completely misses one thing which, I believe, contributes in some degree at least to his unsettled state of mind. The single point is not all of it, but it is important.

That is the nature of the girl, Curley's wife.

Mr. Krutch is not alone in failing to understand her. The *Literary Digest*'s reviewer, for example, calls her a "harlot." Mr. Krutch calls her a "nymphomaniac." What they both miss is that Curley's wife is neither of these things. She is simply a stupid young girl with a good-sized dash of the tart in her. Tens of thousands of technically "good" girls are no better.

And, missing this, you miss much more. You miss, chiefly, the truth about her hanging round the bunkhouse. Steinbeck explains it clearly: "Curley's wife a little wearily, dropping her coquetry: 'I'm jus' lookin' for somebody to talk to. Don't you never jus' want to talk to somebody?'" Certainly. The girl wanted just that: to talk to somebody. With that type, "talk" implies a more or less unconscious emphasis on such cheap physical charm as the subject may possess. That was all Curley's wife knew. But that doesn't make her a harlot, nor (of all silliness) a "nymphomaniac."

What I'm driving at, is that, having missed this you would be bound to miss Steinbeck's tenderness toward the girl who was Curley's wife; a cheap, not very bright little thing, not vicious in the true sense at all but just, so to put it, a poor little tart, as Steinbeck meant her to be and knows she is. And if you miss his understanding of the girl and tenderness with her, then you may as well miss it elsewhere, and so come to wonder (as Mr. Krutch does) whether there is "really" any tenderness in the play.

Certainly Steinbeck is adroit, as Mr. Krutch suggests. Certainly he writes skillfully and brilliantly. But that the quality of either the book or the play proceeds out of any idea of deliberately giving a particular public the particular thing it wants at the moment—that simply isn't so.

Mr. Krutch may be sure that the "eerie power and tenderness" are there—"really." The notion of giving a particular public what it wants at a particular moment is not in Steinbeck's book or play anywhere. If any writers have that idea nowadays you are more likely to find them among the "proletarian" writers on "proletarian" themes, from whose agitated typewriters come the "literary in the bad sense" novels and plays for which the leftist critics are so fond of finding good words.

"Theatre: A Completely Satisfying American Play." *Literary Digest*, 124 (18 December 1937), 34.

A great play has reached Broadway—a play of lowly, cast-off men, whose stark emotions have tamed testy critics and tired audiences into stunned reverence. It is the dramatization of John Steinbeck's best seller, *Of Mice and Men*. The millions whom the novel hypnotized have but one question: Does the play make George and Lennie and their friends real with the mighty brutality and overpowering tenderness of the book? It does.

The hulking, stupid, well-meaning brute, Lennie, creates the situation in his first speeches. "Guys like us," he observes to George, "guys like us what work on ranches are the loneliest guys in the world. They got no family. They don't belong no place."

Then, breaking off with the look of a trusting animal, he says: "With us it ain't like that. We got a future. We got somebody who gives a damn about us. An' why? Because I got you to look after me and you got me to look after you, and that's why."

The tone is set. With that Mr. Steinbeck and his actors proceed relentlessly to unfold the tragedy of loneliness that errs unwittingly in its immense craving for affection. Lennie wants love and beauty so desperately that he takes a field mouse and the stroking of his giant hands kills it. Lennie loves the warmth of young animals, so he nestles a puppy until his caresses choke it. Lennie worships beauty in women, and it is natural to him to run his hands through a woman's silken hair. But she (the boss's son's wife, played by Claire Luce) is a harlot. When she screams, suspecting the usual thing, her screams terrify him. He tries to keep her quiet. Lennie is a big and stupid man. He doesn't know his small gesture has crushed her to death.

This is the point toward which the play drives mercilessly. George, Lennie's small, smart friend who has always cared for him and gotten him out of scrapes, has but one course. He spares Lennie a vengeful lynching by shooting him in the back while he talks happily of the rabbit farm George has promised to get them. A rock would crack at that scene.

The scenes take place in and around a California ranch. Men come when there is work, move on to the next spot when the job is done. Their language is lusty and forthright, but never obscene. In the words of Richard Watts, Jr., *New York Herald Tribune* critic, "there is no line in it that does not possess the true ring of authenticity." It is a play for adults, not for children or bigots seeking the secret thrill of naughty words.

A fair share of praise goes to the versatile and prodigious George S. Kaufman, for his directing. He has stressed every chance for realism. Wallace Ford, once of Hollywood and *The Informer*, fires George with the deep and unaccountable friendship which caused him to waste his life protecting Lennie. The robust, kindly mule skinner, the disillusioned Negro who reads books in the barn because the whites won't have him, and particularly Candy (played by John F. Hamilton) are fine and moving characterizations. Broderick Crawford, son of the famed comedienne, Helen Broderick, takes what must be the most difficult acting assignment in recent years, as Lennie, and makes it a creation of stature. There would be no play if Lennie lost the affection of the audience.

The author, John Steinbeck, at thirty-five, lives in California with his wife. As a boy he worked on ranches with these very tramp laborers. He came to New York in 1920 as a reporter, ended up carrying bricks, and went back west to be a watchman.

Of Mice and Men has been justly described as "the first completely satisfying American play of the season."

Isaac Goldberg.
"Drama and Dramatists."
One Act Play, 1
(January 1938), 858–9.

Not being of that gentry whose opinions, to them, are sacred, I can with the greater ease discuss deviations from those opinions. I am immensely interested in the differences that divide the critics in the case of John Steinbeck's play, *Of Mice and Men*. Gentlemen such as Messrs. Krutch and Gassner, for example, are among those to whom I always look for stimulating discussions of the current drama. When one of them finds the Steinbeck play "literary" in the bad sense of that term and when the other finds a character such as Lennie too abnormal, too psychopathic, for the dignity of tragedy, it is to me, as a critic, interesting and even important. Agreement with one's own opinion is, naturally, flattering; moreover, it soothes. Disagreement, however, is stimulating, and by no means always in the disagreeable sense.

My feeling about *Of Mice and Men* is that it is one of the most important dramas to have reached our stage in many years. I can see, I can feel, the force of Mr. Krutch's and Mr. Gassner's respective objections. I can appreciate, from both the book and the actual production, those elements of the piece that lend themselves to sensationalism and to false emphasis. (Are these not often the same thing?) And yet (to underscore a more violent disagreement with virtually the whole sanhedrin of New York critics), as in the case of Ben Hecht's unlucky *To Quito and Back*, I feel that the faults are far outweighed by the virtues. In the case of Steinbeck's play, indeed, I feel that we have, with whatever reservations may be made, a true tragedy.

As I see it, *Of Mice and Men* is a fable of human aloneness, complicated by human incapacity and misunderstanding. There is not a truly "evil" person in the story; there is not a truly "evil" motive. All the harm that is done comes, not from human perversity, but from human ineptitude. The embrace of love becomes the embrace of strangulation. Wilde, writing his ballad in Reading Gaol, knew that fatal caress. The case of Lennie is, in its way, a pathological symbol. It reaches deep down into the human psyche, however. It has its patent reference to the sanest of us, just as the criminal in the cell has his patent reference to the most law-abiding.

For these people, even for the blusteringly self-revealing Curley and for his wife whose frustrated tenderness takes the form of an inciting snarl, one feels a sad pity. The end of the play is foreshadowed at the very beginning, not only in the structural skill with which the action is articulated, but in the impossible goal that these derelicts have all set for themselves: a goal that becomes communal in its aims as it becomes, in the end, communal in its defeat. It is not strange that Lennie's vision of a Utopia should infect the others. They all have a touch of Lennie in them. So—and this is one of the points—have you and I. It is, to me, a serious mistake to sit back from these misfits in the belief that they are too far removed from us to have relevancy. This is a cycle of human destruction—destruction of others, and of self. A theologian might say that each wanted love, but wanted it not enough, or wanted not enough of it. A psychologist might say that they feared love too much. They are at that stage in civilization when the stranger is the enemy because he has not yet proved himself the friend. It is a stage—witness Europe and Asia and the United States—that we have not yet outgrown. But surely no one who cannot forget the action of the children in Lawrence's *Sons and Lovers*, when they hasten the death of their doomed mother, should misunderstand the end of Steinbeck's tale, when George kills Lennie. It is possible to kill from love as well as from hate. George is more articulate than Lennie, but almost as confused. And every other man in the action is quite as guilty as George—just as guilty as if he, and not George, had pulled the trigger. Just as guilty, and, who knows, just as merciful.

There is, in the tale as it unfolds a healing terror, a scarifying pity. Although the play takes place upon the deceptive plane of reality, it does achieve, for many spectators, and with a cast of humble toilers, that tragic effect which the Greeks achieved with a cast of gods and almost superhuman beings. These lowly figures tread their way to a predestined doom as surely as any Oedipus, any Electra. Not since the coming of O'Neill has any American playwright so infused his drama with a seemingly inevitable catastrophe.

I am not a box-office critic, nor do I take it that one of the functions of criticism is prophecy. But my eye is upon Mr. John Steinbeck. And some of my hope.

Euphemia Wyatt. "The Drama." *Catholic World*, 146 (January 1938), 468–9.

... Few recent books have raised such stormy arguments. The eloquent reviews lured me to open it last spring but the first few pages so nauseated me that I couldn't bear to keep it in my room over night. But all summer, gentle elderly ladies would declare that it was one of the most beautiful stories they knew. When it came to reviewing the play the Harris office advised my taking a shock absorber with me....

Technically the play has the simplest and best construction of any on the boards and has quite enough inherent power and atmosphere to make its oaths and its starkly naked dialogue so much excess horror. Twice I put my fingers in my ears when I was afraid of a story told in the bunkhouse so I will never know just how bad it is. The sacrilege of the oaths is something that should be discussed by some Christian Committee with the Producing Managers' Association.

The hunger of the three men, George and Lennie and old crippled Candy, for a home, cuts to the heart and the pause that is held when Candy's old lame dog is taken out to be shot, breaks records for length and intensity. Wallace Ford, Broderick Crawford and John F. Hamilton all do extraordinary characterizations. If *Of Mice and Men* is a hit it will not necessarily mean that this generation is depraved in its tastes but it does mean that it has strong nerves for suffering and no shame. The play has the sense of impending doom of the old tragedies and all the pitifulness of the present....

Grenville Vernon.
"The Prize Plays."
Commonweal, 28
(3 June 1938), 161.

... [Of] Mice and Men is a tragedy, but despite the fact that it deals with the flotsam and jetsam of life, and that there are passages offensive to good taste, it is informed with a sense of pity and a suppressed poetry of feeling. Mr. Steinbeck, unlike his brother proletarian writers, is not a materialist; it might even be asserted that he is not a realist. He has an acute feeling of the spiritual quality in the submerged, and he writes dialogue which while realistic is often poetic. He has moreover an unusual power of making his characters one with their surroundings, of permeating them with the life of nature. In his depiction of life in flux, without bearings, and without foundation, he expresses as no other writer the tragic side of the America created by an industrial civilization. His people have fled the city, and yet have found no rest or haven in their rural stopping places. They are not lovely, and they are appallingly dumb, but despite their impotence they are blindly groping toward the light. Some have even a nobility, though a nobility twisted and inhibited. They suffer, not only in their bodies but in their souls. It is this realization that a human being has a soul which raises Mr. Steinbeck head and shoulders as a thinker and an artist above the herd who have stemmed from Hemingway....

A.D.
"Music, Stage, and
Films."
Manchester *Guardian*,
13 April 1939, p. 11.

Mr. John Steinbeck's dramatisation of his own short novel *Of Mice and Men* was presented to-night at the Gate Theatre. Doubt is expressed whether the censor will ever be persuaded to license for public production a play which is wholly couched in the strong language of a Californian ranch. A censorship which has already permitted Mr. Eugene O'Neill's stokehold exchanges can hardly raise objections to Mr. Steinbeck's dialogue. There are land mice as well as water mice, as Shylock so nearly said, and it would not be logical to find one more offensive than the other.

The gist of Mr. Steinbeck's play, as of his tale, is that passage in which the short, wiry, nimble-minded George describes to his fellow-wanderer, the vast, iron-handed, half-witted Lennie, exactly the order to which both, in spite of their mental and physical dissimilarity, belong. "Guys like us that work on ranches are the loneliest guys in the world. They got no family. They don't belong no place. They come to a ranch an' work up a stake, an' then they go inta town and blow their stake, and the first thing you know they're poundin' their tail on some other ranch. They ain't got nothin' to look ahead to."

George and Lennie do, however, nourish a fond prospect of owning a cottage, a cow, and a couple of acres all their own. There must also at the heart of this mirage be rabbits in a hutch, because

Lennie has a childish urge to fondle soft things like rabbits, puppy dogs, velvets, and the heads of young women, who screamingly misunderstand him and get him into trouble. When Lennie finds himself in trouble he has not mind enough to do anything but squeeze the protesting object. He has been in trouble before the play begins and he meets a spot of dire trouble in the shape of the far-too-elaborate young wife of Curley, his new boss. Lennie, in his stumbling way, breaks this insidious siren's neck, and George at the end is obliged to shoot his friend rather than let the husband do it. The scene of this sacrifice is the woodland pool at which the story opened.

This gives the play, as it does to the novel, an admirable pattern. The novel itself being brief, tense, and highly dramatic, the transition to the stage has been almost direct with hardly any addition, subtraction, or adjustment. But whereas the book quite masterfully avoids sentimentality the play splashes into the morass at least twice. The episode, for example, of an aged dog having to be shot is quite embarrassingly irrelevant in the play and the production overstresses the emotion of this convocation of tough ranchers at so necessary an event. The tenderness, the grief and pain, and the promised joy of all the essential part of the story are, on the other hand, surpassingly well communicated. Mr. Norman Marshall has here directed a cleverly chosen cast with notable skill. Mr. John Mills is right as George, Mr. Niall MacGinnis has a large amount of the dumb pathos necessary for Lennie, Miss Claire Luce repeats her New York success of the wild carnation of a woman, and Mr. Nicholas Stuart is absolutely authentic as the most amiable of the maudlin toughs. But perhaps the present theatre is too small for so vivid and violent a play. Its minuteness makes it almost impossible for Miss Luce to lie convincingly strangled for twenty minutes and quite impossible for us to believe that these moilers and toilers and slayers on a Californian outpost could have hands so white and finger-nails so well tended.

"Gate Theatre."
London *Times*,
13 April 1939, p. 10.

The strength of this play, which has won for itself a high reputation in the United States, lies not in any subtlety of thought, but in the plainness of its statement and in the impression it unfailingly gives of adhering to fact without embroidery or distortion. If it were to be compared with certain French plays that have been given at the Gate Theatre—with the work of Monsieur Mauriac, for example—it might appear young and crude, young aesthetically in its love of violence, and crude in the simplicity of its comment upon the nature of man; but such a comparison would be unjust to it, for Mr. Steinbeck's work is different from Monsieur Mauriac's, not only in treatment, but in purpose. His desire is, above all else, to stir his audience by direct and simplified narrative to obtain his effects by the use of swift and vigorous dramatic outline.

He is writing of two Californian tramps, George and Lennie, who obtain work on a farm. Lennie is a good-natured giant with a sub-normal mind. His great strength is dangerous, for he is incapable of controlling it, and George has made himself responsible for this vast babyish man. On the farm is a girl, the young wife of the Boss's son, who, being lonely, seeks the company of the labourers, not wishing to stir desire or jealousy in them but inevitably doing so. Only the extreme directness of Mr. Steinbeck's writing and of Miss Claire Luce's admirable performance could make this character persuasive, and persuasive it is. That there will be a clash between Lennie and the girl is foreseen from the outset. Neither wishes harm to the other; neither loves or desires the other; when, at last they are alone together, the girl talks of her life and Lennie of his, neither listening to the other. It is a brilliant piece of dialogue and a good example of Mr. Steinbeck's method. Lennie touches her hair in curiosity and his clumsy fingers become entangled in it. She cries out in fear, he, frightened in his turn, tries to stop her crying and breaks her neck by mistake. He escapes, is pursued, and, by the time his friend George finds him, has completely forgotten what he has done. He is happy, is looking forward childishly to the future, when George mercifully shoots him.

Mr. Niall MacGinnis performs the giant's part with the innocence of a flawless simplicity. Miss Luce brings to the girl an energy of attack and an emotional economy that are of great value to the play. The events in which they are concerned remain nevertheless open to the criticism that they are over-simplified, and it needs the sympathy and charity of Mr. John Mills's treatment of George to give the piece light and shade. George, whose single purpose is to save Lennie from himself, and who is to him at once nurse and brother and friend, brings to the tale a warmth and sentiment that are its salvation.

Derek Verschoyle. "The Theatre." *Spectator* [England], 162 (21 April 1939), 668.

Of Mice and Men is an entirely unsubtle and extremely effective play. It describes an episode in the lives of two young American casual labourers who arrive to work on a Californian ranch. . . .

Of this story a play crude to the point of vapidity might easily have been made. The material of *Of Mice and Men* is crude, and it is not subtle in its methods; but it is effective because it is never inflated and always gives the impression of being honest and truthful. In its construction there is no flaw: granted that from the moment that her existence is mentioned it can be foreseen that the play is going to depend on a clash between the girl and Lennie, the way in which this theme is developed is perfect. The actual scene in which the two are alone is the best written part of the play. Hitherto the girl has made an impression less as a specific character than merely as an automatic cause of trouble; when she enters the barn she becomes for the first time a distinct character; she talks excitedly of her future (she is proposing to run away from her husband), Lennie talks of his; quite disinterestedly she invites him to feel the softness of her hair, his clumsiness makes her panic, there is a short struggle, and in five seconds she is dead. It is a beautifully written scene, so tactful in its handling that what might have appeared melodramatic seems genuinely tragic. The real tragedy in this play is not that of the girl who dies nor that of the man who kills her; it is that of George who has striven so long to save

Lennie from disaster; but while the play lasts it seems that the tragedy is also theirs.

In this production every part is well performed. Mr. John Mills and Mr. Niall MacGinnis, who play George and Lennie, act extraordinarily well together; and if Mr. MacGinnis's is the more spectacular performance, it is by the touches of warmth and sentiment with which Mr. Mills invests his part, that the play is relieved from the threat of a monotony of mood and temper. Miss Claire Luce played the solitary girl with beautiful tact, and for lack of space Mr. Sydney Benson must be singled out from the remaining members of a consistently talented cast for a portrait of an old man which enshrined a legitimate sentiment but avoided mawkishness. Mr. Norman Marshall's production and Mr. Gower Parks's settings were, within the limitations of the small Gate Theatre stage, as good as one could wish.

There is apparently no truth in the rumour that *Of Mice and Men* has been denied by authority the chance of presentation in a London theatre. For it to be refused a licence would be fantastic; and while vapid suggestiveness is habitually given the run of more popular stages, it would be bare hypocrisy to require that a line of it should be altered. It is doing the play no service to overpraise it; it is not, as it has been declared to be, a masterpiece, if by that overworked term one means a play which achieves the most distinguished effects of drama. But its obvious failings are venial compared with the mortal sins which beset the generality of modern plays, and its merits are precisely those which are today most desirable and most uncommon on the English stage. It ran for nearly two years in New York, so the relative powers of discrimination in American and English audiences being what they are,

one can hope for at any rate six months for it in London.

Desmond MacCarthy. "The American View of Human Nature." *New Statesman and Nation* [England], 17 (22 April 1939), 605–6.

Of Mice and Men by John Steinbeck is admirably acted at the Gate Theatre. The play, founded on a successful novel in which, I am told, the Simple Simon has more time to endear himself to readers, is American; so is the cast. This is fortunate since the scene is laid in central California, and the types are indigenous. Neither the atmosphere nor the characters would have been convincing had they not been interpreted by actors entirely at home with them. The play itself is a sentimental tragedy. By that I mean that it touches us rather than moves us deeply, and that the climax (too easy to foresee) does not awake that strange, still exhilaration which springs from looking fate in the face. It is not the passion of man that brings about the catastrophe, but the accident that the central figure is a congenital half-wit. Lennie, with his gigantic muscular strength, was—to use the words of the sister of a lovable village simpleton I knew myself—"not exactly quite all right." And when George, who loves him, is forced to shoot him, because Lennie has absent-mindedly strangled a girl—the chase is up and he would be lynched unmercifully—we, the audience, feel: "Well, it is sad. But in a rough world where no man has time to be his brother's keeper, Lennies are a danger and better dead." *Of Mice and Men* is a play hard on the surface and tender underneath; it is about "tough guys" with warm hearts. The confidence of its appeal to the conviction that at bottom plain human nature is sound and splendid is characteristic of America. This is the deepest difference between America and Europe. In Europe such a feeling is apt to be merely sentimental—a pretence which people leading sheltered lives nourish in themselves because it looks kind and is comforting. But in America it is instinctively believed and common property. It is the main prop of their traditional passion for equality and of their generosity. To-day, it is speaking through the mouth of President Roosevelt. It is the most heartening element in the make-up of a suspicion-ridden modern world. The grudging response it meets here (often to the dismay of practical Englishmen who are eager to make use of it) is due to the reproach generosity of faith conveys. A by-effect of this faith in human nature is that it leaves the American playgoer free to revel in a surface cynicism of comment and laughter such as horrifies English audiences; for he cannot be frightened— *Man* is all right. This is not the theme, but it enters into the spirit of this play.

The lives of the men who compose the wandering mass of casual labour in America are very lonely. They have no roots; few are married. They compete against each other for temporary jobs, well-paid enough to dangle before them perpetually a seldom realised hope of some day settling down on a piece of land of their own and of being at last their own masters. They seldom hunt in couples, for each must take his chance as it comes; a pal may be as great a drawback as a wife in finding one. The curtain goes up on two such men, a big one and a small one, who are exceptions. Evi-

dently they are bound together; they are on their way to a farm where they hope to get a job together. . . .

Well, thanks to George's speaking up for him, they both get the jobs they are seeking. Lennie as a worker gives full satisfaction, doing the work of four. But unfortunately the son of the "boss" employing them has married a poor little floosey of a girl, whose only notion of getting into friendly contact with the men about her is to give them the glad eye. Her husband, Curley, is a bully who can use his fists and is fiercely jealous. George and the other hands on the farm are terrified of getting involved with Curley's wife, and George warns Lennie against speaking to her. You can guess what happens. . . . The great merit of *Of Mice and Men* is the way in which it conveys that these "tough guys" need above everything some outlet for affection.

. . . Mr. John Mills plays the part of George, Mr. Niall MacGinnis, Lennie, Mr. Sydney Benson, Candy, admirably; and I cannot imagine the parts of the old negro and Curley's wife (Miss Claire Luce) being more completely filled. I have indicated the limitation of this sentimental tragedy, and that the spirit of it is something to be grateful for. I can only repeat that the interpretation leaves very little to be desired.

Derek Verschoyle. "Stage and Screen and Theatre."
Spectator [England], 162 (26 May 1939), 901.

. . . *Of Mice and Men* was fully reviewed in this column about a month ago when it was produced at the Gate Theatre. It has now been deservedly transferred to the Apollo. It is a rather unsubtle but entirely honest and extremely effective play describing a tragic episode in the lives of two young labourers who arrive to work on a Californian ranch. It is recommended as one of the few plays running in London that is genuinely worth seeing.

Eric [Keown]. "Of Mice and Men (Apollo)." Punch [England], 196 (7 June 1939), 640.

I always dread seeing the stage versions of books which I have very much enjoyed; and so in honesty I must say about this play that I cannot remember any more successful dramatisation.

Mr. John Steinbeck's story, which took America by storm, and even shook the book-shelves of this country, went deeper and got further in the writer's job of revealing human nature than most of its fatter brethren which have moved the pundits to immoderate ecstasies. It went straight for the subject of loneliness like a terrier and bit hard from the beginning, with an exquisite economy of sentiment which allowed it to expose the most intimate feelings of simple people with never a touch of the maudlin. Here is the whole essence of the book transferred without evaporation or dilution, here are Lennie and George exactly as they appeared in its pages, and here even is the same end, out in the wood by the river, and still the purest tragedy. Mr. Steinbeck has written the play himself, and has scored a double triumph. . . .

[The] play moves quickly in a series of tersely written commentaries on its main theme of loneliness. The scene in the bunk-house when the men have persuaded old Candy to let them shoot his ancient dog is very good indeed, and so is that in which the crippled negro is at home. There is not an inch of padding in any of the dialogue.

The casting is wonderfully accurate. Mr. John Mills gives George just the quality of nervous intensity which is wanted, Mr. Niall MacGinnis plays the childish mountain (*ridiculus mus* in pocket) so that Lennie is always lovable and never silly. These are both notable performances. Miss Claire Luce cleverly brings out the vamp's unhappiness, and the men on the farm are all well taken.

Mr. Norman Marshall must be given credit not only for so good a production but for having launched the play at the Gate.

Anthony Merryn. "Of Mice and Men." Life and Letters To-day, 22 (July 1939), 92–4.

Of Mice and Men has no propaganda, no criticism of society, no plumbing the depths of human experience. Yet that most difficult of modern achievements— true tragedy—has almost been realized. I say almost, for while there is pity and terror, there is little suffering on the part of the principal character, Lennie, who is half-witted and not responsible for his actions. The suffering is rather in the mind of his friend George, who feels so strangely attached to him as to take his protection upon himself, though he thereby handicaps his own career.

But the sense of inevitability is there—the doom of a man essentially lovable but with the brain of a child. There is a poetic sensitiveness in the drawing of his character which is thrown into powerful dramatic relief by the complete absence of poetry in the setting—a background of tough Californian ranch-men with primitive ideas of justice.

Lennie loves to handle soft things—mice and rabbits and puppies, and women's dresses and hair. In his childish ecstasy he forgets his colossal strength (an ironic compensation for wit) and chokes the life out of the only woman who has ever taken any notice of him. To save him from a fearful vengeance, George sets him dreaming of the happy days that are to be, and, when his head is turned, shoots him. The last scene, in its overwhelming poignancy, is perhaps unique in dramatic literature.

Niall MacGinnis's portrayal of the clumsy, simple Lennie is a carefully studied piece of artistic interpretation, entirely convincing and full of imaginative subtleties. John Mills, as George, in a more straightforward, and therefore rather more difficult part, is equally sure of touch. The production, with its superb timing and pregnant silences (helped by a fine economy of dialogue), lifts the whole significance of the drama far beyond the narrow confines of its setting. . . .

Checklist of Additional Reviews

Michael Sayers. "New Plays by Messrs. Howard, Steinbeck, et al." *New Masses*, 7 December 1937, p. 26.

John Hobart. "John Steinbeck, a Convert to the Stage." San Francisco *Chronicle, This World* magazine, 12 December 1937, p. 19.

Burton Rascoe. "John Steinbeck." *English Journal*, 27 (1938), 205–16.

Edith J. R. Isaacs. "When Good Men Get Together." *Theatre Arts*, 22 (January 1938), 11–22.

"*Of Mice and Men* Wins Critics' Prize." New York *Times*, 19 April 1938, p. 23.

Brooks Atkinson. "Critics Circle Play." New York *Times*, 24 April 1938, Section 10, p. ix.

Mark Barron. "Two Candidates for the Pulitzer Prize." San Francisco *Chronicle, This World* magazine, 1 May 1938, p. 19.

Gilbert E. Govan. "Roamin' the Book World." Chattanooga *Times*, 29 May 1938, p. 10.

John Mason Brown. "Mr. Steinbeck's *Of Mice and Men*." *Two on the Aisle: Ten Years of the American Theatre in Performance* (New York: Norton, 1939), 183–7.

Frank H. O'Hara. "Melodrama with a Meaning." *Today in American Drama* (Chicago: University of Chicago Press, 1939), 142–89.

Charles Morgan. "Steinbeck in London." New York *Times*, 30 April 1939, Section 11, p. 3.

"*Of Mice and Men*." *New Masses*, 5 March 1940, 29–30.

"Plays and Pictures." *New Statesman and Nation* [England], 19 (13 April 1940), 493–4.

Louis Calta. "Theatre." New York *Times*, 5 December 1958, p. 38.

THE LONG VALLEY

JOHN STEINBECK

THE
LONG
VALLEY

THE VIKING PRESS

NEW YORK

1938

Wilbur Needham. "New Steinbeck Book: Event of Autumn." Los Angeles *Times*, 18 September 1938, Part 3, p. 6.

John Steinbeck has published nothing that was beneath himself, and he never will. Curiously, he also gives you the impression that he has printed nothing that is quite up to himself; there is a sense of reserve power in all his novels and stories, of material deliberately withheld, of ideas that will some day be unleashed. Yet nothing is gone from any of his work, just as nothing is there that ought not to be.

His books are effortlessly right. His work has perfection, but not the precious perfection that is sterility. Everything he writes has the perfection of finality, even the stories he does not like himself. His pages are as uncluttered as those of Robert Nathan, as rich as Thomas Wolfe's.

He can be delicate, shy, mystical; he can be vulgar, brutal, even horrifying; he can be quiet like a mouse, light of step as a deer on the Salinas hills, warm as the sun on a lazy *paisano*'s back. And he can laugh, ah, how the man can laugh! Low and soft and bending over to hear little people laughing back at him; loud and boisterous with drinkers making tavern walls shake down; sly and chuckling when satiric laughter struggles in his throat.

All these moods and tones are in the sixteen tales of *The Long Valley*; and they are there without spoiling the book's essential unity. Reading *The Pastures of Heaven* was not like going through a group of short stories; and the common locale did not alone give forth that effect, any more than it does in these tales of the Salinas Valley and the Bay of Monterey.

Something else ties together varied techniques, colorings, tonal qualities. Behind each story, inside it and surrounding it, there is a presence you do not often find in the work of writers with more than one string to the bow. It is a fragile presence, but with surprising strength, in that borderland story of this world and the mind's world and maybe another world, "The White Quail." Mary Teller, for all she lives in her garden unaware of a backstage presence, has got some subtle fragrance that is not wholly hers.

It is a clinical presence, a pathological, that comes forth with snakes in its hands in the story of a scientist interrupted at his work by a woman whose aura has Freudian gleam to it. When Peter Randall's wife dies and leaves him alone on the farm she ruled invisibly, a laughing presence enters and the old man is ruled by it. A grotesque presence shambles in with "Johnny Bear;" a quietly bitter one, shocking in its gestures, takes command of "The Vigilante;" a boyhood presence animates "The Red Pony." All these presences are different, and they are all the same.

Whenever I read John Steinbeck, I am in the presence of a man. That is a feeling I have had only at rare intervals during my twenty years of book-reviewing peonage.

William Soskin.
"Varied Art of John
Steinbeck."
New York *Herald
Tribune*, 18 September
1938, "Books" section,
p. 7.

John Steinbeck is certainly one of the most richly promising novelists of the younger American group, and yet he is popularly honored for a work of doubtful value, *Of Mice and Men*. His genuinely tragic *In Dubious Battle* is generally neglected. He is known to part of his audience as a realist to whom human blood is merely ketchup, to another part as a mellow, leisurely observer of his Western *paisanos*, to some as a psychological analyst, to others as a proletarian writer with class consciousness. Many readers and critics are observing his work anxiously, for they feel that he will emerge as a writer of impressive stature, but they also are inclined to regard his present writing as material still in the crucible, still undergoing the chemical processes that will ultimately produce pure artistry.

It is therefore especially interesting to weigh the various merits and faults of so large a variety of his work as appears in a volume of Mr. Steinbeck's short stories, *The Long Valley*. Reading these stories is very much like studying a subject by the case-method—a purely inductive process whereby the law student finally arrives at his knowledge of contracts or torts or real property though an analysis and discussion of already existing decisions that illustrate fundamental principles. Here, in a single volume, are stories which demonstrate intimate, delicious communion with the Salinas Valley land of California that nourishes Steinbeck's art, as well as stories theatrically set in mystic gardens and castles which seem to have no rooted strength. Here are exquisite studies of childhood, poetic and fresh, as well as brutal accounts of mortal struggles with Nature and mercilessly true descriptions of violence. Here are portraits of workers and peasants and farm wives with genuine vitality and truth about them, and over-subtle studies of emotional women which seem false and lacking in understanding. Here are dramas of the class struggle, pictures of hangings and social aberrations that conform to the best sociological patterns, yet contain individual studies of character and human behavior which take them out of the rut of official proletarian writing.

From this bewildering variety of material a transcending body of work emerges in a group of stories under the general title "Red Pony," stories of the growth of a small boy, Jody, on a Salinas Valley ranch. These stories, magic with the child's sensitive observation of the animal life about him, of the smell and feel and sound of the stables, the farmyard, the pigsty, the corral, the kitchen, the mountains, the California skies and dews and nights, and brilliant and simple in the boy's forthright understanding of adult character, certainly sound a major chord and a harmony dominant over all of Steinbeck's work to date.

Coincidentally, the name of the boy in these stories is that of the equally delightful child in Marjorie Kinnan Rawlings's novel, *The Yearling*, and the boys have a great deal in common. But whereas Mrs. Rawlings's story sometimes borders on romantic sentimentality, and is saved from such a fate by her virtuosity in the sheer writing, Steinbeck's boy and the tragedies of his pets and the ordeal of his adolescence seem somehow closer to a bedrock honesty and a thoroughly realistic grasp of life in the child's perspective. Even when one bears in mind the ruthlessness of Richard Hughes's writing of children in *The Innocent Voyage*, as well as Mrs. Rawlings's lovely story, it is hard to recall a work so impressive as "The Red Pony."

Steinbeck is at his comfortable best in stories that demand careful reporting of detail—the agonizing detail of a hunted youth's flight into the mountains after he has killed a man, of increasing pain and thirst and desperate struggle and fear that remind you of one of William Faulkner's hunted creatures and of Eugene O'Neill's terror-stricken Emperor Jones. This same gift for concrete realism makes a gripping little horror playlet out of an incident in which a woman in a biological laboratory identifies herself with a rattlesnake and watches it devour a rat. The weakness in this tale lies in the obvious symbolism whereby the woman's sexual abnormalities are dramatized. Equally weak is a story called "The Chrysanthemums" wherein one of those atavistic women who garden passionately, but inefficiently, discovers that life is passing her by. Another story in the same vein, about a woman who identifies her "pure" self, the mystic self which eludes her blunt husband's understanding, with a white quail in her garden, also seems synthetic and psychologically phony. It is significant, I believe, that Steinbeck's traffic with sophisticated women and female emotion in these stories is his weak point. The only women he does well are mothers, ranch wives, eccentrics and clods like the Jugo-Slavic wife in "The Murder" who becomes devoted and faithful after she is beaten.

In "The Raid" Steinbeck gives us a tense portrayal of an attack upon a couple of Communist organizers by a vigilante mob, but his point is an ironic one—this despite the complete compassion of his story. The young Communists behave exactly like Christian martyrs in their heroism. When the boy who has been virtually murdered says, drowsily, "Forgive them because they don't know what they're doing," his companion replies: "You lay off that religion stuff, kid. Religion is the opium of the people."

The humor in Steinbeck's writing seems healthier and more sturdy in these stories than in the rather sweetish, soft stuff of the novel *Tortilla Flat*. The story of "St. Katy the Virgin," a pig who became a saint, is a riot of hilarious iconoclasm, and the tale of the farmer in "The Harness" who relaxed his belly after his wife died and grew acres of sweet peas for the smell instead of practical crops, is a lovely job.

All the lavish comment that has been made about Steinbeck's conciseness and the economy of his style in regard to his novels may be repeated and emphasized in the case of these short stories. The medium requires just those qualities of composition, and Steinbeck has practiced his art carefully and efficiently.

Lewis Gannett. "Books and Things." New York *Herald Tribune*, 19 September 1938, p. 11.

The Long Valley ... is a sort of sample room of John Steinbeck.

Here is one story of a halfwit, "Johnny Bear," which will remind you at once of *Of Mice and Men* and of William Faulkner. Here is a raw lynching story, and a picture of two young Communists waiting for the mob they know is on their trail, which are somewhat in the mood of *In Dubious Battle*. Here are two sketches of *paisanos*, echoes rather of the *Pastures of Heaven* than of *Tortilla Flat*. Here is the ribald "St. Katy the Virgin," privately printed some years ago, but never put on sale. Here are three or four less successful studies of more sophisticated people, which I suspect were written long ago. And here are the famous Jody stories, "The Red Pony," published in a limited edition last spring, and a new Jody story, never before printed anywhere, and as good as anything John Steinbeck has ever written, suggestive, possibly, of the mood in which he is writing his new novel.

"Why do I have to listen to it?" Carl Tiflin cried out angrily at breakfast, tired of his father-in-law's endless stories of the crossing of the plains. "That time's done. Why can't he forget it, now it's done? Why does he have to tell them over and over. He came across the plains. All right. Now it's finished! Nobody wants to hear about it over and over!"

Carl did not know that his father-in-law had opened the door, and was listening. Jody knew—Jody, the ten-year-old boy who was Grandpa's only eager audience. Later, sitting tired in the sun, Grandpa talked to Jody. It wasn't just the stories, he said; he wanted people to feel those westering days. Every man wanted something for himself in those days, he said; but the big beast that was all of them together wanted only to move on, westward. "The westering was as big as God," he said, "and the slow steps that made the movement piled up and piled up until the continent was crossed." Now "there's no place to go. There's the ocean to stop them. There's a line of old men along the shore hating the ocean because it stopped them. . . . Westering has died

out of the people. Westering isn't a hunger any more. It's all done. Your father is right. It is finished."

But still the wanderers fill the roads of the West, some of them hardly aware that they are hungry. And some of them, squatting in their California valleys, are caught up in some such quick mob as John Steinbeck tells of in "The Vigilante," help drag a man from jail and burn him, and go home with a light in their eyes which makes their wives look up and say, "You think I can't tell by the look on your face that you've been with a woman?"

John Steinbeck can pack into a few paragraphs what many novelists stretch out over a whole book. Sometimes, I think, he packs almost too much. There is an almost climactic monotony in some of these sultry, slow-moving, dry-country stories which suddenly break out in a cyclonic last paragraph; it becomes, in the weakest of them, almost a trick.

The Jody stories are almost miraculously good. No one, I think, has ever caught the ecstasy of a small boy with his first horse more movingly; beside "The Gift," even Lincoln Steffens's story of his small-boy passion for a pony seems long-winded and amateurish. In "The Great Mountains" and "The Leader of the People" Mr. Steinbeck maintains with rare precision the balance of a small boy's intuitions—the uncanny insights into an old man's mind, the decent unspoiled sympathies, and the utter unawareness which go with these.

"St. Katy the Virgin" is such a ribald, blasphemous story (of a pig who became a saint) as only a man brought up among primitive Catholics, to whom blasphemy is real as well as dear, could tell. It might have been born in France in the days of Romain Rolland's "Colas Breugnon"; it grew, obviously, out of whispered stories told at *paisano* campfires in the half-Mexican uplands of Monterey County, Calif., where John Steinbeck grew up.

That is a violent and beautiful country. These are, more than half of them, violent stories, and all of them beautiful stories. John Steinbeck has some strange affinity for violence, but he is never lost in it. There is always a warm sunshine in the background; and such an understanding of the simple belly satisfactions of life as crops out in the four simple, satisfying pages here called "Breakfast."

Harry Hansen.
"The First Reader."
New York *World-Telegram*, 19 September 1938, p. 19.

Case of John Steinbeck—Think of Sherwood Anderson sitting at the feet of Katharine Mansfield and absorbing some of her sophisticated understanding of the short story as an artistic expression, and you get near an explanation of John Steinbeck. Like Anderson, Steinbeck knows people who live close to the earth and are affected by its moods, and, like him, he is absorbed with their inner turmoil. Like Mansfield, he watches the effect of every word, every sentence, and, so far, this has not stood in the way of his originality.

In *The Long Valley* he gives us a book of superb short stories. In each one, whether he writes of gardens, snakes, ponies or radicals, he is interested in what goes on inside the human actors. He shapes them quickly—cuts the cloth into a single pattern. Don't miss "The Red Pony," three stories of the boy Jody and

his pal Billy Buck, and the effect on Jody of the gift of the pony and the tragic episode of the mare—tales of a boy's hopes told with a deep knowledge of ranch life in the Salinas country of California, and a high sense of drama.

Other highlights:—"The Raid," a brief episode telling how two radicals feel when they know that they are about to be beaten up for their activities (excellent); "Flight," the curious inverted psychology of Pepe and the Torres family, with a careful analysis of Pepe going toward his death; "The Leader of the People," the story of the old grandfather, whose tales of the westward movement angered his anchored son-in-law, a story splendid for characterization and rich in meaning. Less successful, to my notion, are "The Snake," a synthetic attempt to identify a mental state with an episode; "The Chrysanthemums," a bit too abrupt at the start but with a good ending, and "The White Quail," which reminds me of Wilbur Daniel Steele. I am also less impressed with "Saint Katy the Virgin," a heavy-footed exercise in irony; Anatole France has spoiled my appetite for coarser fare.

This is Viking's first book by Steinbeck; good jacket by Elmer Hader.

Ralph Thompson.
"Books of the Times."
New York *Times*,
21 September 1938,
p. 29.

John Steinbeck has almost as many manners as there are letters to his name. He can be tender. He can be tough. He can be waggish, cunning, sentimental, callous.

He can turn on the weeps or the heat with equal ease, and combine the saccharine and the sordid without batting an eye.

He is an exciting writer with a curiously catholic taste. Its variety is well displayed in *The Long Valley*, a collection of fifteen (not, as the jacket says, sixteen) stories, all but two of which have been published before in one form or another.

Here is the "Red Pony" sequence issued a year ago in a limited edition, plus a new Jody story called "The Leader of the People." Here is the fumbling "Chrysanthemums," the powerful "Vigilante," the chilling "Snake," the casual "Breakfast," the pretentious "White Quail"; also a half dozen other tales including "St. Katy the Virgin," privately printed by Covici, Friede as a Christmas book for 1936, and "Flight," the second of the pieces now published for the first time.

He is an exciting writer always, but so far as I am concerned much at his best when he doesn't work too hard at it. The callous Mr. Steinbeck, describing a cold-blooded shooting ("The Murder") or a fatal manhunt ("Flight"), is impressive but artificial. The cunning Mr. Steinbeck, dealing with sex symbols ("The Snake") and feminine neuroses ("The White Quail"), is artificial and not impressive. The waggish Mr. Steinbeck, pushing his tongue hard against his cheek and writing of a thirteenth-century pig and two pious monks ("St. Katy the Virgin") is all right but something of a shock. It is quite as though Ernest Hemingway had come forth with an Uncle Remus story.

And the sentimental Mr. Steinbeck, who takes all sorts of unfortunate freaks of nature to his bosom, is something else again. This happens to be the best-known Mr. Steinbeck—the author of *Of Mice and Men*—but I doubt exceedingly that it is the best. He is represented here with a yarn called "Johnny Bear," in which a huge halfwit, shambling, stupid, smiling, with arms like a gorilla and brain like a mayfly, does everything but choke a girl to death. This big Johnny has a peculiar talent: he can repeat anything he hears, whether he understands it or not—anything, in any language, including the Greek. And not only the words but the inflections, so that when he has a couple of drinks under his belt and gets started he can reel off whole conversations that he has overheard. About this monster the author builds a story and all but weeps when he has to conk him with a bungstarter to get him out of the way.

It is admittedly dramatic, etc., but hardly scrupulous, and I for one pray that Mr. Steinbeck will avoid cretins, fools, imbeciles, boobies, idiots, dolts and particular boneheads in the future. He seems to do far better with normal people or with people who could pass for normal in a sizable crowd. The best stories in this collection, at any rate, are those revolving about the quite ordinary small boy named Jody Tiflin, who grows up on a ranch in a California valley and has for a time a pony of his own.

There's not much more to say about Jody than was said after his debut last year except that Mr. Steinbeck's combination of toughness and tenderness makes him a memorable figure. In "The Leader of the People" he is more interested in his grandfather than in any one else; he even invites Grandfather, who has come to the ranch for a visit, to hunt mice in the haystacks with him and his two dogs. But the old man happens to have something on his mind, and the hunt never comes off. Jody learns what that something is with much the same sort of emotion that he had when he saw his red pony lying dead in the sage brush or when Billy Buck pulled the colt out of Nellie one night in the stall.

Elinor Davis. "The Steinbeck Country." *Saturday Review*, 18 (24 September 1938), 11.

Steinbeck is one of the few American writers who refuse to be backseat-driven by success; he writes what he wants to write, instead of letting the expectations of his public push him into a groove. Yet in this collection of fifteen short stories there is less variety than you would expect, after his last three novels; which may be just as well. The one distinctly off-the-trail story of the lot is a burlesque hagiography, which might better have been left in private circulation. The others all deal with what will soon be known as the Steinbeck country, the regions around Monterey and Salinas, which seems to be populated by suppressed husbands, frustrated wives, brides who cheat unless you horsewhip them, old men who are no good any more, sex-starved spinsters of good family who fool around with Chinamen and then hang themselves, etc. About the only people in the book who are pointed in my direction are a couple of communists who go looking for martyrdom under orders; and even them Steinbeck regards with a faintly ironic eye.

However, if that is what he sees that is what he has to write about; and here is certainly some of the best writing of the past decade. Outside of one or two stories you won't find an ounce of fat in his style; and you could pick forty paragraphs out of this volume that would be fit to appear as models in any textbook of composition. Steinbeck makes his country live and the people live as part of it, as much a part as the horned toads or the buzzards. It is not so much the malice of man that gets them down as Nature, internal and external; the pity you feel for them is the pity you would feel for an animal trapped and doomed. But Steinbeck is not too proud to pity them himself; and if his vision is perhaps limited in scope there are no blind spots in the areas where it operates. He sees clear down through these people, and reproduces them in as many dimensions as they have.

Preferences among the fifteen stories will differ, of course; but perhaps most readers would agree that the best are the three episodes in a boy's life which have already been published, in a limited edition, as *The Red Pony*. The same boy and his grandfather, a wornout pioneer to whose repetitious reminiscences people no longer want to listen, appears in "The Leader of the People." How much autobiography there may or may not be in all this does not matter; those stories are packed with truth, that would have been just as true in the Stone Age. Notable among the others are "The Raid"—how it feels to be beaten up by vigilantes, and to have to wait for it; "The Vigilante"—after-effects of a lynching on a member of the mob; and "Johnny Bear," in which a half-wit with a trick of reproducing overheard conversations catalyzes both the good and evil emotion of a whole community. A collection of short stories does not always add much to the stature of a successful novelist; but *The Long Valley* leaves Steinbeck still the best prospect in American letters. . . .

Clifton Fadiman.
"Books."
New Yorker, 14
(24 September 1938),
71–3.

... I can't understand why some reviewers persist in classing John Steinbeck as a hardboiled writer. I guess it must be because he uses homespun English and because so many of his characters are socially submerged—as if itinerant workers and tramps necessarily exuded a more hardboiled atmosphere than, let us say, Captain Anthony Eden. Actually, if resistance to emotion is the true mark of the hardboiled writer, Steinbeck is softboiled, and no bad thing either. Far from being tough, he is exceptionally sensitive, not merely to the cruder, or what one might call large-muscle, emotions but to those subtleties of feeling that are the stock in trade of writers like Chekhov, D. H. Lawrence, and Katherine Mansfield.

Try his book of short stories, *The Long Valley*, to test whether this is so. Note particularly such tenuous tales as "The Chrysanthemums," "The White Quail," "Breakfast," and "The Harness." All four stories are beautifully written, though I think that in them Mr. Steinbeck is trying just a mite too hard to be sensitive and Open to Beauty. But about such matters it is easy to disagree.

The best thing in the book is the three-part story, "Red Pony," a heartbreakingly true picture of boyhood. I think it's a masterpiece. It has something intimate, unworked-over, that the other stories, fine as some of them are, lack. "Johnny Bear," for example, is a horror story; it's subtle, it's highly original—but there is that touch of contrivance which some shrewd critics felt, I think rightly, marred *Of Mice and Men*. On the whole, however, a remarkable collection by a writer who so far has neither repeated himself nor allowed himself a single careless sentence....

Stanley Young.
"The Short Stories of John Steinbeck."
New York Times Book Review, 88
(25 September 1938), 7.

Of late John Steinbeck has had some pretty high adjectives hoisted above his name. But he will not have to strike his colors with this collection of short stories. As a group they are neither profound nor passionate stories of great stature—that is, they do not illuminate an age or a people either emotionally or intellectually, and they are occasionally flagrantly sentimental, as was *Of Mice and Men*. Yet all have one rare, creative thing: a directness of impression that makes them glow with life, small-scale life though it is.

The background is again Salinas Valley, Monterey, with ranch hands, *paisanos*, farm boys objectively observed as they struggle with one primitive emotion after another. In "Flight" the emotion is fear, and the long, agonizing hours in which Pepé the Indian boy rides from his first murder into the shelter of the mountains become as terrifying and as vivid as the flight of Reynard the Fox as Masefield set it down. Pepé's escape is the only thing that matters, one narrow slit of time with a boy in it running for his life.

The story of Mike the vigilante has

the same emotional undertow. Mike has helped at a hanging, and after the wild mob fury is over he is left with a dull tiredness and loneliness, pathetically empty and fearful. It is hard to believe that a man who has stormed a jail and pulled a rope around a neck can be so filled with remorse or made so sympathetically understandable. It's sentimental stuff, but try to resist it as Steinbeck tells it!

"The Raid," a courageous but bitter little story of two union organizers in a California town, is the only piece in the book that has any topical political implication. Two men, one experienced, the other young and fearful, schedule a meeting. When they hear of the coming of the raiders they stand their ground and are beaten mercilessly. They go down smiling a "tight, hard smile," which makes it another fictional raid for this reviewer.

The most exciting thing about this collection lies in the stories that step outside the usual emotional province of this author. The superb story, "The White Quail," has a delicacy and symbolism and design that recall Katherine Mansfield. Mary, whose frozen purity presided over the garden and the house and drove her husband to desperate loneliness, sees in a white quail all the cool lovely essence of herself. The way this self-knowledge affects her and her husband makes for a story of subtlety and grace unlike anything Steinbeck has yet written.

Equally new is the author's capacity to tell a fine, humorous, mocking fable such as "Saint Katy the Virgin," a rollicking, grand story of a pig that became a saint. *Tortilla Flat* suggested the broad Elizabethan mirth of Steinbeck, but the imaginative doings of Katy the pig clinch the matter for all time. Voltaire would have loved Katy, but Disney will get her.

Completely in contrast to Katy's happy story is a grotesque and haunting character study of one "Johnny Bear."

Johnny is as pathetic as the groping half-wit of *Of Mice and Men*, and as menacing. He is a peeping Tom who has a photographic memory which allows him to repeat entire conversations while catching the intonations of voice of the characters he has seen. For a whisky he will talk, and the way in which he reveals the tragedy settling over two respectable maiden ladies in a small town is storytelling oblique and effective to the highest degree.

Finally there is "The Harness" and "The Red Pony," two stories that fulfill the fine promise of the author's best novel, *In Dubious Battle*. The first tells of a man trying to escape the domination of his dead wife; the second gently and effortlessly recreates the day-by-day routine life of a farm and a small boy's love for horses. They leave nothing to be desired. They cannot be talked about. They must be read.

It comes down to this: out of sixteen stories John Steinbeck has written a good dozen that are memorable. He shows more emotional range than he was suspected of having and a maturing craftsmanship. Fortunately he is not working to prove any pet notions. He is writing about people, beautiful or nauseating, as they come. He knows his people and his scene without being bogged down by realistic detail. Beyond that he has a tremendous and abiding sympathy for human beings on all levels of experience. With time and experience and discerning criticism he may become a genuinely great American writer.

"More from Steinbeck." *Newsweek*, 12 (26 September 1938), 29.

The rich Salinas Valley of California is a world in itself. It abounds in all sorts of people—barley ranchers, Mexicans, fruit pickers, and farmers. The self-appointed historian of this little world is John Steinbeck, who sticks close to his elected territory, eating, drinking, and working; out of it he has wrought the stories that have made him a writer of first importance.

In *The Long Valley* are thirteen short stories treating, for the most part, of the same people of his novels, the agricultural workers of *In Dubious Battle*, the *paisanos* of *Tortilla Flat* and the ranch hands of *Of Mice and Men*. When Steinbeck does stray out of his terrain he wanders far; one tale about a pig named Katy is set in fourteenth-century Europe.

There are all kinds of stories here, violent ones, horrible, funny, poignant, and tragic ones. One or two are mere sketches but, like everything the author does, they are watertight. Particularly outstanding is "Flight," the story of Pepé, a Mexican boy, rudely thrust into a man's shoes and a man's fate by a sudden crime. "The Red Pony," almost a novelette, shows Steinbeck in a tender mood, evoking the idyl of a farm boy's life and his love for a horse. "The Raid" seems to be something left out of *In Dubious Battle*—a brief and terrifying description of a beating administered by vigilantes to two Communist organizers.

No one needs be told that John Steinbeck is a master craftsman; these tales reaffirm it.

Joseph Henry Jackson. "A Bookman's Notebook." San Francisco *Chronicle*, 28 September 1938, p. 13.

This volume is a kind of cross-section of Steinbeck—a collection of shorter pieces chiefly, and most of those published before in one form or another.

Several of the 15 have appeared in *Esquire*, one or two in *Harper's*. The three related stories under the single title, "The Red Pony," were brought out last year in a limited edition, and "St. Katy the Virgin" only saw print as the publisher's Christmas gift to friends, and in an edition even more strictly limited. One story, "The Chrysanthemums," was included in the O'Brien "Best Short Stories" annual; two pieces, "Flight" and "The Leader of the People," are here published for the first time. So much for the mere physical description of the volume.

Out of the 15 tales "The Red Pony," to my mind is by far the most important.

As you will remember, it is about a small boy, his passion for his pony, his agony when it is lost to him, his reactions to his first encounter with the harshness of the world into which he is growing up, his feelings when he is faced, one after the other, with the perpetual miracles of death and birth. No, it isn't a "nice" story; but it is an immensely powerful one. Manifestly it is drawn from full understanding of small boys and small horses and the casual cruelties of ranch life. It remains (I think) top-level Steinbeck, ranking with the best he has written.

Supplementing it, in a way, is a new Jody story, one of the two never before printed, "The Leader of the People." This tenderly told tale of an old man who forgot himself and told over and over again his stories of crossing the plains is another fine piece of work. In it, too, Steinbeck expresses through the mouth of old Grandfather something about which he has been thinking more and more. "It wasn't the Indians that were important," says Grandfather, "nor adventure, nor even getting out here. It was a whole bunch of people made into one big crawling beast. . . . It wasn't getting here that mattered, it was movement and westering. . . . Then we came down to the sea and it was done."

Unquestionably it is Steinbeck's knowledge of the new westering, today's machine-economy-driven migratory movement, that leads him to say this. Because it is plain as a pikestaff that though the old kind of westering is done with, there must be a new kind, something to take the place of the old—a westering of ideas perhaps.

For the rest, they vary from the frankly ribald and blasphemous "St. Katy" all the way to the short "sketch" (it's hardly more) called "Breakfast." There is the "Johnny Bear" piece that *Esquire* ran— a creepy tale of an idiot whose mind and voice functioned like a phonograph record. There is "The Vigilante," also a magazine piece, in which Steinbeck lays bare (in a manner that should please the Freudians) something of the underlying sexual motive behind such things as lynchings. There is "The Snake," which I like least of all of them, and there is "Flight," in which the emotion of fear is traced to an almost hysterical pitch. And there is "The Harness," wherein the author demonstrates very plainly that you can't run away from what you can't run

away from. These, with the remaining three, make up the book.

That it is good Steinbeck has already been said. It is also completely characteristic Steinbeck. Like everything he writes, these tales are compounded of brutality and tenderness, beauty and ugliness, because (as I am quite convinced) Steinbeck sees these contrasts as equal parts of the same thing—which is life. There is in them, too, some of the best writing Steinbeck has done; as witness, not to make too great a point of it, "The Red Pony." As for "St. Katy," I'm a little curious to see what the reactions will be. The world sometimes seems completely filled with people crying "Ah, why doesn't Steinbeck do another *Tortilla Flat?*" Well, let them (as Marie Antoinette didn't say), read Kate.

"*The Long Valley*." Booklist, 35 (1 October 1938), 48–9.

Thirteen short stories, most of them set in the long Salinas Valley, California. Two have not been printed before; one, "Saint Katy the Virgin," which may offend Roman Catholics, appeared in a private edition, not for sale; the finest, *The Red Pony*, in three parts, appeared only in a limited ten dollar edition, now out of print. The characters are mainly people of the land; the writing is economical and vivid.

T[homas] K[ing] Whipple. "Steinbeck: Through a Glass, though Brightly." *New Republic*, 96 (12 October 1938), 274–5.

The Long Valley carries its readers back to Steinbeck's first published volume, *The Pastures of Heaven*. Here is the same beautiful countryside, with the same inhabitants—the half-wits, the delightful Mexican peasantry, the Americans who are either healthy normal farmers or interesting psychological freaks. It is true that in *The Long Valley* there are also vigilantes and Communists, to remind us that times change, but since Steinbeck is concerned not with external facts, but only with their odd states of mind when lynching or being lynched, they do not jar against the general tone of the picture. They take their place in the immemorial spectacle of the ill fated race of men.

Surely no one writes lovelier stories, yielding a purer pleasure. Here are tragedy and suffering and violence, to be sure, but with all that is sharp and harsh distilled to a golden honey, ripe and mellow. Even cruelty and murder grow somehow pastoral, idyllic, seen through this amber light, as one might watch the struggles of fishes and water snakes in the depths of a mountain pool. Beyond question, Steinbeck has a magic to take the sting out of reality and yet leave it all there except the sting. Perhaps it is partly the carefulness of his art, with endless pains devising and arranging every detail until all fits perfectly and is smooth and suave as polished ivory. But probably it is more the enchantment of his style, of that liquid melody which flows on and on until even such an experience as a man's dying of thirst in the morning sunlight among remote and rocky hills can seem not altogether ugly, because it has become a legendary thing that happened once upon a time.

Proper distance, I think, is the secret of this effect—to place people not too close or too far away. In the middle distance they cannot touch us, and yet we can see their performances with the greatest clarity and fullness. Detachment, of course, is the essential: we are here to contemplate only, like the Lucretian gods but less remote. We feel the appropriate emotions—pity, sympathy, terror and horror even—but with the delightful sense that we are apart, in the audience, and that anyhow nothing can be done or needs to be done. Such a form of contemplation—which some would like to have the function of all art—is so agreeable, presumably, because it frees us from all responsibility. It is a tremendous relief to get rid of our ordinary burden of feeling implicated in human destinies.

Such seems to me the attitude that is induced not only by Steinbeck's earliest and latest work, but by almost all of it, and that largely accounts for his popularity. *Tortilla Flat*, with its rococo comedy, ironic and romantic, ornate and mannered, may be a photographically accurate portrayal of the poor Mexicans of Monterey, but it leaves its readers amused and incredulous onlookers. Is *Of Mice and Men* an exception? It has more reality than *Tortilla Flat* of course; its dialogue is extraordinarily lifelike and lively, as is most of Steinbeck's talk, for he is amazingly observant; but George and Lennie seem to me unbelievable—the flavor of grenadine is too strong. In any case, even if there have been half-wits as amiable as Lennie with friends as devoted as George, the question is not of reality, but of the attitude toward reality. Does anyone, in reading the book, participate in the fate of these men as their inevitable doom rolls upon them? Or does one watch merely, without sharing?

Steinbeck's reticence threatened to give way at least once: in his least successful novel, *To a God Unknown*, a strange and puzzling version of the Joseph story, full of myths and symbols and mystical identification with the earth. The hero, who is one with the processes of life in nature and men, finds himself comprehending all people so thoroughly that he can have relations with none. After his brother's murder, he says to his father's spirit:

> Thomas and Burton [his other brothers] are allowed their likes and dislikes, only I am cut off. I am cut off. I can have neither good luck nor bad luck. I can have no knowledge of any good or bad. Even a pure true feeling of the difference between pleasure and pain is denied me. All things are one, and all a part of me. . . . Benjy is dead, and I am neither glad nor sorry. There is no reason for it to me. It is just so. I know now, my father, what you were—lonely beyond feeling loneliness, calm because you had no contact.

So might Steinbeck's reader, whether rightly or wrongly, be tempted to speak to him. In *To a God Unknown* he seems for once to commit himself to a point of view, of identification with everything and detachment from everybody.

A reader of the passage just quoted can hardly help thinking of Steinbeck's neighbor, Robinson Jeffers. As writers the two have little in common, but they do share this detachment, and furthermore they share a preoccupation with physical suffering, cruelty and violence. Are these two qualities related? When a man be-

comes too aloof from mankind, so that the life of men turns for him into a mere esthetic spectacle to be exploited for its various notes and colors, does his human nature revenge itself by forcing upon him an obsession with power in its most repulsive forms? Is a surrender of humanity and an assumption of godhead likely to lead to such a result? Perhaps one observation might be permitted to a reader: that a taste for books which place one in the situation of a superior being above the fever and the fret and apart from one's fellows may be an undesirable taste. Apparently many people reconcile themselves to being human only with great difficulty and would much prefer to be almost anything else—a mountain or a beast or a god—in order to escape the limitations and troubles and obligations of humanity; but the literature which encourages these impossible fancies may not be very good literature.

It will be objected that these are social and moral considerations: so they are, but none the less appropriate to literature, a social and moral art. But to take the esthetic view, and to return to Steinbeck, it may be asked whether detachment is good for a writer's writing— or whether "detached" writing makes the best reading. To stand aside and contemplate these creatures with pity or with admiration—it is not so interesting as to get inside them and participate in their living. For one thing, the detachment is relatively monotonous, and leads to monotony—as well as to languor and softness, however seductive—of style. No first-rate novelist or playwright, I venture to say, has gone in for detachment or imposed it upon his readers, but quite the reverse: the best impose the most complete participation.

Steinbeck's finest work affords a case in point. *In Dubious Battle* tells of a fruitpickers' strike led by Communists.

To be sure, one may surmise that the author speaks through the mouth of the doctor who sees little difference between men and microbes, who doesn't "want to put on the blinders of 'good' and 'bad,' and limit" his vision, yet who wishes to give help to men who need it simply because they need it. But, however that may be, *In Dubious Battle* achieves an effect that none of Steinbeck's other books does: the reader does not stand by and look on; he lives through the strike, he shares it and takes part in it. To be sure, there are stiff and awkward passages of philosophizing, and the hero does not come out at all clearly, but these are minor blemishes. The strike and the strikers are directly and immediately conveyed, with none of the magic or the safety of distance.

In Dubious Battle is by all odds Steinbeck's best book because it is far and away the best written. Perhaps for once his material ran away with him; at any rate his style disappears into the material and they become indistinguishable. Here is none of that mellifluous and silky flow, of that saying that things were fierce and harsh and savage in the sweetest and most musical of words. The writing, sharp, energetic and unnoticeable, follows and fits the stuff, and is worthy of it: more could hardly be said. For the story is the tragedy of not one but of many individuals—it is a national tragedy told through individuals. The theme is great, the execution excellent. And incidentally it has more excitement than anything else of Steinbeck's. Yet the American public would have none of it. The public probably does not want to get too close to any reality that amounts to anything. It prefers rococo Mexicans and saccharine half-wits carefully kept in the middle distance.

It must be said, however, that *In Dubious Battle* now shares its excellence, though nothing else, with the series of four stories which conclude *The Long Valley*. These stories concern a little boy and his ponies, his parents, his grandfather and the hired man. They are so well told it is hard to see how they could be better. Delicate and sure, they attain perfection in their kind. And here is no detachment, no distance. The writing is reserved and economical, but it leads straight into the characters and the relations among them. In this respect "The Red Pony" shows a gain over *In Dubious Battle*, in which necessarily the emphasis was upon external action. That *The Long Valley* should close so well is auspicious.

Ralph Thompson.
"Outstanding Novels."
Yale Review, 28
(Winter 1939), x.

... Mr. Steinbeck, as hardly needs saying, is as native as sagebrush, and when he is good he is as good as he is native. Certain pieces in *The Long Valley* don't come off, but others, notably those dealing with the small boy named Jody Tiflin, who lives on a California ranch, are superb. ...

"The Long Valley."
Times Literary
Supplement [London],
4 February 1939, p. 75.

With every book Mr. Steinbeck moves forward in the ranks of America's outstanding younger writers. This collection of fifteen short stories is one of the most

146

brilliant, as it is one of the most distressing, published in a long while. Its author is pitiless. Seeing life as made up far more of despair and frustration than of beauty or even courage, he spares his readers nothing, refusing to blink an eyelid at whatever climax of horror, or to soften in the least degree that fine clarity of vision which gives the slightest of his pieces their distinction and their fascination.

Some of the situations are relatively commonplace. Wives and husbands hate each other with sour distaste, inescapable even after death. Mr. Steinbeck treats this comically in "The Harness," and a rather similar case poetically in "The White Quail." But comical or poetic, bitterness is predominant. A murderer runs from his pursuers through the bleak mountains, hampered by his slowly poisoning arm—how often has it been done before, and how freshly here it is done again, and with what chilling starkness! Nor is the laughter exactly gay when a man murders his wife's lover, and the two of them thrive on it.

Other tales have an air almost pathological. One describes scarcely more than a woman avidly gloating over the killing and swallowing of a rat by a snake. In another a man who has taken part in a lynching realizes that he feels exactly as though he had "been with a woman." Cleverest of all, repellent yet unforgettable, is "Johnny Bear," the story of a deformed half-wit, who automatically mimics voices and repeats conversations secretly overheard.

Only in the shortest sketch of all does beauty manifest itself unshadowed. It appears again, more sustained and more effectively, in the three tales making up "The Red Pony," but mixed here with harsh brutality. No, Mr. Steinbeck is not a happy writer. But he is an extraordinary artist, and not to be shirked on any excuse.

Thomas Moult. "Short Stories." Manchester *Guardian*, 14 February 1939, p. 7.

... The woman in Mr. Steinbeck's opening story, "The Chrysanthemums," is neurotic about life—through loneliness. The woman In "The White Quail," the story that comes next, is also neurotic about life—through an obsession about her garden. Later on there is a story entitled "The Snake" in which the woman is neurotic in a more horribly perverted way—she purchases a snake so that she can watch the reptile devouring his meal, a live rat. The imaginative treatment of these and other variations of his theme and the craftsmanship by which it is exploited make each story not only tolerable but readable in a way that leaves an effect almost unique among present-day short-story writers. If we are reminded of D. H. Lawrence it is to mark a contrast; here is a successor—in a sense—to Lawrence without his forerunner's lack of balance and sentimentality. Lawrence was subjective; he re-created himself. Mr. Steinbeck is objective, clinical. He has the detachment of the scientist. Our confidence in him is the confidence we feel in a scientist. Again we are taken away from the cities to the parched, wide-open spaces, where every shack and farmstead gives up to him its secret history, unique and ruthless, and its cruelty, suffering, and tragedy. Here and there among the sixteen stories that compose the volume we come upon a few pages of relief, sardonically humorous relief, as in a crazy description of how legend was created— "Saint Katy the Virgin." But immediately afterwards we are overwhelmed by the raw actualism of "The Red Pony," the longest piece in the book, which, outdoing Lawrence in some respects, is rank with the atmosphere of buzzards hovering over carrion on a ranch, of pig-killings, and a pony's death. But much of the story is Steinbeck, not Lawrence, especially the rancher's boy Jody, a charming youngster, and the tender-hearted Billy, the farmhand, not to mention Nellie, the ill-starred mare, who remains a beautiful thing until the very end of this powerful epic of birth and life at the cost of death.

J.S.
"American Tales."
London *Times*,
17 February 1939, p. 9.

The most original and thoughtful story in Mr. John Steinbeck's collection is "Johnny Bear." As in several of the other stories in *The Long Valley*, the scene is a Californian township, where farmers and roadmakers and others who have business in the country gather at night in the one saloon and amuse themselves by plying the local halfwit with whisky in return for mimicked excerpts from what he has overheard during the day. In this way the story comes out of the disgrace to the big house in the valley, where ladies live who behave, to the great encouragement of their neighbors, "as though honesty really is the best policy." "The White Quail" is a bitting note on selfishness, "Flight" a remarkable account of a young Mexican fleeing from a blood feud into the mountains, and "Saint Katy the Virgin" a lively piece of nonsense on a theme of Anatole France. Few of the stories are

sentimental and few exaggerated, and it is altogether a notable collection.

John Mair.
"New Novels."
New Statesman and Nation [England], 17 (18 February 1939), 250.

... *The Long Valley* is a collection of short stories, most of which have already been published, though some only in limited editions. The themes are very simple: the death of a fugitive in the hills; a man walking home after taking part in a lynching; a small boy's love for his pony (the best of all, this); but the stories are far more than those "authentic glimpses" of experience that offer a facsimile rather than attempt understanding. Without affectation of style or any of the numerous narrative tricks that mark such a book as *Hope of Heaven*, Mr. Steinbeck possesses that directness of feeling and expression that is coming to be regarded as distinctively American, yet he never falls into the complementary error of making his characters—even the oddest—stock figures from a feature reporter's notebook. Mr. Steinbeck is not a great writer—he has too little passion for that, and his mind seems too observant to be really creative—but in his own way he is as perfect a craftsman as Hemingway and his disciples. But whereas Mr. O'Hara has mastered merely a peculiar idiom, Mr. Steinbeck has learnt the trick of the short story and given each of his tales the polish and poise of a sonnet.

"*The Long Valley*." London *Mercury*, 39 (March 1939), 564.

These short stories by the author of *Of Mice and Men* centre round a valley in California, and the humble people, mostly agriculturists, who live there. They are dexterously told, and though seemingly slight, handle confidently the more uncomfortable aspects of human relationships. In spite of Mr. Steinbeck's tender, almost whimsical, attitude towards his characters, there is a vein of stark brutality in nearly all these tales.

Checklist of Additional Reviews

Sterling North. "A Modern Writer Who Dares to Be Sensitive." Chicago *News*, 21 September 1938, p. 23.

Laurence Hartmus. "A Western Bookshelf." *Frontier and Midland*, 19 (Winter 1938), 140–1.

Herbert J. Muller. "Farrell and Steinbeck." *Kenyon Review*, 1 (Winter 1939), 99–101.

"Spring Books." *Times Literary Supplement* [London], 25 March 1939, p. xiv.

THE GRAPES OF WRATH

The
Grapes of
Wrath

JOHN STEINBECK

THE VIKING PRESS · NEW YORK

Charles Poore.
"Books of the Times."
New York *Times*,
14 April 1939, p. 27.

Their covered wagons are antique jalopies and the gold of their Eldorado hangs on trees in California orchards. If they lived a hundred years ago—these salty, brave and enormously human wanderers of John Steinbeck's magnificent new novel, *The Grapes of Wrath*—we should call them heroic pioneers. We should admire their courageous will to survive in spite of nature's elements and man's inhumanity. We should relish their Rabelaisian candor, their shrewdness and their humor. We should undoubtedly say their spirit made this country great.

Well, we can admire those great-hearted qualities all the more, knowing that they belong to contemporary Americans, and that novelists need not go to the past to find them.

For within recent years thousands upon thousands of people like the Joads in *The Grapes of Wrath* have been rolling westward, carrying all they own in perilous cars of strange vintages, hungry, restless, the children riding on top of the tents and the blankets and the cooking pots, their desperate elders hanging on wherever they can. . . .

Out of the dramatic elementals of this great American migration (there is, by the way, an excellently illustrated article about it in this month's *Fortune*) Mr. Steinbeck has created his best novel. It is far better than *Of Mice and Men*, where the overmeticulously orchestrated theme of loneliness gave certain artificiality to the story's course. Here, his counterpoint of the general and the particular—the full

sweep of the migration and the personal affairs of all the Joads—has the true air of inevitability.

Mr. Steinbeck did not have to create a world for the Joads. It is there. What he did have to do is to make you see it and feel it and understand it. And he does this in the one way a novelist can give life and truth to his story: through the creation of character. It is in Tom Joad (who learns at last what Harry Morgan learned in *To Have and Have Not*, that standing alone will do nothing much to move impressively united opponents) that the story makes Mr. Steinbeck's eloquently presented point.

But our belief depends, in great measure, upon our belief in them all—from the rare and garrulous grandfather who dies on the way, or Rose of Sharon, whose child is born much later, after her whippersnapper of a husband has deserted, or sin-haunted Uncle John, or the mother, who is the best man of the lot, or the father, who is slowly losing his grip, or Casy Strange, the ex-preacher who joins their caravan for a time, or Al, the born mechanic, or Noah, who makes his separate peace—to Ruthie and Winfield, the two most completely credible children we've seen in any recent novel.

For, as MacLeish once said in a totally different connection, out of the vigor of emotions may well come a new art: "But to mistake the art for the emotions is to perform no service to criticism. Only the art matters. The emotion lights the stove." And Mr. Steinbeck's triumph is that he has created, out of a remarkable sympathy and understanding, characters whose full and complete actuality will withstand any scrutiny.

When his characters hold the stage the story has a superb drive and force. It is only in his commentary on the migration, the chapters interleaving the story of the Joads, that he is apt to be a little too

153

hortatory. Here, in a grave, stately prose that seems to be half Jacobean and half Hemingway, he occasionally obscures the story with the moral—which is better borne out in the lives of his characters.

One believes in them absolutely because one sees every side of their natures. And their natures are shown in every possible kind of test and confrontation, in words that can offend only the squeamish and in scenes you will never forget.

The most memorable scene is the last one. . . .

Everything in the book leads up to it. From the time when Tom Joad (who'd been in jail for killing a man who had planned to kill him) came home to the Oklahoma farm, where his family was getting ready to go in search of the land of oranges and grapes and promise, to the book's ending the march of events is as relentless as it is absorbing to read. The scenes along Route 66, the wanderer's trail, in Hoovervilles, in the government camp—where the Joads found the humanity and courtesy almost unbelievable, after what they'd been through—are wonderfully realized. You can't help believing in these people, in their courage and in their integrity.

Clifton Fadiman.
"Books."
New Yorker, 15
(15 April 1939), 81–3.

If only a couple of million overcomfortable people can be brought to read it, John Steinbeck's *The Grapes of Wrath* may actually effect something like a revolution in their minds and hearts. It sounds like a crazy notion, I know, but I feel this book may just possibly do for

our time what *Les Misérables* did for its, *Uncle Tom's Cabin* for its, *The Jungle* for its. *The Grapes of Wrath* is the kind of art that's poured out of a crucible in which are mingled pity and indignation. It seems advisable to stress this point. A lot of readers and critics are going to abandon themselves to orgies of ohing and ahing over Steinbeck's impressive literary qualities, happy to blink at the simple fact that fundamentally his book is a social novel exposing social injustice and calling, though never explicitly, for social redress. It's going to be a great and deserved best-seller; it'll be read and praised by everyone; it will almost certainly win the Pulitzer Prize; it will be filmed and dramatized and radio-acted—but, gentle reader, amid all the excitement let's try to keep in mind what *The Grapes of Wrath* is about: to wit, the slow murder of half a million innocent and worthy American citizens.

I don't know and in truth I don't much care whether it's the "work of genius" the publishers sincerely believe it to be. What sticks with me is that here is a book, non-political, non-dogmatic, which dramatizes so that you can't forget it the terrible facts of a wholesale injustice committed by society. Here is a book about a people of old American stock, not Reds or rebels of any kind. They are dispossessed of their land, their pitiful, little homes are destroyed, they are lured to California by false hopes. When they get there, after incredible hardships, they are exploited, reduced to peonage, then to virtual slavery. If they protest, they are beaten, tortured, or their skulls are smashed in. Even if they do not protest, they are hounded, intimidated, and finally starved into defeat. The industrial and political groups that do these things know quite well what they do. Hence they cannot be forgiven.

Along Highway 66, ribboning from

154

the Mississippi to Bakersfield, California, these disinherited, in their rickety jalopies, have been for the last five years streaming into the Far West. Driven off their farms by the drought, dust, or the juggernaut of the tractor, the small farmers and sharecroppers of half a dozen states, but mainly Oklahoma and Arkansas, have been staking their salvation on the possibility of work in California.

Steinbeck creates a family—the Joads of Oklahoma—and makes them typify a whole culture on the move. At the same time he gives us this migrant culture itself, in all its pathetic hopefulness, its self-reliance, the growing sense of unity it imparts to its people.

If ever The Great American Novel is written, it may very possibly be composed along the lines here laid out by Steinbeck. No one since the advent of Sinclair Lewis has had so exact a feeling for what is uniquely American. This feeling Steinbeck shows not only in his portrayal of the Joads themselves, in his careful notation of their folk speech, folk myths, folk obscenities, but in a thousand minor touches that add up to something major: the description of the used-car market, of the minds of truck-drivers and hash-house waitresses, of Highway 66, of the butchering and salting down of the pigs. It is this large interest in the whole lives of his Oklahoma farmers that makes *The Grapes of Wrath* more than a novel of propaganda, even though its social message is what will stick with any sensitive reader.

The book has faults. It is too detailed, particularly in the latter half, Casy, the ex-preacher, is half real, half "poetic" in the worse sense of the word. Occasionally the folk note is forced a little. And, finally, the ending (a young girl who has only a day or two before given birth to a dead child offers the milk of her breasts to a starving man) is the tawdriest kind of fake symbolism. Just occasionally Steinbeck's dramatic imagination overleaps itself and you get a piece of pure, or impure, theatre like these last pages. One should also add that his political thinking is a little mystical. The sense of unity that his migrants gradually acquire is not necessarily, as he implies, of a progressive character. It is based on an emotion that can just as easily be discharged into the channels of reaction. In other words, are not these simple, tormented Okies good Fascist meat, if the proper misleaders are found for them?

It is unlikely, however, that such misgivings will occur to you in the reading of the book. Its power and importance do not lie in its political insight but in its intense humanity, its grasp of the spirit of an entire people traversing a wilderness, its kindliness, its humor, and its bitter indignation. *The Grapes of Wrath* is the American novel of the season, probably the year, possibly the decade. . . .

Louis Kronenberger.
"Hungry Caravan."
Nation, 148
(15 April 1939), 440–1.

This is in many ways the most moving and disturbing social novel of our time. What is wrong with it, what is weak in it, what robs it of the stature it clearly attempts, are matters that must presently be pointed out; but not at once. First it should be pointed out that *The Grapes of Wrath* comes at a needed time in a powerful way. It comes, perhaps, as *The Drapier's Letters* or *Uncle Tom's Cabin* or some of the social novels of Zola came. It burns with no pure gemlike flame, but with hot and immediate fire. It is, from any point of view, Steinbeck's best novel, but it does not make one wonder whether, on the basis of it, Steinbeck is now a better novelist than Hemingway or Farrell or Dos Passos; it does not invoke comparisons; it simply makes one feel that Steinbeck is, in some way all his own, a force.

The publishers refer to the book as "perhaps the greatest single creative work that this country has produced." This is a foolish and extravagant statement, but unlike most publishers' statements, it seems the result of honest enthusiasm, and one may hope that the common reader will respond to the book with an enthusiasm of the same sort. And perhaps he will, for *The Grapes of Wrath* has, overwhelmingly, those two qualities most vital to a work of social protest: great indignation and great compassion. Its theme is large and tragic and, on the whole, is largely and tragically felt. No novel of our day has been written out of a more genuine humanity, and none, I think, is better calculated to awaken the humanity of others. . . .

In the fate of one such family—the Joads of Oklahoma—John Steinbeck has told the fate of all. Their fate is the theme of an angry and aroused propagandist, but the Joads themselves are the product of a lively novelist. A racy, picturesque, somewhat eccentric tribe, with certain resemblances to Erskine Caldwell's Georgia exhibits, the Joads—mean, merry, shameless Grandpa; brooding, conscience-stricken Uncle John; strong, tough, understanding Ma; Al, a squirt thinking only of women and cars; Tom, who has been in prison for killing a man in a brawl—the Joads, with their salty, slanting speech, their frank and boisterous opinions, their unrepressed, irrepressible appetites, would, in a stable world, be the stuff of rich folk-comedy. But suddenly uprooted and harassed, they are

creatures forced to fight for their very existence. During the first half of Steinbeck's long book the Joads, both as people and as symbols, have tremendous vitality. Steinbeck's account of this one family leaving home and journeying forth in a rickety makeshift truck is like some night-lighted, rude Homeric chronicle of a great migration. It has a vigor, as of half-childlike, half-heroic adventuring, that almost blots out the sense of its desperate origins and painful forebodings.

But after the Joads reach California, something—a kind of inner life—disappears from the book. The economic outrage, the human tragedy are made brutally clear. The chronicle of the Joads remains vivid; the nature of their fate becomes ever more infuriating. As a tract, the book goes on piling up its indictment, conducting the reader on a sort of grand tour of exploitation and destitution. And all this has, emotionally at least, a very strong effect. But somehow the book ceases to grow, to maintain direction. It is truly enough a story of nomads; but from that it does not follow that the proletarian novel must fall into the loose pattern of the picaresque novel. Artistically speaking, the second half of *The Grapes of Wrath*, though it still has content and suspense, lacks form and intensity. The people simply go on and on, with Steinbeck left improvising and amplifying until—with a touch of new and final horror—he abruptly halts.

The Grapes of Wrath is a superb tract because it exposes something terrible and true with enormous vigor. It is a superb tract, moreover, by virtue of being thoroughly animated fiction, by virtue of living scenes and living characters (like Ma), not by virtue of discursive homilies and dead characters (like the socialistic preacher). One comes away moved, indignant, protesting, pitying. But one comes away dissatisfied, too, aware that

The Grapes of Wrath is too unevenly weighted, too uneconomically proportioned, the work of a writer who is still self-indulgent, still undisciplined, still not altogether aware of the difference in value of various human emotions. The picturesqueness of the Joads, for example, is fine wherever it makes them live more abundantly, but false when simply laid on for effect. Steinbeck's sentimentalism is good in bringing him close to the lives of his people, but had when it blurs his insight. Again, the chapters in which Steinbeck halts the story to editorialize about American life are sometimes useful, but oftener pretentious and flatulent.

But one does not take leave of a book like this in a captious spirit. One salutes it as a fiery document of protest and compassion, as a story that had to be told, as a book that must be read. It is, I think, one of those books—there are not very many—which really do some good.

George Stevens. "Steinbeck's Uncovered Wagon." *Saturday Review*, 19 (15 April 1939), 3–4.

It is exciting to watch the steady unfolding of a real writer's talent, to follow his development from promise to achievement, with the sense that he knows what he wants and knows what he is doing. It is particularly exciting because it is rare. Van Wyck Brooks pointed out long ago that the blighted career, the unfulfilled promise, is the rule in American writing, and his statement turned out to be as accurate in prophecy as in diagnosis. Writers who produced one or two good books; writers who abandoned literature to go to Hollywood, or to go to Spain, or to write plays, or to attend meetings, or simply to retire on their earnings; writers who exhausted their resources and kept doing the same book over and over—one after another they have left their overexcitable discoverers holding the bag: a bag full of words like "genius" and "masterpiece," to be taken three times a day, with meals.

Among the novelists of his generation, the most notable exception to this state of things is John Steinbeck. He has never yet flashed in the pan. ... Steinbeck tore up the manuscripts of his first two novels, and retired the third. Since his first published book, *The Cup of Gold*, each successive one has revealed a new facet of his ability. *Tortilla Flat* was the humorous and sympathetic story of some attractive and disreputable Mexicans. *In Dubious Battle* was a serious labor novel, remarkable of its kind in presenting the issues in terms of animate characters, who had the vitality to take the story over for themselves. *Of Mice and Men* was a miniature tragedy which lost none of its effectiveness for being written with an eye on the stage, which was just as poignant whether you took it straight or symbolically. Different as these novels are (and Steinbeck's variety is further manifested in the stories in *The Long Valley*), there has been a constancy of flavor which is impossible to define: something deeper than the "personality" of the author, which never intrudes; something more impalpable than "ideas"; something in the style, but in a style of which one is almost never conscious.

For these reasons Steinbeck's reputation is unique. All our reviewers, and such critics as we have among us, are pretty consciously in the "watch Steinbeck" movement. If it is turning into a bandwagon, that is not Steinbeck's fault.

He has already survived some fairly indiscriminate adulation. His activities, outside of writing novels, have managed to remain his own affairs, to a remarkable degree in the great American goldfish bowl; and nothing has interfered with his serious production. The lively curiosity which Steinbeck has inspired is a legitimate curiosity about his work. Because of his variety, nobody can put him in a pigeon-hole; nobody has been able to say, "Steinbeck has done it again," but rather, "What is Steinbeck going to do next?" Since it became known that Steinbeck had a new novel for spring publication, and that it was by far his longest and most ambitious production to date, it is safe to say (for whatever it may mean) that no other book on the current lists has been so eagerly looked forward to by the reviewers.

The Grapes of Wrath is worth it, worth all the talk, all the anticipation, all the enthusiasm. Here is the epitome of everything Steinbeck has so far given us. It has the humor and earthiness of *Tortilla Flat*, the social consciousness of *In Dubious Battle*, the passionate concern for the homeless and uprooted which made *Of Mice and Men* memorable. These elements, together with a narrative that moves with excitement for its own sake, are not mixed but fused, to produce the unique quality of *The Grapes of Wrath*. That quality is an understanding of courage—courage seen with humor and bitterness and without a trace of sentimentality; courage that exists as the last affirmation of human dignity. To convey that understanding with passionate conviction, in human terms and also in terms of mature intelligence, so that we respond integrally and without reservation, is a very considerable thing for a novel to do. That is what *The Grapes of Wrath* does. It is by no means perfect, but possibly its faults (one of which is egregious)

are a measure of its worth, in that it triumphantly lives them down.

The Grapes of Wrath is the story of the new American nomads, of the migrant farmers who have lost their few acres in the Oklahoma dust bowl to the onward march of tractors and foreclosures. It is in particular the story of one family, the Joads from a farm near Sallisaw. You have seen them going west through Texas and New Mexico on Route 66, or you have seen them in Resettlement Administration photographs: three generations in a second-hand truck, piled high with everything they own. Car after car, from Arkansas to California; people with no home but the road, no prospects but hope, no resources but courage: the thirty-niners in their uncovered wagons.

With this material Steinbeck has done what, according to at least one theory, cannot be done: he has made a living novel out of the news in the paper, out of contemporary social conditions. In "Land of the Free," Archibald MacLeish wrote a sound track to the Resettlement Administration's documentary stills. He looked at the pictures of the plowed-under farmers and wrote a poet's abstract statement, pared down to gaunt monosyllables, of a seemingly insoluble problem. Steinbeck has looked at the Oklahoma farmers themselves—the "Okies" in Salinas County, California, driven from camp to camp, finding no work, not allowed to settle. What he has written about them is a narrative: colorful, dramatic, subtle, coarse, comic, and tragic. For *The Grapes of Wrath* is not a social novel like most social novels. It is instead what a social novel ought to be. When you read it, you are in contact not with arguments, but with people. . . .

Others will see in it a different and more immediately sociological value. Unquestionably *The Grapes of Wrath* states

158

the problem of the southwestern tenant farmer in a form that will bring it home to the imaginations of thousands who have hitherto looked on it with comparative unconcern. Unquestionably, also, Steinbeck sees his material both as a narrative and as a condition calling for action. At regular intervals in the book he inserts general chapters stating the problem in terms of pure non-fiction. For my own part, I found these chapters at best superfluous, occasionally sententious, and in one instance downright bad (this is a very windy passage indeed, in which the author coins the word "Manself," which I hope no one will ever use again). It is not these chapters, but the story of the Joads, that makes you want to do something about the migratory tenant farmers.

There remain one warning and one major criticism. It is only fair to say that there are conservative readers whom the language used by the Joad family will offend. In my opinion, all the dialogue is necessary and right; Steinbeck's ear is perfect, and he lets the Joads talk with uninhibited coarseness. I think this is vital in a serious book like *The Grapes of Wrath*, and that it would be obscene to write the dialogue otherwise; but I realize that some readers will feel differently.

As for the criticism—a point on which another group of readers will disagree—I think that the last scene of the novel is bathos. It describes a physically possible but highly unusual event which even if palatable would be unconvincing; and even if Steinbeck had made it convincing, he would have added nothing to the story. The fact is that the story has no ending. We are left without knowing what happens to the characters. That is a necessary condition of writing about the immediate situation of the tenant farmers' odyssey, and we could put up with the absence of a satisfactory ending. But

the final episode in the book seems to me a trick to jar the reader out of the realization that the story really does not end. It takes away a little of the effectiveness, and there will be many readers to wish Steinbeck hadn't done it.

But *The Grapes of Wrath* is good enough to live down more than this. Mrs. Roosevelt spoke recently of the need for a novelist who can interpret what is going on in this country among the kind of people of whom book readers in general know little—people like the Joads. John Steinbeck is the novelist. He knows what the country is doing to the Joads, and what goes on in their minds and emotions.

Peter Monro Jack. "John Steinbeck's New Novel Brims with Anger and Pity." *New York Times Book Review*, 88 (16 April 1939), 2.

There are a few novelists writing as well as Steinbeck and perhaps a very few who write better; but it is most interesting to note how very much alike they are all writing. Hemingway, Caldwell, Faulkner, Dos Passos in the novel, and MacLeish in poetry are those whom we easily think of in their similarity of theme and style. Each is writing stories and scenarios of America with a curious and sudden intensity, almost as if they had never seen or understood it before. They are looking at it again with revolutionary eyes. Stirred like every other man in the street with news of foreign persecution, they turn to their own land to find seeds of the same destructive hatred. Their themes of pity and anger, their styles of sentimental elegy and scarifying denunciation may come to seem representative of our time. MacLeish's *Land of the Free*, for instance, going directly to the matter with poetry and pictures—the matter being that the land is no longer free, having been mortgaged, bought and finally bankrupted by a succession of anonymous companies, banks, politicians and courts, or, for the present instance, Steinbeck's *The Grapes of Wrath*, as pitiful and angry a novel ever to be written about America.

It is a very long novel, the longest that Steinbeck has written, and yet it reads as if it had been composed in a flash, ripped off the typewriter and delivered to the public as an ultimatum. It is a long and thoughtful novel as one thinks about it. It is a short and vivid scene as one feels it.

The opening scene is in Oklahoma, where a change in the land is taking place that no one understands, neither the single families who have pioneered it nor the great owners who have bought it over with their banks and lawyers. As plainly as it can be put, Mr. Steinbeck puts it. A man wants to build a wall, a house, a dam, and inside that a certain security to raise a family that will continue his work. But there is no security for a single family. The cotton crops have sucked out the roots of the land and the dust has overlaid it. The men from the Bank or the Company, sitting in their closed cars, try to explain to the squatting farmers what they scarcely understand themselves: that the tenants whose grandfathers settled the land have no longer the title to it, that a tractor does more work than a single family of men, women and children put together, that their land is to be mechanically plowed under, with special instructions that their hand-built houses are to be razed to the ground.

This may read like a disquisition by Stuart Chase. There is, in fact, a series of essays on the subject running through the book, angry and abstract—like the characters, "perplexed and figuring." The essayist in Steinbeck alternates with the novelist, as it does with Caldwell and the others. The moralist is as important as the story-teller, may possibly outlast him; but the story at the moment is the important thing.

The most interesting figure of this Oklahoma family is the son who has just been released from jail. He is on his way home from prison, hitch-hiking across the state in his new cheap prison suit, picking up a preacher who had baptized him when young, and arriving to find the family setting out for California. The Bank had come "to tractorin' off the place." The house had been knocked over by the tractor making straight furrows for the cotton. The Joad family had read handbills promising work for thousands in California, orange picking. They had bought an old car, were on the point of leaving, when Tom turned up from prison with the preacher. They can scarcely wait for this promised land of fabulous oranges, grapes and peaches. Only one stubborn fellow remains on the land where his great-grandfather had shot Indians and built his house. The others, with Tom and the preacher, pack their belongings on the second-hand truck, set out for the new land, to start over again in California. . . . Californians are not going to like this angry novel. . . .

The beauty and fertility of California conceal human fear, hatred and violence. "Scairt" is a Western farmer's word for the inhabitants, frightened of the influx of workers eager for jobs, and when they are frightened they become vicious and cruel. This part of the story reads like the news from Nazi Germany. Families from Oklahoma are known as "Okies." While they work they live in what might as well be called concentration camps. Only a few hundred are given jobs out of the thousands who traveled West in response to the handbills. Their pay is cut from 30 cents an hour to 25, to 20. If any one objects he is a Red, an agitator, a trouble-maker who had better get out of the country. Deputy sheriffs are around with guns, legally shooting or clubbing any one from the rest of the Union who questions the law of California. The Joad family find only one place of order and decency in this country of fear and violence, in a government camp, and it is a pleasure to follow the family as they take a shower bath and go to the Saturday night dances. But even here the deputy sheriffs, hired by the banks who run the Farmers Association, are poking in their guns, on the pretext of inciting to riot and the necessity of protective custody. The Joad family moves on through California, hunted by anonymous guns while they are picking peaches for 2 1/2 cents a box, hoping only for a little land free of guns and dust on which they might settle and work as they were accustomed to. The promised grapes of California have turned into grapes of wrath that might come to fruition at any moment.

How true this may be no reviewer can say. One may very easily point out that a similar message has been read by the writers mentioned above, and that Mr. Steinbeck has done the same thing before. It is easy to add that the novel comes to no conclusion, that the preacher is killed because he is a strike-breaker, that Tom disappears as a fugitive from California justice, that the novel ends on a minor and sentimental note; that the story stops after 600 pages merely because a story has to stop somewhere. All this is true enough but the real truth is

that Steinbeck has written a novel from the depths of his heart with a sincerity seldom equaled. It may be an exaggeration, but it is the exaggeration of an honest and splendid writer.

Joseph Henry Jackson. "The Finest Book John Steinbeck Has Written." New York *Herald Tribune*, 16 April 1939, "Books" section, p. 3.

"You never been called 'Okie' yet? 'Okie' use' ta mean you was from Oklahoma. Now it means you're scum. Don't mean nothin' itself; it's the way they say it. But I can't tell you nothin'. You got to go there. I hear there's three hundred thousan' of our people there—an' livin' like hogs, 'cause ever'thing in California is owned. They ain't nothin' left. And them people that owns it is gonna hang on to it if they got ta kill ever'body in the worl' to do it. An' they're scairt, an' that makes 'em mad. You got to see it. You got to hear it. Purtiest god-damn country you ever seen, but they ain't nice to you, them folks. They're so scairt an' worried they ain't even nice to each other." . . .

Multiply the Joads by thousands and you have a picture of the great modern migration that is the subject of this new Steinbeck novel which is far and away the finest book he has yet written. Examine the motives and the forces behind what happened to the Joads and you have a picture of the fantastic social and economic situation facing America today. Cure? Steinbeck suggests none. He puts forward no doctrine, no dogma. But he writes. "In the souls of the people the

161

grapes of wrath are filling and growing heavy, growing heavy for the vintage." I have no doubt that Steinbeck would not enjoy being called a prophet. But this novel is something very like prophecy.

The Joads were only one family to learn that a bank was not a man. It was made up of men but it was a bigger thing and it controlled them, even though sometimes they hated to do what the bank-monster said they must. That monster moved out the Joads and other thousands. Little farms, even tenant-farming wouldn't work any more on the worn-out land. Only huge land companies and tractors could make it pay. It happened all at once, and they had to go somewhere; thousands and tens of thousands were in the same boat.

Angry and puzzled, the heads of families tried to figure. When the little handbills appeared in the lost country, they thought they saw a way out. If they sold everything, they might buy an ancient car and move to California where the handbills said there was a chance for pickers. The second-hand car dealers cheated them right and left, but they bought the rattletraps; they had to. And they took to the road, headed westward over Highway 66. . . .

What happened to the Joads is the immediate story of this novel. What happened and is happening to the thousands like them is the story behind the story; the reason Steinbeck wrote *The Grapes of Wrath*. What may happen—must happen, he believes—in the long run is the implication behind the book. "Whereas the wants of the Californians were nebulous and undefined, the wants of the Okies were beside the roads, lying there to be seen and coveted; the good fields with water to be dug for, earth to crumble in the hand, grass to smell. . . . And a homeless, hungry man, driving the roads with his wife behind him and his thin children in the back seat, could look at the fallow fields which might produce food but not profit, and that man could know how a fallow field is a sin and the unused land a crime against the thin children." There is the hint. And here again: "And the great owners, with eyes to read history, and to know the great fact: when property accumulates in too few hands it is taken away. And that companion fact: when a majority of people are hungry and cold they will take by force what they need. And the little screaming fact that sounds through history: repression works only to strengthen and knit the repressed." Prophecy perhaps. Certainly a warning.

For the story itself, it is completely authentic. Steinbeck knows. He went back to Oklahoma and then came West with the migrants, lived in their camps, saw their pitiful brave highway communities, the life of the itinerant beside the road. He learned what was behind the handbills. And he came back with an enormous respect for the tenacity of these dispossessed, and with the knowledge that this migration is no less a forerunner of a new way than was that migration of those earlier Americans who took California from another group of landholders who had grown too soft to hold it.

It is a rough book, yes. It is an ineffably tender book too. It is the book for which everything else that Steinbeck has written was an exercise in preparation. You'll find in it reminders of *Pastures of Heaven*, of *In Dubious Battle*, of *The Red Pony*, even of *Tortilla Flat*. But here there is no mere exploration of a field, no tentative experimenting with a theme. This is the full symphony, Steinbeck's declaration of faith. The terrible meek will inherit, he says. They will. They are on their way to their inheritance now, and not far from it. And though they are the common people, sometimes dirty people, starved and suppressed and disappointed people, yet they are good people. Steinbeck believes that too.

It is easy to grow lyrical about *The Grapes of Wrath*, to become excited about it, to be stirred to the shouting-point by it. Perhaps it is too easy to lose balance in the face of such an extraordinarily moving performance. But it is also true that the effect of the book lasts. The author's employment, for example, of occasional chapters in which the undercurrent of the book is announced, spoken as a running accompaniment to the story, with something of the effect of the sound track in Pare Lorentz's *The River*—that lasts also, stays with you, beats rhythmically in your mind long after you have put the book down. No, the reader's instant response is more than quick enthusiasm, more than surface emotionalism. This novel of America's new disinherited is a magnificent book. It is, I think for the first time, the whole Steinbeck, the mature novelist saying something he must say and doing it with the sure touch of the great artist.

"Okies."
Time, 33 (17 April 1939), 87.

On California's highways during the last few years a tourist sometimes encounters a mysterious and appalling sight—thousands of jalopies, driven by hungry-faced men, bulging with ragged children, dirty bedding, blackened pots and pans. Hated, terrorized, necessary, they are migrant workers who harvest the orchards and vineyards, the cotton and vegetable fields of the richest valleys on earth. Their homes are filthy squatters' camps on the side roads, beside the rivers and irrigation ditches. Their occupational diseases are rickets, pellagra, dysentery, typhoid, pneumonia, starvation, sullen hatred exploding periodically in bloody strikes. Old American stock, they are mostly refugee sharecroppers from the Dust Bowl of the Southwest and Midwest. They are called the "Okies." There are 250,000 of them—a leading U.S. social problem, and participants in one of the grimmest migrations of history.

The Grapes of Wrath is the Okies' saga. It is John Ernst Steinbeck's longest novel (619 pages) and more ambitious than all his others combined (*Tortilla Flat, In Dubious Battle, Of Mice and Men, et al.*). The publishers believe it is "perhaps the greatest modern American novel, perhaps the greatest single creative work this country has ever produced." It is not. But it is Steinbeck's best novel, *i.e.*, his toughest and tenderest, his roughest written and most mellifluous, his most realistic and, in its ending, his most melodramatic, his angriest and most idyllic. It is "great" in the way that *Uncle Tom's Cabin* was great—because it is inspired propaganda, half tract, half human-interest story, emotionalizing a great theme. . . .

Between chapters Author Steinbeck speaks directly to the reader in panoramic essays on the social significance of the Okies' story. Burning tracts in themselves, they are not a successful fiction experiment. In them a "social awareness" outruns artistic skill. Steinbeck is a writer, still, of great promise. But this novel's big audience of readers will likely find in it one of the most impassioned and exciting books of the year.

Burton Rascoe.
"But . . . Not . . . Ferdinand."
Newsweek, 13 (17 April 1939), 46.

Many years hence, maybe a new bunch of Baconians (who think Shakespeare wasn't Shakespeare) will rise up with learned theses to prove that John Steinbeck was not John Steinbeck, but was, in fact, Charlie McCarthy.

They will have much to go on. If the Bard of Avon can be called "myriad-minded" and accused of being two other fellows on the available evidence, then Steinbeck's chances of being known as Steinbeck are certainly slim; for, even if you wouldn't want to call the man "myriad-minded" (maybe you wouldn't want to call anybody that), you have to admit that not one of his books, except in the superficies of idiosyncratic cadence, remotely resembles any of his other books. He is not a school, as Hemingway is. . . . He is always different.

I know of no top-notch other writer in my time, including Cabell, Dreiser, Anderson, Jeffers, and Robinson, who had as many bad breaks at the start of his career as Steinbeck. For a long period, every time he had a new book coming out, the publishing house folded up ten minutes after the book was off the press. Thus he got no publicity, no advertising, little distribution of his wares. He earned less in royalties than he earned as a hod carrier in the construction of Madison Square Garden.

His first big success was *Tortilla Flat*, which went begging for months among the publishers until Ben Abramson of the Argus Book Shop, Chicago, told Pat Covici of Covici-Friede that Steinbeck was a good investment. Pat was delighted with the manuscript Ben turned over to him, saw *Tortilla Flat* become a best seller, published *In Dubious Battle* (which also got high praise and became a best seller), *Of Mice and Men* (which was a great success both as a novel and as a play), *The Red Pony* (issued in a limited, high-priced edition), and *The Long Valley* (also issued in a limited, high-priced edition). And then Covici-Friede was forced to the wall and Pat, an able editor-publisher, went over to Viking Press, taking Steinbeck with him.

Viking Press has just issued Steinbeck's *Grapes of Wrath*. . . . Reports are that advance orders for the book are more than treble the advance orders on all the other Steinbeck books put together. It is a book of 619 pages, which is to say, about 195,000 words or about twice the length of both *Tortilla Flat* and of *Of Mice and Men*.

It is about tenant farmers in Oklahoma, who got pushed off their land by the wicked landlords and struck out in a jalopy for California, where they thought you didn't have to work but could just live on oranges picked from somebody else's trees. They found out different. The book has beautiful and, even magnificent, passages in it; but it is not well organized; I can't quite see what the book is about, except that there are "no frontiers left and no place to go."

The title is from Julia Ward Howe's "Battle Hymn of the Republic" with its line "He is trampling out the vintage where the grapes of wrath are stored." In chapter 25, he explains what he means by the title, in an impassioned essay about the California vineyards, which, he says, have fallen into the hands of the banks: "The decay spreads over the state, and the sweet smell is a great sorrow in the land. Men who can graft trees and make the seed fertile and big can find no way to let the hungry people eat their produce . . . The works of the roots of the vines, of the trees, must be destroyed to keep up the price, and this is the saddest, bitterest thing of all. Carloads of oranges dumped on the ground . . . etc." (Secretary Wallace, please take note: Steinbeck is predicting a revolution from the vicious circle that has grown up around crop destruction for price maintenance.)

M[arjory] L[loyd]. "Off the Book Shelf." Carmel [Calif.] *Pine Cone*, 21 April 1939, p. 5.

. . . It is a powerful novel, written by a man who for a time lived among these migratory workers of our valleys in order that he might himself fully understand their plight. In an old Ford truck Steinbeck moved from camp to camp and listened to their stories and saw their plight. They are Americans for six and seven generations back, Americans who have lived in pride on their own land and been forced from it by the merciless forces of nature and the equally remorseless forces of the economic system. In telling the story of the Joad family who left their land and journeyed to California, Steinbeck has written a novel powerfully strong, strikingly beautiful and full of human sympathy. The story is intensely gripping and once the family starts on their way it is almost impossible to leave them till the end of the book. At the end their story is unsolved. It is unsolved because there is no solution. They are still

with us in our valleys and on our highways. What is to become of them? . . .

Whether or not we agree with the economic views of Steinbeck we must bow to the power of his writing, its force, sheer beauty and splendid characterization. He is peculiarly our own in California, born of the country, steeped in its beauty and cruelty. He has written a great book about a great people, a people who are now, due to circumstances, Californians. No Californian should disregard this book and its message. It is for us and it is one of the greatest of American books.

In the style of the writing, Steinbeck has made a new departure. Lest we should get a too particularized picture of these migrants through only the association of the Joad family, he has written in each alternate chapter a generalized picture. Also in these chapters he has set forth the views he holds lest the characters themselves fail to give the message.

No doubt Steinbeck will be criticized for so strongly presenting this message but we feel that it is needed. It is no use shutting our eyes to conditions which surround us. There is one thing, however, that this reviewer hopes. We as Californians shall and will do something about these conditions and give to a people proud and worthy a chance to work out their destiny. Surely we are not heartless and surely there is something to be said in defence of the picture of the seemingly heartless landowners of our state. They, too, have their problems.

Philip Rahv.
"A Variety of Fiction."
Partisan Review, 6
(Spring 1939), 111–12.

... From Mr. John Steinbeck—whose inspired pulp-story, *Of Mice and Men*, swept the nation like a plague—one expects nothing. It is therefore gratifying to report that in *The Grapes of Wrath* he appears in a more sympathetic light than in his previous work, not excluding *In Dubious Battle*. This writer, it can now be seen, is really fired with a passionate faith in the common man. He is the hierophant of the innocent and injured; and his new book, though it by no means deserves the ecstatic salutations it has received in the press, is an authentic and formidable example of the novel of social protest.

The book is at the same time a detailed exposure of dreadful economic conditions and a long declaration of love to the masses. It is an epic of misery—a prodigious, relentless, and often excruciating account of agrarian suffering.... Mr. Steinbeck spares us not a single scene, not a single sensation, that could help to implicate us emotionally. And he is so much in earnest that a number of times he interrupts his story in order to grapple directly with his thesis. Thus several chapters are devoted to outright political preaching from the standpoint of a kind of homespun revolutionary populism.

But the novel is far too didactic and long-winded. In addition to the effects that are peculiar to his own manner, Mr. Steinbeck has assembled in this one book all the familiar faults of the "proletarian" literary mode. There are the usual idealized portraits and the customary conversions, psychologically false and schematic as ever, to militant principles. Moreover, the technical cleverness displayed in *Of Mice and Men* is lacking in this novel, which should be credited with valid political observation and sincere feeling, but which fails on the test of craftsmanship. Its unconscionable length is out of all proportion to its substance; the "ornery" dialect spoken by its farmers impresses one as being less a form of human speech than a facile convention of the local-color schools; and as to problems of characterization, Mr. Steinbeck does not so much create character as he apes it. For aping, too, can be turned into a means of "recreating" life. It would appear from this and similar novels that on a sufficiently elementary level, and so long as a uniform scheme of behavior—however simple—is imposed upon characters, all a fiction writer requires to make his people seem real is the patience to follow them everywhere, the perseverance to copy down everything they say and everything they do....

Malcolm Cowley.
"American Tragedy."
New Republic, 98
(3 May 1939), 382–3.

While keeping our eyes on the cataclysms in Europe and Asia, we have lost sight of a tragedy nearer home. A hundred thousand rural households have been uprooted from the soil, robbed of their possessions—though by strictly legal methods—and turned out on the highways. Friendless, homeless and therefore voteless, with fewer rights than medieval serfs, they have wandered in search of a few days' work at miserable wages—not in Spain or the Yangtze Valley, but among the vineyards and orchards of California, in a setting too commonplace for a color story in the Sunday papers.... The novel, which has just appeared, is John Steinbeck's longest and angriest and most impressive work....

The second half of *Grapes of Wrath*, dealing with their adventures in the Valley of California, is ... good but somewhat less impressive [than the first]. Until that moment the Joads have been moving steadily toward their goal. Now they discover that it is not their goal after all; they must still move on, but no longer in one direction—they are harried by vigilantes, recruited as peach pickers, driven out again by a strike; they don't know where to go. Instead of being just people, as they were at home, they hear themselves called Okies—"and that means you're scum," they tell each other bewilderedly. "Don't mean nothing itself, it's the way they say it." The story begins to suffer a little from their bewilderment and lack of direction.

At this point one begins to notice other faults. Interspersed among the chapters that tell what happened to the Joads, there have been other chapters dealing with the general plight of the migrants. The first half-dozen of these interludes have not only broadened the scope of the novel but have been effective in themselves, sorrowful, bitter, intensely moving. But after the Joads reach California, the interludes are spoken in a shriller voice. The author now has a thesis—that the migrants will unite and overthrow their oppressors—and he wants to argue, as if he weren't quite sure of it himself. His thesis is also embodied in one of the characters: Jim Casy, a preacher who loses his faith but unfortunately for the reader can't stop preaching. In the second half of the novel, Casy becomes a Christ-like labor leader and is killed by vigilantes. The book ends with an episode that is a mixture of allegory and melodrama. Rose of Sharon, after her baby is born dead, saves a man from starvation by suckling him at her breast—as if to symbolize the fruitfulness of these people and the bond that unites them in misfortune.

Yet one soon forgets the faults of the story. What one remembers most of all is Steinbeck's sympathy for the migrants—not pity, for that would mean he was putting himself above them; not love, for that would blind him to their faults, but rather a deep fellow feeling. It makes him notice everything that sets them apart from the rest of the world and sets one migrant apart from all the others. In the Joad family, everyone from Grampa— "Full a' piss an' vinegar," as he says of himself—down to the two brats, Ruthie and Winfield, is a distinct and living person. And the story is living too—it has the force of the headlong anger that drives ahead from the first chapter to the last, as if the whole six hundred pages were written without stopping. The author and the reader are swept along together. I can't agree with those critics who say that *The Grapes of Wrath* is the greatest novel of the last ten years; for example, it doesn't rank with the best of Hemingway or Dos Passos. But it belongs very high in the category of the great angry books like *Uncle Tom's Cabin* that have roused a people to fight against intolerable wrongs.

L.A.S.
"Flight from the Dust Bowl."
Christian Science Monitor Weekly Magazine Section, 6 May 1939, p. 13.

John Steinbeck became known to a considerable public with his collection of stories, *Tortilla Flat*. His public was enlarged by the story *Of Mice and Men*, and by the play that was made from it. *The Red Pony* and *The Long Valley* increased his reputation. Now, in *The Grapes of Wrath*, he seems to have achieved the scope and the sweep toward which he has been moving.

This is an epic account of the migration of sharecroppers from the Dust Bowl to the mirage of a free and happy life in California. The canvas is as big as half a continent. The rhythm is that of American life. The characters are living people, presented without apology as they appear to the author. The language no doubt is that of the people portrayed, but its blasphemousness and indecency may obscure the real value of the novel for some readers.

The characters are memorable. Clearly individualized, they are consistent in their behavior, and their interaction appears inevitable to the reader. . . .

The hero of the story, if it has a hero other than the downtrodden one third of a nation, is Tom, eldest of the children, who at twenty-six returns home from a four-year prison term for manslaughter. That is, he returns to the site of his home, only to discover that his people have vanished and the place is given over to tractor-handled cotton raising. He finds his

family at the shack of an uncle; but this place, too, is doomed, and the family is just moving on toward California.

It is a numerous family. Besides Pa, Ma, Uncle John, and Tom, it includes the Rabelaisian Grampa and his wife; Tom's younger brother Al; another brother, Noah, not quite bright; a sister, Rose of Sharon, and her husband, Connie; two small children. They take along also the Preacher, Casy, another unforgettable character. They all start out, with a dog, in an old Ford truck. Grampa and Granma do not survive the journey. Noah wanders off by himself. Connie deserts.

The rest arrive in California, to be met by deputies. Thereafter their life is one disillusionment after another.

So far as surface facts are concerned, it is a sordid, gloomy story. But under the surface it is a saga of high courage and of human brotherhood. Those who have almost nothing share it with those who are even worse off. There is a fine loyalty to the family, and to those others who are kind. There is always a reaching out for something better, a fumbling of untutored minds to understand the forces that are pushing them around so mercilessly. In the end Tom, having seen Casy slain in the labor war, and having avenged him, becomes an underground worker for labor. The family are left to carry on as best they can. But there is always striving, and always hope, and always courage.

Earle Birney.
"A Must Book."
Canadian Forum, 19 (June 1939), 94–5.

This is a MUST book. It is not only the novel by which Steinbeck steps from the fashionable second-raters to the front ranks of living American fictionists. It is not only a work of concentrated observation, folk humor, and dramatic imagination playing over the whole American continent. It is, more importantly, what Milton would call a "deed"—the act of a man out of the pity and wrath of his heart.

It is a rebellious protest, tempered but by no means obscured by art, against the gradual murder of a half-million southwest farmers by the human instruments of an inhuman and outworn economy. When the land their grandfathers had wrested from the prairie grass is taken from them by drought and the banking system, and pooled for tractor cultivation, they pile their goods and kids in pathetic jalopies and struggle west to California, lured by lying promises of work and land. They arrive, as the big California ranchers had planned, in such myriads and in such extremes of need that they are forced to work for no more than what will keep them half-alive. When the picking is over, and while unsold fruit is destroyed, they are hounded into the highways and left to starve, unprotected by law, unaided by humanity. "And children dying of pellagra must die because profit cannot be taken from an orange."

The book is not free from Steinbeck's old faults. In the ending especially there is theatricality; pain and cruelty are sometimes sensationalized in the manner of Faulkner and Hemingway. There are overtones of mysticism and sentimental individualism which occasionally confuse the dominant social philosophy. The feel of dirt in the farmer's fingers seems at times more important than tractors. The central character, Ma Joad, is too infallibly heroic and sybilline, the preacher too shadowy for his important role. The crudities of American folk-speech are perhaps exaggerated. Middle-class Toronto,

speaking through the word-drunk Mr. Bridle, has already denounced the book, in consequence, as "the most unblushing parade of naturalistic indecency so far Nordized since the war," "more elemental than the worst of Dos Passos," etc.

But the sweep of the book's vision and the controlled passion of its style will carry away all but the most hardened prudes. In one short sentence, Steinbeck can catch the whole human tragedy of an abandoned farmhouse: "The wild cats crept in from the fields at night, but they did not mew at the doorsteps any more."

This is no "proletarian novel." It is rather the only thing a class-conscious artist can write so long as the working people of the earth—of our Canadian prairies too—suffer and die like this under their economic overlords. Steinbeck has no pseudo-Marxist hero from the *Daily Worker* office organizing the farmers along with their bosses into Leagues for Peace and Democracy. These proletarians of the soil are in the bitter process of learning for themselves in their own terms what wage-labor and capital mean, of creating for themselves fire-hardened leaders and cadres for the coming revolution.

That the end will be revolution is implicit from the title onwards. Self-interest dictates that the Haves will not concede; self-preservation and the ultimately superior power of numbers means that the masses will win, so long as they retain the will to "turn their fear to wrath." The inevitable fruit of the system are the bitter grapes of wrath, and there will one day be a trampling out of the vintage. The book will not, as Clifton Fadiman hopes, "effect something like a revolution in the minds ... of overcomfortable people," as he assumes *Les Misérables* and *Uncle Tom's Cabin* did. *Les Misérables* did not prevent the Paris Commune nor *Uncle Tom's Cabin* the Civil War. Steinbeck is not so much warning the rich, whom he sees cannot help themselves, as arousing the poor, who can, to courage, endurance, organization, revolt.

Edward Weeks. "The Bookshelf." *Atlantic*, 163 (June 1939), 16.

I should like to say why I think *The Grapes of Wrath* is a landmark in American literature. I think it is quite as important in our time as Sinclair Lewis's *Main Street* was in the early '20s. I think it is an almost perfect illustration of the changes which have occurred in our fiction since the depression. I think it is a story whose characters—if they be not opposed by convention—will come nearer the heart than any other family of Americans I have read of since the war.

In his novels Mr. Lewis was working with characters typical of our middle class: the mediocrity in business, the small-town wife, the doctor and preacher. In his six books Mr. Steinbeck has identified himself with the migratory American and the insecure. *Tortilla Flat* pictured the luck of the laughing *paisano; In Dubious Battle* was the story of a strike fermented for good reasons among the fruit pickers in California; *Of Mice and Men* showed us the aspiration, humor, and pathetic dependence of the "hands" in any ranch house. I think this is suggestive of the change which has become increasingly evident in the short stories and novels since 1930. Every editor knows that the sympathy of his writers has extended downward as the succession of lean years beat into our conscience the inequalities in American life. This feeling for injustice, this compassion for the dispossessed,

is the driving force within *The Grapes of Wrath*. . . .

You have to go back to Dickens to find a story which so plays upon your emotions, which makes you so indignant. Tom Joad's first meeting with his mother after his parole from prison; Ma as she strips her room before the departure; the death of Grampa—such scenes are to me irresistibly moving. Less emotional but no less vivid are the daily circumstances of the caravan—Ma's vigilance, the rough humor, the tinkering of the old car, the ominous rumor of what awaits the Okies in California. As a means of relief and objectivity, the author skillfully injects interludes of impersonal description so that our mind travels, as it were, on two planes—westward bound. To tell the personal story Mr. Steinbeck uses language unadulterated, words which are profane and which in some companies would be lewd. I submit that he could not have written truthfully of the Joads without them, and that in his hands such words are as sanitary as they are relevant to the book. I am again reminded of Dickens as I notice the excessive touches in *The Grapes of Wrath*—how the preachment becomes increasingly intrusive in the second half, and how the book ends on a note of almost mawkish sentiment. I myself would have been better pleased to see the final period on page 477. But these are small points.

Steinbeck has the common touch, and the ability to dramatize it in action and in lingo. His novel is more than the summation of realism: it holds the hunger and the humor, the anger and the poetry wrung from deep feeling, which characterize our life in the uncertain 1930's.

A[rthur] D. Spearman, S.J. "Steinbeck's *Grapes of Wrath* Branded as Red Propaganda by Father A. D. Spearman." San Francisco *Examiner*, 4 June 1939, Section 1, p. 12.

The Grapes of Wrath may be summed up as a brief, written in terms of human misery, for the adoption of the philosophy of life called Communism. The arguments are selected from the customary communistic sources and strategy; a highlighted appeal for the behaviouristic philosophy of sex-indulgence; an animated cartoon of the useless, discouraging influence of religion upon human welfare, a tincture saturating the whole book, and made personal in the warping sin-remorse of Uncle John, brooding upon his past; a portrayal of law enforcement officers as the tools of the rich with no care or interest in protecting the legal rights or life and limbs of the poor worker.

Consistency is not, and any informed thinker knows that it can not be, a quality either of the Communistic mind or of Communistic propaganda. It is not found in Steinbeck's portrayal either of problem or solution in *The Grapes of Wrath*. Lack of consistency in this book should not, however, blind the reader to the definite trend of the writer's sympathies and ideology. *Grapes of Wrath* is a plea for a fundamental "change." It does not see any possibility of restoration of American life on a basis of the Ten Commandments, liberty under law, guidance from true religion, or a relationship of mutual duty and right of employee and employer.

It is a summons to revolution as the only way out of the complex social problem of our time. It points to collectivism in its longings, voiced by Ma Joad, and Casy, and Tom Joad for "our" land, worked by "our" tractors, and enjoyment in "our" communal socials and civic life.

The book ridicules those who see "reds" threatening American life. It honors and appeals for the adoption of Communism, but tractfully refuses to use or accept the name.

Charles Angoff. "In the Great Tradition." *North American Review*, 247 (Summer 1939), 387–9.

There should be rejoicing in that part of Hell where the souls of great American imaginative writers while away their time, for at long last a worthy successor to them has appeared in their former terrestrial abode. With his latest novel Mr. Steinbeck at once joins the company of Hawthorne, Melville, Crane, and Norris, and easily leaps to the forefront of all his contemporaries. The book has all the earmarks of something momentous, monumental, and memorable: universal compassion, a sensuousness so honestly and recklessly tender that even the Fathers of the Church would probably have called it spiritual; and a moral anger against the entire scheme of things that only the highest art possesses. The book also has the proper faults: robust looseness and lack of narrative definitiveness—faults such as can be found in the Bible, *Moby*

Dick, Don Quixote, and *Jude the Ob-scure.* The greatest artists almost never conform to the rules of their art as set down by those who do not practice it. The critics of Bach's time upbraided him severely for not writing fugues as perfect as those of Georg Philipp Telemann.

Apparently nothing much happens in Mr. Steinbeck's tale. A poor white family, the Joads, evicted from their home in the Middle West by the banks, pile into an old automobile and head West toward the land where oranges grow, seeking work of any kind, finding it occasionally at about five cents an hour, but most of the time hounded by the police, and in the end get stuck in thick California mud, which looks no more like oranges than Kansas mud. Nothing much happens, but before one has gone a hundred pages into the book, one finds oneself in a whole world of stress and strain, love and hate, charity and cruelty, cowardice and the most sublime heroism.

The dreadful, almost incredible poverty of contemporary American life, which the New Deal has been trying to combat, beats mercilessly against the Joad family, who can't understand why they should be so hungry in a land so rich. . . .

But the people, with the patience of Christ, keep on going, helping one another to the last bite of bread and the last drop of milk. As Ma Joad, one of the most noble characters in American fiction, says, "I'm learnin' one thing good. Learnin' it all a time, ever' day. If you're in trouble or hurt or need—go to the poor people. They're the only ones that'll help—the only ones."

So the Joads exchange help with their fellow wanderers, and they give sustenance and sympathy to one another in the family, especially to those among them whom an indifferent world has treated harshly and stupidly: son Tom, who served a term in jail; Uncle John, whose wife died because he couldn't afford medical care for her; Preacher Jim Casy, who finally saw the folly of his sermonizing; and daughter Rose of Sharon, whose unemployed husband left her in the middle of her pregnancy.

Ma Joad watches over all of them and dozens of others. She has particular fear for the men lest they collapse inwardly, and she rejoices when she notices rage in their faces, for she knows that "the break would never come as long as fear could turn to wrath." Her final act of magnificence comes at the very end of the book, in a barn, where she has taken her shivering daughter who had just delivered herself of a dead child. Both notice a man not far away, dying of starvation.

"Ma's eyes passed Rose of Sharon's eyes, and then came back to them. And the two women looked deep into each other. The girl's breath came short and gasping.

"She said, 'Yes.'

"Ma smiled. 'I knowed you would. I knowed!'"

Ma and Pa and Uncle John and the younger Joads leave the barn.

"Rose of Sharon sat still in the whispering barn. Then she hoisted her tired body and drew the comfort about her. She moved slowly to the corner and stood looking down at the wasted face, into the wide, frightened eyes."

Rose of Sharon offers him one of her breasts. "'You got to,' she said." And thus he was saved from a stable rat's grave.

Some of the literary Episcopalians have already complained about such passages, wholly oblivious to the eternal heartbreak in them, as their predecessors complained about similar passages in the works of Flaubert, Zola, and Hardy. Steinbeck need not worry. His book offers more praise to God than a dozen Cathedrals of St. John the Divine.

M. L. Elting.
"Fiction Review."
Forum, 102 (July 1939),
iv.

James N. Vaughan.
"The Grapes of Wrath."
Commonweal, 30
(28 July 1939), 341–2.

This has been a vintage year for novels, particularly novels about our nervous, tugging present days. There's a summer's fiction reading at hand that at last measures up to *Personal History* and Paul de Kruif's books and *Red Star Over China*.

First on any list comes *The Grapes of Wrath*, John Steinbeck's magnificent story of dispossessed Oklahoma farmers and their search for new beginnings in California.

The Joad family, a healthy, lusty, cussing lot of Oklahomans came across the desert believing that in a little while they could earn enough by picking fruit to get an orchard of their own and a little white house. But they found that two or three hundred thousand others had the same idea.... The Joads got hungrier and more puzzled. They were pushed around by cops and deputies, and that made them mad. And finally they began to ask why—why can't seven willing pairs of hands fill seven stomachs in the fattest land on earth?

The answer, large and portentous, is part of the story but not all of it. There is humor, too, and pathos and love and fine yarn-spinning. Mr. Steinbeck has written the kind of novel that touches you with an almost personal pride, because it is so exactly what you want to see written.

... His tale of pain, starvation, wretchedness, and death Mr. Steinbeck relates with tenderness and even with detachment so far as the mere story is concerned. If his realism is at times vulgar to a revolting degree, it must be admitted that it offends in this respect on so few occasions that it may be passed over without further mention.

Besides being a novel, *Grapes of Wrath* is a monograph on rural sociology, a manual of practical wisdom in times of enormous stress, an assault on individualism, an essay in behalf of a rather vague form of pantheism and a bitter, ironical attack on that emotional evangelistic religion which seems to thrive in the more impoverished rural districts of this vast country.

The structure of general ideas found in the book is for the most part elaborated by a very effective device consisting of interruptions in the story of the Joads for short excursions into the implications of that story. The argument is this: Here are representatives of the seventh American generation of solid people who are driven to destitution and death by the forces of "capitalism." In the day of their distress no help is extended to them. On the contrary they are regarded with fear and loathing by possessors of property. The loathing which they inspire in the Californians on whom they descend arises from fear that they constitute a threat to property. Ownership of property freezes a person into an "I" which is incapable of joining with others to constitute a "we." Notwithstanding the force and terror devices used by the Californians (by property holders) for keeping these migrant starvelings in their place (in a cowed condition) some day they will band together to take by violence what will not now be peacefully surrendered, viz., some of the owners' superfluity of goods and unneeded acreage. The inevitability of the day of violence is expressly asserted. Meantime to arm themselves for the coming struggle, the downtrodden must be spiritually prepared. This preparation will involve the creation of a collectivistic mentality which will prize the cause of the "people" and will view the perils and death of individuals as well as the rights of individuals as of minor significance.

Some fundamental ideas are overlooked by Mr. Steinbeck. In the first place the relief of the conditions he describes does not require violence—as our experience of the last six years has shown. In the next place the doctrine that the spirit of the beehive must supersede a society of persons who are unique, independent and responsible is the absolute negation of the American way of life viewed in its ideal evolution. Moreover, the spread between the truly horrible conditions here faithfully depicted and the deduction in favor of collectivism is really boundless. Again alternatives in the life of the spirit are not even explored when an author contents himself with juxtaposing the acrobatical Christianity typified in the earlier life and doings of his preacher Casy and the wholly vague kind of pantheism which is expounded by Casy in his post-exodus manifestations.

The impact of this book is very powerful. Whoever reads it will find he has gained a better total grasp on the need in this country for rectification of any and all conditions which now or hereafter may correspond in any degree with the terrible plight of the dust bowl tenant farmers.

"Grapes of Wrath."
Collier's, 104
(2 September 1939), 54.

Some say that John Steinbeck's best-selling novel, The Grapes of Wrath, is a twentieth-century Uncle Tom's Cabin and then some. Others call it a despicable piece of propaganda. The debate is moving a lot of people to read the book, so we'll tell what we think of it.

For one thing, we think The Grapes of Wrath is a very moving book, crammed with human tragedy and comedy (plus considerable dirt), and written in an extremely graphic style. It has to do with poor, broken Southern share croppers forced out of Dust Bowl cotton fields into a flight to California by drought and tumbling cotton prices. You can't help feeling sorry for the poor, harassed devils. A social system that can work such hardships on any substantial number of people unquestionably has its rotten spots.

But we also think that The Grapes of Wrath, as charged by many critics, is propaganda for the idea that we ought to trade our system for the Russian system. It is Mr. Steinbeck's or anybody else's privilege to publish such propaganda in this country—which fact is one of the glories of America.

But it is also anybody's privilege, of which we here avail ourselves, to point out that a similar novel could be written about Russia.

The locale would be the Ukraine, Russia's best wheat and farm area; time, winter 1931–32. The characters would be salty Russian peasants, in place of

Mr. Steinbeck's hymn-roaring, hell-raising share croppers.

Instead of American deputy sheriffs dusting around to shoo evicted hiders-out off foreclosed cotton lands, there would be droves of Red army soldiers and OGPU operatives beating up and down the Ukraine. They would be stripping the peasants of every movable foodstuff, and simply leaving the peasants to starve. Selected peasants would be sent to Siberia.

The score in the end would be between three and four million Russian peasants actually and literally dead of starvation— as against perhaps 300,000 American share croppers forced out of the Dust Bowl and into a California which, while it didn't welcome them with glad cries, at least didn't let them starve to death.

Responsible for the Russian tragedy would be the government at Moscow— quite a contrast to the government at Washington, which strives endlessly to prevent or alleviate such miseries as *The Grapes of Wrath* depicts.

The reason for the tragedies in our imaginary Russian *Grapes of Wrath* would be that the Moscow government had had no luck in selling the peasants the idea of socialized farming, with nobody but the government really owning anything. Hence, the peasants had gone on a sit-down and kill-the-cattle strike, and were raising nothing beyond their own needs. So the government was forced to confiscate everything it could find on the farms to feed the city populations— city populations being harder to keep down than scattered farmers.

As we say, we don't defend the flaws in our system that are to blame for the share-cropper tragedies.

But we do suggest that a country where everybody is free to think, talk, write and act (short of violence) against every social ill has a better chance to work out a just economic system even-tually than has a country where all power resides in one man, and where you are shot or tortured or exiled or starved to death if you are caught as much as thinking that things might be a little better run.

Wilfrid Gibson. "Three New Novels." Manchester *Guardian*, 8 September 1939, p. 3.

Although the reading of novels as a relaxation may help one through a period of suspense, when the world is actually crashing into war it is difficult even for the most conscientious reviewer to give to the consideration of works of fiction the undistracted concentration that is essential to a just assessment of their values. I, personally, have been all the more bothered because I feel that the two American books which head my list are both works of remarkable achievement; and that more especially the second, which is a novel written in verse, I should have liked to have reread, as I must always hesitate to pronounce judgment on poetry after a single perusal.

Yet, although I have been unable to give any of these books a wholly undivided attention, I have no hesitation in saying that *The Grapes of Wrath* is one of the most vital stories that I have read for some time, a story that under any other circumstances would have held me utterly absorbed. It is a tale of immediate contemporary significance, as it deals with the present-day ruthless, and possibly ultimately ruinous, rationalization of American agriculture. The cottonlands of Oklahoma have become gradually exhausted and can now only be made to yield a margin of profit to their owners, the banking corporations, if they are worked on a sufficiently large scale—that is, if they are cultivated by tractors that can drive at least four-mile-long furrows; so that all the small tenant-farmers are being turned off the holdings which their forbears have worked for generations—even their very homesteads falling before the onset of the mechanical jugger-nauts—and forced to seek a livelihood elsewhere. Meanwhile the agony of these disinherited farmers is being exploited for their own purposes by scoundrelly con-tractors who distribute among them leaflets extolling the golden opportunities of California and the certainty of finding work there—though such work, being mainly fruit-picking, is at most sea-sonal,—with the cruelly calculated result that the farmers of Oklahoma are trek-king there in such vast hordes that they must work for starvation wages or per-ish; and rapidly these hitherto respectable countryfolk are being transformed into homeless vagabonds whose desperate condition is already becoming a menace to American civilisation.

Though Mr. Steinbeck is acutely con-scious of the economic and social conse-quences of this revolution in American conditions, he tells his tale in terms of the vicissitudes of a single family, and is mainly concerned with the destruction of the human values. He is a conscientious realist; and if at times, after the fashion of the modish novelist, he would seem to dwell unduly on the description of the operation of the ordinary bodily func-tions, with him this preoccupation is seldom offensive because his presentation of the lives of these primitive people is in all respects so authentic. This is a terrible and an indignant book; yet it is not with-out passages of lyrical beauty, and the ultimate impression conveyed is that of the dignity of the human spirit under the stress of the most desperate conditions. . . .

"New Novels."
London *Times*,
8 September 1939, p. 6.

Money, which began as a convenience, is now an incubus. This is the thesis of Mr. John Steinbeck's long new work, which shows how land in parts of the United States is gradually coming into the possession of the banks and finance com-panies and how a whole population of dispossessed tenant farmers is being turned into the agricultural labour mar-ket. Before we look at the story itself, here is a quotation from one of the inter-chapters that provide the general scene and circumstances: the reference is to banks and companies.

"They breathe profits; they eat the in-terest on money. If they don't get it, they die the way you do without air, without side-meat." That is the text, and the ser-mon is fiery.

The Grapes of Wrath has the excite-ment and the display of character to be expected of the author of *Of Mice and Men*. Against the general background of dusty and exhausted fields and a migrat-ing population and the inevitable com-mercial crows we have the story of the Joads. These are tenant farmers whose grandparents cleared and claimed the ground, whose only knowledge of life has been picked up on this farm and the neighbouring farms, whose whole experi-ence makes it hard for them to believe that the invisible workings of money have the power to deprive them of the visible land.

On this land they have grown their

crops, begot their children, danced, fought, seen their parents die, cooked food, observed the ways of animals and weather, and seen at last the tractor run an impersonal furrow even across the farmyards and where the farmhouse stood. With all their fellows the Joads set out now in a new, unromantic but not less heroic exodus to California, where advertisements of work for fruit and cotton pickers attract thousands of similar families. They go in a motor-car bought at an exorbitant price from the scrap-heap, and on the road they find the mixed kindliness and coldness the poor have to expect. In California they meet with ruthless exploitation and consequently fear. They face hardship with endurance and the bewildering tyranny of money with an astounding courage.

Yet the interest of his sociological theme has not betrayed Mr. Steinbeck into neglecting his men and women. Indeed, it is from the vigour and variety of these as much as from the angry excitement of the narrative that the novel takes life. The Joads—Ma, with her fight to keep the family together, young Tom, whose imprisonment for manslaughter has taught him unexpected lessons, the bickering, impish, and devoted grandparents, the fatuous and pathetic younger couple, the preacher whose fanatical evangelism has changed into pious study of his fellow-men—are characters who hold an interest for us at least commensurate with that of the general theme. Their history has a rough, humorous tenderness that distinguishes it from all the volumes of the second rate.

"Victims of Mammon." *Times Literary Supplement* [London], 9 September 1939, p. 525.

Mr. John Steinbeck's new novel is a campaign, and Mammon is the enemy. While lesser American writers complacently recall their country's past, Mr. Steinbeck is anxiously in touch with its present. He, too, describes an exodus to the West, but this is made in ramshackle motor-cars instead of lumbering wagons. Here there are no battles to bring glory, and at the end the land of promise is a bitter disappointment. There, sure enough, are the farms and orchards and well-watered lands, but others are in possession of them. Yet this the travellers expected: all they hoped for was work; and the indecent exploitation of their necessity to work is shown with cold and precise justice. Mr. Steinbeck's theme, indeed, is twofold. One part of it is the endurance of the common people in conditions of great hardship; and the other is concerned with the tyranny over all classes of economic laws that were framed only to record certain movements and not, in fact, to be the pretext for compelling them. When the movements change, the laws change with them.

From a background that is stated chiefly in short interludes wherein the anger only gives pace to the dramatic rhythms, one group of people stands out. These are the Joads, tenant farmers of Oklahoma, whose land has been mortgaged little by little and forfeited at last to the bank, which controls its own farming corporation. The forty-acre farms are run into one, the tractors plough up the dusty fields to make a final profit before the land is ruined, and the tenants are turned out to find a living somewhere else. Like all their fellows, the Joads can only fasten their hopes on the Californian advertisements for labour. The memories of several generations they must leave behind them with the land, but ahead at least is the chance of work and a new home. Their implements and beasts go for nothing to opportunist buyers; for their wagon they get five dollars towards the purchase of a scrapheap car; and into this precarious transport are piled the essential household goods. They have begun to be at the mercy of opportunists of all kinds.

Mr. Steinbeck looks beyond his people and he sees the universal reverence for profits, but he sees his people first. If he despises and derides Mammon, he does so not because he dislikes a theory but because he sees the practical effect in human misery. Are not his Joads the victims of a system for which no man will take the responsibility? The Joads are certainly not the puppets of a theory. Their essential decency and good citizenship are evident beneath their various raffish surfaces, but they are not mere personifications of these qualities. The grandparents whose love for each other shows itself in continual verbal sparring, the mother who can endure anything so long as the family holds together, the son who has been in prison for manslaughter and knows that he would defend himself again, and the young married daughter fussing about the safety of the child she carries—these are individual men and women. When they speak, it is not to fill in an extra paragraph but to express or conceal their thoughts. When they act, their actions are their own. If they do not rebel, it is because money has become a despot against which rebellion is hopeless.

It is not pretended that this passion is sustained unbroken for the whole course of a long book. At their most wretched, these people have the refuge of memory and humour, and in their recollections of past raciness we are enabled to see the superior colour and variety of a society in which the owners lived on their land, worked it themselves and measured their prosperity directly against its prosperity. There is, besides, the tedium inseparable from any long work pledged to a single idea; but here the tedium is at its lowest. Against such falling off as there is may be set those passages in which the author makes still more transparent the barrier between his mind and our own. We know his mind now for an original one. He has passages in this book that restate the idea of the interlude in *To the Lighthouse* in terms of another country; but his just understanding of character, the candour and forcefulness of his dialogue and his mastery of climaxes are all his own and inimitable.

Kate O'Brien.
"Fiction."
Spectator [England], 163 (15 September 1939), 386.

Some weeks ago the whole British public was counselled emphatically over the air to read a forthcoming American novel called *The Grapes of Wrath*. The gently pontifical tones of Mr. Alexander Woollcott, breaking over our Sunday supper tables, informed us that, along with Franklin D. Roosevelt's, John Steinbeck's is at present *the* American voice, the representative one, through which America should be heard and judged. Here it is, then—immensely ushered in, and accompanied, for the encouragement of reviewers at least, by a whole booklet of acclamation of the man behind the voice, to say nothing of a full-length studio portrait of him.

All this is very nice, but is the booklet necessary, or even advisable? Surely we have heard of John Steinbeck, even in darkest England? Have we not admired *Tortilla Flat* and *The Cup of Gold*, and was not *Of Mice and Men* a Shaftesbury Avenue success until Hitler put out the town's lights? But Mr. Woollcott's claim is that "a young writer who had already written several good books . . . has now written a great one." I do not agree with this. I think that "a young writer, &c.," has now written another good book, but one in which he has had the courage, if you like, to give fuller rein than formerly to a sentimentality which for some of us disfigured his early work.

The theme of *The Grapes of Wrath* is quite magnificent; so is its documentary informativeness; so are its moral and its desolate warning. It is indeed a vivid, generous sermon on modern misery, on the crassness and savagery of some who create it, and the nobility of its victims. Mr. Steinbeck's heart is passionately fixed in the right place, but it would be unfair to the great variety of his talents to suggest that perhaps his trouble, *qua* writer, is that he is all heart.

The story is of the present-day destruction of the land of the Western States of America, and so of the people who, in both senses of the word, live on it. "The land company—that's the bank when it has land—wants tractors, not families, on the land. Is a tractor bad? Is the power that turns the long furrows wrong? If our tractor turned the long furrows of our land, it would be good. Not my land, but ours. We could love that tractor then as we have loved this land

when it was ours. But this tractor does two things—it turns the land and it turns us off the land. There is little difference between this tractor and a tank. The people are driven, intimidated, hurt by both. We must think about this." And in this book we can read about it and see, through the desperate sufferings and adventures of one decent, outcast Oklahoma family, how big business, industrialisation, is destroying the United States.

The Joad family, captained by Tom, the elder son, who is a *parole* man, having done time for manslaughter, have to flee from their long-held forty acres which the inexorable tractor is tearing up. They depart, a large troupe of all ages, in the shakiest of trucks, perilously loaded. They "aim to" start a new life in California. They have read handbills, have heard of the universal trek West, to the peach-pickin', orange-pickin' sun, fertility and fortune in the West. Their journey is heroic, nothing less; and their subsequent slow disillusionment, though immense, actually does not quite use up their common stock of fortitude. When we leave them at the end, somewhat reduced by death and desertion and with their courageous Tom forced on the run again because of another manslaughter, they and their chance friends of the road are more destitute, more weary and directionless than it is easy to convey—but in spirit they are "a fambly" still, their patient hearts still beat, with "Ma," great creature, driving death off, Heaven knows why—saving the starved, dying stranger in the wayside shed with the unneeded milk of her young daughter's breasts.

Mr. Steinbeck gives us an enormous, vivid setting; he fills it with odd and lively characters; he uses an attractive Western States *patois*, and he tells a terrible, moving story of universal and immediate significance. Why, then, am I not

179

enthralled by his book? Simply because, right or wrong, I dislike his manner of writing, which I think epitomises the intolerable sentimentality of American "realism." I think he wrecks a beautiful dialect with false cadences; I think he is frequently uncertain about where to end a sentence; I think his repetitiveness is not justified by emotional result; and whereas the funny, niggling coarseness which he jovially imposes on his pathetic migrants may be true to type, it seemed to me out of tone, and to offend against the general conception. But the book is good, interesting and generous, and its wide popularity would be a beneficial thing.

Anthony West.
"New Novels."
New Statesman and Nation [England], 18 (16 September 1939), 404–5.

The story of *The Grapes of Wrath* is very simple. Prior to 1820 the smallest acreage which the settler could buy from the United States Government was 320, which had to be paid for at the rate of two dollars an acre and paid for in four years. Subsequent to 1820, however, the Government policy changed, and it became possible to buy lots of as little as eighty acres, and after the Civil War the policy was further modified and settlers were able to take up these small farms for nothing. An eighty-acre farm is uneconomic without highly developed local markets and without very skilful farming; the Middle West never developed any sort of regional economy and even the smallest farmers went in for wheat as a main crop. The result was that the farmers were wholly at the mercy of world prices without local standbys, and the consequence of the unending cropping of wheat was soil exhaustion. After the war a succession of drought years accelerated the slow draining of the fertility of the soil, the top soil began to break up into dust and to blow away. The farmers fell into debt and failed to keep up the payments on their mortgages, the banks took over the farms. This is where Mr. Steinbeck's book begins; the Joads, a family of small Oklahoma farmers, have had their notice to quit and have decided to move on westwards in obedience to the lemming-like compulsion which is the vestige of the American pioneer tradition. Like hundreds of thousands of other families, they buy an old car and set off for California; their sufferings on the road and their situation when they arrive at the promised land where they find there is nothing for them but casual labour on an overstocked market make the story of the book. It is a horrible story told with passionate earnestness, distressing and moving, but completely as one is compelled to realise the plight of this human refuse in California the book has great defects as a novel. It is to be compared with Upton Sinclair's novel about the Chicago Stockyards, *The Jungle*. When Sinclair's book first appeared it created the same sort of stir that *The Grapes of Wrath* has made; the working conditions and the brutalised lives it described were as shocking, the case against the meat packers was as strong as the case against the fruit growers, and it was made with the same passion, the same earnestness. People were intensely moved by it. Time has stolen away its force, it is as wholly "1906" as an automobile of that year and as suitable for contemporary use. This old scandal has lost its urgency and cannot horrify one into forgetting that the same thing is being said over and over again and that the book ends when it does because the reader cannot be expected to stand any more. The fact that the sun will look on the puzzled, desperate and utterly defeated people in Mr. Steinbeck's book a few hours after it has looked on us tempts one to overlook similar failings. In form *The Grapes of Wrath* is astonishingly awkward; it combines the novel about the Joads with a generalised account of the experiences of the small farmers of whom the Joads are typical. These two books run concurrently and in such a fashion that a chapter of the generalised account precedes two or three chapters of the novel and forecasts pretty closely what is going to happen. Thus when the Joad family buys its car for the migration first Mr. Steinbeck explains how the Oklahoma farmers who go to California buy bad old cars which use too much oil and go wrong. Then the Joad family buy a car, and they talk about it and decide that they have probably been swindled and that the car is going to use too much oil and that they'll be lucky if it doesn't break down on the road. Then they set out and the car burns up too much oil and breaks down on the road. The Joads, moreover, are slow-thinking people, and they have to hear a thing several times before they believe it, and when they believe it they don't feel easy about it until they've told someone. But they can't bring themselves to say anything straight out; they work up to it by hints and suggestions, by devious back alleys which Mr. Steinbeck follows as enthusiastically and faithfully on page 535 as on page 35. Mr. Steinbeck makes his points with the delicacy of a trip hammer, the book lacks form and ends simply because the characters have reached the ultimate believable degradation and the length has reached the limit which pub-

lishers and public can stand. Pity and sympathy tempt one to suspend purely artistic standards, but this cannot be called a good novel. Its virtue lies in the burning sincerity which has captured the imagination of the American public and awakened them to the human aspect of the dust-bowl disaster. *The Jungle* is dead mutton as literature but it is alive in the American legislation which has amplified the Meat Inspection Bill and the Pure Food Bill of 1906, which the novel called into being within a few months of publication. *The Grapes of Wrath* will take a place beside it in the social history of the United States, but it is its literary fate to lie in that honourable vault which houses the books that have died when their purpose as propaganda has been served. . . .

Paula Snelling. "Snow White and the Share-croppers." Clayton *North Georgia Recruiter*, 19 November 1939, pp. 29–30.

Few readers would fail to concede that *Grapes of Wrath* is an exceptionally good book. But those who claim that it is a masterpiece tread more treacherous ground than do those who call it masterly propaganda. The making of which distinction may or may not be quibbling. I think not. The book is definitely written with the aim of arousing the reader's sympathies for a group of people because of their economic plight. It points the corollary that the group will profit by uniting to meet their enemy. So far so good. For theirs are desperate needs, prolonged callousness to which may easily wreck the civilization in which they occur. And the man whose pen rights these wrongs may well decide that he has chosen the best use to which his talents could be put. Nor can any writer of this generation lay claim to first consideration who fails to recognize economic maladjustments and their disastrous effects on human beings. It is also true that one book cannot do everything. An artist must select. And whether the feeling that no novel can be unequivocally first-rate which fails to give new or deeper insights into human emotions and the intricacies of personality and personal relationships is bias on my part or a fundamental basis of criticism, I do not know. But I am certain that a novel which, even if only implicitly, weights the dice towards the conclusion that when economic evils (or any other single category of evils) have been eliminated people will live happily ever after, thereby proves itself romantic. And there is something a little confusing, too, about combining with the premise that poverty is an evil, the thesis that poor people are better than rich people; if there is truth here, it is truth that needs meditating on.

Grapes of Wrath tells the story of the Joad family, generically derogated in California today as "Okies." They are one small unit in that west-moving horde of former farmers, later share-croppers, finally homeless destitutes ejected from the Dust Bowl area of our country by those impersonal, imponderable forces which have evolved out of our unplanning and uncaring economy.

We see the farm, including the tenant house, mowed down by that double-barreled machine, the tractor and the bank. We take the precarious worn-out-truck trip across the continent. We stop to patch threadbare tires and replace burned-out bearings. We watch the mirage, induced by rosy handbills, of a white cabin, green shade trees, free-fruit-for-all, fade inch by inch into a reality grimmer and more barren than that from which the migrants fled.

Though the book has many points of superiority over Harriet Beecher Stowe's, someone has, with acumen, called it the *Uncle Tom's Cabin* of the Dust Bowl.

It is one of the many stories our country needs to be told in these days when America is girding self-righteous loins against the evils overseas; for in each section, each state, each town of our democracy, man blindly perpetrates against man, class against class, injustices and callousnesses which over a period of time are as lethal as the more dramatic implements of death employed today in Europe. And these stories need to be told by people who, like Steinbeck, can draw out of the reader sympathy at the same time as he pours in knowledge. Only propagandists who are more concerned with human beings than with a Cause, and who also are talented artists can hope to open the eyes of a people to those evils which are a part of its own mores. And the texture of America's sins is so varied that a prophet is needed in each geographic region, each economic sphere, each psychological area of our country.

Steinbeck's device of using only a portion of the book to tell us about the Joads and employing alternate chapters to give in poetic prose the broader sociological current which uproots them and sweeps them on to destruction, is splendid and gives the book its epic quality. Their style resembles, in part, that of Lorentz's *River*. The chapters concerned directly with the Joads are good, but not good enough. When a writer deals with a group of a lower cultural level than that of the potential reader of his book, there

182

is the temptation to rely too heavily upon their uncouthness, upon their quaintness, upon the tang of their speech and to bait the reader overmuch with the baldness of their sexual talk. Though Steinbeck does not capitalize on this in the manner that Caldwell does—that is, such seducing as he does is employed toward the end of saving our souls, not of exploiting them— I believe he assumes (along with so many of our generation) that there is a basic incompatibility between hardboiledness and romanticism; that the crustacean is immune to sentimentality; that when an author has depicted the crude manners of his characters he has attained a realistic attitude toward them. Whereas realism demands the probing for and accepting of truth, palatable or unpalatable, at every level of the human soul and of its relationships.

And Steinbeck is so intent on rousing us to action to save Ma and Tom that he has made Snow Whites out of them. They stand forth primarily as symbols of Goodness-in-Distress;—Goodness nonetheless that it comes garbed in sharecropper idiom and sharecropper mores, and that Tom himself is an unrepentant murderer. The author seems to feel that we won't want to save them if he reveals them as having those inner conflicts and family frictions which we do not yet forgive our artists for revealing to us in ourselves, and which he may be justified in assuming would not make more palatable to us beings from another cultural stratum. It is not that he, like many of our writers, is totally unaware of subterranean pressures in his people's lives: safely distant from his immaculate major characters are the Seven Dwarfs, who each contribute a devious phase of human personality: Muley, clinging to the shadows of his old life when the substance of it is taken from him; Granpa, full of four-letter-words and vinegar, re-

duced to ignominy by buttons he can no longer master; Uncle John, tracked across the desert—tracked across all the deserts of his life—by Sin, and making for himself intermittent oases of drunkenness; Pa, haunted by his initial clumsiness with Noah. But Steinbeck the propagandist is too concerned with showing us the goodness of Ma and Tom and Casey to let Steinbeck the artist have his way with them. Or, judging by the author's other books, it may be a shade nearer the truth to suggest that Steinbeck the almost-artist is not yet wholly freed from those shackles of sentimentality which make us all reluctant to see how inextricably bound together are good and evil at all levels of our lives; that Steinbeck can face truths in minor characters which he cannot also concede to those characters that mean more to him.

Be that as it may, Steinbeck is as interesting a writer as we have in America today. And as talented. He deserves the wide reading and acclaim he is getting. It is just that when a writer has as much as he has, one wants him to have more. And there is a chance that he has, potentially.

Edmund Wilson.
"The Californians: Storm and Steinbeck."
New Republic, 103
(9 December 1940),
784–7.

... John Steinbeck [like Hans Otto Storm] is a native Californian, and he has occupied himself more with the life of the state than any of these other writers. His exploration in his novels of the Salinas Valley has been more thoroughgoing and tenacious than anything of the kind in our contemporary fiction except Faulkner's intensive cultivation of the state of Mississippi.

And what has Mr. Steinbeck found in this region he knows so well? I believe that his virtuosity in a purely technical way has tended to obscure his themes. He has published eight volumes of fiction, which represent a great variety of forms and which have therefore seemed to people to be written from a variety of points of view. *Tortilla Flat* was a comic idyll, with the simplification almost of a folk tale; *In Dubious Battle* was a strike novel, centering around Communist organizers and following a fairly conventional pattern; *Of Mice and Men* was a compact little drama, contrived with almost too much cleverness, and a parable which criticized humanity from a nonpolitical point of view; *The Long Valley* was a series of short stories, dealing mostly with animals, in which poetic symbols were presented in realistic settings and built up with concrete detail; *The Grapes of Wrath* was a propaganda novel, full of preachments and sociological interludes, and developed on an epic scale. Thus attention has been diverted from the content of Mr. Steinbeck's work by the fact that whenever he appears, he puts on a different kind of show. He is such an accomplished performer that he has been able to hold people's interest by the story he is telling at the moment without their inquiring what is behind it.

This variability of the form itself is probably an indication that Mr. Steinbeck has never yet found the right artistic medium for what he wants to say. But there is in his fiction as a whole a substratum which does remain constant and which gives it a certain basic seriousness that that of the mere performer does not have. What is constant in Mr. Steinbeck is his preoccupation with biology. He is a bi-

ologist in the literal sense that he interests himself in biological research. The biological laboratory in the short story called "The Snake" is obviously something which he knows at first hand and for which he has a strong special feeling; and it is one of the peculiarities of his vocabulary that it runs to biological terms. But the laboratory described in "The Snake," the tight little building over the water, where the scientist feeds white rats to rattlesnakes and fertilizes starfish ova, is also one of the key images of his fiction. It is the symbol of his tendency in his stories to present life in animal terms.

Mr. Steinbeck almost always in his fiction is dealing either with the lower animals or with human beings so rudimentary that they are almost on the animal level; and the close relationship of the people with the animals equals even the zoöphilia of D. H. Lawrence and David Garnett. In *Tortilla Flat*, there are the Pirate's dogs, with which he lives in a kennel and which have caused him practically to forget human relationships. In *In Dubious Battle*, there is another character whose personality is confused with that of his dogs. In *The Grapes of Wrath*, the journey of the Joads is figured at the beginning by the progress of a turtle, and it is accompanied and parodied all the way by animals, insects and birds. When the expropriated sharecroppers are compelled to abandon their farm in Oklahoma, we get an extended picture of the invasion of the house by the bats, the weasels, the owls, the mice, and the pet cats that have gone back to the wild. Lennie in *Of Mice and Men* likes to carry around animal pets, toward which as well as toward human beings he has murderous animal instincts. The stories in *The Long Valley* are almost entirely about animals and plants; and Mr. Steinbeck does not have the effect, as Lawrence or Kipling does, of romantically raising the animals to the stature of human beings, but rather of assimilating the human beings to animals. "The Chrysanthemums," "The White Quail" and "The Snake" deal with women who identify themselves with respectively chrysanthemums, a white quail and a snake. In "Flight," a young Mexican boy, who has killed a man and run away into the mountains, is finally reduced to a state so close to that of the beasts that he is taken by a mountain lion for one of themselves; and in the fantasy of "Saint Katy the Virgin," where a bad pig is made to repent and become a saint, the result is not to dignify the animal as the "Little Flowers of Saint Francis" do with the Wolf of Agubbio, for example, but to reduce human religion to absurdity.

The chief subject of Mr. Steinbeck's fiction has been thus not those aspects of humanity in which it is most thoughtful, imaginative, constructive, but rather the processes of life itself. In the natural course of nature, living organisms are continually being destroyed, and among the principal things that destroy them are the predatory appetite and the competitive instinct that are necessary for the very survival of eating and breeding things. This impulse of the killer has been preserved in a simpleton like Lennie in a form in which it is almost innocent; and yet Lennie has learned from his more highly developed friend that to yield to it is to do something "bad." In his struggle against the instinct, he loses. Is Lennie bad or good? He is betrayed as, Mr. Steinbeck implies, all our human intentions are: by the uncertainties of our animal nature.

And it is only, as a rule, on this primitive level that Mr. Steinbeck deals with moral questions: the virtues like the crimes for Mr. Steinbeck are still a part of these planless and almost aimless, of these almost unconscious, processes of life. The preacher in *The Grapes of Wrath* is disillusioned about the human moralities, and his sermon at the grave of Grampa Joad, so lecherous and mean during his lifetime, evidently gives expression to Mr. Steinbeck's point of view: "This here ol' man jus' lived a life an' jus' died out of it. I don't know whether he was good or bad, but that don't matter much. He was alive, an' that's what matters. An' now he's dead, an' that don't matter. Heard a fella tell a poem one time, an' he says 'All that lives is holy.'"

The subject of *The Grapes of Wrath*, which is supposed to deal with human society, is the same as that of "The Red Pony," which is supposed to deal with horses: loyalty to life itself. The men who feel the responsibility for having let the red pony die must retrieve themselves by sacrificing the mare in order to bring a new pony into life. And so Rose of Sharon Joad, with her undernourished baby born dead, must give her milk, in the desolate barn which is all she has left for a shelter, to another wretched victim of famine and flood, on the point of death from starvation. To what good that ponies and Okies should continue to live on the earth? "And I wouldn' pray for a ol' fella that's dead," the preacher goes on to say. "He's awright. He got a job to do, but it's all laid out for 'im an' there's on'y one way to do it. But us, we got a job to do, an' they's a thousan' ways, an' we don' know which one to take. An' if I was to pray, it'd be for the folks that don't know which way to turn."

This preacher who has lost his religion does find a way to turn: he becomes a labor agitator; and this theme has already been dealt with more fully in the earlier novel, *In Dubious Battle*. But what differentiates Mr. Steinbeck's picture of a labor movement with radical leadership from most books on such subjects of its period is again the biological point of view. The strike leaders, here as in other novels, are Communists, but the book is not really based on the formulas of Communist ideology. The kind of character produced by the Communist movement and the Communist strategy in strikes (of the Communism of the day before yesterday) are *described* by Mr. Steinbeck, and they are described with a certain amount of admiration; yet the party member of *In Dubious Battle* does not talk like a Marxist of even the Stalinist revision. The cruelty of these self-immolating revolutionists is not palliated any more than the cruelty of the half-witted Lennie; and we are made to feel throughout that we are witnessing examples of human behavior from which the only conclusion that the author seems confident in drawing is that this is how life in our age is behaving. There is developed in the course of the book—especially by a fellow-traveler doctor who seems to come closer than the Communist to expressing Mr. Steinbeck's own ideas—a whole philosophy of "group-man" as an "animal." . . .

This animalizing tendency of Mr. Steinbeck's is, I believe, at the bottom of his relative unsuccess at representing human beings.

The *paisanos* of *Tortilla Flat* are really not quite human beings: they are cunning little living dolls who amuse us like pet guinea-pigs or rabbits. A special convention has been created to remove them from kinship with the author and the reader. In *The Grapes of Wrath*, on the other hand, Mr. Steinbeck has summoned all his resources to make the reader feel his human relationship with the family of dispossessed farmers; yet the effect of this, too, is not quite real. The characters of *The Grapes of Wrath* are animated and put through their paces rather than brought to life; they are like excellent character actors giving very conscientious performances in a fairly well written

play. Their dialect is well done, but they talk stagy; and, in spite of Mr. Steinbeck's attempts to make them figure as heroic human symbols, you cannot help feeling that they, too, do not quite exist seriously for him as people. It is as if human sentiments and speeches had been assigned to a flock of lemmings on their way to throw themselves into the sea.

I do not mean to say, however, that this picture of human beings as lemmings hasn't its partial validity or its pertinence at the present time. In our time, Shakespeare's angry ape, drest in his little brief authority, seems to make of all the rest of mankind angry apes or cowering rodents. The one thing that was imagined with intensity in Aldous Huxley's novel of last autumn was the eighteenth-century exploiter of the slave trade degenerating into a fetal anthropoid. All the world is today full of people like the Joads deprived of the dignity of a human society, as they had previously been deprived of the dignity of human work, and made to flee from their houses like prairie-dogs driven before a prairie fire.

Huxley has a good deal to say, as our American Humanists did, about the importance of distinguishing clearly between the human and the animal levels; and, like the Humanists, he has been frightened back into one of those synthetic moral cults which do duty for our evaporated religions. The doctor in *In Dubious Battle* deprecates even those elements of religion that have entered into the labor cause; and he takes no stock in the utopianism of the Communists.

For myself, I prefer Mr. Steinbeck's naturalistic point of view toward the animal-man to Mr. Huxley's mysticism. We may conceivably learn something and get somewhere by studying humanity in a biological spirit; I am skeptical about our doing either by the methods of self-contemplation advocated by Mr. Huxley.

For the rest, Mr. Steinbeck has invention, observation, a certain color of style which for some reason does not possess what is called magic. I have not read the first three of his novels, but none of the ones that I have read seems to me precisely first-rate. *Tortilla Flat*—perhaps by reason of the very limitations of its convention—seems artistically his most successful production. Yet there is behind the journalism, the theatricalism and the tricks of most of his other books something that does seem first-rate in its seriousness, in its unpanicky questioning of life. . . .

Checklist of Additional Reviews

Leslie Moore. "Powerful Tale of Poor Okies." Worcester [Mass.] *Telegram*, 9 April 1939, Section 4, p. 10.

"The American Bookshelf." Waterbury [Conn.] *American*, 14 April 1939, p. 4.

Randolph Bartlett. "The Book of the Day." New York *Sun*, 14 April 1939, p. 17.

Joseph A. Belloli. "Book Angles." Pacific Grove [Calif.] *Tide*, 14 April 1939, p. 8.

May Cameron. "Steinbeck Writes Truly Great Novel." New York *Post*, 14 April 1939, p. 15-A.

Lewis Gannett. "Books and Things." New York *Herald Tribune*, 14 April 1939, "Books" section, p. 17.

Harry Hansen. "The First Reader." New York *World-Telegram*, 14 April 1939, Section 2, p. 27.

Michael March. "Page after Page." Brooklyn *Citizen*, 14 April 1939, p. 5.

John Selby. "Books." Daytona Beach [Fla.] *News-Journal*, 14 April 1939, p. 10.

David H. Appel. "Books." Cleveland *News*, 15 April 1939, p. 12.

Charlotte Becker. "Steinbeck Presses Poison from His *Grapes of Wrath*." Buffalo *Evening News* ("Sunday Magazine"), 15 April 1939, p. 7.

"Books and Book Folk." Portland [Me.] *Evening Express*, 15 April 1939, p. 6.

"Bookworm Sees a New Steinbeck." San Francisco *Call-Bulletin*, 15 April 1939, p. 3.

Fanny Butcher. "New Steinbeck Novel Employs an Epic Theme." Chicago *Tribune*, 15 April 1939, p. 14.

Jack Conroy. "The Story of a Grim Pilgrimage." San Francisco *People's World*, 15 April 1939, Section 2, p. 10.

"Fiction." *Booklist*, 35 (15 April 1939), 271.

E. B. Garside. "Steinbeck Reaches the Mountain Top." Boston *Evening Transcript*, 15 April 1939, p. 2.

Marian Murray. "Steinbeck Tells Story of Joads of Oklahoma." Hartford [Conn.] *Times*, 15 April 1939, p. 9.

W.T.S. "In *The Grapes of Wrath* Steinbeck Writes Vividly." Providence [R.I.] *Journal*, 15 April 1939, Section 6, p. 6.

Charles Wagner. "Books." New York *Daily Mirror*, 15 April 1939, p. 10.

Ruth Hinman Carter. "A World Without Neckties." Atlanta *Georgian*, 16 April 1939, Section C, p. 7.

Bennett Davis. "*The Grapes of Wrath*." Buffalo *Courier-Express*, 16 April 1939, Section 4, p. 4.

"*The Grapes of Wrath*." Washington [D.C.] *Evening Star*, 16 April 1939, Section F, p. 4.

"Great Novel About Modern Trek Westward." Akron *Beacon Journal*, 16 April 1939, Section D, p. 9.

J[oseph] H[enry] J[ackson]. "Steinbeck Treads '*Grapes of Wrath*.'" San Francisco *Chronicle* (*This World* magazine), 16 April 1939, p. 15.

R. Alton Jackson. "John Steinbeck Is at His Best in New Novel." Winston-Salem [N.C.] *Journal-Sentinel*, 16 April 1939, Section 2, p. 12.

William Kingsbury. "Fire and Power and Beauty and Pitiless Reality." Nashville *Tennessean*, 16 April 1939, Section D, p. 6.

Ralston Matheny. "John Steinbeck Turns Out One of World's Great Books." Knoxville [Tenn.] *Journal*, 16 April 1939, Section 4, p. 8.

Max Miller. "Steinbeck Discusses Influx of Needy." San Diego *Union*, 16 April 1939, Section C, p. 7.

Wilbur Needham. "Steinbeck Tells Inspiring but Tragic Tale of America." Los Angeles *Times*, 16 April 1939, Part 3, p. 8.

Louis Nicholas. "Steinbeck Scores a Bull's Eye." Philadelphia *Record*, 16 April 1939, p. 8.

Alicia Patterson. "The Book of the Week." New York *Daily News*, 16 April 1939, p. 72.

J. S. Pope. "Reviews." Atlanta *Journal*, 16 April 1939, "Sunday Magazine" section, p. 10.

R.W.N. "John Steinbeck's *Grapes of Wrath*." Springfield [Mass.] *Union and Republican*, 16 April 1939, Section E, p. 7.

Kenneth D. Tooil. "Books." Columbus [Ohio] *State Journal*, 16 April 1939, Section B, p. 3.

Virginia H. Trannett. "John Steinbeck's Newest Work Is a Fascinating Story." Columbus [Ohio] *Evening Dispatch*, 16 April 1939, "Graphic Section," p. 6.

P.G.F. "Latest Books." Jackson [Tenn.] *Sun*, 17 April 1939, p. 4.

Edith K. Dunton. "Read 'Em or Not."

Rutland [Vt.] *Daily Herald*, 18 April 1939, p. 8.

D.K.L. "Brought to Book." New Haven [Conn.] *Journal-Courier*, 19 April 1939, p. 6.

Sterling North. "Book of the Week." Chicago *News*, 19 April 1939, p. 25.

Robert Rutson. "It's in the Books." Concord *Daily Monitor and New Hampshire Patriot*, 21 April 1939, p. 11.

Charles Lee. "*The Grapes of Wrath*: The Tragedy of the American Sharecropper." Boston *Herald*, 22 April 1939, Section A, p. 7.

"People From the Dust Bowl." Oakland [Calif.] *Post-Enquirer*, 22 April 1939, p. 14.

Kathryn James Vogel. "*Grapes of Wrath* May Be the *Uncle Tom's Cabin* of Our Day." Milwaukee *Post*, 22 April 1939, p. 5.

Albert Goldstein. "Literature and Less." New Orleans *Times-Picayune*, 23 April 1939, Section 2, p. 11.

S.R. "Steinbeck's Novel." Durham [N.C.] *Morning Herald*, 23 April 1939, Section 2, p. 2.

Harry Schofield. "Today's Book." Macon [Ga.] *Telegraph*, 23 April 1939, Section A, p. 4.

Robert E. McClure. "Books Worth Reading." Santa Monica [Calif.] *Evening Outlook*, 28 April 1939, p. 8.

Wilbur Needham. "The Great American Novel Has Been Written." Hollywood *Tribune*, 28 April 1939, p. 12.

Helen E. Haines. "*The Grapes of Wrath*, John Steinbeck's Tragic Epic of America's Great Migration." Pasadena *Star-News*, 29 April 1939, p. 12.

Pearce Davies. "*The Grapes of Wrath*." San Jose [Calif.] *Mercury-Herald*, 30 April 1939, Section 2, p. 12.

Gladys Solomon. "Steinbeck Writes of Jobless Vagrants." New Haven

[Conn.] *Register*, 30 April 1939, Section 4, p. 5.

John Chamberlain. "The New Books." *Harper's*, 178 (May 1939), advertisement section, n.p.

Vincent McHugh. "John Steinbeck Branches Out." *American Mercury*, 47 (May 1939), 113–15.

Edward Weeks. "The Atlantic Bookshelf." *Atlantic*, 163 (May 1939), 33 (separate pagination at back of issue).

Edrie Ann Morse. "Book Review." Altoona [Pa.] *Tribune*, 1 May 1939, p. 5.

Burton Rascoe. "Excuse It, Please." *Newsweek*, 13 (1 May 1939), 38.

Granville Hicks. "Steinbeck's Powerful New Novel." *New Masses*, 31 (2 May 1939), 22–4.

"Bound To Be Read." Westfield Valley [Mass.] *Herald*, 4 May 1939, p. 4.

Anna Mary Smits. "Moving, Forceful, Poetic, Steinbeck Story Appalls." Salt Lake [City] *Tribune*, 7 May 1939, Section D, p. 4.

Betty Lou McKelvery. "John Steinbeck Book Is Strong." Green Bay [Wisc.] *Press-Gazette*, 13 May 1939, p. 11.

Willis Bugbee. "Latest Steinbeck Novel Is Powerful Work." Dayton *Journal-Herald*, 14 May 1939, "Spotlight" section, p. 7.

K.J.M. "At the Library of Hawaii." Honolulu *Advertiser*, 14 May 1939, p. 8.

Emilie C. Keyes. "The Book Nook." West Palm Beach [Fla.] *Post-Times*, 14 May 1939, p. 10.

K.W. "Steinbeck to New Heights in *The Grapes of Wrath*." Milwaukee *Journal*, 14 May 1939, Section 5, p. 3.

Rose Loveman Brewer. "*The Grapes of Wrath*: An American Classic?" Chattanooga *News*, 20 May 1939, p. 4.

J. Homer Caskey. "Letters to the Editor." *Saturday Review*, 20 (20 May 1939), 9.

Sidney Lindauer. "Book Chatter." Red Bluff [Calif.] *Daily News*, 20 May 1939, p. 3.

Theodore Smith. "Steinbeck Puts Grim Picture in New Book." San Francisco *News*, 20 May 1939, p. 8.

"Library Notes." Belfast [Me.] *Republican Journal*, 25 May 1939, p. 7.

Olett Levau. "Tale of the Dust Bowl." Atlanta *Constitution*, 28 May 1939, "Sunday Magazine" section, p. 4.

Robert Work. "Editorially Speaking." *Spartan Daily* [San Jose State University], 29 May 1939, p. 2.

Gertrude Binder. "The Joads." *Social Work Today*, 6 (June 1939), 46–8.

Wilbur Needham. "Racketeer Reviewers of John Steinbeck." *Black and White*, 1 (June 1939), 28–31.

Leon Whipple. "Letters and Life." *Survey Graphic*, 28 (June 1939), 401–2.

"*The Grapes of Wrath*." *Life*, 6 (5 June 1939), 66–7.

Lewis Gannett. "John Steinbeck's Latest Tops List of 1939 Novels, in Reviewer's Estimation." Oakland [Calif.] *Tribune*, 11 June 1939, Section B, p. 2.

Evelyn Hart. "Truth Is Uncomfortable." Dayton *Daily News*, 11 June 1939, "Society" section, p. 7.

Arthur D. Spearman, S.J. "Marxist Taint in Steinbeck Book." Albany [N.Y.] *Times-Union*, 11 June 1939, Section D, p. 7.

Charles Lee. "*The Grapes of Wrath* Tops Year's Tales in Heart and Art." Boston *Herald*, 17 June 1939, Section 1, p. 9.

Hazel Selby. "Books to Talk About." Riverside [Calif.] *News*, 20 June 1939, Section 2, p. 8.

Donald MacRae. "A Western

Bookshelf." *Frontier and Midland*, 19 (Summer 1939), 280.

Ralph Thompson. "Outstanding Novels." *Yale Review*, 28 (Summer 1939), viii, x, xii.

Louise Long. "*The Grapes of Wrath*." *Southwest Review*, 24 (July 1939), 495–8.

Richard Peters. "*Grapes of Wrath* Leads Vacation Book Lists." Cleveland *Press*, 8 July 1939, p. 5.

W. W. Withington. "Books of the Times." Santa Rosa [Calif.] *Press-Democrat*, 15 July 1939, p. 5.

S. "Farm Tenancy Central Theme of Steinbeck." Greensboro [N.C.] *News*, 16 July 1939, Section D, p. 6.

Larry Barretto. "Book Talk." Goshen [N.Y.] *Republican*, 18 July 1939, p. 3.

"KC Libraries Ban *Grapes of Wrath*." Bakersfield *Californian*, 18 August 1939, p. 1.

John Walton Caughey. "Current Discussion of California's Migrant Labor Problem." *Pacific Historical Review*, 8 (September 1939), 347–54.

"Attempts to Suppress *Grapes of Wrath*." *Publishers' Weekly*, 136 (2 September 1939), 777.

Philip Jordan. "War or No War, Read This Book." London *News Chronicle*, 8 September 1939, p. 4.

Ralph Straus. "Mr. Steinbeck's Success." London *Times*, 10 September 1939, p. 5.

Frank Swinnerton. "Topical and Timeless." London *Observer*, 10 September 1939, p. 5.

Phyllis Bentley. "An American Voice." Yorkshire [England] *Post*, 13 September 1939, p. 2.

Charles Poore. "Books of the Times." New York *Times*, 15 September 1939, p. 27.

Edwin Muir. "New Novels." *The Listener* [England], 22 (19 September 1939), 543.

Christopher Isherwood. "The Tragedy of Eldorado." *Kenyon Review*, 1 (Autumn 1939), 450–53.

Helen Cockburn. "Californian Mirage." Burton [England] *Observer*, 21 September 1939, p. 9.

John Brophy. "Mr. Steinbeck's Epic Story." London *Daily Telegraph*, 22 September 1939, p. 4.

"A Powerful American Novel." Inverness [Scotland] *Courier*, 22 September 1939, p. 3.

Lettice Cooper. "New Novels." *Time and Tide* [England], 20 (23 September 1939), 1256–7.

V. S. Pritchett. "*The Grapes of Wrath*." *Bystander* [England], 143 (27 September 1939), 472.

E.C.H. "Steinbeck's Story of a Great Trek." South Wales *Evening Post*, 30 September 1939, p. 4.

Vernon Fane. "An Oklahoma Farmer's Fight with Fate." *Sphere* [England], 153 (30 September 1939), 500.

"*The Grapes of Wrath*: John Steinbeck." *Time and Tide* [England], 20 (30 September 1939), 1287.

"Literary Calendar." *Wilson Library Bulletin*, 14 (October 1939), 102.

S.J.K. "Wine Out of These Grapes." *Wilson Library Bulletin*, 14 (October 1939), 165.

"Red Meat and Red Herrings." *Commonweal*, 30 (13 October 1939), 562–3.

"Books of the Day." Southport [England] *Guardian*, 14 October 1939, p. 7.

Richard King. "With Silent Friends." *Tatler* [England], 154 (18 October 1939), 74.

Edgar Bernstein. "An Epic of the Dispossessed." *South African Jewish Times*, 20 October 1939, p. 10.

"Our Bookshelf." *Education* [England], 74 (27 October 1939), 366.

W. E. Cockburn. "Defeating

Depression." Liverpool [England] *Echo*, 28 October 1939, p. 3.

Art Kuhl. "Mostly of *The Grapes of Wrath*." *Catholic World*, 150 (November 1939), 160–5.

Frank J. Taylor. "California's *Grapes of Wrath*." *Forum*, 102 (November 1939), 232–8.

J. H. C. Laker. "Books for Perthshire Readers." Perthshire [Scotland] *Constitutional*, 3 November 1939, p. 11.

"Companionship of Novels." *Times Literary Supplement* [England], 18 November 1939, p. xlix.

Margaret Marshall. "Writers in the Wilderness: I., John Steinbeck." *Nation*, 149 (25 November 1939), 576–9.

Wilfrid Gibson. "Reviewer's Choice." Manchester *Guardian*, 1 December 1929, "Supplement" section, p. iv.

"Reader's Christmas Signpost." *New English Weekly* [England], 16 (14 December 1939), 138.

W.L.A. "News and Views." Yorkshire

[England] *Post*, 29 December 1939, p. 4.

Ralph Straus. "The Year's Fiction." London *Times*, 31 December 1939, p. 5.

Bernard De Voto. "American Novels: 1939." *Atlantic*, 165 (January 1940), 66–74.

Lyle H. Boren. "*The Grapes of Wrath*." *Congressional Record*, 85 (10 January 1940), Part 13, 139–40.

Horace Westwood. "'*The Grapes of Wrath*.'" *Unity*, 124 (5 February 1940), 170–3.

Thomas Quinn Curtiss. "John Steinbeck." *New English Weekly* [England], 16 (21 March 1940), 331–2.

"Wait For the Other Side of the Story." Los Gatos [Calif.] *Times*, 22 March 1940, p. 4.

"Mrs. Roosevelt Tours Mecca of Migrants." New York *Times*, 3 April 1940, p. 25.

Samuel Levenson. "The Compassion of John Steinbeck." *Canadian Forum*, 20 (September 1940), 185–6.

THE FORGOTTEN VILLAGE

The FORGOTTEN VILLAGE

BY ROSA HARVAN KLINE AND ALEXANDER HACKENSMID.

WITH 136 PHOTOGRAPHS FROM THE FILM OF THE SAME NAME

STORY BY JOHN STEINBECK

NEW YORK · 1941 · THE VIKING PRESS

Ralph Thompson.
"Books of the Times."
New York *Times*,
26 May 1941, p. 17.

... *The Forgotten Village* is ... graphic, being in fact 95 per cent stills from a forthcoming documentary film made in Mexico by Herbert Kline, Alexander Hackensmid and associates.

It seems that Mr. Steinbeck wrote the story before anything else was done, and that Mr. Kline (who produced *Crisis* and *Lights Out in Europe*) and a camera crew then went down across the border, found a village to suit the purposes of the script, and began taking pictures. The film is to be released this Autumn, and if it is half as effective on the screen as *The Forgotten Village* is in print, it will be the finest thing of its kind since Eisenstein's *Thunder Over Mexico*.

Magnificent as it was, the Eisenstein had no particular continuity, or at any rate didn't have much of any by the time it was shown to the public. This one will be almost wholly "story," with the so-called documentary detail minor rather than major, and flag-waving and political speech-making left out altogether. In a broad sense, the story is that of Ibsen's *Enemy of the People* retold in terms of the Mexican peon. Specifically, it is an account of a dramatic clash between medical superstition and medical science in an isolated mountain town.

Mr. Steinbeck's sympathetic text runs but a few lines to the page, and serves as captions for the pictures, of which there are 136 in all, reproduced in photogravure.

Richard F. Crandell.
"Steinbeck, Not a Bit
Hard-boiled."
New York *Herald
Tribune*, 1 June 1941,
"Books" section, p. 6.

It is difficult to write on the inside of an eggshell without breaking the egg. So with a man's mind. And his heart. The shell resists men bringing the truth. If a man comes into a small village, one which is everywhere, with the truth, the shell resists and the man, be he a Steinbeck, an Ibsen, a Schick or a Noguchi, must contrive cunningly to get into the shell with the truth.

John Steinbeck tells us this story, a simple little story and one of the most important in the world, of the fight of the Mexican government to bring sanitation into the distant and superstition-ridden villages of our beautiful neighbor of the south. If it inspires only two, or even one, young American doctor to go down and help with this work, it will not have been written in vain.

First he wrote the text, drawing on his travels in untouched Mexican villages. In the little pueblo of Santiago, where the coming of babies and of the corn are the thrilling and important things of life, superstition and death lurk. The water which brings life to the corn brings death to the babies. The charms of the Wise Woman, all the snakeskins and herbs and magic, cannot drive the deadly little animals from polluted water. Children writhe with the stomach pains; their lips are dry, their breath hot. At the funerals mothers are proud and smile at the birth of a new angel, yet their bellies are full of dread.

To illustrate Steinbeck's story of this "Enemy of the People" in the torrid zone thousands of feet of motion pictures were made in the mountain towns, with Mexican Indians taking the parts. From this film 136 still pictures point up the Steinbeck text in the book. Many of them are superb. Agustin Delgado and Filipe Quintanor took the pictures under the direction of Mr. Kline and Alexander Hackensmid. The film itself will be released in the fall with Burgess Meredith as the "voice."

If the stills are indicative of the true merit of the film, it will have high rank in the documentary world. The cameramen for this book have brought out something in these carbon black reproductions that give full credence to the Steinbeck text.

As the camera focuses on Trini, the Wise Woman, looking with fear at the coming of the "horse-blood men," you feel the fear and suspicion of a thousand years of ignorance peering out of those heavy-lidded eyes. These actors are genuine and their sorry problems are translated to film as carefully as Steinbeck fashions his words.

Steinbeck of "the hard-boiled school" drops his guard again in this gatheringly powerful story. With his pen he has gone out to rally help for another bewildered and suffering group of the little people. Increasingly as he calls attention to the Okies, the sufferers of the flats and now the ignorant of rural Mexico, it appears that, far from being "hard-boiled," this writer is a Francis in store-clothes. The "muchas gracias!" of the overworked doctors and nurses of the Mexican rural health service for this gringo visitor and his picture entourage will be more sincere than a thousand phony good-will tours.

"John Steinbeck's Mexican Village." *New York Times Book Review*, 91 (1 June 1941), 8.

This is the book of photographs from Herbert Kline's motion picture of life in a Mexican village, with John Steinbeck's story and explanatory foreword. That it is beautiful and evocative almost goes without saying; but a feature to be pointed out is that, it is a simple transcript of individual reality. As Mr. Steinbeck puts it in his preface, the film's makers reversed the usual process of documentary pictures, and set their suggestion of the general in wholly particular terms. What they—and John Steinbeck in his narrative—show us is one village, one family, one Mexican boy, "who live in the long moment when the past slips reluctantly into the future," and in knowing whom our own minds can take steps to a wider knowledge. . . .

It is a moving, enlightening story, and in its elemental simplicity it shows us, too, the daily pattern of the people's lives: work and festival, field and cottage, joy and sorrow, and birth and death. And as it was photographed in a real village, among the people who really are the "characters" we see, so the pictures are as vitally revealing as they are strong and beautiful. These are the people to whom, in their natural dignity and friendliness and their unbelievable poverty, the new knowledge is bringing change and hope. Even if they cling at first to their age-old spells and fatalisms, there is their own Juan Diego to guide them. They are not forgotten any more.

Joseph Henry Jackson. "The Bookman's Daily Notebook." San Francisco *Chronicle*, 2 June 1941, p. 13.

Something over a year ago John Steinbeck joined forces with Herbert Kline, who made the picture *Lights Out in Europe*, to do a documentary movie about Mexico. Steinbeck wrote the story; Kline photographed it. There are other screen credits and so on, but these apply chiefly to the movie when it is released, which will be some time this autumn.

An offshoot of the picture is what concerns us here. From the 8000 or more feet, 136 stills have been chosen and combined with portions of the Steinbeck text to make a book, just published under the title, *The Forgotten Village*. It is not a major Steinbeck work and is not presented as that. It is an attempt, merely, to tell the story of how, in today's Mexico, the mores of yesterday persist in the face of the knowledge of today. As Steinbeck puts it, this is a tale of "the long moment when the past slips reluctantly into the future."

The scene of the little story is a forgotten village somewhere in Mexico's high mountains. . . .

Plainly, this is a very simple tale, told with a purpose and, naturally, to be written with simplicity and directness. Plainly, too, one's opinion of such a book—a tour de force of a kind must be an opinion on how it is handled rather than a discussion of the subject matter, which is good enough material in itself.

I am sorry to say that it is my opinion that Steinbeck got off on the wrong foot in approaching this whole business and has managed to remain firmly planted on that foot throughout.

In a laudable effort to be simple—like the people about whom he is writing, perhaps—he has gone too far. His mystico-poetical text succeeds only in talking down to the reader. Give it another half inch, and the simple tale would be outright silly. As it is, it's much too close to the border-line for the comfort of any reader who has admired Steinbeck's work in the past.

I have a notion, as it happens, about the reasons for this. Some day a critic will take time to analyze the curious, fatherly-godlike love that Steinbeck manifests for his characters, to examine the chastiseth-whom-he-loveth attitude implicit in so much of Steinbeck's work, the insistent diminishment of his human characters (no, not his turtles) by which the author-creator unconsciously magnifies himself in relation to them.

That, of course, is another matter. It's mentioned here because when that job is done, this *Forgotten Village* will be one of the keys to the puzzle. You have only to read it to see the point. Before you're done, you wonder how these poor, dear idiots Steinbeck describes have managed to survive at all, let alone to produce their several great cultures, to absorb the best conquering Spain could send, to conceive and bear a Juarez, a Cardenas.

In the meantime, this picture-book just won't do. You can say that it's fearfully well meant, if you like, in a wide-eyed sort of way. But that isn't much help.

My suggestion would be just to clear your throat politely, look the other way and pretend that *The Forgotten Village* hadn't been published. Steinbeck has a big book coming this autumn, his *Sea of Cortez*. Whatever it turns out to be like, there'll be something in it to sink your teeth into. And it should be interesting to see what a late-in-life enthusiasm for marine invertebrates (the reason why *Sea of Cortez* came to be written) produces in a writer of Steinbeck's caliber.

"Spring Books."
Time, 37 (2 June 1941), 88.

A picture-textbook heralding a movie made by Steinbeck. Herbert (*Crisis*) Kline and others, in rural Mexico. Steinbeck's story—medicine *v.* magic for sick children—has warm beauty; so have the peasant actors. But his skilfully timed script sometimes goes pseudo-Biblical.

"Brief Mention."
New Yorker, 17
(7 June 1941), 77–8.

The Forgotten Village, story by John Steinbeck, photographs by Rosa Harvan Kline and Alexander Hackensmid. Mr. Steinbeck's first book since *The Grapes of Wrath* [is] a dramatic documentary narrative in pictures and captions, showing how the conflict between a traditional Indian healer and the government's men of science impinged on one family during a typhoid epidemic in a remote Mexican village. With very few exceptions, the numerous photographs—stills from a motion picture written by Mr. Steinbeck, directed by Herbert Kline, and acted by Mexican villagers against their own background—are lustrous and handsomely composed. One of the better picture books. . . .

Edwin Seaver.
"Books."
Direction, 4
(Summer 1941), 41.

Presentation of a film, in the form of a book, this story of one family in a Mexican village comes as near achieving great art as any documentary book we have yet examined. Stills run through the book as an organic part of its make-up, *bleeding* through each page, the accompanying text neither too long nor too short (as is often the case with such treatment). The effect produced transcends the simple facts of medical services finally reaching a village where natives still lived under the spell of a "medicine" woman. It becomes symbolic of the whole streaming of life, from the old to the new, from tradition-bound fear to hope in the future.

"The Forgotten Village."
Booklist, 37
(1 July 1941), 513.

The introduction of medical science into a remote Mexican village, and the opposition of frightened, superstitious natives, told in fine photographs and brief text.

Margaret Marshall.
"*The Forgotten Village.*"
Nation, 153
(12 July 1941), 36.

Philip T. Hartung.
"*The Forgotten Village.*"
Commonweal, 34
(25 July 1941), 329–30.

The Forgotten Village..., another picture book, concentrates on one remote pueblo in Mexico. It consists of 136 stills from a motion picture made by Herbert Kline and Alexander Hackensmid with a script by John Steinbeck. A Mexican boy, Juan Diego, is the central character. The story tells of an epidemic that strikes the village and of the struggle between old magic and new medicine for the minds and bodies of the villagers. It is a dramatic narrative in pictures with the natives as actors. In the end the doctors are driven out by the villagers under the sway of the Wise Woman and her spells. Juan himself is turned away from his father's house for going over to the "poisoners," who have put white powder in the well and tried to inject horses' blood into the children, and is taken to Mexico City by his new friends to go to school and learn how to help his people. Mr. Kline has caught the feeling of Mexico, with its thick undergrowth of ignorance and superstition and its thin layer of modernity. He has even managed to convey, as few photographers of Mexico do or care to do, the squalor and dirt. As a result the reality comes through—and the reality of Mexico is far more moving than any soap-and-water interpretation. The writing is typical Steinbeck—eloquent and sentimental but suited to the subject.

You can read *The Forgotten Village* in a half hour. But for a much longer time you will study its 136 photographs and contemplate its message. In the narrow sense, it is a tale of the little pueblo of Santiago in Mexico and the story of a boy and his family and people, "who live in the long moment when the past slips reluctantly into the future." In a broader sense it is the story of modern Mexico with the clash between medicine and magic used as a symbol....

John Steinbeck, temporarily forsaking the hard-boiled writing and editorializing of *The Grapes of Wrath*, uses a straightforward, simple narrative style that is an excellent complement to the beautiful photographs of Rosa Harvan Kline and Alexander Hackensmid. If the purpose of this book is to whet our appetites for the forthcoming film, *The Forgotten Village*, for which this Steinbeck prose is the script and from which these photographs are taken, it most assuredly succeeds in this intention. However, the evocative book stands on its own merits as an interesting sociological study and as a revealing picture of renascent Mexico.

Barker Fairley.
"Books of the Month:
Symbolisms."
Canadian Forum, 21
(August 1941), 153–4.

It isn't easy to say in a word who is the author of this volume. It is made up of one hundred and thirty-six photographs from a not yet released motion picture directed by Herbert Kline, depicting life in a Mexican village and bearing the same name as the book, along with story or letter-press by John Steinbeck.

Thus the authorship is mixed, but the book will probably rank as another Steinbeck, because Steinbeck is the contributor we are most likely to be curious about. Those who know Steinbeck well enough are eager to know in what direction he is travelling as a socialist or leftish writer. Has he withdrawn or come further into the open? Is he becoming more modern or less?

The book leaves you in this respect where you were before. Reading and looking at its pages the whole thing seems at first a bit romantic and makes you suspect Steinbeck of yielding once more to his weaker tendencies. The plot turns on a clash between superstition— in the form of the local wise woman who "cures" children with charms—and emancipation—represented by the progressive young Mexicans who believe in modern medicine. It all seems not quite contemporary, since this is not, for us, an acute phase of the social problem. On the whole—except for holes and corners— modern medicine has won out.

Nevertheless the final impression of the book is more actual than its plot suggests. The struggle with the wise woman becomes symbolical of all the struggle and it is made very real by being concentrated in one person—Juan Diego, who leaves the village for the first time and goes to the city and sees for himself. It is above all this "concreteness" which seems to pull the book over into today. It remains to be seen whether the film will bear out the impression. Certainly the book gives it strongly. . . .

Remembering his use of the Joad family in *The Grapes of Wrath* it begins to look, after all, as if Steinbeck had had a major hand in the book—and the film too.

Checklist of Additional Reviews

Lewis Gannett. "Books and Things." New York *Herald Tribune*, 27 May 1941, p. 23.

SEA OF CORTEZ

Sea of Cortez

*A LEISURELY JOURNAL OF TRAVEL
AND RESEARCH*

WITH A SCIENTIFIC APPENDIX
COMPRISING MATERIALS FOR A SOURCE BOOK
ON THE MARINE ANIMALS
OF THE PANAMIC FAUNAL PROVINCE

BY

John Steinbeck

AND

Edward F. Ricketts

NEW YORK

THE VIKING PRESS

1941

Charles Poore.
"Books of the Times."
New York *Times*,
5 December 1941, p. 21.

There is an elusive analogy between the work of Steinbeck and the work of Hemingway that continues this morning with the publication of *Sea of Cortez*.

It is a matter of linked opposites as much as it is a matter of similarities. The impact of *The Grapes of Wrath* and *For Whom the Bell Tolls* may have been similar; the contents were different enough. Yet both men like to fight for people who need help in their battles.

Both turn naturally to Hispanic themes: the one in Mexico, the other in Spain. Both have tried their hands at making what are rather sententiously called "documentary" films: *The Spanish Earth* and *Forgotten Village*. When the Pulitzer laurelers give a prize to one of them, it causes almost as much excitement as when they withhold it from the other.

Both like to go on safaris: the one for pure science, the other for pure pleasure. Though there are elements of the opposite, again, in each case. (Compare Steinbeck on trying to harpoon a giant manta ray with Hemingway on the picador's technique.)

And both have written books about their expeditions (made "patterns" of them as both specifically say): *The Green Hills of Africa* and *Sea of Cortez*. Which brings us back to the main subject of today's column.

I shouldn't have said that Mr. Steinbeck had written *Sea of Cortez* because he didn't write it alone. He wrote it in collaboration with Edward F. Ricketts, who is director of the Pacific Biological Laboratories. Mr. Steinbeck and Mr. Ricketts together went on the expedition into the lonely, treacherous and amazing Gulf of California—once called the Sea of Cortez—to study and collect innumerable specimens of the marine life there, and together they wrote this book. You aren't allowed to know who wrote which line, though you may have your suspicions. Instead, you are told from time to time that "one of us" had this characteristic and "one of us" did that, which creates a curiously amalgamated joint personality.

This joint personality has a notable gift for writing with vigor, relish and precision on practically any subject you might care to bring up. And a lively diversity of subjects—sacred, scientific and profane— were brought up on board the seventy-six-foot *Western Flyer* in the course of those six weeks of scientific voyaging in the Spring of 1940.

Marine life was the object of the expedition. Marine life scrupulously studied is the subject of the book. Marine life seethes through its pages in impressive classifications and compilations whose value in filling gaps in the knowledge of Gulf fauna is apparent. But there are also helpful notations on life at large.

While still emphasizing the primary scientific importance of the book, we might notice a few of these. Speaking of the modern thrill-seeker, they—Mr. Steinbeck and Mr. Ricketts—suggest that "it is possible that his ancestor, wearying of the humdrum attacks of the sabertooth, longed for the good old days of pterodactyl and triceratops." Of the mule they sagely observe that "he knows he can out think a horse and he is pretty sure he can out-think a human. In both respects he is correct."

And describing the time that a member of the crew who shirked his part in dishwashing was drastically punished by having all the dirty dishes on the boat piled in his bunk, they say of the broken man: "Some joyous light had gone out of him, and he never did get the catsup out of his blankets."

They go rather weightily into such matters as teleology, early race memories, taboos and war. They have interesting things to say in condemnation of the mosquito and in praise of beer and laziness. They make a superb running narrative out of the day-to-day activities and discussions of the expedition, and while playing down their own characters make great characters out of the members of the crew. . . .

Mr. Steinbeck and Mr. Ricketts have written one of the most unusual books of the year, and their publishers deserve some praise for having given it such an effective embodiment. Putting all this material together coherently must have seemed, in the early stages, only slightly less difficult than building Boulder Dam.

Clifton Fadiman. "Books." New Yorker, 17 (6 December 1941), 107–8.

John Steinbeck, the novelist who doubles in biology, and Edward F. Ricketts, a scientist, chartered the ship *Western Flyer* (76 feet, Diesel engine) in March, 1940, and set out on a six weeks' trip along the shores of the Gulf of California. The objective was to collect, preserve, and classify as many of the marine invertebrates of the littoral as were amenable to such collection, preservation, and classification. Mr. Steinbeck came back not only with his specimens floating in alcohol but with a flock of general ideas floating in his mind. The result is a book, *Sea of Cortez*, a prettier name for the Gulf of California. The title page says it was written by Mr. Steinbeck and Mr. Ricketts, but I think we may safely assume that Mr. Ricketts contributed some of the biology and Mr. Steinbeck all of the prose. Like each of the rest of his books (except, I suppose, the first), it is a complete departure from the previous one.

Perhaps, however, it isn't so much of a departure at that. In a brilliant essay, Edmund Wilson recently interpreted Steinbeck as a biological novelist, one whose vision of life derives from his sensitivity to its animal manifestations. This would explain why Steinbeck writes even better about beasts than about men. It also explains that curious detachment which, despite the warmth of his social sympathies, prevents him from being ticketed as a propaganda novelist.

Sea of Cortez would seem to drive home Wilson's thesis to the hilt. It was obviously written not merely to tell us— and interestingly, too—about how the marine invertebrates of the Panamic faunal province are killed, preserved, labelled, and classified. Nor was it written as a simple narrative of the small adventures, many of them quite comical, that befell the crew on the expedition. It was written primarily to explain Steinbeck's view of life and mode of thinking.

Steinbeck is an intellectual anti-isolationist. He is interested in interrelationships. His aim, whether as novelist in *The Grapes of Wrath* or as amateur philosopher in *Sea of Cortez*, is to arrive at the total pattern—he calls it the "design"— of any experience. Anyone interested in total pattern is apt to be amoral in his judgments, for all moral judgments proceed out of the isolation of experience, the statement "*This* is more important or more valuable than *that*." Thus, Steinbeck is anti-teleological in his thinking, as all good biologists should be; his eye is on the thing as it is, not on the thing as it should be. This is-thinking, as Steinbeck calls it, means to him what the killing of large animals does to Hemingway. It has religious, even mystical overtones for him, overtones that may be inaudible to other ears. It makes him aware not only of the ecological connection between man and the Lightfoot crab but of the evolutionary relationship. His mind is attuned to the survivals in us of previous existences. He believes in biological memory (more than a trace of Jung here), and some of the finest passages in the book have to do with atavism in man. . . .

The scientific supplement to the book contains an annotated phyletic catalogue, eight pages of color plates, sixteen pages of drawings, sixteen pages of photographs, and two isothermic charts. All very forbidding and scientific, and calculated to increase our awe of Mr. Steinbeck.

Beth Ingels.
"*Sea of Cortez* New Picture of Steinbeck."
Monterey [Calif.]
Peninsula Herald,
6 December 1941, p. 2.

Out of the pages of *The Sea of Cortez* slowly emerges a picture of John Steinbeck, the man. He has been shown in other works as the novelist, the playwright, the reformer, but here, for the first time, is a picture of the man who in a few years . . . became one of America's more important writers, if not the most important.

Careful readers will find some of the reasons for Steinbeck's literary stature in *The Sea of Cortez*. They will find one of them to be his enormous curiosity about everything—from sea-life to William Randolph Hearst—and his thoughts and reflections on a thousand and one subjects undoubtedly raise heated arguments from here to Portland, Maine.

Written in collaboration with Edward Ricketts of the Pacific Biological Laboratories in New Monterey, the book is ostensibly an account of a voyage taken by the two men and their crew on a chartered purse seiner down the coast to the Gulf of Lower California for the purpose of collecting and classifying marine specimens.

But the actual trip, amusingly recounted, is merely an excuse to express the combined ideas of two men who for many years have shared their efforts to find the basic truths in all aspects of life.

The result is one of the most unusual books ever published in this country. Its keynote is Ricketts "non-teleological" thinking, and evolving from that idea comes a lucid account of the processes of the minds of two extremely intelligent and sensitive men.

In the course of the book it becomes obvious where Steinbeck leaves off and Ricketts begins. Sometimes it is at the beginning of a chapter, other times in the middle of a paragraph, but always the contrast in both the style of writing and ideas of each is there. Often the change is so definite as to be startling, almost shocking. Each man is tops in his own way, but where one is impulsive, sympathetic and gloriously human, the other is a scientist who builds up his ideas in cold, mathematical intensity.

Steinbeck's short chapter on ships and men is one that won't be quickly forgotten. The beauty of the words and emotions in that piece of writing make it a classic of its kind.

"This strange identification of man with

boat is so complete that probably no man has ever destroyed a boat by bomb or torpedo or shell without murder in his heart.... Only the trait of murder which our species seems to have could allow us the sick, exultant sadness of sinking a ship, for we can murder the things we love best, which are, of course, ourselves."

Half of the book is given over to photograph reproductions and drawings of specimens collected on the voyage, and [to] a complete indexing of them by Ricketts. For marine biological students and scientists, this catalogue should prove invaluable, for it is the most complete ever attempted for the tidal regions covered by this expedition.

The sketches of specimens which could not be photographed were done by Albert Spratt of Carmel. The unusually beautiful color photographs are by Russell Cummings of Pacific Grove, and through an unfortunate publisher's oversight, he was not given by-line credit for them. He is mentioned, however, in the acknowledgment. Other photographs were provided by professionals.

The book, naturally, will cause a great deal of comment. What Steinbeck book does not? But all in all, I believe it to be one of the most exciting and diverting books, in thought and text, that has ever come off an American press.

Of interest to all, but particularly to Monterey readers, will be the account of the trip from the day the charter was signed, the crew assembled, the good-byes said at the old wharf. The crew consisted of Sparky Enea, Ratzi Colleto, Tex Travis and Tony Berry. These men are used as characters throughout the book, while the principals—the writers—are never mentioned by name. The closest identification comes with an account of one of the experiences of "the bearded one."

Humour, both obvious and subtle,

runs through the book in surprising fashion—surprising because, almost in the midst of an erudite observation on the Madonna in the church at Loreto, will come a tale of the exploits of a crew member, Rabelaisian or otherwise. The description and subsequent stories about the "Hansen Sea Cow," the perverse outboard motor, cannot fail to delight all readers, whether or not they are familiar with the variables of such a piece of machinery....

Howard N. Doughty, Jr. "John Steinbeck's Fine Biological Notebook." New York *Herald Tribune*, 7 December 1941, "Books" section, p. 3.

The Sea of Cortez is the Gulf of California, and John Steinbeck and Edward Ricketts went there on a six weeks' cruise to study the gulf fauna and collect specimens. Their boat, the *Western Flyer*, was a charted sardine seiner, manned by a crew of four—Tony, the skipper, quiet, cautious, dry-witted, a hater of variables; Sparky and Tiny, inseparable "bad Boys" from Monterey, whose steering was one of the variables Tony most hated; Tex, the engineer, master mechanic and, recalcitrantly, master dish-washer. Steinbeck (with Ricketts checking the facts) has recounted the voyage of their floating laboratory in a book that is at once a biologist's report and a record of impressions and ideas. The purely scientific data are relegated to an appendix, together with 100 black-and-white photographs and fifteen colored plates. The rest of the book is for the general reader.

And an attractive book the general reader will find it—the holiday book of a person doing something he likes and enjoying it thoroughly. Marine biology is Steinbeck's hobby; his passion for it is contagious. He liked working till he was dog tired, collecting all day and sorting and pickling in the evening. He liked the sea creatures whose lives and habits the expedition had come to study. He liked the gulf region, isolated, primitive, remote from the complexities of industrial civilization. Of all these things, the day's work, the people and scenery of the gulf, the swarming life of the tide-line, he writes with sensitive precision. *Sea of Cortez* is a fine-flavored sketch of travel and biological field work....

Steinbeck had a good time. But *Sea of Cortez* is not only the pleasant record of a scientific outing. It is also the notebook of John Steinbeck, author of *In Dubious Battle* and *The Grapes of Wrath*, and a reading of it gives one a deepened insight into the nature and quality of Steinbeck's work as a writer. It is no accident that Steinbeck is a biologist. As Edmund Wilson has pointed out, a substratum of biology runs through all his novels and stories: a reaching down past human beings to more rudimentary forms of life, a preoccupation with fundamental life processes as such. He chooses primitive or "backward" types for characters in his fiction, not simply out of sympathy for the underdog, but because in them the basic biologic urges are more directly felt and more directly perceptible. In *Sea of Cortez* he is able to dispense with human beings altogether and enter a world where life, uncomplicated by thought, is lived in fullest urgency solely for its own sake.... "Life has one final end, to be alive." It is the spectacle of this abounding biological activity, free of the dis-

guises with which human consciousness clothes it, that for Steinbeck gave ultimate meaning to the trip....

Scott Newhall. "John Steinbeck's Chioppino of Biology and Philosophy." San Francisco *Chronicle*, 14 December 1941, *This World* magazine, p. 26.

John Steinbeck, of course, can write a great novel. But *Sea of Cortez* is by no means a work of fiction. Rather it is a sort of chioppino of travel, biology and philosophy.

A year and a half ago, Mr. Steinbeck, Mr. Ricketts and a crew of four—Tony, Tiny, Sparky and Tex—sailed from Monterey for the Gulf of California. For six weeks they were to collect and preserve the marine invertebrates which infest the tidal sands of the Gulf coast.

When the party returned they had collected 550 different species, they had consumed 45 cases of beer and the two leaders of the expedition each had enough information to write half a book. Mr. Ricketts was to assemble the biological information gathered during the trip; Mr. Steinbeck was to help collect and label, to observe the country, and then after speculation, to translate the meaning of the expedition for the lay mind. This review is concerned with the first half of the book, Mr. Steinbeck's.

Certainly, *Sea of Cortez* is far from Steinbeck at his ablest. This is probably because he has subordinated his very real ability as a writer to his desire to be first a philosopher, and second a naturalist. . . .

In attempting to write a book about anything so prosaic as voyaging to the Gulf of California, or so disciplined as collecting biological specimens, or so confusing as philosophical speculation, John Steinbeck accepted perhaps a far greater challenge than even he realized. He may not have lost the battle, but at least he is badly battered. He becomes inaccurate when he dogmatically states that Padre Clavigero visited the peninsula of Lower California, he is out of date when he illustrates a scientific principle by referring to the ancient decommissioned liner *Majestic* and he is simply small-boy vulgar when he reports on Tiny's collection of Phthirius pubis.

It is unfortunate that John Steinbeck should write anything but a very good book. But, of course, any great writer faces that trap. And it is only fair to report that parts of *Sea of Cortez* come much closer to what the author can really do.

Who else could so understand and admire the small fry of Mexico? Who could speculate better whether "a nation, governed by the small boys of Mexico, would not be a better, happier country than those ruled by old men, whose prejudices may or may not be conditioned by ulcerous stomachs . . ."?

Who else could have appreciated the terrible moral decay eating into the expedition, when one of the party succumbed to the perfidy of stealing slices of lemon pie and devouring them in bed after the lights were out?

It's just too bad that the whole of Mr. Steinbeck's half is not as good. That all of it is not of the same stuff as the following communique:

"On the beach at San Lucas there is a war between the pigs and the vultures. Sometimes one side dominates and sometimes the other. On occasion the swine feel a dynamism and demand Lebensraum, and in the pride of their species drive the vultures from the decaying offal. And again, when their thousand years of history is over, the vultures spring to arms, tear up treaties, and flap the pigs from the garbage. And on the beach there are certain skinny dogs, without any dynamisms whatsoever and without racial pride, who nevertheless manage to get the best snacks."

Joel W. Hedgpeth. "The Scientific Second Half of the *Sea of Cortez*." *San Francisco Chronicle*, 14 December 1941, *This World* magazine, p. 26.

To the general reader, lured this far by the narrative part of the book, the second half of the *Sea of Cortez*, may seem a wilderness of uncouth nomenclature and meticulous minutiae, leavened somewhat by a generous section of photographs and drawings of some of the commoner animals. To the marine biologist, however, this is the important part of the book, for these seemingly unpronounceable names and the annotated bibliographies which accompany them are signposts and traveling directions for one of the world's most interesting faunal provinces, and this appendix will hereafter be indispensable for students of the marine invertebrates of the Gulf of California.

The authors make no pretense that

this annotated list is complete, but prefer to call it "a scientific appendix comprising materials for a source book on the marine animals of the Panamic faunal province." The same careful searching of the literature (as the technical papers are capriciously called) and consultations with specialists which made *Between Pacific Tides* so valuable a book are evident in this work, and it may in some ways be considered a complementary volume to *Between Pacific Tides.* Indeed, the revised edition of the latter book may include cross references to *Sea of Cortez*. It is no reflection upon the authors but upon our incomplete and haphazard knowledge of the fauna of our own backyard that the first general account of this fauna is not much more than an outline.

Although restricted principally to the littoral fauna of the Gulf of California during a period of six weeks, over 500 species of animals were collected, a far better record than that made by several more formal and handsomely endowed expeditions which have invaded the region. The echinoderms, larger mollusks and crabs are especially well represented and a fair collection of shore fishes was also made. There are omissions, inevitable because of the limitations of time and energy as well as the scarcity of good papers on certain groups. The limitation to a single short collecting season may account for the interesting failure to collect any sea spiders, as well as for other less obvious gaps in the collections. The sea anemones are omitted entirely from the appendix although frequently mentioned in the narrative, and several other groups are touched but lightly, yet on the whole the authors have succeeded in the intention of producing a source book rather than a handbook.

Popular accounts of expeditions have long been staple reading fare, but the actual results have too often been lost in the dusty tomes of libraries and museum cubbyholes. This is the first large-scale attempt to include both phases of this particular sort of human activity in one volume, and it would be interesting, if it were possible, to learn what influence this book may have on the development or formation of coming generations of biologists. Certainly no reader can look at this appendix and still entertain the delusion that a scientific expedition is nothing more than an affair of moonlit nights and enraptured contemplation of new and strange animals, a delusion that Dr. Beebe has done little to dispel. Not that scientific expeditions are devoid of their romantic moments, but such popularization has all too often prevented the reader from realizing the vast amount of work yet to be done to bring together and correlate the widely scattered information in order that it may assume its proper place in our knowledge. Neither John Steinbeck nor Edward Ricketts believe that the study of biology, especially the amazingly varied and complex life of the tidal regions, should be the exclusive fare of indefatigable museum drones, and that conviction is the inspiration of *Sea of Cortez*, enlivening even the remoter sections of the technical appendix.

Charles Curtis Munz. "Fishing Trip." *Nation*, 153 (20 December 1941), 647.

In the spring of 1940, about the time that the war was passing from phoniness to reality, Mr. Steinbeck and Mr. Ricketts did what practically everybody would like to do at one time or another—as the time honored phrase has it, they got away from it all. They chartered a seventy-six-foot fishing boat with a crew of four and set out for a six weeks' expedition to the Gulf of California, which was once called by the more romantic name of the Sea of Cortez because the conqueror of Mexico was instrumental in having it discovered and explored. Naturally no American would dare to set out on an expedition like this for the pure fun of it, and so Messrs. Steinbeck and Ricketts also had a scientific purpose— they would collect marine fauna on the gulf's littoral. With becoming modesty, however, the authors confess that their expedition was something of a makeshift. They collected a great many specimens, to be sure, but it would appear that they were less interested in the specimens than in the fun of collecting them.

This book is a leisurely journal of the expedition. The authors maintain a rather curious joint personality; so that it is difficult or impossible to tell when Steinbeck leaves off and when Ricketts begins. There are a few passages that must be almost pure Steinbeck, and a few that are perhaps pure Ricketts, but for the most part the book is written in a combination prose—possibly it would be more exact to say a compromise prose— that throws off few sparks and is hardly adequate to the occasion. The expedition must have been more exciting than this account of it would indicate.

An important contributing reason for the lack of communicated excitement is that the authors have seen fit to drag in a great many Reflections on Life. Thus the reader will be enjoying the chase of *Tethys* the sea-hare when all of a sudden he will find himself becalmed in a soupy discussion of teleology. Most readers, one suspects, will prefer *Tethys* the sea-hare.

The book contains a great number of illustrations, drawings and photographs, and a specific appendix.

"Artist in Wonderland." *Time*, 38 (22 December 1941), 64.

Novelist John Steinbeck and his biologist friend, Director Edward F. Ricketts of the Pacific Biological Laboratories, decided to make an expedition to the Gulf of California, Mexico's long Pacific arm which used to be called the Sea of Cortez. They wanted to find out all they could about the sea creatures, especially the teeming invertebrates along the shores—how they changed in numbers, size, form from place to place, how they lived, loved, ate, fought, fled, hid, died.

Their itinerary lay down a thousand miles of Lower California coast, around Cape San Lucas and up into the gulf of treacherous repute. They collected fish, snails, crabs, sea worms, sea cucumbers, sea cradles, sea urchins, sea hares, starfish, octopi, mussels, anemones, shrimps, limpets, conches, sponges, hundreds of other creatures with fancy Latin names. Although they were not looking for rarities, about 10% of their 550 species proved to be new. They were stung by urchins, morays, anemones, sting-rays, and stinging worms. Their hands, cut by barnacles, became first a welter of sores and then horny-callused. They caught and ate tuna, skipjack and sierra, tried unsuccessfully to eat a turtle; they drank beer and whiskey; they bathed by jumping over the side; they had a wonderful time.

Steinbeck bathed, too, in a heady stream of life-force. At Cape San Lucas he observed that the rocks were "ferocious with life.... Perhaps the force of the great surf which beats on this shore has much to do with the tenacity of the animals here. It is noteworthy that the animals, rather than deserting such beaten shores for the safe cove and protected pools, simply increase their toughness and fight back at the sea with a kind of joyful survival. This ferocious survival quotient excites us and makes us feel good, and from the crawling, fighting, resisting qualities of the animals, it almost seems that they are excited too."

The leaping tuna and the frolicking dolphins were beautiful, but to Steinbeck all the animals, even the repulsive ones, were beautiful with life. As he traces the interaction of men and animals there is never the slightest hint that men might be "superior."

Everywhere Steinbeck finds atavistic hints and murmurs which carry men far back into their brute heritage. When he uses such phrases as "the deep black water of the human spirit" he sounds like D. H. Lawrence, as he does in his subhuman enchantments. Yet Lawrence's animal-love was a negation, a retreat from human modes of thinking and acting; Steinbeck's is an inclusion. Steinbeck also enjoys the syllogisms of philosophers and the constructions of theoretical physicists—it is all right, all part of life.

William Beebe.
"Sea of Cortez."
Saturday Review, 24
(27 December 1941), 5–7.

This six-hundred page book is the joint work of the learned Edward F. Ricketts, author of that excellent manual of marine biology *Between Pacific Tides* (which stands on my science reference shelf here in Santa Barbara), and of boisterous novelist John Steinbeck, author, if you happen to recall, of *Tortilla Flat*, *The Grapes of Wrath*, and *Of Mice and Men*. And presumably it is going to be enjoyed by three sorts of people: first, those who will read anything that Steinbeck writes, no matter what it's about; secondly, that more limited group who want to learn more about the tunicates, ascidians, holothurians, arthropods, echinoderms, coelenterates, porifera, and chordates of the Gulf of California—no matter who writes it. To this, add a third class who are definitely interested in almost anything about Mexico and might well prefer to have the versatile Mr. Steinbeck write it. These will be able to travel, in their arm-chairs, to one of the most unvisited and inaccessible parts of our nearest Latin-American neighbor, where Steinbeck and Ricketts went in the modest little fishing boat *Western Flyer* to collect marine animals and new impressions....

As soon as an American discovers such a place, whether in Bali, the Marquesas, Tibet, or Tepoztlan, he writes a come-hither book about it. And next year we send an Expeditionary Force of our citizens who want to tread the holy ground where Americans have never yet set their heels....

Baja California is definitely doomed, as of December, 1941, on which date Messrs. Ricketts and Steinbeck published their alluring book. I regard it as a departure date fateful not only in the sociology of this state, but in the literary career of Mr. Steinbeck. For he certainly never wrote a book like this before. In fact nobody has done so. In its content it will stagger the Steinbeck fans. Which one of them expected him to indulge in a long self-argument on teleological thought (heresy to the scientist, ortho-doxy to the divinity student) exactly as if his habitual admirers were of the mental stamp of St. Augustine or President Hutchins? The Steinbeck imagined by la-dies who keep bookstores in Connecticut villages, and by middle-aged men who have to read *Esquire* in the barber's chair because they don't dare bring it home, are going to revise their notions of a man whose tears for humanity come out as sweat on his brow, when they find him floundering in tidal pools of the mys-terious Gulf of California, dredging with bleeding hands in order to capture tropi-cal sea worms that sting like hell, and turn to ink and stink before you can pop them in mortician's solutions. Those who want to hear how many bad words this boy from the Lettuce Belt of Salinas, California, has learned from the naughty little Mexican boys born within whiff of the Monterey fish canneries, will find here 250 pages or about 100,000 words of an Annotated Phyletic Catalogue of the marine life of this memorable cruise. . . .

But the colleagues of the learned Mr. Ricketts will find out something they didn't know about him, either, I bet. They will learn that he and his five com-panions of the six weeks cruise of *The Western Flyer*, consumed 2,160 quarts of beer, and unspecified or uncounted quan-tities of whisky. They will find that he either wrote, or concurred in . . . reflec-tions on aphrodisiacs. . . .

. . . The two utterly disparate sections of the book are not assigned to separate authorship. The title page claims shared collaboration between these two unex-pected friends, presumably on all parts of the book. I find nothing inconceivable about an artist taking a distinct interest in the niceties of systematic zoölogy; and not every scientist is foe to beauty, censor of nonsense, chaste in all his thoughts, and sober on both sides.

There can't be a doubt, for instance, that Ricketts has opened Steinbeck's eyes to the rewards and delights of Natural History, or that he has earnestly and meticulously coached him in scientific thought—habits and viewpoints. He has given his ebullient friend a biological phi-losophy—the best kind a man can have, to my way of thinking, the most real-istic, and yet the kindest. Mr. Steinbeck appears to have discovered it only yester-day, in its full implications and deep per-spectives, and he is wildly excited about it. He runs up and down the echoing cor-ridors, paced by Aristotle, Lucretius, Goethe, and the Huxley boys, each in their day, turning cart-wheels of mental liberation from Final Causes, shouting at the marble walls, enchanted by the echoes that they throw back of his own voice, and stopping, sometimes, to whistle through his teeth at the scholastic dignitaries. . . .

Ricketts (or is it Steinbeck?) has dis-covered that you can argue along about a school of tuna fish, and the glandular, psychical, evolutionary, or ecological rea-sons why sardines, who travel in schools, vary so little, even in the normal speed-capacity of their locomotion—and then suddenly switch over to humans, and see why men who go to certain schools, as Harvard, Yale, and Stanford, differ so little from each other "in speech, cloth-ing, haircuts, posture, or state of mind." From here it is but a short step to some reflections on the Collectivist State and to speculations on the probable effect it will have, through Natural Selection, on the human species. There are hundreds of pages of this, in fact; the authors find a hundred sermons in barnacles, and books in sea-urchins.

Frankly, I would say that about one-tenth of this rabbit-out-of-hatting would have sufficed this reader. It is done with versatility, with nimbleness, with humor, sometimes eloquence; but we do, some of us, know how the trick is performed. That to perform it is the chief aim of biological field work, in the Gulf of California or elsewhere, or of Nature writing or popularization, some of us would not admit. Probably the authors would agree; but they seem to think this is what the public expects of them, or of Nature for Victorian audiences.

Either Steinbeck or Ricketts (or all-two-both-of-them) is—are?—potentially a great poet, or poets, of Nature. The grandest passages in this strange bargain-buy of two full-length books under one cover (but for the price of two) are some of the descriptions of the sea, the tide, mirages, wind or dead calm, Indians, tidal pools, or simply night, or dawn, or the barking of a dog, or loneliness on a hot and empty shore. Style, reality, *Stimmung*, at these moments, all deepen and intone. More of this, and less sheer cleverness will make somebody, whichever he is, a writer as lasting in the future as he is brilliant today.

Checklist of Additional Reviews

Eugene D. Hart. "*Sea of Cortez.*" *Library Journal*, 66 (15 October 1941), 903.

John Chamberlain. "The New Books." *Harper's*, 184 (December 1941), advertisement section, n.p.

"Voyage for Fun and Fauna." *Newsweek*, 18 (8 December 1941), 75–6.

Harry Hansen. "The First Reader." Norfolk [Va.] *Pilot*, 9 December 1941, p. 6.

Sterling North. "Jap Shrimp Fishers Most Dangerous Form of Sea Life, Steinbeck Reveals." Chicago *News*, 10 December 1941, p. 28.

"Steinbeck Writes of Gulf of California." Boston *Herald*, 10 December 1941, p. 14.

R. L. Duffus. "John Steinbeck Makes an Excursion." *New York Times Book Review*, 91 (28 December 1941), 3.

"*Sea of Cortez.*" *Booklist*, 38 (1 January 1942), 153–4.

Harold D. Carew. "In the Sea of Cortez." Pasadena [Calif.] *Star-News*, 24 January 1942, p. 18.

Stanley Edgar Hyman. "Of Invertebrates and Men." *New Republic*, 106 (16 February 1942), 242–4.

THE MOON IS DOWN (THE NOVEL)

THE MOON
IS DOWN

A NOVEL

By John Steinbeck

NEW YORK : THE VIKING PRESS : MCMXLII

Frances Alter Boyle.
"*The Moon Is Down*."
Library Journal, 67
(15 February 1942), 182.

Quisling has done his fifth column work so well that the little coal mining seaport is invaded with the loss of only six lives. The insoluble problem for the Nazis is to police the village and secure the good will of the inhabitants, so that the coal can be mined and transported to the Reich. Excellent psychological study, recommended for purchase. . . .

L.A.S.
"Masters of Their Fate."
Christian Science Monitor,
6 March 1942, p. 22.

Like *Of Mice and Men*, John Steinbeck's new book, *The Moon Is Down* . . . is a short novel written in the form of a play. And like the former book, it will be transferred to the stage (on March 31) with little alteration.

The Moon Is Down will have a wider appeal than its predecessor in this form. Its theme is both topical and universal; dealing with the resistance of the people of a small invaded country to their conquerors, it sings the unconquerable courage and strength of liberty-loving human hearts. . . .

There are some superb character sketches: the gentle, scholarly mayor of the occupied town; his friend the doctor; his defiant cook who throws hot water over the soldiers tramping mud into her kitchen; the young widow who avenges her slain husband; the boys who flee to England to carry on the fight.

These on the defenders' side. On the other no less vivid portraits: the popular storekeeper who turns out to be an enemy agent; the invader officers, sharply differentiated in background and character, but all dominated by the totalitarian philosophy to which they have been bred.

Deliberately, inevitably, the denouement comes: It is the invaders, not the invaded, whose morale cracks. In the end the mayor goes out to execution, quoting Socrates' last words, "Crito, I owe a cock to Asclepius; will you remember to pay the debt?" And the doctor replies, "The debt shall be paid." If the individual perishes, the people live.

The book is beautifully written, with restraint, dignity, humor, and calm conviction. The style fits the matter in its Apollonian simplicity and purity. The drama is in the events, and there is no theatricalism of language. A masterpiece in little.

Clifton Fadiman.
"Two Ways to Win
the War."
New Yorker, 18
(7 March 1942), 52.

For all its qualities, John Steinbeck's *The Moon Is Down* strikes me as unsatisfactory on two counts. Its form is deceiving and its message is inadequate.

The publishers, presumably with the author's knowledge, call it a novel. At the most lavish estimate, the story hardly runs beyond forty thousand words, all quite short and simple words, too. Many current novels, it may be argued, would gain by reduction to forty thousand words, but it does not follow that forty thousand words make up a current novel. I fear *The Moon Is Down* is a novel only in a Steinbeckian sense.

The deception, however, goes deeper. The fact is that Mr. Steinbeck's book is not a narrative at all but a play equipped with a few casual disguises. The entire construction is dramatic. The dialogue is play dialogue, not novel dialogue (and there is a sharp difference); the whole affair settles naturally into scenes and acts. It reads well but it plays much better than it reads, and you're apt to find yourself puzzled, as you turn the pages, by the absence of footlights. Indeed, I feel strongly that a dramatic critic would be far better equipped to review the book and that it has strayed into these columns through some error. Come to think of it, Mr. Steinbeck's *Of Mice and Men* was also a play disguised as a story, and was rather more effective after the false whiskers had been removed.

This lack of candor about the form of the book may not bother you at all. What may well be worrisome, though, is the inadequacy of the story's central feeling. *The Moon Is Down*, like *Of Mice and Men*, is a melodrama. It says with great dexterity things every one of us would love to believe, but for all that it remains a melodrama, which would not be to its discredit were it not obvious that Mr. Steinbeck is aiming at something loftier.

The Moon Is Down demonstrates, in terms of sound and even momentarily moving action, that the free spirit of man is unbreakable. The scene is never named (I find this annoying; others may find it an effective device), but it seems to be Norway. The invaders are not named, either, but we may as well come out with

it: Mr. Steinbeck means the N-zis. The town with which the story deals is delivered up by Fifth Columnists, and the totalitarians settle down to what they call the "engineering job" of gearing it into their military-industrial economy. In the course of this effort they shoot, maim, torture, and rape, but to no avail. They are opposed by subtle sabotage, by weapons dropped into the natives' hands from English planes, by a free spirit which is so much stronger than the slave spirit of the invaders that in the end it is the conquerors who grow afraid of the conquered, it is the ruthless soldiers who grow neurotic. As the Nazi Colonel Lanser broodingly puts it, "We will shoot this man and make twenty new enemies. It's the only thing we know, the only thing we know."

Now, I submit that this is simply too easy, that it is a melodramatic simplification of the issues involved. The simplification is based on the notion that in the end good will triumph because it is good and evil will fail because it is evil. With all our hearts we would like to think this true, and that is why melodrama is a popular form of literature. But it is hardly the most elevated form.

Many of us perhaps have been wondering of late why plays such as *Candle in the Wind* (of which Mr. Steinbeck's book is a more professional version) are, for all their splendid sentiment, somehow unsatisfactory. I suppose it is because this war is bigger and more terrible than their authors seem to admit. How shall we put it? If we cease to love freedom, we are lost, but the love of freedom alone cannot win for us. That appears to be the gray truth of the matter, and it is, let us confess, not the kind of truth that inspires exciting plays and novels. Most of our imaginative anti-Fascist literature has rested upon the stirring reiteration of sentiments to which our hearts give allegiance. But it is becoming increasingly clear that this form of spiritual patriotism is not only not enough but may even impede the war effort, because it fills us with a specious satisfaction, it makes our victory seem "inevitable," it seduces us to rest on the oars of our own moral superiority.

I like a fine phrase as well as the next man. I would like to believe, with Mr. Steinbeck, that "it is always the herd men who win battles and the free men who win wars." In the long run perhaps that is true, but everybody now alive is a short runner, and it is perfectly possible for Hitler to annihilate most of us. Once we get interested in winning this war for our remote posterity, it is half lost. Why not win it for ourselves? And if we are to win it for ourselves, we will, I fear, hardly be helped by the noble message in *The Moon Is Down* and in dozens of similar works full of high intentions; we can be helped only by the blood, toil, tears, and sweat of which Mr. Churchill has spoken. We no longer need to be told we are in the right, for we know it. We wish to be told only how we may make that right prevail.

I fear this sermon has obscured the fact that *The Moon Is Down* is a tense story (or play), written with great economy and with a certain grim humor, too. Its characters we have met before in other anti-Nazi books and dramas, but here they are more sharply minted and their dialogue is recorded with precise, if limited, insight. If you read the book quickly and do not reflect upon it, it seems extraordinarily powerful. If you read it slowly and with deliberation, it seems merely extraordinarily skillful. . . .

Margaret Marshall.
"Notes by the Way."
Nation, 154
(7 March 1942), 286.

John Steinbeck's latest book, *The Moon Is Down*, . . . is a fable of the occupied country cast in the dramatic form he employed in *Of Mice and Men*. The action takes place in "any conquered country in any time," and the theme is the slow undermining of the morale of the conquerors. The invaders take over the island without a struggle, thanks to the expert preparatory work of a local fifth columnist—the popular storekeeper. They try to conciliate the people in the person of Mayor Orden; they see no reason why an orderly people should not remain orderly, especially since they are unarmed and helpless, and go on operating the mines which made their island important in the first place. But the islanders, who have been free for four hundred years, refuse to accept their role. They are helpless, yet they manage to disrupt the work at the mines; even worse is their ostracism of the invaders, to whom they deny in innumerable and quiet ways the status of human beings. Shootings have no effect, and in the end it is the invaders who are on the defensive.

The theme is important, timely, universal. It is closely bound up with prevailing emotions. It would seem, therefore, to be the stuff out of which a modern fable might emerge. Yet I found the book curiously unmoving despite my own preoccupation with the subject. The trouble lies, I think, with the method Mr. Steinbeck has affected—studied understatement, simple, unaccented language, matter-of-fact tone. Such writing depends for its power on the concentration and maturity of feeling with which it is charged. In this case the charge is not sufficient. The form, therefore, seems contrived, the simplicity becomes pretentious, the understatement and matter-of-fact tone sentimental. The sprawling yet effective eloquence of *The Grapes of Wrath* seems to me much better suited to Mr. Steinbeck's particular gifts.

R. L. Duffus.
"John Steinbeck's Heroic Tale."
New York Times Book Review, 91 (8 March 1942), 1, 27.

Wars are fought by people. Nazis are people. Their victims are people. War psychology and Nazi psychology are the strange flowers that blossom from the unchanging, or very slowly changing, stalk of human nature. In the end it is human nature that counts. Hate, fear, love, lust—none of these can distort it completely. It has moments when it shines, and is a light that cannot be put out. These are the truisms, never so badly stated (for John Steinbeck is an artist from crown to toe), which are implicit in this remarkable novel.

So strong, so simple, so true, so dramatic in its values is this story, indeed, that its present form is obviously only one of its phases. It is as plainly destined for the stage as was *Of Mice and Men.* Mr. Steinbeck very carefully composes the acting directions for his drama of a little town (supposedly a Norwegian town, but not so stated) under Nazi rule.

He visualizes like a camera: the drawing room of the Mayor's "five-room palace," even to the red-and-gold wallpaper and the "large curly porcelain clock" on the mantel; the "warm, poor, comfortable room" in which Molly Morden, whose husband has been shot, awaits and invites fate; the gestures of a man trying to use a drawing board without a tripod; a man closing his eyes for a moment as he braces himself for death; the vision of an unseen patrol passing by night, in the snow, along a street of shuttered houses. This is a novel, a stage play, a motion picture, a radio drama. It is all those things, and merits being all of them.

For in this story, without hate, with utterly no heroics, almost idyllically, in a tone not less tense and vibrant because it is almost hushed, Mr. Steinbeck has recited the creed that all of us desire to maintain. "You know, Doctor," says Mayor Orden, "I am a little man and this is a little town, but there must be a spark in little men that can burst into flame. I am afraid, I am terribly afraid, and I thought of all the things I might do to save my own life, and then that went away, and sometimes now I feel a kind of exultation, as though I were bigger and better than I am." To believe in the victory of the anti-Axis forces in this war one has to believe in little men, in what they have done, in what they may still do, in what they will not tolerate, and Mr. Steinbeck does make one so believe.

The complexity of the story is not on the surface. Motives and emotions are reduced to their simplest terms. The characters are not shown in the round. All that they are, by birth and training, by growth or stuntedness, is applied to the exigencies of a situation limited in time, space and detail. They have no time to change. They are revealed. Nevertheless, one perceives within these limitations all that the Nazis are doing to conquered

Europe and all that conquered Europe is doing to the Nazis. One perceives, without argument. So economical is Mr. Steinbeck, so intent on dramatic content and so averse to the theatrical, that a syllable, even a gesture, tells a story. . . .

Step by step, with the inevitable march of events in *Of Mice and Men*, but with far more significance to us in this day, the drama proceeds. Mr. Corell, the popular storekeeper, has been helpful, lending his boat to the policeman and postman and arranging a picnic for the local troops ("all twelve of them") on the very day of the invasion. After the first regrettable gunfire the invaders are correct. "You are the authority," says Colonel Lanser to the Mayor. The Mayor smiles. "You won't believe this, but it is true: authority is in the town. I don't know how or why, but it is so. This means that we cannot act as quickly as you can, but when a direction is set we all act together."

Little by little the "direction" appears. The professionally sophisticated Lanser, Captain Bentinck, "a family man, a lover of dogs and pink children and Christmas"; the militant, heel-clicking Captain Loft; Lieutenant Prackle, "a gay young man who nevertheless could scowl like the Leader, could brood like the Leader"; Lieutenant Tonder, the "bitter poet who dreamed of perfect, ideal love of elevated young men for poor girls"; likewise the good, simple Mayor Orden; Dr. Winter with his sardonic touch; likewise Mrs. Orden, who tries in vain to keep her husband neatly brushed; the servants, Joseph and Annie—stock figures in a way, but true to life in a world chiefly populated by stock figures; likewise the anonymous town from which comes the "authority"—these people move toward doom without any choice. Being what they are, they cannot do otherwise. Thus Mr. Steinbeck sticks to his feeling for fate. . . .

. . . There can be no cheerful end to such a story, but there can be a hopeful end. The debt to Asclepius will be paid—the words of Socrates are still good and true.

If the novel were as rigid a literary form as the play it might be proper to ask whether Mr. Steinbeck, in his hurry to get a play into rehearsal, has actually produced a novel. But a novel must probably be defined as any story between covers, and a good novel as a story which sensitive and discriminating people will like to read. Mr. Steinbeck's novel is that, though it is not *War and Peace*, or anything like it.

Mr. Steinbeck is making a point. He is letting off steam. He is providing a composed fury of the sort that seems to be necessary to win this war. Many a reader may sit down to his book sad with the news from Burma or Java and get up resolute and confident. For this episode in an unnamed village in an unnamed country is the heart of the matter.

Wallace Stegner. "Steinbeck's Latest Is an 'Idea Novel.'" Boston *Daily Globe*, 11 March 1942, p. 19.

Undoubtedly this story of a peaceful people overrun, conquered, and eventually driven to underground resistance by an invader will receive both lavishly commendatory and inordinately harsh criticism. It deserves neither. It is neither a great book nor a bad book, though reviewers drunk on the timeliness of the theme may call it the first, and reviewers holding up *The Grapes of Wrath* as a measuring stick may call it the last. . . .

Technically the story is neat, tight, craftsmanly. Like *Of Mice and Men*, it is designed for immediate conversion to the stage, and beyond a doubt it will be a successful play. There is a good curtain line for every scene, the chapters group themselves naturally into acts, the final scene is one calculated to move almost any audience.

Yet for all that, I find *The Moon Is Down* a rather disappointing book, not because it fails to live up to *The Grapes of Wrath*, but because it fails to live up to itself. The theme of the simple courage of simple people is an old one with Steinbeck, and a perennially good one. But it doesn't come off here as it does in *The Grapes of Wrath*, in *In Dubious Battle*, or even in *Of Mice and Men*. I think there is a very sound and recognizable reason why it does not.

An embattled novelist who has produced a monumental best seller on a crucial and timely subject is in a hole. He can't go back to writing novels which are not socially-conscious, for fear of looking like a renegade. He can't repeat himself without dropping into the role of mouthpiece for reform. He must go on. But to what? He must find a problem graver and more pressing than the last one.

There is no difficulty in finding the problem. Any facet of the war problem is the automatic choice. But in choosing to write of the little people being crushed by and resisting the war, Steinbeck had to go out of his own experience. He had to fake, and he faked very well. Still, the people haven't the three-dimensional reality that his other people have had, and the horrors through which they live have been so constantly before us in the headlines and radio reports that, to put it quite bluntly, we are calloused to that variety of pain. War can hardly move us now in the way that fiction must move us

if it is to succeed. The wider the headlines stretch our sympathy for suffering humanity, the less we believe that suffering, the more we spring back into our own personal problems, the more the war becomes an abstraction.

That is the trouble with this careful, honest, skillful, and essentially true book. It deals with problems so terrible that our minds—yet—repudiate them. And I suspect that those problems are abstractions even to Mr. Steinbeck. He has never in the past evidenced any inability to move his reader, even if his reader is hard to move. But this novel will move only the easy ones. The hard ones will see even in the technique, even in the writing, signs of Mr. Steinbeck's own hesitancy.

Steinbeck is an artist, and a fine one, but he is not the infallible artist that some critics have called him, and here he makes mistakes. He uses two servants who are so plainly stock characters that they are almost ham. He cannot resist making Mayor Orden a mouthpiece of the democratic way. He is guilty of having two men on the verge of death by firing squad hold the stage for minutes quoting to each other the *Apology* of Socrates, so that the audience will know they are dying in the cause of intelligence and civilization.

The Moon Is Down is not, thank God, as talky, emotional and dishonest as Robert Sherwood's *There Shall Be No Night*. There are magnificent scenes in it, such as the one in which Lieut. Tonder of the invaders turns hysterical under the steady, silent hatred of the villagers, and the passage (unfortunately impossible on the stage) in which the inevitable growth of that hatred is recreated. But the ending seems to me false and literary, and the people are not real enough to save the book from being exactly what it is, an idea novel, about abstractions. And this I say with some sorrow, because Steinbeck is still one of the two or three best novelists writing in America, and this book under any other name would warrant roses.

Norman Cousins.
"The Will to Live and Resist."
Saturday Review, 25 (14 March 1942), 6.

It would be easier to write two separate reviews of this book than to attempt the usual single account. Because when you put it down (it is a small book, a very small book, and you can read it at a single sitting), you seem to carry away two distinct sets of impressions. The first is your feeling about the book up until a dozen pages from the end. The second is your feeling about it just after you have finished it. In short, the ending, though dramatic enough, seems not of a piece with the story itself, and thereby mars as satisfying a novelette as has been published in many seasons. This is why:

This is a story whose hero is a people—the people of a small town, an honest, reasonable, slow-going people who believed that peace was the language of mankind, that one had only to speak it anywhere to be understood and respected. They believed it when the invader came, speaking the language of fascism. They learned right away that part of that language meant treachery, for they were to discover that a man they had thought to be one of themselves, the once-popular storekeeper, had proved himself the wedge which enabled the small invading force to move into the town almost unnoticed and to fasten its grip on the people so quickly and so effectively that immediate resistance was impossible.

Yet even this early lesson disturbed only slightly the unstrained quality of their mercy, nor did it inflame a bitterness measured in terms of quick violence. They had been speaking one language for centuries, and it was difficult to learn that deceit could mean deceit; and so they could not help it if they tended to see even their enemies in their own image.

Their spokesman—and he was a spokesman in the truest sense of the word—was the Mayor, a rather solid but generally inarticulate character who, seemingly, had been Mayor as far back as anyone could remember, and whose chief virtue was that his mind and the collective mind of the people were one. It wasn't that he had deep powers of insight or vision or imagination; it was that an affinity existed which enabled him to express better than any other person the public will. His job was not to create public opinion but to feel it—sometimes even before the people themselves.

Around the Mayor there were other persons as much a part of the town as the Mayor's old mansion. There was the good doctor—fireplace philosopher and friend and confidant of the Mayor; there was the Mayor's wife, a somewhat fussy and ceremonious little woman who made all the decisions except the important ones; there were the servants, a cook and a butler, both strongly individualistic, whose courage and resourcefulness seemed limitless.

But the Mayor's "palace"—once the invasion took place—also became the headquarters of the occupation forces. The Mayor stayed on in a section of the palace, and retained his nominal authority. The officers occupied another section. Off by themselves, the officers were a human and average lot, so human, in fact, that we can understand them and see them as part of a vaster tragedy. But they had been trained to speak the language of fascism, and even though some of their number realized that this language must always be unintelligible to a free people, theirs was not to question or reason, but to order. They ordered the people to obey. To work the mines. They even ordered them to be friendly.

The people are slow and they are reasonable but they are not fools. Orders spoken in the language of fascism are not reasonable orders. They will work because they have always worked but they will work out of their own free will and not because they are slaves. And when one of them strikes out and murders an officer, the others come to understand that they have a job to do: the enemy must be destroyed at any cost. This wave of resistance starts as a little stream, picks up strength and grows and broadens and becomes a flood. There is no mistaking its force or its size. This is a Niagara of resistance let loose. The people are not armed and open warfare is impossible. But in their own way they have come to understand what the language of fascism means and will have none of it. They hold back at work. They sabotage. They communicate with Britain and get the ally to drop hundreds of sticks of dynamite by parachute.

They cannot be stopped. They cannot be stopped even when retaliation strikes back swift and deep. The Mayor is ordered to stop them, but he does not, because he knows he cannot, because he knows they are doing what he would do. But the Mayor is a symbol. He is loved and respected. The people must be punished. They must be hurt. They must pay the price of their resistance. That price is the life of the Mayor. That is the language of fascism, which twists the knife instead of withdrawing it, and yet expects the wound somehow to close. . . .

That is the rough story. As you read it, you have the sense of participation. You feel the tempo rising in you, even as it rises in the spirit of the townsfolk. You keep preparing yourself for the smashing climax. You are psychologically attuned to an ending of the proportions of *For Whom the Bell Tolls.*

But the last dozen pages do not seem to come off. It is not only that the story is not resolved—we may have to wait a long time until events themselves will justify stories such as these being resolved in the way we should like to see them resolved—but that the technique itself of the ending seems at odds with the overall pattern. The Mayor is a heroic character, certainly, but he is not the hero. And yet the hero's role is thrust upon him suddenly and a hitherto rather inarticulate old man goes off at the final curtain reciting the *Apology* from Socrates. Such a device is obviously better suited to the theatre. In fact, *The Moon Is Down* would make an even better play than it does a book. It divides itself nicely into three acts, and action is described mostly in group conversation, rather than by the direct method. Then, too, the coming and going of the characters, the development of the dramatic situations, the continuing emphasis upon strong, colorful characters—all this seems to add up to drama of the first magnitude.

But play or no play, as a book *The Moon Is Down* is a unique reading experience. Steinbeck tells his story with simplicity, force, dignity, and even beauty. I cannot recall another novel of comparable size that has achieved so much of the sense of vital suspense, so strong a feeling of reality. Steinbeck's images are strong and closely knit. Except for one or two slips, he comes as close as any author to making himself unobtrusive and leaving you free to lose yourself in the story. Which you do.

James Thurber. "What Price Conquest?" *New Republic*, 106 (16 March 1942), 370.

There is, I regret to say, a kind of lamplight playing over the mood and style, the events and figures, of Mr. Steinbeck's new short novel about the people of a small conquered town and its conquerors. I suspect that if a writer conceives of a war story in terms of a title like *The Moon Is Down* he is likely to get himself into soft and dreamy trouble. Maybe a title like "Guts in the Mud" would have produced a more convincing reality. Anyway, this little book needs more guts and less moon. An impatient friend of mine who had read it, too, said to me, "It is probably Robert Nathan's best book." Whomever you may be reminded of, the vastly talented Mr. Steinbeck has definitely taken on here a new phase and a new temper. One wonders what kind of thing he will do next.

The reader of this book does not have to be told that the author had a stage version in mind as he wrote it (the play has gone into rehearsal as I set this down). This has had the unfortunate effect of giving the interiors in the novel the feel of sets. I could not believe that the people who enter Mayor Orden's living room come from the streets and houses of a little town. They come from their dressing rooms. The characters and the language they speak are in keeping with the theatrical atmosphere, from Annie, the irate cook, to Colonel Lanser, the leader of the invaders and his staff. If these are German officers, if they are anything else

but American actors, I will eat the manuscript of your next play.

The point upon which Mr. Steinbeck in these pages has so lovingly and gently brooded is that there are no machines and no armies mighty enough to conquer the people. "The people don't like to be conquered, sir," says Mayor Orden to Colonel Lanser, "and so they will not be." This shining theme is restated a great many times, principally by one of the invading officers whose nerves have been worn thin by the cold eyes and the silent faces of the little people of the little town. Lieutenant Tonder in *The Moon Is Down* goes to pieces and raves, and this scene demands comparison with the going-to-pieces scene of Lieutenant Moore in *What Price Glory?* and that of Lieutenant Hibbert in *Journey's End*. Apparently Laurence Stallings and Maxwell Anderson, who did the scene first (and best), have contributed a convention to the war play of our time. I can only say after reading the three scenes at one sitting that if the German lieutenants of today are really like Lieutenant Tonder, then the American Moores and the British Hibberts will be able to rout the pussycats merely by shouting "Boo!"

Let us listen to Lieutenant Tonder in *The Moon Is Down*:

"I want a girl. I want to go home. I want a girl. There's a girl in this town, a pretty girl. I see her all the time. She has blond hair. She lives beside the old-iron store. I want that girl. . . .

"That's it! The enemy's everywhere! Every man, every woman, even children! The enemy's everywhere! Their faces look out of doorways. The white faces behind the curtains, listening. We have beaten them, we have won everywhere, and they wait and obey, and they wait. Half the world is ours. . . .

"What do the reports say about us? Do they say we are cheered, loved, flow-

225

ers in our paths? Oh, these horrible people waiting in the snow! . . .

"Conquered and we're afraid; conquered and we're surrounded. . . . I had a dream—or a thought—out in the snow with the black shadows and the faces in the doorways, the cold faces behind curtains. I had a thought or a dream. . . .

"Conquest after conquest, deeper and deeper into molasses. . . . Maybe the Leader is crazy. Flies conquer the flypaper. Flies capture two hundred miles of new flypaper!"

Now listen to Lieutenant Moore in *What Price Glory?*:

"Oh, God, Dave, but they got you. God, but they got you a beauty, the dirty swine. God DAMN them for keeping us up here in this hellish town. Why can't they send in some of the million men they've got back there and give us a chance? Men in my platoon are so hysterical every time I get a message from Flagg, they want to know if they're being relieved. What can I tell them? They look at me like whipped dogs—as if I had just beaten them—and I've had enough of them this time. I've got to get them out, I tell you. They've had enough. Every night the same way. (He turns to Flagg.) And since six o'clock there's been a wounded sniper in the tree by that orchard angle crying 'Kamerad! Kamerad!' Just like a big crippled whippoorwill. What price glory now? Why in God's name can't we all go home? Who gives a damn for this lousy, stinking little town but the poor French bastards who live here? God damn it! You talk about courage, and all night long you hear a man who's bleeding to death on a tree calling you 'Kamerad' and asking you to save him. God damn every son of a bitch in the world who isn't here! I won't stand for it. I won't stand for it! I won't have the platoon asking me every minute of the livelong night when they are going to be relieved. . . . Flagg, I tell you you can

shoot me, but I won't stand for it. . . . I'll take 'em out tonight and kill you if you get in my way. . . ."

At one point in *The Moon Is Down* the little people of the little town are aided by the falling of a curious manna from Heaven: small blue parachutes come drifting to earth, carrying dynamite and chocolate. The little children of the conquered town go hunting for the candy with as much excitement as if they were searching for Easter eggs. The Steinbeck story will make a very pretty movie.

I keep wondering what the people of Poland would make of it all.

Charles Duffy. "*The Moon Is Down.*" *Commonweal*, 35 (27 March 1942), 569–70.

Mr. Steinbeck combines something of the technique of the drama with the purpose of the essay in his new novel. An invading enemy, striking with care and competence, quickly overcomes an unnamed country. So well-planned and executed is the attack that the defenders are vanquished before they know what has happened. Mr. Steinbeck is not interested in describing the war but in depicting the plight of the conquered and . . . the conquerors. Readers will, of course, identify Colonel Lanser and his staff with nazi soldiers and Mayor Orden and Doctor Winter with civilian Americans. But there is no need to do so, for the occupation of a once-free country by a hostile force is a timeless situation. The question propounded is this: can force overcome freedom?

The sullen obedience of the conquered

at length breaks into sporadic revolt. The familiar devices of oppression such as starvation, slavery and the firing squad serve only to consolidate the insurrection of a few, which, toward the end of the book, threatens to become open rebellion. Force, then, does not defeat a free people, it merely goads them to action.

Mr. Steinbeck's faith in the people is deeply intuitive. Mayor Orden, Doctor Winter, and Annie, the cook, possess some means of communication with those pools of wisdom lying deep in the consciousness of men and women. In critical moments they are able to draw upon this source, confuting the guile of their oppressors by means of their simple but subtle understanding of right. There are no heroics in their retaliations; there is rather that quiet heroism of Socrates, whose noble words to his accusers are quoted. About to be led to the wall, Mayor Orden remembers his school-boy declamation: "'I prophesy to you who are my murderers that immediately after my departure punishment far heavier than you have inflicted on me will surely await you.'" That there will be others to take up the responsibilities of continuing resistance is covertly suggested in his final words to Doctor Winter, "Crito, I owe a cock to Asclepius. . . . Will you remember to pay the debt?"

Alvin Adey.
"Victims of Conquest."
Current History, 2
(April 1942), 143–4.

Steinbeck's new novel presents a picture of a small town occupied by a ruthless and brutal invader. It might be actually in Norway or hypothetically in northern Britain, but that does not matter, for the whole point of the story is the situation that arises anywhere when a conquered people refuses to accept defeat and resorts to the sullen resistance and whatever sabotage and terrorism can be devised to make things even more horrible for the conquerors than for the conquered.

Beginning with a striking description of how the town is betrayed by a fifth columnist, and by bringing the situation to a head in a group of truly conceived and sensitively portrayed characters, Steinbeck succeeds in fashioning profound and moving drama out of the experience that is widespread in the Europe of today. It is hard to say which is more finely delineated—the mayor of the town who not merely symbolizes but embodies the democratic system, or the commander of the occupation troops, a toughened veteran of the last war who in his own way fully realizes the tragic futility of using armed force to break the spirit of a free people. Excellent too is the portrayal of the townspeople and the commander's staff officers, one of whom becomes infatuated with the pretty young widow of the invader's first victim and is killed by her.

The commander has no alternative but to carry out his mission, and as the provocations and reprisals of the defeated people continue, he is finally compelled to order the heroic mayor to be shot. Steinbeck's conclusion is indicated by making the mayor, before he faces the firing squad, quote the last words of Socrates: "If you think that by killing men you can prevent someone from censuring your evil lives, you are mistaken." But long before this it has been made clear that the invaders have been subjected to much more than censure, for they suffer as acutely from the oppression of which they are the instrument as the oppressed people themselves. This is the psychological situation that gives the story its unity and significance and in the handling of which Steinbeck exhibits his insight and literary power.

The style is excellent—a well sustained, evenly measured prose that is never trite and yet avoids overwriting and melodrama. The form is of interest because the story—only about a fourth of the length of the average novel—has the compactness of a play and has been apparently designed so that it can be easily dramatized for the stage. Whatever qualms anyone might have about Steinbeck's previous work will disappear upon reading this nobly conceived and deftly handled story of one of the grimmest aspects of war and conquest. *The Moon Is Down* is both first-class fiction and a valuable document and, one is inclined to think, a little masterpiece.

vader, Colonel Lanser, is not happy: a veteran of 1917, he knows that the community will not remain as calm and passive as his lieutenants imagine. "Defeat," he says wearily, "is a momentary thing . . . we will shoot this man and make twenty new enemies"—and the conflict which follows proves that he is right. Like *Of Mice and Men*, this narrative obeys the discipline of the theatre: the timing, the telling dialogue, the absence of introspection, all accentuate the sharply defined scenes. By confining the action to a single household—the mayor's—Steinbeck localizes the immediate feeling of defeat; then in the slow antagonism of the military and the conquered he reduces to very human terms the terrible vindictiveness that must now be underground in Europe and Asia.

Edward Weeks.
"First Person Singular."
Atlantic, 169 (April 1942), [p. 7 at front of issue].

Last winter I asked Mr. Somerset Maugham where he thought the best writing of this war would come from. It would come, he replied, from the defeated—just as it did in the last war. John Steinbeck's short novel, *The Moon Is Down*, tells the story of a tiny little community which has just been overwhelmed by the Nazis. The village (it could be anywhere) with its coal mine and its dock has been skillfully betrayed by a fifth columnist, the home guard (of twelve men) wiped out, the mayor, the doctor, and the people hopelessly confused. But the in-

W. E. Garrison.
"The Unquenchable Spirit."
Christian Century, 29 April 1942, pp. 561–2.

Cynics and superior persons who find pleasure in believing that wide popularity for a novel is always a sign that there is something cheap and nasty about it, and that the public's taste is always wrong, are invited to read this chaste miniature masterpiece and then to reflect upon the fact that half a million copies of it were sold within a month from its date of publication, which was March 6.

This is an idyll of the unquenchable human spirit—the indefatigable moral resistance of the conquered and, no less, the persistent reassertion of human qualities in the conquerors, who cannot reduce themselves to the purely military mechanisms they would have to be to carry out effectively their ruthless assignment. . . .

This is not history; it is prophecy. It is the affirmation of a high faith in humanity—which is the same thing as faith in the ultimate triumph of freedom over force. That faith has not been more beautifully stated than in this novel.

E. M. Butler.
"New Books."
Catholic World, 55
(May 1942), 253–4.

. . . *The Moon Is Down* tries to describe the German war machine as it takes over a small country and the disintegration of the German mentality subjected to the scorn of a hostile population. No matter how superior a man may feel himself to be, he must have someone to talk to, if only to pass the time of day, and these soldiers read nothing but scorn in the eyes of their victims. The book's narrative skill and economy of means are undeniable, but the art with which the rather slight story is told is too self-conscious to be convincing. The laughs are all calculated in advance, "planted," as they say in the theater; the characters are types, and the whole effort is to poke fun at their simplicity, much as radio commentators and columnists have poked fun at Hitler, but Hitler *in absentia*. Steinbeck has a serious subject and real ability in using it; he destroys the validity of both by introducing elements that throw the story out of key, as his efforts to be whimsical, which confuse the mood of the book and are repeated too often for comfort. Nevertheless this is a vivid

and dramatic work, much the best thing Steinbeck has done so far, and written with a restraint he seemed incapable of in his earlier books. . . .

"The Moon Is Halfway Down."
New Republic, 106
(18 May 1942), 657.

A few weeks ago we predicted that the controversy over John Steinbeck's new novel would be prolonged and bitter, but we didn't realize at the time that it was going to develop into all-out warfare on the literary front. Clifton Fadiman has assumed command of the Blue, or anti-Steinbeck, forces. John Chamberlain has lately enlisted in the Green army, so called by its opponents because it is defending Steinbeck's moon, which they insist is really green cheese. Hard names are flying back and forth between the opposing ranks like dumdum bullets. Reading Lewis Gannett's usually even-tempered column in the New York *Herald Tribune* one day last week, we were amazed to learn that *The New Republic* has been conducting "a totalitarian crusade" against the book; that we talk as if we were trying to get it suppressed; and that our logic would lead "to the conclusion that the whole German nation, down to ten-year-old children, must be annihilated forever. That," Mr. Gannett concludes, "is propaganda gone mad; it winds up as a racialist philosophy in reverse, as artistic totalitarianism."

And that—referring this time to Mr. Gannett's article—is triumphant and total nonsense. *The New Republic* as a magazine has so far taken no stand in the great Steinbeck war; we have been neutrals, or at most non-belligerents. It is true that the book was unfavorably reviewed by James Thurber, but like our other reviewers he was expressing his own honest opinion. Many books are unfavorably reviewed in *The New Republic*—including a few that the editors admire—and so far not one of them has been suppressed; the fact is that most of them thrive under the treatment. The play fashioned from the novel—or was it vice versa?—was pretty well liked by Stark Young. In our correspondence columns, we printed eight letters about *The Moon Is Down*, and they happened to be equally divided, four Blue and four Green. Does Mr. Gannett really think that we should have censored the review and suppressed the unfavorable letters? Just who is being totalitarian?

On the great question whether Steinbeck was right in depicting his German officers as frustrated and rather likable human beings, we occupy a safe middle position. We believe that he was right to depict some of them in that fashion. On the other hand, he was wrong not to depict any of them as genuine and therefore essentially hateful Nazis. Captain Loft comes nearest to being one of Hitler's real soldiers, but even Loft is less a Nazi than a simple careerist; his great prototype is Lieutenant Alphonse Karlovich Berg, in *War and Peace*. Prackle was intended by the author to be a Nazi, but he didn't work out that way; his adoration of the Leader remains nothing more than a stage direction. All in all, Steinbeck presents a somewhat idealized picture of our enemies.

As for the literary qualities of *The Moon Is Down*, we agree with Mr. Thurber's adverse judgment. Steinbeck has always been one of those authors who start from literature instead of life; who try to make their literary emotion lifelike by finding the words that ordinary people would use to express it and by setting it against a real background. In *The Grapes of Wrath* he was successful because he knew his people and how they lived. In *The Moon Is Down* he does not know his people or his background, and the result is that the literary emotion never becomes quite real. The characters make admirable speeches, but they do not talk like human beings.

If Mr. Gannett wants us to go beyond these casual comments and really take an editorial stand, we shall be glad to oblige him. In that case, we should say to our readers, "Pay careful attention to everything we say, for we are Taking an Editorial Stand. We want you to read *The Moon Is Down*; we want everybody to read it. But please don't confuse it with Shakespeare or even with *The Grapes of Wrath*. And don't think that Mr. Steinbeck's Nazis are the people who actually invaded Norway. If they were, the free nations wouldn't need planes, tanks and gasoline rationing to defeat them. The job could be done effectively with dynamite and bon-bons."

Paul Bixler.
"The Moon Is Down . . . Is Up . . . Is Down . . . Is . . ."
Antioch Review, 2 (June 1942), 322–3.

Although there is much in Stanley Edgar Hyman's article on John Steinbeck in this issue with which we sharply disagree, with one of his conclusions we are in perfect accord—that the heated controversy raging in the press over *The Moon Is Down* has been concerned almost wholly with misleading or extraneous issues. Perhaps fiction published in war time cannot hope to receive a coherent appreciation unless it obviously belongs on the one hand to the school of pure escape or on the other to the school of blood and guts. Perhaps the screaming events of a world war make of the inventions of serious fiction a pale insignificance. However this may be, the reviewing of Steinbeck's short novel entered the silly stage almost on the day of publication and with one or two exceptions has remained there ever since.

Max Gissen's apt phrases, "punch drunk reviewing" and "an excess of uncritical good will" (see his article in this issue) are mildly descriptive of the sort of thing to come from newspaper row; and with the exception of Margaret Marshall, who despite a sound critical approach gave the book little more than a lick and a promise, the liberal press was almost as bad. One gathered from the newspaper boys that here was the book of the century—and from the thinkers that by a stroke of the pen John Steinbeck had lost us the war. To cap this impasse and to pile one confusion upon another, letters began to come to the editors pointedly seeking to re-establish the good character of the denizens of Mr. Steinbeck's "mythical" country; and as a climax too good to be imagined, articles appeared in at least two of the "information" sheets put out in America by representatives of lands now under the Nazi heel heatedly denouncing the Steinbeck opus for traducing the sacred honor of their countrymen. At this point, we believe, criticism ought to turn the page and begin afresh.

If *The Moon Is Down* is not the typically great war story which the critics have been hoping for, surely it cannot help to *lose* the war. If it deals most obviously with an invasion, it can hardly be said that its story is without indications of assistance from abroad. If Mr. Steinbeck's Nazis fit none of the stereotypes we now hate, if it is admitted that there may be something of the stage character about them, one can hardly contend beyond this that they are the central figures of the book, or that they are more in fact than the stooges for the people Mr. Steinbeck is really interested in. As for the title, what does it mean beyond the fact that the night is dark? Let us admit that the novel is essentially a drama, that it is not perfectly contrived, that it does not employ Steinbeck's gifts so well as a longer, fuller form. There yet remains beyond all other considerations the chief theme—the heroism and will to resist of the people of the invaded town. This last is important enough to bear much more elaboration than we can give it here.

The Moon Is Down is Steinbeck's first novel since *The Grapes of Wrath*, and it is hardly strange that the central theme of both is the same. Hundreds of thousands of Americans were awakened to the humanity and the will to democracy of the common man by the impact of *The Grapes*, and other hundreds of thousands were reawakened. Though *The Moon Is Down* does not come with the force of first discovery, its belief in the strength of the common man is patent and should make new converts. The critics may say that Steinbeck's central idea is overlaid with mystical talk about "group men," with an almost religious or metaphysical fervor; they may note that his common man is predominantly rural. But if these overtones do not make for a completely clear-cut ideology, they surely make for a very moving novelist—perhaps the most moving of our time. Is it too much to ask that liberal thinkers who have been thumping for the idea of the common man these many moons accept

231

in Steinbeck a powerful fellow-advocate and cease trying to make neurotic a public already convinced of his humanism by suggesting that he is somehow, wittingly or unwittingly, playing ball with the Axis? For the strength and the will of the common man *is* the chief idea of our time. It is so big and so important that if the little people of *The Moon Is Down* have no validity in real life, then there is small validity in our war.

"Invasion."
Times Literary Supplement [London], 20 June 1942, p. 305.

A short novel or a long short-story, in some sort a fable of contemporary history, *The Moon Is Down* has truth and dignity of sentiment and a sincere accent of homage. It is a simple tale, told with studied simplicity of phrase....

. . . And from it all emerges once more the idea of freedom, an undying idea, a deathless idea. The one impossible job in the world, says Mayor Orden, is to break man's spirit permanently. It is to this statement of belief that Mr. Steinbeck addresses himself, and in the result he is honest, unaffected and full of admiration for the things men will do in the cause of freedom. The invention of the tale is soberly realistic. The Mayor and his old friend, the local historian, receive Colonel Lanser, who is grey, hard, tired-looking and who has reason to remember the military occupation of Belgium and France twenty years earlier. The Colonel is a curious and perhaps romanticized study; at moments, like Milton's Satan, he seems to be the real hero of the piece, a profound and dutiful soul gone astray. He explains the invader's need of the coalmine at the edge of the town and of the local fishing; he deprecates the thought of resistance; he asks for the Mayor's collaboration in maintaining order. The Mayor himself doubts whether the Colonel knows what to expect from the townspeople in their own good time, and these doubts are strengthened when his cook Annie throws boiling water over one of the soldiers observing her too closely in the kitchen and bites another who goes to the rescue.

There are neat and suggestive sketches of the members of the colonel's staff. Major Hunter is a dry, precise formalist; the elderly Captain Bentick is a family man, a lover of dogs, children and Christmas, who in the past has always liked to be mistaken in Paris or Budapest for an Englishman; Captain Loft clicks his heels as perfectly as any dancer; and Lieutenants Prackle and Tonder are witless and sentimental young fire-eaters. Gradually an invisible net of hatred closes round them all. The colonel knows that to maintain order and discipline it is necessary to learn what is in the minds of the conquered. He learns soon enough. Captain Bentick is the first and almost innocent victim, struck down by a blow from a miner's pick, and in ordering the man to be shot the colonel realizes that he is raising twenty new enemies. Occupation grows steadily more arduous. The miners are clumsy and slow, costly machinery is broken, there are accidents on the railway, young men escape to England, there are bombing raids at night; the defeated wait in slow, silent, watchful hatred. And the troops themselves, thinking always of home, their nerves stretched to breaking-point, begin to fear what awaits them when they crack. In a fit of hysteria young Tonder, before the shot miner's wife takes her revenge, protests his loneliness in a world already half conquered. So to the arrest of Mayor Orden as a hostage and his final testimony to the faith of a free man. Defeat is momentary, he says, for even in defeat free men fight on. "It is always the herd men who win battles and the free men who win wars."

Mr. Steinbeck's tribute is warm and sincere, and the slight fiction built round it is of nice balance and proportion. Whether he gains from the half-hearted anonymity of his narrative is doubtful; his model, presumably, is the Nazi invasion of Norway, and in the circumstances so nameless a rendering of the event gives it a rather hollow character. Worse still, if we may say so, there is too little imagination, too complacent a vision in what seems to be his shock of pride in the resistance of the occupied countries of Europe. The sentiment of the tale always rings true, but was it necessary to draw quite so comforting a moral from the oppression and torture of the history, or the European history, of our times?

Philip Toynbee.
"New Novels."
New Statesman and Nation [England], 23
(20 June 1942), 408–9.

Novels of the last war suffered from two besetting faults—self-pity and a devotion to hysterical detail. Many of them screamed so shrilly that they passed, in the end, quite beyond the range of human earshot. Stench, mud, corpses, gas— how little that is really moving has remained! The error was that most of these books were written in a passion, either of rage, despair, or exhibitionism. This may

explain why the best novel yet produced by this war has come from the relative detachment of America.

As if to disclaim any pretension to the particular, Mr. Steinbeck has clothed his book in a most effective anonymity. "By ten forty-five it was all over. The town was occupied, the defenders defeated, and the war finished. The invader had prepared for his campaign as carefully as he had for larger ones."

This is the opening of *The Moon Is Down*, and there are few occasions where more specific terms are used than these. At the same time there is no dream or fable atmosphere to blur the many sharp points and edges. It is soon clear that this is a Norwegian town and these are German invaders, but we are spared any exuberance of local colour.

The story is a short and extremely simple one. It is summed up in the hysterical outburst of a young invading officer, driven mad by months of friendless isolation. "Conquest after conquest, deeper and deeper into molasses . . . Flies conquer the flypaper. Flies capture two hundred miles of new flypaper."

One of the unique merits of *The Moon Is Down* is that both invaders and invaded, both flies and flypaper, are presented intelligibly and sympathetically. The heroes, in the modern sense, are the people of the town: the miners who dynamite railway lines, the hostages, and, above all, the mayor. But in the tragic sense the heroes are the invading flies.

Colonel Lanser, the commanding officer of the invading battalion, is a conventional but beautifully convincing character. His eyes are always tired, his mind struggling perpetually and fruitlessly against the memories of other wars. He knows precisely what he must do, and precisely what will happen. His efforts to persuade Mayor Orden to co-operate can never succeed, and he knows this. The people will resist whatever measures are taken against them, while his own officers will quickly disintegrate. He is the man wise by experience, hopeless by situation.

The mayor is a contrast. He is the ordinary respectable man, at times pompous, at times humble, wise by a sort of bewildered communal instinct. As the people's elected representative, he becomes the people. His understanding springs directly from the collective knowledge of the community, and his resolution from the collective will.

Consequently the mayor is never a tragic figure, for he is never alone. The Colonel, amused or disgusted by his own officers, is always alone. His only moments of human contact are with the mayor, whom in the end he is obliged to shoot.

Mr. Steinbeck rightly pays more attention to the invaders than to the invaded. The resistance of the town is made to seem inevitable: it is taken for granted. But the decay, the terrible galloping consumption of the conquerors can seldom have been more vividly described. The young officers hunger for girls, but when they appeal to the girls of the town for sympathy, they are murdered as they kiss.

They hear music from a café, and eagerly pursue it. But at their appearance the music stops, the couples break apart. And all the time comes the desperate booming of news from home, of victories and occupations which make no difference whatever to their plight.

In the description of the invaded there is hardly a moment of false sentiment or adulation.

Annie [the cook] was always a little angry, and these soldiers, this occupation, did not improve her temper. Indeed, what for years had been considered simply a bad disposition had suddenly become a patriotic emotion.

How convincing this is of all the cooks one knows! Mr. Steinbeck can write authentically about ordinary people without a hint of the abominable Little Man, London-can-take-it, attitude which has perverted English taste for years.

"Baying at the Moon." *Time*, 39 (22 June 1942), 88, 90.

John Steinbeck's *The Moon Is Down* (*Time*, March 9) has stirred up (as book and play) the year's liveliest literary fight. By now the battle has become a general war, involving book reviewers, theater critics, editors, people who write letters to the newspapers, diplomats, college professors and Dorothy Thompson. Two great questions are at issue: 1) Does Steinbeck put too much faith in the moral superiority of democracy? 2) Is Steinbeck wrong in portraying German soldiers as human beings?

It has even been suggested that *The Moon* is veiled Nazi propaganda. In Manhattan the Belgian Commissioner of Information objected to Colonel Lanser, one of Steinbeck's Germans who recalls how, in World War I, an old Belgian woman killed twelve Germans with a long black hatpin. Said the Commissioner: "Mr. Steinbeck . . . does a disservice to the Belgian reputation for dignity and fair play."

Prominent among those who think that the Steinbeck moon is made of green cheese are:

• *New Yorker* Critic Clifton Fadiman ("It seduces us to rest on the oars of our own moral superiority").
• Humorist James Thurber ("This lit-

tle book needs more guts and less moon.... If these are German officers ... I will eat the manuscript of your next play ...").

- The pinko *New Republic* ("Don't think that Mr. Steinbeck's Nazis are the people who actually invaded Norway. If they were, the free nations wouldn't need planes, tanks and gasoline rationing to defeat them. The job could be done effectively with dynamite and bonbons.").

Warmest defenders of *The Moon* are Novelist Pearl Buck, Drama Critic Brooks Atkinson, Dorothy Thompson, Book Reviewer Lewis Gannett. Gannett called the "totalitarian crusade" against the story "a depressing example of wartime hysteria."

Said Dorothy Thompson: "I know dozens of German officers who were thoroughly mature when last I enjoyed friendly relations with them, and they were just like [Colonel Lanser].... The enormous power in Mr. Steinbeck's drama is that it is *not* an attack on *Nazis*. It is an attack on *Naziism*."

Meanwhile *The Moon Is Down* is doing quite nicely. As a novel, it has sold 450,000 copies. As a play, it has entertained when it closed last fortnight, some 56,000 theatergoers. Producer Darryl Zanuck, who paid $300,000 for the film rights, is rushing production of the movie version.

Harold Brighouse. "Books of the Day." Manchester *Guardian*, 26 June 1942, p. 3.

... Mr. John Steinbeck, previously emotional in his advocacy of the inarticulate,

the witless, and the luckless, is evenhandedly Galsworthian in his fantasy of freedom *The Moon Is Down*.... A coal harbour, obviously Norwegian, though Norway is never named, is betrayed to the invaders by the popular Mr. Corell; the protagonists are Colonel Lanser and Mayor Orden, and the tolerance of the colonel is extreme. Orden's cook throws boiling water over soldiers, and Lanser merely removes them. A miner kills an officer with a pickaxe; he is executed, but there is no other reprisal. Lanser's country wanted coal, and his orders were to obtain collaboration. He was not to be provoked, even by Corell, who resented his mildness, nor by the local people, who taught his men what ostracism means. He had, however, finally to shoot Orden. They understood each other perfectly, and Orden and the doctor, recollecting the last words of Socrates, are assisted by Lanser. A soldier and a gentleman obeyed orders, a freeman and a gentleman obeyed the dictates of conviction, and both are finely conveyed in this terse novel, which already has been produced as a play in New York. ...

Kate O'Brien. "Fiction." *Spectator* [England], 169 (10 July 1942), 44.

The first thing to be said of *The Moon Is Down* is that it is, for these times, better value than most new pieces of fiction, for it is a deft, well-written, economical story; it deals with something which must go straight home at present to all imaginations; it is nicely bound and printed, and it costs only two half-crowns. Mr.

Steinbeck tells of the seizure by a company of German soldiers of a little town on the coast of an unnamed country that clearly is Norway; he shows how easy it was to take the town, and how impossible to subjugate it; he gives us clean little character sketches of six German officers and of a number of simple people whom they can neither manage nor understand; in particular he gives us the heroic, modest story of the Mayor, and shows how thoroughly that humble man understood the nature of his office and his duty. It is quiet, ironic and tender, recalling somewhat in manner Alphonse Daudet's tales of the Franco-Prussian War. Yet somehow it falls short of its opportunity. It is as if written at too long a range and too closely to a preconception. The characters of the German officers are differentiated with a crispness which is too effective to capture life, and which tends therefore to indicate sentimentality; and by an odd use of irony, the author understates in the wrong places, and in unconscious correction of this sometimes overstates embarrassingly. An example of the latter kind of lapse is in the awkward straining, in the brave little Mayor's last hour of life, of his and his old friend's recollections from school of Socrates' *Apology.* This is taken much too far—to make the irresistible but quite untrue curtain. It is a pity, for the Mayor was fine and simple and needed no high-flown parallels. Anguish is missed somehow, and what might have been, taken with entire simplicity, a microcosm of the present courage and present woe of millions of the innocent, is turned by too many clever graces into a wry little story, perilously near to the whimsical. . . .

"*Pravda* Likes Steinbeck." New York *Times*, 22 December 1942, p. 23.

Pravda, the Communist party newspaper, devotes almost a half page today to a review of the American edition of John Steinbeck's *The Moon Is Down.*

The reviewer praises the book for its universality and the exposition of the hatred of the inhabitants of occupied lands for the Germans. He judges the book to be of literary and social importance and defends the author against criticisms "that he drew the German characters in too human a light." It is just that combination of human and inhuman features, the reviewer states, that makes the Germans beasts.

However, the discussions that the book has provoked show that the American intelligentsia has a healthy hatred for the enemy and desires that the Hitlerites be described with hatred, the reviewer adds. In Mr. Steinbeck's "objectivity" the reviewer sees not a sign of lack of hatred but solely the effect of his not having personally witnessed the events described.

Checklist of Additional Reviews

John Chamberlain. "Books of the Times." New York *Times*, 6 March 1942, p. 19.

Lewis Gannett. "Books and Things." New York *Herald Tribune*, 6 March 1942, p. 17.

John Gunther. "'One of the Best Short

Novels I Ever Read.'" New York *Herald Tribune*, 8 March 1942, "Books" section, p. 1.

Joseph Henry Jackson. "Books and Their Writers." San Francisco *Chronicle* (*This World* magazine), 8 March 1942, p. 12.

"Viewpoint of Victory." *Time*, 39 (9 March 1942), 84, 86–8.

"*The Moon Is Down*." *Booklist*, 38 (15 March 1942), 252.

"A French Quisling Opens the Gate, and Hate Rises around an Invader." Youngstown [Oh.] *Vindicator*, 15 March 1942, p. 8.

Robert V. Johnson. "*The Moon Is Down*: Steinbeck Writes Story of Free People Who Would Not Be Enslaved." Houston *Post*, 15 March 1942, "Magazine" section, p. 10.

"Problem of Conquering Free People Is Pictured." Asheville [N.C.] *Citizen*, 15 March 1942, Section B, p. 5.

Cara Green Russell. "The Literary Lantern." Greensboro [N.C.] *News*, 15 March 1942, Section 4, p. 5.

Robert Littell. "Outstanding Novels." *Yale Review*, 31 (Spring 1942), viii, x.

Benjamin Howden. "Nazi Conquerors Fall under Steinbeck Pen." Los Angeles *Times*, 25 March 1942, Part 3, p. 5.

Clifton Fadiman. "Books." *New Yorker*, 18 (4 April 1942), 63–4.

"*The Moon Is Down*." *Life*, 12 (6 April 1942), 32–4.

Corrine Sussman. "Letters to the Editor." New York *Times*, 15 April 1942, Section 2, p. 18.

"Steinbeck Tells Poignant Tale of an Invasion." Sacramento *Bee*, 18 April 1942, p. 17.

Wolcott Gibbs. "This Wasn't It." *New Yorker*, 18 (18 April 1942), 33–4.

Edwin Seaver. "Books." *Direction*, 5 (April–May 1942), 18–19.

Lewis Gannett. "Books and Things." New York *Herald Tribune*, 4 May 1942, p. 11.

Max Eastman. "The Library." *American Mercury*, 54 (June 1942), 754–6.

Stanley Edgar Hyman. "Some Notes on John Steinbeck." *Antioch Review*, 2 (June 1942), 185–200.

"The Controversy over *The Moon Is Down*." San Francisco *Chronicle*, 18 July 1942, p. 7.

"*The Moon Is Down*." *Bookmark*, 3 (May–August 1942), 17.

David Daiches. "Fiction and Rhetoric." *Kenyon Review*, 4 (Autumn 1942), 416–18.

THE MOON IS DOWN (THE PLAY)

THE
Moon is Down

PLAY
IN TWO PARTS

By John Steinbeck

THE VIKING PRESS · NEW YORK
1942

Brooks Atkinson. *"The Moon Is Down."* New York *Times*, 8 April 1942, p. 22.

Even if the Broadway theatre had not been moribund for most of the season, it would be easy to like and respect John Steinbeck's *The Moon Is Down*, which was acted at the Martin Beck last evening. For Mr. Steinbeck is telling a calm and reasonable story about the immortality of freedom in terms of a tiny village—probably Norwegian—that every one can understand.

Since the war has yet to be won in the face of terrible and immediate odds, *The Moon Is Down* is not a play to please the propagandists of today. It is assured; it is not rousing and provocative and it does not remind us of the stupendous job that has to be done now and tomorrow. But Mr. Steinbeck apparently feels that a free people do not have to be manipulated by half-truths and tactful evasions. Without raising his voice or playing tricks on a plot, he has put down some of the fundamental truths about man's unconquerable will to live without a master. It is a remarkably convincing play because it is honest in its heart.

Since he is dealing with basic principles, Mr. Steinbeck has refrained from defining his town as Norwegian or the invaders as German. But let us assume that this is the story of the German invasion of a small Norwegian mining town after the ground had been prepared by a local traitor. Although the young German officers are flush with victory, their colonel is a mature man who has tried invasion before. If the people do not submit he knows that the rule of terror merely increases their resistance—that every hostage shot makes a hundred additional enemies, that the more ruthless his rule, the deeper the grave he digs for himself. Everything he does to strengthen his position increases the silent, penetrating resistance that weakens his power and breaks his nerves until he is the one who is surrounded. All this Mr. Steinbeck tells in terms of ordinary people who are face to face with realities.

Although *The Moon Is Down* lacks some of the gaudier excitements of the theatre, it has something better. It has the inner strength of sincerity. As a man of reason, Mr. Steinbeck believes what he is saying, for he also believes in the intelligence, tenacity and strength of an enlightened humanity. It will be a long time before the German commanders share the misgivings of Colonel Lanser, who is as much a man of reason as Mr. Steinbeck. At first glance that reasonable character in the invader's uniform seems to be the weakness of the play. But perhaps Mr. Steinbeck is right even in this characterization. For the play rings true in every detail, and arrives at an inevitable conclusion by an orderly, cumulative progress of concrete details.

Under Chester Erskin's direction it is acted that way. Otto Kruger's Colonel Lanser is lucid and manly without excess detail. Ralph Morgan's Mayor of the town is plain, earnest and selfless. As the benign village doctor, Whitford Kane, one of the best pipe-smokers on the stage, presides in cheerful humor. Among the invaders there are some contrasting qualities that complete the picture—the pedantic officiousness of Alan Hewitt's captain, the drawling patience of Russell Collins's major and the nervous hysteria of William Eythe's skeptical lieutenant. And among the villagers there are also some other tones—Joseph Sweeney's fussy servant, Jane Seymour's sullen cook, Maria

Palmer's coldly revengeful widow of a murdered miner, Leona Powers's bustling, long-headed wife of the Mayor. As the local traitor, E. J. Ballantine is giving a skillful performance.

But the style of both the writing and the acting is unadorned and unimpassioned. Howard Bay's dark-toned settings repeat it. And the effect on the theatre is that of a great truth simply spoken. Mr. Steinbeck is writing out of a conviction that he can prove by the strength of his mind, heart and muscle.

Brooks Atkinson. "John Steinbeck's Story of a Military Invasion Appears on the Stage." New York *Times*, 12 April 1942, Section 8, p. 12.

Take Mr. Steinbeck on his own terms. In *The Moon Is Down*, which finally turned up at the Martin Beck last week, he is making a confession of faith in a style of practicable reality. Using a small mining town as his laboratory, he has written the story of a brilliantly organized military invasion that gradually breaks down in the face of elusive resistance by free men who are ingenious and angry.

The Moon Is Down is not a rhetorical play. Using words and phrases sparingly Mr. Steinbeck underwrites his heroics. To him an ounce of conviction is worth a ton of sound and fury. But he has a talent for vivid imagery that cuts deep and stays there. "Flies conquer the flypaper," screams one of the invaders who is beginning to realize that every victory increases the

hazards of conquest. "Flies capture two hundred more miles of flypaper," he laughs hysterically. Contemplating the irony of conquering a town that continues furtive resistance he bitterly exclaims: "Conquered and we are afraid. Conquered and we are surrounded." For the invaders start losing security the moment they capture the town; every step they make forward takes them two steps back. At the end of the play they are left clinging to the tail of the whirlwind they recklessly set in motion when they took over the mayor's house and started administering the town.

Mr. Steinbeck is a realist of genuine integrity. *The Moon Is Down* is a small play, deliberately. Part of the strength it has comes from the commonness of the men and women who are in it. The invaders are not supermen; they are human beings, subject to human limitations. Despite their armored swank and the omniscience of their military technique, they covet love and sociability, like any one else, and their capacity for living in a state of military correctness is not inexhaustible. The ordinary doubts of human beings weaken their bravado. Nor are the people of the town fabulous heroes. They are miners and fishermen with wives and families, subject to the usual needs. In the long run the conflict lies between character. Pit efficient inhumanity against humanity that has tasted freedom and the inhumanity finally crumbles because it is at war with the living universe. That is the theme of a quiet and sober drama that is well acted by players who are scrupulously refraining from exploiting it. To this theatregoer it is an impressive and heartening play.

Although no one doubts the high-mindedness of Mr. Steinbeck's motives, some people regard *The Moon Is Down* as a dangerous play for these times. By implication it is too much like passive resistance, they say. "Give the Axis powers enough rope," Mr. Steinbeck seems to think, "and they will hang themselves." As a matter of fact, Mr. Steinbeck is no ivory tower prophet. But the reception his play and novel have had poses a troublesome problem in contemporary writing. The long view toward the war and the short view are not identical.

In spite of the grave perils that surround the United Nations this year, most of us believe that the ultimate victory will be ours. That is the long-term faith; we cannot win without it. But the immediate problem is not the same. We cannot win the ultimate victory unless we are driven to action now by the fear of losing the war this year while the Axis powers are at the peak of their strength and we are barely on the threshold of our potential. In short, confidence in ultimate victory may be the sleeping dram that will lose the war before we know it. . . .

And this brings us to the character of Colonel Lanser, commanding officer of the invading detachment. Far from being a cold-blooded despot, he is tolerant and forbearing, disillusioned about the military science of conquest; and, as a veteran of the last war, he understands the psychology of an invaded nation more thoroughly than the people of the town. He is a martyr to a cause in which he does not believe. Mr. Steinbeck has given his most attractive character to the enemy. Although this sympathetic characterization of a representative of tyranny violates popular expectations, it is justified by the results. For it proves that the technique of invasion fails even when it is administered humanely. Colonel Lanser's reluctance to arouse resistance in the townspeople delays sabotage, murder and

reprisals. But, soon or late, the result is the same and inevitable. The town refuses to be mastered.

Take Mr. Steinbeck on his own terms. Although he is no virtuoso dramatist, he knows what he is doing. Under the casual surface of *The Moon Is Down* there is firm tension. It represents the inner serenity of a man whose mind is clear about basic things. He believes in human beings.

Mark Van Doren. "Monster Modified." *Nation*, 154 (18 April 1942), 468.

John Steinbeck's *The Moon Is Down* . . . gets nowhere with its novelty, which consists in the suggestion that a Nazi conqueror may be a man with heart and human memories after all. Its hero-villain, one Colonel Lanser who is played by Otto Kruger, is old enough to remember the other war and to know in his individual mind that this one cannot be won against the odds of universal hatred. Coming into a town, apparently Norwegian, which it has been his duty to invade, he encounters in the mayor (Ralph Morgan) and indeed in every citizen except the Quisling Corell (E. J. Ballantine) the simple and unkillable courage his private experience had schooled him to expect. He knows before he arrives, for instance, what one of his lieutenants will go all but mad with learning, namely, that at the most his army has "conquered flypaper."

Mr. Steinbeck does of course make something of this novelty, and the play has its points of interest, one of these furnishing the somewhat ghastly spectacle of the Colonel proceeding to order executions not only of persons whom he respects and likes more than he does his own people but of persons whose deaths he is certain will do no military good. The spectacle is perhaps too ghastly, too inexpressible, to be of use in tragedy, which cannot afford to leave too much of its meaning unspoken. At any rate Mr. Steinbeck is unable in the writing to put his finger on the point of conflict which will yield him as dramatist the maximum effect of power. The entire town hates the invader, yes; but the invader is divided and obscure, so that, at what should be the climax, we have the Mayor walking out of his house to be shot as a hostage by one who is merely bored with shooting, not to say sick of slaughtering good friends. The Colonel so far agrees with the Mayor as to be one who can prompt him as he rehearses the farewell speech of Socrates; the conflict is not between them at all, any more than it is in the mind of the Colonel alone, which remains a mind that Mr. Steinbeck has not concretely or intensely imagined. The Colonel, in other words, is no more a man than is the customary monster of the anti-Nazi drama. He has been modified in idea only. The ingredient added has been added to what is still an abstraction. So with the Mayor, who is nothing whatever in addition to what he needs by formula to be; and so with all the others who assist in the working out of a humanely conceived but woodenly written play.

The wood is partly in the dialogue, which rarely sounds natural or is spoken with the peculiar personal emphasis we can miss so much when it is not there. This is probably the reason that so many commentators have been free to discuss the tendency or moral of the play; to wonder, for example, whether Mr. Steinbeck has done well to suggest that all a conquered country has to do is wait until the conqueror remembers his humanity. It does not matter that much. Were the play better than it is, we should simply believe it; were it worse than it is, its effect would not matter at all. Just as it is, it seems to me to prove nothing either about its own characters, whom I do not believe, or about Norway in 1942, which it leaves hypothetical and remote.

"New Play in Manhattan."
Time, 39 (20 April 1942), 36.

... Primarily intended for the stage, *The Moon Is Down* was first rigged up as a novel ... and inside five weeks sold almost half a million copies. Theoretically the tailor-made play should beat the make-shift novel all hollow; actually it can't come near it. Steinbeck's fable of how some unnamed but obviously Nazi invaders take over an unlocalized but obviously Norwegian mining town, meet with icy resistance and are themselves worn down, never really comes to life in the theater.

Part of the blame lies in the production's slow-footed pace, heavy-handed direction, weak acting. But part of the trouble is the play itself. The dialogue, more like subdued rhetoric than human talk, often seems stilted and formal when spoken aloud. The play lacks sustained action and commits the dramatic crime of having almost everything exciting take place offstage. Finally, though the townspeople's heroic resolution is made clear, their flesh-and-blood sufferings are not.

Nevertheless, the play, like the novel,

should provoke a hot debate as to how sound, and how salutary, is Steinbeck's thesis: that a free people cannot be conquered. Heartening and lofty though this message may be, right now it can also be over-reassuring to a still-too-optimistic U.S. If Steinbeck is civilized enough to make his Nazis human beings rather than monsters, he is naive enough to picture them as weak, unable to stand up to a cold shoulder. In defeat, the Nazis will probably crack up in a hurry; but there are no grounds for supposing that they go to pieces in victory.

Steinbeck's already famous phrase, "The flies have conquered the flypaper," is a memorable slogan and, taking a very long view, a valid observation. But in terms of here and now, it has still to be proved.

"Steinbeck's Faith." Newsweek, 19 (20 April 1942), 72–3.

John Steinbeck's short novel, The Moon Is Down, was a best seller almost from the first day it was published early last month. At the time reviewers called it a play masquerading between covers, and many sagely predicted that it would reach the peak of its effectiveness behind footlights. That it fails to do so is one of the major disappointments of a disappointing theater season.

Oscar Serlin's production is a faithful transcription, and Steinbeck, the playwright, retains the book's warm feeling for little people. His faith in the ultimate triumph of free man over herd men is still touching and inspiring, but the drama, as directed by Chester Erskin, is surprisingly deficient in impact and plausibility. Although Steinbeck's heroes are the plain, democratic inhabitants of a Norwegian town (the author identifies people and places only by implication), their heroism is largely an off-stage phenomenon.

Steinbeck feels that Nazism is self-defeating, and to prove his thesis, concentrates on a small group of invaders who are average, unextraordinary human beings momentarily deluded by their leaders. The protective coating of Nazi superiority is merely ersatz in the face of the unrelenting hostility and hatred of their victims.

Colonel Lanser takes on added charm and civilization as impersonated by Otto Kruger. Similarly—with the exception of Alan Hewitt's ferocious Captain Loft, and E. J. Ballantine's local Quisling—Lanser's aids are personable and more than a little pathetic. At the same time, Ralph Morgan—miscast and misguided as Mayor Orden—projects the white-haired hero of the people as a bewildered, sentimental old dodderer.

While the novel was generally a critical as well as popular success, there were readers and reviewers, like James Thurber in The New Republic and Clifton Fadiman in The New Yorker, who questioned the wisdom of Steinbeck's lofty tolerance in midwar, and attacked as dangerous the gratifying conclusion that the Nazis would defeat themselves.

With the drama playing to a packed house nightly, controversy engaged the drama critics. Richard Lockridge of The New York Sun and Louis Kronenberger of PM took the view that Steinbeck's charitable conception of the Nazi superman may be the accepted verdict in the days to come, but they both said that the play would be more credible if Hitler's men had ever demonstrated, in their conquests, any spiritual inability to survive a snubbing by their victims. Lockridge termed the author "tolerant to a fault. . . . Maybe we'd better start forgiving [the Nazis] after we have licked them." Kronenberger attacked the play as misguided propaganda for "a nation that is still too complacent."

On the other hand, Burns Mantle of *The New York Daily News* and Wilella Waldorf of *The New York Post* took comfort in the hope that the drama portrays, while Brooks Atkinson of *The New York Times* tipped his hat to a "calm and reasonable story." Richard Watts, *New York Herald Tribune*, applauded the tribute to gallant Norway, but objected to the nicety of Steinbeck's Nazis which "feeds us on the false hope that the Germans are not the strong, determined, terribly powerful people that they are."

David Burnham. "*The Moon Is Down.*" *Commonweal*, 36 (24 April 1942), 14–15.

Like *Of Mice and Men*, *The Moon Is Down* is a virtually word-for-word transcript by John Steinbeck of his own short novel of the same title. The stage version of *Of Mice and Men* was more effective than the fiction version. The reverse, it seems to me, is true of *The Moon Is Down*. For this, the casting and direction are considerably to blame. But it goes deeper than that. The core of *Of Mice and Men* was emotion, arising directly out of action. The core of *The Moon Is Down* is aspiration, arising chiefly out of rhetoric. The former is dramatic method; the latter, literary.

Judging from the enormous popularity of the fiction version, the theme of *The Moon Is Down* must be already familiar to most readers of this column. . . . The invaders learn that "herd men" may momentarily dominate but cannot conquer free men.

I don't intend to enter the controversy regarding the expediency of Steinbeck's message. The propagandists object that Steinbeck's long view of the power of democracy makes for complacency, blinds us to the need for immediate decisive aggression. I delegate this complaint to Mr. Archibald MacLeish. It is also objected that Steinbeck's totalitarians aren't sufficiently villainous. I object to the motive of this complaint, but it touches the play's chief dramatic defect.

Steinbeck's thesis postulates a conflict between "free men" and "herd men." And yet the herd man is never adequately represented. Only one minor character is truly a herd man, and him his own fellows ridicule. The chief nazi (or whatever Steinbeck chooses to call them), the commanding Colonel, is reasonable, self-deprecatory, cynical. I don't say that a totalitarian colonel might not be so, but as such he is an insufficient symbol of what Steinbeck meant to attack. His reasonableness and cynicism preclude dramatic conflict. It might have become a dramatic situation if this officer had been introduced flushed with victorious confidence and crusading zeal, and been gradually broken down, as several of his subordinates are, by underground resistance which retaliatory violence only aggravates; but instead of this, he reveals in his first scene that an experience in Belgium twenty-five years ago, before Hitler was invented, had already sided him with Steinbeck.

Is it, then, the author's message that the totalitarian method is not sympathetic even to its followers? But if there are, when we probe them sympathetically, no herd men, what is the point in proving that free men cannot be conquered by herd men? One face of Steinbeck's message would appear to be high-minded tolerance; the other face equates heroism with sabotage and, in one case, the cold-blooded murder of a homesick boy by a lonely young widow.

To avoid melodrama, Steinbeck has located all physical action off stage. And his dialogue is for the most part studiously anti-heroic. When I spoke above of his rhetoric, I didn't mean the sort of purple bombast that word often connotes. Understatement is no less a device of rhetoric than overstatement. The direction aims at the same anti-heroic tone, but the device is more effective on the printed page. As I have indicated, the casting of the leading rôles is not happy. Otto Kruger's Colonel Lanser is military in dress only; his qualities and mannerisms are those of a reserved, cultivated Englishman. So small a matter as a crisper accent might have vivified the whole play. I can't think of a better comment on Ralph Morgan's performance as the local Mayor than the remark of a young lady sitting behind me when at the end he was led off to be executed: "Isn't he *cute?*"

like the play even more. But the fact remains that what Mr. Steinbeck has to say about the good people inheriting the earth (eventually) is more convincing on the printed page than it is heard from the stage. This is due partly to the fact that the reader of the book gets more satisfaction from his own imagined characterizations, suggested by Mr. Steinbeck's economical and beautiful prose, than the casting in the play affords. We did not, for example, see Colonel Lanser, head man of the invaders and representative of the ruthless Nazi system, the way Otto Kruger played him. Nor did we visualize Mayor Orden (Ralph Morgan) as the consistently bewildered leader of a group of people so slow to take fire.

Mr. Steinbeck's long-view thesis, in both play and book, that no free people can be permanently conquered, that "herd men may win battles, but free men will win wars," isn't enough for a time like ours. It's a comforting thought, something to keep our undying faith pinned to during the next terrible months and years, but meantime, freedom-loving people all over the world have been, and are being conquered every day.

"The Play's the Thing." *Scholastic*, 40 (27 April—2 May 1942), 19.

Those of you who have read John Steinbeck's new novel, *The Moon Is Down*, have also read his new play, now on view at the Martin Beck Theater in New York, produced by Oscar Serlin. The play is the book, almost verbatim. . . .

We liked the book, and expected to

John Gassner. "*The Moon Is Down* as a Play." *Current History*, 2 (May 1942), 228–32.

It took John Steinbeck to jog the increasingly dormant theatre during its first wartime season. Just as it had settled down to nearly uninterrupted somnolence, Mr. Steinbeck came along with the production of *The Moon Is Down*, and instantly the air was filled with controversy, people began to consider again what the art of theatre really is, and playgoers had, at long last, a play that they could attend without feeling foolish.

The story is by now familiar to both the playgoing and the reading public, for Mr. Steinbeck's novelette has been bought by nearly half a million Americans and the book reviewers everywhere have discussed it. Invaders easily identified as Nazi soldiers capture a mining town in a country that is unmistakably Norway. . . .

But they are quickly disillusioned, for a free people does not lightly accept enslavement. . . . Before long, railroad tracks are blown up, communications interrupted incessantly, and the conquerors are harassed continually. The flies, as a hysterical officer remarks, have conquered the fly-paper. Free men are easily taken unawares, and they are slow to act in concert. But their spirit is invincible; for this reason herd men win all the battles, and free men all the wars.

That is Steinbeck's affirmation in these days of darkness, and who can fail to respond to his good tidings or fail to be moved by them? The author's message is all the more appealing since it is delivered without heroics or fustian. He has employed the method of understatement, and the bedrock simplicity of the townspeople gives justification to his approach, which is notably limpid and restrained. Moreover, he has cast his parable in the mold of human beings, among whom the two prominent figures are the wonderfully understood Colonel Lanser, a gentleman and thinker though a relentless soldier in the line of duty, and Mayor Orden, a mild and simple person whose strength runs deep and never froths on the surface. Out of them emanates Steinbeck's confident prognosis for civilization—not merely because they remind us that there are civilized men even in the midst of outrage and oppression, but because both the Colonel's well-founded doubt as to the efficacy of the force he is ordered to apply and the Mayor's stubborn courage signalize the inevitability of defeat for the conquerors.

A good deal of the beauty and power of the novelette translates itself into the theatre. Mayor Orden, played by Ralph Morgan, and Colonel Lanser, by Otto Kruger, invest Steinbeck's leading characters with their proper humanity; and it is also gratifying to see several other characters in the flesh, and to hear their voices. Snow falling, the tramping of a patrol through the dark streets, the lights going off as sabotage begins, a shot through the window immediately after the execution of a miner, the infernal little British parachutes spread on the Colonel's table, and finally the sound of distant bombardment—all these give visual and audible reality to the story in the time-honored manner of the theatre. We learn from this production what we have always known—that the stage, which is so vulnerable to inclement social weather and to the fumbling that can arise in a collaborative art, has been able to hold men's hearts and imagination because in it literally the word becomes flesh.

But the stage is a platform, and everything that occurs on it is, so to speak, on exhibition. And what an exhibition! Lights, scenery, costumes, curtains rising and falling, sound, and music attend the spectacle. Therefore, flaws in a work of art, though occasionally glossed over by the magic of theatrical effects, become highlighted. The experience resembles that of watching a complexion under kleig-lights. It is on the stage of the Martin Beck Theatre that the potential weaknesses of Steinbeck's novelette become actual.

His dialogue sounds frequently pedestrian from the platform. His Nazi soldiery seems painfully unrepresentative, for all but one of the officers seem so mild as to lead one to wonder how they could have conquered nation after nation and perpetrated the verified brutalities of Warsaw. Worse still, our sympathies are not only divided, but unequally divided, so that the issue is beclouded. Although we admire Mayor Orden and everything he represents, we are compelled to pity the fly-paper more than the flies. We are constantly made sensible of their pathos of bewilderment, longing for home, and desire to be liked and accepted. The most dramatic situation in the play is the murder of the lonely Lieutenant Tonder by the woman whom he has treated with great delicacy, and from whom he wanted a little sympathy.

Colonel Lanser is the most fascinating character in the drama because it is in him, and not in his opponent, the Mayor, that a genuine dramatic conflict is projected. And as we watch him torn between his tired wisdom and his sense of duty we even admire him. We admire the Mayor, too, but in the last analysis we expect him to behave as he does, since he is by definition representative of what we consider the spirit of freedom. Colonel Lanser must be regarded as either atypical, in which case the drama becomes a special case, or as typical, in which case the argument against the Nazis loses much of its force. The one personally reprehensible character in the invader's camp is Captain Loft, and he is more comic than sinister. Since, moreover, the veteran Colonel regards him with contempt, we get the impression that the military leaders of the Nazi war-machine dislike the behaviour of their subordinates instead of fostering it with virtually machiavellian deliberateness. It is true, of course, that all oppressive and ruthless measures are attributed to some central office in Berlin, but in a play off-stage re-alities are shadowy realities, and the impression they leave is invariably secondary to the impression created by what is shown on the stage.

This, finally, is also true of the resistance of the conquered. Not a single case of such resistance is concretely dramatized for the audience. A miner is brought in for a very polite trial; Mayor Orden refuses to be one of the judges, and later he refuses to tell his people to stop their sabotage, and in neither instance does his action precipitate a climactic scene. It is true that he goes out to die after quoting Socrates, but the actual conflict tapers off. Indeed, the concluding scene, though touching in its own right, winds up the dramatic situation with almost perfunctory brevity.

If Mr. Steinbeck could be charged with writing the mere outline of a novel in his published book, it could be maintained, with greater justification, that he created the mere sketch of a play. As a novelette, *The Moon Is Down* is a distinguished minor work; minor because even a novelette can have greater density of experience, as Edith Wharton showed in *Ethan Frome*, Tolsoy in *The Death of Ivan Ilyitch*, and Balzac in *The Succubus*. As a play, *The Moon Is Down* is still distinguished, because of the penetrative characterization of Colonel Lanser, the noble pathos of Mayor Orden, and the agony of Lieutenant Tonder; and one must respect the dramatic version for its avoidance of obvious melodrama and pyrotechnics, and for the occasional positive values of understatement, as in the quiet final scene. But the play produces a confusing alignment of forces, a divided effect, and a somehow incompletely precipitated dramatic experience. In the theatre, Steinbeck's story is consequently ineffectual.

The blame, however, must be shared by the production. The casting of the actors was curiously unintelligent. Instead of compensating for such shortcomings as the mildness of the minor officers, the director actually brought them to the fore. The officers were played by young men whom the feminine portion of the audience must have wished it could mother, and the comportment and bearing assigned to them was utterly innocuous. The pace of the entire production kept the drama crawling along with incongruous peacefulness and only the quiet moments in the text were effectively staged. Climactic actions were treated as though the director had been ashamed of them. When the miner is taken out to be shot in the first act, the firing squad gets to work without any suggestion of charged suspense in the Mayor's drawing-room. When immediately after the execution, a shot is fired through the window, young Lieutenant Prackle receives it in his shoulder as though somebody had hit him with a bean-shooter, and on his next appearance in the play he gives no indication whatever that he was wounded. Most of the real theatrical effects that added something to the written page are to be credited, not to the director, but to the exigencies of the stage, to the fact that reality represented on a platform acquires dimension and aliveness. . . .

Rosamond Gilder.
"Moon Down, Theatre Rises."
Theatre Arts, 26 (May 1942), 287–92.

"The people are confused and so am I." So speaks the Mayor of the little snow-embowered town on a northern sea which has suddenly and inexplicably been conquered by a murderous, military power. The people are confused, but not for long. Little by little, inexorably, with slow, relentless pace, the people learn, the people know. And in their bitter, silent, devious ways the people become unconquerable. In *The Moon Is Down* John Steinbeck unfolds before our eyes the blind, the almost silent struggle of the free spirit of man against oppression. His little mining town is a microcosm of the universe. Here the battle of the forces that are ripping the earth apart is played out in miniature and in a minor key, as though muffled by the cold and snow, but no less epically than in the major battle-fields of Russia, Burma or Bataan. . . .

With an extraordinary economy of means, Mr. Steinbeck has given each of his "herd men" an individuality that makes them far more convincing than the cardboard figures of the average anti-Nazi play. One young Lieutenant is driven to the verge of insanity by the tension and horror that slowly invade the snow-locked village, crying out hysterically that he has had a dream—or a thought—that the leader is insane—that the communiques might well read, "the flies have conquered the fly-paper!" The fact that Mr. Steinbeck's invaders are people, not bogies, makes the shooting of hostages, the starving of children to make their fathers work, the fear and hate engendered on both sides all the more devastating. Though the Colonel may be a humanist and listen and even prompt the Mayor as the latter whiles away his own last moment recalling Socrates' denunciation of his murderers, he orders the execution of the Mayor just the same.

Mr. Steinbeck's vivid apprehension of people, as well as his ability to create mood, to set his stage in time and space, provides the actors who interpret his characters with excellent material for performance to which they do full justice. Both the leading roles, the Mayor and the Colonel, sensitively handled by Ralph Morgan and Otto Kruger, present their difficulties. The Mayor, with his early hesitancies and uncertainties, must not appear uncertain as an actor, nor must the Colonel's unorthodox humanity soften too much the harsher outline of his ruthless procedures. The other characters are less complex but equally rewarding in their various ways. Whitford Kane plays the doctor, friend and confidant of the Mayor, with his accustomed warmth and understanding. Russell Collins as the engineer, Alan Hewitt as the complete Nazi, E. J. Ballantine as the fifth columnist, and William Eythe and Carl Gose as the young Lieutenants all give excellent performances which carry this quiet play of violent events forward to its heartbreaking and exultant close.

The power and the poignancy of Steinbeck's play lie in its immediacy, its ability to express world issues with the terrible nearness of little things, its affirmation of the dignity and nobility of man. This place and these people might be in Norway or New England, China or Australia; on the stage they are ourselves: we tremble as they do, our rage boils within us, we almost cheer from our aisle seats when the little parachutes, sent by friendly planes, drop dynamite (and chocolate bars) to help in the fight against the invader. Whether or not, politically speaking, Mr. Steinbeck is over-optimistic about the amount and strength of resistance in occupied countries; whether or not, strategically speaking, his ingenious method of arming the unarmed masses, "writhing and starving under the oppressor's heel," is sound, there is no doubt that he has succeeded in expressing in pure theatric terms an eloquent plea for democracy, a stirring call-to-arms to all free fighting spirits.

Euphemia Wyatt.
"The Drama."
Catholic World, 155
(May 1942), 212–14.

. . . The most unexpected thrill for American History came to me on the little bridge at Concord, Massachusetts. Mr. Steinbeck's play gives you the same tingle of pride. It is the essence of Bataan. *The Moon Is Down* takes up the story of free men where Mr. Sherwood left it in *There Shall Be No Night*. The invaders have come. This time the country may probably be Norway but the tragedy is the same—tragedy, that is, in its grandest sense. It is tragic that men must die for an idea but glorious that the idea survives them. When a man writes with complete conviction he can afford to be simple. The people of Mr. Steinbeck's mining town are commonplace people who are not ashamed to own that they are frightened. The conquerors are no inhuman brutes but soldiers obeying harsh orders. The lieutenants are boys who look forward to peace time. The Captain may be the thorough party man who swells as a conqueror but the Colonel has lived through the years of Belgian occupation and he knows the price exacted by conquest.

The Assyrians, after all, were the most intelligent world-conquerors. They took no chances with captive nations but transported them at once to other countries. There was plenty of room in those days in Mesopotamia and the Assyrian lion opened his jaws wide enough to digest a great many of them. Only two Jewish tribes returned to Palestine where they found aliens rooted in Samaria who had already shed their own paganism and acquired local customs—such is the power of the soil. Lacking world-space the present conquerors are forced to leave their captives where they are and the Colonel foresaw only too well the consequences. Five hostages shot for every soldier killed would make just five times five more implacable enemies. The struggle began at once. Three months later it is the defeated people who are stealthily defeating the conquerors; hemmed in by the cold and the snow, surrounded by covert hate, teased by never-ending annoyances: broken dynamos, broken rails, bitter coffee, constant suspicion.... It is a little difficult to say whether *The Moon Is Down* is more a story with the stage directions amplified or a play with the explanatory paragraphs omitted. Most likely everyone will like it best in the form in which they first knew it. Both begin with the first visit of the Colonel to the Mayor; both end on the Mayor being taken out to be shot as the town roars defiance with a new explosion. Many of the lines common to both versions will be endlessly quoted. "Free men can fight on in defeat ... so it is always the herd men who win battles and the free men who win wars."

There has been some criticism about the officers not being convincing. It may be that we have been so used to having foreign actors play them that an accent has become a tradition. It is also against stage tradition to have these "super leaders" ordinary homesick boys. Personally we can find nothing unpatriotic in having the Colonel an intelligent, broadminded soldier who hates his particular job.... Otto Kruger is exceptional in the part. Ralph Morgan's Mayor has for some too much gentleness but he suggests a background which makes his Socratic quotation at the end quite natural. Alan Hewitt has the effective part of the dogmatic Captain but Whitford Kane, Russell Collins

and Joseph Sweeney all have parts incommensurate with their abilities, but do much to strengthen the general picture.

The Moon Is Down has been said to instill a dangerous degree of optimism but is fear or pictured horror any surer incentive to action than an increased pride in the heritage of freedom? No actual act of brutality may be shown but for all the people's bravery and determination, the price that they are paying in their souls for the struggle is made clear when the unfortunate girl-widow is driven to a cold-blooded murder. Mr. Steinbeck's play is the fresh wind in a stale season.

Stark Young. "Serious Images." *New Republic*, 106 (11 May 1942), 638–9.

The theme and situation of the new Steinbeck play are by now too well known to dwell on here. The novel has had a vast sale and the play a very considerable amount of attention.... In the end it is the invaders who are surrounded by the village, and broken down emotionally, the younger officers most of all.

The point of this theme depends, of course, to a certain extent on the nature of the colonel heading the invasion; since a perhaps younger and more ruthless leader might have annihilated the village. This possibility, however, the dramatist has partially countered by making the Germans dependent on the native miners for the coal, without which the invasion would have been a waste of time.

There is, accordingly, implicit in the

play no essence of inescapable logic that would help to make it significant. For this final logic it depends a good deal on the persuasion of the character combinations, the acting and the mood established. But the elevation of the dramatist's mind and intention and the nobility of his approach do much to reinforce our conviction toward this thesis he offers regarding men's souls; so that the play, though it is not the proof, is at least the evidence of the truth of its faith and belief.

The basic limitation of *The Moon Is Down* lies most in the writing itself. A certain economy, a stripping down and simplification, is attempted which may go well enough in a printed novel but which on the stage leans too much on the director and the players, to whom it gives very little really to do or say and then expects them to create something around and into it. This type of economy in writing may come off well in the high epic manner or in writing essentially poetic and rooted in imagery, like that of John Synge. But on the realistic plane it runs toward monotony; in a style so close to life and nature we require more living rhythms to speak. It would seem that many of the situations and characters could, as the play stands now, be filled out and further developed; though to what extent and how this would affect the total impression would remain to be seen. *The Moon Is Down* must, nevertheless, be ranked far above most contemporary plays in its purpose, its central inner quality, its serious and quiet application to the world today, and its hold on us.

"*The Moon Is Down.*" *Library Journal*, 67 (1 September 1942), 739.

Play form of best-selling novel about group of simple people under Nazi yoke. Judged by some critics the best play of 1941–42 season. Suitable for little theater production. . . .

"Steinbeck in Sweden." *Time*, 41 (19 April 1943), 42.

Opening in Stockholm last month, John Steinbeck's anti-Nazi, inferentially Norwegian *The Moon Is Down* proved such a smash that it speedily moved to a bigger theater. Swedish critics, speaking of ever-growing Norwegian resistance, praised Steinbeck for prophetic insight, remarked that *The Moon Is Down* is truer today than when it was written.

Judging by reports which have sifted through, the widespread U.S. criticism that the Nazis in the play are too weak has not been voiced in Sweden.

"Whitehall Theatre." London *Times*, 9 June 1943, p. 6C.

The special quality of this moving play seems to spring from the author's surprise and pleasure in his discovery of how much ordinary people will do for freedom. "You cannot," says the honest old mayor, facing the Nazi invaders in his tiny palace, "you cannot break man's spirit permanently."

It is as though Mr. Steinbeck had found in contemporary history proofs he hardly expected to find of the truth of this statement; and from his sudden new pride in the spirit's power of endurance the play draws its freshness and its theatrical impetus. Extraordinary as it may seem, a cook will throw boiling water over one conqueror who has irritated her and bite another who goes to the rescue; a hot-tempered miner ordered to get on with his work will strike the foreign foreman dead with his pickaxe; and his execution will raise 20 new enemies of the occupying forces. In time the triumphant troops themselves, thinking always of home, hating the invisible net of hatred they have drawn about themselves, their nerves stretched to breaking-point, will begin to fear what awaits them when they crack. Then the flies will have conquered the fly-paper.

It is this chain of consequences which fascinates the dramatist. He works it out in the soberly, realistic way of one who is so sure of his spiritual theme that character and incident must be made even at the cost of minor falsifications to explain it. Colonel Lanser, the grey, hard, tired-looking German officer who has reason to remember the military occupation of Belgium, is deliberately romanticized for this purpose. He knows how ruinously wrong are the things he is ordered to do, and dutifully he does them. The character disturbs the realistic values, but it is theatrically most effective, and Mr. Karel Stepanek plays it well enough to suggest that he might encompass a fascinating Hamlet. The mayor, on the other hand, is no less effectively conceived in terms of realism, and Mr. Lewis Casson gives the part all the unstrained simplicity which is

its due. The least plausible episode is that in which the miner's wife takes her revenge on her husband's executioner. Here Mr. Steinbeck seems momentarily to forget his enthralling chain of consequences while he writes a conventional and too protracted love scene.

The audience last night included King Haakon.

James Redfern. "The Theatre." *Spectator* [England], 170 (18 June 1943), 567.

... Not much need be said here about John Steinbeck's play on his novel *The Moon Is Down*, which has some excellent forceful dramatic scenes marred by the unreality and sentimentality of the women's acting—particularly in the scene in the miner's wife's house—for which the producer must be held partly responsible. There is some excellent acting by Lewis Casson as the Mayor and Karel Stepanek as the cleverly drawn German Colonel....

"*The Moon Is Down.*" *New Statesman and Nation* [England], 25 (19 June 1943), 400.

... *The Russians* isn't a satisfactory play, but its material is authentic and it kicks to the end, which is more than can be said of *The Moon Is Down*. This

Steinbeck piece, a generalised picture of the invasion of Norway, was far more convincing as a novel. On the stage, it looks unreal in the extreme; the Nazis arrive in a state of mental breakdown, the Mayor holds firm, his wife wonders whether to give them wine, the upstart business-man has paved the way for the invaders, and months of occupation bring jitters and sabotage in the night. Lewis Casson gives a dignified performance in the rôle of the Mayor, but the whole production goes at a snail's pace. Unlike *The Russians*, this play has no genuine background, and anyone who thinks of visiting the Whitehall would do better to stay at home and read the account of invasion in *The Mountains Wait*.

A[lan] D[ent]. "At the Play." *Punch* [England], 204 (23 June 1943), 532.

... Both *The Moon Is Down* and *The Russians* say that there is a tremendous and thornily complicated war waging, and say it with the most lurid and resonant effectiveness. The one gives Mr.

John Steinbeck's American view (stated before America's entry) and the other M. Konstantin Simonov's Russian view (set down when its young author was in the actual field of battle). If these plays have to be compared one would say that the first is better art and the second better melodrama. But both plays are rich in momentous incident, and in both the enemy is not made to seem improbable. There are, too, some sterling performances. In the Steinbeck Mr. Lewis Casson as a martyred Mayor, Mr. W. E. Holloway as his gentle doctor-friend, and Mr. Karel Stepanek as a Nazi Colonel with some hopeful misgivings about him. In the Simonov Mr. Michael Golden and Miss Freda Jackson as guerrilla fighters, Mr. Russell Thorndike as a quisling, Miss Olga Lindo as his harrowed wife who feels obliged to betray him, and Mr. Arthur Hambling who walks to certain death as proudly as Fortinbras's army.

Checklist of Additional Reviews

Milton Bracker. "Note on Colonel Lanser." New York *Times*, 19 April 1942, Section 8, p. 1.

BOMBS AWAY

Bombs Away

THE STORY OF A BOMBER TEAM

Written for the U. S. Army Air Forces by

JOHN STEINBECK

With 60 Photographs by John Swope

NEW YORK · THE VIKING PRESS · 1942

Joseph Henry Jackson. "The Bookman's Notebook." San Francisco *Chronicle*, 26 November 1942, p. 11Y.

Since the move into Africa, Americans have become more than ever conscious of the great bombing planes that have been coming off the production lines for months past. The terms "Fortress" and "Liberator" are common words today; we regard those magnificent engines of destruction almost with affection.

The fact is, however, that we know more about the planes themselves than about the men who operate them. There have been magazine articles—a few—and there have been some newspaper stories. But until now the whole extraordinary story hasn't been told.

John Steinbeck's new book tells that story. *Bombs Away* . . . is its title. It's no romance, no fictionized yarn, but a book of actualities, written specifically at the request of the U. S. Air Forces. To write it, Steinbeck toured for months, visiting training fields all over the country. With him went John Swope, himself a flyer, to take the 60 fine photographs that illustrate the book. Text and photographs together, this is as completely American a book as the war has produced. It's the story of something very specially and peculiarly U. S. A. In a way it epitomized America at war—as you'll see the moment you open it.

There are six jobs that make up a bomber crew, six tasks that must be performed with all the precision, all the *élan* of, for example, a crack basketball team

executing a carefully thought-out play.

The men that do these jobs are the pilot, the navigator, the bombardier, the crew chief, the gunner, the radio man.

How are these men selected? How are they trained? After individual training, how are they welded into the compact, hard-hitting, smooth team that they must be in order to function properly?

The answers to these questions are the material of *Bombs Away*!

To tell his story, Steinbeck selects six typical Americans, young fellows who wanted to fly, and tells the story of each, from his boyhood up through his selection for the air forces, his individual training, his team practice.

Here, step by step, you may follow what's happening, perhaps, to your son, your nephew, to thousands of young Americans, the pick of the Nation.

. . . It's a dramatic, admirably told, crystal-clear narrative that Steinbeck has put together, and it will tell Americans for the first time the whole story of that enormously important arm of our fighting forces, the thousands of bombers that are our spearhead in the kind of war we must fight. . . .

Lewis Gannett. "Books and Things." New York *Herald Tribune*, 27 November 1942, p. 19.

John Steinbeck is half-Irish, and he has a conscience, perhaps inherited from the New England missionary who was his grandmother on his other side. When an Irishman gets mad he wants to fight, and when a New Englander gets mad he begins by preaching. Steinbeck, moreover, started out to be a biologist before he took to writing stories; in his way he is still a biologist. And he is forty years old. Put that all together and you may understand how John Steinbeck came to write *Bombs Away: The Story of a Bomber Team*. . . .

Bombs Away is the meticulously precise life-history of a bomber team: a scientifically precise account of what it is, and how it gets that way, written with passion by a man who deeply regrets that he cannot be part of one. It isn't what you would expect from the author of *Tortilla Flat*, of *Grapes of Wrath*, or even of *Sea of Cortez*. But then, nothing that Steinbeck has written has ever been just what the readers of his previous books expected of him, which is one of the things which proves that he is a writer. It isn't a story; it is at times more like a textbook, and sometimes like a sermon. Steinbeck wanted to do something about this war; *Bombs Away* is one product of that urge. . . .

I talked with John Steinbeck about this book early last summer, when the magazines were full of stories about bad morale in the training camps. "It isn't true," he said, if I remember him aright. "We've never had a better Army. I've been around a little. The officers are good; the men are good; the people making weapons are good; and they aren't excited. They are doing the job, and it is a good job. The young men of today are as good as any young men ever were—perhaps better."

This book is written in that faith, and in the further faith that the best of them are in the bomber teams, whom John Steinbeck watched training, with whom he flew over the Gulf of Mexico. It is written with a conviction that it was not to our discredit that no nation in history

had ever tried more passionately or more thoughtfully to avoid fighting than we did; that it was not to the discredit of the depression generation that they did not know where they were going; that Pearl Harbor set in motion the most powerful biological drive known—that of survival; that air war is a natural channel of expression for young America; and that the nation is entitled to feel a kind of fierce joy in the experience and training of our young aviators. Wandering around the country, Steinbeck met grumblers and doubters; so he sat down, first to study, biologically, the "greatest team in the world," the American bomber team, and then to preach about it. *Bombs Away* is the result. . . .

The United States Army . . . has developed some amazing gadgets for perfecting the training of those lads. Steinbeck tells about some of them—and also about the excruciating discipline of "parachute parades" gayly imposed on the boys when they first go out of bounds. He leads you, conscientiously and patiently and proudly, through each stage of that training. He gives you an extraordinary picture of the sensation of first flight, when the little training plane seems balanced in the air, "tippy as a canoe and as dependable in the hands of a flyer," and of the mystical sense of brotherhood among flying men. (All Irishmen are part mystics, and Steinbeck is part Irish.) He says that these flying men of ours go through an experience which "has the impact of religion, and while most of them are never able to say it, never want to say it, they all understand it."

Navy flyers may feel that John Steinbeck has acquired not only a religion of flying, but a religion of Army flying, and dispute his assertions about the role of land-based bombers. But they will understand and respect the spirit in which he wrote this book. The bomber teams, to whom the book is dedicated, will not, Mr. Steinbeck thinks, want or have time to read his book, for to them it would be primer work. He wrote it as a primer for parents—and as a sermon.

Orville Prescott.
"Books of the Times."
New York *Times*,
27 November 1942, p. 21.

"The nation is at war. There isn't time for ceremony and parade. This isn't a war of flags and marching. It is a war of finding the target in the cross-hairs of the bombsight and setting the release, and it isn't a war of speeches and frothy hatred. It is a technical job, a surgeon's job. There is only time for hatred among civilians. Hatred does not operate a bombsight."

In this mechanized war, dependent for its successful conclusion on many men's professional mastery of many complex techniques, the supreme example of just such a scientific, objective manner of waging war is to be found in the United States Army Air Force Flying Fortress and Liberator bomber crews. As war can be fought rationally, coolly and precisely, so can books about it be written in the same manner. John Steinbeck has done so in his *Bombs Away: The Story of a Bomber Team*, which is out today and from which the above opening lines are taken.

As a nation we are intensely proud of our Air Force. Mr. Steinbeck shows how well justified that pride is. The finest young men in this country, physically, mentally and morally, are in it. Their training and their equipment are the best in the world. . . . In this book, written as a public service at the request of the Army Air

Force, Mr. Steinbeck describes how the members of the bomber crews are selected, how they are trained for their various duties and how they are welded into the greatest example of team work in the world. Sixty photographs by John Swope are closely integrated with the text. The author's and photographer's royalties and the publishing profits will all go to the Air Forces Aid Society Trust Fund. . . .

Bombs Away is a book to stir you to the core with a warm glow of patriotism. With men and machines like these our country can look forward to the future as boldly as when similar men with no machines were conquering the wilderness. It is a book of clear, clean, exact expository writing, with only occasional traces of manner to suggest that it is written by the author of *The Grapes of Wrath*. It has as little use for the more creative literary virtues as a purely factual article in a trade journal. With no pretensions of doing anything else, *Bombs Away* offers "the story of a bomber team" to all those who are interested in just such timely information. Their number undoubtedly will be enormous.

Clifton Fadiman.
"Books."
New Yorker, 18
(28 November 1942),
80–2.

. . . The Army Air Forces did a smart thing when they got John Steinbeck to write *Bombs Away*. They are a first-rate outfit and there is no reason in the world why a first-rate writer should not handle their recruiting propaganda. For that is essentially what *Bombs Away* is—an extraordinarily fine job of recruiting propaganda which achieves its effect by telling the truth in words that have life in them.

It's pointless to say that Steinbeck has written better books than this. This is not a "book" in the book-reviewer's narrow sense at all. It aims "to set down in simple terms the nature and mission of a bomber crew and the technique and training of it." This clear, useful aim Steinbeck accomplishes by telling the complete story of a hypothetical crew from the moment six young men from various corners of the land shamble tiredly into an induction centre as Army Air Forces candidates to that superb moment when "the greatest team in the world" takes to the vast night air to accomplish its first true mission.

The whole story is told by personalizing the six-man team (navigator, pilot, bombardier, gunner, crew chief, radio engineer), by sketching their conceivable backgrounds, filling in their probable temperaments, describing in as full detail as possible their exact régime of training. In the course of his exposition, Steinbeck quietly demolishes a number of civilian myths: that the average survival time of a pilot is twenty minutes of combat, that the gunner's job is suicidally dangerous, that the pilot is the most important man in the outfit.

If you have a son in the Army Air Forces or preparing to enter, this is the book for you and for him to read. If you haven't, read it in any case and get the lowdown on the young men who, without much talk about it, with their hands at the controls, their eyes on the bomb sights, touch and glimpse the future.

John Swope contributes sixty honest, unspectacular photographs. All his royalties, like those of the author, and all publishing profits will go to the U.S. Army Air Forces Aid Society Trust Fund. . . .

Harry Hansen. "The First Reader." New York *World-Telegram*, 28 November 1942, p. 11.

Among books on military training those dealing with aircraft and flying lead all others two to one, and the public interest holds out in the same proportion. The latest author to describe a phase of this fighting arm is John Steinbeck, whose story of a bomber team, *Bombs Away*, is a labor of love and the result of many visits to United States Army airfields all over the country. Illustrated with excellent photographs of men in training by John Swope, the book is intended to augment the Air Forces Aid Society Trust Fund, which provides emergency aid for families of fliers lost in action: hence no royalties or profits are accepted by author, photographer or publisher. . . .

The outstanding merit of Steinbeck's book is its emphasis on the human factor. He knows how reluctantly we adopted the idea of the big bomber, which means destruction. But when its use was forced, we recognized it as the backbone of air power. "The puncher is the heavy bomber." And even though factories turn out bombers on the assembly line, each ship has its own eccentricity and becomes intimately known to its crew, which gives it such names as Little Eva, Elsie and Alice.

To describe the training and the attitude of the men Steinbeck takes individuals, putting them through their paces, and showing not only what they accomplish but how they feel. The pilot also has a co-pilot. Pilots, navigators, bombardiers and gunners are commissioned officers. Aerial engineers (crew chiefs) and radio operators are technical sergeants. Steinbeck says the nation has a great reservoir of men who are familiar with gasoline engines: "It is not nearly so great a jump from Ford engines to the great power plants of the B24 as it is from no engine to Ford engine.... We have a wealth of partly trained men, garage mechanics who know gas engines inside out, high school graduates who have kept the motor running when it should have been dead." He also emphasizes the co-operation of the ground crews, who also are carefully trained. When these airships go out to bomb the Nazis or the Japs, they are formidable engines, manned by intelligent, highly trained young men who know exactly what is at stake.

S. T. Williamson. "The Crews of the Big Bombers." *New York Times Book Review*, 92 (29 November 1942), 1, 30.

One of those four-engine bombers which occasionally fly overhead with motors singing in the deep tones of a basso profundo choir costs a quarter of a million dollars to build and carries a crew of nine men. That crew is really a team with human coordination as delicate and as sturdy and as dependable as the bomber's complex mechanism. Pilot and co-pilot have cool yet hair-trigger minds. The bombardier must be right the first time; he may never again get the target between the hairlines of his bombsight. The navigator must know in three dimensions the way from here to there and back here again. The chief mechanic knows each one of his four motors better than he knows any living being. The radio man is the human link between the frontier of the sky and land and home. And three bantam-weight, gimlet-eyed gunners are the aerial inheritors of the American dead-shot tradition of Dan'l Boone and Buffalo Bill.

What a team this is, drawn from college classrooms, repair garages, store counters and the fields of America! And given such material, what a theme for John Steinbeck, master molder of the sensitive and the hard-boiled and of intricate detail into rhythmic prose. A new form of dialogue fills the mouthpieces and earphones of our warplanes' communications systems—all of which should be Steinbeck meat.

The idea appealed to the Army Air Force. It asked Mr. Steinbeck to report to prospective airmen, to their families and to the rest of us upon the quality and training of the men and the excellence of the equipment of the Air Force, and it arranged for special visits to training camps and flying fields to enable him to gather the fullest material....

All royalties and publishers' profits on this book go to the Air Forces Aid Society Trust Fund, and motion-picture rights sold for $250,000 also go to the fund. Since he was asked to do this job and responded handsomely, the question arises: Shall Mr. Steinbeck's work be judged as charitably? His last book, the moving novel *The Moon Is Down*, apparently dealt with the German invasion of Norway, and among its characters were one or two *Herrenvolk* who showed considerable distaste for the dirty work they were ordered to perform. And because he depicted some Nazis who were not thoroughgoing beasts some critics, who should have behaved better because they had been loudest guardians of artistic integrity, did their worst to make Mr. Steinbeck out as a near fifth columnist. Now that he has undertaken an unrewarded assignment to publicize the Army Air Forces, Mr. Steinbeck employs types for which he was given the devil for not doing in his novel. If such a device seems mechanical and artificial, then here is the best answer to those who got such high blood pressure over *The Moon Is Down*. . . .

[Steinbeck provides] an enormous amount of detail. For when the text is read without reference to the capital action photographs by John Swope it seems as if War Department training schedules and recruiting pamphlets had been rephrased in John Steinbeck prose. The excellent, distinctive prose is there, but at few points does Mr. Steinbeck let himself go. He is informative, he gives a careful, fulsome report—a polite report, if you please—but only the style is Steinbeck.

William Bradford Huie. "Executioners of the Air." *Saturday Review*, 25 (5 December 1942), 22.

When the Army Air Force began building crews for our clouds of big bombers, the most persistent difficulty was that every boy wanted to be a pilot. The pilot was the glamor boy, and the public thought of the Air Force as "a group of lordly pilots with valets to service their planes." The rumor got around that a bombardier or a navigator was always a frustrated, washed-out pilot, and when an officer suggested to a cadet that he be trained for a bombardier, the cadet's face fell almost to the floor.

Into this psychological breach stepped John Steinbeck with his talents, and when you have finished *Bombs Away* you will know that the nine men who operate a big bomber are a team—"an association of experts each dependent on the other." Indeed, as I read the chapters devoted to the various crew members, I concluded that the gunners, the bombardier, the navigator, the engineer, and the radio operator are the really important, glamorous figures and the pilots are only the "truck drivers."

Mr. Steinbeck, who handles words and paragraphs like a stone-cutter handles fine marble, must have been deeply affected by the clear-eyed, firm-handed young Americans of our Air Force during the weeks he spent with them. His book is a labor of love and duty, since all royalties and publishing profits are to go to the Air Forces Aid Society Trust Fund. . . .

Mr. Steinbeck makes us remember that we are a nation with mechanical know-how; that if our sons are not born with steering wheels in hand they soon acquire them; and that our enemies have made the mistake of choosing weapons with which we are most proficient. If the energy to defeat Napoleon came from the playing fields of Eton, it seems likely that the genius to defeat Hitler will have come from the Model-T Ford. . . .

During his weeks with the boys of the Air Force, Mr. Steinbeck apparently found confirmation for some of the conclusions expressed in *The Moon Is Down*. He says: "This isn't a war of flags and marching. It is a war of finding the target in the cross hairs of the bombsight and setting the release, and it isn't a war of speeches and frothy hatred. It is a technical job, a surgeon's job. There is only time for hatred among civilians. Hatred does not operate a bombsight." There are some who will decry his refusal to give emotion a proper place in this war, but, in my opinion, Mr. Steinbeck has all the better of the argument.

Bombs Away is illustrated with sixty photographs taken by John Swope, himself a flier. Royalties from the photographs have also been contributed to the Air Force Trust Fund.

In its simplicity, restraint, and superb workmanship, I found *Bombs Away* as exciting as any Steinbeck novel. The characters are Al and Abner and Joe and Bill and other Americans who make up a bomber team. They are men who know what they are doing, and thus they "are the best fighting instruments in the world." They learn to handle a great soaring product of American genius called "Baby, Baby" and, with no trumpets blowing, go roaring off into the distance to make the world safe for the things dear to a free race of men.

Wolfgang Langewiesche. "John Steinbeck's Manual for Bombers." New York *Herald Tribune*, 6 December 1942, "Books" section, p. 3.

This is an unusual type of book. It is a little like those flossy airline advertisements recently in magazines, signed by philosophers and archbishops: a recruiting pamphlet which is at the same time a genuine Steinbeck! . . .

Steinbeck puts his great skill as a novelist to work and creates the persons of six boys who are to be a bomber crew. Without any fictional story-complications but with all the sympathetic insight of the *Grapes of Wrath*, he follows these boys from their civilian life through several training schools, describes how they become airmen and soldiers. Finally they come together, assigned to one big bomber. He tells of the further training which welds them together into a team, and how finally one dark night they take off for distant parts of the world, and action. . . .

It is not, of course, a new story. Most magazines have recently run stories, slanted to time-tested formulae, on the various phases of air crew training. Even the point that Steinbeck stresses (or that the Air Forces stress through Steinbeck), that all air crew members are equally important members of a team and that the pilot is not the fair-haired boy, has been clearly brought out. What distinguishes this book is the author's superior insight. At last this process down here at the training fields is described as the men to whom it is happening might describe it. . . .

What there is in this book is simply a truthful statement of what happens to a man, what air training feels like. Steinbeck has sensed the one thing which actually does take up two-thirds of the mind of the boys down here at these training schools. . . .

It is a moving book: at least down here at the training fields it is moving. Perhaps rather inexplicably so. It may be that Steinbeck uses tricks of the writing trade that we don't notice, but more likely it is that truth of any kind has an electric quality, and a book that assays as high in truth as this one does is bound to be moving.

It certainly is an important book. The process which it describes alone would make it important. Steinbeck has much to say about the things in the American culture that make this country produce great bomber crews. . . .

A. C. Spectorsky.
"John Steinbeck's Stirring Portrait of a Bomber Team."
Chicago *Sun*, 13 December 1942, Section 5, p. 1.

To John Steinbeck the teamwork of the bomber crew is the salient fact with which he emerged from his study of our Army bombers and the crews that man them. These men, Steinbeck tells us, function as a highly integrated, complex, precision unit; the crewman's is a trained brain and a trained body; he is a thinking and smoothly working member of a team made up of men like himself, not a brainless cog that runs true but merely as an automaton. The team is symbolic of the *democracy* for which the bombers fight; the conscious controlled working-together toward a common goal within the bomber is democracy in microcosm.

To me, one of the most impressive things about *Bombs Away* is that its author, too, engaged as a team member in a democratic act when he wrote the book. Steinbeck the artist, the cerebral lone performer, the dreamer of *The Moon Is Down*, the angry, articulate critic of our American scene in *The Grapes of Wrath*, responded to the call of the U.S. Army Air Forces, toured the country for weeks and studied the way in which our bomber crews live, learn and work. With

him went John Swope, flier-photographer, whose pictures illustrate the book. Viking Press published it. It is a democratic work, democratically produced: *all* royalties and profits go to the Air Forces Aid Society Trust Fund.

Everything about this book is fine and encouraging. The writing isn't superartistic but it is a superb professional job of explanation—explanation of a technical and intricate kind of work and training. It's interesting and often inspiring; some of the most painstakingly detailed passages have the same appeal as Hemingway's best (and earlier) meticulous descriptions of bullfighting, or his story of Nick's fishing trip in *In Our Time*. . . .

It is hard not to sound fulsome about this book which, considered purely as literature, might not warrant so much praise. But another aspect of the democratic life is the emergence of books from their ivory tower. Books are a part of life today; we don't judge *Bombs Away* on its literary merits alone, but neither do we approach it from an exclusively esthetic point of view. To every American it will appeal in many different ways; it will surely make all its readers feel proud—and more determined than ever that when the bomber crews come home for good, at last, we here will have a better world for them to come home to, a world rebuilt within the safety they have preserved for us.

"*Bombs Away.*" *New Republic*, 108 (18 January 1943), 94.

. . . In this book, Steinbeck is frequently eloquent and always clear in describing technical stuff, but his passion for writing down to his presumed readers (prospective fliers and their parents) has simplified his style to the point where it reads like a parody of Hemingway; reduces his characters, the hypothetical fliers, to the baldest stock types; and debased his ideas to a rather dangerous level, as when he says of the bomber team: "They had no patriotic sentiments. Those were for politicians." The book will probably raise a great deal of money for the Air Forces Trust Fund, but it bears about the same relationship to literature that a recruiting poster does to art.

Richard Graef.
"New Books: Shorter Notices."
Catholic World, 156 (February 1943), 635.

... More interesting than any of his novels is this story of John Steinbeck, telling us how our boys from every state are being trained into the bomber teams that are fighting in Europe, the Near East and the Pacific. After visiting the training corps and flying fields of the United States, he tells us how our government educates for action the pilot, navigator, bombardier, crew chief, gunner and radio operator, who make up a bomber crew. . . .

Checklist of Additional Reviews

"Books." *Newsweek*, 20 (30 November 1942), 68.

Fanny Butcher. "John Steinbeck Makes Worthy Contribution to War Effort in His New Book." Chicago *Daily Tribune*, 2 December 1942, p. 21.

Beth Ingels. "Steinbeck Writes Another Fine Book." Monterey [Calif.] *Peninsula Herald*, 3 December 1942, p. 2.

Raymond Krank. "Bomber Crews of America Dump War in Enemy's Lap; Steinbeck Tells the Story." Brooklyn *Citizen*, 7 December 1942, p. 9-B.

"*Bombs Away*." *Booklist*, 39 (15 December 1942), 132.

"*Bombs Away*." *Library Journal*, 68 (1 January 1943), 37.

CANNERY ROW

Cannery Row

BY

JOHN STEINBECK

1945

THE VIKING PRESS · NEW YORK

Nathan L. Rothman.
"A Small Miracle."
Saturday Review, 27
(30 December 1944), 5.

When you have finished reading *Cannery Row* you know that John Steinbeck has passed another of his small miracles. It is the best thing he has done since *The Grapes of Wrath*, although it is not quite like that, in ways that we shall discover. This goes back in style and substance to those other brilliant little tales he wrote, to Monterey County in California again, where once we met Lennie and George, and Danny and the *paisanos*. Add to these the people of Cannery Row: Doc, and Mack, and the boys, and the bright-haired Dora, for they are likely to seem as memorable. They are caught up alive for us, stirring and functioning, in the whole, integral atmosphere of their shacks along the shore line, the canneries, and the flophouse, Lee Chong's store, Doc's marine laboratory, Dora's Bear Flag Restaurant.

There is one fairly consistent thread of plot that runs tenuously through the book. It will seem trifling when it is mentioned: the blundering and fantastic attempts of the other inhabitants of the Row to show their love for . . . Doc, to throw him a party, to serve him in their untutored ways, like the fabled Juggler at the altar. But more important is the series of individual and group portraits revealed along the way, and most important of all the spiritual correspondence between place and people. Lines of force and sentiment run between them; the places breathe and suffer changes of mood, the humans assume the gnarled dualities of salt air and rickety structure, and the whole thing runs together fluidly,

people and place, into a vital organism, Cannery Row. We have seen Steinbeck do just this at least once before, with his *Tortilla Flat*, but it is still a revelation to see it done again, in the strictest, easiest, and most beautiful economy of line.

In the presence of this craftsmanship, of what I have termed a small miracle, it must seem irrelevant, certainly ungrateful, to point out that it is not a great one. Yet there must be some accounting for the gnawing dissatisfaction that one may feel along with admiration for the finesse of this little book. There is something Steinbeck is doing, consciously, with his power, that seems to point him, I hope tentatively, in the wrong direction. I can show this best by quoting a few lines from one or two places and making what I can of them. Chapter Two is a kind of rhapsodic interpolation, of which there are a few. He is speaking of the Row and what it means to him. He says:

> The Word is a symbol and a delight which sucks up men and scenes, trees, plants, factories, and Pekinese. Then the Thing becomes the Word and back to Thing again, but warped and woven into a fantastic pattern. The Word sucks up Cannery Row, digests it and spews it out, and the Row has taken the shimmer of the green world. . . .

Steinbeck is explaining the wonderful thing that happens when he looks upon his materials and feels stirring within him the power to transmute them into the evocative word. It is the intoxication of a god looking upon his handiwork, and of a good writer in the realization of his re-creative talents. This kind of consciousness is a natural prelude to the work to be done, yet we expect the work itself to blot it out. We do not expect to see the writer rear up among the pages to watch himself functioning, lift his people up and turn them over before our eyes like a conjuror. He can write an essay on how he wrote his novel—as Wolfe did—but he cannot do both simultaneously without casting a film of self-consciousness over some of the bright and natural and sincere qualities of immediacy.

In the very presence of the contriving god, some of the art will become artifice. (Was he not aware of this, writing, "warped and woven into a fantastic pattern"?) Here is an example. In one episode, William, the doorman at Dora's Bear Flag, falls prey to melancholy, contemplates suicide, and actually performs it. The chapter ends as follows:

> His hand rose and the ice pick snapped into his heart. It was amazing how easily it went in. William was the watchman before Alfred came. Everybody liked Alfred. He could sit on the pipes with Mack and the boys any time. He could even visit up at the Palace Flophouse.

Now this is cold, cold as a puppetmaster. This is reaching for insouciance. See—the man dies, and we slip away at once on an oblique angle, to Alfred, for effect. But Steinbeck's powers have not sprung from angles and effects, from being a contriving literary god. They sprang out of love and pity and understanding of the men he knew, Danny, Jim Nolan, Tom Joad. He is using William, effectually, without sympathy, and this is the measure of our discomfort about *Cannery Row*.

The Grapes of Wrath was a big book because it was big with love for its people. There is much of that here too, in such chapters as the tenth, about Frankie, and the twenty-fourth, about Mary Talbot, each of them compressed and poignant with unimaginable tenderness. But they seem hardly to belong to the tale;

they are supernumeraries very much like the starfish, the anemones, and the octopi in Doc's marine lab, upon which Steinbeck lavishes, similarly, some of his easiest and finest pages. It is Doc, the central figure, whose bearded face is described as "half Christ and half satyr," and you can see the trouble with that right away, the masking and contrivance that will go into making this man interesting and mystical and complex, at the expense of simple reality. The story will focus upon Doc, yet some of the simple things at the periphery, the way an anemone expands or the way Mary Talbot talks to her husband, will come out with the most clarity and freshness, because Steinbeck wasn't toying with transmutation and the Word, wasn't trying to do anything but give them to us unaltered, with original vision.

We don't have to have *The Grapes of Wrath* every time, but we do need the original vision, and the loving, intimate identity of author and subject that made *Tortilla Flat* and some of the short stories and the parts of this book that are best. *Cannery Row* is exciting for the way in which this key problem in a writer's development is spread before us visible in its workings, like a tinted cross-section of one of Doc's specimens, as well as for the characteristic, lusty excitement of a Steinbeck narrative.

272

Joseph Wood Krutch.
"In an Atmosphere of
Good Will toward Men."
*New York Herald Tribune
Weekly Book Review*, 21
(31 December 1944), 1.

Perhaps Mr. Steinbeck's new sketches of life among the lowly and disreputable were definitely planned as a "Christmas book." If they were not then publication at this particular moment is a lucky accident indeed, for despite the very thin veneer of "realism" and "toughness" his *Cannery Row* ought to be read in an atmosphere favorable to that good will toward men which it is calculated still further to promote. Inevitably reviewers will say that he here returns to the manner of *Tortilla Flat*, but that will be something of an understatement. He has passed that manner by to go on in a direction which takes him still farther away from *The Grapes of Wrath* and brings him close to an unexpected convergence with William Saroyan who would find himself reasonably at home among the people of good will in *Cannery Row*.

Possibly Steinbeck never really belonged by nature or inclination among the hard-boiled writers. Perhaps his love for people was always more vivid than his hatred of that Society which he has denounced in his turn. But in any event he now lets himself go in delightfully grotesque humor, grotesque sentiment, and grotesque pathos. Despite the four letter words which appear with some frequency this one reader at least found himself reminded at times not only of Saroyan but of books written before the latter was born. *Cannery Row*, I kept thinking, is, if

we make due allowance for the change in our literary manners, in mood more than a little like *Mrs. Wiggs of the Cabbage Patch*.

The community in question is described as "a poem, a stink, a grating noise, a quality of light, a tone, a habit, a nostalgia, a dream." It is "the gathered and scattered, tin and iron and rust and splintered wood, chipped pavement and weedy lots and junk heaps, sardine canneries of corrugated iron, honky tonks, restaurants and whorehouses, and little crowded groceries, and laboratories and flophouses. Its inhabitants are, as the man once said, 'whores, pimps, gamblers, and sons of bitches,' by which he meant Everybody. Had the man looked through another peep-hole he might have said, 'Saints and angels and martyrs and holy men,' and he would have meant the same things." . . .

Cannery Row has no plot in any ordinary sense of the word. It is lyric almost as much as it is narrative and the incidents which fill the two hundred brief pages have no unity except that of tone and that supplied by the repeated appearance of the same dramatis personæ. A male employee at the whorehouse kills himself when the other members of the community make their dislike of his character an excuse for calling him pimp—though they have no real feeling about the profession which he practices; "the girls" make themselves useful in an unaccustomed way when they sit up nights with the victims of an epidemic; the bums stage so successful a party to celebrate a frog-hunting expedition in the interests of Doc that they let all the frogs get away. And so it goes. Mr. Steinbeck writes vividly, breathlessly and with great gusto. Some of the incidents are genuinely pathetic; some are genuinely funny. And over the whole broods so boundless an enthusiasm for human nature and the individuals in whom it is embodied that the reader who resists it is in danger of considering himself a Scrooge or worse. Most, I predict, will not resist.

In what I have long thought the most entertaining book of criticism I ever met with, G. K. Chesterton discusses the fact that the contemporaries of Charles Dickens found "realistic" those same passages in his novels which our own generation is inclined to dismiss as exaggerated and "cheap" optimism. The explanation, he says, lies in a consideration of the difference between what is customary for us and what they were accustomed to. We are thoroughly used to writers who make everything out a great deal worse than it is. When a gloomy Russian or an exasperated Anglo-Saxon exaggerates the depravity of human nature or the unhappiness of most people's lives we do not call it exaggeration. We call it Art. But when we find Dickens presenting characters rather more benevolent than people generally are and insisting that life is an astonishingly jolly affair, we not only accuse him of exaggeration but go on to call his optimism "cheap," despite the fact that there is no obvious reason why exaggerated optimism should be any "cheaper" than exaggerated gloom. "Realism," one may add, is a tricky term. To accuse an author of not being true to life is to imply that one knows what life is really like and that is a staggering implication.

I think that Mr. Steinbeck "exaggerates." But I can only think so; and I very seriously doubt that he exaggerates any more in one direction than many of the tough-talking pessimists, hailed as truth-telling realists, have exaggerated in the other. I am also reasonably sure that the public is about ready for a bit of exaggeration in the direction which Mr. Steinbeck has taken. That benevolence, self-sacrifice, heroism and kindliness are actually more commonly met with among prostitutes and drunkards than among respectable people is, I believe, a romantic delusion. But that a novelist like Mr. Steinbeck can find them anywhere at all will probably be cheering to those who assume that serious novelists are of necessity concerned only with total depravity. It would not be too surprising if the virtues of the middle class were rediscovered before too long.

F. O. Matthiessen. "Some Philosophers in the Sun." *New York Times Book Review*, 94 (31 December 1944), 1, 18.

If you picked this book up without the author's name on the title page you might guess that it was by someone who had read *Tortilla Flat* and had decided to write a Steinbeck novel. The scene this time is along the waterfront at Monterey, where the chief points of interest are Lee Chong's grocery, Dora's "stern and stately" brothel, Doc's one-man marine biological laboratory and the Palace Flophouse and Grill. This last had served as a warehouse for fish meal until it was taken over by Mack and the boys, who act the roles formerly played by Steinbeck's slap-happy *paisanos*. They are lovable bums encumbered with no money and no ambition—and not much characterization beyond their names and a fondness for getting a skinful. The author uses them for his now familiar reversal of values. In a cash-ridden society where "the sale of souls to gain the whole world" is almost unanimous, Mack and the boys are shining exceptions. They work only when it's absolutely necessary. They are "the Beauties, the Virtues, the Graces" of the "hurried, mangled craziness of Monterey," and our only wonder is that they seem entirely free of lice or cirrhosis of the liver or other occupational diseases.

Steinbeck has always been at his best when he has had a powerful narrative to command his energies, as that of the strike in *In Dubious Battle*, or of the trek to California in *The Grapes of Wrath*. The story here is as simple as a Grade-B scenario. The boys are warmed by the desire to give a party for Doc, since he is "the nicest fella" you ever knew. First they must make enough money by catching and selling to him the four or five hundred frogs that he needs. Then, since it is to be a surprise party for him in his own place, they have to plan it while he's away on an overnight expedition down the coast. They collect the liquor and the decorations and the guests, but unfortunately Doc doesn't get back when they expected him. With the laboratory all lighted up, some strangers mistake it for Dora's. In the fight that repels this insult, Doc's place is pretty well wrecked, and even the frogs get away from the packing case into which Mack had knocked one intruder.

Such is the beginning and the middle, but the end turns, of course, upon another reversal. The boys are under a cloud for weeks, but when their pup, Darling, catches distemper and Doc consents to tell them how to cure her, they feel themselves pariahs no longer. They plan another party. This time Doc gets wind of it and manages to be there. About the same things happen again. Everybody gets drunk, and the fights start. But now everybody enjoys them, and the evening has reached its happy climax when Doc

read[s] aloud "Black Marigolds," a translation of a Sanskrit love poem, and Mack, exclaiming, says, ". . . that's pretty. Reminds me of a dame."

James T. Farrell found *Of Mice and Men* to have "all the mannerism and none of the substance of genuine realistic writing," and thus to occupy a sort of intermediate position between serious fiction and slick entertainment. There is no battle between kinds here, since the ever-increasing influence upon our novelists of Hollywood conceptions of oversimplified situation and character has won in this novel a complete victory. Steinbeck remarks in his foreword that when you collect certain delicate marine animals you have to ease them gently into your bottle of sea water, and adds: "perhaps that might be the way to write this book—to open the page and to let the stories crawl in by themselves." He thus provides a frame for several interchapters apart from his main theme, for a series of further grotesques, such as an adolescent Lennie, the man and his wife who live in a boiler, and a bogus painter who works chicken feathers into his medium. But these sketches, instead of possessing any of the tender life that Sherwood Anderson, say, might have endowed them with, fall inertly on the pages. Many of them, like the speculations as to how the Monterey flagpole sitter satisfied the needs of nature, are cheap without even being robustly coarse.

The best pages are the coarsest, those in which Steinbeck enjoys Mack's animal heartiness and his gift for blarney. The repeated assertion of how wonderful all the boys are soon runs very thin, since it is backed up with no more evidence than a similar strain in Saroyan—from whom Steinbeck now seems to be borrowing. The only other one of the boys who has anything like a distinct individuality is

Gay, the handy man, "the little mechanic of God, the St. Francis of all things that turn and twist and explode." Such a character provides Steinbeck with a chance for a soliloquy on the Model-T, how most of the babies of its period "were conceived in Model-T Fords and not a few were born in them. The theory of the Anglo-Saxon home became so warped that it never quite recovered." Such lively folklore was one of Steinbeck's chief delights in *The Grapes of Wrath*, but here it is crowded out by the succession of noble sons of nature and madams with hearts of gold. And when we recognize in wily Lee Chong no other than the Heathen Chinee, we realize that, in spite of the whiff of Saroyan, we are really back in the bright and false realm of Bret Harte.

But the most revealing evidence of the author's tastes and intentions in this book is provided by Doc, the philosophic scientist who has appeared in one idealized guise or another in several Steinbeck novels. He has not grown more real through repetition. His face is "half Christ and half satyr," and his nature accords with it. He is a sufferer over humanity, and his lonely love of truth is balanced only by his love of girls and music. Steinbeck admires him as a spokesman for the mind, as Mack is a spokesman for the body. But when Doc plays Gregorian chants on the phonograph to entertain one of his sleeping companions, or reads aloud at the end that poem about "the citron-breasted fair one," he seems as arty as any half-baked "intellectual" of Carmel.

It's a puzzler why Steinbeck should have wanted to write or publish such a book at this point in his career. Some of his pieces as a war correspondent had a freshness of observation which seemed to promise that he was growing beyond the streamlined view of anti-Fascism that bothered so many readers of *The Moon Is Down*. But he has not returned from an all too imaginary Norway and from the actual Italian beach-heads to the California he once examined with so much vitality. His most integrated book, *In Dubious Battle*, appeared almost a decade ago, in 1936, the same year as Dos Passos' last successful novel, *The Big Money*. Such a lapse of time and of talent on the part of our two most influential social novelists of the Thirties suggests again that the novel of social protest can be written only so long as the writer is responding deeply to the forces and movements of his time.

That has proved to be particularly difficult in a decade as rapidly changing and confused as the past one. The most notable social novels of the current year have been produced by less gifted writers than Steinbeck or Dos Passos, but they have gained their strength by concentrating on our most pressing issues, which are no longer quite those of the depression. They are the issues of racial inequality as Lillian Smith handled some of them in *Strange Fruit*, and of our own threatened brand of fascism, as John Hersey touched on it more briefly in *A Bell for Adano*—a novel greatly indebted to the earlier Steinbeck.

Orville Prescott.
"Books of the Times."
New York *Times*,
2 January 1945, p. 17.

There was a heat wave last summer in New York. The sidewalks felt hot through the soles of your shoes; the subways were like ovens where passengers baked slowly; the air-conditioning units worked at full blast and the citizens sighed for January. Each bright, sweltering morning for six weeks a tall Californian took refuge from New York's climate in the air-conditioned offices of the Viking Press. He would arrive about 10 o'clock and settle down in the sanctum of one of the Viking executives then absent on urgent military business. With occasional time out for coffee and contemplation, he would pound the office typewriter until 3 in the afternoon and then depart. After six weeks a novel was completed, as far as I know the first novel ever to be written in a publisher's office by a refugee from a heat wave. The novel is published today, *Cannery Row*, by John Steinbeck.

Ever since his triumph with *The Grapes of Wrath* Mr. Steinbeck has been coasting. He still is. This little tribute to a waterfront block in Monterey and its indecorous inhabitants has some of the Steinbeck mannerisms, much of the Steinbeck charm and simple felicity of expression, but it is as transparent as a cobweb. For all its 208 pages it is less substantial than a short story. There just isn't much here, no real characters, no "story," no purpose. Instead, with considerable pointless vulgarity and occasional mildly humorous scenes, a series of loosely connected incidents is thrown casually together.

The general atmosphere is one of biological benevolence, a sort of beaming approbation for human activities conducted on an unthinking level far below the demarcation line of pride, honesty, self-respect and accomplishment. Mr. Steinbeck has always shown a great love and sympathy for ordinary, run-of-the-mill people without necessarily respecting their intelligence. In *Cannery Row* he has allowed his affection to boil over into sentimentality, into pathos and even into whimsy. The *paisanos* of *Tortilla Flat* were men of charm and individual flavor, but the

bums of *Cannery Row* are just bums. . . .

Cannery Row, because John Steinbeck wrote it, is greater than the sum of its parts. If its characters have no personality, *Cannery Row* itself has some of its author's personality. One feels in it Mr. Steinbeck's scientific interest in marine fauna, his love of life in its simplest manifestations, his mastery of words. But this is John Steinbeck in an off moment. There is no driving idea, no creative energy, no living juice in *Cannery Row*. It may be an accurate picture of one block in Monterey, but it doesn't seem as if it could be. The real block would be more interesting.

John Steinbeck has gone back to California, where they don't have heat waves like ours of last summer. The man who could create the magnificent and pitiful Joad family, who could tell the wonderful story of Jody and his pony, is one of our ablest living writers. Perhaps in his own country he will find again the power and passion of his best books and escape the confusion of thought and artistic futility that weaken *Cannery Row*.

Frank Daniel. "New Books." Atlanta *Journal*, 3 January 1945, p. 6.

John Steinbeck has returned to the scene and the mood of *Tortilla Flat* to tell, with affection and gusto and abundant suavity, a story entirely foreign to his famous news accounts of American men during the Allied invasion of Sicily and Italy.

Cannery Row may be the means by which Mr. Steinbeck, after witnessing war, turned his mind from the impact of new scenes and withdrew to gain perspective on those experiences and emotions. He has cast over his story the special light of reflection and reminiscence which gives its timelessness and removes it from the harsh lights of today's events. It is in that case escape literature for both writer and reader. . . .

Edmund Wilson.
"Books."
New Yorker, 20
(6 January 1945), 62–3.

John Steinbeck's new novel, *Cannery Row* . . . is one of the least pretentious of his books, but I believe that it is the one I have most enjoyed reading. It deals with a community a little like that of the same author's *Tortilla Flat*: a cannery neighborhood in Monterey, with a biological laboratory, a brothel, a Chinaman's general store, and a scattering of shacks and old boilers, in which various nondescript characters live. *Cannery Row* is amusing and attractive in the same way as *Tortilla Flat*: here again Mr. Steinbeck has created a sun-soaked Californian atmosphere of laziness, naïveté, good nature, satisfaction in the pleasures of the senses and indifference to property rights, in which the periodical failures and suicides hardly disturb the surface with a momentary eruption of bubbles. But the new book is more complex than the earlier one, in which the characters were mostly "Mexicans," "*paisanos*," all on the same level. The characters in *Cannery Row* represent a mixture of races and a variety of social levels. It would be impossible to give an account of the book by disengaging and retelling a "story": it is a series of little pictures and incidents that are often not

related in any direct way. . . . But there *is* a central interest in *Cannery Row*: it is that of the relations of Doc, who runs the biological laboratory, with the other, more rudimentary members of the community. The man of science, living alone with his phonograph and his books, takes his neighbors for what they are and as they come. . . .

This is the fable: a dramatization of the point of view already implicit in most of Steinbeck's fiction. A curious and perceptive mind is situated among simple human beings and scrutinizes their activities with the same kind of interest that it finds in the habits of baby octopi, sea anemones, and hermit crabs. It is capable of sentimentalizing about them but it has difficulty convincing itself or us that it accepts them on its own level. It may let them climb all over it, but it always brushes them off. Doc does, as I have said above, feel some genuine warmth of contact with his neighbors, and it may be that *Cannery Row* is Steinbeck's most satisfactory book because it attempts to objectify and exploit the author's own relation to his characters; but it is characteristic of the author as well as of his protagonist Doc that the moments when Doc feels emotion are the moments that are least well done. When Doc finds the dead girl in the surf, he can only hear imaginary music, and this music is none too well described; when the loafers and the trollops of Cannery Row give him their bang-up party, the author must rely, like Doc, on long passages of quoted verse. It is hard to put one's finger on the coarseness that tends to spoil Mr. Steinbeck as an artist. When one considers the brilliance of his gifts and the philosophic cast of his mind, one keeps feeling that it should not be so. Yet it is so: when this watcher of life should exalt us to the vision of art, he simply sings "Mother Machree." . . .

A. C. Spectorsky.
"Steinbeck Reaches New
Heights in His Best
Earlier Manner."
Chicago Sun Book Week,
2 (7 January 1945), 6.

I don't say it *did* happen this way, but it could have. A group of people were sitting around discussing books and such. Said one, in a nostalgic mood, "What I'd like to read now is a book that has nothing of the war and yet is modern; something full of fun, life, warmth and just a touch of philosophy to round it out. Something maybe a little like Steinbeck's *Tortilla Flat*."

Said another: "That would be swell, but Steinbeck couldn't write it. It would need the unreal reality of Saroyan. . . ."

A third member of the group interrupted; "That's true," he said, "but you'd want some of the native American toughness of the earlier Hemingway, and. . . ."

A fourth chimed in: "Personally, I'd like some Mark Twain in it, too; some of his fabulous folklore quality. . . ."

And so the conversation went, each person adding a touch of his favorite author, until the last speaker said, "Well, it's a nice idea, but no one man could do it, especially today."

Now, it so happened that John Steinbeck was listening to the whole thing, though no one knew he was there. He smiled to himself, went home and sat down at his typewriter. The name of the book is *Cannery Row*. It has all the elements the speakers wanted, plus a score more. It's somewhat slight, quite short, episodic, inconclusive—but it's one of the most thoroughly enjoyable and delicious books you'll ever have the fortune to read.

Steinbeck has taken as his locale a place called Cannery Row, a few blocks of buildings and vacant lots on the Southern California coast. It's a tawdry, ugly, wonderful, bawdy and luminous place, as Steinbeck paints it, especially in the hours just before dawn and just before dark.

You will find yourself exulting with Steinbeck in the stench of fish meal, the sight of wild weeds growing up over rusted boilers discarded by the cannery, the smells of "kelp and barnacles when the tide is out and the smell of salt and spray when the tide is in."

For his characters Steinbeck has chosen as motley and human a crew, collected from the nether rungs of the economic ladder, as you'd ever be scared by if you met them in real life. . . .

Doc is a character complex and simple; complex as a sensitive highly organized personality; simple in a philosophy of life which is easy-going, yet rigidly ethical; ethical, yet never coldly so. He is the father confessor, beer supplier, voice of authority and guardian to Cannery Row.

Doc's relationship with Mack, and the two parties Mack organizes for Doc, hold the book together. Within these confines you will find: A restful and lively attitude toward life and the earning of money; more impressively artistic, seemingly effortless writing than occurs in most books five times as long; humor to send you into gales of audible laughter. Priceless in this last category are the episodes surrounding a frog hunt, a beer milkshake and the question everyone wanted to ask the flagpole roller skater.

Some critics will, no doubt, accuse Steinbeck—surely one of the major luminaries in the writing firmament—of retrograde motion, claiming his preoccupation with the prewar lower strata (economically speaking for his characters and biologically for his protagonist's specimens) reveals him to be fugitive from a world he couldn't come to grips with in *The Moon Is Down*. But *Cannery Row* is a fine small art, a miniature gem, a verbal minuet—and who is there to tell Steinbeck he should have composed a symphony?

I'm afraid *Cannery Row* won't have even the considerable incidental value that three of his earlier books had—of providing the fable for the fine movies: *The Grapes of Wrath* (John Ford), *Of Mice and Men* (Lewis Milestone) and *The Forgotten Village* (Herbert Kline).

George Mayberry.
"Reading and Writing."
New Republic, 112
(15 January 1945), 89–90.

Margaret Marshall.
"Notes by the Way."
Nation, 160
(20 January 1945), 75–6.

... The non-book club, or independent, first big-seller of the year is John Steinbeck's *Cannery Row*, in which the race between the author's admitted talents and his undoubted meretriciousness finishes another lap with the latter taking a long lead this time around. As even the Boston Booksellers' and Bookburners' Association knows by now, this is an episodic ramble along the Monterey waterfront and an examination, but not a very deep or meaningful one, of its "whores, pimps, gamblers and sons of bitches" and/or "saints and angels and martyrs and holy men." Mostly it is about Doc, "a hell of a nice fella" who runs a marine laboratory, and a bunch of bums (read saints and holy men) who try to throw a swell party for him and keep tripping up on their failings. It is a readable book, and there are moments when Steinbeck removes his beer-colored glasses to write savagely and truly and with love, as he has done intermittently before in *In Dubious Battle*, *The Grapes of Wrath* and in some of the stories. But technical archness, superficial characterization and boozy metaphysics are seldom absent.

Intrinsically it is unfair to subject John Steinbeck's latest book, *Cannery Row* ... to the standards of serious (I do not mean unhumorous) literature, as unfair as it would be to judge glass jewelry, or what the department stores call simulated gems, by the standards that apply to precious stones. But the responsible critic, who is presumably jealous of the good name of art and whose function, if he has any at all, is to engender discrimination in the reading public, is forced to undertake the thankless exercise of demonstrating that *Cannery Row* is the chaff and not the wheat of literature because the book is being talked about as if it were, *a priori*, an authentic work of art.

Let it be said at the start that the subject of *Cannery Row*—the life and the attitude toward life of a group of ne'er-do-wells in California—seems to me a perfectly good subject for literature; and I don't think it's "too bad" that Steinbeck doesn't write about the war.

A good book, even a great book could be fashioned from the materials Mr. Steinbeck has used. I say could be; I should say has been, by a writer named Mark Twain. For, unhappily for Mr. Steinbeck, this book reminds one of Mark Twain—as fake jewels remind one of real ones—if only because it is essentially a string of anecdotes, some of them all [tall?] tales, of the sort Mark Twain delighted in.

The writing, to begin with, is factiously simple, after the fashion of the moment; it is at the same time highflown and flyblown, cheap, fancy, and false. . . . The whole book is written in this daydream prose which devitalizes everything it touches and has the same relation to the force of life, and of good writing, as the iridescent foam on the edge of a river has to the main current. . . .

The first defect of the characters is not that they are "typed" but that Steinbeck endows them with no motive power of their own. They do not move but are moved about. Often he achieves a good imitation of the behavior and speech of bums and ne'er-do-wells—but at fatal moments the hand and voice of Steinbeck become all too apparent. As a result *Cannery Row* lacks reality—either the reality of a fairy tale, which can be devastating, or the reality of straight fiction.

The great defect grows out of Steinbeck's attitude toward the people he has chosen to portray. He professes to love them; he probably thinks he does. But his real attitude, except in the case of Doc, is nine parts condescension and one part sentimentality. In *Cannery Row* Mr. Steinbeck handles human beings as if they were a species of small animal life. They exist and have their being on the same level as the frogs and dogs, the cats and octopuses he is so fond of watching. Their "happiness" is that of insects, and his "love" for them is that of a collector. Conversely, and significantly, he humanizes frogs and dogs, cats and octopuses in a way that becomes at times repellent as well as embarrassing. . . .

Aside from its negative failures, *Cannery Row* also has its positive vices. If proof were needed that sentimentality and cruelty are the two sides of the same coin, it may be found in this book. The unpleasant pleasure with which Steinbeck describes the killing of a mouse by a cat, the "murder" of a crab by an octopus, the sadism of a small boy toward a smaller boy, is disturbing, to say the least. As for the vulgarity which is a by-product of sentimentality, it is all too manifest here. Steinbeck's maudlin celebration of the automobile leads him to speak of one of his characters as "the little mechanic of God," the St. Francis of coils and armatures and gears. It also leads him to the "philosophical" statement that "two generations of Americans knew more about the Ford coil than the clitoris."

His social criticism in general is of this stripe. For *Cannery Row* has "social significance" of a curious kind. It seems to be written out of a violent hatred of modern life, particularly of our money civilization. Mr. Steinbeck uses strong language on this score. "What can it profit a man to gain the whole world and to come to his property with a gastric ulcer, a blown prostate, and bifocals?" ". . . a generation of trapped, poisoned, and trussed-up men. . . ." He calls the parties given by professional hostesses "about as spontaneous as peristalsis and as interesting as its end product."

Hatred can be creative. Steinbeck's is not. And in the end it defeats itself. His picture of Monterey is certainly meant to be a protest against the futile busy-ness, the greed and ugliness of modern life. If he had captured the reality of *Cannery Row*, in fantasy or otherwise, it *would* have constituted a protest, and might have been far more hilarious than it is. What he has actually accomplished, by turning his characters into happy and inferior creatures who live in a non-existent Monterey, is an irrelevant and rather smug escape from modern life. Bankers will love it.

Cannery Row is a "simulated gem" which has neither intrinsic luster nor permanent worth. It would not be worth the space I have given it if it were not, along with many another of the same sort, being currently passed and accepted, as the genuine article.

C. G. Paulding. "*Cannery Row.*" *Commonweal*, 41 (26 January 1945), 378–80.

... *Cannery Row* has a plot: the bums think that "Doc" is the kindest man they have ever heard of and they try to give him a party, but they get it started too soon and it wrecks the laboratory and all the beautiful disks which play Gregorian and the "Pavane" and "Daphnis," and "Doc," when he gets home and finds the mess, smashes the kindest of the bums in the mouth and then everybody is very sad about human misery. After this there is a great deal about the life, murders and voracities of the little animals that hide in the rocks and are discoverable when the tide is low; there are several short stories complete in themselves; again the tide recedes and this time there is the body of a young girl caught in the rocks, and "Doc" is very sad again about human misery; there is the story about Henri the painter and the girls who never can live with him for long because it is too uncomfortable in the boat he has built to live in on shore because he does not like a boat on water; there is a story about the man who roller-skates to a record on a platform on top of a pole; there is a suicide, and the story of how the bums manage to live in a sort of community house of their own, and how they get enough to drink, and how a man takes pride in his house whenever he can feel that his house is his own; there is the story of how the brothel functions and this includes the sad story of how sometimes a man can be very unhappy if he is the bouncer in a brothel, but even this is not a hopeless story because after this bouncer has killed himself there is another bouncer who is very happy and makes many friends. This sounds as if the plot had been lost sight of, and it would sound even more so if some more of the stories were here recapitulated, but the plot is all right and so Mack and the bums plan another party for the kindest man in the world and, this time, they are very much more careful about it, and it works out fine. The laboratory is wrecked again but this time "Doc" thinks it is fine because he has been right in on the party all the time. Dora and her girls are at the party, everybody in the book is at the party, unless he killed himself before the party; "Doc" reads out loud a long and beautiful poem from the Sanskrit—no less— and everybody weeps, but all this is so wonderful that there must be a "release" somehow for this wonderful purity of the moment and fortunately the crew of a San Pedro tuna boat who are looking for Dora's girls try to break in and so there is a lot of wonderful fighting in which everyone fights to save everyone else's feelings or honor, and in the morning everyone is strewn round everywhere.

Then comes the sad story about a gopher who builds a wonderful home and cannot find a mate so that he has to move to a less wonderful home.

It all smells of fish and reeks with kindness.

Is there any use in reading this book?

It is as sentimental as a book can be. It oozes sentiment. And of course the confusion comes in because it is written in the technique of realism. The tripes are described. (Literally. A small boy and a dog find them in a gulch. They are supposed to be those of the late Josh Billings.) So that one might make a mistake; one might take this book for a scientific, true and complete picture of life. But that would be a false impression produced by the sound of the words, the hard, harsh words, and the sound of the cursing, also by the sound of broken bottles. But all this method, all the technique is not used for description or employed in a realistic search for the truth; it is used to make us weep. Read it and weep. The technique of realism is used by an impressionist.

As for Mr. Steinbeck's philosophical interests they are not usable for anything. There is something about "Our Father who art in nature" in a passage in which "The Thing becomes the Word," but this is not usable even for blasphemy because it seems so obviously well-intentioned and so certainly is stupid.

So that the realism is false, the thinking unimportant, and all that is left is the weeping all over everything. Tears through joy or the other way round. Well, what is it worth? It is not worth much for anyone who has seen man's pity for man expressed by any of the great and honest writers of world literature. Or for anyone who through God's grace knows that the prostitute, the miserable and the lost remain for ever inseparably bound to him in the brotherhood of man. But for those who have tried to break that link considering the prostitute an animal, the miserable remote, and the lost for ever irrecoverable, then anything which may bring them to tears would be worth reading. Maudlin tears are better than no tears at all. The trouble is that such people would think that *Cannery Row* is funny.

Mark Longaker. "New Books: Shorter Notices." *Catholic World*, 160 (March 1945), 570–1.

This book—for really tough and strictly sophisticated readers—comes from a man who is a skillful weaver of words, gifted with more than an ordinary share of poetic fancy and deeply, sincerely sympathetic with the little people. His tale centers in a group living among the sardine fisheries which give the book its title. The scenes are laid in the grocery store of Lee Chong; in the Palace Flophouse and Grill of Mack and his friends; in the marine laboratory of the overdrawn Doc, and in other less reputable establishments. Steinbeck's characteristic powers of observation and description justify, at least in part, the ballyhoo which has greeted the appearance of his latest contribution to the amusement of the "emancipated." But the critical-minded will still perceive his unfortunate tendency to let himself be carried along a single track—human nature is much too complex to be summed up in the formula that there is good in the worst and bad in the best of us. Mr. Steinbeck moreover suffers from an apparently irresistible urge to exaggerate general statements and to draw upon the medical dictionary for his vocabulary. His admirers, invited to take part in a sort of treasure hunt for unsuspected beauty and unappreciated goodness, run the risk of being suddenly pushed into a bog or over a precipice. He would be a greater writer if his originality and courage were balanced by decent restraint and a good sense of proportion.

N[orman] C[ousins].
"Who Are the Real People?"
Saturday Review, 28 (17 March 1945), 14.

John Steinbeck likes to get a rise out of his readers. He likes to ruffle them and startle them with the unexpected and the bizarre. He likes to write, for example, of a brothel as a "decent, clean, honest, wholesome" place (as in *Cannery Row*), where the customers get their money's worth and where the working girls are decent, clean, honest, wholesome, etc., in contrast to the "twisted and lascivious sisterhood of married spinsters whose husbands respect the home but don't like it very much."

Our purpose here is not to take issue with Mr. Steinbeck's high regard for decent, clean, honest, wholesome persons or institutions. After all, he isn't the first to call attention to or glorify the career bed. It was pretty much of a literary chestnut even when DeMaupassant wrote about it in "Madame Tellier's Establishment." It is pertinent only as it illustrates Mr. Steinbeck's unfailing devotion to the reverse twist under any circumstances. So much so that his unpredictableness becomes almost predictable. It is a familiar literary device having a certain effectiveness but sometimes it wears thin and shows through. When it does, it has all the charm and winsomeness of an old hangnail.

If you grant that Steinbeck's own ideas or beliefs may frequently be subordinated to the requirements of his literary devices or technique, you can avoid either the bother or the pleasure of rising to his bait; that is, you are willing to give him a liberal allowance because of his perquisites as a novelist. But there comes a point where you are certain that his technique represents an authentic and precise vehicle for his own convictions. At such a point, it is both legitimate and pertinent to ask questions.

In particular, we should like to ask questions about Mr. Steinbeck's obsession with what he likes to call "real people." It is not a solitary obsession, to be sure: other writers in what has been termed the school of modern realist writing share it. Ernest Hemingway, particularly in his novel of thugs, rum runners, and murderers, *To Have and Have Not*, and in many of his other novels and short stories, demonstrates a predilection, if not an admiration, for his own brand of real people.

But who are these real people, what are they like, that they should thus command the attention and affection of these writers? In Steinbeck's case, the answers are both available and explicit in *Cannery Row*—even more, perhaps, than in its atmospheric predecessor, *Tortilla Flat*. Steinbeck's "real people" are the well-meaning, big-hearted, coarse, ignorant bums, boobs, castoffs, and misfits of both sexes. "They survive in this particular world better than other people. In a time when people tear themselves to pieces with ambition and nervousness and covetousness, they [the castoffs, etc.] are relaxed. All of our so-called successful men are sick men, with bad stomachs, and bad souls, but Mack and the boys are healthy and curiously clean. They can do what they want. They can satisfy their appetites without calling them something else."

These "real people" of Steinbeck's are amusing enough and make good copy, but we are neither impressed nor convinced. Mr. Steinbeck has made special pets of them, and exhibits them as though they were anything but real. They are big, rough, and tough, and know how to guzzle pot likker, even if they don't know the difference between drinking and soaking. They're innocent as babes and delightfully dumb, and they have an instinct for kindness and gratitude that is as touching as it is menacing. Beware that gratitude as you would a bear-trap. The "real people" get tied into knots and they slide unsuspectingly into the gol-durndest brawls you ever saw, with split heads, bashed faces, and broken ribs as common as frogs in a pond at midnight. F'rinstance, they want to do something nice for a friend, whom they all love and respect, so they throw him a party while he is away and smash up his laboratory until the place looks like a heap of broken glass. The highspot of the evening is a "long, happy, and bloody battle that took out the front door and broke two windows."

Now this is all very stirring and refreshing. It is good to see decent, clean, honest, wholesome human beings acting in such a natural and unrepressed manner. They don't "tear themselves to pieces with ambition and nervousness and covetousness," and they know how to relax. There is no point in bringing Freud into all this, but you can't help admiring their magnificent lack of self-restraint—the real tonic for the real psyches of real people. Consider, too, their superb constitutional equipment. Contrast them with the unreal people who have stomach ulcers and various other disorders as the result of nervous living. Mr. Steinbeck's people are invariably healthy. Not an instance of cirrhosis of the liver, delirium tremens, polyneuritis, Korsakoff psychoses, or Saturday-night-paralyses in the carload. Doubtless, all his castoffs, bums, procurers, deadbeats, sporting girls, and madams die in the sublime beauty of their old age. But don't bet on it.

Apart from the ludicrous, there is something both curious and perilous about Mr. Steinbeck's preoccupation with and worship of these "real people," as distinct from all others. Curious, because he himself treats them more as phenomena than as the substance of reality; perilous, because there are inevitable concomitants of anti-culturalism and anti-intellectualism that cannot be separated from the original obsession. These by-products are more than vaguely reminiscent of a remark by an incipient hasbeen who once said that when he heard the word culture he reached for his gun. Maybe Adolf H. never actually said it; maybe it was Hermann or Little Joseph or one of the others. But whoever said it, everyone knows or should know what it meant.

We admit the urgency for a novelist to break away from the stuffy and synthetic atmosphere of penthouse cocktail parties, and to associate himself with the more valid feel of large numbers of people living a less glorified life. But there is also a danger that he may lose his balance in going in the other direction—the danger that he may become patronizing and try to turn people into something special or freakish. It should be at least possible to write about the mainstream of humanity without putting a halo on the half-wit, deifying the drunk, or canonizing the castoff.

We are not saying that Mr. Steinbeck's gallery is not filled with real people. They may be real enough, but we'll be hanged if we will genuflect before them or regard them as a master race. Besides, we have devised our own test for determining whether people are real. It is infallible. You take a long, sharp pin and jab it into the arm. If blood comes out, and if the blood is red, then the person is real.

John Hampson.
"Fiction."
Spectator [England], 175
(2 November 1945),
418, 420.

... What is to be said about *Cannery Row*? On both sides of the Atlantic all sorts of people, including some who should know better, have shouted themselves hoarse in cracking up Mr. Steinbeck. He, they have told us, is a "classic," a "poet," and a "genius." Their views about his short new novel may be a little more guarded, since the tale is not merely slick but also very thin, and has to be bolstered up with a few anecdotes, sentimental character studies and quite a few chunks of very flabby padding: "Doc had driven slowly. It was late afternoon when he stopped in Ventura, so late in fact that when he stopped in Carpentaria he only had a cheese sandwich and went to the toilet. Besides, he intended to get a good dinner in Los Angeles, and it was dark when he got there. He drove on through and stopped at a big Chicken-in-the-Rough place he knew about. And there he had fried chicken, julienne potatoes, hot biscuits and honey, and a piece of pineapple pie and blue cheese. And here he filled his thermos-bottle with hot coffee, had them make up six ham sandwiches and bought two quarts of beer for breakfast."

The puff on the jacket urges: "Go to the party which the boys and girls of Cannery Row give that quaint old philosopher Doc...." "The boys" are hoboes and "the girls" are from the local brothel. "Doc has the hands of a brain surgeon, and a cool warm mind. Doc tips his hat to dogs as he drives by and the

dogs look up and smile at him." Mr. Steinbeck is an iconoclast, who conceals his sentimentality under a snappy husk of toughness, which may explain why he is so highly esteemed by a large section of the fiction-reading public. Perhaps they will enjoy, too, his recently developed streak of whimsey, which, if less refined than the average English variety, is not the less nauseating: "Mary Talbot gave a pregnancy party that year. And everyone said: 'God! a kid of hers is going to have fun.'" Lush mush.

"The Dickensian Flavour."
Times Literary Supplement [London],
3 November 1945,
p. 521.

"Cannery Row in Monterey in California is a poem, a stink, a grating noise, a quality of light, a tone, a habit, a nostalgia, a dream." Thus Mr. Steinbeck in the first sentence of a short novel of an artificially boisterous and somewhat rhetorical character, so sketchy and episodic in plan as to seem not much more than a hasty improvisation. The poem, the stink, the grating noise to which he refers leave one, indeed, unimpressed; they seem to have little connexion with the sardine fleet in the background of the picture he has drawn on this occasion or with the collection of stock types of the American comic and picaresque in the foreground.

... Mr. Steinbeck has a shrewd popular touch here and there in this short book, but his feeling for the grotesquely human or the humanly grotesque has frequently landed him in a sort of perverse prettiness and sometimes in a fling of disappointingly cheap philosophy.

Hugh I'A. Fausset. "Books of the Day." Manchester *Guardian*, 9 November 1945, p. 3.

... Miss Meredith is a good story-teller, and composes a character as carefully as she does a period [in *The Beautiful Miss Burroughes*]. What she rather lacks is "the hot taste of life," to quote from John Steinbeck's new story, *Cannery Row*, ... which abounds in just this quality. This is a riotous comedy, at once coarse and kindly, staged in a small town where fish is tinned on the Californian coast. A group of genial reprobates who have learnt the trick of living easy on others cause most of the fun, and an odd old collector of frogs and starfish, who is both philosopher and philanthropist, is in his original way the one moral figure in a world in which vice and virtue have come to the happiest terms with one another....

Rintaro Fukuhara. "Steinbeck's *Kanzume Yokocho [Cannery Row]*." *Eigo Seinen* [The Rising Generation] [Japan], 92 (1 February 1946), 35–7.

[Review translated by Kiyoshi Nakayama.]

The setting seems to be a fishing port in California. There is a street called Kanzume Yokocho [Cannery Row] in Monterey. *Cannery Row*—this is the title of Steinbeck's novel published by Viking Press in 1945.

One of the inhabitants of this street is, first of all, a Chinaman by the name of Lee Chong. He sells groceries—alcoholic beverages, foods, and so forth. Once he sets the price of a commodity at 20 cents, he never changes the price even 10 years later, when it is covered with dust. He is a solid merchant. He never declines what others offer or request, and he looks like what one would expect a Chinese merchant in California to be. Lee Chong's is a long-established store.

Another Chinese appears. He walks by with a basket every evening, and goes back at dawn holding the basket with water dripping from it. He looks as if he has been gathering something from the sea. He wears heavy shoes, one sole of which is loose, and passes with clocklike regularity. Nobody ever approaches, and even children keep away from him in fear. When a boy who comes from another town taunts him, singing: "Ching-Chong Chinaman sitting on a rail," he has a vision of a lonely countryside. In an instant, however, the vision disappears and he finds himself in Cannery Row.

Although this old Chinaman is not a main character, he walks by from time to time in the novel.

The Palace Flophouse and Grill, the name of which makes it sound like a gorgeous place, is nothing but a tenement house. Mack, the elder and the leader, draws five oblongs on the floor with a piece of chalk to indicate the simulated beds for the boys. These five boys play the leading roles. Mack keeps a puppy, and one day she gets distemper. The boys quit their jobs to take care of her. Finally they ask Doc, the central character of the novel, to take a look at her. Doc is the owner of the Western Biological Laboratory, which sells small animals for students' experiments. He examines the dog, says, "You'll have to force feed her," and returns home. And the puppy gets well.

Doc is respected and loved by everyone; they all think, "I really must do something nice for Doc." He lives together with mice, rattlesnakes, frogs, and octopi in the big house, and is celibate. He graduated from college, but is not at all puffed up. He is kind and humane, and like a wise hermit. He likes music, and his hobby is listening to masterpieces on a big electric phonograph. He himself collects marine animals to sell. Once he gets an order for hundreds of frogs. The boys of the Palace Flophouse promise to collect frogs, drive out into the mountains, and catch a thousand of them.

The story, as it develops, basically centers on Doc, Mack, and the boys. It is not, however, the ordinary kind of novel one usually comes across. Rather, Cannery Row itself is a leading character. The novel, portraying the various aspects of the life in the Row, conveys the breath of humanity prevailing in it.

There is a whorehouse called the Bear Flag Restaurant. The girls are also inhabitants of the Row. When the influenza epidemic comes to the whole town, they run about the town with pots of soup and sit with the families. There is a vacant lot nearby in which large pipes lie abandoned. People living in the pipes are also respected citizens. A boiler has been abandoned among the pipes as well. In it lives a couple. The entrance is low and narrow, so they enter it on their knees, but once inside there is room enough for them. One day, when the husband comes home and enters through the narrow door, the wife says, "Holman's are having a sale of curtains." His reply, ". . . for Christ's sake what are we going to do with curtains? We got no windows," seals his fate. The wife cries and cries: "Men just don't understand how a woman feels." Later, when the husband reappears in a different chapter, he simply says to Mack, "You know any kind of glue that you can stick cloth to iron?" This careful ground-laying on the part of the writer is worthy of admiration.

It seems that this novelist's world is composed of the heart-warming stories of these lower-class people. I found *Of Mice and Men* a story of the subtleties in human nature that could be played by such Kabuki actors as the late Hikosaburo and his brother Kikugoro, and it surely has two major characters. The story develops via the two heroes' dramatic conflicts. But *Cannery Row* has no similarly complicated plot, although, as mentioned, it has as protagonists Doc, Mack, and the boys. It is a story of the whole Row, including the whores, the Chinamen, and the couple living in the boiler. In short, it is a story of a world of good-natured people. No evil-minded people appear in it. Everyone is good-natured. When drinking, they drink heartily. When angry, they readily start a fight. But they are simply happy-go-lucky, and good by nature. No one strives for success in life, and there is no competition. Just leading a life without much trouble is sufficient for them. Their lifestyle seems to be leading a happy life by living together, and getting along with one another.

The writer portrays these people in brief cuts, scene by scene, as if *Cannery Row* were a movie. As the scenes change without any interrelations at all, the reader understands the life of these people, develops an intimacy with them, and keeps reading quite naturally. This might be a technique of the new novel.

A painter lives in a boat that is never completed, even after a ten-year work of building. He lives in the cabin, in which he bumps his head when he stands up. Sometimes he gets drunk to be mellow. Once he saw with drunken eyes a vision of the ghosts of a young man and a baby sitting together in the cabin. The young man cut the baby's throat with a razor, and the baby went on laughing. The drawback of this boat is that it has no toilet.

I wonder if the novelist has a particular interest in depicting illusions. Doc also feels astonished to find a floating young girl's face looking up at him among the rocks on the shore where he goes out collecting little octopi. Do these lower-class people generally believe in supernatural things? In Mokuami Kawatake's Kabuki play, one has the same kind of feeling. In Tomoji Abe's *Fusetsu* [Wind and Snow], there is a scene in which an old statesman happens to see a vision. It seems to be an abrupt appearance of romance in a novel dealing with social and political issues. I wonder what the novelists think of these problems. In *Cannery Row* the scenes are incorporated in so natural a way that none will feel them strange. One might speculate that the supernatural suggests the depth of intuition of such men of simplicity in the world, a depth lacking in intellectual people.

That Mack and the boys go out collecting frogs comes from their goodwill, as they want to do something nice for Doc. They plan to have a party for him, bringing the frogs as gifts. They go into Doc's place with wine and a thousand frogs while Doc is away from town collecting octopi. Doc's lab has never been locked. Unfortunately Doc does not come home that night. Mack and the boys get drunk, and break the phonograph and the windows until the whole place is devastated. To make matters worse, the frogs crawl out one by one, and pour out in growing numbers onto the stairs and into the street. Cars pass by, and run over many of them. It is a somewhat pleasing and agreeable scene.

In spite of this failure, once again they try to throw a party for Doc. It is a birthday party. Everyone comes over, as in the finale of a play: Lee Chong, the painter, the girls of the Bear Flag, and of course Mack and the boys, who are the organizers. And Mack says a few words to open the party. Everyone brings a gift for Doc. The gifts from Mack and the boys are 21 cats, and there is a patchwork quilt from the girls. This party is a great success. The dancing starts. After the pleasant moments, Doc reads aloud stanzas from a poem called "Black Marigolds," translated from Sanskrit. When the party gets mellow in sweet sadness, there is a tramp of feet on the stairs. The group, shouting, "Ain't this a whore house?" turns out to be the crew of a tuna boat. In an instant, a big fight starts. Each girl slips off a shoe and holds it by the toe, and Dora grasps a meat grinder she finds in the kitchen. By and by the fight ends. The crew comes humbly back and joins the party. The next morning Doc awakens to find himself under the brilliantly colored quilt. He gets up slowly and picks up a book. It is the one he read the previous night.

Even now
I know that I have savored the hot
taste of life
Lifting green cups and gold at the
great feast.
Just for a small and a forgotten time
I have had full in my eyes from off
my girl
The whitest pouring of eternal light—

Checklist of Additional Reviews

"The Bowery of Monterey." *Time*, 45 (1 January 1945), 62.

"*Cannery Row*." *Booklist*, 41 (1 January 1945), 140.

"Steinbeck Straight." *Newsweek*, 25 (1 January 1945), 78–9.

Harold A. Wooster. "*Cannery Row*." *Library Journal*, 70 (1 January 1945), 32.

David Appel. "Turning a New Leaf." Chicago *News*, 3 January 1945, p. 13.

Ritch Lovejoy. "*Cannery Row* Is Monterey's." Monterey [Calif.] *Peninsula Herald*, 3 January 1945, p. 9.

Joseph Henry Jackson. "Assorted Orphans of the Storm in a Kind of Near-Fantasy." San Francisco *Chronicle*, 7 January 1945, p. 14.

Ted Robinson. "Steinbeck's *Cannery Row* Dissects a California Slum." Cleveland *Plain Dealer*, 7 January 1945, p. 12.

Josephine Gardner. "Book Angles." Pacific Grove [Calif.] *Tribune*, 12 January 1945, p. 6.

J. Donald Adams. "Speaking of Books." *New York Times Book Review*, 94 (14 January 1945), 2.

Malcolm Cowley. "Steinbeck Delivers a Mixture of Farce and Freud." *PM*, 14 January 1945, p. 15.

John Chamberlain. "The New Books." *Harper's*, 190 (February 1945), advertisement section, n.p.

Margaret Marshall. "Notes by the Way." *Nation*, 160 (3 February 1945), 131–2, 134.

W. F. Cody. "Steinbeck Will Get You If You Don't Watch Out." *Saturday Review*, 28 (7 July 1945), 18–19.

Philip Toynbee. "New Novels and Stories." *New Statesman and Nation* [England], 30 (24 November 1945), 356–7.

THE WAYWARD BUS

The
Wayward
Bus

JOHN STEINBECK

THE VIKING PRESS · NEW YORK · 1947

Harrison Smith. "John Steinbeck Does It Again." *Saturday Review*, 30 (15 February 1947), 14–15.

In the new novel we have all been waiting for John Steinbeck has abandoned the familiar, odorous waterfront of Monterey with its cannery row. Gone are the doctor and the docks, the warm-hearted girls who were all whores, and the drunks and the bums who were all more delightfully human than any man could possibly be who has money in his pockets and a balance in the bank.

The setting for *The Wayward Bus* is a neat and shining little lunch room, garage, and gas station set down under a clump of lofty trees forty-two miles below San Ysidro, where the highway meets a lesser road that rambles for forty-nine miles across the farms or mountainous landscape to meet the great coastal thoroughfare. From the beginning Steinbeck creates the illusion of complete reality. The little establishment of Juan Chicoy and his wife stands four-square and solid, the battered old bus he shuttles from one highway to the other is real, the landscape is the good earth itself, the drenching rain is wet. Mr. Steinbeck had expected to have the book ready for publication many months ago, for the scene and the nine characters who play their parts have lived in his mind for several years, and have, according to Lewis Gannett, excited and stirred him as they developed.

What he has attempted and has accomplished is to present the natural man, *homo simplicimus*, and to a lesser extent the natural woman, in glaring contrast to the artificial and glazed products of middle-class civilization. This theme has fascinated writers since Rousseau and a hundred devices have been used to illustrate it: the single man or whole families cast away on desert islands, the enthronement of the noble savage, the love battle between primitive man (*homo erectus*) and sensitive, cultured woman; what else, indeed, is Tarzan but a crude attempt to glorify the vestigial animal in man, for the more extravagantly complicated civilization becomes the more we will yearn for the man creature that nature designed to walk erect and dangerous over the earth. Not that Juan Chicoy, half Irishman, half Mexican, is by any means an animal, or dangerous, except to women. He is the free man, the man who cannot be held in bonds of any sort, the man who will at any moment leave a woman who loves him too jealously, or an enterprise in which after toil and frugality he has succeeded, who will walk away with only the clothes on his back, to begin again anywhere else. The natural man and the free man have been constant in Steinbeck's work, from the abysmal brute in *Of Mice and Men*, to the simple and gentle heart and mind of the peasants in *Tortilla Flat*, who are as incapable of understanding what civilization is doing to them as the ape riding a bicycle in a vaudeville show.

If it has sometimes seemed possible to satirize John Steinbeck for sentimentalizing the underdog, though never so grossly or ludicrously as Saroyan, there is no trace of this weakness in *The Wayward Bus*. Juan is all man, sturdy, passionate, capable, a fine mechanic, loving and understanding people, as magnetic to women as nectar to a bee. His wife knows his virtues, but the tension under which she lives with the knowledge that she may some day lose him is a rasp to her temper and often when he is away she has to drink herself into a stupor.

Two very human underdogs live with them, an anemic, homely girl—madly in love with a picture of Clark Gable—who looks after the customers in the lunch room, and a youthful mechanic called Pimples to whom adolescence had given itching sensuality and the mottled and pustulate mask of a bad case of acne. Four customers arrive and wait through a rainstorm for Juan to drive them in the old bus to the western highway. One of them is an honest girl so luxuriously seductive that her days are cursed by every man she meets, so that it is impossible for her to hold a job or to find a man who would not prefer to rape her than to marry her. She earns her living by offering her naked body at stag parties to the stares of respectable businessmen, ending her act by sitting in and rising from an enormous glass filled with red wine. You can make what you want of the ancient role in society of this depressed bacchante, for Mr. Steinbeck likes to play with symbols. There is a second honest girl, healthy and unfulfilled, who sometimes hopefully dreams that her parents have suddenly died. The wealthy Pritchards, with their daughter, are on their way to Mexico so that when they get back home they can boast of their little adventures. The N.A.M. should sue the author for this portrait of an American manufacturer and the Association of Women's Clubs must protest the description of his wife in the sacred name of the American woman and of motherhood. A more poisonous and mean couple have rarely been achieved in fiction. Mr. Pritchard is dirty-minded, boastful, dishonest, and hag-ridden by his wife; she has remained an aging little girl who has doubtless by immaculate conception produced a child, and who brings her family to heel by imaginary illnesses. The fourth paying customer is a sprightly little man who sells tricks, gadgets, and mildly obscene devices to amuse people with a perverse sense of humor. Perhaps he represents the pixies and malign sprites of ancient folklore among this collection of straight, twisted, or thwarted human beings.

And so eight of them wait through a rainstorm that is like a cloudburst for the bus to start. Mrs. Chicoy has to stay to look after the business, and Juan knows well that her nerves are on edge because he has been eyeing the Pritchards' daughter and knows too that she will be blind drunk when he gets back home. At the end of the journey a bridge is down so Juan recklessly takes the lumbering bus over an unused and dangerous road into the mountains. Why Juan does not abandon everyone and walk straight down into Mexico, why Mrs. Pritchard tears at her baby face with bloody nails, how her daughter finds that she loves the way a free and natural man makes love, and how Mr. Pritchard gets what is coming to him from the girl he had once seen naked, her thighs dripping with wine like purple blood, all of this must be left for the reader to discover.

The Wayward Bus cannot be coupled with any of Mr. Steinbeck's previous novels. It has not the tenderness of *The Pastures of Heaven* and *Tortilla Flat*, or the fierce brutality in *Of Mice and Men*, and it is not a novel of bitter social strife like *In Dubious Battle* and *The Grapes of Wrath*. But every page of it carries the unmistakable seal and signature of John Steinbeck's mind and style. Nor can one say that it is better or worse than this book or that book of his. It stands by itself, the work of a writer as distinctively American as Mark Twain, who has developed in power and dramatic talent for almost twenty years, and who is deeply concerned with the second greatest problem of our day, how to preserve the essential simple virtues of human beings from the catastrophe that mechanized civilization is bringing upon all of us.

Carlos Baker.
"Mr. Steinbeck's Cross-Section."
New York Times Book Review, 96 (16 February 1947), 1, 31.

Five hundred years ago Englishmen used to gather round a rough outdoor platform to watch, both for amusement and the good of their souls, the enactment of a simple allegorical drama called *Everyman*. Facing the title-page of Steinbeck's first full-length novel since *The Grapes of Wrath* is a quotation from this medieval morality play:

I pray you all gyve audyence,
Here this mater with reverence,
By fygure a morall playe.

The Wayward Bus may confidently be taken as a twentieth-century parable on the state of man. Although Steinbeck is not quite so insistent on his moral as Jonathan Swift, the underlying conception in what he has to say was succinctly summarized by the King of Brobdingnag in *Gulliver's Travels*: "I cannot but conclude the bulk of your natives to be the most pernicious race of little odious vermin that nature ever suffered to crawl upon the surface of the earth." Steinbeck's moral is therefore hardly new, and it has been occasionally exploited in our own day by such artists as John O'Hara and such polemicists as Philip Wylie. But in recent years the subject has rarely received so searching a treatment as Steinbeck gives it. Both because of the richness of its texture and the solidity of its structure, this new novel, unlike many parables, makes good reading. And it might even be good for one's soul.

The wayward bus is an ancient, aluminum-colored conveyance which serves the public as connecting link between two great arterial highways in central California. But its chief importance is that it serves Steinbeck as a vehicle of thought and action. He assembles in it eight members of his cast, carefully graded as to age and sex, and sends them talking and fighting across the forty-nine miles of rain-sodden and flood-swept country which lies between Juan Chicoy's lunchroom-filling station at a crossroads named (perhaps significantly) Rebel Corners and a point within eye-shot of the lights of a town called (perhaps significantly) San Juan de la Cruz.

The device of assembling a number of divergent characters and making their mutual attractions and repulsions produce the inner tensions of a book is as old as Chaucer's *Canterbury Tales* and as new as *The Iceman Cometh*, with both of which *The Wayward Bus* could be profitably compared. Steinbeck makes the bus ride an excuse for a long look at the internal substance of his characters. What he finds beneath the skin will not cause members of the Book-of-the-Month-Club to jump out of theirs, but it may well cause them to squirm in their chairs at the partial but painful truth of Steinbeck's implied conclusions.

The passengers in the bus are none of the pleasantest, possibly because Steinbeck examines their respective constitutions with such meticulous care and clinical exhaustiveness that one gets to know them from the inside out. . . . If the reader sniffs closely between the lines he may catch from time to time a gamy odor which will recall that of the Yahoos in the last book of *Gulliver's Travels*.

What prevents Steinbeck from swinging completely over into a savage indignation like Swift's is, however, a saving sense of humor and a deep strain of pity. . . .

Yet readers will do well to handle this parable with care. It is loaded—with the powder of longing and the lead of vice. Norma, the waitress, aspires to Hollywood stardom, and adopts, as her unwilling idol, Camille, the stag-dinner girl. Camille dreams of a peaceful apartment where predatory males will let her alone. Bernice Pritchard wants an orchid house and the admiration of her friends; her daughter Mildred wants a husband, and her husband Elliott would like nothing better than to out-Babbitt his most Babbitt-like business associates. Kit Carson, when he is not eating pie, dreams of a career in radar, and the gadget salesman of a money-making patent. Alice Chicoy would like to arrest the fading of her looks, and even Juan grows nostalgic for the old days in Mexico when he was free of a wife and of responsibility. The vices are equally typical. Gluttony and sloth gnaw at Pimples Carson, envy and hate and covetousness at the Pritchards, and lechery at all the males and some of the females. "My little friend," says the King of Brobdingnag ironically to Gulliver, "you have made a most admirable panegyric upon your country." Steinbeck's panegyric carries a heavy charge of buckshot.

Those who were mildly troubled that so good a book as *The Grapes of Wrath* should have been marred by structural defects may take heart in the assurance that *The Wayward Bus* has an even more solid unity than that which distinguished

In Dubious Battle. The long build-up to the bus ride begins before dawn at the lunchroom, and the darkness of evening settles over the bus as it nears its destination. Those harrowing tensions which develop in the course of the ride are established during the breakfast hour, heightened at mid-day by the dangers of the flood-racked bridge, and brought to climactic explosion in mid-afternoon when Juan skids the bus into a ditch and vanishes up the road. But in the end, with their passions spent and Juan as their conductor, the passengers arrive. The novel has as subtle and neat a horizontal structure as Steinbeck has ever evolved.

Of equal interest, though less for formal than for philosophical reasons, is what may be called the vertical structure. The route of the bus is through a clean and rain-washed countryside, and Steinbeck often, though quietly, draws the reader's eyes outward to the rich, calm beauties of the springtime land. Across the scene chugs the vehicle with its mundane human freight, while above its dashboard, like an unheeded and enigmatic guardian angel, hangs Juan's "connection with eternity," a small metal Virgin of Guadalupe painted in brilliant colors of gold and blue. The vertical structure of God, man and nature is not the less powerfully effective for being underplayed.

Among the hints by which Steinbeck enlightens his audience, readers may observe the bumpers of the wayward bus, where its modern name, Sweetheart, is boldly painted. Still dimly visible beneath the newer lettering is an older and far more serious inscription: El Gran Poder de Jesus—the great power of Jesus. This modern version of a medieval palimpsest will provide, for the thoughtful, one more handle to Steinbeck's parable of Everyman.

Ralph Habas. "Steinbeck's People Wayward as His Bus." Chicago *Times*, 16 February 1947, p. 55.

Here is John Steinbeck's first full length novel in eight years. And it is too bad he wrote it; it is so inferior to his previous creations, such as *Grapes of Wrath*, *Of Mice and Men*, *Tortilla Flat*, *Cannery Row*. Those stories were accomplishful, revealing. This is nothing but a report of the thoughts and actions of a small group of people—pretty low class, most of them—in a bus. . . .

All of these characters except Juan's wife—she stays behind at the lunch room and gets drunk—board Juan's old bus for the trip to San Juan de la Cruz. A heavy storm had swept the valley and bridges are unsafe. A detour is taken and the bus gets stuck. Juan, who is extremely attractive to women and well liked by men, seizes the opportunity and walks off, determined to return to Mexico and a new life. He gets only as far as a barn a mile distant and stops for a nap in the hay. Mildred catches up with him there.

All of the action of the novel takes place in one day. There is no plot, and not much action. A good portion of the story deals with the thoughts of the characters, who are portrayed in typical Steinbeck manner; no holds barred, life stories, desires, habits and appetites laid bare. The descriptions—character and landscape—are excellent.

Howard Moria. "Latest Novel Tells Ability of Steinbeck." Los Angeles *Times*, 16 February 1947, Part 3, p. 4.

Steinbeck is always an event but this is something special—his first full-length novel since 1939 was topped by *The Grapes of Wrath*.

It will disappoint social-minded readers who expect Steinbeck to do a *Grapes* every year but it is not without significance and it brings back the depth and richness so largely missing from his work while the turmoil of war and his war work threw him off stride as a major novelist.

Right at the start, Steinbeck's bus passengers begin to live with you, even the ones you don't like; and the owner of the wayside garage, lunchroom and bus station and his people live with even greater vitality.

Except for Proprietor Juan Chicoy of Rebel Corners, where the bus drops north and south passengers to take Juan's vehicle across to the California coast, the novel's characters are frustrated, some to the point of madness—as we are today. And Juan himself has anger lurking beneath.

Mishaps overtake the bus travelers; rage and madness leap out of their politely restraining cages. In the midst of all this excitement John Steinbeck loses neither his head nor his slyly uproarious sense of humor.

Orville Prescott. "Books of the Times." New York *Times*, 17 February 1947, p. 17.

Eight years ago John Steinbeck's *The Grapes of Wrath* established its author as one of the most powerful and interesting of living American writers. Since then Mr. Steinbeck has written nothing worthy of comparison with his one major triumph. None of his earlier books has anything like its stature either. Is it possible that Mr. Steinbeck is a one-book author whose reputation has been so inflated that it has intimidated critics and readers alike into a mood of respectful admiration which his books do not deserve? On the evidence supplied by his new novel, *The Wayward Bus*, the answer must be an emphatic if reluctant yes.

This is a tired and tiresome reworking of a shopworn formula, the arbitrary throwing together of a group of strangers into one common danger so that each of them may reveal his character under stress. Fires, floods, hurricanes and blizzards have been used times without number to isolate ill-assorted groups on ships, trains, mountain peaks, islands and in caves and grand hotels. Mr. Steinbeck uses a flood and a bus. . . .

The characters in *The Wayward Bus* are socially several cuts above the worthless riffraff of *Cannery Row*. But Mr. Steinbeck doesn't seem to admire them as much. His fond affection for the social pariahs of his last book has been replaced by a sort of contemptuous pity. Weak, frustrated, bitterly unhappy, most of his characters are haunted by the biological aspects of nature. Sex itself is always preying on their minds. And two sexual episodes provide the only climax, or conclusion, that there is to *The Wayward Bus*.

So the general atmosphere of *The Wayward Bus* is sordid, petty and vulgar. If this were one of those relentless studies of the super-naturalistic school in which every dark corner of character and environment is exposed its insistence on biological urges would be justified as part of the general philosophy of the book. But Mr. Steinbeck has not written a social document, or even a serious study of character, as he did so magnificently in *The Grapes of Wrath*. He has only provided a scenario, which, after scrupulous cleaning up, might make a passable Grade B movie.

There are two characters in *The Wayward Bus* who are credited with strength and courage. "The Blonde" is one. She is bitterly resigned to her lot, but she is no dummy and no weakling. Juan is the other. Capable, kindly, bursting with animal vitality, he puts up with his hysterical, drunken wife because he knows that he can always find other women whenever he wants to. Is there a conclusion to be drawn from Mr. Steinbeck's choice of these two as his superior characters? Is he suggesting that intelligence and courage are dependent on physical strength? Sandow rather than Keats?

One can't be certain. But *The Wayward Bus* at least raises such a question. Since it is a Book-of-the-Month Club selection, quite a few people may be trying to find the answer in the next few weeks.

George E. Helmer. "Aboard a Bus—with Steinbeck." Sacramento *Bee*, 22 February 1947, p. 15.

In his first full-length novel in eight years, John Steinbeck takes you for another auto ride. But apart from the ride and distinctive Steinbeck style, there's not much similarity between *Grapes of Wrath* and *The Wayward Bus*.... For one thing Steinbeck's dominant concern in his new opus isn't sociology.

His major interest here is the business of how men make fools of themselves over women and vice versa. Nearly all of his latest batch of characters carry on in such a way as to bring this point home to you.

These carryings-on begin when an old bus operating between two small California towns breaks down, marooning its passengers overnight at a dinky crossroads restaurant-garage-service station. And they continue for less than 24 hours.

But that's time enough for you to get thoroughly acquainted with the dark, handsome, good-natured, half-Mexican and half-Irish owner-driver of the bus and proprietor of the crossroads place; his wide-hipped, loose-lipped, insanely jealous wife; the pathetically homely and self-conscious youth who helps around the garage; the restaurant's shy daydreaming waitress; and the passengers including a Babbitt-like businessman; his too-sweet wife; their sensuous 21-year-old daughter; a smoothie novelties salesman; and a blonde tart who earns her living as a stag party stripper.

It's also time enough for the business man and salesman to make a play for the blonde, the youth for the waitress and the b.m.'s daughter for the bus driver. And the author provides adequate opportunity for each of these amorous pursuits to reach a climax of a more or less dramatic sort.

J. M. Lalley. "Books." *New Yorker*, 23 (22 February 1947), 87–90.

A half-dozen lines from *Everyman* chosen by Mr. Steinbeck as the motto of his new novel, *The Wayward Bus*, ... warn us that the book is intended to be a kind of allegory. Indeed, the author has put aside his favorite role of Prometheus for that of moralist; here is no defiant lover of mankind, in agony on the Caucasian crag of compassion, but an inverted Puritan, wrestling grimly with the mysteries of Grace. Of the ten characters Mr. Steinbeck has brought together, after the example of the Canterbury pilgrims and the famous fugitives from the Florentine plague, only one has the marks of sanctity; the others are reprobate and damned by his strange, priapic deity.

... And now, perhaps, we should ask ourselves why there need have been any of it. I have already said that *The Wayward Bus* is clearly intended as an allegory. The characters are not definite individuals, like Ma Joad, for example, or Casy the Preacher, but personified generalities, or, if you prefer, types. They are presented with an accuracy that testifies to the acuteness of Mr. Steinbeck's observation, but you can observe them for yourself on buses almost anywhere. You might while away your journey by attempting to guess what lies behind these familiar masks, but you would have to be a particularly apt disciple of Krafft-Ebing or of D. H. Lawrence to see what Mr. Steinbeck sees in a busload of travellers. I'm very much afraid that Juan Chicoy is simply the projection of Mr. Steinbeck's notion of the Righteous Man in an evil society, a man who is nevertheless enough of a primitive to be free of the mortal neuroses of his civilized passengers, enough of an animal to enjoy his women when he wants to, enough of a man to let them alone when he doesn't. This makes for a sermonizing book, which those who are not of Mr. Steinbeck's priapic persuasion may find fairly tedious. For many readers, no doubt, the moralizing will be well compensated for by the waywardness of Mr. Steinbeck's vocabulary and by his cheery touches of naturalism, such as a little scene in the ladies' comfort station. But even these are veins that others have already worked, I suspect, almost to exhaustion.

Edward Weeks.
"California Bus Ride."
Atlantic, 179 (March 1947), 126, 128.

In *The Wayward Bus*, John Steinbeck is writing about a busload of assorted Americans who are marooned overnight at a California crossroads. The driver and his pimply mechanic patch up the rear end in the early dawn, but as day breaks and the rain comes down, the journey is further imperiled by a spring flood which deluges the San Juan valley, threatening the bridges and turning the old stagecoach road into a slithery morass.

This is Mr. Steinbeck's first full-length novel since *The Grapes of Wrath*. In the intervening eight years he served as a war correspondent with the American troops in Europe. He has been decorated by the King of Norway for the writing of his war book and play, *The Moon Is Down*, and he has published a novelette loosely tied together with the title of *Cannery Row*. But *The Wayward Bus* is a novel of much the same architecture as *The Bridge of San Luis Rey*, and to those of us who admire Mr. Steinbeck, it is refreshing to see the warm flow of vitality which surges up in his pages, and to mark such changes as have occurred in his style and in his philosophy since he wrote his great story of the Okies. . . .

Juan sets the keynote of sex, and to it Alice, his blowsy wife, and the passengers respond or recoil. The adventure of these people as they intermingle and feel each other out is told with a close perspiring intimacy which may seem repellent to nice readers, but it is only fair to suggest that with such sharp anatomical details the novelist is cutting away the gloss, the hypocrisy, the over-advertised glamour of American daily life. He is indeed using the very details which advertising stresses, but with a sharp knife instead of soft soap. He is vulgarly intent on identifying human nature for what it is. To Mr. Steinbeck feminine beauty is no deeper than the make-up. His portraits of Mildred Pritchard and Camille are a repudiation of "those bright, improbable girls with pumped-up breasts and no hips," those Hollywood visions of mediocrity.

There are five noticeable women in this book: Alice, Juan's wife, with her rage ("the uncontrolled pleasure rising in her chest and throat"), her jealousy, and her alcoholic self-pity; Bernice Pritchard ("one of the sweetest, most unselfish people you will ever meet"), as pretty and as untouchable as dry ice; Mildred, her myopic,

300

man-hungry daughter; Norma, the pathetic infatuate of Hollywood; and, last of all, Camille, a wise, defiant tramp with her musky heritage. To Camille, as to Mrs. Pritchard, sex is repellent, though for quite opposite reasons. To the reader the intensification of this instinct among this jostled and confined company may seem forced and a little tedious. Are we all really so possessed? Would we too have caught the contagion of that bus? Is there no motive, no gratification, more compelling in a California spring? I sound like a rock bound Puritan, but the question persists in my mind.

Very lovely, very sensuous the country is in Mr. Steinbeck's rippling prose. . . .

Very natural and funny, and at times very candid, is the talk, as when, for instance, Camille turns down Mr. Pritchard with the remark that she "is not going to be nibbled to death by ducks," or when Alice exclaims that Pimples "could eat pies standing on his head in a washtub of flat beer on Palm Sunday." But, for all this animal magnetism and photographic reality, one ends by wondering if American life is actually so empty, so devoid of meaning, so lonely for the Juans, the Pritchards, and the Camilles of today. God help us if it is.

N[orman] C[ousins].
"Bankrupt Realism."
Saturday Review, 30
(8 March 1947), 22–3.

Unless we miss all the signs, John Steinbeck's new novel, *The Wayward Bus*, will touch off some enlivened literary controversy on at least two separate levels.

On the first level, there is already some argument concerning Mr. Steinbeck's intentions. Is the novel allegory or isn't it? Several reviewers, including our own, have said that it is; they see in it an artful and commanding attempt to point to the greatest tyranny of all—the self-torture of self-inflicted restraints, the surface adherence to artificial values of morality, the inevitable disintegration of the individual when exposed to the corrosive acids of a fabulously complicated social organism.

Other reviewers, equally persuasive, claim to have found no more than meets the reading eye. Whatever the merits of the book may be—and there is considerable disagreement here—these reviewers profess to have penetrated through to no subterranean allegorical vaults; they seem to regard it as nothing more complex than a theme ideally suited to the Steinbeck method. (By way of parenthetical substantiation, we are reminded of his peculiar fondness for people trying to get from one place to another, especially as it may involve automobile museum pieces and their inevitable but literarily convenient breakdowns.)

The controversy on this first level is pleasant but largely academic, since it can only be resolved by Mr. Steinbeck himself, who of course will not tell. But there is no reason why both groups should not have the satisfaction of their own impressions. Allegory, like gold, is where you find it, and any reader who is prospecting for a shiny Message should feel rewarded whenever and wherever he recognizes a glint. Similarly, those who take the book at face value need not feel they are showing symptoms of arrested mental development if their senses fail to detect any profound allegorical implications.

But there is a second and more fruitful level of controversy over the Steinbeck book. John Steinbeck, if he is not the superintendent of the modern school of literary realism, is at least in joint possession of the keys with Ernest Hemingway, although Faulkner, Farrell, and Dos Passos are able to get in and out without knocking. And if that particular school seems to be fading, then it is not inappropriate if the superintendent himself should furnish us with indications of significant weakness.

Our contention, then, is that the dominant mood of American fiction is due for an important change. "Realistic writing," which has prevailed so emphatically for more than twenty years, is now revealing points of critical insufficiency.

Before examining this insufficiency, it may be in order to review some of the principal characteristics of the realistic school. A relentless and frequently ruthless frankness was combined with a sharp ear for dialogue and a still sharper eye for strong off-colors. The tempered-steel hardness of the images contrasted violently with, and was indeed a bitter reaction away from, the lavender-pillowed softness of much of American fiction in the generation before World War I. Realism in writing involved much more than technique: it was fiercely purposeful. Every line, every image, had to carry an assigned payload of social purpose. Which was all to the good. War, slums, unemployment, sharecroppers, Okies, the proletarian artist—these were among the more favored subjects to be dramatized.

More recently, however, realistic writing has gradually lost in strength and vitality, even as it has enlarged on its defects—defects which were inherent in the technique to begin with but which were heavily overshadowed by the drive and flavor of the medium itself. The writers of the realistic school took a calculated risk: if they failed to tie realism to purpose, tie it clearly and definitely, then they stood in danger of robbing their work of its very validity.

And that is just what is happening today. Realism is being divorced from purpose. The attempt is being made to regard realism as an end in itself. It makes no difference, apparently, where the novelist holds his mirror so long as he can be pungent and graphic about what he wants the reader to see. Thus we have had a weird procession of literary curiosa and erotica. It is not fooling anyone to reply to this by raising the cry of prudery. What is offensive is not the use of a word, but the strained, artless, and unrelated nature of extraneous situations brought in to capture the snicker market. Realism of this sort is about as appealing as an old goat emerging from a wet thicket.

Now, John Steinbeck is not to be confused with the more glaring examples of bankrupt realism. In terms of sheer literary talent and command of his materials, he is excelled by few if any living American writers. We had looked forward to *The Wayward Bus*, hoping that he would get back on the track again after his amusing burlesque in *Cannery Row*, and after his long recess following *The Grapes of Wrath*. We had looked to him to put realistic writing back into business, to restore its validity, to prove, as he did in *The Grapes of Wrath*, that realism can be an effective tool but must not master the writer himself.

Despite all the good things that have been and can be said about *The Wayward Bus*; despite its sustained brilliance, the striking power of its images, its grasp of situations, the complete credibility and vividness of its characters, its dramatic staging and effects—despite all this, there are sizable indications that Steinbeck has been infected with what is at least extraneous realism. He has a passion for itemization, and you marvel at the awareness of detail which enables him to walk into a lunchroom and take a descriptive inventory of every item over or under the counter, down to the last box of

Wheaties. But this passion has become an undisciplined obsession unrelated to all reasonable purpose. When, for example, he takes the reader inside a ladies' toilet, minutely describing the fixtures and the postures and conversations of the occupants, you have not the slightest doubt that he is being realistic, but you are not impressed. Instead, you wonder why a mature writer should parade his ability to satisfy the curiosities and compulsions of an adolescent.

A Steinbeck supporter may object that such evidence as this is much too slight for a general indictment. What we are describing, however, is not an example but a characteristic. It is a symptomatic indication of the recent general trend of his work—a work that shows signs of undiscipline and unevenness, so much so that the book as a whole, with or without its ascribed allegorical significance, fails by far to measure up to the ability of *The Grapes of Wrath* to equate realism with purpose. By that much, too, does it fit in with and lend momentum to the present drift towards corrupted naturalism.

Why does a fashion or a period or a school of writing die out? Sometimes the writers just become too tired; sometimes the public mood changes and only the new writers are sensitive enough to anticipate it and respond with proper energy at the propitious moment; sometimes the books slide into patterns falsely created by the best-seller lists; sometimes the public itself is fed up and a reaction sets in. Sometimes, a combination of all these and more is responsible, which is what seems to be happening today. We are in a transition period, but it is too early to tell what will take the place of the pioneering realism of the twenties, the radical realism of the thirties, and the stilted realism of the forties.

But if the needs of America in particular and humanity in general are to be consulted, then the job of the writer is clear: let him first restore his respect for the craft of writing. Let him pour all his talents into the handling of a theme much more fundamental and dramatic and challenging than any problem human evolution has yet known—the need for individual man to find a way of changing the general direction of his mind so that it turns primarily outward rather than inward. Such a change would automatically fulfill what all through the ages was the dream of the philosophers and the poets, but what is today the very specific and crystallized prerequisite for continuation of the human species on this particular planet—the creation of a Group Conscience.

Richard Watts, Jr. "The Wayward Steinbeck." *New Republic,* 116 (10 March 1947), 37–8.

... This is not, it may be remembered, the first time that a Steinbeck work has caused vigorous disagreement among critics. In the case of *The Moon Is Down,* however, the controversy was based rather more on war issues than on literary merit, and involved reviewers of both books and plays. On the whole, the novel about the Nazi invasion of Norway was first received with praise and only a few violent dissenters like James Thurber and Clifton Fadiman objected to its political aspects. But by the time it had reached Broadway as a play, the majority critical comment was against it, considering its German officers too susceptible to human feelings and the passive resistance in it too glowing, and it was soon a theatrical failure.

The matter of the varied and frequently unfriendly critical attitude toward Steinbeck's works is of importance because it supplies one clue to his standing as an American writer. It is certainly not remarkable to find novels that have been roundly condemned achieving tremendous popular success, but it is a little more striking to find books and plays that are critically pilloried for soggy sentimentality later accepted, by the public and a fair section of the critics, as something close to classics in their field.

It is an impressive accomplishment for an author, and the Steinbeck record in this respect is clear: *The Moon Is Down*, which was often regarded as a shallowly sentimental libel on the Norwegian resistance movement, became a treasured document among resistance movements throughout Nazi-occupied Europe. Steinbeck was officially honored in Norway for his tribute to the national heroism, while *Tortilla Flat, In Dubious Battle, The Grapes of Wrath* and *The Red Pony*, which were received with hearty charges of immature sentimentality mixed with the majority critical praise, are now recognized additions to modern American literature. And the dramatic version of *Of Mice and Men* is one of the realistic masterpieces of the American theatre, as well as one of the few motion pictures of genuine quality. This reviewer can attest that during the recent war Steinbeck was one of the three or four American authors, along with O'Neill and Hemingway, that the intellectuals of embattled Chungking and neutral Dublin wanted most to find out about.

Of course, the fact that some of Steinbeck's earlier books have come to be regarded as approaching classic status in their field, despite their detractors, doesn't indicate that the more unfriendly critics are wrong about his latest novel. It merely means that one of the qualities which makes his fiction important is its capacity for taking the ordinary struggles of ordinary people in some period of modern emotional and social strain, giving them moral import and significance and, without losing their realistic simplicity, capturing a quality that makes them at once symbolic, poetic and, at best, of an almost epic nature. Thus his most significant works, *The Grapes of Wrath, In Dubious Battle, Of Mice and Men*, become, among other things, symbolic epics of characteristic phases of American social maladjustment. They are set down with such emotional forcefulness that defects of sentimentality, untidiness and extravagance cannot interfere with their essential integrity. If these books are more successful than *The Moon Is Down*, it is in part because the essential Steinbeck quality is so indigenously American, in characterization, physical setting and mind and emotion, that anything of his which strives to deal with other lands suffers from absence of the soil that nourishes his writing and gives it its spirit.

Yet *The Wayward Bus*, which is completely indigenous, lacks something of the quality of his major works, although in one way it probably marks an advance: the sentimentality is missing. The new novel possesses many characteristic virtues. Its prose is as lean, vigorous and direct as ever; its dialogue, its descriptions of people, places and things and its revelation of a great natural gift for narration are as distinctive and impressive as before. The perhaps less important, but not-to-be-ignored, quality of being immensely readable is always present. The physical feeling for America is there, as well as the rootlessness, inner loneliness and neurotic discontent which Steinbeck sees as melancholy symptoms of a national ailment. The plot device about widely disparate people, unexpectedly thrown together on an adventure, has been a familiar one from the time of Boccaccio and Chaucer to Vicki Baum and Thornton Wilder, but it is purposely familiar and effectively handled. And the characters are interestingly assorted; Camille, the girl with the fatal lure for men, is one of the author's most engaging creations.

If the final effect, although it makes for a striking novel, is less than completely satisfying, it is in great part because we had come to expect another major Steinbeck advance in breadth and power, such as was marked in turn by *In Dubious Battle* and *The Grapes of Wrath*, while *The Wayward Bus* does not reveal such development. Furthermore, the central character of Juan Chicoy, the Irish-Mexican "natural man," does not quite come off, and the climax somehow lacks the expected dramatic force. But there is enough in the novel to make one anticipate Steinbeck's next book as hopefully and eagerly as this was awaited. His is a notable American talent.

Eleanor Clark. "Infantilism and Steinbeck." Nation, 164 (29 March 1947), 370, 372–3.

From the popular practice of honoring the makers of half-truths in order to stay clear of whole ones probably no living writer has profited more than John Steinbeck; and probably as good a way as any to indicate the diseases of the time would be to analyze the particular combination of narrative skill and dishonesty of mind involved in this triumph. Of the most obvious aspect of the dishonesty a good deal has been said already, and more will be for Steinbeck's various falsifications of the "lower depths" of this country—swinging from one social sentimentality to another that cancels it out, and back again—have to do with more than the faulty vision that shows up in any ten pages of *The Grapes of Wrath*, however effective the tear-jerking of which he is a master. There is also a will to irresponsibility which is never missing in this author's work, though it takes many forms, literal idiocy and immersion in the Communist Party being only two of them, and in which lies the root of more political troubles than Steinbeck will ever dramatize. But there is another aspect of this infantilism, and of its appeal in some quarters, too, no doubt, that is not so easy to stop and that bears more directly on *The Wayward Bus*. That is the question of sex and the relations between men and women in general, and it is relevant because the only conceivable purpose of this otherwise trite and meaningless book is to express an eruption of sexual interest so crude and obsessive as nearly to swamp even the technical talent that Steinbeck has usually had at his command.

This seems surprising only because the nature of his subjects until now has drawn attention chiefly to his social meanings, such as they are, and somewhat obscured the much deeper escapism in his treatment of adult human relations. But the process is embarrassingly clear, even to the glorification of the mother. His other women are the merest sex objects, usually rather comical and the stupider the better; and when he speaks of "love" he is referring to an association of men, at least two of his books being quite literal fantasies of escape into a world without women, that is, a world without the main component of adult responsibility. This was the childish charm of *Tortilla Flat* as well as the basic distortion in *Of Mice and Men*, in which he made it quite plain that he was not even retreating into homosexuality but was simply abandoning the problem of sex as an integral part of life altogether. It is a separate, biological matter, so desperately kept apart from Steinbeck's thoughts of human beings in general that if women are capable of any personality or intelligence aside from bed and motherhood, no one would know it from his books, as witness the young moron who passes for a woman, and even an admirable one, among the male Communist heroes of *In Dubious Battle*; and even she is kept apart by having just had a baby. It is also suggestive that a writer so concerned with social injustice should never, as far as I can remember, have spoken of prostitution as anything but amusing.

All this adds up to one of the commonest, and saddest, maladies of the time, and it expresses itself in *The Wayward Bus* in a fashion that will be equally recognizable, especially to anyone who has ever traveled in a club car. This time the social implications, if there are any, are lost in the hay; the contrivance of throwing an assortment of characters together in a public vehicle has an air of being a stock one. Even if it is not, the characters have the same air, and the only overt motivation of the whole business is to show, as the blurb says and with no more irony, that we all have our heartaches, etc. But the real purpose is to lead up to the moment toward the end when the bus breaks down on a lonely mountain road, and all its occupants except one old man who is having a stroke can scamper or be dragged off into the bushes. It is a story of sexual polarity, the two main forces in which are a kindhearted "cookie" named Camille, who causes all men to lick their lips and say "Whew!" and who makes her living sitting in large wineglasses at stag conventions, and the half-Mexican bus-driver Juan, representing what is perhaps the noblest effort Steinbeck has ever made to create a grown-up man. But he is spoiled, too, by being paired off in the crisis with a stereotyped college girl, who felt "swollen and itchy" at her first sight of him, and who when she feels sexually rebuffed says to herself, "Basket-ball . . . that's the stuff"; so that the D. H. Lawrence episode we have been led up to through 200 pages turns out to have more the quality of peanut brittle. Other figures in the parade are an unattractive waitress dreaming, of all things, of Clark Gable; an adolescent youth with acne, called Pimples; a well-off business man borrowed whole from Sinclair Lewis—"Wherever he went he was not one man but a unit in a corporation, a unit in a club, in a lodge, in a church, in a political party"—and his wife, who provides what ought to become some kind of classic among writings on the female mind: "Bernice too could draw a magic circle around herself, with motherhood, or, say, menstruation, a subject like that, and no man could or would try to get in."

This extraordinary performance is by the man who is reported to be one of the two or three modern American writers most highly regarded in Europe and Russia, and who has been praised at length by some of the most astute critics in France. It is also a current Book-of-the-Month Club selection; if it were not, at least if it were not by Steinbeck, it is doubtful whether anyone would have reviewed it. And yet though its cheapness is easier to see, not being hidden behind picturesque personalities or a righteous cause, essentially it is of a piece with the rest of his work, and ought to inspire a little sober questioning of the nature of

306

the author's popularity. For the reputation he enjoys in Europe, aside from the French respect for some of the technical equipment he shares with and may have learned from Hemingway, there are presumably some extra-literary reasons such as curiosity about American life, because, unlike Saroyan, Steinbeck has known how to make the most of his California surroundings. To some extent the same curiosity probably operates here. But it is not on those grounds that he is most discussed, and this latest book makes one wonder again whether the Steinbeck phenomenon may not represent above all an increasing yearning in people to be either morally incapacitated or, what amounts to the same thing, the victims of some insuperable force.

Frank O'Malley.
"The Wayward Bus."
Commonweal, 46
(25 April 1947), 43–4.

By this time everybody knows about John Steinbeck. Some of the more forthright reviewers have dismissed the haplessness of The Wayward Bus without any words of assuagement. Other critics, although disturbed by the novel's astonishing weaknesses, have still tried to find in it the allegorical significance which Steinbeck's epigraph from Everyman would impose on the work. I think that this effort, stimulated perhaps by Steinbeck's reputation, by the remembrance of past glory, has been wasted. For Steinbeck's dreary, prurient pilgrimage has no real human or universal significance. It is nothing more than an unusually dismal bus ride—more dismal, depraved and

meaningless than any man anywhere has ever taken.

Steinbeck appears to have been affected somewhat by the D. H. Lawrence idea of the Natural Man. At least I think that he attempts to realize it in the figure of Juan, the bus driver. But the wisdom, dignity and strength of the primitive of D. H. Lawrence are not in Steinbeck. Juan is just a satyr. And a good deal of Steinbeck's writing about him is ridiculous, stereotyped, hardly a cut above the sleazy sentimentalizing of the passion magazines.

There is also Pimples, a kind of lascivious idiot, conceivably patterned after some of the odd, unnerved inhabitants of William Faulkner's wonderful jungle. But the authentic symbolism, the insight of Faulkner as well as the greatness of his art are missing from Steinbeck's drawing. There is also Mr. Pritchard, a vapid, busy hypocrite. But Sinclair Lewis has given this sort of man-of-affairs his best, warmest and most thorough embodiment. And Steinbeck, in this characterization, does only a feeble imitation of the achievement of Lewis. A scrutiny of other characters: Juan's vulgar, distracted, alcoholic wife, the stupid waitress, both presented without a vestige of subtlety, the gadget salesman, very much like something out of the comic strips or possibly William Saroyan, and Camille, the decoy, whose mysterious attraction Steinbeck is unable to make very baleful—such a scrutiny would only repeat the judgments already passed and prolong the not especially pleasant task of assessing this book.

The publication of this latest work of Steinbeck does raise a very grave question: why do so many of our serious American writers deteriorate? Is it the lure of Hollywood or the submission to the point-of-view, the literary fascism of the New York dictators over literature that vulgarizes and enfeebles them? Certainly there is a depressing lack of distinction, a dead-leveling in current American fiction. And one cannot help wondering why our free citizens—the writers of talent and the literate reading public—do not resist the sinister attempt to exploit them. Banal and venal influences upon our culture and literature have, of course, entrenched themselves. Gorging themselves upon our souls, they have grown rich, fat, big and powerful. But it may not be too late for honest men to go to war against them.

Samuel Roddan. "*The Wayward Bus*." *Canadian Forum*, 27 (May 1947), 45–6.

This is John Steinbeck's first full length novel since the publication of *The Grapes of Wrath* eight years ago. The old Steinbeck craftsmanship is still very much in evidence—in fact, his work now is so beautifully refined that it comes dangerously close to being synthetic, perhaps even cunning.

In *The Wayward Bus* Steinbeck presents us with an assorted group of Americans marooned overnight at a San Juan Valley crossroad. The bus is nicknamed "Sweetheart" and its driver Juan Chicoy is that uncomplicated, intelligent type of personality who through sex or initiative can usually dominate most situations. It is really not important what happens in the bus for it is simply a "vehicle" through which Steinbeck can explore and identify human nature. Naked and unabashed portraits of each of the passengers are skillfully manoeuvred into a tiny mosaic of American life. As one writer has put it, "the adventures of these peo-

ple as they intermingle and feel each other out is told with a close, perspiring intimacy." *The Wayward Bus* is not deficient in entertainment. But to what extent Steinbeck has been successful in reproducing an intelligible and authentic microcosm of our culture is another question.

Harold Brighouse. "Novels and Stories." Manchester *Guardian*, 28 November 1947, p. 3.

... A now familiar device is used by Mr. John Steinbeck in *The Wayward Bus* ...; persons, ordinarily unconnected, are thrown together for a few hours when, in California, a cross-country bus breaks down. Among the passengers inconvenienced by the stoppage and, later, by a flooded river are a Babbitt; his repressed wife and his uninhibited daughter; a man who after doing well in the war is proud to be a commercial traveller in "novelties"— small, offensively silly adult toys; a waitress infatuated with Clark Gable; an amorous, pimply youth; and Camille, a professional of "strip-tease." And either Mr. Steinbeck, persuasively, is sentimental about Camille or she was naturally, inevitably, philosophically, and through no fault of her own an incitement to men. She and the owner-driver of the bus, Mexican-Irish by origin, are accorded chief attention in an ugly, if an able, novel. ...

"Insufficient People."
*Times Literary
Supplement* [London],
29 November 1947,
p. 613.

Americans are sometimes critical of manners and customs of other countries, but it cannot be said that their own writers are, on the whole, any less severe in their attitude towards representative American failings. Mrs. Trollope, Dickens and the rest who did not find the United States to their liking never managed to be so damaging from the outside as Mr. H. L. Mencken or Mr. Sinclair Lewis have been from the inside, and for the last thirty years, at least, there has been a steady flow of American books which depict in no uncertain terms the disagreeable aspects of American life.

The theme of *The Wayward Bus*, for example, is the emotional, social and intellectual barrenness of a group of persons who find themselves thrown together during twenty-four hours in a little service-station-*cum*-restaurant in California, kept by Juan Chicoy, who also drives a motor-coach. Half Mexican, half Irish (with Indian blood) Chicoy is treated by the author with more respect than the rest of the characters, and "because he was a man, and there aren't very many of them," he plays a role familiarized by D. H. Lawrence. In contrast with Chicoy are various examples of a commercialized civilization: his wife, Alice, eaten up with hatred; his employees, Pimples and Norma, the former a garage hand with a taste for sweet cakes, the latter a "hired girl" whose sole interest is her love for Mr. Clark Gable; a fifty-year-old company director called Pritchard who "looked like Truman," with his wife and bespectacled Left-Wing daughter, who "also knew herself to be a young girl of strong sexual potential"; a young man travelling in tricks and novelties; Camille, almost irresistible to men (also treated fairly kindly); and some others, all frustrated to a greater or lesser degree.

Mr. Steinbeck sometimes seems inclined to rag American sentimentality about, for example, the Chinese or the Mexicans, and to ridicule the standards expressed by, "And what a guy at parties! He knows more dames, he's got more phone numbers than you ever saw. A big thick black book full of phone numbers"; but he never succeeds for long in achieving an objectivity that might set these matters in some perspective. "The road ran straight towards the little foothills of the first range," he writes, "rounded, woman-like hills, soft and sexual as flesh. And the green clinging grass had the bloom of young skin." After this we can feel no surprise at Miss Pritchard's pursuit and seduction of Chicoy, her father's unbecoming conduct *vis-à-vis* Camille and his own wife, and the uncontrolled, or uncontrollable, antics of the remaining passengers of the motor-coach which brings them all together.

The Wayward Bus will not add greatly to Mr. John Steinbeck's reputation. In earlier novels he has shown his ability for describing the lives and preoccupations of the half-baked, a subject he treats with zest and confidence though without much humour. Here something more seems required; the book, although readable and competently put together, never rises above the level of the better sort of film to which some uplift has been added.

Robin King.
"Fiction."
Spectator [England], 173
(19 December 1947),
782–4.

... Mr. John Steinbeck's new book comes as something of a surprise. Here again is technical brilliance of a high order; here too is excitement; here, in fact, is almost everything that made Mr. Steinbeck so popular a writer. The characters in *The Wayward Bus* come to life with a facility and an aptness that one can only admire and enjoy.... They are all allegedly American types and they are brought together, rather artificially and slenderly, by means of a bus. The bus is lovingly described (Mr. Steinbeck has a passion for vehicles as well as for animals and insects), and the journey these people take, each one wrapped up in his own world, sealed off from one another by their selfishness as effectively as though they were behind prison bars, can be taken as an allegory of the journey through life. Here comes the cynicism and here, I suspect, comes the flaw. Mr. Steinbeck plunges his characters into danger and boredom and he shows them at their worst. He is quite ruthless in ferreting out the despicable quality in each. In the end one hates the people in the "wayward bus," if not for the same reason that Mr. Steinbeck hates them. He despairs of human motives and he expresses his despair under a surface of flashy cynicism. "What do I care?" he seems to say. "Life is hell, people are greater hells, but there you are—there isn't much choice." All this comes to the surface when the bus breaks down. Mr. Pritchard brutally outrages his wife in a cave; Pimples assaults Norma by means of a trick appeal to her maternal sympathies; Mr. Van Brunt falls fatally ill; and Juan seduces the Pritchards' daughter Mildred. "Aren't they hell?" Mr. Steinbeck seems to say again, with a scornful laugh, and to do him justice we see that they are hell and suspect that we ourselves stand equally condemned.

Jules Strachey.
"New Novels."
New Statesman and Nation [England], 34
(20 December 1947),
496–7.

In the case of Mr. Steinbeck I must admit that it is a sort of technicolour unity that is achieved, of the kind one sees in American advertisements for tobacco, cigarettes, or silver spoons. His eight characters that meet on a Californian highway, at the little restaurant-garage called "Rebel's Corner," and who all finally jump into the "wayward bus" together, certainly have just that glossy, simplified, crudely tinted, sexy, and bouncingly animal look. The setting too—the lunch room with every physical detail, every hamburger, ice-cream unit and glass of coca-cola so defined that it fairly bludgeons one in all its sterile, stolid prose; and the Californian macadamized highway outside with its petrol pumps and garage accoutrements, all done in three block process.

This is a highly professional picture that Steinbeck paints. What a firm hand! What an eye! The latter like a telescope showing us a scene of unnatural clarity, where all the middle distances, and all the mysterious chiarioscuro of a living landscape are eliminated for our convenience.

What are we shown? Eight types. The American business man, goggling sideways at the silk-stockinged thighs of the blonde at the next table, where her tight skirt has wrinkled up. The fat and ageing proprietor's wife behind the counter, who has taken to drink. The college girl, lusting after the proprietor. The drab servant Norma, dreaming of marrying Clark Gable, the spotty young garage help who thinks only of one thing. And now I come to think of it, everybody here thinks only of "one thing." Except the salesman of Novelties, who concentrates on earning his bread-and-butter. Anyway, after they've all lusted and fed, they hop into the bus together (which is appositely named "sweetheart") and drive off. On the high road—but I won't reveal the plot. If only for the reason that I haven't been able to make it out myself. I only know that this is a very skilful, randy, wonderfully easy book to whisk through.

Checklist of Additional Reviews

H. Gilbert Kelley. "*The Wayward Bus.*" *Library Journal*, 72 (15 February 1947), 321.

"*The Wayward Bus.*" *Booklist*, 43 (15 February 1947), 186.

Fanny Butcher. "Intensified Emotions in New Steinbeck." Chicago *Tribune*, 16 February 1947, pp. 3, 15.

Annie Calhoun. "They Got Stranded at Rebel Corners." Dallas *Times Herald*, 16 February 1947, Section 6, p. 7.

Malcolm Cowley. "Steinbeck Brings 'Em Back under Glass." *PM*, 16 February 1947, pp. 12–13M.

Bernard De Voto. "John Steinbeck's Bus Ride into the Hills." *New York Herald Tribune Weekly Book Review*, 16 February 1947, pp. 1–2.

Robert Halsband. "Steinbeck Turns Back to a Serious Theme." Chicago *Sun*, 16 February 1947, Section 5, p. 3.

Joseph Henry Jackson. "John Steinbeck Writes His First Long Novel in Eight Years with the Story of a Bus Ride." San Francisco *Chronicle*, 16 February 1947, pp. 17–18.

Daphne Alloway McVicker. "Book Mark." Columbus [Ohio] *Citizen* (*Citizen* magazine), 16 February 1947, p. 6.

Lewis Gannett. "Books and Things." New York *Herald Tribune*, 17 February 1947, p. 15.

"Steinbeck on a Bus." *Newsweek*, 29 (17 February 1947), 104, 106.

Samuel Sillen. "Steinbeck Skids Downhill in *The Wayward Bus.*" *Daily Worker*, 21 February 1947, p. 11.

Theodore Smith. "Of Making Many Books There." San Francisco *News*, 22 February 1947, p. 10.

"Repent!" *Time*, 49 (24 February 1947), 118, 120.

J. Donald Adams. "Speaking of Books." *New York Times Book Review*, 96 (2 March 1947), 2.

Frances Baker. "Turns with the Book Worm." Jackson [Miss.] *News*, 2 March 1947, Section 5, p. 2.

John Mason Brown. "Seeing Things." *Saturday Review*, 30 (19 April 1947), 24–7.

Orville Prescott. "Outstanding Novels." *Yale Review*, 36 (June 1947), 765–8.

THE PEARL

The Pearl

JOHN STEINBECK

WITH DRAWINGS BY JOSÉ CLEMENTE OROZCO

THE VIKING PRESS · NEW YORK

1947

Robert E. Kingery.
"*The Pearl.*"
Library Journal, 72
(1 November 1947), 1540.

Retelling of an old Mexican folk tale—
the finding of the Great Pearl by Kino, a
fisherman and what then happened to
him, his wife Juana and their baby Coyotito,
before Kino threw the pearl into the sea
again. Within that simple frame, Steinbeck
achieves a major artistic triumph full of
subtle overtones, large fundamentals and
universal significance. This is Steinbeck in
full stature and in culmination, and is,
therefore, without reservation, absolutely
essential in all collections. . . .

Maxwell Geismar.
"Fable Retold."
Saturday Review, 30
(22 November 1947),
14–15.

This is an old Mexican folk tale which
John Steinbeck has recast in his familiar
paisano vein. It originally appeared in
The Woman's Home Companion under
the title of "The Pearl of the World" and
now, with full-page original drawings by
Orozco, it forms a modest and attractive
little volume. But it also raises some serious questions about almost all Steinbeck's
recent books and his work as a whole.

The story deals with a Mexican fisherman named Kino who is devoted to his
wife, Juana, and his child, Coyotito. The
child is bitten by a scorpion and the
white doctor refuses to treat it. Kino discovered a huge pearl, the greatest pearl
in the world according to his Mexican
neighbors. The doctor tries to steal it, the
pearl merchants (also white) try to cheat
him out of it, and Kino is forced, in what
is apparently an inevitable sequence of
tragic consequences, to flee from his village and to murder the "trackers" who
come after him. In the end he has lost his
home, his child, and his happiness, and
he flings the pearl back into the sea.

"If this story is a parable," Steinbeck
says, "perhaps everyone takes his own
meaning from it and reads his own life
into it," and indeed, as in most of Steinbeck's
allegories, there are several meanings
implicit in *The Pearl*, not all of which,
perhaps, are what the author consciously
intended.

The writing is very good, as are the
descriptions of village life and Mexican
types, and the Gulf scene itself: the land,
the climate, even the various hours of the
day. There is less of Steinbeck's romantic
whimsicality, too, although one still could
do without quite so many of his Mexican
"songs." And what one notices again is
how much more interested Steinbeck really is in the natural scene, and in animal
life, than in the people or the human
emotions of his narratives.

It is not particularly important that
the "whites" of his primitive tales are always complete villains. "As with all retold tales," Steinbeck also tells us, "there
are only good and bad things and black
and white things . . . and no in-between
anywhere." But the quality that has marked
Steinbeck's work as a whole is precisely
the sense of black and white things, and
good and bad things—that is to say, the
sense of a fabulist or a propagandist rather
than the insight of an artist. Moreover,
we have now come to understand that even
primitive souls are highly complicated—it
is probably harder for a modern writer to

understand a man of his own time and place. The doctor of *The Pearl* speaks to all of Kino's race "as though they were simple animals." But the doctor's main fault is that he apparently considers all Mexican Indians bad, while Steinbeck considers all Mexican Indians good.

In the climax of this fable, too, it is interesting to notice that Steinbeck describes his native fisherman as "a terrible machine"—in Kino's moment of anger he becomes "as cold and deadly as steel." One has only to compare Steinbeck's primitive types with those of D. H. Lawrence, say, or his studies of peasant character with those of the Italian writer Silone, to realize his limits. Of all the ranking modern writers who have gone back to primitive material as a protest against and a solace for contemporary society, Steinbeck is, as a matter of fact, the least well-endowed; what he usually does is to ascribe a peculiar sort of suburban American romanticism to these native types. "Go with God," Juana says to her husband as he prepares to murder the trackers, but one wonders just which God Kino is supposed to go with.

The most important point in Steinbeck's earlier career was the change, around 1935, from such pagan excursions as *To a God Unknown* or *Tortilla Flat* to the novels of social criticism, *In Dubious Battle* and *The Grapes of Wrath*. It is interesting to speculate on the reasons why Steinbeck has now returned to this earlier and less satisfactory vein of his work. And, without stressing the fact that our national history did not end with the Second World War, one would like to remind this gifted and volatile American novelist that his recent works do mark a sort of reversionary tendency in his career.

One might say that the artist, too, must discover and cherish his own pearl—he cannot reject it for a state of false innocence.

Ralph Habas. "Steinbeck at Top of Form in Old Mexican Folk Tale." *Chicago Sun Book Week*, 7 (23 November 1947), Section 2, 7.

As unpredictable as he is versatile, John Steinbeck has sprung more than one surprise in his writing career. Now, with his present offering, he springs another. This time he tries his hand at retelling an old Mexican folk tale he picked up around the Gulf of California.

The story, actually, is a parable. Hence it's rather short. But it's long enough to give Steinbeck an opportunity to bring into play some of his most distinctive talents, notably his knack for infusing a kind of dynamic rhythm and lyric quality into his prose, his dramatic use of the vernacular, and rare ability to convey direct sensuous impressions.

The narrative is of a sort, moreover, that gives him a beautiful chance to express his well-known sympathy for society's underdogs and indulge his fondness for primitive and symbolical characters. . . .

Despite its rather rudimentary plot, *The Pearl* succeeds in stirring the emotions profoundly. It succeeds, too, in giving eloquent testimony with regard to Steinbeck's integrity and maturity as a literary artist.

Orville Prescott. "Books of the Times." New York *Times*, 24 November 1947, p. 21.

Two years ago a novelette by John Steinbeck was published in *The Woman's Home Companion*. It was a good novelette, infinitely superior to the wretched novels which Mr. Steinbeck was writing at about the same time and which have done so much to damage his literary reputation. It was called "The Pearl of the World" and it seems to have been written after *Cannery Row* and before *The Wayward Bus*. Now, after a long delay during which Mr. Steinbeck wrote a movie version of his story which will soon be released with an all-Mexican cast, his novelette is finally published as *The Pearl*.

This is a Mexican folk tale which Mr. Steinbeck heard on the Lower California peninsula when he was down that way a few years ago on the scientific expedition studying marine life which he described in *Sea of Cortez*. It is as stark and simple as folk literature generally is. But it is permeated with the special sort of impotent and sullen bitterness which only an oppressed and subject people know. There is no cheerful, nursery atmosphere to this tragic folk story, as there is to so many European tales of equally pathetic circumstances ("Hansel and Gretel," for instance). And that may be why it attracted Mr. Steinbeck.

For much of his writing career Mr. Steinbeck has devoted his attention to simple, childlike and fairly primitive people. His admiration for them seems to have been a conscious protest against the decadence and cruelty and stupidity which have been so prevalent in this century among so-called civilized peoples. So when Mr. Steinbeck wrote of the gay, irresponsible and charming *paisanos* of *Tortilla Flat*, he struck a note which appealed greatly to many readers. But when he glorified the worthless and debased riff-raff of *Cannery Row*, he seemed perversely to be denying the essential human decencies—pride and honor and loyalty and self-respect—to be finding life best at its lowest biological level.

In *The Pearl* Mr. Steinbeck has written about people who are primitive but who are admirable. The Indian fishermen of La Paz, on the Gulf of California, whom he describes are ignorant, illiterate, superstitious and brutalized. They live in brush houses little better than those in an African kraal. They subsist on an inadequate diet of corn meal and fish. But they know love and loyalty, pride and ambition, hope and fear. Their sufferings are of the spirit, not just of the flesh, and so their misfortunes are tragic as well as pitiful.

With an artful simplicity exactly suitable to his theme, Mr. Steinbeck has told the story of Kino and his wife, Juana, and their baby son, Coyotito, and what happened to them after a scorpion stung the baby. . . .

Like all folk tales, *The Pearl* is simple and direct. It is not concerned with subtleties of characterization or profundities of thought. Yet its emotional impact is powerful. Kino, who fought that his son might have a chance, by which he meant a chance to rise so far in the world that he might learn to read, is a heroic figure. His devotion to his family and his courage in the face of death are deeply moving. They give *The Pearl* a universally human quality, for they are the virtues which men everywhere have always admired above all others.

It is interesting to note the resemblance of *The Pearl* to Kipling's wonderful Mowgli story, "The King's Ankus." Both stories concern symbols of fabulous wealth, the evil they loose on the world and the decision to return them whence they came made by primitive persons. Kipling's is the more exotic, colorful and dramatic. But since Mowgli was only an observer, not a victim, of the evil the jeweled ankus caused, it lacks the poignancy of Mr. Steinbeck's pitiful story of Kino and the unholy treasure he found in the depths of the sea.

The Pearl, I believe, is much the best book which Mr. Steinbeck has written since *The Red Pony* and *The Grapes of Wrath*.

Carlos Baker.
"Steinbeck at the Top of His Form."
New York Times Book Review, 97 (30 November 1947), 4, 52.

Seven years ago, during a trip to the Gulf of California (the same which provided materials for his *Sea of Cortez*), John Steinbeck heard a Mexican folk tale about a pearl as big as a gull's egg and the woe it worked in the lives of those who found it. A mature and skilled writer, whose tastes had always run toward the fable and the parable, needed no more than time and the broad outlines of this folk tale to fashion a work which fits as neatly into the list of Steinbeck's books as the last gem in a carefully matched necklace. When the substance of the tale had settled into that limpid prose of which Steinbeck is a notable master, he dramatized it, as *Of Mice and Men* and

The Moon Is Down have been dramatized. *The Pearl* has been filmed with an all-Mexican cast and is to be released in this country. The 30,000-word version appeared in magazine form in December, 1945, and now first becomes a book.

In turning from the background of this story to what the Middle Ages would have called its "mystery," one is chiefly struck by the number of points at which the tale impinges, through Steinbeck's artfully simple rendering of it, on the unkillable folklore of Palestine, Greece, Rome, China, India and the whole sweep of western Europe from the Scandinavian to the Iberian peninsula. For the pearl which the Mexican fisherman Kino dug from the Gulf of California was concealed in the center of the golden fruit of the Hesperides, and its seeds were at the core of another apple in a fair Mesopotamian garden called Eden. Its death-dealing luster glinted in certain fabulous gold coins in the hands of beggars in ancient Baghdad; King Midas knew its power and felt its pain. It was guarded by fire-spewing dragons in the lonely stone cairns of the Norsemen; certain German princes found its prototype in the treasure boxes of bewhiskered cannibalistic giants; and one heard of something like it in the smoky longhouses of the Algonquin Indians. In a hundred metamorphoses it nestled among the foliage on Frazer's *Golden Bough*. One of its names is the power of good and evil.

With such a ubiquitous associational potential at the center of his fable, Steinbeck needed only the developmental skills which his long experience had taught him how to supply. He found the setting where he heard the story—among the brush huts of the Mexican fishermen near the town of La Paz on the shores of the Gulf of California. His protagonists were in his mind and in his other books already, needing only new names; Kino the fisherman, Juana his wife, Coyotito the baby. He found simple antagonists in the gluttonous village doctor who dreamed of returning to a life of ease in Paris, in the scheming pearl brokers who fleeced the Indian pearl divers as a matter of professional pride, in the nameless night crawlers who came to rob Kino of his pearl of great price, and in the impersonal, relentless trackers who hunted the man, the woman, the child and the pearl across the desert and into the stone mountains north and east of the Gulf.

He had in the fable itself a rough structural blueprint: the finding, hiding, defending and casting away of the pearl. He knew how to employ, as his story shifted from low to high gear, the ancient formula of the chase, and the climactic moment of the overtaking. He knew how to elicit the reader's sympathy for his protagonists by showing the growing threat of the innocent joys of family life, the loved child at its center who may die of the bite of a scorpion, as the parents may die from the bite of the Pearl.

Whether because his story was to appear first in a woman's magazine or because he really wished it to be that way, Steinbeck made no allusions offensive to the taste and carefully measured in certain proportions of sentiment. He knew how to keep his little family in the central spotlight. He was lucky to have his book adorned with five powerful myopic line drawings by the Mexican muralist Orozco. And he had long trained his prose style for such a task as this: that supple, unstrained, muscular power, responsive to the slightest pull on the reins, easily moving from walk to trot to canter, never breaking through to gallop.

Edward Weeks. "The Peripatetic Reviewer." *Atlantic*, 180 (December 1947), 138.

... To the short novel John Steinbeck brings simplicity, the power of suggestion, and naturalness, which convey a great deal within a limited space. To his fine trio, *Of Mice and Men*, *The Moon Is Down*, and *The Red Pony*, we now add *The Pearl*, the story of Kino, a Mexican fisherman, his wife Juana, and their baby Coyotito; the story of how the baby was bitten by a scorpion and of how Kino— to pay the doctor's bill—dived for and brought to the surface a pearl beyond price. What happens thereafter is for you to read.

Within the lineaments of this Mexican folk tale and with silk-smooth, deceptive simplicity Mr. Steinbeck is doing what he most enjoys: laying bare the human nature of primitive people, showing us their capacity for endurance, their resistance to domination (the supercilious doctor, and the pearl dealers who try to cheat); showing us the peasants' instinctive love and protectiveness, their wisdom (as in the old beggars), and the songs which best express their emotion. One can take this as a parable or as an active and limpid narrative whose depth, like that of the tropical waters which Steinbeck so beautifully describes, is far more than one would suspect.

Thomas Sugrue. "Steinbeck's Mexican Folk-Tale." *New York Herald Tribune Weekly Book Review*, 24 (7 December 1947), 4.

In the Gnostic fragment known as the "Acts of Judas Thomas" there is a passage called the "Hymn of the Soul," which says that "If thou goest down into Egypt, and bringest the one pearl, which is in the midst of the sea, hard by the loud-breathing serpent, then shalt thou put on thy toga, which is laid over it, and with thy brother, our next in rank, thou shalt be heir in our kingdom." Among the Indians of Mexico the story is that Kino, a fisherman, found the pearl, and that Juana, his wife, and Coyotito, his infant son, were with them [him?] when the discovery was made. John Steinbeck, hearing the tale while on an expedition to the Gulf of California in 1940, decided to write it. His story was published in *The Woman's Home Companion*. It was also made into a movie, as yet unreleased, and now it is a book.

... Mr. Steinbeck, faithfully re-telling what he heard, left the ending as it was. Had he not done so he would be writing yet, and the incident of an Indian fisherman's surrender to the challenge of experience would be growing into the saga of man's search for a soul. As it is, the action of the story is brief, and in it, as in all folk tales, there are, as Mr. Steinbeck says, "only good and bad things and black and white things and good and evil things and no in-between anywhere."

It began one morning when a scorpion bit the baby Coyotito (the biting of the child by the scorpion, or scarab, signifies the entrance of the divine nature into the mind; the pearl of great price, the knowledge of spiritual growth, must then be found so that eventually the divine nature can be set free). The white doctor would not treat the child, so Kino and Juana and Coyotito got into Kino's canoe and went to the oyster bed, hoping to find a pearl that would pay for the medicine that was needed. Kino stepped into the water and let his diving rock carry him to the bottom; he filled his basket with oysters; under a lip of rock he found a very large oyster, and he carried this up in his hand. When he opened it he found that it contained the great pearl, the pearl of the world, the pearl of great price.

Almost before Kino's canoe was beached every one in the town knew of his find, and by nightfall ninety per cent of the population were scheming to get the pearl away from him. The doctor came to Kino's hut and insisted on treating Coyotito, who had been saved ten hours before by his mother, who sucked the unbearable portion of the poison from him (in the black and white of folklore Juana, or woman, is the emotion nature). Kino was attacked in the night. When he tried to sell the pearl next day prices were rigged against him. He told Juana that he would go into the mountains, to the capital, to ... bring its true price, so that Coyotito could be sent to school (the mind must be trained and filled with wisdom).

Juana made the classic gesture of the emotion[al] nature; she tried to throw the pearl into the sea. Kino restrained her, and then, after he had again been attacked, and after his house had been burned and his canoe wrecked (his assailants were nameless shadows; he recognized none of them), he set out in flight with Kino, Coyotito and the pearl. But he did not strike for the city in the hills; he did not face his dream and attempt to re-alize it. He followed the coast, and eventually he was found by a man on horse-back; he killed the man and the two trackers who were with him, but Coyo-tito was shot and died. Kino and Juana returned to the town, and Kino threw the pearl into the sea.

That is the end of the story as Mr. Steinbeck heard it; the horseman is easy to identify as the Spaniard who conquered the Indian, though horsemen representing desires of the lower mind normally in folklore pursue the ego in quest of the soul. Kino, refusing the adventure of the spirit, renouncing his opportunity for re-alization and understanding and identity, returns to the rim of the unconscious, the primitive state wherein responsibility re-sides in nature and wherein man nurses, like a tree, at the breast of earth. He thought once of the city in the hills, shook briefly with the dream of the grail, then gave up in fear and ran away.

In the past Mr. Steinbeck has demon-strated an affection for this acceptance of defeat, this philosophy of rejected realiza-tion, this refusal to face up to ownership of the pearl of great price; two of his novels, *Tortilla Flat* and *Cannery Row*, were concerned with it. He has also writ-ten of those who keep the pearl and who fight for it, those who strike out for the city in the hills and who, if they are cut down on the way, fall forward. This pre-sent reversion to the theme of negation is a simple task of tale-telling, complete with biblical rhythms and repeated pat-terns of prose melody; it probably indi-cates, on Mr. Steinbeck's part, no more than the average man's recurrent inner wish that he had let well enough alone and never begun the lonely journey through awareness toward the crest of identity.

The Pearl, as distinguished from the Gnostic "Hymn of the Soul," is the story of a man who turned his back and walked away when his name was called and he was told to bring up out of Egypt, which is the mind of the world, the pearl whose price redeems the soul. Kino has many brothers.

"*The Pearl*."
Booklist, 44
(15 December 1947), 152.

A short, somber tale about a Mexican pearl fisher who finds a fantastically large pearl. Instead of being the means to a better life for the fisherman, the pearl arouses envy and greed, leads to murder and the death of the fisherman's child, and is at last given back to the sea. Sup-posedly a folk tale, the story may be in-terpreted as a parable. . . .

"Counterfeit Jewel."
Time, 50
(22 December 1947),
90, 92.

"It was as large as a sea-gull's egg. It was the greatest pearl in the world," and Kino had found it. How the pearl brought grief to its finder is a Mexican legend which Novelist John Steinbeck first heard on a trip to Mexico in 1940. Seldom has an old tale been made to pay off so richly. Steinbeck expanded it into a long short story for the *Woman's Home Compan-ion*, has adapted it as a Hollywood movie script to be released next spring, and now has issued *The Pearl* between covers with powerful but hurried illustrations by famed Mexican Painter Orozco. . . .

Steinbeck has a field day with this simple tale. "Kino squatted by the fire pit and rolled a hot corncake and dipped it in sauce and ate it. And he drank a little pulque and that was breakfast. . . . Kino sighed with satisfaction—and that was conversation." The style is simple and effective when Steinbeck is describing things; turned on people it acquires a stickiness that is rapidly becoming the trademark of Steinbeck's prose: "And the baby was weary and petulant, and he cried softly until Juana gave him her breast, and then he gurgled and clucked against her." Steinbeck's *Pearl* will seem a little jewel only to those readers who find important meanings in calculated ambiguities, and mistake manipulated sentimentality for emotion.

John Farrelly.
"Fiction Parade."
New Republic, 117
(22 December 1947), 28.

John Steinbeck's latest novel, *The Pearl* . . . was first published two years ago in the *Woman's Home Companion*. Since then, it has been worked into a motion-picture script. Its first appearance in book form serves very well as Steinbeck's bid for a position on the Christmas list. Although it would be doing him a disservice to suppose that he took *The Pearl* seriously, its publication is not without significance in his career. For when the public will buy this story under Steinbeck's name, his reputation has achieved that immunity in which an author may be said to endorse, rather than to write, his book.

As a seasonal item, it is in a familiar pattern: a rewritten Mexican folk tale, complete with all the stock elements of the genre. . . .

An appropriate solemnity is supported by a lackluster, almost iambic, prose, which suggests, more than anything else, the boredom of the writer. The characters speak in that kind of monumental grunt which has become, in our fiction, the conventional *patois* of the noble savage and the proletariat. And finally, if he needs it, the reader receives his cue in Steinbeck's instructions to "take his own meaning from it and read his own life into it."

"Briefly Noted."
New Yorker, 23
(27 December 1947), 59.

. . . A parable of Mexico, told in the humble, almost Biblical manner that Mr. Steinbeck habitually employs when dealing with the Mexicans. There is nothing extraordinary about this story of a poor Indian fisherman who finds a magnificent pearl and is thereafter driven by the forces of evil and avarice to a tragic end (which you can see coming on the first page); some such tale is in the folklore of every land. Mr. Steinbeck's version of it, however, has the distinction and sincerity that are evident in everything he writes. Illustrative drawings by José Clemente Orozco.

Anne Hunter.
"The Pearl."
Commonweal, 47
(23 January 1948), 377.

... The tale is of a Mexican diver who found a pearl of great size and of how it brought him calamity and perhaps wisdom. It is a legend of simple people, a piece of folk music which Steinbeck transformed into an art song.

Form is the most important thing about him (Steinbeck). It is at its best in this work. The story moves with simplicity and direction, with ease and polish. Because of the writing there is a remoteness, a pearl-like quality in it. It comes between the characters and the reader. Kino and Juana, his wife, are figures on a tapestry, fitting into a pattern. In this tale it is suitable. One wishes sometimes that the people in Steinbeck could take over as people. So often they are Steinbeck's people before they are people, and then they lack complete authority. But in this tale it is fitting.

And besides his form what else is there in Steinbeck? And why is there not more? There is much else in him. He is a man of many arts and causes, and somehow there is no whole greater than these parts. But he does write well. Maybe too well. This is a very good story; not a great story.

The drawings by Orozco are dramatic but not very good. More interesting are Peggy Worthington's illustrations of Viking's recent edition of *Tortilla Flat*.

Stevie Smith.
"Short Stories."
Spectator [England], 181
(29 October 1948), 570.

... Mr. Steinbeck is not quite at home with his old Mexican "folk" story—"fake" would be better—of Kino, his wife Juana and their child Coyotito. Kino finds a great pearl, tries to sell it, learns that merchants cheat, keeps the pearl, commits murder, runs away with his family, is hunted and when the baby is killed comes home and throws the pearl away. Mr. Steinbeck tries hard to be simple, but he only manages to be embarrassing: "Coyotito whimpered and Juana muttered little magics over him to make him silent." The book is really a fine example of what the Germans call *erstklassiger Kitsch*. It is difficult to find an adequate English translation for these withering words and kinder perhaps not to try.

"At Home and Abroad."
Times Literary
Supplement [London],
6 November 1948, p. 621.

A Pacific Coast Indian finds a giant pearl and everyone tries to rob him of it. The dealers tell him it is a monstrosity worth only a thousand pesos as a museum exhibit. Thieves, spurred on by an avaricious French doctor, break into his little hut. He kills one and takes to the mountains with his wife and child. He ambushes his pursuers, but the child is shot.

He and his wife return to the sea and throw the pearl away. That is the story of Mr. Steinbeck's short novel. *The Pearl* is written with studied simplicity and some quasi-biblical touches intended to reinforce its allegorical effect. The exact location and the nationality of the exploiters except that of the doctor, are left indefinite. Mr. Steinbeck makes a strenuous attempt to get right inside the mind of Kino, the finder of the pearl, and produces a vivid, touching little picture of his humble family life. The result is a taut and, on the whole, very effective piece of story-telling even if it leaves the impression of being a story told to a prearranged pattern rather than one that grows, pearl-wise, out of its own material. . . .

"New Novels." *New Statesman and Nation* [England], 36 (6 November 1948), 400–1.

. . . No doubt, Mr. Steinbeck is one of the most accomplished narrators in our time; and these days the dying gift of narrative is not to be despised. His latest work, a short parable called *The Pearl* is a commendably spare piece of storytelling. Returning to the world approximately of *Tortilla Flat*, it recounts the misfortunes of a Mexican peon when faced with the prospect of wealth. A pearl-fisher living on the Gulf is quietly eating his breakfast when he sees a scorpion bite his baby, Coyotito. The distracted couple appeal vainly for aid to the local doctor—the usual portrait of a heartless Mexican capitalist which seemed all right in Eisenstein's day, but now strikes one as hardly less

strange than Henry Wallace's picture of an imperialist England. Having without knowing it already cured Coyotito by their simple native remedy, a seaweed poultice, the fisherman and his wife go out pearl-fishing, in the hope of luck bringing them enough to pay the doctor's fees.

But their luck is too good. The father finds a pearl of fabulous size and beauty. At once evil closes in upon them; thieves burn their house, drive the fisherman to murder; the unfortunate, fortunate couple fly with Coyotito by night in an attempt to reach Mexico City, and there sell the pearl. They are followed by trackers and killers—this is the best part of the book. The fisherman kills all three of his tormentors, but in the struggle Coyotito also dies. The mother carrying the bloody bundle of their little son on her head, the couple return to their town, and throw the jewel, now grown odious even for the fisherman, back into the sea.

An effective, if not entirely original, theme. But three-quarters of one's pleasure in it is offset by the desperate archaism and the portentous reflections of his prose. The continued misuse of the conjunction "and" with which to start a sentence: phrases such as: "a town is a thing like a colonial animal," "a school of great fishes dove in . . . ." Why must so sensitive an artist as Mr. Steinbeck, just because he writes of peasants, employ this patronizing, semi-Biblical jargon? He is not, after all, Miss Pearl Buck.

Checklist of Additional Reviews

John Hersey. "Books and Things." New York *Herald Tribune*, 24 November 1947, p. 19.

Sterling North. "He Likes the Common Man." Washington *Post*, 30 November 1947, p. 7B.

R. C. Whitford. "Avarice and Love in Allegory." Brooklyn *Eagle*, 30 November 1947, "Christmas Book Number," p. 3.

Ritch Lovejoy. "Round and About." Monterey [Calif.] *Peninsula Herald*, 9 December 1947, p. 4.

Donald Weeks. "Steinbeck's Slightly Tarnished Pearl." San Francisco *Chronicle*, *This World* magazine, 14 December 1947, p. 16.

Bill Bedell. "John Steinbeck, Story-Teller." Houston *Post*, 19 September 1948, Section 4, p. 16.

A RUSSIAN JOURNAL

John Steinbeck

A RUSSIAN
JOURNAL

WITH PICTURES BY *Robert Capa*

1948

The Viking Press • NEW YORK

"*Russian Journal*." *Time*, 51 (26 January 1948), 58–9.

In London's Savoy Hotel, John Steinbeck overheard a Chicago *Tribune* man snort: "Capa, you have *absolutely no integrity!*" That wartime remark, says Steinbeck, "intrigued me—I was fascinated that anybody could get so low that a Chicago *Tribune* man could say such a thing. I investigated Capa, and I found out it was perfectly true." Photographer Robert Capa and Author Steinbeck became great friends.

Last March, in a Manhattan bar, they met again. Over two drinks they decided to go to Russia to record, not the political news, but the private life of private Russians. Last week, in the New York *Herald Tribune* (which had jumped at the chance to pay their way) and in twoscore other U.S. and foreign papers, the first chapters of their *Russian Journal* appeared. According to plan, they had brought back no headlines but an unexcited (and sometimes unexciting) report that, like any proof that the Russians are people after all, would make the brazen voice of the Kremlin all the more disheartening.

The Soviets admitted them—with some misgivings about Capa (who, in any country, talks and looks like an enemy alien) and his cameras. "The camera is one of the most frightening of modern weapons," says Steinbeck, "and a man with a camera is suspected and watched." To a polite, but suspicious young man at VOKS, the cultural relations office in Moscow, they tried to explain their mission.

"Your own most recent work," the Russian told the hulking, hearty Steinbeck, "seems to us cynical." Steinbeck explained the job of a writer was to set down his time as he understood it. He tried to make clear the unofficial standing of writers in America: "They are considered just below acrobats and just above seals." Eventually, Capa and Steinbeck were given an interpreter and approval to go to the Ukraine, Stalingrad and Georgia, where the interpreter himself needed an interpreter. They went by air, always in U.S.-built C-47s, and never found a stewardess who did anything but carry pink soda water and beer to the pilots. In restaurants, of all places, they found red tape as endless as spaghetti.

Amid the ruins of Kiev, they found German prisoners helping clear up the rubble. "One of the few justices in the world," wrote Steinbeck. "And the Ukrainian people do not look at them. They turn away...." At the museum there were crowds staring wistfully at plaster models of the future Kiev. "In Russia it is always the future that is thought of. It is the crops next year... the clothes that will be made very soon. If ever a people took energy from hope...."

In the fields around shell-pocked Shevchenko, they found cheerful bands of women picking cucumbers. They were barefoot, "for shoes are still too precious to use in the fields." Everywhere, they found dogged, friendly people, willing to share their bread and cabbage, anxious to hear about America and full of misconceptions about it, instilled by the Russian press. Again and again they were asked: "Will the U.S. attack us?" Again and again they had to explain why the U.S. does not believe in controlling its press or regimenting its people.

Capa was refused permission to shoot the antlike activity at the Stalingrad tractor plant (and later had 100 of his 4,000 negatives confiscated). They came home convinced that the Soviets, who keep the permanent foreign correspondents cooped up in Moscow, have the world's worst sense of public relations. "The Embassy people and the [regular] correspondents feel alone, feel cut off. They are island people in the midst of Russia, and it is no wonder that they become lonely and bitter," Steinbeck wrote. "But if it had been part of our job to report news as they must, then . . . we too could never have left Moscow."

William McFee.
"Book Reviews."
New York *Sun*,
16 April 1948, p. 24.

"It is our belief," says John Steinbeck in his *A Russian Journal*, illustrated with photographs by Robert Capa . . . "that the Russians are the worst propagandists, the worst public relations people, in the world."

This is not an encouraging statement at the beginning of a book about the Russian people, but Steinbeck, of course, is speaking not of the common people but of the Russian bureaucracy. What he went to Russia to report on was the people in the towns and villages, Capa assisting with some of the most magnificent photography we have had of late. In this they succeeded. Steinbeck has drilled a few holes in the Iron Curtain and given us a glimpse of Russia's working classes. He found that Russia was full of Russians, and the Russians were human beings. He got on very well.

At first Steinbeck and Capa, instead of being shadowed by suspicious police, could not find anybody who was willing

to take care of them or even admit that they had arrived. Steinbeck and Capa began to doubt their own existence. It began to seem as if they had dreamed they were in Russia.

They found a little distrust at first among the Russian officials, in spite of the nonpolitical nature of their assignment. Karaganov, the head of Voks, the cultural relations bureau, explained that a number of Americans had come to Russia, and after praising Russia to the Russians, had gone home and written what he regarded as anti-Russian books. Eventually, after interrogating Steinbeck and his photographer, he cleared them and gave them an interpreter, a young lady named Svetlana, which the Americans instantly converted into "Sweet Lana."

It will be seen that Steinbeck and Capa had their tongues in their cheeks. They refused to be stuffy. Steinbeck mentions, with disarming candor, that he uses the personal pronoun "I" by special arrangement with John Gunther. He pokes a lot of fun at Capa's personal habits and assigns him a chapter, in which Capa does a nice job on Steinbeck. But make no mistake. This is one of the best books about Russia since Maurice Baring wrote his *Puppet Show of Memory* in 1922. We can only regret that Steinbeck lacks Baring's command of the Russian language. But he has a most observant eye, a deadpan humor and a command of the English language unsurpassed by any American of our time. The Steinbeck style is one of the marvels of the age. It is entirely unpretentious; it would seem anybody could write like that. But it is an instrument of the greatest delicacy and of extraordinary versatility. It can be used for any purpose.

Steinbeck has fun with Simenov's play, *The Russian Question*. It is the most popular play in Russia. It is a grotesque caricature of American life which is accepted as literally true. Steinbeck wrote a synopsis of a play called *The American Question*, which was a travesty of Russian life.

Fear of the camera is a psychopathic symptom of Russian bureaucracy. Capa wanted to photograph the interior of the Stalingrad tractor plant, which the Americans were permitted to go through, but no pictures were allowed. All the machinery was American and the assembly lines had been designed by American engineers. It had been a tank plant while the Germans bombed the city and the tanks were being turned out under fire. Capa wanted to show the faces of the people. Permission refused.

Steinbeck thinks Russia's secret weapon is hospitality. The Americans were nearly fed to death with immense banquets wherever they went in the country. They visited Georgia, and speak with reverence of the Georgian wines and cakes. The people do not fear the atom bomb. Stalin has told them it will not be used and will not do any harm, and Stalin, according to the Russians, has never been wrong. The Russian people do not want war, Steinbeck insists. They want to be friends with Americans. He has no solution for this paradox. He went to Russia on a nonpolitical mission and he succeeded brilliantly.

Orville Prescott.
"Books of the Times."
New York *Times*,
16 April 1948, p. 21.

. . . As books about Russia go, *A Russian Journal* is a lot better written than most, but it is more superficial than many. Mr.

Steinbeck has written it in a smooth, casual, informal manner that always is readable and frequently entertaining (in spite of several lapses into a clumsy and forced jocularity at Mr. Capa's expense). With a keen eye for pictorial detail and a warm friendliness for individual Russians, Mr. Steinbeck has described people, places and travel adventures. Like a letter from a traveling friend, *A Russian Journal* is pleasant reading, but it doesn't add up to much. . . .

Ben Clare.
"Iron Curtain Penetrated by Steinbeck."
Los Angeles *Times*,
18 April 1948, Part 3,
p. 5.

Steinbeck saw more of Russia, and Capa photographed more of the land and people than anyone who has gone behind the so-called Iron Curtain. That was because they went to Russia with only one thing in mind: to see the country and talk with the people and watch them at their herculean tasks of rebuilding, and to have no thought of politics.

They took with them no preconceived notions, favorable or unfavorable, and they convinced the Russian official who handled their request that they would report only what they observed, not what they might imagine.

In the book, there is very little about Communism or officialdom, and some of that is favorable, some angry or puzzled—but it is all understanding, for they tried to put themselves in Russian caps and figure out how they would feel toward foreigners in the land, and they also knew that we do some things in America to exasperate visitors.

There is a great deal about the Russian people, living in rubble and yet able to smile in the towns and villages smashed so wantonly by Nazis; rebuilding houses, public buildings and apartment houses; working with millions of willing hands to plant and harvest crops, to replace and tend orchards cut down by Nazis, to erect farmhouses, to save the children from starvation—working, man, woman and child, with crude farm implements and with what hands, arms, legs, eyes the war did not rob them of, even the small youngsters. . . .

Steinbeck's companion, famed Photographer Capa, has illustrated the book with splendid shots of the country and the rugged, good-natured people. And Steinbeck makes his story always readable because he loves real people and because he has a sense of humor that never lets him down.

Richard Watts, Jr.
"The Eye of the Observer."
New Republic, 118
(19 April 1948), 22–3.

It is another small but ugly symptom of the sensitive state of Russian-American relations that John Steinbeck's sympathetic account of his recent travels in the Soviet Union should be denounced so violently by Moscow commentators. *A Russian Journal* . . . certainly is not rhapsodic about the USSR; some of its criticisms of

the censorship, bureaucracy, inefficiency and the regimenting of writers are sharp and outspoken.

Steinbeck frankly prefers the unregulated confusion of American life to the austere and moralistic Russian planning. But he is a warm and friendly man, as well as a charming writer, and he loved the exuberance and vitality, the expansive hospitality and the hopeful dreams of the Russian people. His book is filled with genuine, if far from uncritical, affection for them and a complete belief in their essential goodwill and desire for peace.

In a world less filled with passions, his travel record would be liked in both the US and the USSR. As it is, he has already been justified in his melancholy foresight that "this journal will not be satisfactory either to the ecclesiastical Left, nor the lumpen Right. The first will say it is anti-Russian, and the second that it is pro-Russian. Surely it is superficial, and how could it be otherwise? We have no conclusions to draw, except that Russian people are like all other people in the world. Some bad ones there are surely, but by far the greater number are very good." It does not seem a sensational statement to make, but, in the current state of violent tempers, it could well be one.

The need for a greater understanding of the Russian people being what it is, it may not be the highest praise to say that the outstanding quality of *A Russian Journal* is its friendliness and its refusal to take itself too seriously. It happens, however, that these qualities arise, not from any triviality or determined jocularity on Steinbeck's part, but from a frank and cheerful admission of his limitations of opportunity and personal equipment.

He set down what he observed and no more, and he admitted his own shortcomings as a commentator. Steinbeck had been in Moscow only once before, for a few days in 1936—he notes that the physical improvements since then have been tremendous—and his traveling companion, the brilliant Robert Capa, who took the superb photographs which accompany the text, had never been in Russia at all. They did not speak the language, although Capa speaks almost every language in some form or other, and their visit was a brief one which took them only to Moscow, Stalingrad, the Ukraine and down into ideally beautiful Georgia.

They might have pretended to the omniscience which comes so easily to travelers in the Soviet Union, no matter how brief their sojourn. A Russian Journal is the more interesting as reading and the more valuable as a report because they did not. It is clearly of the first importance today to understand the Russians emotionally, to see them as human beings not very different from ourselves, and the Steinbeck book, in its modest way, makes a definite contribution to just that sort of understanding.

In setting down the reasons why A Russian Journal offers no startling inside revelations or new material, it should be stated immediately that Soviet guile and deception are not responsible. If there was anything Steinbeck and Capa failed to see, it was not because Kremlin agents were keeping it from them or were deceiving them by elaborate window-dressing.

Steinbeck found that the Russians are the worst propagandists in the world and the people the least skilled at the art of window-dressing. The travelers saw good things, friendly people and the hope of a peaceful future in the USSR, because they were there to be seen. It was the individual Soviet citizen, in Moscow, Stalingrad, Tiflis, Batum and the collective farms of the Ukraine who convinced them that the Russians "had a hatred of war, they wanted the same things all people want—good lives, increased comfort, security and peace."

Like all travelers in the USSR, Steinbeck and Capa found that they were happier outside of Moscow and in the Russian countryside. Moscow seemed to them a somber city, with a sense of strain about it and even the jokes were sharp and critical, with no warmth in them. In the Ukraine and in Georgia they found gayety and high spirits. They were least comfortable with the intellectuals, whom they found individually engaging, but as a group excessively earnest and intense.

The Russian literary man may be, as Stalin desired, the architect of the soul, and his contribution to the task of building the new Soviet society has been a tremendous one; but it was made at the sacrifice of his racial high spirits and his creative independence. Steinbeck did not like the extreme artistic conservatism which caused the abstractionists and experimenters to be regarded with disdain and moved their girl interpreter in Moscow to say that Picasso "nauseated her." The author found a prevailing puritanism, which made him at times almost suspect that the Russians, despite cheering evidence to the contrary, were becoming a "stuffy, non-alcoholic, non-lecherous people." Nor was he happy about the virtual worship of Stalin that he found everywhere.

As such comments suggest, A Russian Journal does not flatter the Soviet Union and its people. The important thing is that the criticisms are made without the captious and snarling scorn characteristic of books on Russia by hostile observers. If Steinbeck sees great flaws in the Soviet picture, it is not in contrast to an ideal and dreamy US, which never existed, but against the reasonable background of the suffering, the struggles and the triumphs of a great, once backward, essentially friendly people, who have made amazing progress against vast odds in a brief period of history. And even in the short time they stayed in the USSR, they noted signs of physical progress in the achievement of a better life for a land that had suffered to an unparalleled degree from the ravages of war.

Irving Pflaum.
"Book Day."
Chicago *Sun*,
26 April 1948, p. 48.

As their Russian journey was to Steinbeck and Capa, this book was for me an amusing disappointment.

I don't know what I expected. But because Steinbeck is unquestionably a very great writer and Capa a talented photographer, I expected more than this.

Through the years, I have had the idea that a liberal American poet or writer should visit Russia and report to our people. I had in mind Carl Sandburg but he always refused the assignment, begging old age, which is obvious nonsense. For Carl can out-sing and out-drink even Stalin's Georgians who beat Steinbeck and Capa at both activities.

After reading what Steinbeck brought back from Russia, I agree with Sandburg. Perhaps no famous American, whose writings are known in the U.S.S.R., could get next to the Russian people. Soviet officialdom stands in the way. He would be shielded from the people by guides, interpreters, officials, receptions and literary societies.

Steinbeck would have done better, I think, disguised as a fur buyer and limited to the confines of Moscow and Leningrad.

John Steinbeck is too good at his trade not to recognize a failure. In the closing paragraph, he calls his book "superficial" and says its only conclusion is "that Russian people are like all other people in the world." But it's doubtful if he proves even that conclusion. For he saw and learned so little of the Russian people. Most of the weeks he had in the Soviet Union, he passed among Ukrainians and Georgians.

(It's interesting that another recent book, *Russia and the Russians* which was highly praised in these columns by Prof. Frederick Schumann, is based on a theory that Russian people are NOT like all other people in the world.)

Capa's contribution to *A Russian Journal* is particularly disappointing. But the book contains only a few of the 3,000 photos he took in Russia and of the somewhat less than 3,000 he was allowed to take out. Surely he has better work to show for his journey.

The book's errors are innocent, amusing and not importantly misleading. It contains much pleasant writing and honest reporting and an occasional Capa shot with just the right shadow and light.

Those who want to find the final answer about the Russians will want this book as another piece of the Russian puzzle. But they won't find in it the complete answer.

Oriana Atkinson.
"John Steinbeck and Robert Capa Record a Russian Journey."
New York Times Book Review, 97
(9 May 1948), 3.

John Steinbeck, author of *The Grapes of Wrath*, *The Red Pony*, *Of Mice and Men*, and a number of other stories and novels which have become American classics, met the famous photographer, Robert Capa, in a bar one day. After a few drinks, they decided to collaborate on a book on Russia.... The result of the collaboration is *A Russian Journal*. Pictures and text were originally published in the New York *Herald Tribune* and elsewhere.

As a reporting job the book is superb. What they saw, they have presented simply and honestly. Nobody can say that they carried chips on their shoulders. But they did find it a little difficult always to remain calm when they met simon-pure examples of Russian bureaucracy; and before they left the U.S.S.R., like everybody else who gets the opportunity, they visited the Kremlin.

This book could only have been written by an American. Although it bears throughout the stamp of Mr. Steinbeck's sincerity, he sometimes breaks into the irrepressible American nonsense that always baffles the Russians. And it is nice to know that even so high-minded an observer as Mr. Steinbeck found some of the aspects of Moscow life as comic and difficult as other Americans who have had to end it....

[Mr. Steinbeck's] descriptions of the Ukraine and the Ukrainian people are illuminating and extremely interesting. They visited Kiev, mother of Russian cities, and saw life and hope struggling up through the appalling ruins. They visited two collective farms there, Svenchenko 1 and Svenchenko 2, and found the workers well fed and well housed. Although there is a pitiful lack of farm machinery, the work goes on, the harvests are garnered.

"They are not a sad people," Mr. Steinbeck says. "They are full of laughter, jokes and songs." Mr. Capa's photographs bear him out. The farm people look sturdy, merry and determined....

Everywhere they went the Americans were asked whether they thought there would be another war. "Will the United States attack us?" the Russians asked. "Will we have to defend ourselves again in our lifetime?" At Svenchenko 1, Mr. Steinbeck found: "They knew no more about their foreign policy than we know about ours. There was no animosity in their questions, only wonder.... Our host said, 'Somewhere in all of this there must be an answer and there must be an answer quickly. Let us drink to the hope that an answer may be found, for the world needs peace, needs peace very badly.'"

Since Mr. Steinbeck did not meet any members of the Politburo, he naturally does not record their opinion on this subject. As Mr. Steinbeck himself would say, "This we do not know." ...

Misery, despair, degradation of the human spirit? The author of *The Grapes of Wrath* saw none of these. Within the narrow circumference of his journey, no political prisoners, no slave laborers, no fear, no poverty-stricken people broken on the wheel of totalitarianism made him pause and reflect. Careful analysis of the trip brings the thoughtful reader to one inescapable conclusion: The farther one gets from Moscow, even within the U.S.S.R., the freer the people, the brighter the outlook.

As far as this book goes, it is forthright, simple and direct. There is, however, a reverse side to the medal which Mr. Steinbeck did not examine. And just as he traveled in accustomed paths while in Russia, so, since his return, has he been accorded the usual, automatic treatment by the Russian press. He has been denounced as bourgeois, and he has been accused of misrepresentation, with free use of the usual odorous adjectives always applied to foreign observers. Except, of course, the Dean of Canterbury.

As for Mr. Capa's part in the collaboration, he took "thousands of flash bulbs, hundreds of rolls of film, masses of cameras and a tangle of flashlight wires," with him from America. It would seem that these supplies, plus the virgin territory of Soviet Russia, plus Mr. Capa, would produce more distinguished pictures. However, since all the film had to be developed in Moscow by unloving hands before being granted clearance, no doubt Mr. Capa thinks so, too.

Louis Fischer.
"Conducted USSR Tour."
Saturday Review, 31
(15 May 1948), 13–14.

Has anybody the right to write a book? Is an author justified in turning out a book simply because he is sure his publisher will publish it? I am inclined to think that this volume should have been suppressed by Steinbeck. Or perhaps he should have surrendered all the excellent heavy paper to Capa's marvelous photographs (one would have liked three hundred instead of only seventy) and limited himself to a few lines of text for each picture. This book was conceived in cocktails and nurtured prenatally with a ghastly volume of vodka and wine and an indecent amount of food. I do not know what stimulated the actual writing but it certainly wasn't loyalty to the original intention of reporting on the "private life of the Russian people."

Under the influence of several green suisses served by Willy at the bar of the New Bedford hotel in New York, Steinbeck and Capa decided that too much had been printed about what the Soviet leaders were thinking and doing and too little about the "private life of the Russian people." "No one wrote about it," Steinbeck complained. Well, in all these 220 big pages there is not a single private conversation between the author and a plain, private Soviet citizen. On the rare occasions he went into a home it was always crowded with visitors who had come for a feast.

Of course, Steinbeck and Capa do not speak Russian so they had to talk through a Soviet government translator, and no Soviet citizen would speak freely in such circumstances. But the book contains no evidence that Steinbeck even tried, despite the interpreter, to get a Soviet workingman or peasant or intellectual to express himself on the problems of private life in the Soviet Union. Most conversations recorded in the book were at public dinners or in groups and then the Russians all orated like *Pravda* editorials. So did officials and prominent authors he met individually. In cases where they spoke English, Steinbeck did not probe at all into matters like friendship, family relations between persons under a dictatorship, relations of persons to the dictatorship, relations of the artist to the state, freedom of speech, of movement, of conscience, etc. Usually they talked about the danger of war and then Steinbeck elicited nice Kremlin clichés.

Steinbeck writes that the American journalists resident in Moscow cannot travel outside the city without special permission, which is rarely if ever granted. Now some of these correspondents are consistently pro-Soviet. Did it occur to Steinbeck why he was allowed to travel through the country though they are not? They could, since they know Russian, establish direct contact with Russians and look into their hearts and minds and really study their private lives. Therefore, they are forbidden to move from Moscow or to maintain friendly contacts with Moscovites.

Steinbeck received permission to go about the country because the authorities knew he couldn't learn anything, surrounded as he was by translators, officials, and big-shot writers who knew what to tell him. This being the case, Steinbeck might have come back to New York and said, "I went to do a really important and revealing book, but I didn't get enough material, so I'll just write a few newspaper articles and pay back the publishers' advance, if any, from the royalties of my next novel."

"Surely it is superficial," Steinbeck admits in his last paragraph, "and how could it be otherwise?" Correct. "We know that this journal will not be satisfactory either to the ecclesiastical Left, nor to the *lumpen* Right. The first will say it is anti-Russian, and the second that it is pro-Russian." This statement reflects the grave error of many fellow-travellers who think that America is either Left or Right. As a matter of fact, neither the Communists nor the Fascists count for much without dupes from the Center, which constitutes the political bulk of the nation. The Center in the United States has a healthy curiosity about the Russian people and, I think, a friendly attitude to it (but not to Stalin's dictatorship), and it would have been satisfied with something that was informative, that had facts, opinions, insights, interpretations. They are wanting in this book.

Steinbeck wished to be fair, and with the exception of very few lapses he is fair. My objection is not that the book is too pro-Russian or too anti-Russian. It just isn't Russian enough. I haven't taken the trouble to count the lines, but my guess is that more space is devoted to Steinbeck's intake of liquor and food and to his teasing of Capa than to any aspect of Soviet life. These personal angles highlight the great Steinbeck's *Russian Journal*. I suspect that a Russian would be offended by the treatment his wonderful country received at the hands of this American celebrity. And the cynics who directed Steinbeck's tour will laugh. But they should cry. For this is the chaff Russia will get as long as those who could do better are denied access to the Soviet population.

Soviet citizens would be charmed to learn of Steinbeck's main conclusion: he discovered that people are people. STEINBECK REVEALS RUSSIANS ARE HUMAN BEINGS. That's the big story of the book. Terrific. But what goes on inside them he never attempted to ascertain.

A Russian Journal is not a portrait of the Russian people. It is merely a portrait of the American artist turned police reporter in a police state. The only thing added is the daily banquet.

"Double Vodka."
Times Literary Supplement [London], 23 April 1949, p. 259.

It is a rather trivial aspect of the journalist in Mr. Steinbeck that is represented in this volume. He and Mr. Capa spent two summer months in Russia some little while ago; there is nothing to indicate the precise year of their visit, but it seems probable that they went in 1946. Mr. Steinbeck went with the no doubt laudable but not very original idea of ignoring politics and reporting on the "private life" of the Soviet citizen. Such a mission, unfortunately, undertaken with a limited equipment of historical or other relevant knowledge, argues a certain naivety on his part. And the evidence of a marked innocence of mind accumulates rapidly from the point where Mr. Steinbeck accepts the explanation offered him by the Soviet Consular authorities in New York for their reluctance to grant a visa to Mr. Capa in the latter's capacity of cameraman. "Why do you have to take a cameraman? We have lots of cameramen in the Soviet Union."

But the truth is that Mr. Steinbeck easily lost sight of the private life of the Soviet citizen in his preoccupation with drinking parties and the ways of American foreign correspondents at the Metropole and the Savoy in Moscow. Of such familiar matters there is a deal too much in this book. Not that it entirely lacks interest. Having been encouraged by a carefully spoken Voks official to be entirely "objective," provided with a pretty young interpreter and shown some of the sights in Moscow, Mr. Steinbeck went off to Kiev and was regaled with the tremendous feasting commonly reserved for eminent foreign authors. Interviewed by the editor of a Ukrainian literary magazine, however, he was somewhat taken aback when he discovered that "the answers I was supposed to have given did not very closely approximate what I had said." This, he hastens to explain, was not done on purpose; the trouble was not a matter of language but of "translation from one kind of thinking to another."

From Kiev he proceeded to Stalingrad, on to Tiflis—that is, Tbilisi—and thence to the Stalin birthplace and museum at Gori. He describes the birthplace, covered by an enormous canopy of stained glass supported on square golden marble columns and set in a vast rose garden. This, perhaps, is his most serious effort of description and interpretation, though scarcely of private life in the Soviet Union; the feasting and drinking predominate in what follows. Mr. Capa suffered agonies of uncertainty before his films, after marvels of official obstruction, precaution and inspection, were eventually returned to him (most of them, anyhow) in a sealed box at the airport just as he was about to leave. The anxiety of the Soviet authorities seems to have been just a little excessive in the circumstances. The photographs, reproduced by lithography, have come out well and are for the most part expertly composed, but a great many merely present the usual scenes of idyllic happiness and few of the others are intrinsically interesting.

Richard Chancellor. "Americans in Russia." *Spectator* [England], 183 (29 July 1949), 152.

In these days, when the Russian obsession for secrecy has reached such a pitch that *Pravda* itself is on occasions withdrawn from foreign circulation, any book, however superficial, from an actual observer of that enigmatic country has a value out of all proportion to its intrinsic merits. *A Russian Journal*, by John Steinbeck, illustrated with photographs taken on the spot by Robert Capa, can be forgiven on these grounds alone for the thinness of its contents, but, in addition, it gives us an opportunity to understand something of the bewilderment which is the chief impression produced by Soviet Russia on two well-known and perhaps typical Americans during their first visit to the U.S.S.R.

Before the war an important weapon in the armoury of the Propaganda and Agitation Directorate of the Central Committee of the Communist Party for conveying to a sceptical world the desired impression of the Soviet Utopia was the "Intourist" organization, which catered efficiently for the needs of foreigners visiting the Soviet Union. Since 1945, however, the system has for various reasons remained in abeyance. It may be that in John Steinbeck the Russians saw a useful means of cutting their Intourist propaganda losses at second-hand, so to speak, and it can only have been some such consideration as this which impelled them to give an entry visa at the same time to the photographer, Robert Capa, with a mountain of films and equipment. Their choice of men, and the final outcome, should be sufficient proof, if proof were needed, that the Russians have lost none of the skill in such matters that has served them so well since the days of "Tsar Boris" Godunov.

It is tiresome, but inevitable in the circumstances, that even in a book of 200 pages, covering six weeks and many thousands of miles of travelling through Russia, far too much space is taken up by "padding." It is equally irritating to have names such as "Svietlana" americanised into "Sweet Lana," and this is typical of a jarring facetiousness which extends throughout the book but which may, of course, be due simply to the author's inward realization of his lack of any real comprehension of a great and ancient race. How else could John Steinbeck have written as he does about the world-famous Lavra and Cathedral of St. Sophia in Kiev, and have coupled his few lines on one of the greatest of Russia's war tragedies with remarks like this of Capa's, "All good churches are gloomy. That's what makes them good"? John Steinbeck found the Sword of Stalingrad "a little absurd in the poverty of its imagination," and it is to be hoped that the ladies of Coventry will disregard his reference to "the tablecloth with the embroidered names of fifteen hundred women in a small British town." But when the Georgian queen Tamara is compared with "the fairy queens of the world, like Elizabeth, and Catherine of Aragon and Eleanor of Aquitaine," one may be forgiven for wishing that some of John Steinbeck's "borscht" [*sic*] had disagreed with him. However, the Russians have time-honoured methods of coping with Western philistines, and the description of their final departure from Tiflis airport is a joy to read, and the best thing in the book.

The authors (for Robert Capa has contributed a short chapter and all the illustrations) were able in six weeks to cover an itinerary which included Moscow,

Kiev, Moscow, Stalingrad, Moscow, Tiflis and back again to Moscow, with a train trip from Tiflis to Batum thrown in. The whole period was spent under the auspices of V.O.K.S., the Soviet Society for Cultural Relations, and it was an inevitable consequence of the peculiarities of the Russian air-transport system that most of their time should have been spent in the Russian capital. Within their limitations they have faithfully recorded what they saw and heard, and many of Robert Capa's photographs are excellent. It was only when they had suffered the full impact of Georgian and Ukrainian hospitality that honesty impelled them to record: "We had the feeling that we were not seeing things sharply any more," and it is perhaps for this reason that they could not do full justice to the celebrations in honour of Moscow's three-hundredth anniversary, nor to the invitation to the Kremlin with which they were honoured before they left. And as they were ushered dazedly into their final aeroplane they came to this conclusion: "We found, as we had suspected, that the Russian people are people, and as with other people, that they are very nice." Most of us who have had the same experience will agree with them.

Checklist of Additional Reviews

Scott Adams. "Subject Books." *Library Journal*, 73 (15 April 1948), 650.

Iris Barry. "Sprightly Report on Russia." *New York Herald Tribune Weekly Book Review*, 24 (18 April 1948), 3.

Victor H. Bernstein. "Family Album of the Russian People." *PM*, 18 April 1948, pp. 12–13M.

"Briefly Noted." *New Yorker*, 24 (1 May 1948), 107.

"*A Russian Journal.*" *Booklist*, 44 (15 May 1948), 311.

James Doull. "For Readers of Varied Tastes." Sacramento *Bee*, 12 June 1948, p. 19.

Geoffrey Gorer. "Press Gang." *New Statesman and Nation* [England], 37 (25 June 1949), 683.

Arthur L. Simpson, Jr. "*A Russian Journal.*" *Steinbeck Quarterly*, 5 (Spring 1972), 53–4.

BURNING BRIGHT (THE NOVEL)

JOHN STEINBECK

BURNING BRIGHT

A PLAY IN STORY FORM

THE VIKING PRESS · NEW YORK · 1950

Orville Prescott. "Books of the Times." New York *Times*, 20 October 1950, p. 25.

For the first time on record a book by a celebrated author is being published in the same week as the production of a play derived from it. Book and play are John Steinbeck's *Burning Bright*. Its merits as a play behind footlights with actors adding the illusion of flesh-and-blood reality to Mr. Steinbeck's symbolical characters were discussed yesterday by Mr. Atkinson on the theatre page. It is the book, to be read by thousands of persons who will not be able to see the play, which concerns us here. As a book, then, *Burning Bright* is artificial and peculiar, but moderately effective.

This is the third example of a literary form of Mr. Steinbeck's own invention, the "play-novelette" as he calls it. The others were *Of Mice and Men* and *The Moon Is Down*. A play-novelette, says Mr. Steinbeck, "is a play that is easy to read or a short novel that can be played simply by lifting out the dialogue." It has two justifications in Mr. Steinbeck's mind: "to provide a play that will be more widely read because it is presented as ordinary fiction, which is a more familiar medium," and to augment "the play for the actor, the director and the producer, as well as the reader." It gives theatre people "the fullest sense of the intention of the writer."

Burning Bright is not only an example of an experimental form; it is a radical departure from all Mr. Steinbeck's previous work. This is a legend, a parable and a folk poem, as far removed from the brawny realism of *The Grapes of Wrath* as a play by J. M. Synge or Lord Dunsany. It is a moral lesson celebrating the virtues of love and loyalty and courage, nearly as far removed from the debased human riff-raff of *Cannery Row* and *The Wayward Bus* as *Pilgrim's Progress*. It is nearer in spirit to Mr. Steinbeck's Indian folk legend, *The Pearl*, than to anything else he has written. The two books together are evidence that John Steinbeck has outgrown his temporary obsession with human worthlessness and enrolled, if not on the side of the angels, at least on the side of individual worth and human dignity.

And it is because of its message of affirmation, its declaration of faith in people and life, that *Burning Bright* deserves respect. A philosophy of life is implicit in all fiction, explicit in much. All art is didactic to a certain extent, whether for good or for ill. If the didacticism is clumsy, the art is damaged. If it is deft as well as sincere, there can be small room for complaint. In *Burning Bright* it seems completely sincere; but it is superficial and awkward.

Burning Bright is the story of a man who passionately desired a son to carry on his family tradition and be his link with immortality. Unfortunately, Joel Saul was sterile. His young second wife, Mordeen, loved Joel so devotedly that she was unfaithful to him to provide him with the happiness for which he desperately yearned. The father of the son was a young and mindless brute, the eternal interloper. Joel's best friend, always called Friend Ed, was loyal, patient and understanding. These four starkly symbolical characters act out Mr. Steinbeck's morality play.

As individuals they are unbelievable. The dialogue they are forced to speak is rigidly stylized and painfully artificial, sometimes sounding like something out of *Hiawatha*—"strong in your wife-loss," "friend-right to ask a question." To make them as obviously universal symbols as possible Mr. Steinbeck has changed the setting and background for the sections of his novel which correspond with the three acts of the version in the theatre.

In the first Joel, Mordeen and Victor, the lover, are circus acrobats and Friend Ed is a clown. In the second Joel and Friend Ed are farmers and Victor is a hired man. In the third they are sea captains and Victor is a first mate. But the story goes on in each section from where it left off in its predecessor.

It is astonishing in view of all these artificialities that *Burning Bright* is interesting. But the reading mind can adjust itself to the most bizarre literary conventions quickly. And when they are used to tell as simple and universally human a story as this they do not distract so much as one might expect. Mr. Steinbeck's four characters may not be interesting individuals; but they are involved in a painfully human situation and they are concerned with the most important of human emotions: love, friendship, pride, self-pity, selfishness, loyalty and self-sacrifice.

These are emotions which matter, which can make an inept and mediocre story or play capable of holding serious attention. Mr. Steinbeck's novel is neither inept nor mediocre. It is adequate within the limitations he has seen fit to impose upon it. The cloud of darkness which surrounded Joel, which he finally threw off to face life with a generosity and courage he had never previously known, hangs over us all. Mr. Steinbeck's sermon is not without eloquence of a sentimental sort.

Maxwell Geismar. "Cosmic Mother and the Gift of Life." *Saturday Review*, 33 (21 October 1950), 14.

John Steinbeck's new "play-novelette" is a flat failure as a novelette at least, and I think it is correct to add that he has not written an important work of fiction since *The Grapes of Wrath*, more than ten years ago.

What has happened to the career of this writer who was, along with Tom Wolfe, one of the major figures to emerge during the 1930's? *Burning Bright*, as you might guess, is actually a play in three acts—a play that is "easy to read," as Steinbeck says, or a short novel that can be played simply by "lifting out the dialogue," and something of this facile and mechanical approach pervades the whole tone of the writing. It is practically a gadget, and you can also lift out any of the central characters without doing great harm to the script.

Another feature: the main characters are a group of circus acrobats in the first act, and remain as the same personages throughout the story. In the second act, however, they are farmers; in the third, sailors. This is symbolic, and at a quick guess the shift in scene from air to land to sea involves the three main areas of human or animal existence in the evolutionary process.

But I am still trying to work out the connection of this symbolism with the story, and why Steinbeck's characters should start out as birds and end up as fish. The hero, Joe Saul, is starvingly in love with his wife, Mordeen, who is, as we are also told, a burning flower in his heart. But he craves a son to carry on his bloodline. Mordeen, who knows that he is sterile, is determined to give him a child by any means, and for this purpose selects Joe Saul's assistant, Victor, another acrobat, who represents animal vitality and complete sterility of spirit.

The drama is now under way, and from this point on everything drops into place with a nice sharp, clean click. There is no attempt to define any of these characters beyond their symbolic roles in the play whatever happens to them is formulated by the plot and not by temperament or character. Mordeen is, of course, one of Steinbeck's recurrent fantasies of the Eternal Woman or the Cosmic Mother—a type I myself have never personally met. Even Victor, the brute-man, is affected by the aura of supreme love that radiates from her; so much so that he quite naturally wants to claim his own son. Jealous, frustrated, and in human terms the only credible character in the play, he has to be murdered, of course, to preserve Mordeen's secret.

What is one to make, incidentally, of this episode in which an innocent human being, however unpleasant, is bumped off so casually—an episode that has undertones of the California vigilantes as well as of maternal bliss? It is good stage, probably, but is it nice? Are the peculiar means of Mordeen really justified by the altruistic climax of the drama, in which Joe Saul discovers (in another improbable episode) that what counts is not his own son, but, as it were, anybody's child, or the gift of life itself, which Mordeen in her infinite, if witless compassion has granted to him.

In the final "big scene" of the drama Joe Saul appears in the hospital, next to Mordeen and the new child, as only a voice and a white facelessness. "Where is your face?" Mordeen asks, "What's happened to your face, Joe Saul?" "It's not important," he says, "just a face," and here perhaps, in the revealing unconscious which so often tells the truth about a writer's work, is the clue to the deterioration of Steinbeck's work in the last decade. For the whole purpose of art, if not of evolution, is to create human faces which are important, and which cannot, as they are here, be lifted off and on in the interests of the loftiest message or the most startling stage effect.

That voice, indeed, and that "white facelessness" are symptomatic of a writer who is concerned only with grandiloquent themes and mechanical people. Steinbeck's work has always been uneven, and one had to measure such an excellent early book as *The Pastures of Heaven* against such poor works as *Cup of Gold* or *To a God Unknown*. The success of his later works was due primarily to the essential force and vitality of the writing which often obscured the false, sentimental, or banal concepts of life which Steinbeck still carried along with him.

And this "success" in terms of the commercial stage, the movie scenario, the best seller, has apparently led Steinbeck to develop the least satisfactory elements of his previous work. One can still hope that he will throw off the adolescent philosophy, the facile emotions, the final subordination of any genuine interest in human beings as such to a tricky theme or a theatrical climax—these typical characteristics, in short, of the California school of writing from Jack London and Frank Norris to Steinbeck himself, and of a cultural atmosphere in which writers somehow never seem quite to grow up. But this is, judging from the present work, a poor and desperate hope.

Richard Lockridge. "Swan Dive into the Heart of the Matter." *New York Herald Tribune Weekly Book Review*, 27 (22 October 1950), 4.

As he did in *Of Mice and Men*, John Steinbeck has here written a play in the form of a novel, relying chiefly on dialogue to reveal character and keeping the action largely within the limits available to the stage, but amplifying stage directions into narrative. That has been, at any rate, his intention; now and then we read such novelistic passages as "Victor's unfortunate choice it was always to missee, to mis-hear, to misjudge," an idiosyncrasy of character perhaps a little difficult to reveal in pantomime or by facial expression. Now and then, too, action takes place off-stage, but that happens in the theater also, or used to. By and large, I guess, Mr. Steinbeck has done what he wanted to, technically.

He has also made one of those swan dives into what he believes to be the heart of the matter which now and then tempt even good writers, particularly when they are thinking in dramatic terms. If Mr. Steinbeck has found his conception too shallow and so bumped his head, that is no more than Sean O'Casey did when, in *Within the Gates*, he made a similar leap into meanings which turned out to be not so deep as he had imagined. The idea, of course, is to tell a simple little story which Sums Up Everything. . . .

What is Summed Up is, more or less, man's desire for continuity of life. What Joe Saul learns—well, a little reluctantly.

I must give you Mr. Steinbeck's own words. He learns that—

"Every man is father to all children and every child must have all men as father. This is not a little piece of private property, registered and fenced and separated. This is *the Child*."

Joe Saul also learns that the human race must go "staggering on" because, if there is nothing else to say for people, "somewhere in us there is a shining." ("What animal has made beauty, created it, save only we?")

Throughout the language is stately, as it so often is when a writer Sums Up. There is hardly a page without its Affirmation. It is all so Universal it hurts. At any rate, remembering some of the things Mr. Steinbeck has done in the past, it hurts me.

If schedules have held, a play named *Burning Bright* is now at the Broadhurst, brought there by accomplished people of the theater. Perhaps they will have found in it something more than appears on the page. I find it, however, pretty hard to guess what.

Alice S. Morris. "Inheritance for a Child." *New York Times Book Review*, 100 (22 October 1950), 4, 34.

John Steinbeck's brief new work is scaled to the heroic dimension. Its theme is timeless and touching: the dilemma of a heredity-possessed man who discovers that he is sterile and must embrace as his own another man's child. Its four solitary characters are neither flesh-and-blood nor stock figures: husband, wife, friend, outsider, they are the legendary arch-types of folklore, speaking a spare, bare-boned language salted with color—a kind of abstract of folk speech that is stilted, poetic and moving.

What it all comes to is a full-scale flight on Mr. Steinbeck's part into the up-per air of the O'Neill genre of morality play; and while he navigates his craft with virtuosity, one returns to earth not quite convinced that one has ever cleared the treetops.

In describing the "play-novelette" form in which his new book is cast (a form which Mr. Steinbeck used more loosely in *Of Mice and Men* and *The Moon Is Down*), the author writes: "It is a play that is easy to read or a short novel that can be played simply by lifting out the dialogue."

Actually, *Burning Bright* in its struc-ture, strictures, tensions and impact is all play and no novel. The embodiment into the "novel" of descriptions usually tele-scoped and parenthesized as stage direc-tions in a play; the substitution of "she said huskily" for "Mordeen (*huskily*)": do not alter the case.

Mr. Steinbeck's most interesting in-novation is also strictly of the theatre. Though from first to last there is an un-broken continuity of action and charac-ter, there is an absolute discontinuity of milieu from one act to the next, from The Circus to The Farm to The Sea. These shifts are something more than a vivid and refreshing piece of theatre; they serve to deepen and extend Joe Saul's tragedy and heroism, since they show him in three guises (acrobat, farmer, sea captain) in which the handing down from father to son of an ancient heritage, of something "in the blood," has a powerful precedent. . . .

It is Joe Saul's hard lesson to learn that it is not the survival of inherited blood lines that matters, but of inherited knowledge. The genes and chromosomes be damned! "Every man is father to all children and every child must have all men as father," he says to his wife. "This [child] is not a little piece of private prop-erty, registered and fenced and separated. Mordee! This is *the Child*."

Two things, it strikes this reviewer, weaken and thin Mr. Steinbeck's moral drama. The crucial whim that brings Joe Saul face to face with the knowledge of his sterility is implausible. The shabby and contemptuous use of the outsider Victor (Joe Saul's circus partner, farm hand, First Mate) by the insiders shakes the framework of the whole morality. (Wasn't he, also, once *the Child*?) To justify this high-minded sacrifice of a fellowman, even if a handsome and lout-ish one, the essential goodness and supe-riority of Saul would have to be proved more guilefully than it is in Mr. Stein-beck's characterization.

Harrison Smith.
"A New Form of Literature."
Washington *Post*, 22 October 1950, p. 5B.

Burning Bright is a drama published con-currently with its opening in New York. For the reading public, Steinbeck has pre-sented it as a novelette in three acts.

"It is a combination of many old forms," he writes in his prologue, "a play that is easy to read or a short novel that can be played simply by lifting out the dialogue." It is true that the average man finds it difficult to read a play; the brief descriptions of scenes and characters in-tended for the guidance of producer and actor, the hints of changes in the mood or action, require an imaginative awareness that the reader may be incapable of giving, so that unless the dialogue is commanding and brilliant it is like finding a path through a dark field.

After reading *Burning Bright*, it would appear that there is also something lacking and unsatisfactory in the play-novelette, or at least in this particular attempt at a new form of literature. The characters are more vivid, the scenes sharper, but on the whole the book is a failure because the reader is often bewildered, as if Mr. Steinbeck's four characters were puppets moved by strings, using words put into their mouths by a ventriloquist.

If the author were writing as a novelist and not primarily as a playwright, you might sense the background for the motives of his people; you would certainly know them better, for the novelist is compelled to tell you a great deal more about them, how they live, where they came from, what their families and friends are like, something of their childhood and of their habits and tastes.

There is a feeling of unreality in *Burning Bright* that may come from his method of handling the story itself. The four characters in the first act are circus people, three men and a woman, who are seen in the dressing room tent of Joe Saul and his beautiful young wife, Mordeen. In the second act the same characters are farmers in a Midwestern farmhouse; in the third act they are in the captain's cabin of a cargo ship docked in New York Harbor.

During these three incarnations of the same people, they do not change their way of speaking to suit the scene; they never speak as would sailors, farmers or, doubtless, circus performers. The book is literally a morality play, and the characters can be labeled as if they were symbols of human virtues and vices, a device

that Mr. Steinbeck has used frequently in his later novels. . . .

Symbolism in his characters and his plots may be vital to the growth or the decline of Mr. Steinbeck as a creative writer, but his rudimentary philosophy, his feverish climaxes and the story as he has told it, in whole or in part, are neither credible to the reader nor successful as the elements of a short novel.

Joseph Henry Jackson. "A Bookman's Notebook." San Francisco *Chronicle*, 27 October 1950, p. 16.

Experimenting with the idea of telling a story in something very close to play form is nothing new with John Steinbeck. All one needs to do is to remember *Of Mice and Men*, for example, or *The Moon Is Down*.

In his new *Burning Bright*, a play-novelette (as he prefers to call it), Mr. Steinbeck tries this for the third time. The result is closer to a play than his other two experiments in this direction, yet it may be read exactly as fiction is read.

What Mr. Steinbeck is saying here is that love as a force is, or can be, a greater matter than people have heretofore made it, relying for definition and understanding, as they always have, on standard concepts—love of a parent, love of a marriage-partner, love of one's own child, and so on. All these and other aspects of life, Mr. Steinbeck suggests, are no more than parts of the whole. The discovery is made by his central character, Joe Saul, when he comes to see that "every man is father to all children and every child must have all men as father. This is not a little piece of private property, registered and fenced and separated. This is The Child." And again: "It is the race, the species, the spark continues."

Mr. Steinbeck's central situation involves an older man, Joe Saul with a young wife, Mordeen, who loves him though he cannot give her a child. Seeing him greatly troubled about this, even beginning to doubt himself as a man, she makes her decision, allows a young man, Victor, to have his way with her. If there is a child, as she is sure there will be, then it must be old Joe Saul's child, to make his life right again for him. No one must know.

But Joe Saul's friend, Ed, does know. The young man, Victor, knows. And with Joe Saul's happiness threatened—for Mordeen thinks of this and not herself—the play-novelette draws to its strong climax, a resolution of the problem which it would not be fair to give away here.

Mr. Steinbeck has his reasons for choosing to develop the form of the play-novelette, and in a brief introduction he states some of them.

For one thing, he believes that many people do not like to read plays as such, and he believes that the play-novelette will provide a "play that will be more widely read because it is presented as ordinary fiction."

He has another reason also. The play-novelette "augments the play for the actor, the director and the producer as well as the reader." This is quite true. In a play, a character is described only briefly by the author: "A businessman, aged 40," or something of the sort. By the method that Mr. Steinbeck is developing, those who bring the play before the audience may know far more of how the author thinks about the characters and setting than the standard play form permits.

A third reason is that although the play-novelette is difficult for the author to write, since the restrictions of the theater remain, these same restrictions operate as a challenge, stimulating the author to keep his action close built, to make his dialogue constantly carry the story forward, as has to be the case in the play proper, and to be sure that by the time the piece has ended, something has actually happened to the characters and to the problem.

Steinbeck, however, writes that despite its difficulties the play-novelette form is highly rewarding to the author. Here he demonstrates that it can be highly rewarding to the reader as well.

Particularly interesting are one or two of the borrowings from stage techniques which Steinbeck uses here—effects to which the theater audience is in some degree accustomed but which the fiction reader may find startling for a moment.

One such effect is his shift of scene and background, his characters being circus performers in Act 1, farmers in Act 2, and sailors in Act 3, yet remaining the same people throughout, faced with the same situation which develops in a straight line independent of the setting. What Steinbeck is after here, I should suppose, is simply to show that his theme is universal.

Another deliberate effect is the author's use of language. As is often the case with the drama, he does not attempt strict or literal realism; he avoids building up sharp distinctions among his characters through choosing distinct styles of speech for them. Instead, all of them talk the "language of the play"—a carefully worked-out, somewhat mannered dialogue, which Steinbeck must have felt best suited to the theme and to his purpose. Whatever you may think of this idea, it is consistent, poetic often, and always effective.

Once the reader allows for both these adaptations from the theater, then, *Burning Bright* can be read easily and with full enjoyment of Mr. Steinbeck's development of his fundamental theme. That he has added, as secondary themes, jealousy, friendship and hate—the unthinking, automatic hate of Victor, who does not know whether he hates or loves—is something else, and so much to the good.

As this is written, no reports on the play are available here, though it opened in New York on the 13th. It will be interesting to see what the theater-wise critics found in the performance. Meantime, this experiment in the play-novelette is not only successful in print, but a very interesting move in the direction of something fresh in fiction.

N[orman] C[ousins].
"Hemingway and Steinbeck."
Saturday Review, 33 (28 October 1950), 26–7.

... John Steinbeck's new book, *Burning Bright*, seems to have been written almost in direct refutation of Hemingway. It, too, is a philosophical summation, but it shows pluses where Hemingway shows minuses. It reveals moral values where Hemingway reveals monomaniac meanderings. It tries to meet deep inner conflicts instead of pampering them.

The truculent, arrogant, prize-fight-conscious, sperm-ridden, perennial soldier-boy of Hemingway's book dies a heroic and glamorous death. The man who meets death in Steinbeck's book is also a pompous and self-willed brute, but there is nothing heroic about him or his

death. He is a pathetic and oafish stud whose typically twisted ego makes it impossible for him to understand that virility alone does not automatically entitle him to the love of a desirable and understanding woman. No man is a real man, says Steinbeck, unless he is first of all a real human being.

Joe Saul, in *Burning Bright*, becomes this real human being. He discovers that love has higher dimensions than he had realized, and that identification with the human family is purpose and fulfillment in life. He can look at a child—any child—and feel the pride of a father relationship. He has, in short, broken through the limitations of mechanical masculinity. What he eats, whom he sleeps with, and how he punches are of less consequence than what he does to justify the gift of compassion and conscience.

But it is unfair to Mr. Steinbeck to cite aspects of his book before describing his full stage. *Burning Bright* is a play-novelette: it can be used directly as a playscript but the story is handled descriptively. Instead of chapters, the book is divided into three acts, each one of which is set against a contrasting background. The book is not to be read, nor is the play to be seen, as a conventional or specific plot with conventional or specific characters. The story, for example, is not to be regarded a tragedy because one of the central characters is murdered. The murder is non-violent in its symbolic presentation. In fact, the characters, story, and setting are used as part of a symbolic whole.

Steinbeck is dealing with universal types and universal situations and makes no effort to invest his people with individual color or substance. To accentuate this purpose his story unwinds through three separate and contrasting backgrounds. The characters and their story names remain constant though they are seen as circus folk in the first act, as farmers in the second, and as mariners in the third.

What does all this symbolism lead up to? It is far from obscure; what it tries to do is to penetrate through to the anchored positions of the human ego, and to release them. It tries to emancipate men from the tyranny of the personal self. It tries to develop an aspect of man's nature, too often hidden, which hungers truly for larger understanding and mutuality in life. It demolishes the supposed importance of a continuing biological immortality, revealing the blazing truth that so long as human beings exist anywhere every man is immortal.

All this has been said before. The greatest literature in all languages has reflected the fundamental reality that all men are brothers. But it hasn't been said with any real skill or frequency in American literature in recent years. Too many of our writers, like Hemingway in his current book, have written thinly of life precisely because they have been too close to the ego and not close enough to the human heart. Too many of them have been engaged in thematic trivia instead of with great ideas and the struggle for higher values.

Steinbeck himself, in many of his earlier books, has been victimized by this obsession with marginal themes. For a long time, it appeared that he had lost or abandoned the gift of inspiration—which comes close to being the worst that can happen to a writer. But in *Burning Bright*, he is restored to his full stature as a major American novelist. He has written his most mature book, a book which, if carefully and slowly read, can be as rewarding a literary experience as any of us is likely to have for a long time. As a vital corrective to the new Hemingway book, it couldn't have been better timed.

Milton Crane. "Steinbeck's 'Play-Novelet' Is Soap Opera." *Chicago Sunday Tribune Magazine of Books*, 29 October 1950, p. 8.

[We find here] a theme of soap opera, orchestrated for the carriage trade by the addition of devices which do not enlist my wholehearted admiration. Thus, for example, in Act I all the principals are circus performers; in Act II they are farmers; in Act III they are sailors. One can see how these transformations are intended to emphasize the universality of the theme, and they certainly must have seemed like a good idea at the time—the kind of idea that might have engaged Eugene O'Neill's attention for about a half hour in 1928.

Mr. Steinbeck has yet other innovations. He complains that the typical play is unreadable in published form, and that the typical novel can gain clarity and concision from the discipline of dramatic writing. So we have the "play-novelet," which uses dialog more dramatically than does the novel, and which supplies background and characterization lacking in the ordinary published play.

It is a great ideal that Mr. Steinbeck offers us, or it might seem so if we did not have such works as the published plays of George Bernard Shaw, who certainly has mastered the art of making plays come alive for the reader. And the "play-novelet" that Mr. Steinbeck has written (he explains that *Of Mice and Men* and *The Moon Is Down* are earlier efforts in the same form) is hardly more than a

351

truncated novel. One is tempted to tell him: don't look now, but your screenplay is showing.

Stephen Longstreet. "Steinbeck Goes Arty in Play-Novelette." Los Angeles *News*, 11 November 1950, pp. 10, 12.

California was fertile earth. It grew big sons and they burst on the world shining and full of meat and talent. Jack London pouring out life, Bret Harte inventing new forms, Frank Norris making the color and sound of things part of the bigger world, beyond the black mountains.

And there was John Steinbeck. It was not easy for him and he had the long darkness of being alone and unknown. For a long time he waited. I remember long ago finding a book by an unknown author, *To a God Unknown*, and finding in the rather bad D. H. Lawrence enough of promise to think this man would be great. *In Dubious Battle* was a touch of life, a man at grip with the shape of things as they are. Then came *Grapes of Wrath*, and the first half was the best modern novel yet written by an American (the second half was trash mixed up with a Message). At this high water mark John Steinbeck stopped and it's been the journey down, and fast. The nonsense about fascism in *The Moon Is Down*, the hot foot humor of *Cannery Row*, the maudlin symbolism of *The Wayward Bus*. And now *Burning Bright*.

Steinbeck is a little ashamed of this 159 pages of large print. He writes a long foreword explaining it isn't a novel and it isn't a play, it's a "play-novelette," whatever that bastard form is. It shows no sign of any talent, it has no form, not one word that sounds real or has any excitement. As I read I kept thinking this sounds like a parody of a bad O'Neill play—done by a rather dull college boy. No one is real in it, every one is a symbol, and talks in that stilted language found only in people who can not think, feel, taste, or enjoy anything. . . .

I can not think of any important writer of our time who had slipped so badly. The dialogue is frankly so arty, overdrawn and so full of fake aches and pains that I felt maybe this is a gag, the whole thing is some bad bit of humor that didn't come off. But under it all I can see Steinbeck grunting and twisting, trying to make something cosmic out of a plot Faith Baldwin wouldn't touch.

One can only hope that the book (these short pages aren't really a book) is only a mistake, that the vitality that Steinbeck showed in his early work will come again. But looking back at London, and Harte, and Norris, I doubt it. They too failed after great beginnings; but they never sank as low as *Burning Bright*.

Carol H. Weiss. "*Burning Bright*." *Commonweal*, 53 (24 November 1950), 178.

As a play, *Burning Bright* lasted eleven days on Broadway. The critics found it artificial, pretentious, and filled with pseudo-poetic dialogue that hit the ears with the effect of "chalk squealing on a slate." As Walter Kerr noted in his drama review, Mr. Steinbeck had junked reality and flown off, rather shakily, into the unrewarding abstract.

Burning Bright has also been published as a novel, or in Mr. Steinbeck's term, a play-novelette. The novel was written first, with the intention of transforming it into a play simply by lifting out the dialogue and turning the descriptive passages into stage directions. Some minor line-changes were made in rehearsal—one of them, Mr. Steinbeck relates, with the help of some Yale students who saw the try-out in New Haven and left a note at the box office—but the book remains substantially the novel version of the play. The same flaws that the drama critics hopped on so vigorously are of course present—the arty dialogue, the removal from reality, the shallowness of characterization reminiscent of an Arbor Day pageant.

But in novel form, some of these faults are less disquieting. The reader, more than the playgoer, is used to poetic language and artificial constructions. He accepts phrases like "I've got a rustle in me" or "the loneliness we wear like icy clothes" or "we were the only gay in that laughter-starving time." And without the painful sound of the play, Mr. Steinbeck's dramatized idea is almost moving. Joe Saul, who is unable to have the child he passionately craves to carry on his line, comes to accept as his son his wife's child by another man; he learns that a child is not "a piece of private property, registered and fenced and separated," but a shining being, a part of indestructible humanity.

Nevertheless, with all the grandeur of the idea, and the greater tolerance of the eye than the ear, the book is hung up on the same basic flaw—the morality-play abstractness of the characters. In one of his earliest novels, the little noted and long forgotten *To a God Unknown*, Mr. Steinbeck had a previous whirl at heavy symbolism. Another guy named Joe, consumed with a passion for fertility—fertility of the land rather than his own fertility—was loaded down with the responsibility of being "a repository for a little piece of each man's soul, and more than that, a symbol of the earth's soul." Mr. Steinbeck recovered to write *Grapes of Wrath* and *Of Mice and Men*.

L. A. G. Strong. "Fiction." *Spectator* [England], 187 (10 August 1951), 196.

... Mr. Steinbeck is at pains to justify what he calls a play-novelette, a short novel of which the dialogue makes a play, since each act, or chapter, keeps to one scene. No justification is needed, provided the result succeeds. *Burning Bright* has a strong theme, the realisation that none of us can claim to possess a living soul. A child is not yours or mine. It is its own, or all men's. Life is sacred. The most we can do is free it, make a home for it. This lesson, which a great many parents have yet to learn ("I have decided to make my boy a lawyer," etc., etc.) is not made easier or more acceptable by the dialogue in which Mr. Steinbeck's characters indulge. Its embodiment is clear enough. The widower Joe Saul, a circus clown in Act One, a farmer in Act Two, a seaman in Act Three, has married a young wife but has no child. This so distresses him that she is moved to show her love by conceiving someone else's. He finds out, is distraught, but at least accepts with gladness the fact that a child has come. Unfortunately some of the language in which these illuminations are recorded is on a different level from the rest. Friend Ed, fellow clown in Act One, has some odd things to say: "Three years it is since Cathy died. You were strong in your wife-loss." ... Oddity is not confined to Ed. Mordeen, the young wife, has her share: "Without that trick you'll go screaming silently in loss."

Have I, I wonder, the admirer-right to tell Mr. Steinbeck that this trick has set me screaming silently in my reader-loss?

"Staging a Story."
Times Literary Supplement [London], 17 August 1951, p. 513.

It has always been clear from Mr. John Steinbeck's writing that the theatre—and perhaps, equally, the film—is rarely far from his thoughts. This is perhaps a dangerous state of mind for a novelist, because the arts concerned are of a very different kind; and, although there have certainly been novels that turned into good plays, there have also been many unsuccessful experiments in that line; while at least a few good novelists have shown a tendency to overdramatize their novels by too keen a grasp of purely dramatic technique. In the case of the work under review there is no question of the "influence" of one technique on another. The book has been, admittedly, written simultaneously as a play.

Burning Bright contains four characters—husband, wife, lover, and *raisonneur*. Husband and wife are getting on in years, and, in spite of passionate desire to have a child, are childless. Accordingly, the woman decides to bear a child to the lover in order to satisfy this lifelong wish of her husband. How this situation

works out is the theme of the book, which falls—like a play—into three acts. There is a further point. In the First Act, the characters are set against the background of a circus; in the Second Act, a farm; and in the Third Act, the *dramatis personae* are on board ship. These changes merely show the action going forward, different circumstances illustrating its different stages of development.

Mr. Steinbeck, by adopting this form of writing begs the whole question posed at the beginning of this review; and it is hard to see how the method can really be justified, at least in the form before us. The story—as a novel—is perhaps possible, the characters on the other hand are not very convincing and the changes of scene appear—in a novel—without any point at all. As a play, on the other hand, the effect might be different. Improbability in drama stands or falls by the conviction of the moment. It is possible, therefore, that *Burning Bright* might convince a theatre audience. As a play, it seems to suggest the influence of Molnar; and the changes of setting might fall into place, just as re-dressing an act can help a show along visually.

Checklist of Additional Reviews

"*Burning Bright.*" *Booklist*, 47 (1 September 1950), 3.

Lewis Gannett. "Books and Things." New York *Herald Tribune*, 20 October 1950, p. 23.

Charles Poore. "New Books." *Harper's*, 201 (December 1950), 102–12.

Maurice Dunbar. "*Burning Bright.*" *Steinbeck Quarterly*, 13 (Winter– Spring 1980), 44–5.

BURNING BRIGHT (THE PLAY)

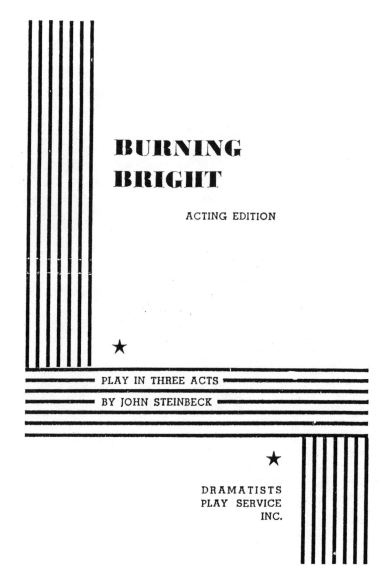

BURNING BRIGHT

ACTING EDITION

★

PLAY IN THREE ACTS
BY JOHN STEINBECK

★

DRAMATISTS
PLAY SERVICE
INC.

Brooks Atkinson.
"At the Theatre."
New York *Times*,
19 October 1950, p. 40.

Credit John Steinbeck with having the courage to try something that is difficult. Credit four actors and a director with a superb performance. For *Burning Bright*, which opened at the Broadhurst last evening, is written in the form of an epic and acted like a poem.

But there is always a "but" at the end of such salutations. Although Mr. Steinbeck is a man of faith, he does not write with the majesty of a prophet and *Burning Bright* does not have much eloquence in the theatre. Mr. Steinbeck has been happier when he has been closer to mice and men and the itinerant Okies. Abstract ideas do not appear to be his medium.

Like the preacher in Ecclesiastes, he says that the earth abideth forever. The human race must go on, though the method does not matter. To illustrate his thesis he offers a middle-aged husband, a young wife, a friend of the family and a young lover. Although the husband is sterile, he longs for children to continue the inheritance he has had from his forebears. Descendants are a religious obligation to him.

To gratify his vanity, the wife secretly takes a lover and pretends that the child is her husband's. When he discovers that he has been deceived, he is crushed and horrified. But in the end, Mr. Steinbeck shows the husband as resigned to any method that keeps the chain of life unbroken.

To give his theme a universal significance Mr. Steinbeck presents his characters first as circus folk, second as farmers and third as sailors. To his way of thinking these are the elemental professions. And to rise above the literary sphere of naturalism, Mr. Steinbeck writes in an impersonal, conscious style.

But somehow the grandeur escapes him; and, despite its admirable intentions, *Burning Bright* is an earthbound play. For Mr. Steinbeck has not demonstrated that he is a poet with his pen, however rhapsodic his dreams may be. The play is cramped, literal and elementary. . . .

Sam Zolotow.
"*Burning Bright* Quits
Tomorrow."
New York *Times*,
27 October 1950, p. 24.

A for Effort: *Burning Bright* flickers out after its thirteenth performance tomorrow night. The sudden departure of John Steinbeck's "play-novelette" makes the Broadhurst available for another attraction, thereby easing the booking jam slightly.

Everything connected with *Burning Bright*, except the script, evoked general commendation, e. g., the four-character cast (Kent Smith, Barbara Bel Geddes, Howard da Silva and Martin Brooks), the sympathetic direction of Guthrie McClintic, the inspired lighting and scenery of Jo Mielziner, and last, but by no stretch of the imagination least, the tender and loving care bestowed upon the offering by Richard Rodgers and Oscar Hammerstein 2d, the producers.

If it weren't for the inordinately high weekly overhead of $18,000, with which the $60,000 venture is shackled, efforts would have been made to prolong the engagement. Here's another instance where a healthy advance doesn't mean a thing unless there's a comfortable window sale.

Commenting on the quick withdrawal, Mr. Hammerstein said yesterday: "We are very proud to have produced it because it's a play that should have been done. Few plays of that type are written or presented." . . .

John Lardner.
"The Theatre."
New Yorker, 26
(28 October 1950), 52, 54.

John Steinbeck's new play, *Burning Bright*, which opened at the Broadhurst last week, is full of noble thoughts, beautiful human emotions, and poetic speech. In the circumstances, it may sound flippant to say that it seems to me that Mr. Steinbeck did himself a disservice by putting it on the stage. His readers know that he has always tended to see a goodness, a shining quality, in man. This view is stated explicitly in the last scene of *Burning Bright*, when an Everyman sort of character named Joe Saul says, "What animal has made beauty, created it, save only we? With all our horrors and our faults, somewhere in us is a shining. That is the most important of all facts. *There is a shining.*" No one can quarrel with the author's right to insist on that shiningness, but I think it's legitimate to object, in his behalf as much as anyone else's, when he goes about it in terms that are sometimes arty, often absurd, and generally misplaced.

The question of misplacing is connected with Mr. Steinbeck's theory of the technique of what he calls the "play-novelette." *Burning Bright* appeared in book form at about the same time it opened as a play. In a foreword to the book, the author explains that a play-novelette "is a play that is easy to read or a short novel that can be played simply by lifting out the dialogue." Earlier examples by Mr. Steinbeck were *Of Mice and Men* and *The Moon Is Down*. A thing he failed to say in the foreword is that the piece ought to be—or so I would figure—pretty nearly equally suitable for print and the stage; otherwise, why not write it in one form or the other and let it go at that? The printed version of *Burning Bright* is not a very good book, especially for a Steinbeck book, but it *is* digestible. We're accustomed, in reading books, to coming across lyric tales, sermons, or fantasies in which the speech of modern people is written in poetic language, though in prose form. So, whether we like the device or not, a book like *Burning Bright* goes down quite easily; it is not disconcerting. But on the stage the talk of Mr. Steinbeck's characters occasionally hits the ear with the effect of chalk squealing on a slate. Granted, the time of the action is described as "any time;" still, it's a contemporary background, with modern details and trimmings, against which Mr. Steinbeck has asked the players to speak such lines as "When he is tired past wakefulness, take him to the sleeping car," "It's time we sing this trouble out into the air and light," "A poisoned thought, lying concealed but toxic," and "You were strong in your wife-loss." It might be interesting to know by what plan Mr. Steinbeck constructed his poetry, or what sources he went to for the archaic tone of some of it. I would guess that there is a good deal of planning in it, aside from the obvious intention to show that the theme and the characters are timeless. In Elizabethan plays, poetry in a person's speech indicated high rank or education. In *Burning*

Bright, it seems to indicate goodness, or, at any rate, moral progress. The story's one ignoble character, as soon as he comes to know true love, turns on like a light and acquires a brand-new tendency to speak of the lashing branches of the pear trees or wild duck driving south over the burning sumac.

The chief figure of the play, Joe Saul, is a sterile husband. Unknown to him, his wife arranges, with the most selfless and loving motives, to give him a child by another man. In the end, after an emotional ordeal complicated by his ideas about his own "blood" and the importance of reproducing it, he comes to appreciate the fact that, as Mr. Steinbeck writes, "every man is father to all children and every child must have all men as father." It is impossible to deny the dignity and grandeur of this thought. However, the play suffers not only from its inconvenient rhetoric but from over-conciseness—it is too tight and jerky for the size of its message—and a couple of creaking hinges in the plot. A young man with plenty of other things to be doing is lured into ambush by one of the season's most abrupt ruses, as follows: "Will you come on deck with me? I have a message for you." "Say it here." "No, it's a secret." Joe Saul learns of his sterility when his rival sells him, in a few seconds' time, the unusual idea of going to his doctor and getting a clean bill of health to hang on the Christmas tree as a present for his unborn son. (In the book, Joe Saul thinks of the idea himself, which makes the scene more convincing.) In each act of *Burning Bright*, Joe Saul is a different person—first a circus acrobat, then a farmer, then a merchant mariner. The same formula was used a few seasons ago, with the same object of achieving an Everymannish, timeless mood, and with at least equal success, in a musical show called *Love Life*. Toward the end of the evening, the sight of Mr. Steinbeck's Everyman (infécund model) in different professions and places, always being called Joe Saul rather than Joe, began to fuddle me a little, and I heard erratic echoes of the old song about Joe Hill, the labor martyr:

> From San Diego up to Maine,
> In any place at all
> Where fathers haven't got no kids,
> That's where you'll find Joe Saul.

Barbara Bel Geddes, Kent Smith, Howard Da Silva, and Martin Brooks do valiant jobs of acting, especially Miss Bel Geddes. They all seem embarrassed at times by what they have to say, but that won't do them any permanent harm. As for Mr. Steinbeck, he can afford to miss a shot now and then, if any writer can.

Margaret Marshall. "Drama." *Nation*, 171 (28 October 1950), 396.

Sterility, no doubt, is a "folk" concern and has been a source of tragedy and dramatic conflict in the lives of individuals. But as John Steinbeck presents it in *Burning Bright* (Broadhurst Theater) it has no reality either as a primal folk concern or as a factor in individual human lives. His handling of the theme is pretentious and crude; his appeal to the universal is forced and false; as for the "poetic prose" in which the piece is written, it is so fancy and bad that its only effect is one of acute embarrassment.

Steinbeck universalizes his play by presenting his four characters as circus folk in Act I, farm folk in Act II, and sailor folk in Act III. And then there are the names he has given them—Joe Saul the husband (and don't think he's ever called Joe), Friend Ed (who is always called Friend Ed), Mordeen, the ever-loving wife, and Victor, who supplies the child the husband can't provide.

The characterizations are rather vague—of course one of the presumed advantages of "folk" writing is that characterization isn't necessary—except that Joe Saul, as the evening wears on, becomes so intolerable with his folk-whining about his blood and his line that you wonder how even a folk-wife could go on loving him.

The cast does far better than you'd expect, given their assignments—particularly Barbara Bel Geddes, who manages to impart an air of flesh and blood to the part of Mordeen and thereby demonstrates her abilities as an actress. Kent Smith as the sterile husband can't quite overcome the hazards of his role, and Howard Da Silva is hard put to it to make palatable the unrelieved sweetness and kindness of Friend Ed. Martin Brooks has the easiest part, that of Victor, which at least has a touch of reality, though it becomes pretty attenuated toward the end.

The settings are nice.

The title is taken from William Blake's "Tiger, tiger, burning bright," and the poem is printed in the program. I have not yet worked out its connection with the play.

Brooks Atkinson. *"Burning Bright."* New York *Times*, 29 October 1950, Section 2, p. 1.

There is a cant critical phrase that applies to John Steinbeck's *Burning Bright*. The experiment does not "come off." For *Burning Bright* is an experiment, available as a "play-novelette" in the text published by Viking and as an allegorical drama which has just concluded a brief engagement on Broadway. It is the third of Mr. Steinbeck's attempts at an art form equally useful in book form or on the stage. Both *Of Mice and Men* and *The Moon Is Down* were published to be read, and produced to be seen and heard on the stage.

As an art form the "play-novelette" is sound enough. It may have less significance than Mr. Steinbeck imagines, but it is a useful medium of expression. In the case of *Of Mice and Men* it resulted simultaneously in a taut, sentient novel and a vivid drama that made history under the masterly direction of George S. Kaufman. Although *The Moon Is Down* came directly out of Mr. Steinbeck's personal convictions in the early stages of the war, he was not so intimately acquainted with the Norwegian characters as he was with the ranch rag-tag and bobtail of *Of Mice and Men*. His first experiment with the "play-novelette" remains his most successful.

To judge by the literary as well as the drama reviews, *Burning Bright* dissatisfies both camps. Those who read and those who look and listen are equally unhappy with it. And this is not because the form is inept but because the material is commonplace. Everything else Mr. Steinbeck has written has been saturated in the sweat of human beings. In *Burning Bright* he has made a conscious attempt to write in a new style and to argue a philosophical thesis. He is saying that the individual ego is less important than the species and that nothing matters except the continuance of the human race.

After a writer has devoted a lot of hard work to trying to say something useful and important, it is all too easy for a critic to come along at the end of the line and denigrate the attempt and the achievement. There is something a little supercilious about saying "no" so casually. From that point of view, the following comments are probably supercilious. But they are set down with respect for Mr. Steinbeck's high-mindedness and also with admiration for the courage of an established author who tries something new and difficult.

But after seeing *Burning Bright* in a sensitive and pulsing performance on the stage and after reading it in book form, one cannot shake off the conviction that Mr. Steinbeck has no ability for expressing abstract ideas in the imaginative form of play or story. To judge by this one instance, he throws away his greatest talent when he abandons the villages, boarding houses and highroads for the library.

There is nothing wrong with his argument that the race is more important than the individual, though a sound argument could be developed on the other side. But Mr. Steinbeck is one of the last men to argue from the general to the particular. He has enormous skill in expressing the particular—the racy, pungent, rather pathetic men and women who drift through the pages of his novels. The particular is his natural bailiwick. When he has written about specific people with gusto or compassion, as in *The Red*

Pony, *Of Mice and Men*, *Cannery Row*, *Tortilla Flat* and *The Grapes of Wrath*, it has been easy enough to draw some general philosophical conclusions from them. Mr. Steinbeck does not have to tell us what they mean. *Grapes of Wrath* proves eloquently that the human race has a genius for survival. Nothing about *Burning Bright* comes anywhere near as close to the point.

If *Burning Bright* "came off" in the theatre or in book form, the symbolic devices Mr. Steinbeck has invented would be saluted as poetic inspirations; and if his dialogue made music in the theatre, the liberties he takes with words would be admired. To give his theme universal scope Mr. Steinbeck offers his characters successively as circus people in the first act, farmers in the second and sailors in the third—these being, in his opinion, the fundamental, timeless professions. And to give his play the stature of an allegory, he writes in a formalistic style that includes a number of factitious phrases— "Strong in your wife-loss," "I am harsh-breathing," "Do I have the friend-right to ask a question?" etc.

But, since *Burning Bright* does not "come off," the dogmatic change of scene from one profession to another seems pretentious, and the self-conscious style, sophomoric. *Burning Bright* emerges as a rather monotonous, and at times a clinically literal story about a sterile man whose wife secretly takes another man to give her a child. It is a humorless play— not merely because it is not funny, but because it lacks the sense of proportion that humor instills in normal people. Mr. Steinbeck would not be so solemn if he were among friends on the home grounds.

To judge by his previous work, he is a warm, humorous, independent, sympathetic member of the human race with a faith in people. In *Burning Bright* he has tried to escape his real talent by putting on the robes of a prophet. Since the play does not "come off," the prophet's robes may as well come off, too. There is a good man underneath.

It remains to be said that the performance, under Guthrie McClintic's evocative direction, was an extraordinarily fine piece of theatre, and that Barbara Bel Geddes' performance as the woman had the fearful symmetry and the passion of the William Blake verse from which Mr. Steinbeck chose his title.

"*Burning Bright.*" *Newsweek*, 36 (30 October 1950), 78.

John Steinbeck's new drama, which preceded by two days the appearance of the same story in novel form, is his third experiment in what he calls the play-novelette technique. The first two were *Of Mice and Men* and *The Moon Is Down*. This time, however, Steinbeck makes the experiment doubly hazardous by writing an allegory within an unusual dramatic framework that is superficially intriguing but ultimately appears to defeat his ends. *Burning Bright* is a clinical and morbid play written in a triumphant innocence. It is passionate with sincerity and frequently eloquent; but, inexplicably, it fails to come to life on stage.

At ground level Steinbeck's plot is a straightforward and simple one that involves only four characters: a proud and physically powerful husband who is sterile but obsessed with the desire to have a child to carry on his heritage; a young wife who loves her husband so much that she sacrifices her own pride to give him a

son by another; the arrogant young lover; and an all-wise friend of the family.

Steinbeck attempts to give his theme a universal significance by garbing his characters as circus folk in the first act, as farmers in the second, and as sailors in the third. He has also written in a poetic mood, avoiding personal distinctions in the dialogue to keep his parable rigidly in the realm of the abstract and the symbolic. The result is to deprive his drama of its emotional substance and leave only the insistent iteration of faith in life and the stubborn survival of mankind.

For Steinbeck the play is summed up as the monumentally self-conscious husband finally overcomes his great vanity to accept the new child as his own: "I had to walk into the black to know—to know that every man is father to all children and every child must have all men as father. This is not a little piece of private property, registered and fenced and separated . . . This is *the Child*."

Despite the repetitiousness and the excessive exaltation of its elementary concept, *Burning Bright* is too courageous to be brushed off for its sins. . . .

"New Play in Manhattan." *Time*, 56 (30 October 1950), 58.

Burning Bright . . . suggests that misused talent can be more distressing than none at all. In this reversible raincoat of a "play-novelette,"[1] Steinbeck tells of a sterile husband (Kent Smith) with a fierce yearning for parenthood. His wife (Barbara Bel Geddes), out of love for him, conspires to have a child by another man.

At first crushed and incensed when he learns the truth, he is at length comforted with a transcendental sense of being the father not of one child but of all children.

Steinbeck has chosen for this theme the sort of treatment that must succeed splendidly or not at all. In an effort to universalize his characters, he has made them successively circus folk, farmers, sea-farers. To exalt them further, he has made them as full of mysticism as philosophers, as lavish with metaphor as poets.

The result is a jumble of the interstellar and the folksy. Characters who are neither living people nor vivid symbols traffic in blown-up emotions and rouged-up words. Besides being high-pitched and mawkish, *Burning Bright* is frequently dull. Steinbeck might have done far better with a few people talking simple prose in a suburb, might have remembered that writers best achieve the universal through the particular. Blake, who gave him his title (*Tyger, tyger, burning bright*) could also have given him a good cue: *To see the world in a grain of sand.*

Note

1   Also published last week in book form. Steinbeck's theory: a short, meaty novel (*e.g.*, *Of Mice and Men*) can be transformed into a play by simply treating descriptive passages as stage directions and dialogue as actors' lines.

Walter Kerr. "The Stage." *Commonweal*, 53 (10 November 1950), 120–1.

The title of John Steinbeck's new play, *Burning Bright*, is derived from William Blake's "Tiger, Tiger," and serves notice on us at once that Mr. Steinbeck has something weighty to say and is going to say it on a pretty elevated level. Apparently convinced that the realistic observation and prose style with which he is identified are inadequate to his new and lofty purposes, Mr. Steinbeck has cast his lot with symbolism and a formality of diction many times removed from the concrete characterization and living speech of *Tortilla Flat*, *Of Mice and Men*, and *The Grapes of Wrath*.

Mr. Steinbeck is determined that his new play shall be universal. Its story is not that of one man's struggle with sterility and failure, but of every man's. Its characters are not persons, but ideas about persons—the Responsible but Impotent Man, the Irresponsible but Creative Man, the Eternal Woman, and the Eternal Friend. They address each other throughout by their full proper names, as though they had heard of one another but had barely been introduced. It is always "Friend Ed," never simply "Ed." Joe Saul's wife always speaks of him as Joe Saul, even to his face. To emphasize the fact that these people are symbols, existing only in the third person, they are transferred to a new milieu with each act. In the first they are circus performers (it may be taken that life is a circus); in the second, they are farmers (fertility, at a rough guess), and in the third, they are discovered on the ever-changing sea (life is fluid, and changes can be made). Their language is not that of common life, but a deliberate and artificial construction, occasionally gilded with a pseudo-poetic word or phrase, designed to carry Mr. Steinbeck's considered profundities.

The curtain has no sooner gone up than someone says, "She wouldn't have gone else," and you know what you are in for. And you are in for it. As the evening goes on you will be treated to Friend Ed telling Joe Saul what a "nervy" thing he has done, to Mordeen (you heard me—Mordeen), speaking of the growing thing within her which will soon be reaching for the sky, and to Friend Ed's climaxing his great verbal assault on Joe Saul by calling him a "nastiness." You are going to be spared nothing this night.

Now it is very possible to sympathize with Mr. Steinbeck's anxiety to increase the dimension and stature of our literary form. The literary method of the twentieth century has been, for the most part, to record in an almost scientific manner the surface phenomena of material reality. Its psychology has been reflexive and behavioristic, and its narrative method has been that of the detached and judicious reporter. While this so-called realistic form has the values of idiomatic accuracy (John O'Hara) and sensitivity to material surfaces (Hemingway on a duck hunt), it finds itself so concerned with the specific as to lose sight of the universal. Great art always has a sense of the universal, and Mr. Steinbeck knows this. The trouble is that he has gone about getting it in the wrong way.

He has junked concrete reality altogether and flown off into the abstract. It is a sophomore's mistake. Anyone who has ever taught playwriting will recognize this play. It comes in from the novice, once every year, in just these words, just

these rhythms, just these pretensions. It is the old mistake of supposing that universality can be imposed from without, just because you want it to be. You decide on some generalized statement you would like to make, and suppose that you will be able to find characters who will willingly jump through hoops for you in order to illustrate it. Good plays, and above all, universal plays, don't get written this way.

They begin with something concrete—a real action, a real character—and stay with it, burrowing deeper and deeper into it, uncovering layer after layer of what is still reality, until the penetration is so complete that we seem at last to grasp the essential spirit which vitalizes it. Half the time I doubt that the artist knows what it is until he gets there. I don't think Shakespeare ever did find out what it was in Hamlet, though there is something half-glimpsed which tantalizes us. Anyway, this is the artist's method of seeking the universal, and it has nothing to do with the mathematician's. To get a little windy about it, it is a sense of immaterial form *within* material reality, not divorced from it. It is Mercutio, not Friend Ed. We do sense a universal of friendship in Mercutio, but it would be hard to put our finger on it, Mercutio is so fluid and so alive.

Graham Greene mentions in his *British Dramatists* that Macbeth is only a step away from the symbolic figure Ambition in the morality plays. But the step is everything. All figures known as Ambition, in fact all labels anywhere, are dead. Mercutio and Macbeth are alive because they are first men, and only finally significant men. The friendship and the ambition are in them, not stamped upon them.

It is unfair to hold Mr. Steinbeck to account for Shakespeare's successes. But it would be equally unfair to treat a man of Steinbeck's talent other than seriously. Further, the flight into symbolism is not a new problem, and it seems to be a particularly thorny one for men reared in this age of scientific realism. All the great realists—Ibsen, Hauptmann, Strindberg, O'Neill—wound up as symbolists, and the last stage was worse than the first. The reason why the problem is so acute in our time is that the scientifically trained mind cannot conceive, or deliberately rejects, the metaphysical possibility that an essential and spiritual form does inhabit, and does animate, each lump of living matter. Why work so hard to penetrate matter when the interior form is not there to be perceived? To the scientifically trained mind, the notion of universal form is only a man-made equation, existing outside and apart from matter, an intellectual construction after the fact. Hence, when the realist has wearied of his literal reporting and yearns for the universal, he can only escape to an equation, to an intellectual construction. He calls his equation The Master Builder, or The Sunken Bell, or Dynamo, or Burning Bright. Having abandoned the reality which might have proved more fertile than he could imagine, and over which he already had a considerable mastery of the surface, he finds himself scratching about on the bare rock of abstraction. That is Mr. Steinbeck's present plight, and it is a sad thing to report that there is not a moment in this more ambitious play to touch any given moment in the earthy *Of Mice and Men.*

No production could help *Burning Bright* very much, but the present one is geared to expose its most artificial and embarrassing qualities. Guthrie McClintic has staged it with reverence, and the effect is stupefying. Kent Smith, a fine actor, is made to seem rigid and awkward. Howard da Silva, another fine actor, is made to bubble friendliness to the point

where he bears an uneasy resemblance to Jerry Lester. Only Barbara Bel Geddes maintains sufficient reserve in the face of the play's pretentiousness to command your respect, and, with it, your sympathy.

"*Burning Bright.*" Theatre Arts, 34 (December 1950), 16.

John Steinbeck has taken the title of his play from *The Tyger*, William Blake's moving poem of awesome wonder at the great mystery of the creation. Like Blake, he has pondered on man's finiteness in a boundless universe and found his answer in the creative richness of love; in man's capacity for good. *Burning Bright* is an affirmation of faith in the human race, an avowal of belief in the dignity of man stated with unmistakable sincerity.

Burning Bright is a modern morality play, a parable told through four symbolic characters; husband, wife, friend and intruder. The story moves continuously against backgrounds that change in each act—the first is in a circus, the second on a farm, and the third on board ship—a device which is intended to emphasize the universality of the play's theme. The effect is artificial; one regrets its use since the basic theme, valid in any setting, gained nothing from the theatrical trick. Similarly, Mr. Steinbeck's use of highly stylized language is awkward rather than poetic and does him a disservice. However one must rejoice at what Mr. Steinbeck has to say, even while regretting that he did not say it better, for he is the very antithesis of the dramatists of despair, the delineators of disintegration. The noblest function of the art of drama is to show life as it might be; to serve, in Shaw's phrase "as a temple to the ascent of Man." This has been Mr. Steinbeck's aim; it commands respect.

Unaware that he is sterile, Joe Saul passionately desires a child to carry on the "blood line" in which he has fierce pride. Mordeen, his young wife, realizes Joe Saul's desperate need to perpetuate himself through a son and, out of selfless love for her husband she conceives a child with another man. Just before the child is born Joe Saul discovers the deception. Basic and base human emotions of love, jealousy, pride, self-pity, and self-sacrifice are encompassed in this human situation. Joe Saul's triumph is his comprehension that all men are father to all children, and every child must have all men as father. William Blake said it this way:

> . . . for Man is Love
> As God is Love; every kindness is a
>   little death
> In the Divine Image, nor can Man
>   exist but by Brotherhood.

Euphemia van Renssaelaer Wyatt. "Theater." Catholic World, 172 (December 1950), 228.

In the much heralded and short lived *Burning Bright*, John Steinbeck made use of the same plot as O'Neill in his *Strange Interlude* but Steinbeck built up to a humanitarian climax a story which, with O'Neill, showed only the stark consequences of sin. In the pragmatic philosophy of Steinbeck, the sin became transmogrified into heroic self-sacrifice.

Rarely has morality been so squarely challenged by literary casuistry.

To give the play the aura of the universal, Steinbeck pictured his four characters first in the circus, then on the farm and finally on a cargo ship and the experiment proved successful. But to illustrate the theme that it is not the individual's but the race's progress which is important, the young wife tries to satisfy her husband's morbid anxiety to preserve his forbears' "lifeline," by giving him a child by another man. She finally convinces her husband of her devotion, and the tag line was "Every man is the father of all children."

Happier to report were the fine performances by Kent Smith and Barbara Bel Geddes; the sets by Mielziner and the good prose of the stylized dialogue.

George Jean Nathan. "Burning Bright." Theatre Book of the Year: 1950–1951 (New York: Alfred A. Knopf, 1951), pp. 67–70.

A middle-aged, sterile man longs for a child to perpetuate his name. His wife, who loves him deeply, gratifies his wish by having relations with a younger, fertile man. The husband, believing the child to be his own, is elated until he discovers the truth. After an explosion, he is reconciled with his wife in the philosophy that the end justifies the means.

That is Mr. Steinbeck's plot, as it has been the plot of various playwrights before him, though impotence rather than sterility—as if it made much difference dramatically—has been accounted the reason for the husband's disability. But whereas the others have treated it with more or less simplicity, Steinbeck has elected to invest it with what he evidently imagines is universal import and has so tortured it into an attempt at immense symbolic, religious significance that the result is a play whose extreme pretentiousness rids the story of what power it might have and previously has had in a less strained telling.

In a conversation the author had with me while he was working on the script of the play, he told me not without evident pride that, though he was not too versed in dramaturgy, he was profoundly gifted in the matter of raw human emotions, and that this was to be envied in a day when the theatre has become emotionally trivial. That raw human emotions are one of his better stocks in trade is true, but at least on this occasion the rawness is carried to such a melodramatic extreme that what drips from it is often less human blood than greasepaint. Like other of the novelists and playwrights of the "guts" school, Steinbeck frequently mistakes the intestines for the brain and heart and is so intent upon being "strong" and "virile" that the hair on his literary chest becomes ingrowing, inflames him out of all poise, and enfevers him and his characters to the point where blood-pressure bursts any conviction they might have if they took things a little more easily. Violent emotion is, of course, not in itself a dramatic sin; but emotion that continues at boiling pitch for too long is bound to make an audience's reaction luke-warm.

In the effort to give his plot a sense of universality, Steinbeck has resorted to the superficial device of shifting the scenery from act to act and showing his characters successively as circus people, farmers, and seamen, his idea being that the circus, farm, and sea represent the oldest professions of man and that, by changing his actors' costumes, he can indicate the timelessness and permanence of man's quest of immortality through offspring. Though he has expressed his belief that in this respect he has achieved something completely novel in the theatre and drama, what he has actually achieved is merely an arbitrary trickery visited on the familiar device of showing the same characters in different settings either down the ages (as in *The Skin of Our Teeth, Love Life*, etc.) or over the period of several generations (as in plays by Bennett, Knoblock, *et al.*). The only small difference is that Steinbeck's span of time is nine months.

He has expressed the further belief that he has hit a new note by having his characters speak not in the vernacular of the three locales but in what he terms a universal language that is not within their own limitations. It is strange that he considers this something strikingly original with him, since the same thing has been done by dramatists for centuries. (Eugene O'Neill, for a later day example, managed such expression very successfully in *Mourning Becomes Electra* by basing his characters' speech on a liberal paraphrase of the language in the King James version of the New Testament.) More, Steinbeck's notion of a universal language—or the notion rather of suggesting a universal language—is peculiar, since it consists in little more than causing his characters stiffly to forego such contractions as "don't" and "won't" in favor of "do not" and "will not," and making them speak in what Orville Prescott describes as rigidly stylized and painfully artificial dialogue that sounds—with its "strong in your wife-loss," "friend-right to ask a question," etc.—like something out of *Hiawatha*. The play, in sum, is one that, despite its author's heroic puffings, gruntings and strainings to lend it more weight than it essentially and naturally has, haplessly suggests the vaudeville comedian with padded muscles under his tights who, after prodigious heavings and much wiping off of perspiration, quiveringly succeeds in lifting aloft a papier-mâché dumbbell marked 2,000 pounds. Aiming at universality, what Steinbeck's gassy exhibit has captured elementally of the cosmos is mainly and only its wind.

Should the reader at this point protest that things can not be as wholly bad as all that with a writer of Steinbeck's ability, he will be right. Some of the play's psychology, notably in the cases of the young wife and young lover, is intelligently plumbed; some of the better lines are not without a lyric essence; and one or two of the situations are well handled. But over-all the effect is one of mechanical intensity, of an overblown toy balloon, of a desperate attempt to pound tin into steel.

Parenthetically, it might somewhat have lessened Mr. Steinbeck's indignant and tragic approach to the problem of sterility had his research been a little more up-to-date and had he become privy to the latest reports on the subject from the Wistar Institute of Anatomy and Biology. He would have learned—and duly conveyed his findings to his characters— that irradiation of the pituitary gland has induced fertility in males believed to be sterile and—his husband and wife characters in particular would have been morally relieved to know—that artificial insemination with the husband's sperm, if the count is not too low and hence reproductively insufficient, will often get results when the customary procedure will not.

The acting company, notably Barbara Bel Geddes, who has developed remarkably as an actress, meets fully the script's demands, though Guthrie McClintic's otherwise satisfactory direction has a tendency at times to make the male players so scream and shout that they would scare the life out of Olsen and Johnson.

P.S. Mr. Steinbeck makes much of the claim that never before has sterility figured as a theme in a play or a novel. It has been embarrassingly pointed out to him that not only did Lorca employ the idea in his play, *Yerma*, but that Elinor Glyn, of all people, also used it in her long ago fiction gem, *Three Weeks*.

Checklist of Additional Reviews

Albert Goldberg. "The Sounding Board." Los Angeles *Times*, 10 December 1950, Section 4, p. 5.

THE LOG FROM THE SEA OF CORTEZ

T H E
L O G
FROM THE
SEA OF CORTEZ

The narrative portion of the book, *Sea of Cortez*, by
John Steinbeck and E. F. Ricketts, 1941,
here reissued with a profile
"About Ed Ricketts"

BY

JOHN STEINBECK

NEW YORK

THE VIKING PRESS · 1951

Harry Gilroy.
"Steinbeck's Living Sea."
New York Times Book Review, 100
(16 September 1951), 6.

At a time when readers are interested in authors who go down to the sea, and come up again with good tales, in sails John Steinbeck as scientist-deckhand on a collecting expedition in the Gulf of California. His journal of these activities will be new to many of his usual audience, but this *Log* appeared in 1941 as part of *The Sea of Cortez*, a joint effort of the novelist and Edward F. Ricketts, the biologist of the collecting trip. Then Steinbeck was sandwiched between hundreds of pages of notes about dreadful little marine animals, with the result that only 3,000 customers had the nerve to take the book from the store. Now the biology text has been dropped and Steinbeck has added an entertaining profile of Ricketts.

The best part of this newly unveiled work of the novelist presents sharply evocative descriptions of the sea and the approaches to shore, plus some interesting accounts of the scuttling, flopping, sucking, stabling, poisoning creatures that were taken on the beaches. To go from Monterey Bay to the hot, dangerous, seldom sailed waters of the Gulf, Steinbeck and Ricketts chartered a seventy-six-foot, Diesel-powered fish trawler. They visited numerous old settlements and timeless bays.

Steinbeck makes the reader feel the relief of coming from the rolling seas inside the sheltering capes and jetties. The local authorities troop aboard, all in their rarely worn uniforms and displaying their ceremonious .45 automatics. The little ship's company of seven goes ashore and attends church, feeling how much the service means to the native communicants; goes also to the *cantina* and realizes that the sad, glistening-eyed young men are waiting for an angel with golden wings who will order drinks for everyone at the bar. Another good section of the book is the profile of Ed Ricketts. It develops that the biologist, who died in 1948 in a railroad-crossing accident, was the original Doc of *Cannery Row*.

Writing his log, the novelist is impelled to supply the philosophical discourse that passed between the friends in the late watches of the night. Their conversations must have brought sound sleep to all aboard the trawler. On this evidence, Steinbeck the philosophical essayist will do well to leave the field to the other Steinbeck; the novelist appears to have a far more penetrating insight into nature.

Charles Poore.
"Books of the Times."
New York *Times*,
22 September 1951, p. 15.

. . . When John Steinbeck published *Cannery Row* half a dozen years ago he said that "the people, places and events in this book are, of course, fictions and fabrications." Then he dedicated it to "Ed Ricketts, who knows why, or should"— and opened the story with a fine sketch of the waterfront in the far from fictitious California town of Monterey.

Now, in a fine book that is both new and old, *The Log from the Sea of Cortez*, Mr. Steinbeck discards the disclaimer, as it were, and expands the dedication. For the new part of this volume is a superb memoir of Edward F. Ricketts, and there is no longer any lingering shadow of a doubt that he was the original of the character called Doc in *Cannery Row*. The jumble of immaculate scientific equipment and uproariously disorderly living arrangements that Mr. Ricketts called the Pacific Biological Laboratories (and in which Steinbeck was an enormously absorbed stockholder) is also true, equally, to life and art.

"I used the laboratory and Ed himself in a book called *Cannery Row*," Steinbeck observes in his memoir. "I took it to him in typescript to see whether he would resent it and offered to make any changes he would suggest. He read it through carefully, smiling, and when he had finished he said, 'Let it go through that way. It is written in kindness. Such a thing can't be bad.'"

It was inadvertently bad, though, because it drew coveys of tourists who had read *Cannery Row* to the real Cannery Row, interrupting the pleasures and duties of the day. They would stop their sticker-embellished automobiles and peer through whichever windows in their cars didn't have coats and dresses hanging in them at Ed and his establishment. The bolder ones trooped through the laboratory asking unlearned questions. This was a nuisance. It had some compensations, though. For, as Ed Ricketts said, "Some of the callers were women and some of the women were very nice looking."

Ten years ago, reviewing the original edition of *Sea of Cortez* in this quadrangle, when the book was issued as the joint work of Steinbeck and Ricketts, I noted that this joint personality had a notable gift for writing with vigor, relish and precision on all sorts of things. The book, as many will remember, was an account of their expedition to the lonely, treacherous and amazing Gulf of California—once called the Sea of Cortez—to collect specimens of the marine life there.

Now that Mr. Steinbeck has reissued the log, the narrative part of *Sea of Cortez*, the secret of who wrote what is cleared up. This will no doubt be a relief to collectors of Mr. Steinbeck's excellent works. For the log is still magnificent reading. And the pages upon pages of scientific data that filled out the earlier book, we hope, have long since been incorporated in the main body of technical knowledge about those Pacific waters. . . .

Ed Ricketts, Mr. Steinbeck remembers, "was gentle but capable of ferocity, small and slight but strong as an ox, loyal and yet untrustworthy, generous but gave little and received much. His thinking was as paradoxical as his life. He thought in mystical terms and hated and distrusted mysticism. . . . Ed kept the most careful collecting notes on record, but sometimes he would not open a business letter for weeks."

It may be, John Steinbeck concludes, that there really was no key to the personality of Ed Ricketts. That may be so, as it may be true of anyone or everyone. But few men have had more understanding memorials than *Sea of Cortez*, *The Log from the Sea of Cortez* and *Cannery Row*—in which the revised flyleaf notation might read: *Everything in this book is imaginative, including these words.*

"Briefly Noted."
New Yorker, 27
(6 October 1951), 117–18.

. . . A re-issue of the narrative part of *The Sea of Cortez*, which was the record of an expedition to the Gulf of

California undertaken ten years ago by Steinbeck and his marine-biologist friend Ed Ricketts. The object of the voyage, made in a seventy-six-foot seiner, was to observe, collect, and catalogue examples of the marine life of the Pacific littoral, as well as to have some fun. The book that came out of it was an unconventional and memorable one, very unlike most reports on scientific exploration. The present volume omits the marine biology, and the author has added an informal biographical sketch of Ricketts, who was killed in an automobile-train collision in 1948. Ricketts, according to Steinbeck (who used him as the central character of *Cannery Row*), was an improvident, irreverent, hard-working man who made up his own moral code as he went along, had odd and interesting ideas of what is diverting in life, and was almost an idol to the citizens of Monterey who knew him. His highly flavored personality, as it emerges from the pages of the new preface, greatly enhance[s] the appeal of the book. . . .

W. D. Bedell.
"People and Crabs Not the Same to Steinbeck."
Houston *Post*,
7 October 1951,
Section 4, p. 14.

John Steinbeck's forte is people: Everyday people like Tom Joad and Danny and George; screwballs like Casy the preacher; twisted people like Lennie; earthy angels like Ma Joad.

It matters not that the movies have transformed these people and that to a generation they are identified with such people as Henry Fonda, John Carradine, Lon Chaney and Burgess Meredith.

What matters is that, if they are as true and genuine people as they seem to be, future readers will be able to see them in the mind's eye and get a very sharp picture of what life was like in the United States in the dusty, hungry 30s of the 20th century.

No other writer has put down such a picture. In his people alone, Steinbeck has contributed a warm, human offering to American literature.

When he gets off of people, precise, exact people, Steinbeck is someone else again. His ideology is leftish, but a modicum muddied by doubt of leftishness. His philosophy is appealing but not quite workable. His writing, deprived of pinpoint description and characterization and talk of people, loses much of its force. He sounds as if he were trying to sell something he doesn't exactly believe in.

This trend started in earnest in 1941 (the year the 30s died with a vengeance) with the publication of *Sea of Cortez*. It continued to some extent in *The Moon Is Down*, increased in *The Pearl*, and reached its height in *Burning Bright*. These last three books were not exactly novels or plays. They were mostly preachments. Steinbeck is a good preacher, but only when he subdues his preaching to his people.

The Wayward Bus and *Cannery Row*, both written in the 40s, do not follow this pattern, although they are not so vivid as his earlier stories dedicated primarily to people.

The Log from the Sea of Cortez is a powerful example of the two Steinbecks.

The *Log* is taken from the book published in 1941. It is simply a narrative of the Steinbeck-Ricketts expedition to the Gulf of California in the spring of 1941. The original *Sea of Cortez*, a joint

373

endeavor of Steinbeck and Ricketts, was heavy with scientific data. In the *Log*, Steinbeck has culled out the purely technical portions and left a story of a group of carefree collectors on a strange junket on a fishing boat.

The Trouble with *Sea of Cortez* and the *Log* which was culled from it is that it has no characters. True, it has an engineer who knows Diesels like his own face and a couple of playful crewmen who can't steer a boat and who have a big time in every Mexican town they come to. But, limited to hard fact, Steinbeck is here somehow limited to anecdote, and nobody ever shines through the morass of brittle stars and all kinds of crabs and all kinds of clams and sea cucumbers that were always interrupting the contemplation and the beer drinking of the expeditionary force.

Even Steinbeck and Ricketts themselves stay in the background of the story.

A great deal of philosophy and observation emerges, some of it concise and good, sentences such as:

"It is possible to work hard and fast in a leisurely manner, or to work slowly and clumsily with great nervousness."

"A Mexican town grows out of the ground. You cannot conceive its never having been there."

"Boredom arises not so often from too little to think about, as from too much, and none of it clear nor clean nor simple."

There is also, in one page, the basic legend from which he later wrote his beautiful but not very-popular allegorical book, *The Pearl*.

All in all it is a good, solid travelogue, a little wordy but creditable—it would be creditable, that is, for a travel writer less expressive than Steinbeck.

He seems to have realized this mediocrity, so he makes up for it in the profile of Ed Ricketts. . . .

Steinbeck pictures Ricketts as a biolo-gist negligent of his clothes, his whiskers and his financial affairs, but rich in matters of love, whether man for man or man for woman.

Before you know it you are back in Tortilla Flat and Ed Ricketts is Danny (on a slightly higher intellectual plane, it is true) and the sun is warm and the beer flows and the world is like the world ought to be.

For Ed Ricketts is Steinbeck's ideal man, the man Steinbeck wishes he himself could have been.

He does a wonderful job of putting down on paper this highly individual specimen of the genus People.

M. R. Levitas. "Steinbeck All at Sea." *New Leader*, 52 (31 March 1952), 10.

The ocean has always provoked the imagination of sailors, poets, scientists, and seaside lovers on a moonlit night. Placid and turbulent, its whispering tides have lisped the enticements of mystery.

Recently, we have been treated to two brilliant and successful attempts at providing the layman with some answers to the riddle of the sea—Thor Heyerdahl's *Kon Tiki* and Rachel Carson's *The Sea Around Us*. Now a third volume seeks to join these two in making the sea more meaningful. Unfortunately, however, John Steinbeck's *The Log from the Sea of Cortez* is unworthy of its predecessors.

. . . Though it is intended for both average readers and marine biologists, it is hard to say which the current *Log* will appeal to less.

For the layman, it is an unconscionably dull chronicle of the comings and goings of the *Western Flyer* as it stopped to pick up various specimens on both coasts of the gulf. Mixed in with this record is a sprinkling of meditative thoughts—equally uninspiring—on many subjects. . . .

For the marine biologist, *The Log* offers its conclusions chiefly in generalized terms of what species of animal lived where and in what number. In detailed form, this is probably valuable information, but why in the world did it take the reissue of the "unscientific" portion of a scientific volume to provide it? Presumably, anyone interested in the marine life of the Gulf of California has read the original *Sea of Cortez*.

By far the best part of the book is that which has nothing to do with the Gulf of California—a profile of Ed Ricketts by Steinbeck, who was his devoted friend. Sympathetic and wise, Ricketts seems to have been one of those rare, intelligent people who are alert to all things, but particularly to individuals. Steinbeck here writes vividly and movingly about Ricketts and his place in the lives of the cannery-row characters of Monterey. . . .

Joel W. Hegdpeth.
"*Sea of Cortez* Revisited, or *Cannery Row* Revised."
Pacific Discovery, 6 (January–February 1953), 28–30.

Toward the end of 1941 a well-known novelist by the name of John Steinbeck, and Edward F. Ricketts, a marine biolo-

gist of less renown to the world at large, presented to the somewhat bewildered world of letters a thick book about a collecting trip to the Gulf of California, under the title: *Sea of Cortez*. . . . To the critics who were convinced that something was wrong with Steinbeck as a writer, this "sort of choppino of travel, biology and philosophy" was full of clues and material for essays, and in recent years three such essays have appeared in the *Pacific Spectator* alone.

At least one well known reviewer of nature books somewhat innocently thought that the "colleagues of the learned Mr. Ricketts" would be surprised to learn that he drank great quantities of beer, and "wrote, or concurred in" certain bawdy speculations. He did not, however, miss the fundamental point that the book was the joint effort of two authors, who had a lot of fun putting it together.

That was ten years ago. Steinbeck and Ricketts had such a good time with this enterprise that they planned another—northward, this time—at first, to the Aleutians, then, more realistically, to the Queen Charlottes; and Ricketts began to develop a scheme to interlock his *Between Pacific Tides* with *Sea of Cortez* and the new book, *The Outer Shores*, which was to be in part the result of this northern expedition. He had an elaborate set of cards in two sizes and several colors printed to record all this information, with spaces for cross references to the other books. In the meanwhile, Ed Ricketts had become the Doc of *Cannery Row* and the legend was beginning to grow. Then one day in 1948 Ed forgot about the afternoon train to Pacific Grove and drove his car into its path. It was not a pleasant or an easy way to die, and the manner of it increased our sense of loss. For many of us, the heart has gone out of Cannery Row now, and only the curious passers-by go down to look at the shack that was once the "Pacific Biological Laboratories." Steinbeck was the hardest hit, because Ed was perhaps the only friend who was not in the least awed by his reputation as a writer and treated him first as a human being. When you become a famous writer, it is something like being rich: it is not easy to be sure that your friends are really your friends. He could never have any doubts like that about Ed Ricketts.

It is for the sake of saying what he had to say about his friend that Steinbeck has published this edition of *Sea of Cortez*. It consists of the narrative portion of the original book, up to page 271, with this long preface or "profile." . . .

Usually a preface to a new edition is not given much space by reviewers, but this 67-page "profile" will be approached by critics as further source material for the "Steinbeck problem," while friends of Ed Ricketts will read it to learn how Steinbeck knew him: "As I have said, no one who knew Ed will be satisfied with this account. They will have known innumerable other Eds. I imagine that there were as many Eds as there were friends of Ed." With such a disclaimer, we are left without too much to say about this portrait by Steinbeck, and are invited, in effect, to write our own, if we are not satisfied. In writing about Ed Ricketts, John Steinbeck has attempted one of the hardest writing jobs he has ever set himself to do. In a way, he has succeeded—at least, the history of this interesting friendship, and something of the personality which has had such an influence on one of our major writers has been set down. But as one who knew Ed as a fellow biologist, and didn't care how he managed his private life, I find some curious gaps in this "profile." . . .

The most conspicuous oversight in Steinbeck's profile is the failure to mention that Ed wrote another book—which

began as a collaboration between him and his friend Jack Calvin (who now runs a printing business in Sitka, Alaska), and which is an enduring contribution to the literature of seashore biology: *Between Pacific Tides*. It was probably the publisher's doing that the listing of this title has been removed from this reissue of *Sea of Cortez*; it should be restored in further printings. This little detail and the general tone of Steinbeck's memoir may leave the impression among uninformed readers that the narrative part of *Sea of Cortez* is even more Steinbeck's doing than it was. . . .

To say that Ed was holistic in his thinking is simply to say that he was by temperament a naturalist, devoted to achieving some synthesis of the world about him. As William Morton Wheeler once observed, such people usually become hard-boiled Aristotelians, but Ed was a soft-boiled one, unable to exorcise his inherent mysticism. He lacked the toughness of mind to adhere to an established intellectual discipline, either as a biologist or a philosopher; he lived and thought as he pleased. Those of us who had to knuckle down to conventions and circumstances envied him at times. Yet he was not always as happy in this manner of living as we who envied or admired him might imagine that we could be in similar circumstances. As Steinbeck says, he was looking for something—most often in love, but in music and in the tidepools as well—that he did not find.

On one plane he was the archetype of the Steinbeck hero (out of the clinically detailed pages of a book for men only), on another, a lost soul. Well, we are all lost souls, seeking salvation of some sort or another, but it is characteristic of Steinbeck that he does not come to grips with this aspect of Ed's character—perhaps he will in some future writing, at least by indirection. Although his critics do not use these words, they do agree that the flaw in Steinbeck's writing is his failure to meet this problem of salvation—like Ed, he is contented to take things as he finds them.

Certainly one does not try to reform one's friends, especially after they are dead, and least of all, to censure them for their faults, whether they be those of glandular imbalance or lack of philosophical discipline. It would be unkind, and not quite true, to say that this profile is simply *Cannery Row* in a new key—it is a portrait of a friend, written in kindness and love. I wish I knew how to say things as well, yet enough has been said, indeed, to demonstrate that he was a rare and lovable personality.

As for his eccentricities, they are all true enough—how many times have we been asked if there really was a beer milk shake, I wonder; he was gravely polite to dogs yet a competent embalmer of cats, and in his attire a veritable wedding guest in mufti. His easygoing attire was the cause of an unpleasant little incident in the library of a certain research foundation, but he got his revenge by making critical remarks about the rich man in science in *Sea of Cortez*. Things happen to—and around—people like Ed, and even Steinbeck, with his love for a good story, has hardly scratched the surface of the store of anecdotes.

But it must be said again that Steinbeck has not said enough about one of the most enduring labors of Ed's life, of how for these last ten or twelve years students of marine biology have found, in the book he started to write for his friends out of the background of those years of hours in the tidepools, their introduction to the seashore of the Pacific Coast. Certainly *Between Pacific Tides* proved that Ed was one of [W. C.] Allee's finest students, and the professor may well remember him as a "sometimes disturb-ing, but always stimulating" student, "one of a group of Ishmaelites."

John Coleman. "Marine Creatures." *Spectator* [England], 198 (26 September 1958), 412.

The Sea of Cortez is an old name for the Gulf of California, a long, narrow, treacherous body of water. In the spring of 1940, John Steinbeck, together with a biologist friend, Ed Ricketts, and a hired crew, spent six weeks there collecting marine fauna. The results of this expedition were preserved in an unusual book that appeared the following year, in which Rickett's scientific data and Steinbeck's journal lay cheek by jowl. It is the lively, literary half of this collaboration we are now offered, prefaced by a long profile Steinbeck wrote after his friend's death in 1948.

One has only to sense the affection he inspired to know that Ricketts was no ordinary man. "Nearly everyone who knew him has tried to define him," writes Steinbeck in his memoirs. "Such things were said of him as, 'He was half-Christ and half-goat.'" But this is somewhat disingenuous, since Steinbeck himself perpetrated the remark in his novel *Cannery Row*, where Ricketts appeared as Doc (and the goat, to be exact, as a satyr). Undergoing this obituary profile is accordingly a weird discomfort, rather like watching Mr. Greene turn a film into a novel and, in the event, no more appealing: for the profile is little more than an extended paraphrase of the "fictional" saga of Doc, and the strange outcome is that Doc, without the romantic framework of the novel, Doc, stepping out of that tough, sentimental, bawdy, incorrigible, private world, is suddenly diminished, almost betrayed, as Ricketts. I suppose there is a moral of sorts in all this, something about acts of piety.

There is a sound enough moral to be drawn from the second part of the book, anyway: go to the ant (or sea-cucumber), thou novelist, and be wise. Why is it that English literary men show, for the most part, such strenuous disinterest in the dance of bees and atoms—as if the human comedy were the only one? In his day-to-day musings and descriptions, as the *Western Flyer* went round the Gulf in a series of hops, Steinbeck is at his most tender and, significantly, his most Lawrentian. The aggressively male anecdotes of thirst, copulation and greed are interrupted while the men wade for sand-dollars and sponges. His passionate interest in all created things, "teeming, boisterous life," leads him on and out; and, if at one minute you are being heartily bored by twenty pages on "teleological" thinking, the little essays on laziness and man's boat-shaped mind that bolster the journal are often more rewarding than the best of Aldous Huxley. The book is indexed and, disarmingly enough, such pieces are listed under "Speculations on. . . ."

"Queer Fish."
Times Literary Supplement [London], 10 October 1958, p. 575.

To say of one of Mr. Steinbeck's writings that it is eccentric is to glimpse the obvious, but the adjective is useful here in describing both the form of the book and its displacement from Mr. Steinbeck's customary lonely orbit. It never swings clear of the field of force of Mr. Steinbeck's Monterey. Indeed if it can be said to be about any one thing, it is hauntingly about the "doc" of *Cannery Row*. But in building this memorial to a remarkable man it contrives to examine almost everything that concerns his species and its mysterious world.

In 1940 Mr. Steinbeck sailed in a sardine boat with his friend the biologist Ed Ricketts to collect marine invertebrates from the beaches of the Gulf of California. This expedition was described by the two men in *The Sea of Cortez*, published in 1941. Eight years later Ricketts was killed in a motor accident, and in 1951 Mr. Steinbeck, having written a profile of his friend in a vain attempt to cut the losses of his bereavement, used this as a preface to the narrative portion of *The Sea of Cortez*, which now appears in an English edition.

These men poked about the inter-tidal shores of a dangerous sea not so much to collect rare specimens as to find out, if they could, how the colonies of life in sand, rock and coral lived together. Ecology was their common interest; how does life go on? their consuming question. And not only the life of worms, crabs, starfish and sea-cucumbers, but the lives of the Mexican Indians in the gulf settlements, of the American citizens bordering it in a state of preparation for war, and of themselves and their seamen, breaking and entering a closed system with their alien desires and awkward questions. The invaders argued as tirelessly as they waded and sorted their specimens. Mr. Steinbeck's index shows oddly what they were after. Clams, Crabs, Fishes, Shrimps, Snails have each a fat entry. But Speculation easily surpasses them all, and if one works through its items one gets a pretty comprehensive exposition of the Steinbeck-Ricketts line on what life is really about. Nothing is too familiar to be looked at twice. There is, for example, much more for us in a boat than we might think:

> A man builds the best of himself into a boat—builds many of the unconscious memories of his ancestors. Once, passing the boat department of Macy's in New York, where there are duck-boats and skiffs and little cruisers, one of the authors discovered that as he passed each hull he knocked on it sharply with his knuckles. He wondered why he did it, and as he wondered, he heard a knocking behind him, and another man was rapping the hulls with *his* knuckles, the same tempo—three sharp knocks on each hull. During an hour's observation there no man or boy and few women passed who did not do the same thing. Can this have been an unconscious testing of the hulls? . . .

At the other end of the scale there is a strong attack on the very basis of teleological modes of thought. Progress, we like to think, is by way of explaining more and more of the phenomena that we observe. Nothing is more soothing to civilized man than to be able to say with finality, "This is so because that is so." But to the ecologist *in excelsis* such statements rarely make sense. To him any situation is the centre of a complex array of inter-related forces. To say "It is because it is" need not be the tautology of the unthinking; it may be the most profound phenomenal statement that it is possible to make. And if one stands on this, few of the most comforting explanations of what is happening to the world, and to ourselves in the process, stand unshaken.

On this cruise one of the arguments concerned the proper function of the biologist. How best to get at the life of a fish? You may with luck watch the flashing colours and the fugitive movements of his voracious and predatory freedom; you may produce its simulacrum by putting him in a carefully controlled aquarium; or, having killed and preserved him, you can make a strict count of his anatomy. In this book Mr. Steinbeck is hunting that queer fish Ricketts. He says he will let his profile come as it will, and it comes as vividly, raggedly and inconclusively as the man himself. "Half Christ and half goat" is only a cartoonist's label; some fraction of him should go to Socrates, for he loved to question fragments of reality. As for his other loves, they were lived out among the bums and whores, the cheap bottles and poverty of Cannery Row. He loved music and some literature, besides honesty and truth; those who knew him found they could not do without him; and yet he could be trusted with no other man's woman. In the narrative of the cruise Ricketts is never mentioned; he is the other half, the sleeping partner, of the narrative "we." But he is awake, alive and boisterously kicking, on most of its pages. Having first been instructed in his anatomy, we have him in his freedom, and Mr. Steinbeck's problem is solved:

> One night soon after his death a number of us were drinking beer in the laboratory. We laughed and told stories about Ed, and suddenly one of us said in pain, "We'll have to let him go! We'll have to release him and let him go." And that was true not for Ed but for ourselves. We can't keep him, and still he will not go away.

Why should he? He was, as Mr. Steinbeck might say, an influential man.

E. D. O'Brien.
"From Childhood and the Sea to Saints and Sorcerers."
Illustrated London News, 233 (11 October 1958), 620.

... Excellent, too, in a quite different genre, is Mr. John Steinbeck's *The Log from the Sea of Cortez.* . . . I am among those who can take any amount of John Steinbeck, and although I cannot claim to be very much interested in the marine creatures which he and Ed Ricketts set out to catch in the Gulf of California, for purposes of biological research, I cruised along very happily with this unusual crew. But it is Ed Ricketts who provides the point. The book begins with a long, detached chapter, "About Ed Ricketts," which is of a much finer quality than the account of the cruise itself. "Detached" refers only to the chapter's place in the structure of the book, for if ever a portrait was lovingly painted, it is this one. Someone said of Ed Ricketts that he was "half-Christ and half-goat." He was a biologist, an eccentric, and a great lover of women. "He could receive and understand and be truly glad, not competitively glad." Mr. Steinbeck is a fluent author, but he stumbles and falters slightly with the authentic accents of deep affection and sorrow at an irreparable loss.

Checklist of Additional Reviews

Elizabeth M. Cole. "*The Log from the Sea of Cortez.*" *Library Journal,* 76 (1 October 1951), 1565.
"*The Log from the Sea of Cortez.*" *Booklist,* 48 (15 October 1951), 68.
Bruce W. Hozeski. "*Sea of Cortez.*" *Steinbeck Quarterly,* 6 (Spring 1973), 57–8.

EAST OF EDEN

JOHN STEINBECK

East
of
Eden

1952
THE VIKING PRESS · NEW YORK

W. Max Gordon. "Steinbeck's New Book, *East of Eden*, Tells of 'His People' in Our Valley." Salinas *Californian*, 14 September 1952, p. 4.

There is nothing truly evil except what is within us, and it is man's own decision whether or not he shall rule over sin. This in essence, we think, is the theme of John Steinbeck's new book . . . which goes on sale today here and throughout the nation.

Mr. Steinbeck has taken some 600 pages to chronicle the story of "his people" and that of an imaginary character, Adam Trask. Much of the story is laid in the Salinas valley. Many will recognize the real and imaginary people he weaves into his long story.

Steinbeck is never dull and, even if you miss his message, you'll not be bored. There is only one Steinbeck and no one writes about "his people" as well.

"His people" in this case are members of his own family. His grandfather, Samuel Hamilton, an easy-going and impractical inventor, tried to eke a living from a poor ranch near King City. He wasn't too successful, but he raised a wonderful family and the impact of his goodness and understanding was immeasurable.

"His people" also are the workmen, the ranchers, the ranch hands, the mechanics and even "the girls." He understands them, knows how they think and how they react. . . .

Steinbeck and his publishers say this is his greatest book. Certainly, it is thoroughly Steinbeck, whose characters talk like such characters should and do. It has many fine passages, one of which is the description of the trip with his favorite uncle. We think the public will like it, and, of course it's a "must" for Monterey county people.

Orville Prescott. "Books of the Times." New York *Times*, 19 September 1952, p. 21.

John Steinbeck's best and most ambitious novel since *The Grapes of Wrath* is published today. It is called *East of Eden* and is a quarter of a million words long. Clumsy in structure and defaced by excessive melodramatics and much cheap sensationalism though it is, *East of Eden* is a serious and on the whole successful effort to grapple with a major theme. The theme is a moral one, good and evil and the mixture of both, which give significance to all human striving. In the thirteen years that have passed since the publication of *The Grapes of Wrath* John Steinbeck has given the impression of a writer exploring blind alleys, wasting his great talents on trivial books, groping and fumbling among his own confused opinions about human character and life itself. Now in *East of Eden* he has achieved a considered philosophy and it is a fine and generous one. Men and women are no longer weak and contemptible animals, as they were in *Cannery Row* and *The Wayward Bus*. They are people, strong and weak, wise and stupid, sometimes vicious; but their lives are made meaningful by "the glory of choice." *East of Eden* is Mr. Steinbeck's testimony to free will and the essential nobility of man.

This long, crowded, violent and desperately earnest novel concerns the affairs of two families through several generations. It is laid in the Salinas Valley of California, where Mr. Steinbeck grew up. Most of its important characters are members of the Trask family. Most of its minor characters belong to the Hamilton family, which is Mr. Steinbeck's own. So there is a curious overlapping of fictionalized, personal family memoirs with outright fiction in *East of Eden*.

Few modern novels have been organized according to so intricate a pattern as that of *East of Eden*. It is filled with parallels in situation and contrasts in character carefully arranged in pairs designed to diagram Mr. Steinbeck's ideas. These seem artificially contrived and they do slow down the course of Mr. Steinbeck's narrative.

East of Eden starts with two brothers, Adam and Charles Trask, Adam loved by his father and Charles rejected by him. Adam is a nobly good man, but a stupid one, who idolizes the vicious woman who is his wife. They have two sons; Aron is also good and loved and an idealist, blind to the realities around him. Cal, like his uncle Charles, feels rejected by his father and is a mixture of good and evil.

In contrast to the good but stupid Adam are two good and intelligent men. And these are two of the finest characterizations Mr. Steinbeck has ever achieved. One is of his own grandfather, Samuel Hamilton, a poor rancher stuck with near-desert lands, a blacksmith, a water diviner, a poet and philosopher. Samuel Hamilton is that exceedingly rare thing in literature, an entirely virtuous man who is also a believable, likable and wise one. Equally wise and equally interesting, but not quite so humanly believable, is Lee, Chinese cook and guide, philosopher and friend to the Trask family.

And, in contrast to these good men, is Adam's wife, Cathy, a symbol of absolute evil. Cathy is a baby-faced monster, a sexual degenerate, a murderer and a caricature of malice, duplicity and depravity. Mr. Steinbeck calls her a monster himself in one of the many interludes, in which he addresses his readers in the first person in the manner of some of the eighteenth and nineteenth century novelists. But, since Cathy is a monster, she never seems human.

Her crimes and her vile career as the madame of a brothel seem grossly out of keeping in a novel so seriously concerned with ethics and character as this. Mr. Steinbeck has piled up horrors in revolting fashion. Cathy may win some readers for *East of Eden* who otherwise would never be attracted by it. But she is sure to sicken and to bore many others, those who respect the art of fiction and who care about the same issues of good and evil that Mr. Steinbeck cares about.

East of Eden, it seems to me, is seriously damaged by Cathy's unreal presence and by the disgusting details of her career. It is also somewhat handicapped by its elaborate balancing of symbolical characters and by Mr. Steinbeck's interruptions of his story to deliver little lectures on Western history, the roles of the railroads, the church and the brothel. But it is proof of the rich vitality and tremendous drive of *East of Eden* that it survives such failings and remains an impressive book.

A fine, lusty sense of life is here, a delight in the spectacle of men and women struggling in the age-old ways to meet their separate destinies, and an abundance of good story-telling. Many of the minor characters, particularly the members of the Hamilton family, are lovingly and amusingly portrayed. John Steinbeck has grown in his respect for his fellow human beings, in his understanding of them. He has reached mature and thoughtful conclusions about them. And he has expressed his conclusions in interesting and thought-provoking fashion.

East of Eden is constructed around a central idea that provides the most important of its many parallels, the story of Cain and Abel. What use Mr. Steinbeck makes of that immortal story and what his interpretation of it is will not be revealed here.

Leo Gurko.
"Steinbeck's Later Fiction."
Nation, 175
(20 September 1952),
235–6.

This is the longest and most ambitious of the six novels by Steinbeck since the appearance in 1939 of his masterpiece, *The Grapes of Wrath*. It shares the distinction with the other five of being unsatisfactory in one important aspect or another and raises anew the question of why Steinbeck's talent has declined so rapidly and so far.

The physical dimensions of the book are quantitatively impressive. Two large families, the Trasks and the Hamiltons, supply the cast of characters across three generations. The time span stretches from 1870 to 1918 and covers, in rapid descriptive interludes, most of the big events of American history between the Civil War and the First World War. The scene is the Salinas Valley in northern California, home territory for the author, which he treats with the minutest geographic and meteorological detail. And the text runs to more than six hundred pages.

Yet the results, artistic and imaginative, are meager. The characters divide into symbols of good and evil, keeping us from accepting them as individuals. Sam Hamilton, who came from Ireland to California, is the embodiment of everything good, sensitive, and true. His polarized counterpart is Cathy Trask, introduced at the start as a monster rather than a human being, who burns her parents to death, cuckolds her husband on their wedding day, shoots him later after the New England Trasks have settled in the Salinas Valley, and abandons her newborn twins to become the impresario of the town's leading brothel, where she operates a ring of murder, blackmail, and sexual sadism.

Mixed in with this moral symbolism is some biblical allegory, centering mainly around the Cain-Abel theme. Old Cyrus Trask has two sons, Adam and Charles, who separate neatly into opposing categories. Adam is sensitive and good, Charles is muscular and bad. Naturally Charles tries to murder his brother out of envy and hatred because Adam is his father's favorite—just as Abel's offerings were preferred by God to Cain's. The drama between them is repeated with Adam's two sons, Aron and Caleb. The result of the struggle is that the evil brother is morally and psychologically conquered, and in the process transformed into his counterpart.

Confronted with these simplified abstractions in the genre of the old medieval morality plays, one remembers that the Joads were none too individualized either. But their private lives were merged with the collective lives of the Okies, with the population drift from the Dust Bowl to the land flowing with milk, honey, and orange groves beyond the mountains, and finally with the lives of the uprooted everywhere. This linkage gave

The Grapes of Wrath its terrific intensity. Here the linkage is with rather vague stereotypes about good triumphing over evil, men being distinguished from animals by their moral sense and the eternal existence of free will. No one will dispute the validity of these concepts, but they are only verbalized clichés as they appear in the novel.

Steinbeck is no great shakes as a moral philosopher, and this novel in terms of action and character is committed to its moral philosophy. He is, or was, at his best when moved by indignation, horror, passionate tenderness, and the other violent emotions that animated the naturalist novelists from Zola down. There is in this story very little emotion that affects the author amid the numerous emotionalizing melodramas through which his characters pass.

Furthermore, various elements fail to relate or cohere. The often lovely and always vivid descriptions of the Salinas Valley are not tied in with the lives of the Trasks and the Hamiltons, who might just as well be living in any valley anywhere; the detailed accounts of nature are purely ornamental. So much time, energy, and drama are invested in the Trasks that the Hamiltons as a group struggle vainly for the attention of the reader. And the narrator, Steinbeck himself, a third-generation Hamilton, since he is only an outside observer of the events he deals with, has a superfluous air.

The brothel scenes aside, the novel might well have been written by Edna Ferber or Louis Bromfield. It is big, sprawling, muscle-bound, full of readily digestible characters involved in sentimental situations in which virtue inescapably triumphs over vice. The Steinbeck who was as much the genius of the 30's as Sinclair Lewis was of the 20's, is scarcely in evidence. The vitality, passion, and folk-communion that made *Tortilla Flat*, *Of Mice and Men*, and *The Grapes of Wrath* a permanent part of our literature are painfully absent in *East of Eden*, as they have been in Steinbeck's fiction since the 1930's came to an end.

Harvey Curtis Webster. "Out of the New-born Sun." *Saturday Review*, 35 (20 September 1952), 11–12.

Perhaps *East of Eden* isn't a great novel according to the strict conventions of formal purity so widely accepted today, but it will take almost equal quantities of pride and stupidity to deny that it is one of the best novels of the past ten years and the best book John Steinbeck has written since *The Grapes of Wrath*. Most people will like it and many will buy it. They should, for it is to be doubted if any American novel has better chronicled our last hundred years, our trek from East to West to discover an Eden that always somehow escapes us and that we as a people yet continue to hope for and believe in.

East of Eden is not a compact novel like *Of Mice and Men*, not brilliant sociological fiction like *The Grapes of Wrath* and *In Dubious Battle*, not a temperately ironical tale of the disreputable who are more lovable than the respectable like *Tortilla Flat*. It belongs really in the tradition of the novels Fielding wrote and Thackeray tried to. It jangles, yet is full of vitality; reading it you realize that Steinbeck has never learned or cared to learn the lesson of Henry James, but that doesn't seem to matter as you are carried forward by a narrative flow that encompasses vulgarity, sensibility, hideousness, and beauty.

In another sense, *East of Eden* can be taken as a long parable expertly told. Mostly it centers about Adam Trask, appropriately and Biblically named. He is a fallible, gullible intelligent man who thinks he has found his earthly paradise in the Salinas Valley, is seduced by his Eve, and comes out of the moral wilderness this sends him into to achieve belief in himself and in the world he must learn to live in.

But as its length of six hundred pages suggests, this parable is as full of incidents and people who deviate from the main line of narrative as *Tom Jones*. Some of the episodes, like the compact and highly interesting story of Cyrus Trask who never forgot the Civil War or learned gentleness, seem at first to be largely irrelevant. One feels that Steinbeck spends altogether too much time on the whores Adam's wife ultimately controls, too much loving description on the Salinas Valley, that he overcrowds his canvas with characters. Yet in the end the reader must conclude that there is little real irrelevance and that even the actual irrelevance is so full of vitality that he is glad Steinbeck did not do a sterner job of pruning.

The novel marks a definite advance in Steinbeck's thinking which has been defined by Edmund Wilson as too barely naturalistic. In his earlier novels, men approach the condition of animals with a uniformity that sometimes becomes monotonous. In *East of Eden*, the animality is still there but it is joined to a sense of human dignity and what it may achieve. There is none of the sentimentality about the outcast you find in *Cannery Row*, none of the unconvincing mysticism of *The Wayward Bus*. The main characters are good-and-bad, good, and bad; and one always has a sense that they

are endowed with a freedom of choice that permits them to change their moral category. . . .

. . . These focal characters who bring meaning and focus into what superficially seems a sprawling narrative full of unguided life are Steinbeck's artful instruments in a novel that convincingly demonstrates that he is still one of the most important writers of our time.

Anthony West. "California Moonshine." *New Yorker*, 28 (20 September 1952), 121–2, 125.

Mr. John Steinbeck has placed the telling of his new novel, *East of Eden*, . . . in the hands of a narrator related to many of the characters. There is nothing especially outrageous about this device, but in this case the choice of instrument is unfortunate. When he wishes to inform us that he nearly died of pleural pneumonia, he chooses to say that he "went down and down, until the wing tips of the angels brushed my eyes." When he is not rolling verbal syrup of this kind around his mouth, he is liable to be toying with phrases that resemble metaphors but in which something bordering on a genius for dissociation may be discerned. When Adam Trask, the hero of the novel, is working hard to clear a neglected ranch that he has just bought near Salinas, we are told that "Adam sat like a contented cat on his land." A little later, with work on the homestead going forward nicely, his happiness is increased by the knowledge that he is to become a father, and his manner grows livelier: "Adam fluttered like a bewildered bee confused by too many flowers." A certain exaltation in an expectant father is only right and proper, but since Adam has served two five-year hitches in the United States Cavalry, fought in the Indian Wars, rubbed elbows with I.W.W. stalwarts in hobo jungles, and done a twelve-month stretch on a Tallahassee chain gang, it is permissible to suggest that the delicacy of his condition is overstressed. The narrator's efforts to transform Trask into a marshmallow of a man, all sponginess, purity, and softness, are at war with Mr. Steinbeck's intentions, which are apparently to get a good man in a tough spot that will test his moral fibre.

The pregnant lady responsible for Adam's flutterings is not altogether a credit to her sex. When she is what is known in the garment trade as a subteen, a baroque quality in her romping gets two of her boy friends sent off to reform school. In her first year at high school, she drives her Latin teacher to suicide with her offbeat fancies, and two years later, hitting her stride, she cracks the safe of her father's tannery and commits arson, patricide, and matricide. This sixteen-year-old voluptuary then takes off to slake her appetite for the rarer forms of fun in the New England sporting houses. While advancing her professional career, she encounters a big-time procurer with a circuit embracing thirty-three towns and wins his simple heart. When he finds out what sort of girl he has fallen in love with, his reactions are the uncomplex ones of a deeply passionate man; he takes the lady into a rural section of upstate Connecticut and tries to beat her head in with a rock. The shady back road on which she is left for dead passes by the Trask homestead, and before long she is in bed there, being lovingly nursed by Adam Trask and cordially detested by his half brother Charles.

In no time at all, the lady is married to Adam, but it is clear from the first that the young people are not made for each other. On the wedding night, the new Mrs. Trask gives her husband a Mickey Finn and tiptoes off to Charles' room. Even before Adam moves out West to the ranch near Salinas, his wife is none too keen on the farming game, and sitting around pregnant while her land-hungry husband ambles about the place with water diviners cures her of it for good. She dislikes breeding just as much as she dislikes farming, so as soon as the twins are born and she is on her feet again, she plugs Adam in the shoulder with a Colt .44 and makes for the nearest bordello. She is a career girl and a hard worker, and before long she is in a position to poison the madam and take over. Her peculiar talents give the place an uncommon atmosphere, and it is soon as widely known throughout the Golden West as that Parisian establishment called "the Enigmatic Miss Floggy's" was known in Europe during the thirties. Adam, who has no idea where she is or what she is doing, settles into a sullen grief in which the reader may well share, as all this takes us only to about page 300 and there are another three hundred pages to go. Mr. Steinbeck and his narrator, however, have got Adam to the focal tough spot of the story, and the point of it all is in sight.

Adam is for a long time unable to bring himself even to name the twins, or to pay them any other attention. The task of caring for them falls upon his Chinese cook, who at last insists they must have names—the least a child can expect of its father. A neighbor naturally suggests Cain and Abel, but Adam compromises with Caleb and Aron. In due course, the boys grow up, the family moves off the ranch into Salinas, and Caleb—to the astonishment of no perceptive reader—finds out what Mama is. In a moment of pique at his father's disapproval of his successful gambling on futures in the bean market, he takes his brother to one of the bizarre exhibitions that are a feature of her establishment. In disgust, Aron joins the Army and goes off to get himself killed in the First World War. Caleb, it becomes clear, is indeed Cain, and the book, it becomes clear, is about the riddle presented by Genesis 4:1–8, an extremely bewildering episode.

Mr. Steinbeck sees this story, which is concerned with the primitive religion of a people halfway between a nomadic and a pastoral life, through a haze of modern psychology, which is almost entirely concerned with the world of experience of the urban middle class. Cain was unhappy because his love was rejected; this made him mean, and his meanness made him feel guilty. To break his feeling of guilt, he became murderous, and thus more guilty, and so on. According to Mr. Steinbeck, this is the story of all mankind and the reason man is the only guilty animal. If this were all, the outlook for the human race would be a glum one, and Adam Trask, perversely depressed more by his wife's departure than by the manner of it, is inclined to take the dim view. His Chinese cook, aided by a philosophic neighbor, argues him out of it. The cook, a Bible student, belongs to a highgrade discussion group run by a San Francisco tong. His master's problems have persuaded him to an attentive study of the Cain and Abel story, and he has put it up to the group for clarification. They produce startling new information about the obscure sentence "And unto thee shall be his desire, and thou shalt rule over him." "Thou shalt," it appears, is a mistranslation of "timshel," which really means "thou mayest," and "him" refers to sin. So the last part of the sentence should read, "Thou mayest rule over sin." This calls for a new deal all round with a new

deck. Spiritually armed by this knowledge, Adam goes off to the brothel to face his wife as she really is, a meeting from which he emerges unscathed, and released at last from the feeling that some vileness of his has driven the delicate creature of his illusions away. In his exaltation, he makes the perfect gesture of a mystic in an industrial society and buys himself a new Ford. The liberation is not simply a passing mood, either, and when the final crisis of the book comes, and his son stands before him stained with his war profits of seven and a half cents a pound on beans and his brother's blood, he is morally strong enough to lift the burden of guilt from the boy by murmuring, "*Timshel*."

"The subject," Mr. Steinbeck declares, "is the only one man has ever used as his theme—the existence, the balance, the battle, and the victory in the permanent war between wisdom and ignorance, light and darkness—good and evil." It is true that this has been the single theme of a certain kind of literature. Mr. Steinbeck has written the precise equivalent of those nineteenth-century melodramas in which the villains could always be recognized because they waxed their mustaches and in which the conflict between good and evil operated like a well-run series of professional tennis matches. Experience would suggest that the conflict is in fact quite different and vastly more interesting, for the forces are not in balance and victory is not guaranteed to the side of the angels. Be that as it may, there is nothing more puerile than a discussion of the subject conducted in terms so naïve that evil is identified with sexual aberration. Compared with the evil that sits smiling in the family group or mingles with the guests at a wedding in a neat suit, the evil that hides behind shutters in the red-light district is neither very deadly nor very interesting.

Paul Engle.
"John Steinbeck's Theme Is Struggle of Good and Evil."
Chicago Sunday Tribune Magazine of Books,
21 September 1952, p. 3.

We all live East of Eden, that country where Cain lived after the Lord had set his mark on him. We are all children of Cain, and thus mingled of good and evil, and wherever men and women live is the land eastward from Eden, whether it is a Connecticut valley, where Adam Trask, the main character of this long novel, was born, or whether it is the Salinas valley in California, to which Adam brought his wife and where he died.

Now, Adam Trask is in many ways the original Adam himself, the man of innocence, the man betrayed utterly by a woman, his wife, Cathy, who brought him perpetual sorrow. Cathy is absolute evil, with no interest except her own pleasure and property. She murders.

But this is no novel of a man and a woman. It is a big, roaming story which moves from Connecticut to the Indian west, to a Georgia chain gang, to a California ranch, to a house of prostitution, to death. It runs in time from the years of the Civil war to the first World war.

In human terms, it includes a crowd of people: Adam Trask, his surly brother, Charles, and their pretentious father, Cyrus, who left them fortunes whose origin could never be discovered; the exuberant family of Samuel Hamilton, poor inventor, rancher, philosopher, and his wife, Eliza, tiny, determined, and their many children; the Chinese servant, Lee, profounder than the reader ever quite believes is possible; the children of Adam, mixed and hard Cal and the gentle Aron, who is killed early. And against all, against the world and life itself, the ruthless Cathy, the lifetaker who ends by taking her own.

The theme of the book is the struggle of the good in some men against the evil in others, and the struggle of the good in each man against the evil in himself. In the end, the good triumphs, but only after appalling loss and pain. The grief that pure evil causes shatters lives, but the delight that pure good causes mends them. One feels that Sam Hamilton and Lee are almost too perfect to be living men, but they are very clear characters and very fine.

There is a great deal of solemn talk in the book and this is its weakest part. When an action is being accomplished it moves crisply and firmly, but when Sam and Lee and Adam discuss great matters, their language is stilted and unreal, utterly beyond any state of language which the reader can accept from these men. The writing is feeble at times in its reliance on the obvious; there are too many trite phrases such as "the fruit of his loins," "an idol was crashing in Mary's temple," and Samuel is described as "beautiful as dawn with a fancy like a swallow's flight."

Like its characters, this is a mixed book in which the good and the bad are about evenly divided. A book which is to be admired for the sweep and range of its conception and the variety of its human qualities.

At the end one feels impressed with the solid weight of experience faced and shaped, but depressed by the heavy literariness at times and the too neat manipulation of such incidents as the death of Adam, at which he utters the single word which has been made into a symbol of the entire book, "*Timshel*," meaning that man may prevail over evil.

Mark Schorer.
"A Dark and Violent Steinbeck Novel."
New York Times Book Review, 102 (21 September 1952), 1, 22.

Probably the best of John Steinbeck's novels, *East of Eden*, is long but not "big," and anyone who, deceived by its spread in space and time (c. 1860–1920), says that it is "epical in its sweep," is merely in the usual grip of cliché. Its dramatic center is a narrow story of a social horror that rests quite disarmingly on the proposition that "there are monsters born in the world to human parents." But through the exercise of a really rather remarkable freedom of his rights as a novelist, Mr. Steinbeck weaves in, and more particularly around, this story of prostitution a fantasia of history and of myth that results in a strange and original work of art.

East of Eden is different from any of the earlier Steinbeck novels. It is, in a sense, more amorphous, less intent on singleness of theme and effect. The story of the development of Mr. Steinbeck's own country, the Salinas Valley, it is yet as devoid of the regional emphasis of *Tortilla Flat* and *Cannery Row* as it is of the sociological emphasis of *In Dubious Battle* and *The Grapes of Wrath* or the political emphasis of *The Moon Is Down*. Its central situation is closest in spirit,

perhaps, to *Of Mice and Men*, with that book's interest in the violence of irrationality, but in total treatment and effect there is little similarity between the two.

Mr. Steinbeck's tightly constructed short novels, in fact, and even such longer work as *The Grapes of Wrath*, have given us no preparation for this amplitude of treatment that enables him now to develop, within this single work, not only a number of currents of story, but a number of different modes of tracing them.

The novel opens in the mood of informal history:

"The Salinas Valley is in northern California. It is a long, narrow swale between two ranges of mountains, and the Salinas River winds and twists up the center until it falls at last into Monterey Bay.

"I remember my childhood names for grasses and secret flowers. I remember where a toad may live and what time the birds awaken in the summer—and what trees and seasons smelled like—how people looked and walked and smelled even. The memory of odors is very rich."

In this mood, the novelist reconstructs the history of his maternal grandfather, Samuel Hamilton, who came to the Salinas Valley in about 1870 with his wife, and there produced a brood of children. From the history of Samuel Hamilton, which, although it is a story of economic failure is also a sunny and exhilarating account of a rich and various family life set against the rigorous background of a recalcitrant land, we move into the dark and violent story of Adam Trask.

In about 1900, Trask arrives in Salinas with a strange and very pretty wife. His own home was a Connecticut farm which he could not share with his brother, Charles, the Cain to Adam's Abel, and when he finds the girl, Cathy, beaten nearly to death on his doorstep, he nurses her back to health, marries her, and takes her to the West. Her own history, for all her apparent innocence, already involves the murder of her parents, and prostitution, but this background is almost mild when we follow her career as Adam's wife. She gives birth to twins, Caleb and Aron, another Cain-Abel pair, and abandons them and Adam to become the most infamous brothel keeper in that part of the world. It is her story that seems most to concern the novelist.

These stories in themselves are less interesting than the whole that they compose, and more especially, than the various ways in which the novelist creates that whole. There is, to begin, the speculative voice of Mr. Steinbeck himself, a kind of democratic chorus that broods on implications of the action but is itself, in this role, entirely separate from the action. ("Our species is the only creative species, and it has only one creative instrument, the individual mind and spirit of a man. Nothing was ever created by two men. There are no good collaborations. . . .") Then there is the narrator when he sinks into narrative, involved in his own ancestral history and even, fleetingly, in his boyhood. ("When I, her only son, was 16 I contracted pleural pneumonia, in that day a killing disease. I went down and down, until the wing tips of the angels brushed my eyes.")

Then there is that family history, particularly of Samuel Hamilton, through whom we are taken into the social history of Salinas County. Hamilton, an eloquent Irishman, and his friend, Lee, an eloquent Chinese servant, are the most moving characterizations in the novel, and both are ancillary to the story.

As we come into that story, we observe further varieties of method: the rapid, impersonal narration of which Mr. Steinbeck is a positive master, a method that has not found much room in the contemporary novel with its Jamesian emphasis on the dramatic unit; then the

narrative method constantly erupting into the jagged intensities of the dramatic, or rather, the melodramatic method.

From the story of Samuel Hamilton, we are led into the Cain-Abel story of Adam Trask, the Biblical situation occurring in two successive generations; and here the method moves again into poetic hesitation and indecision, mythic implication rather than dramatic definition or narrative explication. With Adam Trask we move, too, into the core story, the incredible story of his wife, the "monster" Cathy Ames, most vicious female in literature, whose story if we accept it at all, we accept at the level of folklore, the abstract fiction of the Social Threat, of a Witch beyond women.

This account may suggest a kind of eclectic irresolution of view which is, in fact, not at all the quality of the book. I have hoped to suggest, instead, a wide-ranging, imaginative freedom that might save the life of many an American novelist.

There are defects in Mr. Steinbeck's imagination, certainly. He has always been fascinated by depravities that he seems helpless to account for; hence the melodrama. Inversely, he has always accepted certain noble abstractions about human nature that his melodrama is hardly designed to demonstrate; hence the gap between the speculative statement and novelistic presentation; or sentimentalism. These qualities cause familiar discontinuities in *East of Eden*, yet the tone of this book, the bold ease with which the "I" takes over at the outset and appears and disappears and reappears throughout, both holds it together and gives it its originality; the relaxations of its freedom. ("There is so much to tell about the western country in that day that it is hard to know where to start. One thing sets off a hundred others. The problem is to decide which one to tell first.")

I am trying to praise the audaciousness with which this novelist asserts his temperament through his material, and the temperamental means by which he defines that material for us.

Joseph Wood Krutch. "John Steinbeck's Dramatic Tale of Three Generations."
New York Herald Tribune Weekly Book Review, 29 (21 September 1952), 1.

Mr. Steinbeck's new novel is described as his most ambitious effort since *The Grapes of Wrath*. That is inevitable, but it is also entirely inadequate because *East of Eden* is a novel planned on the grandest possible scale. In some of his recent books the author may have seemed to be letting himself off easy, but in this he spares nothing. Here is one of those occasions when a writer has aimed high and then summoned every ounce of energy, talent, seriousness and passion of which he was capable. The most unfriendly critic could hardly fail to grant that *East of Eden* is the best as well as the most ambitious book Mr. Steinbeck could write at this moment.

The scene is mostly the Salinas valley in California; the action mostly events in the lives of three generations of two families. In each generation two brothers in one of the families play the leading roles and in each case there is some sort of Cain-Abel relationship between them. Obviously the action is intended to be significant on three levels. In addition to being the story of certain individuals it is a story supposed to illustrate and typify

certain phases in the cultural development of America. But that is not all or even the most important intention. Besides being individuals first and types second the characters are also something else—they are also symbols.

Here, so we are being told, is not only the story of certain families and the story of a frontier, but also the story of mankind. Mr. Steinbeck is not, either as man or writer, very much like Thomas Mann, but one thinks of *The Magic Mountain* as the most obvious example of another modern novel which operates upon the same three levels. And like Thomas Mann, Mr. Steinbeck employs almost the whole repertory of novelistic devices. Besides highly dramatized scenes there are panoramic descriptions, philosophic dialogues and interpolated disquisitions in which the author, speaking in his own person, discourses ironically upon such subjects as the whore house as a social institution or what goes on when women meet at the village dressmaker's.

Leaving aside for a moment the question of symbolic meaning, the first thing to be said is that the whole ramifying narrative holds the attention to an extraordinary degree throughout the six hundred long pages. Quiet, almost idyllic, passages alternate with scenes of extravagant violence. There are sadistic beatings, a rape, murders and even worse horrors almost too numerous to count. But considered at least as separate self-contained episodes they nearly always come off because Mr. Steinbeck's talents seem to be under that disciplined, self-critical control too often absent in his lesser works, which often degenerated into sentimental melodrama. The violent scenes are, moreover, thrown into high relief by the consequences of the fact that Mr. Steinbeck seems to know when, as narrator, to participate in the hysteria of the scene, when to withdraw into the detached, faintly ironical spectator. Never, I think, not even in *The Grapes of Wrath,* has he exhibited such a grip upon himself and upon his material. If one has sometimes been tempted to dismiss him as merely a routine manipulator of the more obvious tricks of the tough-tender, hardboiled-softboiled school, he cannot be so dismissed here. There is seriousness as well as violence; passion rather than sentimentality. He is also, when the occasion requires, master of a quietly and humorously deft little phrase of description or comment which strikes precisely that note of serenity necessary to highlight the violence. When a wet year came to the Salinas valley "the land would shout with grass." Samuel Hamilton's Irish wife was "a tight hard little woman humorless as a chicken."

What is most likely to disturb a reader, at least during the first third of the book, is the tendency of the characters to turn suddenly at certain moments into obviously symbolic figures as abstract almost as the dramatis personae in a morality play. This awkwardness—and awkward it certainly is—becomes less and less noticeable as the story proceeds. Whether that is because Mr. Steinbeck learns better how to fuse the individual and the symbol or because the reader comes to accept his method I am not quite sure. But in any event it is not because the symbolic intention becomes any less clear or important. In each generation the Abel-Cain relationship is symbolized by a childish gift offered by each brother to the father and always in one case seemingly rejected. And in each generation one of the pair carries a scar on his forehead. Indeed, Mr. Steinbeck states explicitly as one of his theses: "The greatest terror a child can have is that he is not loved, and rejection is the hell he fears. I think every one in the world to a large or small extent has felt rejection. And with

rejection comes anger, and with anger some kind of revenge for rejection, and with the crime, guilt—and there is the story of mankind." Furthermore, the central character in the whole story, a son in the second generation, is named Adam despite the fact that he is also Abel, and his wife (intended perhaps as Lilith) is a figure of pure evil outside the reach of all good human impulses. She was a whore and murderess before she married Adam and she leaves him to become both again.

Mr. Steinbeck does not stop with this attempt to embody a meaningful myth in the chronicle history of a modern family. He goes on to draw a further moral and to pronounce a further thesis. Stated in the barest and most abstract terms this thesis is, first, that Good and Evil are absolute not relative things and, second, that in making a choice between them man is a free agent, not the victim of his heredity, his environment, or of anything else.

This thesis is first announced parenthetically, casually, and without any hint of its importance on page twelve, where it is remarked in passing that the first settlers survived their trials because they were more self-reliant than most people seem to be today, "because they trusted themselves and respected themselves as individuals, because they knew beyond doubt that they were valuable and potentially moral units." Nearly three hundred pages later it receives its most explicit discussion in a dialogue between two of the characters concerning the meaning of a phrase in the Cain-Abel story which refers, apparently, to "sin."

In the King James version the phrase reads "and thou shalt rule over him"; in the American Standard Bible it appears as "Do thou rule over him." But according at least to one of Mr. Steinbeck's characters, the crucial Hebrew word is *timshel* and it means "thou mayest." "'Don't you see?' he cried. 'The American Standard translation *orders* men to triumph over sin, and you can call sin ignorance. The King James translation makes a promise in "thou shalt," meaning that men will surely triumph over sin. But the Hebrew word, the word *timshel*—"Thou mayest"—that gives a choice. It might be the most important word in the world.' " And lest we might possibly fail to see that upon this point the whole meaning of the book is intended to depend, its last sentences are: "Adam looked up with sick weariness.—His whispered word seemed to hang in the air: 'Timshel!' His eyes closed and he slept."

Moral relativism and some sort of deterministic philosophy have commonly seemed to be implied in the writings of that school of hard-boiled realists with which Mr. Steinbeck has sometimes been loosely associated. It is difficult to imagine how any novel could more explicitly reject both than they are rejected in *East of Eden*. The author, who was acclaimed as a social critic in *The Grapes of Wrath* and sometimes abused as a mere writer of sensational melodrama in some subsequent books, plainly announces here that it is as a moralist that he wants to be taken.

The merits of so ambitious and absorbing a book are sure to be widely and hotly debated. The final verdict will not, I think, depend upon the validity of the thesis which is part of a debate almost as old as human thought or upon any possible doubt concerning the vividness of Mr. Steinbeck's storytelling. On the highest level, the question is this: Does the fable really carry the thesis; is the moral implicit in or merely imposed upon the story; has the author recreated a myth or merely moralized a tale? There is no question that Mr. Steinbeck has written an intensely interesting and impressive book.

"It Started in a Garden." *Time*, 60 (22 September 1952), 110.

John Steinbeck, now 50, has run a wobbly literary path for nearly a quarter of a century. Signposts along the way read: charming sentimentality (*Tortilla Flat*), left-wing melodrama (*In Dubious Battle*), maudlin blather (*Of Mice and Men*), tender innocence (*The Red Pony*), honest social indignation (*Grapes of Wrath*), meretricious sex (*The Wayward Bus*). His latest novel, *East of Eden,* comes under none of these labels, although it courts most of them for long stretches.

In 1938, while working on *Grapes of Wrath,* Steinbeck wrote in his journal: "I must one day write a book about my people [family]." He got around to it in 1951. Steinbeck's intention was to write a story that would tell his sons, now aged eight and six, about their forebears and the Salinas Valley in California where they settled. But on the way, fiction ran riot and took over from fact so brazenly that much of the story is hardly fit reading for moppets. . . .

Perhaps Steinbeck should have stuck to his original idea of telling just the family history. As it stands, *East of Eden* is a huge grab bag in which pointlessness and preposterous melodrama pop up as frequently as good storytelling and plausible conduct. Cathy's story, gamy, lurid, and told at tedious length, is all but meaningless. Almost as tiresome is the figure of Lee, the Trasks' trusted Chinese houseman, whose warmed-over Oriental wisdom and too gentle heart give the whole California story an overdose of stickiness.

Ironically, Novelist Steinbeck has done some of his best writing in *East of Eden.* As always, he describes his Salinas Valley with fidelity and charm. Moreover, individual scenes and yarns are frequently turned with great skill. But whether as a novel about pioneers in a new country or just men and women working out their private, earthly fates, *East of Eden* is too blundering and ill-defined to make its story point. That point, says Steinbeck, is "the never-ending contest in ourselves of good and evil." *East of Eden* has over-generous portions of both, but a novelist who knows what he wants channels them, he doesn't spill them.

Robert R. Brunn.
"'You Must Master It.'"
Christian Science Monitor,
25 September 1952, p. 15.

In this rambling and ambitious novel spread out over more than half a century, John Steinbeck wrestles with a moral theme for the first time in his career, certainly a hopeful sign of the times. Yet his obsession with naked animality, brute violence, and the dark wickedness of the human mind remains so overriding that what there is of beauty and understanding is subordinated and almost extinguished.

This is true to such an extent that to read the book can be a punishing experience. His portrayal of Catherine Ames alone, "a monster" in his own words without a spark of humanity or sensibility, is so hopelessly evil as to make her incredible and the book a chamber of horrors. His excursions into the mellow light of normality with their wit and joy and poetry are clouded and often blotted out by

the shadow of the revolting Ames theme.

Yet the book is worth considerable discussion, for Mr. Steinbeck, obviously, is trying to say something which reaches a higher level than the plane of bitter frustration and senseless brutality upon which such books as *Of Mice and Men* and *The Grapes of Wrath* moved. To do this, he has gone back to the story of Cain and Abel, to the ancient problem of good and evil. This dominates the book. Two sets of characters at various times act out the parts of the brothers, and indeed the title of the novel is taken from the passage in Genesis which tells how Cain "dwelt in the land of Nod, on the east of Eden" after being "cursed from the earth."

Late in the book Mr. Steinbeck, in one of many asides, states the belief which is at the bottom of his characterization and is the foundation upon which the book is laid: "Humans are caught—in their lives, in their thoughts, in their hungers and ambitions, in their avarice and cruelty, and in their kindness and generosity, too—in a net of good and evil. I think this is the only story we have and that it occurs on all levels of feeling and intelligence."

Believing this, Mr. Steinbeck takes for his central theme the passage from Genesis in the King James version where Jehovah speaks to Cain of overcoming sin: "If thou doest well, shalt thou not be accepted? and if thou doest not well, sin lieth at the door. And unto thee shall be his desire, and thou shalt rule over him."

His characters are overjoyed at one point to discover a translation of the Hebrew which has this passage read "thou *mayest* rule over him," that is, thou *mayest* overcome evil or sin, not thou *shalt*. To Mr. Steinbeck, believing that man is enmeshed in a web of good and evil this latter translation offers boundless hope—for in it he sees man with a private mind or intelligence, free to choose between a real good and a real evil.

The "thou *mayest*" with its intimation of dignity for the human mind and the reality of evil is transcendent to him. It is the last thing said in the book. Yet the Standard Revised Version of the Bible, to be published this month after more than 20 years of painstaking research and the use of early manuscript never before available gives this translation of the passage: "If you do well, will you not be accepted? And if you do not well, sin is couching at the door; its desire is for you, but you *must* master it."

Now this is not a carping discussion. The implication of the word *must* denies man the choice between good and evil, affirms the King James translation, and implies the inescapable fact of man's perfection as "the image of God" as stated in Genesis. Can this perfect man know sin or have a private mind to know it?

And it is his belief in the gloomy philosophy of good *and* evil and of a human mind apart from God, the divine Mind, that seems to have caught Mr. Steinbeck in the net to which he refers, a mesmeric net from which he has not yet broken free—free of its arguments of violence, bestiality, and compulsive wickedness.

Arthur Mizener. "In the Land of Nod." *New Republic*, 127 (6 October 1952), 22–3.

After I had struggled through to the last of *East of Eden's* 602 pages, I began to think I must be wrong about the earlier Steinbeck, that it couldn't possibly be so good as I remembered it: one of the worst things about a bad book is the way it infects your recollection of the author's good work. So I went back and reread some of the stories in *The Long Valley* and it was a great comfort; they are every bit as good as they seemed originally, maybe better. The animals, the people, the places, the weather are all there (in about that order of importance), realized with a remarkable delicacy and humor. And out of this fully realized material there emerges imperceptibly Steinbeck's feeling for life, a feeling that only the continuity of life itself is sure, and that it is enough. This feeling allows him to face things like suffering and death and especially that part of growing up which consists in recognizing and accepting these things, with an odd but impressive dignity. They are part of the process of life and therefore, however painful, justified and fine. Steinbeck's sense of the process controls his sympathy for the individuals involved and keeps it genuine.

In a story like *The Red Pony*, even the touch of third-rate mysticism about old Gitano's riding Easter off into the strange mountains and the melodramatic and bloody climax when the colt is born are absorbed by the story because Jody's awareness of the life around him is completely convincing. You ascribe the Shangri-la stuff to Jody's boyhood imagination (though Gitano and Easter are unavoidably Steinbeck's) and the bloody violence to the shock of his first experience of birth. No good story is ever written without risks like these; *The Red Pony* is so very good because Steinbeck takes them and on the whole gets away with them.

But I suppose it was possible to see even in these stories how dangerous the limitations of Steinbeck's feelings were and to guess what would happen if he tried to write in the usual way about people and got to dwelling on the foggy visions and flat moralizing which are his substitutes for a response to adult humanness. Edmund Wilson pointed out a long time ago that Steinbeck had a

> tendency . . . to present life in animal terms . . . [and his characters] . . . in spite of Mr. Steinbeck's attempts to make them figure as heroic human symbols . . . do not quite exist seriously for him as people. It is as if human sentiments and speeches had been assigned to a flock of lemmings on their way to throw themselves into the sea.

Well, the best of the characters in *East of Eden* are these talking animals. Not that you believe in characters like Adam's wife, Cathy, for example; there aren't really animals like this. But until the moral turns her into an illustration for a Salvation-Army speech, Cathy is, like the characters in good animal epics, a fine macabre fancy. Most of the characters are not that interesting. They are comic-strip illustrations of Steinbeck's moral, like Adam and Cal, or they are stock figures who act as mouthpieces for the moralizing—a philosophical Chinaman from some novel by Earl Stanley Gardner or a merry-and-sad Irish blacksmith who says things like, "In a bitter night, a mustard night that was last night, a good thought came and the dark was sweetened when the day sat down." (If you don't believe this, it's right there on page 258.) Steinbeck is always catching this old gentleman posed against the sky with "his white hair shining in the starlight"; and his manner keeps spilling over onto the other characters so that they begin to say things like, "In some strange way my eyes have cleared. A weight is off me."

The book's action is always getting lost in a swamp of solemn talk from these philosophers. The Chinaman even reads aloud from Marcus Aurelius and the Irishman from Genesis—the whole Cain and Abel story. It isn't enough that Steinbeck's title is from the passage in Genesis ("And Cain went out from the presence of the Lord, and dwelt in the land of Nod, on the east of Eden"), or that his hero is named Adam, or that Adam's brother tries to kill him and has a scar on his forehead, or that Adam's sons are named Caleb and Aron (Aron likes hunting but Caleb is a gardener). Steinbeck is far more interested in bludgeoning us with his hopped-up commonplaces about abstract evil and abstract good than he is in making us see his people and their lives.

Luckily he cannot fill six hundred pages with Deep Thoughts from the Best Thinkers. *East of Eden* was apparently conceived as an epic about the Salinas Valley and Steinbeck seems to imagine that the basic principle of the epic is "plenty of everything." He doesn't even get the hero to the Valley for over a hundred pages. One of the fortunate results of this catch-all method is that he puts in a number of things which, though they are never effectively related to the action, are entertaining in themselves. There are amusing scenes like Olive Steinbeck's airplane ride and Dessie Hamilton's return to King City; there are a few spare, exciting episodes like Adam's escape from the chain gang or Cathy's murders of her parents and of Faye. Occasionally Steinbeck's old ant-hill-observer's feeling about humans and their institutions asserts itself and we get wryly sympathetic accounts of how difficult it is to run a good whorehouse and how Kate does it. And once in a long while his fine feeling for the animals and plants and weather of the Salinas Valley emerges. Most of the time the characters and events are forced into stagey postures and well-made-play situations by the moral, and sometimes they are forced off the stage altogether while Steinbeck himself lectures us about Life. . . .

There is evidence even in *East of Eden* of what is quite clear from Steinbeck's earlier work, that so long as he sticks to animals and children and to situations he can see to some purpose from the point of view of his almost biological feeling for the continuity of life he can release the considerable talent and sensitivity which are naturally his. As soon as he tries to see adult experience in the usual way and to find the familiar kind of moral in it, the insight and talent cease to work and he writes like the author of any third-rate best-seller. Let us hope that some day he will go back to the Long Valley he really knows and maybe even find Jody Tiflin there.

Riley Hughes.
"*East of Eden*."
Catholic World, 176
(November 1952), 150–1.

There have always been at least two John Steinbecks—one who writes feelingly of old men and young boys and natural beauty; the other, a strident and fatuous theorist, who explores the grotesque. The latter clearly has control in *East of Eden,* a huge mish-mash of a book. In it Mr. Steinbeck embraces, and embarrasses, the cause of free will; his novel sharply demonstrates the baleful consequences of an anti-Thomistic concept of evil. Once again the author is attracted to the story of Cain and Abel as the story of Everyman. In Mr. Steinbeck's handling of the struggle of good and evil the latter rages through his book with the progress of a disease.

Evil in this novel is not the absence of good, but absolute principle and entity. It is embodied in Cathy, the most fully drawn character. Cathy starts her career by murdering her parents and faking her own suicide. A willing whore, she is trapped into marriage, escapes to Salinas to commit another murder—to gain control of a brothel which she makes a hell of sadism and masochism as well as of lust. Meanwhile her husband rears their two boys, not knowing that they are his brother's sons. Cathy dies (in the book's second justified suicide) at the invitation of Alice in Wonderland! ("Eat me," says the poisoned capsule.)

East of Eden is not without its passages of human warmth, particularly those which characterize old Sam Hamilton (Steinbeck's maternal grandfather). But the impact and impress of the book—whatever the author's intention—are on the side of evil, of an exploitation of a mad, inhuman lust and a cruelty that lacerates and degrades.

"New Fiction."
London Times,
26 November 1952,
p. 10.

. . . Mr. Steinbeck's enormous book has to engulf some 40 years of time and stretch from Connecticut to California in order to inflate a series of anecdotes about some very elementary people to the proportions of a novel. . . .

Mr. Steinbeck is . . . ambitious. His characters are in the throes of love all the time, except when devoured by hate. With an attention to detail worthy of Richard Strauss, he has produced a kind of Domestic Cacophony, scored mainly for percussion and wind, yet constantly breaking into piquant and observant detail. He might claim that by an exhibition of sustained vitality he can bludgeon the reader into accepting *East of Eden* in a mood of constant anticipation. But still a doubt must remain. For although the novel of delicate nuance has been grossly overworked in the past 30 years, and although a conscious assumption of high art can be as irritating as too obvious an artlessness, it is hard to justify any novel the apparent purpose of which is to report an imaginary experience without bestowing a real one.

R. D. Charques.
"Fiction."
Spectator [England], 189 (28 November 1952), 744.

Never, I think, a writer who has let imagination get the better of his considerable powers of contrivance, Mr. Steinbeck has yet deserved serious attention here as a representative American novelist. Dos Passos, Hemingway, Faulkner, Steinbeck—for some time now those have been the accepted older names. And no doubt all in this respect is entirely as it should be. Only what in the name of reason and courtesy does one say about *East of Eden*, Mr. Steinbeck's latest novel? I have not the least doubt that it will be hugely, dizzily successful and even in some degree merit success, but at the same time it seems to me a quite shockingly crude, meretricious and trumped-up piece of work....

... There is scarcely a word of this long, fluent and industrious novel in verbal technicolour that I could believe. The story-telling energy is there, I admit, but the dramatic passages seem to me preposterous, the philosophising a tissue of platitude and tinsel rhetoric. In spite of the unmistakably serious purpose of Mr. Steinbeck's conjuration of episodes of his family-history in northern California, almost the only thing to be said in favour of the whole rich and absurd farrago is that one does go on turning the pages in order to find out what happens next....

Paul Bloomfield.
"Books of the Day."
Manchester *Guardian*, 5 December 1952, p. 4.

Judges, whose burdensome but circumscribed business it is to administer the law as laid down, took a long time to become fluttered by the problem of responsibility. As private individuals they have no doubt often, like others of us, been deeply puzzled by the meaning of good and evil. In *East of Eden* ... John Steinbeck writes a story about good people and evil ones. This long book sheds no light. Was Cathy so wicked because she had let herself be seduced as a child? Or had she been so ready to let herself be seduced because of a congenital sensuality? And is it to be understood that congenital sensuality is much the same as evil—"original sin"? But Mr. Steinbeck proves that he knows that austerity can be dangerous too. Some of the most mischievous people in the world are the positively undersexed ones, whose self-esteem needs more than a little love to nourish it.

Mr. Steinbeck, like John O'Hara, has, however, got some bee in his bonnet about the special devilishness of tender, slender, fair girls. If he has, it is a medieval attitude, respectable without being clarified: he can shed no light if he has no light to shed. As drama the book falls very much short of a carefully designed classic like *The Mayor of Casterbridge* (Cathy's husband, Adam Trask, here in a rôle remotely like that of Henchard); as realism it is not to be compared with such a grand book about a bad woman as Balzac's *Cousine Bette*, or the lesser but still superb *Belchamber*, by Howard Sturgis, which one person has read for every hundred or more who will read this. . . .

"Larger than Life."
Times Literary Supplement [London], 5 December 1952, p. 789.

Everything that grows in California is slightly larger than life, and this applies to stories as well as oranges. Under that fecund sky Mr. Evelyn Waugh and Mr. Aldous Huxley gave free rein to their fancy; it is not surprising that Mr. Steinbeck, a native son, fills *East of Eden* with the most extraordinary characters. . . .

Each incident is possible and even plausible in itself, but the continual piling up of eccentric characters and arbitrary disasters eventually surfeits the reader, until if another lovable old philosopher walked up on three legs he would pass unnoticed in the crowd. From time to time there are hints that this is a retelling of the story of Cain and Abel; but one succinct incident from Genesis cannot fill out such a rambling chronicle. Although the total effect is not boring for there are

charming descriptions of scenery and shrewd estimates of personality, Mr. Steinbeck has tried to say too many things at once, and his message is hidden under superfluous decoration.

J. D. Scott.
"New Novels."
New Statesman and Nation [England], 44 (6 December 1952), 698–9.

Like a school of stranded sea-elephants— long, slow and wet—the Great American Novels are also hard to tell apart. How like, for instance, is Mr. Steinbeck's latest offering to Mr. John Dos Passos's recent *Chosen Country*! The recipe is simple; it is to take one or two diverse families in different parts of the country, to put them into the American Melting Pot, and simmer. Mr. Steinbeck has followed this recipe closely. In *East of Eden* the Hamiltons, for instance, give the stew the necessary Irish flavour, while the Trask family perhaps represent the genuine home-bred beef. A less usual flavour is added by the soya sauce of the Chinese philosopher-servant, Lee. This book is not, however, so deliberately "the American Story" as *Chosen Country* was; it purports to be a drama of good and evil, with evil represented by a girl called Cathy, who begins her career by burning down her parents' house with her parents in it, and carries it forward by combining brothel-keeping with further murders. Cathy represents direct evil; hers is a character with the good simply left out. Evil is supported by the rather bumbling kind of falseness of the eldest Trask, who, having played an exceedingly inconspicuous part in the Civil War, creates a legend of his prowess which he comes to believe in, and lives by swindling the veterans' organisation for which he works. Good, however, is represented by the barrelful in Adam Trask, Samuel Hamilton, and Lee, who, if Cathy is a kind of Satan of the Digests, are a kind of Trinity for Rotarians.

Is there any point in saying that this best-sellerish novel has the virtues of its type? Competently told, readable, occasionally forceful, it provides characters who are credible enough so long as one is actually reading about them. As a piece of American commercialism it is not offensive; but with literature it has only the most tenuous and accidental connection.

Checklist of Additional Reviews

"*East of Eden.*" *Booklist*, 48 (15 July 1952), 369.

Eleanor Touhey Smith. "*East of Eden.*" *Library Journal*, 77 (August 1952), 1303.

Paul Pickrel. "Outstanding Novels." *Yale Review*, 42 (September 1952), viii, x.

"Evil in Salinas." *Newsweek*, 40 (2 September 1952), 119.

Lewis Gannett. "Books and Things." New York *Herald Tribune*, 19 September 1952, p. 15.

Patricia McManus. "Steinbeck Uses 300 Pencils on Novel." Los Angeles *Daily News*, 20 September 1952, p. 6.

Don Guzman. "Steinbeck's Latest Held Sure Best Seller, But——." Los Angeles *Times*, 21 September 1952, Part 4, p. 6.

Joseph Henry Jackson. "Books." San Francisco *Chronicle* (*This World* magazine), 21 September 1952, pp. 20, 22.

Sterling North. "Wordy but Good." Columbus [Ohio] *Citizen* (*Citizen* magazine), 21 September 1952, p. 20.

Thomas B. Sherman. "Reading and Writing." St. Louis *Post-Dispatch*, 21 September 1952, p. 4C.

Harrison Smith. "Steinbeck Writes New Masterpiece." Santa Barbara *News-Press*, 21 September 1952, p. C–2.

Irene Alexander. "Steinbeck Writes Long Promised Saga of Salinas Valley." Monterey [Calif.] *Peninsula Herald*, 23 September 1952, p. 4.

Emerson Price. "Steinbeck Writes Pageant about Search for American Eden." Cleveland *Press*, 23 September 1952, p. 12.

George F. Helmer. "The New Steinbeck Novel Is a Great One, to Rank Alongside *The Grapes of Wrath.*" Sacramento *Bee*, 27 September 1952, p. 31.

"*East of Eden.*" *Bookmark*, 12 (October 1952), 10.

Gilbert Highet. "New Books." *Harper's*, 205 (October 1952), 101–5.

William Phillips. "Male-ism and Moralism." *American Mercury*, 75 (October 1952), 93–8.

Charles Rolo. "Cain and Abel." *Atlantic*, 190 (October 1952), 94.

Clyde Beck. "Books of the Day." Detroit *News*, 2 November 1952, "Home and Society" section, p. 19.

Delmore Schwartz. "Long After Eden." *Partisan Review*, 19 (November–December 1952), 701–2.

Robert O. Foote. "Steinbeck's Salinas Story." Pasadena [Calif.] *Star-News*, 21 September 1953, p. 39.

Claude-Edmonde Magny (trans. Louise

Varèse). "Magny on Steinbeck." *Perspectives USA*, 5 (Fall 1953), 146–52.

Harold C. Gardiner. "Novelist to Philosopher?" *In All Conscience: Reflections on Books and Culture* (New York: Hanover House, 1959), 136–8 (reprint of unlocated review).

SWEET THURSDAY

JOHN STEINBECK

Sweet Thursday

1954

THE VIKING PRESS · NEW YORK

Hugh Holman.
"A Narrow-Gauge Dickens."
New Republic, 130
(7 June 1954), 18–20.

John Steinbeck's latest novel, *Sweet Thursday*, is both a sequel to *Cannery Row* and an implicit comment on Steinbeck's career—a career which has been one of the most baffling in recent literary history. He has appeared to be a naturalist of the Biological Determination persuasion and a celebrator of the simple joys of life; the author of effective social propaganda and of mystically symbolic and wryly comic parables. Certainly a fair portion of those who read him as a social critic in the 1930's are not among the still large numbers who read him as a writer of picaresque comedy or of romantic parables.

Among the fifteen volumes of his prose fiction that preceded *Sweet Thursday*, Steinbeck has produced an impressive strike novel (*In Dubious Battle*), a powerfully effective propaganda novel (*The Grapes of Wrath*), three stylized experiments with plays in novel form (*Of Mice and Men*, *The Moon Is Down*, and *Burning Bright*), a volume of distinguished short stories (*The Long Valley*), an "epic" prose poem of too great length (*East of Eden*), and a group of picaresque, comic novels on the delights of poverty and lawlessness (*The Pastures of Heaven*, *Tortilla Flat*, *Cannery Row*, and *The Wayward Bus*).

The ideas which help to shape these books are as diverse as the books themselves. They include a pervasive and informed interest in marine biology, a fund of late transcendental mysticism, a Rousseauistic belief in the innate goodness of man and the inherent evil of social systems, a faith in social progress through better social structures, and an anti-intellectualism so intense that it is most likely to find truth in the mouths of half-wits and the demented.

These ideas, together with remnants of Steinbeck's earlier interests are discernible in *Sweet Thursday*, together with an added concern about writing and an attack on current standards of criticism. The novel is the account of the return of Doc, the marine biologist, to Cannery Row in Monterey after the war, his attempt to deal with his loneliness through scientific experiment and the writing of an article, and the way that Mack and the boys from the Palace Flophouse and the girls from the Bear Flag brothel, through the inspired instrumentality of the half-wit Hazel, bring together Doc and Suzy, a hustler from the Bear Flag. This plot is certainly older than the soil on which it is laid; the basic tone of the novel is the charmingly picaresque folksiness for which *Cannery Row* has prepared us, and the optimism about man's basic nature is consistently that which Doc expresses when he tells an insane but suggestively Christ-like "seer," "I'm surprised they don't lock you up—a reasonable man. It's one of the symptoms of our time to find danger in men like you who don't worry and rush about. Particularly dangerous are men who don't think the world's coming to an end."

These elements entitle us to dismiss *Sweet Thursday* as a minor episode in an erratic career. But the biologist Doc often seems suggestive of his author in his interests, his dilemma, and his statements about life; and the comments on writing are too consistent to be casual; while the tone of half-disparaging banter often seem directed against the author himself. These qualities encourage us to look at the book as one in which Steinbeck has taken a trial balance on his career—implicitly if not explicitly.

Steinbeck apparently cares little for much of our contemporary fiction, and he criticizes it for a quality he was once thought to have—that of blood, darkness, and symbolic evil. Joe Elegant, the cook at Bear Flag, is writing a modern symbolic novel, *The Pi Root of Oedipus*, filled with myth, Freudian symbols, and a grandmother who "stands for guilt . . . the reality below the reality."

Doc is tormented by the question: "What has my life meant so far, and what can it mean in the time left to me?" He is haunted by a sense of debt: "Men seem to be born with a debt they can never pay no matter how hard they try. It piles up ahead of them. Man owes something to man." He declares this to be his objective, a goal which his creator seems to share: "I want to take everything I've seen and thought and learned and reduce them and relate them and refine them until I have something of meaning, something of use." His attempt to do this through scientific writing appears doomed to failure, but the efforts of his friends force him into realizing it through action and human relationship. Yet the answer, when he finally arrives at it, seems to be:

> "What did Bach have that I am hungry for to the point of starvation? Wasn't it gallantry? And isn't gallantry the great art of the soul? Is there any more noble quality in the human than gallantry? . . . Everyone has something. And what has Suzy got? Absolutely nothing in the world but guts. She's taken on an atomic world with a slingshot, and, by God, she's going to win! If she doesn't win there's no point in living any more."

Set briefly against Cannery Row is Prairie Grove, a typical bourgeois community, against which Steinbeck levels two chapters of obvious satire which tend to spoil the tone of the book at the same time that they point up with unconscious irony the extent to which Steinbeck's characters develop bourgeois patterns for their own lives. The whores from the Bear Flag cherish and cultivate the middle class virtues however much they may depart from middle class ideas of morality. Mack and the boys from the Palace Flophouse, in their sense of social structure and social obligation, seem to differ from the unhappy people of Prairie Grove most in that they are warm, loving, and happy; so that these social and economic grotesques serve finally not to condemn the total social structure (as one feels that they were intended to do) but to criticize its failures through the examples they yield of success.

This book, however thin and unconvincing its central situation is, does make an emphatic and clear-cut statement of Steinbeck's greatest single theme: the common bonds of humanity and love which make goodness and happiness possible. The Christ-like seer declares, "There are some things a man can't do alone. I wouldn't think of trying anything so big . . . without love."

W. H. Frohock has pointed out that Steinbeck's characters are all essentially the same good, improvident, and gentle folk, and that they are happy, as in *Cannery Row*, or miserable, as in *The Grapes of Wrath*, depending upon the degree of external pressure exerted upon them. The point is valid. Steinbeck seems to see man as basically noble, with a gentle goodness like that pictured in *Sweet Thursday*. Without the pressure of social indignation he writes of such men in idyls of pastoral happiness. He can, too, portray with fury the distortions of this goodness and the piteous suffering which society can inflict. But he shares with Charles Dickens the failure to subject his people under either situation to an organized and logically consistent philosophy. Louis Cazamian has called Dickens' solution *"une forme vague et sentimentale du socialisme chrétien,"* which was rooted in human love and sympathy on the individual level. Steinbeck's solution may well be called *"socialisme chrétien"* too.

The comparison with Dickens is more than casual. Steinbeck is a modern Dickens, limited in range and theme, a narrow-gauge Dickens, but properly in the tradition of sentimental social criticism of which Dickens is the greatest master. The parallels between the men are interesting. Both are notoriously tender-spirited, sensitive to suffering, easily moved to pity, forgiving of weakness and failure, the fascinated and marvelously successful portrayers of children and child-like states of mind. Both have made sympathetic use of the wisdom of the demented. Hazel in *Sweet Thursday* with his fear of having to be President has striking parallels to Mr. Dick and his King Charles' head. Both writers are keenly sensitive to social and economic injustice, without maintaining any really consistent framework within which to judge it. The failure to recognize or to follow the party-line in Steinbeck's strike novel, *In Dubious Battle*, a failure he justified by saying of men such as his characters, "They don't believe in ideologies ... They do what they can under the circumstances," is comparable to the "plague on all your systems" attitude in Dickens' fictional social tract, *The Chimes*.

Steinbeck shares with Dickens, too, a tendency to picture eccentrics and grotesques, a fascination with the abnormal in people, and a delight in folk speech. *Sweet Thursday* consists almost exclusively of grotesques: Fauna, who left a Mission to become madam of the Bear Flag (her real name was Flora); Joseph and Mary Rivas, a Mexican in the rogue tradition; Mack, who recites snatches from Shakespeare, Tennyson, and the Bible; the "seer," who can't resist candy bars; Hazel, the half-wit who worries because his horoscope says he will be President. Every one of them moves with Dickensian extravagance; everyone is presented with Dickensian verve; not one, I hazard a guess, would Dickens have scorned.

Dickens' two most effective novels for contemporary readers are probably *Bleak House*, with its passionate indictment of social injustice through the imbittered examination of one institution, and *David Copperfield*, wherein goodness and warmth and humanity, particularly among the lowly and the simple, are celebrated. And always the imperishable but unreal glow of transcendent goodness gleams through Dickens' Christmas books. Steinbeck's *The Grapes of Wrath* is comparable to *Bleak House* both in its indictment of society and in its lack of a solution. *Tortilla Flat* and *The Long Valley* echo the nostalgic charm of *David Copperfield*. It is probably coincidence that both men were fascinated by the drama in their middle years, but I believe it is no coincidence that *Cannery Row* and *Sweet Thursday* belong in the same world of bright dreams that Dickens' Christmas books belong in: they are beautiful to contemplate, they are inspiriting, but they are not dependable indices to any actuality we may ever meet.

I think we have been wrong about Steinbeck. We have let his social indignation, his verisimilitude of language, his interest in marine biology lead us to judge him as a naturalist. Judged by the standards of logical consistency which naturalism demands, his best books are weak and his poorer books are hopeless. Steinbeck is more nearly a twentieth century Dickens of California, a social critic with more sentiment than science or system, warm, human, inconsistent, occasionally angry but more often delighted with the joys that life on its lowest levels presents. I think *Sweet Thursday* implicitly asks its readers to take its author on such terms. If these terms are less than we thought we had reason to hope for from *The Grapes of Wrath*, they are still worthy of respect.

Charles Poore. "Books of the Times." New York *Times*, 10 June 1954, p. 29.

Although John Steinbeck is increasingly eminent, he shows no signs whatever of becoming appropriately stuffy. The pomposities of prestige arouse in him a genial hilarity. He apparently allots little time to brooding over where his books will rank in literature. He made his mark, once for all, with *The Grapes of Wrath*, and anything he has had to tell us since then has been bounty. That bounty gives us fine rewards again in *Sweet Thursday*, a rhapsody in blue about the rare and raffish characters who live on Cannery Row. I'm not certain that you could call *Sweet Thursday* a novel. It is awash with plots, excursions and uproars. But, when all is said and done, the most prudent thing to do would be to say that it is a welcome continuation of that earlier Steinbeck saga, *Cannery Row*, with certain elements that link it biologically to *Sea of Cortez* and *The Log from the Sea of Cortez*. At any rate, *Sweet Thursday* is Steinbeck at his best and magnificently entertaining. There hasn't been a better

incitement to summer reading since the decline and fall of the hammock. Such changes as have come to Cannery Row since we were all last there a dozen years ago or more only deepen and enrich its antic folklore and preposterously sentimental mythology.

World War II rescued Cannery Row from the threat of prosperity. In a sustained burst of profitable patriotism the wartime fishermen caught just about all the fish along that part of the improbable California coast. Now no one needs to dabble in the perils of excess profits taxes. They have nothing to take with them from that cabbage patch.

The hero of this libretto for a musical comedy is, once more, Doc, troubled by a failure to concentrate on his marine scientific research and by the love of a prostitute with a heart of gold that Mr. Steinbeck has borrowed from a lit'ry public domain older than Egyptology. The girls at the Bear Flag, the boys of the Palace Flophouse, all the hospitable locality's freaks, fools and men of destiny unite to further that rocky romance. And, in the meantime, they live their own wild lives, in groups and alone.

Mr. Steinbeck's most peculiar character is willowy Joe Elegant, a sort of offshoot of the new collegiate criticism, who is writing a novel to be called *The Pi Root of Oedipus*, rife with myths and symbols, wounds and bows. Then there's Fauna, once a revivalist and now a madam, who likes to recall the days when she managed a welterweight called Kiss of Death Kelly. And a wacky wanderer whose faulty horoscope burdens him with the threat that he is destined implacably to become President of the United States. And a man who mixes a drink (a martini made with chartreuse instead of vermouth) called the Webster F. Street Lay-Away Plan. And a mad millionaire who operates as a sort of cut-rate robber baron. To meet them all you have only to set your calendar to *Sweet Thursday*.

Harold C. Gardiner. "Vulgar Irresponsibilities." *America*, 97 (12 June 1954), 302.

Mr. Steinbeck's wide-eyed discovery in *East of Eden* of the agonies and the glories that come with personal responsibility and the terrible freedom of the human will now seem to have been a mirage. Or perhaps he found that such a discovery laid too heavy a burden on his art—that he could not carry on so smoothly and devil-may-careishly if he had to be facing up to the eternal problem and to the only really valid theme of a serious novel, that life and its temporal and final destiny is shaped by an individual's free acts.

At any rate, Steinbeck is here back with his beloved friends of *Cannery Row*. Anyone, accordingly, who knows the earlier book will know what to expect here. There would be little point in any extended review, were it not for the fact that this new visit to the Row will undoubtedly rocket the book into the best-seller lists. It prompts, therefore, some lengthier remarks on public taste, publishers' tills and the relationship of sentimentally ribald novels to both.

Cannery Row is, in Steinbeck's loving Baedeker, almost, if not quite, the skid-row section of Monterey. It is inhabited by bums, small-time racketeers, ladies of what is politely called "easy virtue," and by one dearly beloved, universally kind-hearted and generous marine-biology "researcher," called Doc, who is the hero of this saga of low life that is at the same time so very warm and generous and human. The heroine of the noble tale is one Suzy, the harlot with the heart of gold, wronged in her youth and now trying with stiff upper lip and stubbornly raised chin to find true love, home and children. . . .

It is only fair to say that anyone who tries this raucous story—provided he can prescind from the foul language and the crude suggestions—will find that it is, in spots, genuinely funny in some of its situations. He may also be lulled into a benign (perhaps "boozy" is the better word) sense of tolerance for the stumble-bums and the failures who do have, it must be admitted, a sort of pathetic and warped dignity.

But no one ought to be hoodwinked into thinking that the sentimentality with which the story is super-saturated springs from anything else than a "philosophy" that believes that environment is what determines character. With the single exception of Suzy, who shows a little self-determination, every one of these characters just can't help himself. He is what he is because the war, poverty-stricken youth, the unfaithful lover or the climate has made him what he is. That the public will eat up this tale probably shows that—if they take Steinbeck as a serious novelist—they think the same way. And that publishers will publish it probably proves that they think that the book trade is just what it is, and there's simply nothing they can do about it.

If you'd like a refreshing contrast, pick up some of Damon Runyon's stories. He wrote about down-and-outers, too, but his style was never billingsgate and if the human dignity of his characters was often forlorn, it was never perverse or perversely defended.

Harvey Curtis Webster. "*Cannery Row Continued.*" *Saturday Review*, 37 (12 June 1954), 11.

John Steinbeck's *Sweet Thursday* evidently is well on its way to becoming a best seller even on its day of publication. It will be widely advertised and reviewed as a continuation of the very popular *Cannery Row*, as another novel about "whores, pimps, and gamblers" who, looked at from another point of view, could be called "saints and angels and martyrs and holy men." Because *Sweet Thursday* is so clearly headed for a "success" very few books have, it's likely to be praised or panned quite as much in terms of the reader's intellectual affiliations as in terms of its merits or demerits. What's certain is that all the brows, from highest to lowest, will have their say about the novel, that the public will become even more aware of *Sweet Thursday*'s existence than they were of *East of Eden*'s.

Like *Cannery Row*, Steinbeck's new novel centers about the activities of Doc, who, you'll remember, was sufficiently at ease with himself to be at ease in the world of Cannery Row. Because of this self-sufficiency he was able to like Fauna, the madam of Bear Flag (the community's best house of prostitution), the girls who worked there, Mack, the amiable cook, Hazel, the mild moron, and a lot of others most readers wouldn't dare to like in real life. But Doc's self-sufficiency has deteriorated since the war. He feels guilty that he's not accomplished more, undertakes a study of the transparent emotions of octopi he hopes will reveal a good deal about human emotions and temporarily loses interest in people who are pleasantly moral. The community, with Fauna and Mack in the lead, manage to get Doc to fall in love with Suzy, a prostitute who doesn't love her work. And so they marry, to live not unhappy ever after, and maybe Doc even completes his study of octopi.

The intelligentsia undoubtedly will ban *Sweet Thursday*. The sentimental assumption that "bad" people really are "good," which invaded all of his best novels except *East of Eden*, pervades this book as it did *Cannery Row* and *The Wayward Bus*. It's another of his bad retakes of *Tortilla Flat*, and maybe the intelligentsia will say, that one wasn't as good as it seemed, either. Doc is a one-dimensional character with no resemblance to any scientist living or dead. All the other characters are as unbelievable as an adolescent's day dreams after he has read Rousseau. In other words, *Sweet Thursday* is simply another concoction of sweetness and sex by an author who has somehow been overpraised.

But there will be intelligent others, who are maybe closer to the truth, who will praise *Sweet Thursday*'s uninhibited gusto and argue that Steinbeck's intentional exaggerations make good reading and good sense. Whores sometimes do become good wives; crooks are often more moral than those who judge them; fellows like Doc represent the perplexity about good and evil that characterizes our anxious age. Anyhow, it's a good yarn, full of good cracks like the one about the crook, Joseph and Mary, who took "a certain pleasure in being partly legal. It gave him the satisfaction most people find in sin."

How strike a balance between these two points of view? As anyone who has followed him from *Cup of Gold* until now knows, Steinbeck is the most uneven excellent writer of our times. Even his worst books are pleasantly readable some of the time; even his best novels are never as thoroughly plausible and illuminating as the best of, say, Faulkner and Hemingway. Sometimes it seems as though Steinbeck can become as great an American writer as we've had in our century (I thought so when I read *East of Eden*); at other times, it appears that he is a gifted writer who can never control his fiction sufficiently to write a first-rate book.

Sweet Thursday makes one feel betwixt and between; it's better than *Cannery Row*, not as good as *Tortilla Flat*, *In Dubious Battle*, *The Grapes of Wrath*, and *East of Eden*. It belongs with his good-and-bad books, like *The Pastures of Heaven* and *Of Mice and Men*. Of course Steinbeck's insight into the civilized and moral behavior one often finds among the disreputable is valid and healthy. Of course Steinbeck is frequently clever, sometimes wise in *Sweet Thursday*. But his latest novel often reads like an unconvincing reiteration of what he's said before and better. All of the characters are flat types, none of them individuals as Danny was, as Tom Joad was, as Adam Trask was. The comedy (and comedy justifies oversimplification but not predictable distortion) depends upon forgetting what you know is going to happen, and there are stretches of pages you can only get through because you know from past experience with Steinbeck that some good scenes will be coming up. . . .

Carlos Baker.
"After Lousy Wednesday."
New York Times Book Review, 103
(13 June 1954), 4.

Sometime we may have a book called *The Two Masks of John Steinbeck*. Using the fashionable critical idiom, it will make the point that for the past twenty-five years Steinbeck has alternately worn the comic and the tragic masks. The latter has perhaps predominated. The corners of the mask-mouth are turned down in books like *The Grapes of Wrath*, *In Dubious Battle*, *The Pearl*, and *East of Eden*. But alongside these, like comic interludes in the vast human drama, come the merry tales of *Tortilla Flat* and *Cannery Row*, farcical *tours de force* on the jovial riffraff of slumside Monterey—those philosophical *paisanos*, golden-hearted females and benignant bums who inhabit Steinbeck's tight little never-never land on the shores of the North Pacific.

Sweet Thursday is probably best described as a sequel to *Cannery Row*. If you liked *Cannery Row* you will certainly like the new novel. . . .

The changes in personnel have been occasioned by the passage of time and the intervention of World War II. *Cannery Row* was pre-war; *Sweet Thursday* is post-war. Gay is gone, killed by ack-ack fallback in a London street. Dora Flood, the Bear Flag's queen, is gone, and the madamship has passed to her older sister Flora, nick-named Fauna. Lee Chong has sold his store to one Joseph and Mary Rivas, and departed in his own trading schooner with a stock of gold-plated collar-buttons, canned goods and rubber boots to the green and palm-strewn islands of the South Seas. As Mack puts it, "the tum-tum changes, giving place to the new. And God tum-tums himself in many ways."

A stranger, though, would find little outward change. The hardworking girls at the Bear Flag still live in tawdry affluence; the nonworking boys in the Palace Flophouse still loll and argue in sybaritic contentment. The big change is inward, and Doc is the first to feel it. He still lives on beer and peanut butter sandwiches, still plays J. S. Bach on his superb phonograph, still journeys to the great tide basin at La Jolla in search of baby octopi. But something is missing. A vacuum develops at the center of his soul. "The worm of discontent," says Steinbeck, is "gnawing at him." Cannery Row, ever sensitive to the incursions of melancholy, becomes uneasy. "Doc acts," says Mack to Fauna, "like a guy that needs a dame."

Enter Suzy. . . . Is Suzy the maidenly answer to Doc's unvoiced prayer? Will Mack and Fauna succeed in marrying off Doc and Suzy? These are the 85-dollar questions asked and answered in a yarn so gaily inconsequential that it might serve as the working script for a musical comedy on the order, say, of *Pal Joey*. Readers who want a hint about the outcome may ponder the fact that Sweet Thursday is the name of the day that follows Lousy Wednesday. Steinbeck's confectional blend of satire and sentiment, of cracker-barrel philosophizing and the comic mystique is probably not to everybody's taste. But for those unregenerate thousands whose intellectual bridgework still permits them to relish salt-water taffy, Monterey style, this sequel to *Cannery Row* can be happily recommended.

Paul Engle. "It's Pure Steinbeck." *Chicago Sunday Tribune Magazine of Books,* 13 June 1954, p. 3.

In his last novel, *East of Eden*, John Steinbeck portrayed as evil a woman as has ever appeared in American fiction. His new novel leaves the area of black night and old sin for the sunnier slopes of his earlier *Tortilla Flat*, to deal with the simple folk of California, motivated by the excellent drives of simple survival and honest feeling for those around them. Just as *East of Eden* suffered from having too much pure evil, hardly compensated for by the too pure rancher, so does this new novel suffer from too much goodness.

The situation revolves around Doc, with his marine laboratory, collecting specimens for selling to colleges, and a crowd of plain people who have an extraordinary softness toward Doc because he has befriended them all.

There are the girls of a certain house called the Bear Flag, and especially one named Suzy. There are the men of the Palace Flophouse, of no apparent occupation. There are the customers of a greasy restaurant called the Golden Poppy. There is a swarthy character named Joseph and Mary. All these are involved by Steinbeck in a touching but at times quite unbelievable story, culminating in the departure of Suzy and Doc together.

The narrative is diverting, often lively, often amusing, occasionally relying too much on a whisky known as Old Tennis Shoes. There is a fantasy about a party at the Palace Flophouse in which a dim witted character called Hazel is persuaded to appear as a Prince Charming, so named in his own words, in as unreal a scene as modern fiction has produced. Other local characters are dressed as a witch, as a dwarf, as Cupid, and it is altogether just too cute and contrived to convince.

This is an interim story in the author's career, written with a heavy effort of lightness, full of fine things about the ocean and warm things about people and forced discoveries of innocence and good will among the humble.

Don Guzman.
"Reviewer Says Steinbeck Slipping."
Los Angeles *Times*, 13 June 1954, Part 4, p. 7.

Dear John Steinbeck:

Your new novel, *Sweet Thursday* . . . is an amusing affair, when it comes off right; and it will of course be a best seller. But is that enough for you? Ever since *The Grapes of Wrath*, you have been taking time out for fun, except where you have done something penny dreadful in a naively serious vein (*Burning Bright* and *East of Eden*), though *The Moon Is Down* was not altogether bad.

You have made readers laugh, upon occasion, in *Cannery Row* and *The Wayward Bus*. But these two novels, and *Sweet Thursday*, dip into the sorghum barrel a little too much; and they labor hard over philosophical interludes between laughter— a philosophy that is sometimes on the verge of being astute but is largely maudlin.

You cannot recapture the satirical-burlesque mood of that little masterpiece *Tortilla Flat*, and you may as well give up trying. Perhaps you cannot go back to the mood of *Grapes* or *To a God Unknown* or *In Dubious Battle*, or even *Of Mice and Men*. Do you need to?

Is there nothing left aside from repeating triumphs of the past? Have you tried looking up from yourself and out into the world, to see whether there isn't something you have missed, notably in a forward direction? Your old readers would like to see such an awakening.

Now you have done a sequel to *Cannery Row*, with Doc and the boys of the Palace Flophouse and the girls of the noble bawdyhouses and a few townsfolk of Monterey and nearby Pacific Grove.

The party to raise money for Doc's microscope and the ludicrous mistake the boys made, the sad figure of Hazel and his weird mental processes, the conversations between Doc and his wealthy but penurious friend, Old Jay; the antics of the boys in their cups—these and a few other matters are going to make a lot of readers laugh. Your old friend, this reviewer, even broke down and cracked a guffaw once in a while.

But his laughter was hushed and spoiled by the interludes of heavy thinking; by the persistence with which you regard a madame or a hustler as one of nature's noblewomen (yes, you did create an evil madame in *East of Eden*, but she was not in your great tradition of the bawdyhouse and she may be discounted as an aberration on your part).

Some of us are getting a little wearied by your obsession with the virtues of sin; we are bored with hazy philosophy and ashamed of too-frequent crying in your beer over your own characters, such as they are.

415

Until you come out of beer fumes and the befuddlement of the phony, many of us will have to drift away from you.

Sincerely, DON GUZMAN.

Milton Rugoff.
"Business as Usual, and Fun, Too, on John Steinbeck's Cannery Row."
New York Herald Tribune Weekly Book Review, 13 June 1954, pp. 1, 11.

As if out of sympathy with the pace and complexity of our time, John Steinbeck returns constantly in his novels to the misfits, outcasts, and primitives—to a simpler, slower civilization. Sometimes he writes of them with great seriousness, as in *The Grapes of Wrath* and *In Dubious Battle*, and at other times whimsically or even farcically, as in *Tortilla Flat, Cannery Row*, and this new novel. He seems almost to alternate between these moods, as though after the tension of tragic or bitter themes he needs the relief of writing about men and women who live carelessly, lustily, more or less spontaneously. For this relief he has created several groups of disreputable but unchastened characters and set them down on the California coast—Mexican Americans in Tortilla Flat and others in a rundown, fishing-wharf area called Cannery Row. He knows these people well and he is thoroughly at home in the vein of low comedy in which he writes of them. But into this ancient and honorable tradition he injects a strain of romance that is perilously close to being cute. Only the up-

bubbling notes of rowdy humor and the occasional broad satiric thrusts save the love story from turning into what might be described as corn.

In *Sweet Thursday* Steinbeck takes us back to Cannery Row, with its Palace Flophouse, a shack shared by several down-and-outers, the Bear Flag, a brothel so wholesome it's prudish, Wide Ida's bar, Lee Chong's grocery (now the property of one Joseph and Mary Rivas), and Doc, a marine biologist and the Prospero of this superbly uninhibited, shamelessly impulsive community. Doc had been a model of the well-adjusted Steinbeck man, dividing his time between Bach and beer, between reluctant cephalopods and willing young ladies. But he has grown depressed, and the inhabitants of Cannery Row, all beneficiaries of his open-handedness, decide to help him. Insofar as this involves collecting money by hook or crook and arranging a party that means well but ends disastrously, the novel is *Cannery Row* all over again, with many an echo of *Tortilla Flat* to boot. The chief innovation is Suzy, a badly bruised but of course not really tainted young hustler who comes to work at the Bear Flag. She and Doc attract each other, although both presumably know better, and *Sweet Thursday* is the record of Cannery Row's efforts to bring them together in, of all things, matrimony.

The spectacle of Doc, wise in the ways of the world no less than of marine life, falling for a saucy trollop would be too pat were it not that Steinbeck so plainly relishes the irony of it. Love, he chortles, is the biggest practical joker of them all. To add to the joke he has the inmates of a flophouse and a bawdyhouse combine to see that love leads to marriage. The fact that they pick a Suzy for Doc is not without its worldly wisdom, but their choice of a masquerade party as a means betrays their irrepressible irresponsibility.

416

Few things seem to give readers and theatergoers more amusement than roughnecks trying to be proper or more satisfaction than seeing them revert to type.

Fortunately the plot in these low-life comedies of Steinbeck's is a good deal less important than the characters and their attitudes—their lack of either ambition or inhibition; their camaraderie; their gusto and capacity for pleasure; their admiration, if not imitation, of the good, the true and the beautiful. If Steinbeck idealizes them outrageously he does so not simply for the sake of humor; he is implying that they are genuinely closer to nature and to those virtues their genteel fellow citizens most admire. Here only the shiftless and no-account seem to have the leisure and the spirit to be good neighbors. Next to them the folks on the more respectable side of the tracks seem dull and furtive; they would, Steinbeck hints, live like Cannery Rowers if only they had the capacity.

Sweet Thursday brims with generous rapscallions, honest whores, good-natured simpletons, a sentimental madam, and an intellectual susceptible to all the fevers of the flesh—nature's noblemen all of them. It is a world conjured out of a wishing-well—the kind that makes very pleasant and amusing reading, particularly for all earnest, hard-working, respected and very frustrated citizens.

They say *Sweet Thursday* is to be made into a musical comedy; it will require very little making; a few songs and dances and it will be ready to take its place as "The Guys and Dolls of Cannery Row."

"Back to the Riffraff." *Time*, 63 (14 June 1954), 120, 122.

John Steinbeck respects the underdog, but he melts uncontrollably before a no-good, boozed-up bum. His sentimental eulogies of riffraff began with his first successful book, *Tortilla Flat* (1935), continued in *Cannery Row* (1945), and appear again in *Sweet Thursday*, which is really a return visit to Cannery Row. It reads like stuff that has been salvaged from the wastebasket. All the characters in *Sweet Thursday* (who live in Monterey, Calif., Steinbeck's home territory) have a lot in common: rotgut whisky in their bellies, leather in their hides, gold in their hearts and bats in their belfries.

In the cast which peoples Steinbeck's skid row are the following weirdies:

- A madam called Fauna who runs the Bear Flag and once masterminded a flourishing South American export trade in shrunken human heads. She keeps a former competitor's noggin in a desk drawer to remind her of the good old days.
- A homosexual cook at the Bear Flag who is writing a novel called *The Pi Root of Oedipus*.
- A middle-aged Ph.D. named Doc, previously characterized in *Cannery Row* by Steinbeck as "half Christ and half satyr," who spends a lot of his non-drinking time stimulating a tankful of octopuses into apoplexy, for research purposes.
- A beachcombing seer who lives on sea lettuce and stolen candy bars.
- A Los Angeles hoodlum named Joseph and Mary Rivas, who graduated from "switch knives, snap guns . . . and, for

the very poor, socks loaded with sand" to ownership of the Lee Chong Grocery, and now keeps busy trying to figure out a way to cheat at chess.

- Hazel, a male deadbeat, who owes his name to a remarkably unobservant mother. He lives with other deadbeats at the Palace Flophouse and is deeply disturbed by his horoscope, which indicates that he is destined to be President of the U.S.

Plot? Yes, there is one, of sorts. Scholarly Doc is in the middle-aged dumps. Hazel, Fauna and the rest of Cannery Row decide that he needs a woman, perhaps even a wife. While guzzling a liquid killer called "Old Tennis Shoes," they pick the girl, a scrappy newcomer at the Bear Flag named Suzy. Suzy is unsure of herself. It seems that she was rejected as a child. . . .

Suzy makes a bachelor girl's flat out of an abandoned 16-ft. boiler and starts slinging ham and eggs at the local hash house. Just when the matchmaking plans appear to be spiked, Cannery Row focuses its cloudy mind long enough to bring the two lovers together by an action as silly as it is surprising.

Sweet Thursday is a turkey with visibly Saroyanesque stuffings. But where Saroyan might have clothed the book's characters and incidents with comic reality, Steinbeck merely comic-strips them of all reality and even of very much interest.

Joseph Henry Jackson. "Bookman's Notebook." San Francisco *Chronicle*, 15 June 1954, p. 21.

In his new *Sweet Thursday* . . . Steinbeck returns to his decade-old setting—Monterey's Cannery Row. It has changed a bit since the war, though not so much as it might. What has not changed is Steinbeck's own pleasure in telling about the economic and social waifs and strays of this special world, the often rowdy humor with which he does this, or the way in which he uses his story to say various things he feels like saying about our contemporary, too-complex, often wildly hypocritical society. . . .

As readers of *Cannery Row* are aware, every time "the boys" try to do anything for Doc the result is catastrophic. That's what comes of it this time, too. The regular tom-wallagaer of a party they throw for him turns completely sour. But out of it good comes—not only for Doc but for Suzy too. And, just incidentally, also good things for Mack and the rest of them in the Palace Flophouse.

As you'd expect, all this is told with extreme adroitness—with, in fact, a technical craft that inescapably suggests the theater. (It's not the first time Steinbeck has written a short novel like a play.)

Indeed, you're likely to feel very much as if you'd had a couple of hours in the theater, during which you've often been highly entertained, often felt the sharp needle of satire, and now and then been given a thought or so to chew on (see Fauna's advice to Suzy), all of this without having been urged to believe too hard in either the people or the events—at least, any more than you'd have to believe in characters or action in any other bit of good theater. *Sweet Thursday* comes out as basically a kind of Christmas-pantomime-in-apparent-reverse, a fable and a fairy-tale in which, encapsulated, are some choice fragments of funny-sad and sad-funny satire.

In the end what? You'll have been marvelously amused, provided you're willing to accept modern frankness to the extent of letting yourself enjoy a tale about types that society calls "no-goods." You'll have been a trifle dizzied by what current jargon knows as "the switch"; i.e., the good people are sometimes so "bad" and "bad" people are, surprisingly, often so good.

And if you let the story take you with it you may even find yourself wondering for a moment or two, until the temporary spell—again, so like that of the theater—wears off, whether your accustomed world or its upside-down reflection in the Steinbeck mirror makes better sense after all.

Robert H. Boyle.
"Boozy Wisdom."
Commonweal, 60
(9 July 1954), 351.

Several years ago, Edmund Wilson, in writing of John Steinbeck, remarked: "... when his curtain goes up, he always puts on a different kind of show." Mr. Wilson couldn't have been more wrong as far as Mr. Steinbeck's latest novel is concerned. *Sweet Thursday* is nothing more than a repeat, albeit post-war, performance of *Cannery Row*.

And it is a pity. Mr. Steinbeck has let his rooters down. Of late, some persons have started to take Mr. Steinbeck and his work so seriously that a number of them felt that his absence from the academic quarterlies was rather poor pool on the part of the critics.

A debatable point. But at any rate, one thing is certain. Mr. Steinbeck has presented both his public and critics alike with a grade-B pot-boiler in *Sweet Thursday*, a sentimental mishmash of a sequel involving the awkward antics of Doc,

Mack, Hazel, and the girls at the Bear Flag. The plot, digressions aside, is simple. Doc is back from the army puttering amongst his rattlesnakes and octopi, all set to rehabilitate himself by writing a scientific paper. But Doc is unable to think of the business at hand. His mind prefers to wander amongst the birds and the bees. Doc is lonely, and there is but one answer in a novel of this sort. Doc needs a woman.

This gives Mr. Steinbeck his chance to play the sugar-coated Maupassant by introducing a tart named Suzy. Needless to say, Suzy reforms and Doc finally wins her. But one really knows this all along. It is only a matter of time and 273 pages. Suzy is too much of a lady to put up with a tart's life, and one knows she never will because, in Mr. Steinbeck's words, "a good hustler is flat-chested."

Cannery Row wasn't one of Mr. Steinbeck's better efforts, but he did manage to write his lyric to the vacant lot with a certain amount of charm. But there wasn't enough to carry over to *Sweet Thursday*.

Brendan Gill.
"Books."
New Yorker, 30
(10 July 1954), 70–2.

In the case of another current self-parody, a novel by John Steinbeck called *Sweet Thursday . . .,* consolation is harder to find [than in Thomas Mann's *Black Swan*]. For here the evidence tends to show that while the author is comparatively young and vigorous, his talent diminishes from book to book. *Sweet Thursday* is intended to be—shouts aloud, in fact, that it *will* be—funny and vulgar and touching, and yet all for kicks; what it proves to be is labored, self-conscious, and drenched with artificial sunlight and good feeling. . . .

Sweet Thursday is a sequel to Steinbeck's *Cannery Row*, and the author himself is one of the boys. He earns this honor first by showing that he can write English two ways, plain and fancy, with and without, and then by showing that he knows all there is to know about people—how, when you get to see them close up, the bums and whores and assorted mavericks (some of them doctors, some of them even writers), why, it turns out that they're the salt of the earth. Maybe yes, maybe no, but in *Sweet Thursday* they're movie salt, and not only salt but sad, because once upon a time it looked as if the man who invented them might end up a major American writer instead of merely a major American writing name. . . .

"A Minor Pleasantry." *Nation*, 179 (10 July 1954), 37.

Sweet Thursday is a minor pleasantry from a major novelist. John Steinbeck has returned to the never-never-land of Cannery Row, and the result is once again unpretentious but relaxing; a cast of intriguing eccentrics bound together by a loose and lazy narrative. . . .

Sweet Thursday, however, is in no way a nostalgic novel. The boys in the Palace Flop House are still free souls; the girls at the Bear Flag House still have hearts of gold; and Doc—the vagabond Ph.D.—is still puttering around with his sea specimens, leading a life that would have turned Athenian philosophers green with envy. If Lee Chong and Gay are lost, Joseph-and-Mary is gained, a double-named genius of immorality and one of Steinbeck's more fascinating creations.

For a time it looks as though the war might have betrayed Cannery Row into thinking about life instead of living it. *Sweet Thursday*, however, is replete with happy ending, as Doc discovers a love for octopuses and a girl named Suzy. The plot is forthrightly sentimental; Steinbeck concentrates on characterization and gentle satire. Even the portrait of Joe Elegant, a pointed burlesque of the moonlight-and-magnolia school of novelists, is not likely to arouse the wrath of any reader. The book was designed to go nicely with a cool highball and a warm sun, and it does.

Riley Hughes. *"Sweet Thursday." Catholic World*, 179 (August 1954), 393–4.

Perhaps the person with the clearest license to make fun of Mr. Steinbeck is Mr. Steinbeck himself. Surely nobody else could hope to parody with such unerring accuracy as can be found in these pages the sentimental absurdities of the Salinas master. *Sweet Thursday* comes close to conscious parody, and not only conscious but deliberate. Most of the inhabitants of Cannery Row are back after the war, engaged in their old occupations: Doc, at the marine lab; Fauna and the girls at the Bear Flag; Wide Ida at the bar; and Mack and all the boys at the Palace Flophouse. Semi-puns, misquotations, and other archnesses abound. Here are two chapter titles: "Tinder Is as Tinder Does," and "Where Alfred the Sacred River Ran." Perhaps Mack expresses the theme of the whole thing when he says: "Vice is a monster of so frightful mien, I'm sure we should all be as happy as kings."

... Mr. Steinbeck's world, it must be admitted, has at times the charm of its absurdity.

Ward Moore. "Cannery Row Revisited: Steinbeck and the Sardine." *Nation*, 179 (16 October 1954), 325–7.

... To both the *paisanos* and the "old" Americans indigenous to the Peninsula, Cannery Row was heaven-sent. Seasonal, irregular cannery work was suited to the temperament engendered by Monterey's climate and tradition. Further, it promoted a dignity on the ancient American go-to-hell basis, unavailable to those in service occupations. If Carmel was a rural Greenwich Village, Cannery Row was a proletarian bohemia.

Inevitably this bohemia had to have its Murger; fortunately or unfortunately— opinions differ among Peninsulans—it turned out to be John Steinbeck. To Steinbeck, who carries to an extreme the Hemingway small-boy nostalgia for the never-never world of comradely masculine society without women save as an occasional convenience, Cannery Row was an ideal microcosm. In it, socially at least, the infantile triumphed; Mother— the realist, the disciplinarian, the stabi-

lizer—was excluded, and Father, if admitted at all, came as a refugee from domesticity. In Cannery Row the locale the small boy as employee justified his restiveness in casual labor; in *Cannery Row* the novel the small boy vindicated his pranks, his misdemeanors, his fear of responsibility in a glorification of perpetual hooky.

How documentary was *Cannery Row*? How faithful to objective reality were the details of the novel; how much license did Steinbeck take in the loosely joined sketches? Since he used an extant geography and characters with readily identifiable models, the legitimate question arises: Did his selection of some material and exclusion of some emphasize the romantic or the "real" aspects of the Row? It is significant that the reader is never taken inside a cannery or introduced to even minor characters directly involved with fish-packing and with wages and work, unions and families. In a proletarian bohemia Steinbeck chose to portray the ultra-bohemian fringe: the bums, whores, and the two professional men—the merchant, Lee Chong, rapacious and benevolent, with a tightly symbiotic relationship to the Row, and Doc, whose presence is socially and economically fortuitous.

Steinbeck's attraction to the bizarre is notable in his depiction of Doc. It is an undeniably legitimate privilege of the novelist to distort his model in order to bring out desired effects; in heightening and foreshortening the original of Doc he was merely exercising this privilege. But "About Ed Ricketts," which is prefaced to *The Log from the Sea of Cortez*, is not fiction, and is therefore subject to restraints not put upon the novelist. Yet in "About Ed Ricketts," Steinbeck departs from objective facts, apparently to sharpen drama. These facts, particularly the manner of Ed Ricketts's death, are on record. To say, as Steinbeck does, "I am sure that many people, seeing this account, will be sure to say, 'Why, that's not true. That's not the way he was at all. He was this way and this.' And the speaker may go on to describe a person this writer did not know at all"—is merely to hedge. The complexity of any man's character is admitted, and no one can write of what is alien to him in another, but this does not excuse, in purported non-fiction, artistic distortions of speech and action, time and circumstance which are proper in fiction. Indeed, a confusion seems to have grown up in the author's mind between Doc of *Cannery Row* and Ed Ricketts on whom Doc was modeled, so that in "About Ed Ricketts" Steinbeck attributes to his friend many of the characteristics and actions which belonged solely to his creation. He could no longer distinguish between the two, not so much because one was based on the other as because the intimacy of creation excluded the intimacy of friendship. The character stood between the author and the man.

This confusion between fact and fancy seems to have been further compounded in *Sweet Thursday*, in which Steinbeck returns to Cannery Row, possibly in dissatisfaction with the justice done to the Ed Ricketts-Doc entity, or as an act of love toward his dead friend. But now the author is no longer drawing from life in order to present his own version of reality, as in the earlier novel. In *Sweet Thursday* he has forgotten that *Cannery Row* was a fiction, an improvement upon and distillation of things seen, just as he has unconsciously forgotten that Ed Ricketts and Doc were not identical, and created by him. He has confused *Cannery Row* with the material which went into it, so that *Sweet Thursday* is drawn, not from life or even his memory of life, but from his own book, second-hand, with a consequent diminution of size and vitality. If *Cannery Row* was farce, *Sweet Thursday* is burlesque; if the first novel was peopled by lovable little men, the sequel is full of leprechauns; if the smell of the sardine was muted in the first, the odor of rendering sugar is overpowering in the second. Cannery Row is no longer softened by a transmuting haze of artistry—it is tidied up and prettified beyond recognition.

Ostensibly *Sweet Thursday* displays the post-war, post-sardine Cannery Row. Doc lives, despite Ed Ricketts's death, but he lives to be the beneficiary of hovering solicitude, the recipient of anxious endowments, from writers' block and a sudden perception of loneliness to the affections of Suzy, a wistful and wholesome whore. Steinbeck ceases to be the poor man's Hemingway and becomes a slightly raffish Faith Baldwin.

The other adult in *Cannery Row* has been whisked from the scene. Lee Chong, Steinbeck relates gravely, has sold out his store and gone to trade with the glamorous Polynesians. In "About Ed Ricketts," Lee Chong is called Wing Chong, in understandable confusion with the name of the store, "Glorious-Prosperous." There was no Chong—neither Lee nor Wing. The founder of Wing Chong was Yee Won; the business was carried on by his son, J. H. Yee, and C. M. Sam, from whom the character Lee Chong was derived. Neither Mr. Yee nor Mr. Sam has departed for the South Seas, though they have dissolved partnership and the "Glorious-Prosperous" store is in the process of what is possibly the slowest and most dignified liquidation in history. It has been selling out, at the moment, for more than nine months, and the end is not in sight. When it finally closes, Cannery Row will no longer have a vestige of communal life; the few who still live there will have to shop in Monterey or New Monterey, like everyone else.

The "Glorious-Prosperous," like the rest of the Row, is the victim of short-sighted greed. The pilchard is going the way of the buffalo and the passenger pigeon. Large catches produced more canneries; more canneries called for larger catches. The number and size of boats and nets grew; the migration stream of the fish was charted; with insatiable zeal the schools were pursued, netted, canned, or reduced to meal—breeding stock, fry, and all. Voices raised for conservation were shouted down; regulation was avoided or evaded. Suddenly and "mysteriously" the sardine disappeared; the searching boats netted handfuls of the survivors instead of thousands of tons. If pursuit of the pitiful remnant were absolutely forbidden, the sardine could come back in time, but this idea is repugnant to those who hold to the "mysterious disappearance" theory and talk of shifting ocean currents and less plentiful plankton for the pilchards to feed on locally, though it must be obvious that the answer to the plaintive query, Where have the sardines gone? is, Into the cans.

Meanwhile the actual Cannery Row enjoys none of the shenanigans of *Sweet Thursday*. Some of the canneries work part time—on anchovies, squid, mackerel, or tuna. One has burned down, leaving a hole in the wall of two-story buildings through which the Bay can be seen from the Row. One has been spruced up to accommodate a moving-and-storage company. Others are talked of as possible homes for light industry—which so far has been reluctant to pay the extra freight costs which are the penalty for not being on the main line. For the most part the canneries are empty, paint-peeling and dusty, with mocking NO ADMITTANCE, APPLY AT OFFICE signs. But the offices are closed, and the obsolete buses

which once took the workers to their jobs stand rusting and flat-tired. A newly decorated "fish and steak house" attempts to lure some of the tourist trade from fishermen's wharf.

People still live on Cannery Row. Two blocks of small apartments and a scattering of weary frame houses shelter a small population. Ed Ricketts's (or Doc's) laboratory, its paint removed by the weather and its windows obscured against the curious, is in use as living quarters, the "B" of "Pacific Biological Laboratories" alone remaining to identify it. Visitors and rubberneck buses detour down the half-mile-long Row. Optimistic business men speak of the return of the sardine, basing their prophecy on a catch of four or five tons in southern waters, trucked swiftly to the canneries, which obligingly open for a few hours to receive them. But the proletarian bohemia is gone.

What does Cannery Row think of John Steinbeck? "Who?" asks one inhabitant. "Wish I had his dough," mutters another.

Anne Duchene. "New Novels." Manchester *Guardian*, 26 October 1954, p. 4.

... And at the bottom of the scale [of feeling and thinking] there is alas, John Steinbeck, nowadays content with counterfeit feeling and thinking. *Sweet Thursday* ... comes off his *Cannery Row* production line. Fauna (real name, Flora), owner of the local "flop-house," wants to marry one of her girls to "Doc," Cannery Row's marine biologist; the joke is about extra-social if not anti-social people behaving with elaborate propriety.

There are chapter-headings like "Whom the Gods Love They Drive Nuts" and "Hooptedoodle (1)" (interpolations to "spin some pretty words, maybe, or sing a little song with language"); the fag-end of a worn-out American convention. It is monstrously sad to see Steinbeck mumbling at it. . . .

Maurice Richardson. "New Novels." *New Statesman and Nation* [England], 48 (6 November 1954), 589–90.

. . . With *Sweet Thursday* Mr. Steinbeck is back in Monterey with his Cannery Row characters. The plot hinges on the wooing of Doc, the shaggy, classless, marine biologist, and Suzy, newest recruit to the local brothel. It is, I suppose, great fun for some, but rather too whimsical and Hollywooden for me, especially when Suzy leaves the brothel and lives in an old boiler.

"Fiction." *Times Literary Supplement* [London], 26 November 1954, p. 753.

Sweet Thursday is a humorous fairy-tale of a specifically American kind. Its people are less characters than specimens of national folklore. The golden-hearted

brothel-keeper, who provides a rest room for her young ladies equipped with a table tennis set, a card table and a parchesi board; a collection of hoboes and eccentrics who live together in the Palace Flophouse and drink immature whisky known as Old Tennis Shoes; a store keeper who cheats as a matter of principle and is genuinely distressed to discover that it is not possible to cheat at chess: these and many others are presented for a reader's amusement rather than his belief. What these people do is less important than what they say and the way they say it. Their language is salty, rich and humorously extravagant. Fauna reproves her girls for gambling in the rest room:

> If a young lady wants to run a few passes with a customer, that's different, but I don't want to find no more pencil marks on the lump sugar. Gambling's a vice. I knew many a good hooker with a future that's throwed it away on games of chance.

The book's plot is like something bred by Damon Runyon out of *Hellzapoppin*. It deals with the efforts of the hoboes to bring about the marriage of Doc, who is dissatisfied with his chosen task of writing a thesis about the habits of octopi, and Suzy, who gives up work with Fauna to go and live in a disused boiler. Suzy paints the curving boiler walls blue and sticks the curtains to the walls with cement. Doc and Suzy are finally brought together through the activities of a hobo whose life has been changed by a horoscope prediction that he will one day be President of the United States. *Sweet Thursday* might have seemed merely silly. Mr. Steinbeck's handling, deft and casual, gives the book very often a quality of inspired idiocy, a genuine harebrained charm.

"Book Reviews."
Dublin Magazine
[Ireland], 30 (January–March 1955), 66.

As a sequel to *Cannery Row*, *Sweet Thursday* is rather disappointing. The Monterey sun still shines down on the old boiler and Palace Flophouse, but the passing years have changed The Row and Mr. Steinbeck with it. The war has intervened, problems are now serious in the laughter-and-tears fashion, and the disreputable characters—now amateur psychologists to a man—have taken on all the charm and quaintness of Workers or Peasants. The result, if it can be imagined, is a sort of *Resurrection* cum *Redemption* novel that combines and nearly parodies both Tolstoy and Francis Stuart. Doc, the marine biologist who held *Cannery Row* loosely together, now returns from the Army full of obscure but rather familiar troubles. He realises in turn that a Man has a Need, that he must learn to Give Himself, and that these are the steps towards Fulfillment. He reaches this happy fulfillment when he rediscovers and applies the great truth that bad hustlers make the good wives. It is much like a film in which we try to forget the plot and the love story in order to enjoy whatever remains.

Checklist of Additional Reviews

"*Sweet Thursday*." *Booklist*, 50 (15 April 1954), 309.

Paul Pickrel. "Outstanding Novels." *Yale Review*, 43 (June 1954), x, xii.

Louise Barron. "*Sweet Thursday*." *Library Journal*, 79 (1 June 1954), 1052.

Lewis Gannett. "Book Review." New York *Herald Tribune*, 10 June 1954, p. 23.

Sterling North. "Steinbeck Back in Cannery Row." Washington *Post and Times-Herald*, 13 June 1954, p. 7B.

"Steinbeck's Philosophers." *Newsweek*, 43 (14 June 1954), 110–11.

Gilbert Highet. "New Books." *Harper's*, 205 (July 1954), 93–6.

Robertson Davies. "For Hammock and Deck Chair." *Saturday Night* [Los Angeles], 69 (24 July 1954), 13–14.

Edward Weeks. "Suzy and the Octopus." *Atlantic*, 194 (August 1954), 82.

Patrick F. Quinn. "Fiction Chronicle." *Hudson Review*, 7 (Autumn 1954), 463.

THE SHORT REIGN OF PIPPIN IV

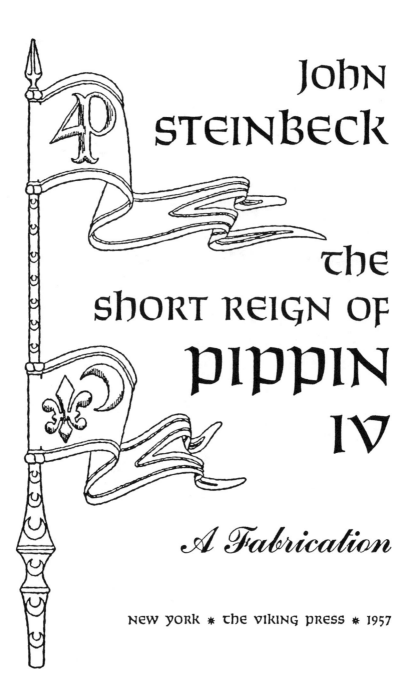

JOHN
STEINBECK

THE
SHORT REIGN OF
PIPPIN
IV

A Fabrication

NEW YORK ✳ THE VIKING PRESS ✳ 1957

Ben Ray Redman. "French Romance." *Saturday Review*, 40 (13 April 1957), 14.

Graham Greene makes a practice of distinguishing between his "novels" and his "entertainments." In a similar way John Steinbeck has set his latest book *The Short Reign of Pippin IV* apart from the bulk of his fiction by dubbing it "A Fabrication." He could have just as well, and perhaps more accurately, have called it a humorous fantasy.

The idea from which *The Short Reign of Pippin IV* springs is one that might have stimulated the playful imagination of Anatole France, one that might have excited Robert Nathan's fancy; and it is tempting to speculate upon what these authors might have done with it. We can be certain, I think, that either of them would have exploited this idea with more inventiveness, and more entertainingly, than has Mr. Steinbeck. He puts very little flesh on the bare bones of his idea; the entertainment that he provides is thin broth indeed; and when we have finished *The Short Reign of Pippin IV* we are left with the impression that it is the sort of thing that Art Buchwald might have written, had he decided to parlay a newspaper column into a short book.

The brief tale begins in the year 19——, when France, as is not unusual, finds itself without a government, and all efforts to form one seemed doomed to failure. "For three days the struggle raged. The leaders slept on the brocade couches of the Grand Ballroom and subsisted on the bread and cheese and Algerian wine furnished by M. le Président. It was a scene of activity and turmoil."

It is a deadlock of the democratic forces that gives the Royalists a chance to propose a restoration of the monarchy; but the Royalists are split among themselves as champions of various blood lines, until an imaginative nobleman provides a common ground for action by proposing that they all "unite under His Gracious Majesty Pippin of Héristal and Arnulf, of the line of Charlemagne." That this famous line is extinct, the nobleman explains, is a misconception. It lives on in Paris today, in the person of "Pippin Arnulf Héristal, a pleasant man, an amateur astronomer," whose uncle, a somewhat shady art dealer, bears the proud name of Charles Martel. Pippin—who has emerged only once before from happy obscurity, as the discover[er] of a comet—is informed of his elevation to the throne, his troubles begin, and Mr. Steinbeck's fragile fable is launched.

How Pippin plays his part of King; how his wife, Marie, "a good manager who knew her province and stayed in it," deals with the housekeeping problems presented by the vast and drafty reaches of Versailles; how his daughter, Clotilde, who at the age of "fifteen wrote a novel entitled *Adieu Ma Vie*," finds happiness with a young American named Tod Johnson, son of the Egg King of Petaluma, California; how Uncle Charlie discreetly carries on his business at the old stand—these are themes that engage Mr. Steinbeck's somewhat pedestrian fancy as his pleasingly written little story makes its way, with few amusing surprises, towards its all too foreseeable end.

"Briefly Noted."
New Yorker, 33
(13 April 1957), 164.

. . . A brief, waggish novel about a pleasant middle-aged Frenchman who is contentedly practicing astronomy in his house in Paris when, to his consternation, he is proclaimed King of France and forced to take up residence in Versailles. The time is now. . . .

Fanny Butcher.
"Slight Sleight-of-Hand by Steinbeck."
Chicago Sunday Tribune Magazine of Books, 14 April 1957, p. 6.

If John Steinbeck's reputation as a great writer (and he is one) had to stand or fall on his latest fabrication (as this tale is labeled) it would topple like the spire of the Old North church in a hurricane.

The author of one of the truly great novels of our day, *The Grapes of Wrath*, of the lusty, funny *Tortilla Flat*, and of the unforgettable *Of Mice and Men* has written in *The Short Reign of Pippin IV* what is meant to be a satire on everything today. It starts with the assurance that in one of the crises of contemporary French politics in 19——, France, in desperation, was returned to a monarchy, with the joyous agreement of all of its warring parties, including the communist, . . . and to the joyous acceptance of all Frenchmen.

Using that internal situation and an equally joyous acceptance of it by other nations of the world, Steinbeck pulls every conceivable satiric rabbit out of the fictional hat. Even skilled legerdemain can pall and, when the rabbits give little hint of being real, tricks for tricks' sake can be boring.

There is a faint thread of story in the book. Pippin, drafted as king, is a simple little man whose greatest joy in life is sitting up all night looking thru a telescope, much to his wife's displeasure. He has a daughter who, still in her teens, has been a motion picture star, has written a best selling novel, and who has captured an American prince, son of the egg king of Petaluma, Cal.

The trouble with this satire—in contrast to the great permanent satires of literature—is that, although the idea is really funny, and some of the contrived situations have hilarious possibilities, the book demands that the reader know thoroughly what is being made fun of if he is to give a whoop—or a hoot.

The publisher of *The Short Reign of Pippin IV* suggests that it "might find a place . . . as a minor classic." In this reader's opinion one of those last two words is superfluous, and that word isn't *minor*.

Elizabeth Janeway.
"A Star-gazing King."
New York Times Book Review, 106 (14 April 1957), 6, 18.

This "fabrication" by John Steinbeck is a froth of a book which must have been great fun to write. In addition, it is one of the purest expressions of true, simple, American affection for the French that has ever been written—compounded with our equally simple conviction that they are also, after all, a funny race. . . .

Reluctantly, Mr. Héristal, now suddenly Pippin the Fourth, is quite as aware as Hamlet that the times are out of joint, but for fifty-four years he has had no inkling that he was born to set them right. Here the moral of Mr. Steinbeck's fabrication—and he is a highly moral writer—begins to show through the joke. For Pippin is both *l'homme moyen sensuel*, and the ordinary citizen, who is suddenly confronted with responsibility. What is he to do? Lend himself to the shabby face-saving that has set him up as a figurehead, or try to be what a king should be? "The purpose of a king," he says, "is to rule, and the purpose of rule is to increase the well-being of the kingdom."

This, however, is not poor Pippin's only dilemma. Does he want to rule? Should he? "A king without power is a contradiction in terms," Mr. Steinbeck has him say, "and a king with power is an abomination." Pippin is thus confronted not only with the practical problem, on the material level, of whether he *can* be king. He is also involved in the moral problem of whether it is right for him to try to be king.

I'm afraid it's too much weight for the book to carry. Pippin's allies, with whom he discusses the alternatives he faces, come from the borders of the realm of farce. Among them are a young American from Petaluma, Calif., the son of the Egg King. This Tod Johnson, the Egg Prince, is an aspirant for the hand of Clotilde, now a princess herself. He talks unfortunate American slang and mixes martinis, and any casting director would try to get Russell Nype to play him. Another of Pippin's cronies is Sister Hyacinthe, who left the world for the cloister after twenty years with the Folies Bergère, a profession which gave her fallen arches and a wide knowledge of men. Another less trustworthy member of the circle is Pippin's uncle, Charles Martel, a seedy art dealer who specializes in selling paintings he won't guarantee.

The last two, at any rate, are amusing conceptions, but if we are to accept them at all, it can only be as figures of farce. When we whizz by them at ninety miles an hour, they are very funny indeed: I was entranced by Uncle Charles' explanation of that seemingly pointless crime, the theft of the Mona Lisa. But when we sit down to discuss moral dilemmas with them, this soufflé of a book threatens to collapse into a sodden crust.

To insist on taking Mr. Steinbeck's fun too seriously is to be a spoilsport. Let us pass over in silence, as Cicero liked so inaccurately to say, that Puritan structure of morality which our author can never quite ignore, and enjoy the fabrication he has draped about it. It is safe to predict, I am certain, that of next summer's crop of outward-bound American tourists, at least two-thirds will have with them a copy of *The Short Reign of Pippin IV* (a dual Book-of-the-Month choice for May); and of these, a good 95 per cent will find themselves laughing happily as they travel with Pippin on the royal motorscooter, or attempt to keep up with Uncle Charles' business arrangements.

Dick Wickenden. "Steinbeck's Extravaganza." *New York Herald Tribune Weekly Book Review*, 14 April 1957, p. 1.

A few years from now, things in France will come to such a pass that the twelve squabbling political parties of that splendid but sorely troubled nation will be reduced to restoring the monarchy. The man destined to be crowned Pippin IV, in a rather confused ceremony at Rheims, is a charming gentleman in his early fifties, M. Pippin Arnulf Héristal....

Such, at any rate, is the glimpse of the future provided by this small and amusing book. The author's name is Steinbeck and his effervescent "fabrication" is an April choice of the Book-of-the-Month Club. Although new to the field of amiably satirical extravaganza he seems happily at home in it. He maintains a firm control over material that might easily have got out of hand; his inventions are never outrageous or his humorous flourishes arch, and his style is cleverly contrived so as to sound, for the most part, like an adroit translation from the French. The climax, though it might have been more incisive and tumultuous, is altogether appropriate.

The Short Reign of Pippin IV probably arises out of a deep if sometimes exasperated affection for France and the French and for the foolish race of man in general. It was clearly a great deal of fun to write, and many thousands of readers, infected by John Steinbeck's high spirits, are going to have at least as much fun reading it.

William DuBois. "Books of the Times." *New York Times*, 15 April 1957, p. 27.

The problem of getting two or more Frenchmen to agree may soon be abandoned as insoluble by most sensible analysts, including Frenchmen. In *The Short Reign of Pippin IV* John Steinbeck, of all people, comes up with a suggestion that Francophiles, to say nothing of wellwishers of the human race, are advised to approach with caution. France, suggests Mr. Steinbeck, could achieve all her former glories (at least for a year or so) if two bold steps were taken. Step one, restore the monarchy—strictly at *roifainéant* level. Step two, let nature take its course. It should be noted immediately that the author has labeled his book "a fabrication" rather than a novel. Written with a deceptive, off-the-cuff zing, and lacking the savage posturings that distinguished his full-dress, Bunyanesque comedies, it will seem a total departure to many Steinbeck readers.

The fun (and we found it a very funny book indeed) is self-generating, oddly exotic. Had the book come to us as a translation, with any of a half-dozen current Parisian labels, it could have been accepted as such without demur. It is only when one puts it aside that the special Steinbeck impact comes through cleanly.

Things start with a bang in this day-after-tomorrow France when the Cabinet finds itself in a crisis to end all crises. After a series of backhanded miracles too complex to be detailed here, the Royalist party blunders into pro tem power. When a member, more in jest than hope, suggests that only a King can serve as a rallying point, it is no accident that not even the Royalists can agree on a possible candidate. Finally, after a deadlock among the Capetians, the Bourbons and the myriad heirs of Bonaparte, the Merovingians sweep the field. Within a few hours they have discovered a descendant of the eighth-century do-nothing, Pippin III—and the fabrication is in high gear . . . .

Fortunately for France, the reign of Pippin IV is too short to bring destruction. How the King grows weary of a do-nothing status, how he eludes the royal guards at Versailles for incognito tours of his realm on a motor-scooter, how he is howled down by his own Deputies after a shy attempt to develop a program for national betterment that would substitute deeds for words—this is the subject-matter of Mr. Steinbeck's final chapters, and the reviewer has no intention of revealing the *modus operandi*. It seems proper to add that M. Héristal returns quietly to his astronomy—and that France lapses once again, wearily but contentedly, into near-chaos.

Early commentators have already objected that this book is slam-bang farce and nothing more, that Mr. Steinbeck has only belabored an obvious victim with his slapstick. The present reader took it at a sitting, and genuinely enjoyed its surface humors. It was only when the meanings-within-meanings began cropping up that he found himself glancing over one shoulder, as uneasily as Pippin's subjects. Clearly Mr. Steinbeck is reminding us that happiness must be earned. Is it barely possible that he has aimed his moral at Washington, no less than at the Quai d'Orsay?

"If I Were King."
Time, 69 (15 April 1957), 126.

At long last, France decided that the French Revolution had all been a big mistake (some readers will say "I told you so"). Caught in a parliamentary impasse to end all parliamentary impasses, the National Assembly decided to abolish the republic and restore the monarchy. *Hourra! Vive le roi!*

This is the central situation of John Steinbeck's latest booklet—an underdone novel and overdone gag which is a long, long way from wrathful Okies and *Tortilla Flat*. . . .

Though *The Short Reign of Pippin IV* (a May co-selection of the Book-of-the-Month Club) is a fable that makes no claims for itself beyond the desire to please, its author waters Aesop with Alsop, mixes persiflage with prescriptions for the ills of modern France. The satiric lapses into the pontifical ("The French are a moral people—judged, that is, by American country-club standards"). Pippin makes a charming king-for-a-day, but the joke goes on for so long that those who come to laugh may stay to yawn. *Hélas*, political reality in France is so preposterous that even better satirists than Steinbeck have a hard time topping it.

David Rey.
"Many Keys to Steinbeck."
Nation, 184
(29 April 1957), 346–7.

... King Pippin's history, as a story, is rather slight. It relates an attempt to remedy the French Republic's instability by restoring the monarchy with an obscure descendant of Charlemagne, an amateur astronomer named Pippin. When he decides to be kingly rather than a mere figurehead, Pippin realizes that "the time for kings is past," something we may have suspected in the first place. He goes back home, leaving us with the conclusion that the people want a patsy, not a leader, and insist on remaining devoted to unstable republics. Perhaps the comparison the publishers make to *Candide* was too much in Steinbeck's mind as he wrote *Pippin IV*, for the style is remarkably like a translation from Voltaire, or more accurately, reads as if it were written to make a translation into Voltaire's French an easy job.

... Within the limited framework of Pippin's circular career from bourgeois to king and back again, Steinbeck has brilliantly, if briefly, lacerated French and American society and politics. When Pippin is made king he is advised that his first "official act should be to request a subsidy for his government from America for the purpose of making France strong against Communism, and an equal subsidy from the Communist nations in the interest of world peace." He also has the benefit of counsel from his daughter's boy friend, a progressive jazz fan. The boy's father, who had gone from rags to riches in the chicken industry, "never blamed President Hoover for the loss of his grocery store, but he could never forgive President Roosevelt for having fed him." Pippin is also advised to turn over the details of the executive office to one of the meat advertising agencies. ...

The book makes us want to see his promised big work in progress, and we are reminded that Hemingway didn't fulfill the predictions of doom after *Across the River*. *Pippin IV* occupies a similar position in the work of a major writer.

Harry T. Moore.
"Steinbeck the Soft-hearted Satirist."
New Republic, 136
(27 May 1957), 23–4.

... Steinbeck shouldn't attempt satire—which is what both he and his blurb writer call this *Pippin IV* novel. Actually, it is a gentle comedy, superficially amusing for a while; but long before its 188th and last page, it begins to pall.

For this *Pippin* story is no more than an extended anecdote about a king who tries to be more democratic than the democrats and thereby gets into trouble of a traditional French-revolutionary kind. The fable is cliché, and most of its language is cliché masquerading as epigram: "There's no snob like a self-made man," and so on. Throughout, the characters are made to speak like those in a phrase book. The king appears to be likeable enough, and his relatives try to be. There is for example the uncle who deals in proverbs and fake paintings, whom the author has, appropriately enough, contrived with painful fakery; and there is the king's daughter, a recognizable cartoon of a teen-age novelist, about as profoundly created as the take-offs, in TV shows, of Brando or Capote. Odd: American writers used to "do" Europeans so well, comically or otherwise, between the times of Irving and Henry James. As for satire, surely Steinbeck is too soft-hearted for the medium: for that, one needs the *saeva indignatio*, or at least the chill upper lip of the author of *The Loved One*. In this category a squashy sentimentalism won't do. Nevertheless, the continuing admirers of Steinbeck will probably hail this soft "satire" as an important mutation in his career and will nourish the book with the usual over-praise. Indeed, it has already received the accolade of the Book-of-the-Month Club.

"New Fiction." London *Times,* 30 May 1957, p. 13.

... *The Short Reign of Pippin IV* is a high spirited holiday excursion into satirical extravagance. The author's sardonic comments on the French political scene to-day pepper the pages of this brief *conte* of how M. Pippin Arnulf Héristal, a shy, middle-aged amateur astronomer, descended from Charlemagne, is crowned King of France. At the root of Mr. Steinbeck's joke is the instability of the French political system. The new king is a placid creature capable of detached observation. He is willing to sacrifice his quiet life for the sake of his country, and up to the day of his coronation the reader will willingly accept him for what he is.

Then the squib misfires, but only because the author persists in flouting factual possibility. It is incredible that the king should slide out of his coronation coach into the crowd without being observed. Impossible, too, that he should make secret trips all over Paris without encountering the press or television cameras. Even when the monarchy falls and Pippin returns to his stargazing no one sees him go. Mr. Steinbeck has great fun at the expense of various French and American institutions. It would have been well worth his trouble to treat his main theme with a decent regard for the probabilities.

Daniel George. "New Novels." *Spectator* [England], 198 (31 May 1957), 726–7.

... John Steinbeck's little fantasy, *The Short Reign of Pippin IV*, is delightful. The publishers' announcement in the *Bookseller* read: "John Steinbeck has been 'having himself a ball,' as his countrymen say. With abundant good nature and a pen, needle-sharp, he has contrived a delicious lampoon of French politics and American big-business and a sly sideswipe or two at the British monarchy." No overstatement here. The position is that in despair of ever again forming a stable government the French have voted the Republic out of existence and proclaimed a monarchy. Disagreeing among themselves, the Royalists nominate an inoffensive amateur astronomer who happens to descend from King Pippin II. The events that flow from this decision are rapturously funny, the broadest humour in the telling of them being tempered with wit that would pass as French.

Patricia Hodgart.
"Books of the Day."
Manchester *Guardian*,
4 June 1957, p. 4.

As an established Old Master, John Steinbeck needs no recommendation, although *The Short Reign of Pippin IV . . .* is an unusual flight of fancy for him. An extravaganza on French politics, it exploits with disarming gaiety every cliché about France and the French. His conception of the return of the monarchy and the national response to it has the witty and loving detail of a René Clair film.

"King for a Day."
Times Literary Supplement [London],
7 June 1957, p. 345.

It is possibly no less surprising for the reader to find Mr. Steinbeck in the role of an entertainer than it was for M. Pippin Arnulf Héristal, a contented middle-aged *rentier* and amateur astronomer, to find himself suddenly called to the throne of France as Pippin IV. But an entertainment, or, in Mr. Steinbeck's own words, "a fabrication," is undoubtedly what his new book is primarily intended to be and what for the greater part of its space it succeeds in being. Only secondarily should it be considered as a satire on politics, French character or the French nation, and even then one must doubt whether it is intended to be taken at all seriously. Mr. Steinbeck in fact is in holiday mood, and if not everybody would choose his type of holiday, his good humour and high spirits are undoubtedly infectious.

Most of Pippin's subjects as well as Pippin himself are very conventionally French. They are, that is to say, very much the sort of people one would expect from a knowledge of French literature, or rather of literature about France, to meet in a book set in Paris but would be less certain of meeting in a Paris street. Pippin himself, for example, is very much the traditional type of leisured individualist, living on the rent from his vineyard, peering at the stars, enjoying what is in the best sense of the term a marriage of convenience, *i.e.,* one that provides him with comfort, companionship and affection, if, perhaps, not a great deal of passion. His uncle Charles Martel, inheriting from his ancestors a taste for ease as well as for pictures, manages to combine both in his profession of art-dealer, his main ambition being to sell dubious Renoirs to rich Americans. He, too, is very much a stock character. But this is not to disparage Mr. Steinbeck's understanding of, and liking for, the French themselves, which shows clearly throughout the book. It is simply that he has chosen to accept a definite literary convention, and obviously expects his reader to do the same.

Within the limits of this convention his characters have individuality and life of their own. He relies perhaps too much for comic effect on the disputes, divisions and disappearances of French Governments—too hackneyed a theme to be acceptable even within a literary convention, and in any case, and particularly at the moment, a rather dubious subject for mirth—and his one characterization of an American in Paris seems surprisingly wide of the mark; even so there will be few readers who do not enjoy Pippin's short reign considerably more than Pippin did himself.

A.B.
"*The Short Reign of Pippin IV.*"
Canadian Forum, 37
(July 1957), 89.

Another innocent goes abroad, this time the novelist of the American dispossessed, the bard of the golden-hearted bawd, the singer of the mouse-loving, mouse-crushing, retarded giant, chronicler of the boiler-dwellers—but why should I keep the reader in suspense? Before this paragraph took its first breath the cat was out of the berry-bushes and everyone knew that the author of this *tourisme de force* was none other than John Steinbeck. How're they going to keep him down on the Flats, now that he's seen Paree?

The central idea of the book is sturdy enough for an excellent skit by Wayne and Shuster, to last no longer than seven and a half minutes of sponsored time. A scion of the race of Charlemagne is called on to become king by a France riddled with political dissension and raddled by indecision. His adventures as Pippin IV have a verve that can only be likened to the whoop of a tourist descending from his train at the Gare du Nord. After some unfruitful dickering with an American millionaire who wants him to achieve national solvency by selling French titles to Texas cattle barons and oil kings, Pippin falls into regal disrepute because he starts taking his job seriously.

His final downfall comes when he addresses a convention of political leaders and proposes a list of reforms that are like as dammit to the New Deal. (Remember?) As Mr. Steinbeck would have it, these reforms are laughed to scorn by Pippin's audience because they are revolutionary and impossible. I suspect that those acute ex-deputies gave their king the bronx cheer because they found his formulas about as exciting as yesterday's fish-course or last week's mistress. But you can never tell with the French.

Me, I can hardly wait for the next depression when a man'll be able to raise a real hungerin' thirst for them grapes o'wrath.

Riley Hughes.
"*The Short Reign of Pippin IV.*"
Catholic World, 185
(July 1957), 312.

Mr. Steinbeck calls this light, 188-page bill of fare a "fabrication." The book is not to be taken seriously, his publishers contend, except as writing. But here is where this utterly sleazy fabric fails most. With only a minimum of imagination, verve, and wit Mr. Steinbeck gets his tale told.

The time is now, or thereabouts, and France has decided to become a monarchy again as a solution to recurrent governmental breakdown. A king is chosen from Charlemagne's line, a man who is an amateur astronomer and a man of middle-class views. Pippin and his family, along with the other characters in this lead balloon, are the veriest shadows, not precise enough to be called cartoons. We are not amused by them, least of all by one Sister Hyacinthe, former burlesque performer now a nun, who is confidante of the new queen. To get back to the plot, Pippin tries to apply American methods ("Royalty is extinct and its place is taken by boards of directors"), and comes to a farcical end.

Our nomination for the silliest book of the year.

Edward Weeks.
"A New King for France."
Atlantic, 200 (July 1957), 83–4.

You can tell from the feel that John Steinbeck was vastly amused at the prospect of writing a satirical novel, *The Short Reign of Pippin IV*, about the restoration of the French monarchy today. He chooses for his hero a gentle French amateur astronomer, M. Héristal. The steps by which M. Pippin Arnulf Héristal, lean, handsome, and fifty-four, is maneuvered toward the glories of Versailles are made more entertaining because of the remonstrances of his wife and the escapades of his daughter, Clotilde, who at fifteen had written a best seller entitled *Adieu, Ma Vie*, and at sixteen and a half had joined the Communists.

Mr. Steinbeck exuberantly caricatures bourgeois finances, the proliferation of French political parties, aristocratic art dealers, and adolescent female novelists. But once *le pauvre* M. Héristal has been crowned, a more solemn note begins to intrude. The new king has some surprising plans in store for the *couture*, the movies, and the tourist trade, but it also appears that he (or his alter ego Mr. Steinbeck) would have the French pay their taxes and correct the housing shortage. But this sudden infusion of transatlantic common sense tends to waterlog the cockleshell fantasy.

Mr. Steinbeck's liberal-humanistic principles are admirable, but when they begin to show through, the fun grows appreci-ably less. The author is at his best in concocting wild musical-comedy ramifications, such as the international furor of chemical analysis provoked by the Soviet government's purchase of several tank cars of perfume. And no matter how semiserious his reflections on the United States may be, this comment on the Martini is worth quoting: "It's not their strength," a young American tells the groggy king, "it's their inherent meanness."

Pamela Hansford Jones.
"New Novels."
New Statesman [England], 54 (13 July 1957), 61–2.

... It is not necessary to brush up on the Carolingians to enjoy *The Short Reign of Pippin the Fourth*, but it adds an extra shade of irony to the joke. Pépin le Bref's attempt to make kingship an effective office was one of the personal successes of history: Mr. Steinbeck's Pippin Héristal, thrust upon the throne of France quite recently by the consent of all parties, tries to do the same thing and immediately provokes a revolution. Mr. Steinbeck's joke is a pretty good one, pointed mainly at the instability and incessant government-destruction of the French, but having a good deal of point for the Americans too. It is an amiable book, sometimes very witty, sometimes just a trifle ham-handed; this kind of thing needs the precise verbal dexterity of Evelyn Waugh or Marcel Aymé to be entirely successful. The Carolingian twist is a funny one, but not quite justifiable: it fits too loosely and sometimes seems, like M. Héristal's court attire, to be held in with safety-pins at the back. It is pleasing for him to have an uncle called Charles Martel, who is a dealer in fake pictures and antiques, but the elaboration is a bit untidy and unmotivated. Still, this is both an engaging and a sensible jape, fun to read, and with all the exhilaration of a sober writer's holiday-piece.

Checklist of Additional Reviews

Harvey Breit. "In and Out of Books." *New York Times Book Review*, 106 (20 January 1957), 8.

Harvey Breit. "In and Out of Books." *New York Times Book Review*, 106 (3 February 1957), 8.

"The Short Reign of Pippin IV." *Booklist*, 53 (1 March 1957), 345.

Eleanor T[ouhey] Smith. "New Books." *Library Journal*, 82 (13 March 1957), 753.

Maxwell Geismar. "Steinbeck Uses Great Talent to No Purpose." Chicago *Sun-Times*, 14 April 1957, Section 3, p. 1.

William Hogan. "Steinbeck Plays an Elaborate Joke with a King." San Francisco *Chronicle, This World* magazine, 14 April 1957, pp. 22, 28.

"New Steinbeck Work Takes Jab at Politics." Los Angeles *Times*, 14 April 1957, Part 5, p. 6.

Lon Tinkle. "Reading and Writing." Dallas *Morning News*, 14 April 1957, Part 6, p. 10.

"John Steinbeck's Latest." *Newsweek*, 49 (15 April 1957), 114.

Phil Watson. "Steinbeck's Whimsy." San Jose [Calif.] *Mercury News*, 21 April 1957, p. 8.

Irene Alexander. "Steinbeck's Pippin." Monterey [Calif.] *Peninsula Herald*, 26 April 1957, p. 20.

Paul Pickrel. "The New Books." *Harper's*, 214 (May 1957), 84.

"The Short Reign of Pippin IV." *Bookmark*, 16 (May 1957), 191.

ONCE THERE WAS A WAR

Once There Was a War

by John Steinbeck

THE VIKING PRESS
NEW YORK
1958

"Once There Was a War." Booklist, 55 (1 September 1958), 8.

A troop ship's Atlantic crossing, an American air base in England, and the invasion of Italy are among the many scenes and events depicted by a World War II correspondent whose immediate, unsentimental prose recaptures time, place, and mood. Originally sent as dispatches to the New York *Herald Tribune* and other newspapers, the pieces deftly underline the human element that survives even in the midst of war's impersonality.

T. Houlihan. "Once There Was a War." Library Journal, 83 (15 September 1958), 2436.

This collection of World War II news dispatches by the noted author brings to mind the journalistic maxim that there is nothing quite so dead as yesterday's news. Nevertheless, these dispatches, written in 1943 when Steinbeck covered England, Italy and Africa as a war correspondent, contain some excellent sketches depicting the humor and tragedy of war, and the fear and courage of men and women in combat. Fans of Steinbeck will enjoy this collection, as will many of those who saw action in the places covered by the author. . . .

John H. Thompson. "Steinbeck's War Stories." Chicago Sunday Tribune Magazine of Books, 26 October 1958, p. 10.

"Once upon a time there was a war," are the first lines written by John Steinbeck in this book, "but so long ago and so shouldered out of the way by other wars and other kinds of wars that even people who were there are apt to forget."

With that Steinbeck, the master story teller, reintroduces a collection of dispatches he wrote as a war correspondent between June and December, 1943. Unless you read the New York *Herald-Tribune* foreign service in those days you will never have seen these beautiful, clean, clear stories of men at war.

In today's world of nuclear weapons, ballistic missiles, satellites, and space travel they almost are period pieces. Steinbeck was not interested in strategy and generals, but in the soldiers, GI or lieutenant, and what they did. No one has ever excelled him in this field. If you have forgotten what that war was like, Steinbeck will refresh you. Age never can dull this kind of writing.

Stan Swinton.
"Period Pieces of a
Terrible Time."
Saturday Review, 41
(1 November 1958), 18.

These dispatches are—as the author says in his introduction—"period pieces, the attitudes archaic, the impulses romantic." Some of them make exciting reading nearly fifteen years later. When Steinbeck tells of a tiny task force capturing the island of Ventotene, off Italy, his ability to describe precisely and to flesh out the incident with literary form is admirable.

But many of the dispatches, particularly those from a troop ship and from wartime London, today hold only curiosity value. A collection such as this was frequent during and immediately after the war. Issuing it today seems a rather pointless exercise. Steinbeck buffs will appreciate it, of course. So will former war correspondents, for many of these dispatches represent extraordinarily good journalism. War reportage either can be very easy or very hard for the journalist, you see.

The war is transcendent news. Even the indifferent correspondent can satisfy a distant editor without stirring too far from the press camp. If the weather is too cold or his hangover too horrendous, there are handouts which can be rewritten. At the worst he can quote the PIO sergeant on life at the front. The number of PIO sergeants who have been identified by name and home town, but not by job, in dispatches bravely datelined "With the 5th Army in Italy" or "With the 7th Army in Southern France" is staggering.

But journalistic malingerers were few. For the bulk of combat reporters, war correspondence was perhaps the most testing and rewarding journalistic form.

It tested the man. You had to be there to write a stirring and honest account. It couldn't be done back at regiment or division or Army.

It tested reportorial skills. The human mind has a powerful tendency toward escapism in combat. It is much easier to keep your head down and think of your wife than it is to observe carefully and precisely so that you can write accurately and honestly later.

It tested writing ability. You reached the press camp at night, tired, dusty, and hungry, headed for the typewriter and wrote. If you were very good the results had the color and form of dispatches by men like Dan DeLuce, Milton Lehman (of *The Stars and Stripes*), or of these by Steinbeck.

It tested the ability to be a human being. The war correspondent was only a partial participant. He did not stay in the line with the infantry company for a week or ride the PT boat every day or fly the mission over Ploesti ten times. He participated, withdrew to write and send his story and left the soldier or airman or sailor behind to stay until death or rotation or peace came along. If an outfit accepted the same correspondent several times or many times it meant he was respected or liked or both. And this was personally important to the successful combat reporter.

Steinbeck's dispatches reflect all these qualities of good war reporting and, in the second half of his collection, great war reporting in the age of pre-atomic war. But reading them is like taking time out in this new hour of crisis to browse through old copies of *The Stars and Stripes*. It tends to be rather meaningless.

"Briefly Noted."
New Yorker, 34
(8 November 1958), 215.

... The author's introduction says that for a long time he resisted the impulse to reprint his war correspondence, believing that "unless the stories had validity twenty years in the future they should stay on the yellowing pages of dead newspaper files." Unfortunately, these thin feature stories—"human-interest" without recreating human beings—about goat mascots, short snorters, the pathos of a shelled rosebush, and the atrocity of English cooking do not pass that admirable test. . . .

Herbert Mitgang.
"Noble Men in Uniform."
New York Times Book Review, 108
(16 November 1958), 12.

In the second half of 1943, John Steinbeck went to England, North Africa and Italy and wrote a series of dispatches for the New York *Herald Tribune* and other newspapers. Now for the first time these sixty-six short pieces are assembled in a book. Because Steinbeck's people in fiction and non-fiction have always been men and women of good-will, it is not surprising that his men at war also shine nobly.

There are some fine little stories and descriptions in *Once There Was a War*. "The men wear their helmets, which make them all look like long rows of mushrooms," and a reader conjures up visions of the Okies of Steinbeck's fiction. In England, Steinbeck discovered several characters, especially an American private named Big Train Mulligan. "You can leave Big Train parked in the middle of a great plain, with no buildings and no brush, no nothing, and when you come back ten minutes later there will be a girl sitting beside him."

In Italy, Steinbeck went out with the Navy on a mission to capture a German radar crew on the tiny island of Ventotene in the Tyrrhenian Sea. Steinbeck here—far from his Sea of Cortez—conveys the emotions of combat with the paratroopers. Watching a handful of men make a landing and bluff the Germans into surrender makes for the most suspenseful part of the book because one can sense the author's own tenseness and excitement.

Long ago, Steinbeck proved that he could report. Indeed, his strong descriptive powers and eye for detail are important in all his big novels. In an introduction, he says that these stories were written in haste to appear as (he adapts the perfect word) "immediacies." As a result, many of the pieces are slight in subject and obvious. The packed emotion of Steinbeck the fiction-writer is missing, for the most part, in these dispatches, but who can consistently sustain excitement in thousand-word stories?

From the same war theatre and time, of course, two truly great books emerged— Ernie Pyle's *Brave Men* and Bill Mauldin's *Up Front*, which upon rereading today remain not merely journalism but fine literature. The Pyle and Mauldin books together stand as the common soldier's story of World War II, in a class by themselves. Steinbeck's short pieces are not so good, but nevertheless they do hold up today.

Herbert Kupferberg.
"Correspondent Steinbeck."
New York Herald Tribune Weekly Book Review,
8 February 1959, p. 10.

Once there was a war and John Steinbeck went to cover it. It was the New York *Herald Tribune* which sent him there, as a matter of fact, and the year was 1943. Some of those dispatches which appeared in this newspaper have now been collected in book form and fitted out with an introduction in which Mr. Steinbeck sets down his memories of soldiers, censors and war correspondents. He resisted the impulse to turn his dispatches into a book at the time, he says, because he felt that "unless the stories had validity twenty years in the future they should stay on the yellowing pages of dead newspaper files."

Well, it has been only fifteen years. But these samples of Steinbeck's journalism decidedly do have validity, both as memory joggers and as artistically wrought pictures of the war that are often quite moving.

It so happens that 1943 was one of those in-between years of the war; the year after the invasion of North Africa and the year before the invasion of France. So although Steinbeck's itinerary covered England, North Africa and Italy, his stories for the most part deal with the everyday war, the less spectacular but more typical aspects of a soldier's life. Those are accounts of what it was like to cross the Atlantic in a silent, darkened troopship (something which nearly every soldier remembers vividly); what it was like in London during the bombings; what it was like at an American bomber

base in England; what it was like when the kids asked for chewing gum and oranges; what it was like when an Italian village fell all over itself trying to surrender.

Scenes such as these retain a surprising immediacy in Steinbeck's recountings, perhaps because after fifteen years of gnawing worldwide struggle one feels almost an acute nostalgia for the days when joyous Sicilians garlanded the G.I.s with grapes, and "Lilli Marlene" wafted its haunting melody between the opposing lines. "It would be amusing if, after all the fuss and heiling, all the marching and indoctrination, the only contribution to the world by the Nazis was 'Lilli Marlene,' " wrote the Steinbeck of fifteen years ago, and he wasn't far wrong.

Unlike some correspondents, Steinbeck saw the war less in terms of military strategy and political objectives than of the people involved in it either purposefully or accidentally. In them, he found, was the stuff of life and of legend. There are both a-plenty in this warm and truthful book.

Harry Klissner.
"John Steinbeck Harks Back to World War II."
Los Angeles *Times*,
22 February 1959, Part 5, p. 7.

The horrors of World War II have been cut into anecdotal morsels in *Once There Was a War* by John Steinbeck. . . .

With the exception of the introduction, Steinbeck makes no attempt to inject his post-bellum feeling. Instead he permits some of the news releases he sent home from Europe and Africa from June 20 through Dec. 13, 1943, to show the mental detachment which man has placed between that period and today.

Many of the stories seem humorous now because there are no men fighting for their lives. The reality of the slaughter has passed into oblivion, and this makes the title of the book particularly apt.

While Steinbeck permits the news releases to speak for themselves, he presents his message in his introduction. Here he points out: "Greece, it was said, had to be at war every 20 years because every generation of men had to know what it was like. With us (20th Century Man), we must forget, or we could never indulge in the murderous nonsense. . . ."

His compassion toward members of the armed forces is amplified in another part of the introduction as he comments ". . . and although all war is a symptom of man's failure as a thinking animal, still there was in these memory-wars some gallantry, some bravery, some kindliness. A man got killed surely, or maimed, but living, he did not carry crippled seed as a gift to his children. . . ."

John Anderson.
"*Once There Was a War*."
Manchester *Guardian*, 11 December 1959, p. 6.

Mr. John Steinbeck is a distinguished writer, and he produced some very good war correspondence in the New York *Herald-Tribune* and other papers during the last war. *Once There Was a War* . . . is a collection of his pieces written as a war correspondent from England, North Africa, and Italy in 1943. They have been republished to mark the twentieth anniversary of the outbreak of war in 1939. Do they still have any relevance to the war? To anything? Mr. Steinbeck himself seems a little doubtful, for he describes them as "period pieces, fairy-tales, half-meaningless memories of a time and of attitudes which have gone for ever from the world." The time has gone—but have the attitudes? That, alas, is less certain, and here is justification for republishing these "period pieces." They offer no more than an anecdotal description of war, nearly always touching, and often quite funny. But their combined effect is to bring out a sensitive writer's conviction that the war he tries to write about and the war that men and women undergo are on utterly different planes of human experience. He records a conversation with a soldier at Salerno, who describes his landing:

We were out there all packed in an L.C.I. (landing craft infantry). . . . I could see the boats land and the guys go wiggling and running, and then maybe there'd be a lot of white lines and some of them would waddle about and collapse and some would hit the beach. It didn't seem like men getting killed; more like a picture, like a moving picture.

That is very accurate reporting: that is what war does look like at a little distance, like a movie; until there is a sudden sick realisation that one is on the wrong side of the screen. Mr. Steinbeck meets an air-gunner who has been reading a newspaper from home. "Well, anyway," he says, "I looked through that paper pretty close. It seems to me that the folks at home are fighting one war and we're fighting another one. They've got theirs nearly won, and we've just started on ours. I wish they'd get in the same war we're in."

Yes, these are period pieces. In an atomic war there would be less doubt about which war people were in.

E. D. O'Brien.
"A Literary Lounger."
Illustrated London News, 235 (26 December 1959), 960.

... Could anything, I asked myself as I picked up his *Once There Was a War*, be more dreary than *another* book about the last war—and that a reprint of the author's dispatches as war correspondent? I deceived myself. If there were sackcloth, I would wear it, or ashes (apart from anthracite clinker in my all-electric house), I would distribute them liberally on my head. This is one of those books which baffle description. I will only say that, reading it alone, with no one to whom to quote the best passages, I found myself at one moment laughing aloud; at another moment, the tears were pouring down my reluctant cheeks. Mr. Steinbeck knows a good deal about war, but he knows much more about human beings. Here is a book as well worth buying as it has been worth publishing.

"Italian Risorgimento?"
Times Literary Supplement [London], 8 January 1960, p. 15.

Mr. John Steinbeck's war-time dispatches from England, Africa and Italy have re-cently been published under the title *Once There Was a War*. ... Mr. Steinbeck has written an excellent introduction to them, describing the hazards and obstructions of a correspondent's life, and this is by far the best piece in the book. The rest—to an English mind, anyway—hardly justify reprinting.

Mr. Steinbeck is an agreeable, relaxed reporter, and one can rely on him to create the real picture without distortion or falsity. His tone is admirable, too. But the fact remains that these reports, which read more like drafts from novels than day-to-day dispatches, seldom say enough to interest at this range.

J. R. Ackerley.
"*Once There Was a War*."
Listener [England], 63 (16 June 1960), 1067.

In 1943 John Steinbeck was attached to the American forces as war correspondent. He visited England, Africa and Italy, and this book collects the dispatches he sent in. He tells us he resisted the impulse to make use of the material when the war ended, "believing or saying I believed that unless the stories had validity twenty years in the future they should stay on the yellowing pages of dead newspaper files." Rereading them lately for the first time since they were hastily written and 'phoned across the sea, he offers them now for other and rather strange reasons, because "I realize not only how much I have forgotten but that they are period pieces, the attitudes archaic, the impulses romantic, and, in the light of everything that has happened since, perhaps the whole body of work untrue and warped and one-sided." Indeed, war and truth are not buddies, as he goes on to confess in an introduction that is really the most interesting part of his book; truth is dangerous to the war effort and deleted by the censor wherever it happens to creep in; these dispatches were true so far as they went, he avers, but they were not the whole truth; that could not be told.

They re-create for us, nevertheless, something of the atmosphere of that black and blacked-out period, and perhaps managed to indicate to homefolk at the time a few convenient lies and to ruffle a few complacencies. As will be expected, Mr. Steinbeck is deeply sympathetic with the private soldier and has decent things to say about his loneliness, his nerves, and his fear. "I read a very nice piece in a magazine about us" (says a tail-gunner: Mr. Steinbeck was then attached to a bomber station). "This piece says we've got nerves of steel. We never get scared. . . . I never heard anything so brave as us. I read it three or four times

to try and convince myself that I ain't scared." "I wish they wouldn't think we're so brave," says another; "I don't want to be so brave." There are useful remarks, too, about Anglo-American relations and some amusing side-lights on the English scene as viewed through American eyes.

But on the whole the reports suffer from the disabilities under which Mr. Steinbeck admits they were written. Inevitably, too, a compilation of scraps, such as this is, suffers from the tedium of scrappiness, and it is a pleasure when some of them form a sequence, as they do in the accounts of the transatlantic troopship voyage and the battle scenes in Italy at the end. Occasionally also they suffer from the triviality of "comic relief" and from a certain over-neatness in design. Yet an air of honesty, so far as honesty could go, pervades them, and, written in quick, short, clipped sentences—a telegraphic style—they do manage to report, with feeling and energy, many aspects of that boring war that happened "once upon a time."

THE WINTER OF OUR DISCONTENT

THE
WINTER
OF OUR
DISCONTENT

The Viking Press · New York · 1961

JOHN
STEINBECK

Peter Harcourt.
"Steinbeck's Fables."
Time and Tide [England],
41 (6 June 1961),
1031–2.

For over 25 years now, John Steinbeck has been a prolific and unpredictable novelist. The first of his works to attract attention were *Tortilla Flat*, and *To a God Unknown*, both published in 1935. Already in these early works, Steinbeck revealed what we now think of as his most characteristic qualities: his warmth, his whimsy, his sense of fun, his mistrust of organised society, his belief in the validity of the simple pleasures of simple people, and if indeed his sentimentality, also his reverence for life of all kinds, for all things that grow. Like so many American writers, Steinbeck is at heart a fablist; and both these novels have all the directness and simplicity of a fable. *To a God Unknown* is undisguisedly a celebration of the forgotten mysteries of a pagan world, of the gods of the earth and the sky, with a blood sacrifice at the end that brings on the required rain. And in *Tortilla Flat*—as some ten years later in *Cannery Row* and its sequels—if the solemnity in the face of the mysterious gods of the earth has disappeared, the simple sense of wonder remains.

The world of the Salinas Valley in California—the world of Monterey that in *Tortilla Flat* produced Danny and Danny's friends and in *Cannery Row*, Doc, Mack, and the boys—is a world virtually untouched by the hustling way of life of the great American continent. In *Tortilla Flat* and in *Cannery Row* the values both praised and embodied are above all loyalty and friendship; then indolence, drunkenness, a playful violence, cheerful drabbing with androgynous whores, and general high spirits and affection. In this world of Steinbeck's fancy, there is nothing so intense or personal as love, because love would involve complexity and tension and the whole of his characters' personalities, while the layabouts of Monterey are all just generalised warmth and good-will. They have the single dimension and immediate appeal of characters in a fairy tale. To drink wine with one's friends, to wiggle one's toes in the sun— this is the core of life and its wisdom. And however unreal this rose-coloured world may appear to us, it is difficult not to respond to these books that have been so warmly, so generously conceived.

But beneath the whimsy and unreality of these particular novels, there lies a serious social concern; and from this concern as again from the Salinas Valley came Steinbeck's two greatest works—*Of Mice and Men* and *The Grapes of Wrath*. These two books can also be seen as fables, but this time the characters have the accent and manners of real people. In *Of Mice and Men*, Lennie is a simpleton, a kind, loving creature who delights in bright colours and in the texture of soft things, but who possesses the strength of a giant. Lennie epitomises all of Steinbeck's characters who are underprivileged in some way. There is simply no place for such creatures in our society, no place for people who are inescapably different. They engender mistrust and suspicion. Lennie's strength is his undoing, and— like the old dog in the middle of the story—Lennie has to be destroyed. There is simply no other way.

The Grapes of Wrath exhibits Steinbeck's most hostile criticism of American society, a society of unchecked technological expansion and exploitation. It is the struggle of the common people to survive starvation in the face of the wasteful abundance of the privately-owned fruit farms of California; and like the turtle at the opening of the book, no matter how many set-backs they experience, they carry on in the same direction. In this book, there is faith in abundance and an affirmative anger: "We've got a bad thing made by men, and by God that's something we can change." And at the close, when Rose of Sharon gives the life in her breast to the starving man in the barn, we realise that this is not only offered as a final indication of how the poor will look after one another, but also we get the sense that Rose of Sharon's baby was not lost completely in vain: as at the end of *To a God Unknown*, Steinbeck seems to be saying, through the loss of some lives, others may continue. Once more we have a kind of sacrifice and then the sense of life going on.

But I began with a reference to the unpredictability of Steinbeck as a novelist, for he has not always assumed the dungarees of an uneducated country people. The list of his complete works is a long one and contains books that are too various both in their treatment and in their success to encourage confident generalisation. *The Moon Is Down*, for instance, is the war-time story of an unspecified occupied country and of the quiet determination of the occupied people to resist the invader. Thematically, it is not unlike *The Grapes of Wrath*, but in manner, completely different. The whole thing is seen at a distance, with none of the immediacy of the world of the Salinas Valley. The tone is measured, cool and exact; and though it achieves a quiet impressiveness by the time we get to the end, the novel as a whole seems rather less than the sum of its individually persuasive moments.

Many readers will make a similar complaint about his most recent novel, *The Winter of our Discontent*. It is the story of a New England gentleman who, through his honesty and goodwill, has come down in the world and who sees a chance, by abandoning his honesty, to regain his fortune and thus the trappings of his social position and self-respect. In the process, of course, something inside him begins to corrode and the corrosion spills over and begins to spoil the lives of the people around him. Like *The Moon Is Down*, the whole thing is seen as if from a long way off, but this time the feeling of distance is largely the result of the discrepancy between the factitiousness of the plot—the clever way it is all made to fit together at the end like a thriller—and the warm humanity and inconsequential humour that enlivens each individual page and which serves to bring his characters so vividly to life.

And yet, although the manner is so different, the perennial Steinbeck concerns are there: the validity of the affections, of decency, even of small talk endlessly indulged in as a valuable transmitter of warmth and goodwill from one person to another. There is the same power of language, the proof of his own sensitive and sensuous response to experience, the ability to compel us not only to see what he is describing but to love it as much as Steinbeck does himself:

No one in the world can rise to a party or a plateau of celebration like my Mary. It isn't what she contributes but what she receives that makes her glow like a jewel. Her eyes shine, her smiling mouth underlines, her quick laughter builds strength into a sickly joke. With Mary in the doorway of a party everyone feels more attractive and clever than he was, and so he actually becomes. Beyond this Mary does not and need not contribute.

And finally, there is the central recognition (so laboriously worked out, I feel, in *East of Eden*) that in some ultimate sense a man *is* his brother's keeper.

But most curiously of all in this novel, there is the pervasive feeling of something intangible, joined with a mistrust of the intellect, a feeling that there is something in life that governs our actions which is much deeper than thought. It is at times close to superstition and is as implicit in this particular novel as it was overt in *To a God Unknown*. It is as if Steinbeck wishes to suggest that in our materialistic pursuits we have lost something meaningful, something perhaps magical, that is able to give life more than a merely day-to-day significance. He doesn't know exactly what it is, or at least, he can't say directly; but he writes about it in such a way that we are made to feel the reality of his sense of loss.

The Winter of our Discontent is a curious book and a strangely moving one, the product of a veteran novelist who throughout his career has managed to retain his faith that out of goodness and simple feelings, more goodness can flow and, as at the end of the novel, the light of life can continue burning.

"Damnation of Ethan Hawley."
Time, 77 (23 June 1961), 70.

In the early, vigorous fiction that brought him fame, John Steinbeck wrote in the language of the outcast and sided with the outsiders. It was an ambiguous form of social protest, since Steinbeck sometimes seemed less at war with the unjust acts of society than with the fact of society. One never quite knew whether his heroes wanted to storm the barricades or take to the woods and play hooky from the machine age. *In Dubious Battle* found him siding with Communist labor organizers, but in *Tortilla Flat* he sided with an amorally jolly bunch of vagrants and winos. In *The Grapes of Wrath* he keened over the suffering Okies in their mass exodus, but in *The Red Pony* he celebrated the vernal innocence of a boy and a colt beyond the reach of civilization's dust bowls. After the '30s, this internal dramatic tension drained out of Steinbeck and his later novels are all rather like Hollywood sets, more to be looked at than lived in.

In *The Winter of Our Discontent*, Steinbeck tries to recover his angry young manner with a blast at the affluent society. Unfortunately, the book contains more pose than passion, and the moral anathema sounds curiously like late-middle-aged petulance.

The book's hero, Ethan Allen Hawley, is a decent sort who loves his wife, has two teen-aged children and seems affably adjusted to failure. He clerks in a grocery store that he once owned for a Sicilian-born boss named Marullo. However, Ethan is haunted by totems of past status. The sleepy Long Island port of New Baytown in which he lives was once virtually the fief of his whaling-captain forebears. He carries one such captain's narwhal stick and lives in his great-grandfather's white shiplap house with its widow's walk. It hurts Ethan when his son pipes up: "I'm going to buy you an automobile so you won't feel so lousy when other people all got one."

Almost black-magically, Ethan's luck and character (but not his dialogue) do begin to change. He discovers that his boss Marullo entered the U.S. illegally, and he tips off the immigration authorities. The unsuspecting Marullo, who admires Ethan for his loyalty, gives him the store before he is deported. Author Steinbeck has other heavy ironies to put in the moral fire, and at book's end, Ethan owns the world of New Baytown but he has, of course, lost his own soul. How does he learn that? He discovers that his son has cribbed from the speeches of Jefferson, Webster, Lincoln and Henry Clay to win a nationwide TV essay contest.

All of this might be funny in a macabre way if it were not so flatly incredible. The novel is not helped by an overworked style that always seems to be asking the reader to finger the rich material of the prose. In Steinbeck's naively symbolic handling, the world of money and business is reduced to a branch of witchcraft, thus vitiating any valid point that Steinbeck might have hoped to make about the state of U.S. ethics. Asked to define business at one point, Ethan calls it "everybody's crime." The guilt for this novel is somewhat easier to localize.

John K. Hutchens. "Daily Book Review." New York *Herald Tribune*, 23 June 1961, p. 21.

A major American novelist's first major effort in almost ten years finds him moving to a new bailiwick and bringing with him, as he does so, an old concern. Across the country from the West in which he set his *Grapes of Wrath*, *Of Mice and Men*, *East of Eden* and their frontier company, John Steinbeck comes to an At-

lantic seacoast town as tradition-haunted as his West is still raw in its newness.

He makes the journey with the easy assurance of the artist he is, instinctively receptive to the subtleties of place and change. That old concern of his, the basically moral concern in *Grapes of Wrath*, the effect on character of the patterns of society—this too is entirely at home in New Baytown (Long Island?), scene of *The Winter of Our Discontent*.

But the truth is that the fact of place, splendidly as Mr. Steinbeck captures it, is not the most important thing here. What happens in New Baytown, as he indicates in a prefatory note, could happen in a large part of America today. For *The Winter of Our Discontent* is essentially a commentary on the ethics of success, or what constitutes the national concept of it; and Mr. Steinbeck's story is of the fate of one man who under sundry pressures succumbs. . . .

Because, given the sensitive cast of mind, the intelligence, the pride with which author has endowed his protagonist, and the absence of some sudden, desperate need, Ethan's surrender is all but incredible—and *The Winter of Our Discontent* is accordingly enfeebled, the surrender being after all the pivotal point of the novel. One suspects that Mr. Steinbeck himself sensed this weakness, unless there are hidden meanings in a misty lot of abracadabra involving fortune cards, a talisman, etc., encountered by Ethan on his new road.

Familiar Steinbeck virtues are happily here—the tang of believable speech, the blend of tenderness and irony, the deft way with minor characters, the gratifying sense of being in the presence of a writer who is writing *about* something. So much about *The Winter of Our Discontent* is satisfying that you can even forget from time to time the implausibility at the heart of it. But it keeps coming back to mind, and it mars the rest.

Orville Prescott. "Books of the Times." New York *Times*, 23 June 1961, p. 27.

The first lines of Shakespeare's *Richard III* are:

> Now is the winter of our discontent
> Made glorious summer by this sun of York.

Richard is talking about the period of exile, frustration, envy and poverty endured by the Yorkists while the Lancastrians held the English throne. In John Steinbeck's new novel, *The Winter of Our Discontent*, the title has a double meaning. It refers to the corruption of our times, to the greed and dishonesty that drive people in politics, business and the professions to take bribes, to demand kickbacks, to accept payola and to cheat the Government, their competitors, their employers and employees and the general public.

Such practices are not new, but they are now so commonplace that many people take them for granted. Mr. Steinbeck's title also suggests that those who steal and betray resemble Richard III, the arch villain, even if they are lesser criminals and would not dream of murder.

With such a topical theme inspired by a host of recent headlines *The Winter of Our Discontent* is the most serious, bitter and angry novel Mr. Steinbeck has written since *The Grapes of Wrath*. But the manner of the writing of this satire robs it of much of its force. Mr. Steinbeck's prose is jocular, gay and flippant.

His hero, whose surrender to the pressures of a grossly materialistic society should be cause for grief or anger, is only an amusing allegorical figure. Likable and even charming, he seems too much like a character in an early Alec Guinness comedy to inspire any sobering reflections on the "there-but-for-the-grace-of-God-go-I" theme.

There are some solemn moments in *The Winter of Our Discontent*, particularly at the end when realization strikes, when the sins of the father are imitated by the son and suicide seems the only solution; but even these cannot make Mr. Steinbeck's parable as effective a protest and warning as it ought to be. When comedy is the prevailing note, moral outrage is a difficult emotion to sustain in the face of the hero's distracting habit of calling his wife by a whole series of dismaying pet names: "Duck Blossom," "My Creamy Fowl," "Flower Feet," "Dimpsy Darling" and "Pigeon-Flake."

It all happened in the village of New Baytown in Wessex County, L.I., which much resembles Sag Harbor in Suffolk County. There Ethan Allan Hawley toiled as a clerk in Marullo's fancy grocery store. This was a comedown for Ethan because his ancestors had all been prominent citizens, privateers and whaling captains. But Ethan's father had lost the family fortune and Ethan had gone broke himself. So now he worked for Marullo and righteously rejected bribes, under-the-counter commissions and opportunities to steal from his boss. But the path of virtue was rocky.

Ethan's simple-minded but nice wife couldn't hold her head up while he was only a clerk. His 13-year-old daughter was "sick of being poor." His 14-year-old son, obnoxious almost past belief, complained: "Do you think I like to live without no motorbike? Must be twenty kids with motorbikes. And how you think it is if your family hasn't even got a car, leave alone no television?"

And all around him Ethan knew that deals were being made, frauds were being perpetrated, suckers were being tricked. "Don't be a fool. Everybody does it." "Grab anything that goes by." "Look out for number one."

So—just to get "a cushion of security"—Ethan abandoned the ethical standards in which he believed and ruthlessly betrayed both his oldest friend and his boss, who trusted and admired him. Ethan even planned to hold up a bank. After his various financial coups paid off he would become respectable again.

In telling Ethan's story Mr. Steinbeck displays considerable ingenuity in contriving unexpected twists of plot. His portrait sketches in silhouette of Ethan's wife, children and neighbors are deft and amusing.

His own pleasure in a sprightly, prancing, frivolous prose style, unlike anything he ever wrote before, is attractive. But this change of literary personality, while diverting enough, diminishes the weight of Mr. Steinbeck's attack on moral corruption. Satire, if it is to draw blood, inspire feelings of guilt and contrition, cannot afford to seem too light and playful. Mr. Steinbeck's anger and bitterness are the underlying forces that drove him to write this book. But, once it was started, a sort of verbal cheerfulness kept breaking in and blunted the edge of his wrath.

Nevertheless, there are clever bits, funny bits and touching bits in *The Winter of Our Discontent*. They make sure that this uneven novel is always pleasantly readable.

Granville Hicks. "Many-sided Morality." *Saturday Review*, 44 (24 June 1961), 11.

In his new novel, *The Winter of Our Discontent . . .*, John Steinbeck has written what he intends to be a tract for the times, a sermon on the decay of moral standards. "Readers seeking to identify the fictional people and places here described," he announces, "would do better to inspect their own communities and search their own hearts, for this book is about a large part of America today." Unfortunately, the book is neither convincing as a piece of fiction nor persuasive as a sermon.

The time is emphatically the present—from Good Friday to the Fourth of July, 1960. The scene is a Long Island community, New Baytown, once a prosperous center of the whaling industry, and the hero is Ethan Allen Hawley, a descendant of whaling captains. The family having lost its wealth, Ethan is currently general factotum in a grocery store owned by a Sicilian.

The most important thing about Ethan as we meet him is that he is an honest man. Indeed, early in the book, several persons assure him that he is too honest for his own good. His employer is one of them. Another is the president of the local bank, an old friend of the Hawley family. A salesman gives Ethan a practical lesson in how to get ahead by offering him a bribe. But Ethan remains steadfast.

Suddenly, under a variety of pressures, Ethan decides to change his ways. In order to gain possession of the store, which he once owned, he betrays his boss, and, to protect his financial future, he takes advantage of a close friend. He also plans to rob the bank, but everything else turns out so well that he doesn't have to. Not only does he get hold of the store; he is in a position to exploit the wealthy men who have for years been exploiting the town.

Then disaster strikes in what if for Ethan, though not for the reader, an unexpected fashion. His fourteen-year-old son, Allen, has entered a national I Love America Contest, and, his essay having won honorable mention, he is to appear on television, which is the height of his ambition. Just in the nick of time, from the point of view of the sponsors of the contest, it is discovered that his essay was plagiarized. Ethan is so stricken that he almost commits suicide.

What is wrong with the novel as a novel is simply that it isn't plausible. In the first place, I cannot believe that Ethan Allen Hawley would do the things that Steinbeck has him do. To give Steinbeck his due, he makes us feel that Ethan is somebody we know. He is a thoughtful man, often amusing in a whimsical way, ashamed that he has fallen so far below the position of his ancestors, but proud of his fidelity to their moral teachings. I can believe that such a man might hold stubbornly to his unprofitable course. I can also believe that his standards might slowly erode under pressure. What I cannot believe is that he would deliberately seek to attain his ends by mean and underhanded methods. He might conceivably rob a bank, but he would not betray his friends.

In the second place, I am puzzled by the climax of the book. It is clear to the reader, and it should be clear to Ethan, that young Allen is perfectly capable of plagiarism. Indeed, he says again and again that all he wants is to lay his hands on some easy money. Ethan yaps at him, but he doesn't understand that the boy

means what he says, and he is stupidly unprepared for what happens. (Ethan strikes me as a pretty poor sort of father.) Moreover, it does seem to me surprising that Ethan, with so much on his own conscience, has so little sympathy for his guilty child.

In the third place, I object to the slick way in which Steinbeck has carpentered the novel. Ethan prospers by virtue of the most extraordinary set of coincidences; even the bank robbery that never comes off is perfectly set up for him. Equally implausible is the way in which Allen almost gets away with his plagiarism; the advertising man who breaks the news to Allen says he can't understand what happened, and neither can I. I also dislike Steinbeck's way of playing with the supernatural, and I distrust his chronology. (Is it likely that Ethan, who was born after 1920, would have remembered, very well indeed, a grandfather who remembered the great days of New Baytown's eminence as a seaport?)

If it is difficult to take the novel seriously as a novel, it is impossible (for me) to be impressed by its message. A novel indicting our low moral state ought, I think, to deal with a representative person in a representative situation. Ethan is about as untypical an individual as one can imagine: a member of a distinguished though now impoverished family, a Harvard graduate, a captain in World War II, who after the war chose unaccountably to set himself up in the grocery business, and, having failed as a businessman, cheerfully spent a dozen years sweeping the store and waiting on customers. Moreover, when he yields to temptation, he does not engage in the kind of chiseling and cheating that we are all so well aware of but behaves in a dastardly fashion.

Steinbeck is not naïve enough to suppose that there was no corruption in

America before 1950, but he assumes that the past decade has witnessed a decline in morality. If he is right, as very likely he is, he ought at least to show how this decline has come about. But his examination of our present situation is superficial. He says nothing, for instance, about the fact that our whole economy depends on the production and consumption of more and more unnecessary goods, and he says nothing about the part that advertising plays not only in creating a demand for these goods but also in shaping our moral standards. If his readers heed his exhortation to inspect their own communities, they will not find that the book has contributed much to their understanding of what they see.

Finally, Steinbeck has failed to resolve the problems he has raised. Ethan decides to go on living, lest another light (meaning his daughter) should go out, but we are not told how he proposes to come to terms with his conscience, or what he intends to do about his son, or what kind of life he and his family are going to lead. Like Calvin Coolidge's preacher, Steinbeck is against dishonesty, but he has not explored at any depth its causes, consequences, and cure, nor has he thrown any bright light on the practical problems of an honest man in our society.

Saul Bellow has written: "In this book John Steinbeck has returned to the high standards of *The Grapes of Wrath* and to the social themes that made his early work so impressive and so powerful. Critics who said of him that he has seen his best days had better tie on their napkins and prepare to eat crow." Having greatly admired Steinbeck in the early years and having expressed disappointment with much of his recent work, I should have been happy to eat a little crow, but that is not what *The Winter of Our Discontent* has put on my plate.

Carlos Baker.
"All That Was in the Cards for a Man Named Ethan Hawley."
New York Times Book Review, 110 (25 June 1961), 3.

The appearance of a new and full-fledged novel from the pen of John Steinbeck after a lapse of nearly ten years is bound to invite speculation. In some quarters it will be seen as a kind of "comeback," achieved at the age of 59, after what looked to be a period of at least partial desuetude punctuated only by the humorous novel, *Sweet Thursday*, the subtle fable on King Pippin the Fourth, and the retrospective collection called *Once There Was a War*.

Then there is the matter of the eastward shift in locale. Never before has Steinbeck-of-California chosen to write about the East Coast village of New England traditions. Never hitherto has he picked as a protagonist anyone quite like the impoverished young Yankee storekeeper whose ancestry goes . . . back to Revolutionary times. Does this account of the change for the better in the fortunes of Ethan Allen Hawley suggest an implicit allegory on Steinbeck's own career as a writer since he left the West Coast to establish a permanent residence in these Atlantic longitudes? Would it be fair to say that, with this return to serious fiction, Steinbeck himself has now emerged at last from the long winter of his discontent into a vernal equinox where the sun once more shines warm and clear?

Possibly so, though it is a speculation not to be ridden too hard. Not since *East* of Eden in 1952 has Steinbeck engaged a theme of such broad social significance as his present one: the threat to personal integrity and right conduct which is imposed on men of goodwill by the modern slackening of ethical standards. Not since *The Grapes of Wrath* in 1939 has he found a subject closer to his heart than this account of one man's resolute rise to self-redemption after a period dominated by sundry forms of inertia, doubt and failure of nerve. . . .

Connoisseurs of vintage Steinbeck will soon recognize that here, as in most of his major fictions, he has chosen to write a fable in the form of a novel. Not for nothing does the action take place between two holiday week-ends in the spring of 1960—precisely the time, we are told, when the first draft of the book was set down. For in the opening Friday-to-Sunday of Easter tide, after some hours of distinct spiritual unrest, Ethan begins to experience a dawning sense of rebirth, a consciousness of fresh beginnings. And the book concludes, wisely enough, with Independence Day, replete with certain climactic emotional fireworks, and reaffirming once more, in an individual instance, the proud old national principle of self-reliance.

Indeed, Steinbeck plays with fabulous elements rather more overtly than is his usual custom. There is, for example, a handsome lady-witch named Margie Young-Hunt who confidently predicts the rise in Ethan's fortunes by reading a pack of Tarot cards. Among the Hawleys' collection of knick-knacks there is also a curiously carved stone talisman to which magical powers now and again seem to be attributed. And the cave of contemplation to which Ethan periodically returns to reassess his values, probe his motivations, or reflect upon the influences of his stars and his ancestors, is almost a Platonic metaphor.

Like the hints of the marvelous in Hawthorne's romances, however, these of Steinbeck's are of less importance in themselves than as a means of exploring the labyrinthine twistings of human psychology. No amount of abracadabra can disguise the fact—as the lady-witch herself puts it—that a good man named Ethan Hawley is traumatically enmeshed in a socio-economic trap from which his whole personality, not to mention the shades of his men-of-action forebears, cries out for release. No matter how we explain it, Ethan reflects, there comes a year pregnant with the possibilities of change, a time "when secret fears" emerge into the open, "when discontent stops being dormant and changes gradually to anger." It is just here, Steinbeck's novel suggests, rather than in the configurations of the stars or the hidden predictions in Tarot packs, that the patterns of fresh action are accountably initiated. Yet who shall say that cards and stars and talismans have not played some obscure role in sparking the prepared mixture and setting the vehicle in motion?

Steinbeck *redivivus* is less ready than he formerly was with the sturdy moral preachment and the pat social answer. This is all to the good. Yet so many half-hidden ironies play through the story of Ethan Hawley that most readers, pausing to reflect, may find themselves baffled or bemused. This is a problem novel whose central problem is never fully solved, an internal conflict novel in which the central issue between nobility and expediency, while it is joined, is never satisfactorily resolved. For this reason, despite its obvious powers, *The Winter of Our Discontent* cannot rightly stand in the forefront of Steinbeck's fiction. Yet it is also a highly readable novel which bristles with disturbing ideas as a spring garden bristles with growing shoots. If this is Steinbeck's second spring, it is a welcome season.

Virgilia Peterson.
"John Steinbeck's Modern Morality Tale."
New York Herald Tribune Weekly Book Review,
25 June 1961, p. 29.

We have come to think of John Steinbeck as a writer with two literary faces, the one gleeful, the other outraged, but both startlingly and memorably alive. It is the angry face, however, the face of the moralist, that commands, *ipso facto*, the more attention, and this is the one that looks out from the pages of his latest novel, *The Winter of Our Discontent.*

Deserting, for the new book, the exuberant California scene he has so often tenanted for his readers, Mr. Steinbeck now takes a sleepy-looking Long Island village named New Baytown for his setting. By-passed by modern industrial development, New Baytown still bears the marks, beyond the new municipal pier, of its Old Harbor, where deep-hulled whalers used to dock, and on its tree-lined streets the facades of Colonial houses still keep vigil among the functional buildings of today. The people in New Baytown know each other's habits, as, too, they know each other's place. The policeman keeps the same beat; the town drunk still begs money for a drink at the same hour of the night; the bank president arrives at the bank at the precise same moment in the morning; the red setter on Elm Street knows whom to salute with his tail. The ground New Baytown stands on has never shifted, you would swear, since its earliest settlers set foot on it. But, according to Mr. Steinbeck, you would be wrong. The real, the moral ground on which New Baytown stands today has cracked and shifted, perhaps irreparably.

The protagonist of this Steinbeck novel is Ethan Allen Hawley, descendant of New England whaling captains, but now, at the threshold of his middle age, reduced, by misfortune, mismanagement, and the chicanery of an earlier generation, to working for his family as a grocer's clerk. . . . Until the moment when the author presents him, he has been resigned to failure. How, at the cost of conscience, he almost achieves money, power, and success, and what happens to make them slip from his grasp, is the burden of this story.

It is on Good Friday—a day that Ethan has always held in awe and dread—that a wholesale grocery drummer offers him a five per cent cash bribe to obtain his employer's business and leaves behind him on the counter a shiny leather billfold with twenty dollars in it. And it is some three months later, on the Fourth of July week-end, that Ethan reaps the whirlwind he has meanwhile been sowing. In that brief span, Mr. Steinbeck undertakes to prove how easy it is to make out of a lamb a shark.

No one who has attempted to breast the tides of our affluent society would dare deny that its waters are shark-infested, nor fail to notice that it is to the victorious shark that the spoils usually go. Even the sharks themselves could scarcely quarrel with the thesis that today in America honesty is losing its reputation. But it takes more than an incontrovertible thesis to make a novel. No matter how right the author is, how fine his wrath, he will not disturb his readers' sleep or trouble their complacency unless he has filled the arteries of his characters with blood. But how much can we believe in this Ethan who makes such sophisticated jokes when in bed with his Boston-Irish wife and who sees through the maneuvers of one of Steinbeck's least probable huntresses, yet has never heard, till the day we meet him, of the bribe? How far can we believe in a man of innocence and principle who finds it so ridiculously easy to outshark the sharks? And if Ethan himself is hard to accept, the rest of the characters—with the exception of Ethan's tender, womanly, foolish wife—are all drawn quite casually from stock.

When serious, John Steinbeck is one of the most serious American writers of our time. Inescapably, therefore, whatever he writes is exposed to a fiercer scrutiny than is given to most of his contemporaries. With each new Steinbeck play or novel, there springs up the question: Is this as good as his best? In the case of *The Winter of Our Discontent*, the answer is, unfortunately, no.

"The Old Steinbeck."
Newsweek, 57
(26 June 1961), 96.

Any critic knows it is no longer legal to praise John Steinbeck. Indeed it sometimes seems that he has been in the doghouse almost since the great days of *The Grapes of Wrath*. When he exuded the heavy molasses of *Sweet Thursday* seven years ago, it looked as though he had glued the door shut. As Steinbeck's first real novel since then, *The Winter of Our Discontent* is bound to stir up that unfragrant memory—the more so since it is destined for vast, popular success in both the mass magazines and the bookstores. Happily, this is Steinbeck in his old, rare form.

In his finest novels, he captured the whole drama of a time by writing about simple hunger. For today, he makes almost as telling a social theme out of a crisis of personal honesty. Fallen aristocrat Ethan Hawley is a grocery clerk in an old Long Island whaling town his family once owned. Ethan can take it, although his upright rearing makes him a poor pupil when his immigrant boss trains him to weigh the meat for sale without trimming off the fat. Poverty lies heaviest on his wife and two teenage children who—the shame of it!—must live without such amenities of the affluent society as a television set or auto.

Under pressure from his friends—and the influence of an everybody-does-it morality—Ethan plots to mend his fortunes by seizing the store. To do so, he has to destroy two men and mutilate his old-fashioned conscience. Lest he be spared any of the pain of the latter, he sees his crookedness mirrored in his son who wins fame through a patriotic essay contest in which he has submitted stolen material. Steinbeck, writing better than he has done for years, gives this story a concentration of emotion and a relevance to the larger scene which make it a sort of prodigy—a preachy novel which is a good one.

Chatting in his bearish basso in the garden of his New York town house the other day, John Steinbeck said he had learned to ignore the report card the critics give him. "I care what is thought about this book," he said, "I don't care what is said." Big all over, including nose and ears, Steinbeck now has one small feature—a becomingly pruned beard. He started it as a joke, then kept it as a decoration when it developed "a skunk streak" and reminded him of "certain relatives." When writing, Steinbeck said in his warm rumble, he never addresses an audience but a single individual—usually imaginary. The new book was written to his father.

At the moment, Steinbeck is halfway through another book based on a cross-country motor tour he took last year to eavesdrop on the American people. They were fearful, he found, at the thought of the old moral codes fading in influence. At the same time, Steinbeck observed: "Every man is moral. It's only his neighbors who aren't." He himself was appalled by American waste—"city dumps twice as big as cities." And everybody, everywhere in this country, he said, was itching to be somewhere else.

What about the uprooted generation which Steinbeck wrote of in his masterpiece, *The Grapes of Wrath*? "Ah, they were different," he said, "they were wanderers because they had to be. Today, the Okies of the 1930s are not only settled, they own land in California—and probably are guilty of some of the same practices they were victims of during the depression."

Steinbeck was puzzled that the magazines were cutting *The Winter of Our Discontent* after he had already cut it to the bleeding point. He learned to do this, he said, from an old Scot whom he once heard declare that, if it were respectable to put water in whisky, "they'd do it at the distillery."

Melvin Maddocks. "Steinbeck's New Novel." *Christian Science Monitor*, 27 June 1961, p. 7.

In his best-known novel *The Grapes of Wrath*, John Steinbeck wrote about how poverty erodes character. In his latest novel he has written about how prosperity does even worse.

The Winter of Our Discontent is partly a protest against the American cult of success, a novelist's tradition that goes back a good way.

Partly it is a comment on what is popularly being dramatized as the moral crisis of our times, a topic that ranges, according to taste, from the Van Doren scandal to juvenile delinquency. Mr. Steinbeck has treated this subject previously in nonfiction forms, most notably in his letters to Adlai Stevenson reprinted in the *New Republic*.

In his novel the Steinbeck who responded so powerfully to the pioneer's mystique in "The Leader of the People" is wondering desperately how the best and the hardiest in American experience can be made continuous today.

But the book often seems as fundamentally confused as it is, fundamentally, earnest. Its indignant diatribe against amorality is incongruously punctuated by trashy paragraphs of titillation and the sort of intolerably arch, smutty chitchat characteristic of meretricious Broadway comedies. It is marred by a badly mishandled religious motif that is both pretentious and disturbingly inappropriate. And its only destination—despite a curious and unconvincing final reprieve—is the *cul de sac* of romantic despair. . . .

With a welter of symbolism Mr. Steinbeck suggests that the committed search for money is a form of witchcraft whose spell devotees are not free to break.

Ethan gets his money all right, but at the price of betraying his oldest friend, his employer, and, of course, himself.

One cannot help reading this story, in a detrimental sense, as a fable. Neither characters nor events seem self-impelling. The rigging hand of the author is irritatingly omnipresent, converting plot into evidence for his opinions, conjuring up a past of white sails and granite-principled Great-Aunt Deborahs to play off against a present, editorialized as a materialistic orgy set to rock 'n' roll. Ironically Mr. Steinbeck's golden age just about coincides with the era William Dean Howells was doing his own lamenting upon in books like *The Rise of Silas Lapham*.

But the basic trouble may be that Mr. Steinbeck is not working to his strength. He writes most eloquently about simple people fingering the rich soil of a California valley. His natural hero is the primitive. Man as a social creature depresses him.

He is the Huck Finn of American novelists. In the city or even the town he loses his certainty as a writer. His whole style suffers. The characters of *The Winter of Our Discontent* fall into flattened stereotypes. Their dialogue becomes by turns embarrassingly florid, cute, and cheap. They are confused people for whom Mr. Steinbeck can feel only a confused compassion.

Though diluted with sentimentality, his goodness of heart is impressive. But the complexities of the contemporary challenge are almost certain to elude a thinker whose most passionate instinct is not for a better civilization but for no civilization at all.

"New Fiction."
London *Times*,
29 June 1961, p. 15.

A deep disquiet about present-day materialism is shown in both this week's American novels. Mr. Steinbeck, the established author, is an optimist, while Mr. Stevens, who wrote *The Double Axe* while he was still at Princeton, is resignedly pessimistic. Mr. Steinbeck, it may be felt, has stacked the cards rather unfairly. The hero (very nearly the anti-hero) of

The Winter of Our Discontent ends up with the best of both worlds. When we first meet him, Ethan Hawley, last of a once-wealthy New England ship building family, has sunk to working in a grocery run by a Sicilian immigrant, and his social position depends on his birth and his reputation for honesty. He is well educated (he has a literary allusion for every occasion), and adores his wife with an endless supply of freshly coined endearments; in fact his aggressive satisfaction with the world and himself constitutes a kind of hubris. So he is tempted. His wife and children drop hints that they want to be more like other families. His boss, understandably irritated by his shining virtue, tries to teach him the sharper points of business. Ethan succumbs, completely, dramatically, and basely, but survives by an ironic intervention of Fate, which is presumably taking his past conduct into account.

The trouble with Ethan is that he is such a windbag. He is all talk and literary moralizing, while inside there is no character at all. This may have been Mr. Steinbeck's intention, but it makes Ethan's lapse into crime absolutely unbelievable. The crucial moment of betrayal comes and goes in a haze of words. . . .

Burns Singer.
"New Novels."
Listener [England], 65
(29 June 1961), 1140.

Call him anybody. He might be your next-door neighbour or the man who comes to read your gas meter. He might even be your boss, certainly any of your subordinates at the office. In the novels under review he is alternately a grocery clerk who comes of a good family, an aging journalist, an accountant, retired, who contributes snippets to the local rag, and a highly articulate bargee. He lives, again alternately, in New England, France, New England (where he evidently flourishes) and Scotland. He is the average decent man, a bit helpless in the maelstrom of modern life but trying valiantly to keep his integrity, to do his best. He is beloved by novelists of all races and all persuasions. Not only does he provide a foil for the more eccentric characters in their books but also, by penetrating into the tensions that lie hidden under his façade, he allows them to grope for the malaise of our time and other such high-sounding social agonies.

Such, anyhow, would appear to be his purpose in John Steinbeck's new novel, an elaborately pretentious and portentous parody of all the other books about the little man. Ethan Allen Hawley has only one notable characteristic. He calls his wife by a multitude of names running the gamut from "My Mary" through "Miss Mousie" to such absurdities as "Darling chicken-flower" and "Pollywog." He also has certain properties, a house, a walking stick, its handle fashioned from a narwhal's horn, and a talisman, "a kind of mound of translucent stone, perhaps quartz or jadeite or even soapstone." (I should have thought that, since he attached so much importance to it, he might have made some effort to discover which it was. There is, after all, a very considerable difference in hardness alone between quartz and soapstone.) The verbal pyrotechnics Hawley address[es] to his wife strike me as a device on the part of Mr. Steinbeck to disguise from the reader the basic poverty of his own life. Indeed, this is a book of disguises, singularly transparent and uninteresting disguises. Thus, Hawley disguises himself, in his own imagination, as a

bank robber and is only saved from carrying out his part by the timely, though accidental intervention of an F.B.I. agent. The plot proceeds by a series of innuendoes, disguised as actions, and actions, disguised as innuendoes, from one Hawley success to another. And each success is a disguise for loss, the loss of a real integrity. Hawley, for example, betrays his best friend by giving him a thousand dollars, in the certain knowledge that one thousand will be quite enough to allow his friend to drink himself to death. He betrays his boss by informing the F.B.I. that he is an illegal immigrant; and his boss, out of respect for Hawley's honesty, gives Hawley the business. And, indeed, the character of this boss, an Italian money grubber, is the only genuine thing in the whole book, the one reminder of what a great writer Mr. Steinbeck used to be, a shade sentimental, perhaps, but essentially noble. In the last few pages, Mr. Steinbeck loses me completely. Their obscurity is such that I have no idea of what is happening or why. . . .

Matthew Hodgart. "Models of Mischief." *New Statesman* [England], 61 (30 June 1961), 1052–4.

Local politics is an ideal subject for the novel. You have a community, public opinion, individuals whose actions matter, complex issues, temptation and fall. In England, despite *Middlemarch*, it seems hard to find out just what is going on (what ever did happen to that chief constable?), but in America all secrets are known. Novelists have long been busy making models, as convincing and as sinister as a toy Polaris. Steinbeck's nest of corruption, in *The Winter of our Discontent*, is a pleasant little port in New England, where almost everyone is discreetly on the fiddle. Ethan Hawley, of good family and education, has come down in the world, to become clerk in the grocery store, which belongs to a Sicilian. Ethan is about the only honest man in town; but tired of being broke he is determined to prove a villain. He gains development land by giving his old friend, the town drunk, enough money to kill him off, he informs on his Sicilian to get him deported for illegal entry, and is even on the point of robbing the bank when he learns that his grateful boss has given him the store for next to nothing. Flushed with victory over the local banker, and on the point of enjoying wealth beyond the dreams of avarice, Ethan finds to his horror that his son has cheated in a TV competition, and so ends in self-disgust and repentance. Mr. Steinbeck, obsessed with the problem of honesty, has written a serious tract, or at least the sketch for one; his grasp of local detail is sure, and he writes of the setting with some charm. But his people remain unconvincing, especially Ethan: I simply cannot believe in his transformation into Richard III; while his wisecracks and domestic endearments are sadly sentimental. Ambition should be made of sterner stuff.

Simon Raven. "False Prophets." *Spectator* [England], 206 (30 June 1961), 960.

... John Steinbeck's *The Winter of Our Discontent*, while sentimental and slow, provides some interesting discussion of honour. Ethan Hawley, scion of an old New England family, a man of scruple and culture too delicate for our greedy age, is reduced as a result of his own honesty to serving in a grocery store. His wife and children could do with less scruple and more money and start making this plain. Looking around him, Ethan realises that indeed he stands alone in his righteousness. So shall he too join the dog-fight? After almost interminable delays, he does—with some quite funny results which prove he was right in the first place. Though a contrived and foreseeable tale, this does have some telling bits of observation and some very quotable remarks scattered through its pages.

Norman Shrapnel. "Routine Steinbeck." Manchester *Guardian*, 30 June 1961, p. 7.

A mixed bag this week, starting with a live and kicking Steinbeck—a big fellow, the biggest since *East of Eden*. The theme of *The Winter of our Discontent* ... is honour and its corruption. The hero, Ethan, is a small and honest shopkeeper who starts to think, and thought is dangerous. "Men don't get knocked out, or I mean they can fight back against big things. What kills them is erosion; they get nudged into failure. They get slowly scared."

Ethan resolves to fight back against the little things, to halt the erosion, to play it the top people's way. The resulting success and dishonour kick back at him with a certain domestic charm; his small son, for instance, catching the general skulduggery in the air, composes a prize-winning "I Love America" essay which turns out to have been written by a team consisting of Henry Clay, Daniel Webster, Jefferson, Lincoln, and some others.

But this is not comedy. It is moral tragedy with too much basic innocence, and too much routine skill, to get very far. Its virtue is atmospheric: the sensuous descriptions such as that of the small-town general store are fascinating: "The seminal smells of flour and dried beans and peas, the paper-and-ink odour of boxed cereals, thick rich sourness of cheeses," and so on. The dialogue is highly individual, as likely to consist of a man talking to himself as to anyone else, or to some old sunbaked dog met on the way to work, or even to the still-life vegetables in the shop. . . .

Robert Poole.
"Resurgent Steinbeck."
Books and Bookmen [England], 6 (July 1961), 19.

It had been said by some critics that John Steinbeck had passed his peak, that he had given his best, and to some extent such works as *The Short Reign of Pippin*

IV, *The Pastures of Heaven*, and *The Long Valley*, with themes as Wayward as The Bus, appeared to justify them. But now, with *The Winter of Our Discontent*, Steinbeck re-emerges as one of America's most subtle and human writers, one whose work gathers enormous power from the calm restraint of the writing, and his detractors will have to think again.

The book is a study of the meaning of honesty and morals in a small town on the U.S. coast. . . .

The character of Ethan Hawley is sharply and clearly drawn, and very early in the book the seeds are set which allow him to become a cool, calculating advantage-taker. The whole cycle of the book is established one morning when Ethan is sweeping the sidewalk outside the store. Mr. Baker passes on his way to the bank, as he does unfailingly just before nine o'clock. Baker knows that Ethan's wife Mary has inherited some money from her brother, and he urges Ethan to put it to use. Ethan is reluctant, and briefly they recapitulate the decline of the Hawley fortunes. . . .

Ethan's hatred of his job is naked and intense. With his knowledge of what by rights should be his social position, stiffened by the goading of his two children and by Mary's need to have her pride in her husband restored, Ethan rationalises himself into making use of his knowledge of the weakness and foibles of his neighbours and friends—even of tragic Danny, the lonely drunk who had been Ethan's school pal.

Shrewdly Ethan goes to work and his plan succeeds. The Dago is deported, allowing Ethan to buy the grocery store for a fraction of its value. Danny drinks himself to death with money Ethan gave him, having first made over to Ethan the deeds of his only possession, his great family home that stands on the only level ground for miles that could be developed as an airport.

As this unfolds we see that Ethan loves his pretty daughter Ellen and his snarly son Allen, but these two are contaminated by the evil that has grown in their father. The book ends with a climax in which tragedy and irony are combined, and which makes it one of the most powerful and telling novels I have read.

Most important from the point of view of new or would-be writers is the establishment very early in the book (the conversation . . . with Mr. Baker) of all the potentialities that are in Ethan's nature. Only too often writers, probably in order to add drama, make their central characters say or do something completely at odds with the character so far established in the reader's mind. It weakens the whole structure they have created. Apart from its value as a book, *The Winter of Our Discontent* is an object lesson in writing technique and control.

Edward Weeks.
"Yankee Luck."
Atlantic, 208 (July 1961),
122.

In *The Winter of Our Discontent* . . . John Steinbeck turns for the first time in his versatile career to the East Coast for his setting and character. Bay Hampton, where on Good Friday morning his new story begins, could be any small seaport on Long Island or on the coast between New York and Boston. It is a village once famous for its Yankee skippers and sea-plucked fortunes, now being run by the new blood from Ireland and Italy. Ethan Allen Hawley, whose name echoes the past, is a gay, unaggressive spirit working as a clerk for Alfio Marullo; like his father before him, Ethan has lost the acquisitiveness of his forebears, and with it what remained of the family fortune. At the age of thirty-six all he has left is the old Hawley place, a couple of frankly envious children, and the nest egg of $6500 which his patient, pretty Irish wife, Mary, inherited from her brother.

The meaning of Good Friday was burned into Ethan as a boy, and it is ironic that on this day a series of small provocations—a bribe offered and rejected, a fortuneteller at her cards, a remark of Mary's that prodded under the skin—should startle him from his rut and even launch him on a new career. Ethan lends himself to the conspiracy of events in such a human, doubting-Thomas way that before he knows it he is in up to his knees. He has two charming accomplices in Margie and Mary, the one tempting, the other pushing, and the gradual debasement of his honesty is absorbing and rather shocking to watch. It all happens so effortlessly.

That his years at Harvard and his prowess in World War II should have left Ethan so feckless and so incompetent must be taken on faith; these phases of his career are touched so lightly as to be superficial, but what is genuine, familiar, and identifiable is the way Americans beat the game: the land-taking before the airport is built, the quick bucks, the plagiarism, the abuse of trust, the near theft which, if it succeeds, can be glossed over—these are the guilts with which Ethan will have to live in his coming prosperity, and one wonders how happily. John Steinbeck was born to write of the sea coast, and he does so with savor and love. His dialogue is full of life, the entrapment of Ethan is ingenious, and the morality in this novel marks Mr. Steinbeck's return to the mood

469

and the concern with which he wrote
The Grapes of Wrath.

Eric Keown.
"New Novels."
Punch [England], 241
(5 July 1961), 31–2.

A man from the moon trying to learn about America from its current fiction would easily get the impression that all its thinking is done in small, cheerfully backward coastal communities, as untouched by progress as, say, East Anglia in 1914.

This significant retreat from the mainstream of American life is part of the new respect for the social courage of the beachcomber and the bum, and I dare say is healthy escapism. Such a forgotten port, left behind in the march of the big machines, is the scene of John Steinbeck's *The Winter of Our Discontent*. This is a study of an innocent whose character is corrupted by the discovery that graft is easy. The descendant of prosperous shipowners who have frittered their money away, he has been to Harvard and is now a grocery-clerk, happily married with two ruthless children. He has odd habits. He makes speeches to his bottles of tomato sauce and pickles, and calls his long-suffering wife by a fresh pet-name every time he addresses her. This is Steinbeck in holiday mood. One gets to know everyone in the town, even the dogs, and all their secret springs; the children come to life with alarming reality, and much of it is entertaining, but the odour of whimsy is strong, and one senses that only a part of Steinbeck's feeling was engaged. I was unprepared for the melodrama of the ending.

"Looking after Number One."
Times Literary Supplement [London], 7 July 1961, p. 413.

Mr. Steinbeck is a versatile novelist and he has achieved several different kinds of success. Now he has written a morality. His tempted Everyman is a grocery clerk in a small New England town. The tempters are his friends and neighbours, who, he suddenly discovers, have no morality or scruples where business and the dollar are concerned and consider him rather a fool for not looking after number one. This apparently contented, whimsically minded and unenvious man thereupon defrauds his employer, drives his best friend to suicide and ably double-crosses the bank manager, who is as bad as himself. Armed with his popularity and his reputation for scrupulous, stick-in-the-mud honesty, he finds it all quite easy to do; and of course, in the end, he finds it does not pay in an ultimate sense. He cannot confide in his wife and seems to be about to slip into the arms of another woman for the sole reason that she understands what he is up to. His son fools a television company in a schoolboy essay contest and he contemplates suicide.

Crime does not pay: the point is a rather obvious one and the book is, indeed, sentimental and rather trivial at heart. The hero is to begin with too good to be true and in the end too wicked. The perfect marriage with which he starts is described with that sentimental impudicity which is a feature of so many fictional happy families; the small town setting and characters seem right out of stock; we scarcely need to be told how it will all end, even to the fact that the hero will remain in possession of the considerable swag. Some of the things he gets up to—the bank robbery that he plans, for example—are quite unbelievable; and the reader could well have been spared, if not some of his conversations with his wife, at least some of his conversations with the groceries. Yet it must be said that Mr. Steinbeck has one or two good comic scenes (the one with the man from the television company, worried about another scandal on top of the payola and the quizzes, for instance) and, when he is not being embarrassing, a sort of affable, relaxed charm.

E. D. O'Brien.
"A Literary Lounger."
Illustrated London News,
239 (8 July 1961), 70.

The advantage of being a literary lounger, as I see it, is that one may, with honest impunity, lounge: that is, one need not be continuously on a nervous look-out for some new masterpiece, or manifest frustrated disappointment if one fails in one's search. We are now beginning what I will not call the "silly" season—that would be unfair both to authors and publishers—but a time of year in which one does not expect (though one sometimes finds) the appearance of any outstanding new work. This has been, from that point of view, a typical week, when I have had before me a number of readable but comparatively unpretentious books, each good in its way, but none eliciting any tremendous response.

The best, I think, is John Steinbeck's new novel, *The Winter of Our Discon-tent*. Here is another long work of American fiction, quite different from those which usually come my way. The hero is a sensitive, loving, intelligent scion of a distinguished American family which has steadily come down in its little world until Ethan Allen Hawley is reduced to working as an Italian-born grocer's assistant. He himself is comfortable and philosophical, steady in his honesty and devoted to his wife and two children. But pressure gradually grows on him to enter the rat-race and become rich. He succumbs, and the art of Mr. Steinbeck has never been shown to better advantage than when he describes, quite casually, the two unutterably mean and despicable actions which open the door to Ethan's prosperity.

But meanness and treachery are catching. The atmosphere spreads its own miasma. Allen, Ethan's fourteen-year-old son, wins an honourable mention in an all-American essay competition. The boy is about to sign TV contracts and launch out on the lucrative career of a prodigy when it is discovered that his essay is a clever pastiche of cribbing. (This strikes the only false note. Can the judges really have been so ignorant of their own country's literature?) The finale is so brilliant that I will not spoil it by a bald summary. But the point, to me, lies in the skill whereby the author maintains the consistency—not the inconsistency—of Ethan's weak but most attractive character. This is a gentle, brave, and humane book. . . .

Harold C. Gardiner.
"The Old Pro and Three Newcomers."
America, 105
(22 July 1961), 554.

... The trouble with this new novel by a man who was once one of the near-greats on the U.S. literary scene is that it poses as a modern morality play, but is at the same time utterly devoid of any firm sense of moral commitment. Pretending to probe into the unraveling moral fiber of America, Steinbeck can summon up only a languidly condemnatory tsk-tsk. What made *The Grapes of Wrath* a notable book was the subdued glow of a type of moral indignation over the social ills so graphically depicted. This book whimpers where it should bang.

The story, briefly, concerns the moral decay of a good man. He is from old native New England stock and counts among his forebears intrepid whaling captains and sturdy traders. His own fortune has declined, and he is just a clerk in the town grocery store. But he is happily married, has two rather stock-character children and is not discontented. He gets the bug of ambition, however, and sets about bettering his economic condition by a series of underhand deals. He even plans to rob the local bank, but a happy accident thwarts that, and anyway he doesn't have to, because his schemes are working out well.

Indifferent to his own moral decay, he is brought up short when he discovers that his son has cheated in winning honorable mention in a nation-wide essay contest. How can he justly rebuke his son when the boy brazenly protests that he has only done "what everybody else does"?

This is just about where the book ends. There is no focus either in the supposed morality or, indeed, in the telling, which is marred by an insufferably cute dialogue, especially when the hero is addressing his everloving wife. If our public morality is declining, this book doesn't shed much light on the whys and wherefores.

Asher Brynes.
"A Man Who Lived with Failure."
New Republic, 145
(21 August 1961), 24.

The curtain rises and we are in the midst of a man-and-wife dialogue. The setting is a bedroom on a sunny morning. It is Good Friday, which commemorates the agony by which man may be redeemed. Ethan Allen Hawley spouts bits from the Bible and the *Golden Treasury* and *Mother Goose*. Mary Hawley protests happily; her responses are a sweet chorus to his flights of fancy. Then the Problem appears.

Ethan is the lone offshoot of a line of grandees who once owned much of this old whaling town, but now he clerks in a grocery store and his employer is a "wop." All that is left of his New England patrimony is the house his ancestors built—and mouthfuls of words in place of the cash in strong-boxes. So he masks his bitterness with a persistent gaiety of speech. Since the Hawleys live in a small community and were once people of wealth, their lack of money is almost unbearably conspicuous. Besides, Ethan's two children have actively average tastes for the consumption of merchandise....

The ... novel is the story of a man

472

who lived with failure for a long time and woke up late, so late that he is obsessed with the idea of neglecting no opportunity to grab what he should have had all along. He literally leaves uncommitted no sin that can profit him. He even tries to perpetrate an unnecessary theft. . . .

As in all his major fiction, Steinbeck wants to instruct and warn the reader as well as entertain him. *The Grapes of Wrath* dealt with rural people in a Western setting; and he knew them so well that despite the fact that he sandwiched a full chapter of generalizations about them between each chapter of the earlier novel, few readers found those digressions objectionable. Here the allegorizing is more obtrusive. Another demerit is the absence of a controlling point of view such as the Jeffersonian agrarianism which served him so well in sorting out the significance of things when he wrote of country people. Here the iron-handed way in which he implements (that *is* the proper word) all omens and ties all strings and punishes all important sins— those which involve betrayals of trust and affection—gives *The Winter of Our Discontent* an unintended pathos. It is clearly a comeback effort, and as clearly a failure.

"Brief Mention." New Yorker, 37 (16 September 1961), 177.

. . . A symbolic novel, an allegory, a parable, a tract—take your choice—that spends three hundred pages telling us that dishonesty breeds dishonesty. The hook the author hangs his sermon on is Ethan Allen Hawley, a young and impoverished member of an old New England–type family. Hawley, who is distinguished only by the non–New England endearments he uses with his Boston Irish wife ("my creamy fowl," "Cheesecake," "my dimpsy darling," "pigeon-flake"), by his insomnia, and by his total lack of humor, embarks on a somewhat tarnished program of financial self-improvement and is one-upped by his own son, who commits an even better misdemeanor. Mr. Steinbeck's style ("She was laughing her lovely trill, something that raises goose lumps of pleasure on my soul") suggests Grand Rapids chartreuse. A Literary Guild selection.

"The Winter of Our Discontent." Virginia Quarterly Review, 37 (Autumn 1961), cxii.

Three hot wars and an interminable cold one, together with a single deep economic depression and several of minor though lasting significance have beyond question left their impress upon the American people who have suffered among other things such intangible losses as a lowered sense of morality and personal responsibility, a weakened concept of integrity, and a tendency to accept material values in preference to the abstractions represented by honor, duty, or even decency. In a complete and invigorating break with his literary past Mr. Steinbeck convincingly demonstrates his skill as a novelist, and his determination not to be shelved as a major contemporary writer, by considering at length the debilitating effects upon character of such currently fashionable traits as disloyalty, dishonesty, infidelity, cheating, and untruthfulness among the inhabitants of a northeastern seaport founded by American pioneers who possessed the very qualities and attributes scorned by their descendants. Mr. Steinbeck's parable is incisive and chilling. His admonitory finger is all the more arresting because it is never shaken in the reader's face. With his technique of understatement and his progressively insidious development of deteriorating standards, both individual and collective, the author adds considerably to his stature as an authoritative commentator on American life. His new novel is certain to be rated with his finest work.

Larry Conterno.
"*The Winter of Our Discontent*."
Catholic World, 194 (November 1961), 125–6.

John Steinbeck, in his new novel, turns to a consideration of the loss of personal, business and political morality in our society. In setting and character this work represents a departure for the author who, heretofore, has written of the Far West and of simple, uneducated people in that area.

The locale of this novel is the Northeastern Seaboard during the time between Good Friday and the early days of July; and the characters depicted are for the greater part wellborn, educated and successful. The story concerns Ethan Allen Hawley, an heir to the upright New England tradition whose forebears have numbered sea captains and men of prop-erty. Ethan, who (like his father before him) has lost the courage and daring of his ancestors and most of the money left by them, dwells in a village known as New Baytown with his wife and their two teen-age children.

Employed as a grocery clerk by Alfio Marullo, an immigrant Italian, Ethan (although aware of the dishonesty and the shady practices engaged in by some of the leading families in the maintenance of their wealth and prestige) is so riddled by the fear that he will be unable to support his family at all, that he takes no chances and lives resigned to his fate.

Good Friday arrives and it is ironic that on this day the moral disintegration of Ethan should begin, prompted by the discontent of his wife who complains that their children have a hang-dog look because they cannot be dressed as well as others. His children in turn express their longing for luxuries their friends enjoy. Disturbed by these outpourings, Ethan is subjected during the following days and months to a series of temptations which could (if he succumbs to them) result in the acquisition of money, property and prestige. It would also mean betraying his employer, cheating a lifelong friend and even holding up the local bank.

Aided by a female witch equipped with fortune-telling cards (and a knowledge of better things for better living through chicanery) Ethan's disintegration is seemingly effortless, remarkably smooth, successful in purpose and horrible to watch. How he is saved from self-destruction makes up the denouement of Mr. Steinbeck's plot.

The theme of the novel is inherently powerful and meaningful and the bare outline of the plot has an undeniable fascination. It is regrettable that the author, in the mistaken notion that additional weight is necessary, has invested the book with a lot of mumbo-jumbo and hocus-pocus involving a talisman, a female witch and ambiguous religious significance that results in a contrived, pretentious story, reduces his theme to a point of dullness and vitiates his moral indignation to a spark where it ought to be a flame burning bright. There is a further lack of conviction in the use of a time span which seems too brief for the disintegration involved, and in the sketchiness of some of the characterizations.

What you have left that is appealing and reminiscent of Mr. Steinbeck's finer works, is his writing about the land and the sea. These passages are lovingly, evocatively and warmly rendered. It is too bad that this is not, as advance ballyhoo would have had one believe, his finest novel since *The Grapes of Wrath*.

D[aniel] A. P[oling]. "*The Winter of Our Discontent*." *Christian Herald*, 83 (November 1961), 100.

This novel is something altogether different from other best sellers of the author, but it is as distinguished in its own right as *Wayward Bus* or *The Grapes of Wrath*. Those who wait for Steinbeck's next will be surprised with this. They may be disillusioned, but hardly will they be disappointed. Mature and not for church libraries.

Benjamin De Mott. "Fiction Chronicle." *Hudson Review*, 14 (Winter 1961–2), 624–5.

. . . Once or twice in his career Steinbeck labored hard at writing, accepted the killing obligation to offer objects instead of comment on objects, places and people instead of complaints. But he has not done this for years, and he does not do it in the novel at hand. His scene is completely unrealized (he explains in a note that "this book is about a large part of America today"). His talk, though bouncy and cheerful, is embarrassingly out of touch (consider the slangy "grapes" above). And his central situation, integrity challenged in a grocery store, never becomes a situation (because it interests its creator merely as an excuse for chatter about how to be really good). Nobody can blame an established reputation for being reluctant to roll the fictional stone any longer up the hill, or for ceasing to regard self-doubt as a powerful primal energy, or for hoping that his name will serve in lieu of illusion. But there is no way of evading the truth that the hope is false, and that the writer who gives himself over to it has the poorest (not the best) chance of getting himself accepted as a sage. . . .

Jarmila Dvorak.
"The Winter of Our Discontent."
Books Abroad, 36
(Winter 1962), 80–1.

After years of silence, John Steinbeck presented us in 1961 with a large novel, set in a small eastern coast town with a famous whaling past. . . . One day in spring of 1960, Ethan decides that he would help to regain the lost family dignity. He plays with the idea of robbing the bank, but finally he uses less spectacular means to help the family back on its feet. He swindles his boss out of his business by denouncing him to the immigration authorities for illegal entry into this country—and gets the last lot of valuable land from his former best friend—now the town drunk who commits suicide. We also learn about Ethan's teenage son Allen, who copies a composition for the contest from a book—and wins. But the end sees everybody happy and well established where they belong—including the Italian grocer, who returns to his native Sicily.

All this may very well illustrate the moral climate of the Fifties but I suspect that the author did not want to criticize, but to praise the "good old American way of life" for which the Hawley family is striving at any price. And this is a very disturbing thought.

Of course, John Steinbeck is a skilful writer and he has proven it more than once in his own great past, first in his classic work *The Grapes of Wrath* (1939). But at that time we had no doubts about the author and his intentions, while today we somehow feel out of place with our own discontent.

J. N. Hartt.
"The Return of Moral Passion."
Yale Review, 51
(Winter 1962), 305–6.

. . . After frolicking in the beery froth of *Sweet Thursday*, Steinbeck comes up clean and dry in *The Winter of Our Discontent*. Here he is moralizing even more vigorously, and with less philosophic pretentiousness, than in *East of Eden*. He rides with a simple story-line: Ethan Allen Hawley, scion of a history-making New England family, has seen his fortunes fall on evil days. He is reduced to clerking in a non-supermarket, and to watching helplessly as his wife and two children struggle to maintain pride and integrity against the multitudinous pressures of community life in our troubled era. Against impossible odds Hawley himself lives by his own code of honesty, fairness, compassion, and courage; and he is able to get in at least one thumping body-blow against moral corruption in high places. But he has to stand by impotent, as his son capitulates to the success-at-any-price attitude; and he is himself partly culpable in the death of a very dear friend. Unable to live faithfully, as he feels, in a world gone dead and rotten at the heart, he is on the verge of suicide when he is brought back to renew the good fight. In this darkling world even the smallest light is worth infinite care: there's the principle.

Steinbeck comes very close to espousing the cause of American small-town virtue against the juggernaut of urbanization. What we call Progress, he tells us through Ethan Hawley, is often a move toward the moral jungle, the noisome wilderness in which the reputation of rectitude is but a ruse for the aggrandizement of the power-lusting ego. Thus the moral tone of *The Winter of Our Discontent* is unquestionably serious, indeed, passionate. I do not believe that any of the characters attain a proportional luminosity and power. The villain is drawn from stock; and his motivations are exposed only for the purposes of excoriation. And sweet and lovely as Hawley's love-affair with his wife is—Steinbeck is prepared, I take it, to endure disbelief and perhaps even contumely in having them faithful to each other—Hawley appears to draw his moral strength from solitude only. But with what does he commune thus? Ancestors of oaken moral fiber. This I find preposterous, for a grown, battle-seasoned man, since it is one of the more inane forms of ancestor-worship. The virtues which have made America great, rather than merely strong, are indeed doomed, if Steinbeck has correctly represented the sources of courage and wisdom in the defense against the evils of this present hour. . . .

J[oan] Didion.
"The Winter of Our Discontent."
National Review, 12 (16 January 1962), 33.

He: *"You're a witch! Why don't you whistle up a wind?"* She: *"I can't whistle. I can raise a puny little storm in most men with my eyebrows. How do I go about lighting your fire?"* He: *"Maybe you have."* Although it is difficult to believe that whoever wrote that dialogue had much more on his mind than something along the lines of *Flying Down to*

Rio, believe it we must. Plucked more or less at random from *The Winter of Our Discontent*, that particular colloquy is the handiwork of Mr. John Steinbeck; and Mr. Steinbeck is quite in earnest, deeply troubled by what the jacket calls "our shoddy attitudes toward honesty and success" (antithetical, as any fool knows), by "the loss of integrity in our world." For both Mr. Steinbeck and his protagonist, a grocery clerk who temporarily wanders down where the money and the primroses grow, the idea of "integrity" is pretty much encompassed in that of not cheating on television quiz programs. It all takes several hundred pages, but in the end, Mr. Steinbeck *is* against cheating. He is for honesty. He is for some other things, too—families, for example, and friendship—but his ideas about *honesty* and *integrity* are far and away the most provocative of all his moral perceptions. Perhaps the most interesting thing about *The Winter of Our Discontent* is that Dr. Carlos Baker, writing in the *New York Times Book Review*, found it a novel loaded with "disturbing" implications. *Nada te turbe*, Carlos.

"The Winter of Our Discontent."
Christian Century, 20 May 1962, p. 693.

Ethan Hawley, descendant of an upright New England family, works as general handyman in a grocery located in a Long Island Sound village. Despite the loss of family fortune, Ethan is happy—happy in his job and in his marriage and family. Then the seeds of discontent begin to germinate. He has no car, no television set, none of the appurtenances which symbolize success and contribute to comfort. He decides to go after the money which he now feels will bring more happiness to his family. He engages in some shady business maneuvers and in the process almost loses his soul. Although this modern morality fable is too contrived to be entirely convincing, Steinbeck succeeds in drawing one devastating portrait, that of a modern teen-ager, in this case Ethan's son. The lad decides to emulate Charles Van Doren's example and cash in on television's prizes. He almost succeeds. Had Steinbeck been less concerned to preach a sermon about the evils of materialism, he might have written a better novel.

Checklist of Additional Reviews

"*The Winter of Our Discontent*." *Booklist*, 57 (1 June 1961), 606–7.

Robert B. Jackson. "*The Winter of Our Discontent*." *Library Journal*, 86 (15 June 1961), 2339.

Emerson Price. "Compassionate Steinbeck Novel Explores Loss of Moral Principle." Cleveland *Press*, 20 June 1961, p. 8B.

William Hogan. "A Bookman's Notebook: Steinbeck—Again the Social Critic." San Francisco *Chronicle*, 22 June 1961, p. 29.

William Hogan. "A Bookman's Notebook: Steinbeck Comments on the New Morality." San Francisco *Chronicle*, 23 June 1961, p. 33.

Fanny Butcher. "Steinbeck Novel Offers a Mental Challenge." Chicago *Tribune*, 25 June 1961, Part 4, pp. 1–2.

Jean Martin. "Steinbeck Wades into Modern Integrity." Chicago *Sun-Times*, 25 June 1961, Section 3, p. 1.

V.P.H. "New Steinbeck Novel Just Literary Pablum." New York *World-Herald, World-Herald Magazine*, 25 June 1961, p. 20.

Paul Pickrel. "The New Books." *Harper's*, 223 (July 1961), 91–2.

"*The Winter of Our Discontent*." *Bookmark*, 20 (July 1961), 234.

"Critics Disagree about New Book." Monterey [Calif.] *Peninsula Herald*, 17 July 1961, p. 5.

Mary Lowrey Ross. "Moral Disarmament." *Saturday Night*, 76 (5 August 1961), 27.

Ernest Gordon. "*The Winter of Our Discontent*." *Princeton Seminary Bulletin*, 15 (Winter 1962), 44–7.

TRAVELS WITH CHARLEY IN SEARCH OF AMERICA

JOHN STEINBECK

Travels
with
Charley

IN SEARCH OF AMERICA

THE VIKING PRESS · NEW YORK

Eric Moon.
"Travels with Charley."
Library Journal, 87
(15 June 1962), 2378.

Orville Prescott.
"Books of the Times."
New York *Times*,
27 July 1962, p. 23.

Charley is "an old French gentleman poodle" with a placid temperament and cultural pretensions. John Steinbeck is an aging writer with a romantic view of himself as a "man of the people," now worried that the America he has been writing about for 20 years has passed him by. This is the crew of Rocinante, a three-quarter-ton pickup truck equipped with a miniature ship's cabin and named after Don Quixote's horse. Their journey of rediscovery takes them through 40 states, but it is really no more than an excuse for Steinbeck to be along, to meet again people on the road, and to muse nostalgically about the way things used to be before "progress" came along. The mood ranges from sentiment (his love affair with Montana), through gentle irony (Texas hospitality), to a rather naïve horror over the mechanical demonstrations by strident women outside New Orleans schools. The prose is, as one would expect, always competent, often self-conscious, sometimes superb. It's a slight, inconsequential book by a nice man rather than a great novelist. But it's a pleasant evening's reading, and it will be deservedly popular.

Soon after Labor Day in the autumn of 1960 a big man with a beard and a large dog with a scraggly mustache set forth together on an automobile tour of the United States. The man was John Steinbeck, one of the most successful of contemporary American novelists. The dog was Charley, an elderly French poodle who understood French better than English and who, Mr. Steinbeck insists, could read minds—his master's mind anyway. They rode in a pickup truck named Rocinante after Don Quixote's famous steed.

On the truck was a small house built to Mr. Steinbeck's specifications like the cabin of a small boat. The riders were off to learn "what are Americans like today?" Mr. Steinbeck was no longer sure because for twenty-five years he had been living in New York and had lost touch with the ranch hands, migrant workers, *paisanos* and such about whom he had written in his best books. A report on the trip of man and dog is now published, *Travels With Charley: In Search of America*.

This is a likable and amusing book. Mr. Steinbeck has not been able to find out what Americans are like today, but he thinks that they are growing more like each other than they used to be and that regional differences are disappearing. He noticed what one would expect: the expanding cities, the roaring superhighways, the good breakfasts and wretched dinners available along the highways, racial strife in New Orleans and the beauties of nature everywhere.

Travels With Charley is lightweight

fare and contains nothing of much significance about the present state of the nation. But Mr. Steinbeck doesn't pretend that he discovered a new America. He had an interesting time. He writes about it in a bright, brisk, bouncy style. Relaxed, informal and chatty, he indulges in whopping exaggerations, tells tall stories, sketches odd characters he met and tosses off a series of capsule essays on scores of subjects. Since Mr. Steinbeck is an intelligent man and a facile writer the result is engaging.

Reading *Travels With Charley*, I found it necessary to keep a volume of state road maps handy. Mr. Steinbeck, who "was born lost and takes no pleasure in being found," rather scorns maps. But I am one who cherishes them. Without them how would I know where he and Charley were when they met the young man in Idaho who yearned to be a ladies' hairdresser in New York? Or when they encountered the roving actor in Montana who was giving a one-man Shakespeare reading, as exactly like Sir John Gielgud's as possible?

Through thirty-four states for more than 10,000 miles, camping out in Rocinante most of the time, staying in motels for the sake of a hot bath some of the time, Mr. Steinbeck journeyed. He was frightened in the dark and amid the woods of northern Maine. He had a terrible time when a rear tire blew out in a rainstorm in Oregon. Charley was alarmingly ill twice. But the lobsters of Maine were delicious. The Wisconsin countryside was beautiful and surprisingly varied. The redwood trees of California were magnificent. And Montana, "a great splash of grandeur," was so wonderful that it is now and forever Mr. Steinbeck's favorite state.

Just to give you a notion, here are a few of the many topics briefly discussed in *Travels With Charley*: French Canadian potato pickers in Aroostook County,

Me.; a sermon in Vermont depicting the fires of hell as awaiting most of us; the habits of truck drivers, who know nothing of the country they pass through; mobile homes and mobile living; the nature of turkeys; the melancholy changes that have transformed Salinas and Monterey since the day of Mr. Steinbeck's youth; the beauties of the Mojave Desert and Texas as a state of mind and as a religion.

I like particularly what Mr. Steinbeck has to say about superhighways:

"Trucks as long as freighters went roaring by, delivering a wind like the blow of a fist. These great roads are wonderful for moving goods but not for inspection of a countryside. You are bound to the wheel and your eyes to the car ahead and to the rear-view mirror for the car behind and the side-mirror for the car or truck about to pass, and at the same time you must read all the signs for fear you may miss some instructions or orders.

"No roadside stands selling squash juice, no antique stores, no farm products or factory outlets. When we get these thruways across the whole country, as we will and must, it will be possible to drive from New York to California without seeing a single thing."

Fanny Butcher. "Steinbeck Rediscovers His Land and People." *Chicago Sunday Tribune Magazine of Books*, 29 July 1962, Part 4, pp. 1–2.

John Steinbeck, who has cut deep into the heart of America more than once with his novels (will you ever forget *The Grapes of Wrath?*), decided he wanted to see what had happened to his native country and fellow Americans since he last had had intimate contact with them across the land. He would make a journey around the world of the United States, he decided, and he would come closest to the American good earth and the American people if he went by truck, avoiding main highways as much as possible.

He bought a three-quarter ton pickup truck, had "a little house built like the cabin of a small boat" constructed on it, equipped it with "a heater, refrigerator and lights operated on butane gas, and a chemical toilet." He called it his "turtle shell" and named the conveyance Rocinante in memory of Don Quixote's steed.

He took shotguns and fishing equipment. "If a man is going hunting or fishing his purpose is understood, even applauded," but, "I no longer kill or catch anything I cannot get into a frying pan." These preparations for making talking to strangers easier proved unnecessary.

Charley, who shared Steinbeck's three months, 10,000 mile trip, was born in France, a "very big French poodle who knows a little poodle English, responds quickly only to commands in French ... a born diplomat, a good watchdog, who roars like a lion."

Charley was not only companion but stage setting, too. For, says Steinbeck, "A dog, particularly an exotic like Charley, is a bond between strangers. Many conversations en route began with 'What degree of dog is that?' " The best way of all of opening a conversation, however, he found was to be lost.

The trip began at Sag Harbor, Long Island, just after Labor Day in 1960. His course went to the tip of Maine, across the northern United States to California, back thru Texas, New Orleans, and the south.

If the reader expects to find here a travel guide to the United States, he will be disappointed. If he hopes to find trenchant observations about life in general and about our country, occasional glowing descriptions of nature, some wonderful, revealing scraps of conversation, a penetrating insight into American mores, searching thoughts on loneliness, all recorded by a master of the writing craft, he will be delighted with *Travels with Charley*.

"Americans are a restless people," says the author, reminding us that this country was settled by people who "hungered to move." "But just moving has obsessed many Americans," he observes, and he wonders wryly if "one goes not so much to see as to tell afterwards."

One thing he noticed about American cities all over the country is that they "are like badger holes, ringed with trash"— all of them "surrounded by piles of wrecked and rusting automobiles and almost smothered by rubbish." He saw divergent tendencies thruout the country, in northern Maine and New England, villages giving way to cities and wild life taking over, in the midwest and the far west, a population explosion and "progress" everywhere. And he says, "I wonder why progress so often looks like destruction?"

"When we get these thruways across the whole country as we will and must, it will be possible to drive from New York to California without seeing a thing," he asserts. He used other roads whenever possible and confesses, "I was born lost and take no pleasure in being found, nor much identification from shapes which symbolize continents and states."

Some of his descriptions of nature are thrilling. Of autumn in New England he writes, "It isn't only color, but a glowing.... There's a quality of fire in these colors." The Wisconsin fall enchanted him. "The air was rich with

483

butter-colored sunlight, not fuzzy, but crisp and clear, so that every frost-gay tree was set off. . . . There was a penetration of the light into solid substances, so that I seemed to see into things, deep in, and I've seen that kind of light only in Greece."

Steinbeck often was asked if he was traveling for pleasure, and he could always answer yes until he went to New Orleans. There he saw a group of women called "cheerleaders" applauded by crowds as they shouted obscenities at two small Negro children entering and leaving a previously all-white school. "They were neither women nor mothers," he says, in what they were doing, and it made him sick at heart. He left the south saying sadly to himself, "I know that the solution when it arrives will not be easy or simple."

His words about his traveling companion (and the human race) are ironic: "Charley doesn't belong to a species clever enough to split the atom, but not clever enough to live in peace with itself."

Lewis Gannett.
"From Coast to Coast, He Met No Strangers."
New York Herald Tribune Weekly Book Review, 29 July 1962, p. 3.

After twenty-five years in Manhattan and Hollywood, Sag Harbor, London, Paris and points East, John Steinbeck decided that it was time for him to go back and feel America, hear its changing speech, look at its hills and water, smell its grass and trees and sewage. So he equipped himself with a three-quarter-ton pickup truck, a "camper" atop it, and set out, accompanied only by Charley. Charley is a French-born blue poodle, companionable and friendly, except for bears.

Now John Steinbeck, as readers know, is a born story-teller with a rumbling chuckle in his way of speech, and a great gift of friendship, particularly for dogs, but also for truck-drivers, bartenders and lonely wayfarers. He was, to be sure, his own bartender on most of his journey, but a small bar in a "camper" is almost as good an invitation to confidences as a dog, and Mr. Steinbeck had still another gadget for making friends along the way. He has, he says, a talent for getting lost, and a lost driver brings out the best in human nature, even in New York City policemen.

The resulting book is unlike anything Mr. Steinbeck ever wrote before, and utterly unlike the usual pseudo-sociological observations on what's wrong with America. Mr. Steinbeck set out in a benign mood, just escaping the hurricane Donna, and he claims that from start to finish he met no "strangers." Even the guardians of absentee-owned estates, who began by questioning Mr. Steinbeck's right to park and camp, quickly turned into friends. The only people Mr. Steinbeck saw that he didn't like were the screeching ninnies, locally known as "cheerleaders," who were shouting obscenities at integrated school children when he passed through New Orleans. Of course, Charley helped. Charley liked people, and people liked Charley on sight, and the friendship quickly extended to include Charley's travelling companion.

New England a little baffled Mr. Steinbeck, who is California-born and accustomed to conversation at breakfast. Breakfast with truckers was one of his delights in state after state. Truckers, forever on the move, are the kind of people who particularly appeal to Mr. Steinbeck's restless soul. But in Maine he discovered that "the natural New England taciturnity reaches its glorious perfection at breakfast." An early morning waitress who condescended to say "Yep" to an out-of-state visitor was, in Mr. Steinbeck's experience, relatively garrulous. In the midwest he found people friendlier. He was startled by the sheer beauty of the Wisconsin countryside, and with the whole state of Montana he fell wildly in love. Sometimes he passed the night in trailer camps, where he discovered the friendly company of the great fraternity who live on wheels. They have no roots, he says, but they all have dogs.

In Chicago Mr. Steinbeck had a good time figuring out the history of the previous occupant of a hotel room whose wastebasket had not yet been emptied: that's one story. The trailer-travelling actor he met on a North Dakota roadside is another. So is the unbelievably co-operative Sunday garage owner on a mud road in Oregon. And so's Thanksgiving dinner with Mr. Steinbeck's wife's friends in Texas. For sheer emotion, though, try Steinbeck on the big trees of his native state, or the story of his return to Johnny Garcia's bar in Monterey, complete with the whole cast of characters from *Tortilla Flat*, including the "American dogs."

It's a happy, relaxed book, devoid of the bitterness and violence of some of the middle-period Steinbeck. But Steinbeck is still Steinbeck—no Pollyanna he. He thinks America, putting cleanliness first, has lost the sense of taste. He doesn't like sprawling cities—always gets lost in them, for one thing, and besides, they lack dogs. The books and magazines on sale along the way, and the local radio stations he listened to, were as tasteless as the food. Mr. Steinbeck is pretty dogmatic about his thesis that Americans are a new breed, whether of Chinese,

British or Negro descent, more like each other than a Lowland Scot is like a Highlander. This, he says, "is an exact and provable thing," but he didn't stop to prove it. He and Charley just kept moving along, and moving along with Steinbeck in this mood is a very pleasant experience.

Eric F. Goldman. "Steinbeck's America, Twenty Years After." *New York Times Book Review*, 111 (29 July 1962), 5.

There are some men, John Steinbeck says, who are born wanderers; when the winds of restlessness seize them, there is nothing for them to do but go. They find reasons for everything, including the need for the trip. In Steinbeck's case, the justification was easy enough. Here he was an American writer, writing about America, but for some twenty years he had known little of the country at first-hand. Shortly after Labor Day, 1960, Steinbeck left his Long Island home for a swing around the United States.

Three months and 10,000 miles later the 58-year-old novelist was back, physically and emotionally exhausted. But it was all decidedly worth the effort. The resulting book is pure delight, a pungent potpourri of places and people interspersed with bittersweet essays on everything from the emotional difficulties of growing old to the reasons why giant Sequoias arouse such awe....

The swing into the Middle West brought out the old agrarian in Steinbeck.

He deplored the superhighways and he abhorred the mammoth cities. He noted too that the road signs were shifting in tone. The New York State signs had shouted at him. The New England ones had a kind of laconic precision. In the Middle West the signs were "more benign.... The earth was generous and outgoing here in the heartland, and perhaps the people took a cue from it."

Once past Chicago, Steinbeck's prose takes on a new lift. This was his kind of country, and the Pacific, his Pacific, was nearing. By the time he reached Montana, he was engaged in an unabashed love affair with nature. The calm of the mountains and grasslands, he was sure, had seeped into the inhabitants. Out here even the casual conversation, in Steinbeck's glowing reportage, has an earthy sagacity. It was beyond Chicago that he talked with a crossroads storekeeper and raised the question that was beginning to bother him. Why didn't Americans argue violently about public affairs any more? ...

On to Seattle and then down into northern California. Naturally the clash between old and new produced the sharpest twinges in the area of Steinbeck's boyhood and of his novels. In Monterey, Johnny Garcia stood behind his bar and went on and on about what a homecoming this was and Steinbeck sat on the stool thinking about the Carmel Valley when he could shoot his rifle where he pleased without disturbing anything but frogs. Suddenly he was on his feet, bolting for the door. "I was on Alvarado Street, slashed with neon light—and around me it was nothing but strangers."

Texas undid Steinbeck. He was determined not to go along with the usually easy denunciations of the state, and in this chapter he leans backward so far that at times he tumbles into saccharinity and even near incomprehensibility. But no one can doubt his meaning as he reached New Orleans and "Cheerleaders" scream at a tiny Negro girl making her terrified way into a desegregated school. Here is the most powerful writing in the book, stinging with the cold lash of outraged decency....

Of one thing Steinbeck became quite sure. For all the stubborn regionalism of the United States, for all the ethnic range of its people, "we are a nation, a new breed.... The American identity is an exact and provable thing." But just what was this exact and provable thing? Steinbeck would try to lay hold of it and more and more he came back to the drive for change in the American character. In a whole series of mullings, he speculated on the exact cause and nature of this characteristic.

Increasingly in his travels Steinbeck caught himself when he wanted to lash out at the most fundamental result of that drive, the rampant industrialization. "It is the nature of man as he grows older to protest against change.... The sad ones are those who waste their energy in trying to hold it back, for they can only feel bitterness in loss and no joy in gain."

For such talk Charley had no comment at all. A wise dog does not try to top wisdom.

George Mills. "Maybe Satchelful of Characters?" Des Moines *Sunday Register*, 29 July 1962, p. 15G.

Can a man take a dog and a mobile home and go out and discover what

America really is like in three months?

That is what John Steinbeck tried to do. Charley is his French poodle. Together they traveled from coast to coast. (Iowa was not on the itinerary.)

If Steinbeck "discovered" present-day America, he doesn't give a deep report of his findings here. Maybe he brought back a satchelful of characters who will spark future *Cannery Rows* and *Sweet Thursdays*.

Nevertheless, this is a lively and refreshing book. Steinbeck's cutting edge is still good. . . . His word artistry is classic. . . .

The comparative brevity of the book, 246 pages, is sufficient proof of the fact that the author is not pretending to provide his readers with a definitive picture of the nation as it is today. One omission: Steinbeck includes no report on the imaginative, strenuous, vital and erudite life of intellectual young Americans on today's college campuses.

"Steinbeck on the Road." *Newsweek*, 60 (30 July 1962), 77–8.

"For many years I have lived in many parts of the world . . . I had not heard the speech of America, smelled the grass and trees and sewage, seen its hills and water, its color and quality of light. I knew the changes only from books and newspapers. But more than this, I had not felt the country for 25 years. In short, I was writing of something I did not know about, and it seems to me that in a socalled writer this is criminal." . . .

Steinbeck's concern with his writer's craft was admittedly not his only reason for mounting Rocinante. A year earlier, at 59, he had suffered a severe illness, and now he meant to prove something. "My wife married a man," he writes. "I saw no reason why she should inherit a baby. I knew that ten or twelve thousand miles driving a truck, alone and unattended, over every kind of road, would be hard work, but to me it represented the antidote for the poison of the professional sick man."

And off he went, curving up through New England, then through the Midwest, the Northwest, down through California, over to Texas and the Deep South, and up the Appalachian line. Steinbeck is very much a visual man, and he responds most vividly to excesses of nature—the autumn riot in New England, the Dakota Badlands, the limitless plains of Montana, and the sequoia forests of California. His taste in people, though, is more subtle, and he finds wonder or pleasure or annoyance or stimulation or anger or amusement in every human he meets, from a hellfire preacher in Vermont to an old Negro hitchhiker in Louisiana.

It is silly to talk about drawing conclusions from a journey like this, because Steinbeck set out simply to see and to hear, and he has done both with a quick mind and an honest heart. If this vigorous, affecting, and highly entertaining book has a flaw, it is only in Steinbeck's self-indulgent loathing of every city he drove through, cities which seemed to him nothing but "a great surf of traffic . . . waves of station wagons, rip tides of roaring trucks." Even Don Quixote knew that you can't begin to judge a city until you get off Rocinante.

Paul Pickrel.
"The Changes That Time Brings."
Harper's, 225
(August 1962), 91–2.

In *Travels with Charley* . . . John Steinbeck tells of a trip he took around the United States to see how time has changed the country in the last twenty years, while he has been too busy writing about it to do much traveling. . . .

What Steinbeck saw turns out to be largely predictable. He found for instance that regional differences in speech are less marked than they once were, a change that is hardly surprising after several decades of radio and television and a vast amount of moving around. He thinks that American speech may be more grammatical than it once was, a piece of speculation that will bring no comfort to the numerous deplorers of the way grammar is now taught (and dictionaries compiled), though they may find some reassurance in the fact that Steinbeck himself is not the most sure-footed of grammarians: he thinks that the word slow in a sign saying "Drive slow" is an adjective, and deprecates its use.

Steinbeck found the American people more subdued and uncertain than they once were, without many or strong convictions, too worried or too indifferent even to exercise their long-established right to argue over the Presidential election. (The one exception—the violent anti-segregationists of New Orleans, who were willing to make a lot of obscene noise about their convictions—shocked him.) On the whole the old New England farmer who spoke to him at the outset of the trip set the tone of what follows: "What good's an opinion if you don't know? My grandfather knew the number of whiskers in the Almighty's beard. I don't even know what happened yesterday, let alone tomorrow. He knew what it was that makes a rock or a table. I don't even know the formula that says nobody knows. We've got nothing to go on—got no way to think about things." Not many people that Steinbeck encountered were that articulate or that much aware of their own predicament, but the sense of being shut off from certainty was prevalent.

In its generalizations *Travels with Charley* is a commonplace, even a trivial book, agreeable enough to read but not really very enlightening. But it comes to life whenever Steinbeck fastens upon the particular. His marvelous ear for dialogue, his skill in revealing character through speech, and his quick sympathy for the disadvantaged raise nearly every personal encounter he reports well above the level of his general observations. So too, though his general impressions are undistinguished, his descriptions of particular objects or prospects are nearly always effective and sometimes brilliant.

Edward Weeks.
"Seeing Our Country Close."
Atlantic, 210 (August 1962), 138–9.

As his books reveal, John Steinbeck is a writer who is happiest when he gets down to earth. He is a rugged, broad-shouldered, six-foot Californian, born in Salinas, and destined to write his first stories about the Valley. He has the gift of identifying himself passionately with other

Americans, with migratory fruit pickers, as in his novel *In Dubious Battle*, and with the Okies, as in *The Grapes of Wrath*. He relishes doing things with his own two hands; in a swift self-portrait he writes, "I have always lived violently, drunk hugely, eaten too much or not at all, slept around the clock or missed two nights of sleeping, worked too hard and too long in glory, or slobbed for a time in utter laziness. I've lifted, pulled, chopped, climbed, made love with joy and taken my hangovers as a consequence, not as a punishment." Gradually his career drew him into the success and confinement of Manhattan and Long Island, and it came to him with a shock one day at the age of fifty-eight to realize that not for twenty years had he seen at close hand the country he had been writing about.

His new book, *Travels with Charley* ... is a one-man, one-dog account of the expedition in which he recaptures his familiarity with America. He set out with some misgiving, not sure his health would stand up to the 10,000-mile journey he envisioned; as he traveled, the years sloughed off him, and the eager, sensuous pages in which he writes about what he found and whom he encountered frame a picture of our human nature in the twentieth century which will not soon be surpassed. . . .

This is a book to be read slowly for its savor, and one which, like Thoreau, will be quoted and measured by our own experience. It holds such happy passages as his love for Montana, his rediscovery of San Francisco, and his surprising new impressions of the Middle West; it holds such horror as he witnessed in the rancid race demonstrations in New Orleans. And as all good journeys must, this one suddenly went flat as he was returning through Virginia. Thereafter, his one desire was to get home, and when a policeman forbade him to drive through the Holland Tunnel with so much butane in the cabin, all the novelist could say was, "But I want to get home. How am I going to get home?" Incidentally, in his passage of over 10,000 miles through thirty-eight states, he was not recognized even once.

Melvin Maddocks. "Westering with Steinbeck." *Christian Science Monitor*, 2 August 1962, p. 7.

In a short story titled "The Leader of the People," young John Steinbeck made a patriarchal survivor of covered-wagon days lament to his grandson: "No place to go, Jody. . . . But that's not the worst—no, not the worst. Westering has died out of the people. Westering isn't a hunger any more. It's all done."

Time's wingèd wagon train rolls on.

It is a quarter of a century later. Mr. Steinbeck, now a prosperous, middle-aged literary celebrity, is surprised by an ancestral westering itch in his traveling shoes.

There are always "reasons" for a trip. Mr. Steinbeck officially justifies his on business grounds: "I, an American writer, writing about America, was working from memory. . . . I was writing of something I did not know about, and it seems to me that in a so-called writer this is criminal."

At Sag Harbor, Long Island, he fitted out his 1960's version of a covered wagon: a brand new three-quarter-ton pickup truck with a custom-built camper top, complete down to its double bed, four-burner stove, heater, refrigerator, radio, 30-gallon water tank, and window screens.

Other items for the well-equipped pushbutton pioneer: padded nylon subzero underwear; sufficient emergency food, one gathers, to service a bomb shelter; tools for repair, tools as spares—tools perhaps to make tools with; several guns; 150 pounds of books.

Waving an admittedly regretful farewell to his wife and his cabin cruiser, Mr. Steinbeck with his French poodle Charley beside him set out to face what he foresaw as "the terrors of the uncomfortable and the unknown."

A man who once banged around the country in an old bakery wagon with a mattress in the rear, he acknowledged an element of self-parody by dubbing his motel-on-wheels Rocinante, after the horse of Don Quixote.

It is quite possible—the allowance must always be made with travelers who rationalize—that part of him did not want to make the trip at all. But once he found himself on the road, the reflexes of an observant writer and an entertaining raconteur took over, ensuring an unpretentious book that is light without being trivial.

Mr. Steinbeck has nothing startlingly new to report, and he wisely avoids straining after ambitious summing-up.

Like most United States travelers since the war, he deplores growing signs of uniformity: the superhighways that soon will make it "possible to drive from New York to California without seeing a single thing"; the hygienic flavorlessness of most roadside restaurants; the radio that blasts "Teen-Age Angel" in California as predictably as in Maine.

On the plus side, he loves Montana and truck drivers and stands in awe of Texas. Though he carefully refuses to play the grizzled reactionary, he leaves no doubt that he prefers country to city, wood to plastic, the old ways to the new. We may grow tired occasionally of Mr. Steinbeck's slightly tough-guy, occasionally profane confidences. All except French poodle owners are likely to weary of Charley and his fairly limited responses to the American wayside.

But even Charley becomes a small, tail-wagging part of America in a subjective travel book—and what travel book isn't?

Or as Mr. Steinbeck puts it: "This monster of a land, this mightiest of nations, this spawn of the future, turns out to be the macrocosm of microcosm me."

Which is perhaps why the westering instinct will never die as long as the urge for self-discovery remains alive.

Rudolph J. Gerber. "Travels with Charley." America, 107 (4 August 1962), 569.

Into nearly a score of major works John Steinbeck has injected varying degrees of the spirit of America, exporting, perhaps, more of that spirit than he imported. *Travels with Charley* issues from his concern that he might have been writing about a nation existing largely in his imagination.

To discover the reality of modern America, Steinbeck set out on a voyage of rediscovery, westward from New York, in the company of his distinguished French poodle, Charley. . . .

His reflections, offered informally to the reader and to Charley, constitute the core of his modern-day travelogue. The booming trailer camps bordering our highways raise questions about where America's roots lie, and Steinbeck wonders if America is perhaps a restless, rootless people.

Friendliness, he finds, increases as the prairies and the Rockies approach, but he shares the artist's concern that television is effacing local color, regional speech and individual custom. Roadside restaurants have shared an analogous fate in sacrificing taste to cleanliness, and he notes that the mental fare of radio across the land is as generalized, packaged and undistinguished as the food of most local restaurants.

Segregation and the tourist trade are criticized, among other things, but there are many moments of pride and satisfaction. From start to finish Steinbeck found no strangers. His one "immaculately inspected generality" is that despite our geographic range and sectionalism and interwoven breeds, we are one country, a new breed, more like our countrymen than our European ancestors.

Travels with Charley reveals the American spirit and culture in its commonplace sources—the "little" people, the small villages, the vast prairies. Its evaluation is objective and penetrating, if not always optimistic, and its observations would be worth-while to any American curious about his cultural environment.

"*Travels with Charley*."
Time, 80
(10 August 1962), 70.

Put a famous author behind the wheel of a three-quarter-ton truck called Rocinante (after Don Quixote's horse), equip him with everything from trenching tools to subzero underwear, send along a pedigreed French poodle named Charley with prostatitis, follow the man and dog on a three-month, 10,000-mile trip through 34 states, and what have you got? One of the dullest travelogues ever to acquire the respectability of a hard cover. Vagabond Steinbeck's motive for making the long, lonely journey is admirable: "To try to rediscover this monster land" after years of easy living in Manhattan and a country place in Sag Harbor, L.I. He meets some interesting people: migrant Canucks picking potatoes in Maine, an itinerant Shakespearean actor in North Dakota, his own literary ghost back home in California's Monterey Peninsula. But when the trip is done, Steinbeck's attempt at rediscovery reveals nothing more remarkable than a sure gift for the obvious observation.

William Rivers.
"The Peripatetic Poodle."
Saturday Review, 45
(1 September 1962), 31.

When the novelist turns to journalism, he may, like Norman Mailer, invest so much of himself in his reportage that every effort is autobiographical. Or he may condescend, as Ernest Hemingway occasionally did in magazine articles, almost to the point of saying: "I need not spend much of my talent on nonfiction."

There is a little of both attitudes in John Steinbeck's *Travels with Charley*, a report on a trip around the United States. The reader learns much more about the author than he does about the country. And, although Steinbeck undoubtedly went through the agony every writer experiences who makes a book sound offhand, one cannot imagine that he gave himself to it in quite the way that he surrendered to, say, *East of Eden*. The result is both better and worse than what a perceptive journalist might have accomplished.

The opening pages are heavy with truisms that a first-rank journalist would have avoided. "I live in New York," Steinbeck writes, "or dip into Chicago or San Francisco. But New York is no more America than Paris is France or London is England." Then, "Thus I discovered that I did not know my own country. . . . So it was that I determined to look again, to try to rediscover this monster land."

There is more of much the same. It is perfectly true that the act of writing—ordering and organizing observation and experience—teaches the writer as well as the reader. But sentences like "I set this matter down not to instruct others but to inform myself" represent humility of a highly self-conscious sort. Few journalists get caught in this net, but Steinbeck is entangled again and again. . . .

But if the self-consciousness . . . rings an occasional loud note of falsity, the novelist's eye and mind are precious. Here is Steinbeck on literary style in highway signs:

> The New England states use a terse form of instruction, a tight-lipped, laconic style sheet, wasting no words and few letters. New York State shouts at you the whole time. Do this. Do that. Squeeze left. Squeeze right. Every few feet an imperious command. In Ohio the signs are more benign. They offer friendly advice and are more like suggestions. Some states use a turgid style which can get you lost with the greatest ease.

And when Steinbeck stops at a crowded Chicago hotel and must for a few hours occupy an unmade room, he analyzes the previous occupant from bits and pieces left behind: laundry slips, a half-written letter, a scent of perfume, a broken comb. Like most of the book, this is highly impressionistic, but it is also a stunning performance. Almost any journalist daring to try it would probably prove himself the victim of a circumscribed imagination.

In the end, the novelist's eye, which sees the droopy, early-morning men in a roadside restaurant "folded over their coffee cups like ferns," makes this book memorable.

E. D. O'Brien.
"A Literary Lounger."
Illustrated London News,
241 (6 October 1962),
534.

. . . The America inspected by John Steinbeck in *Travels with Charley* is rather different. Charley is a poodle, incomparably the most charming character described by the author in his travels through forty of the States. The trouble is that Mr. Steinbeck has travelled almost too far. His delightful vignettes of people, places, and incidents whet the reader's appetite, but never satisfy it. The segregationists of the South come in for a tousling. On the other hand, the Texans—here they are again!—emerge as funny and furry creatures, to be commended, like the yak, "as friends to the children. . . ."

Nicholas Wollaston. "In Continents and Islands." *Spectator* [England], 209 (19 October 1962), 604–5.

To touch the fringe of an unknown country, without the chance of penetrating it, is a tantalising thing. Like an encounter with a stranger, those brief, guarded moments of curiosity offer a prospect of disappointment but also a promise of love, and it is little comfort to be told afterwards, by another traveller, just how much one missed.

John Steinbeck, of course, missed nothing. My experience of the United States is limited to a night at Miami airport, but now I know all I want to know about the rest. It is the grand country I always hoped it might be, and *Travels with Charley* . . . is a fine, generous, loving book. As Steinbeck himself says, "there's absolutely nothing to take the place of a good man," and for the author of a travel book I would add that there's absolutely nothing to take the place of a writer. A self-confessed bum in search of America, he drove a truck with a boat's cabin built on the back through forty States, and the only sorrow he brought back to his cottage on Long Island was the memory of the screaming white women outside a school in New Orleans where a little black girl was being escorted to her lessons by the US marshals. And Charley? The only sorrow he brought back was the memory of the giant forest redwoods in the State of Oregon. For Charley was a big blue poodle, and those redwoods were like no trees he had seen before.

"Exploring Home." *Times Literary Supplement* [London], 2 November 1962, p. 843.

John Steinbeck's new travel book describes a tour of the United States which he made late in 1960 in the company of his French poodle, Charley. Like many middle-aged writers, particularly in such a vast country, he feared he had lost touch with his raw material and so he set out self-consciously, yet, conscientiously, "in search of America." Earlier in his career—when he resisted all the many attempts to make him a public personality—he would have produced a reporter's account of what he saw and heard, with a minimum of generalizations and personal references. But Mr. Steinbeck has mellowed since then and his new book—like some of his later novels—reflects this change in him.

He becomes the chief character of his *Travels*, Charley is his Fool, and the United States—nearly forty of them—fly by like a backcloth to a sketch of a writer in search of material. Mr. Steinbeck's deepest impressions of modern America will probably not be put on paper until he has had more time to digest his experiences for future novels. They will presumably be the real reward of an often arduous tour. This book in that sense is a mere byproduct, an amiable ramble from New York through the Middle West and the Far West—with a family reunion in the home of *Cannery Row*—through the Deep South and then back home to New York. Mr. Steinbeck even relaxes enough to fall for the temptation of a generalization now and then, and some of them are as bad as:

> It is a fact that Americans from all
> sections and of all racial extractions
> are more alike than the Welsh are like
> the English, the Lancashiremen like
> the Cockney, or for that matter the
> Lowland Scot like the Highlander.

Yet with his novelist's eye, he also hits off in reports of casual encounters a few home truths that will make him the envy of some experts on America who have devoted much more space to saying much less. He is particularly telling in the Deep South, for segregation to him—a native of Salinas, California—is as foreign as it is to an Englishman, and as a middle-aged man he can observe it in a detached way impossible for the latest generation of Americans who have grown up in a period more aware of the Negro's struggle. This section shows that when he is sufficiently gripped by his subject Mr. Steinbeck is still a superlative reporter.

But the essential superficiality of his book as a study of America can be seen in his passing glance at the school integration conflict in New Orleans, for he arrived there while the mobs were still active and yet paused only long enough to look at them. Having been there at the same time one would have thought a novelist particularly would have wanted to remain long enough to gain a complete understanding of this complex tragedy. But perhaps he did not want his picture of America as a whole to be thrown off balance by too long in one place and in one situation. Or perhaps his deepest conclusions will come only in a future novel.

At least in *Travels with Charley* there are two excellent conversation pieces. One of them reflects the Louisiana Negro's unwillingness to trust any stranger with a white face. There is also a memory of a Negro family he grew up with in Salinas

which helps to put the Deep South into perspective. And even if these scattered gems of reporting do not compensate for the more whimsical exchanges between Charley and his master, the book as a whole has the warmth of an extended personal essay, that fast-disappearing and much-missed form of literature: an essay, moreover, written in Mr. Steinbeck's deceptively simple style, that odd blend of precision and the colloquial, which provides a lesson in how to write modern prose.

Francis J. Thompson. "Travels with Charley." *Florida Historical Quarterly*, 42 (July 1963), 59–60.

Comparison of our Nobel Prize winners, though odious, may be instructive. John Steinbeck, for example, is more akin to Pearl Buck than to either William Faulkner or Ernest Hemingway.

Steinbeck's latest book, a beatnik grand tour of the United States, starts out with an exciting account of "Donna" walloping his Sag Harbor, Long Island, cottage. The hurricane did extensive damage in the peninsula state, too, but this doesn't fit into his picture. In fact, when he gets his gear stowed away after the blow, he embarks for Bangor musing about how much he prefers autumn sight-seeing in exciting, chilly Maine to October in uneventful, warm Florida. The horrible vision of "sitting on a nylon-and-aluminum chair out on a changelessly green lawn slapping mosquitoes in the evening" hurts him until he drinks a tumbler of vodka and forgets it.

As long as he follows the Canadian border towards the occident, Steinbeck's reactions are eager, and interested, but when he turns from Seattle, he begins to yawn. Later, still, levanting from Salinas to Texas, he transmits his boredom by repeating tiresome, old jokes about the size of the lone star state, its cowboy boots, chauvinism, and so on.

Reviving as he approaches Louisiana, he gradually works himself into such a rage at the puerility of some segregationists that he appears willing to turn Dixieland over to the Black Moslems. The outward and visible signs of his agitation attract public attention. So on the edge of New Orleans he warily parks Rocinante, his mobile home, and Charley, his pet poodle, where they will be relatively safe from suspicious white tribesmen and takes a taxi to within a block of the school where the disturbances have been taking place. There he is able to spy on the natives without being detected until, outraged beyond endurance by the naughty war cries of some pale-face "cheerladies," he scurries away to safety north of the Mason-Dixon line.

Some twenty-odd years ago Edmund Wilson spoke disapprovingly of "Mr. Steinbeck's tendency to present human life in animal terms." In *Travels with Charley*, the pooch and Rocinante, his "three-quarter-ton pickup truck equipped with miniature ship's cabin," are closer to *genus homo* than his representative Southerners are, and more *simpatico* than any bipeds observed during the journey.

En fin, just as Pearl Buck took us to China to see the truth about mankind as she knew it, so Steinbeck would have us go to canines and cars, consider their ways, and be wise. Hemingway and Faulkner on the other hand chose daring Americans for their heroes although there is evidence that the Nobel Prize was awarded the Mississippian in the mistaken belief that he, too, hated the South.

Checklist of Additional Reviews

"New Steinbeck Book Is Story of His Travels through 40 States." Salinas *Californian*, 20 June 1962, p. 16.
"*Travels with Charley*." *Booklist*, 58 (1 July 1962), 748.
John Harris. "John Steinbeck's Sentimental Trek." Los Angeles *Times*, 22 July 1962, "Calendar" section, p. 15.
William Hogan. "Class Tells in Steinbeck's Diary." San Francisco *Chronicle*, 29 July 1962, p. 24.
Robert L. Perkin. "One Man's Pegasus." Denver *Rocky Mountain News*, 29 July 1962, p. 22A.
"Reading the Editors Have Liked." *Holiday*, 32 (August 1962), 13.
Van Allen Bradley. "Rediscovering America." Chicago *News*, 1 August 1962, p. 12.
Hoke Norris. "Good Steinbeck Trip Despite Whimsy." Chicago *Sun-Times*, 5 August 1962, Section 3, p. 2.
"Books." *New Yorker*, 38 (8 September 1962), 152.
Alistair Cooke. "Steinbeck's New Found Land." Manchester *Guardian*, 21 September 1962, p. 6.

AMERICA AND AMERICANS

Text by
John Steinbeck

AMERICA and AMERICANS

Photographs edited by the staff of
Studio Books, The Viking Press

The Viking Press

New York

Maurice Dolbier.
"World of Books."
New York *World Journal Tribune*,
24 October 1966, p. 37.

A little over five years ago John Steinbeck went off in a truck with a tall dog named Charley to rediscover America. He traveled over 10,000 miles and through 34 states, and he wrote a book about the places he saw and the people he met and what they said.

"From start to finish," he summed up in *Travels with Charley*, "I found no strangers.... For all of our enormous geographic range, for all of our sectionalism, for all of our interwoven breeds drawn from every part of the ethnic world, we are a nation, a new breed.... This is not patriotic whoop-de-do. It is a carefully observed fact.... It is astonishing that this has happened in less than 200 years and most of it in the last 50. The American identity is an exact and provable thing."

In his new book, Steinbeck makes a deeper examination of that identity— what historical institutions and accidents have helped to create it, what paradoxes are present in it, what dangers threaten it, what powers of survival it may have against them. It is, he writes, a book of "opinion, conjecture and speculation" about a country that is "complicated, bullheaded, shy, cruel, boisterous, unspeakably dear, and very beautiful."

Steinbeck is not a patriotic whoop-de-doer. There are shameful pages in our national history; he does not overlook them. There are symptoms in today's society of an illness that could bring us to the verge of moral collapse; he describes them in grim detail. But he loves his country

and his people and he has faith in them— faith that the energy, the driving dissatisfaction with things as they are that has been an integral part of the American story will enable us to survive "the danger which in the past has been most destructive to the human: success—plenty, comfort, and ever-increasing leisure."

The varied components that make up the unity that is America are richly displayed in the photographs that fill so many pages of the Steinbeck book—photographs by a stellar group of 55 artists....

Conrad Richter.
"America Appreciated, Especially New England."
Harper's, 233 (November 1966), 132–3.

... It's stepping out of the distinctions of New England in more ways than one to come to *America and Americans*. There is almost a confusion of photographs, of which some emerge memorably from the mill run. Perhaps the latter must be expected when choice lies in the hands of a committee or panel able to agree most equably on a common denominator. Steinbeck's text, while not of the quality of Charlton Ogburn's, stands clear of the panel, is individual and independent as it can well afford to be, one man's responsibility and to hell with the blame. He declares at the outset that his writing is opinionated. He is most convincing in his judgments on civilization, politics, despoliation, and lack of principle today as well as in the past. But it's in telling a story that we get the best glimpse of him, the account of his Great-Aunt Carrie, his Faulkner-like tale of a miser in Salinas, that of a piano in a sod shanty ("Professor, could you play the Maiden's Prayer?"), and the meaningful incident of Jimmy, the Indian, and the mermaid. Reading these, even the dullest reader should feel that here is the hand of an accomplished storyteller. . . .

Robert J. Cooke.
"Books."
Social Education, 3 (December 1966), 673–4.

A good picture book is very seldom the victim of a cleaning off of shelves—its detail is infinite and its appeal is timeless. One returns to a picture book because it makes no demands, its message is emotional rather than intellectual, yet it fills the spaces left after reading printed words. . . .

John Steinbeck's *America and Americans* is clearly a labor of love and he describes his work as "a book of opinions, unashamed and individual." The pictures are rather ordinary (with one or two notable exceptions such as "Schoolgirl" by Declan Haun on page 65) and most of them have been seen before in *Life* or *Time* or some such magazine. The almost book-length text is, indeed, Steinbeck opinion; whimsical, superficial, idle observations such as "Sometimes we seem to be a nation of public Puritans and private profligates," or "But we are an exuberant people, careless and destructive as active children." The book is disappointing. Steinbeck, like Dos Passos, grows older. . . .

S[ister] M[ary] L[ucille] [McCreedy].
"Books for Young Adults."
Catholic Library World, 38 (December 1966), 273.

Nobel prize winner, John Steinbeck, writes affectionately about the government, the American people in their pursuit of happiness and Americans and their land, their relationship to the world, and their future. Magnificently illustrated with 136 pages of photographs, twenty-four in full-color, by a distinguished group of photographers and edited by the staff of Studio Books, The Viking Press. Recommended for those collections which can afford this expensive, beautiful volume.

"America the Beautiful."
Times Literary Supplement [London], 1 December 1966, p. 1120.

From one point of view, this is a picture book, an excellent picture book but rather conventional in that it stresses too much America the Beautiful. But it is a picture book whose accompanying text is not a rivulet but a river and the text is by that famous and idiosyncratic author (and Nobel Prizeman), John Steinbeck.

The pictures, adroitly chosen, are by some of the most famous American cameramen and some are dazzlingly beautiful and some have special kinds of fascination. But it is the text that matters. Mr. Steinbeck still thinks of the United States as "the last, best hope of earth" but in some ways, this brief commentary is as disconcerting for the 100 per cent American as was *The Grapes of Wrath*. Mr. Steinbeck has no sacred cows. Indeed, he dares attack a cow more sacred even than Mom, the rule by what he calls the "paedarchy." The "alienation of youth" does not impress him, although it does depress him.

> The reign of terror, which is actually a paedarchy, increases every day, and the open warfare between adults and teenagers becomes constantly more bitter. . . . I do not blame the youth; no one has ever told him that his tricks are obvious, his thoughts puerile, his goals uncooperative and selfish, his art ridiculous. Psychoanalysts constantly remind their little patients that they must find the real "me." The real "me" inevitably turns out to be a savage, self-seeking little beast.

Mr. Steinbeck notes the importance of the fact that the Americans have always been, to quote from Professor David Potter, "a People of Plenty." He knows the importance of the forest, the *antiqua silva* that dazzled Pastorius in the late seventeenth century. Mr. Steinbeck is worried by "the Negro question." He tells us of the quick and prudent reaction of a Negro who might have been accused of rape. And of his reply to Mr. Steinbeck's congratulations—"I've been practising to be a Negro for a long time."

Mr. Steinbeck has his quirks. The longbow was a Welsh, not an English invention. The Japanese in California are taller and heavier than their parents were, but so are the Japanese in Japan. The *Nisei* no doubt "look American,"

but it is not a matter of features but of a score of ways of behaving that marks all Americans, white, black, yellow. The Cornish-speaking miners Mr. Steinbeck met ought to be shipped back to the Duchy, to teach the modern Cornishmen their ancestral tongue.

The pictures are brilliant, but not representative. The Middle West is nearly neglected. The antiques and ruins that Americans are so good at building are excessively represented. There is an almost total absence of academic scenes. Why not a picture of a midwestern college with a fine site like Marietta? Why, if we are to have Vanderbilt chateaux, not Biltmore rather than The Breakers? Why not some rural slums like the decayed mining villages of Pennsylvania and West Virginia or decayed textile towns like that New Hampshire town that proudly boasts it is the original of Peyton Place? But it is a pleasure to see some of the great natural sights, to realize that the power of wonder New York once had is not exhausted, to recognize a fine restaurant in San Francisco by the wallpaper and to see a member of the (Boston) Athenaeum holed up in his natural habitat. This is an expensive book but it is worth the money.

Tetsumaro Hayashi. "America and Americans." *Visvabharati Quarterly* [India], 31 (1965–6), 404–6.

John Steinbeck, a Nobel Prize winner, one of the greatest living American authors, recently spoke out again forcefully in his *America and Americans*, a collection of informally written essays of serious nature about his beloved country and people. His essays are illustrated by beautiful, selected photographs of American people and typical American festivals, events, and scenes.

Like his *Travels with Charley in Search of America* (1962), this book attempts to recapture the diversified images of America and her people and to tell Americans how they stand and look to others. To a great extent, however, what he discusses seems to be an assimilation of what many sociologists, psychologists, theologians, and philosophers have argued in the past. Therefore, this book will not shock the reader, nor will it impress you with strikingly new ideas and interpretations. Yet it is the straightforwardness and honesty with which Steinbeck talks about the realistic human condition in the United States that make the work significant and captivating.

He is, for instance, unashamed when he praises his country for her greatness. At the same time, he is equally unrestrained when he points out the evils and hypocrisies of his country and people. It is this honesty and boldness as well as this fairness and insight in his critical appraisal that makes this book worth reading, for the conscience of America is revealed in the person of John Steinbeck throughout this book.

Steinbeck sees America as a country full of contradictions, conflicts, tensions, and paradoxes. Thus he dares, though sympathetically, to discuss various problems and subjects in their intricate and mysterious dichotomies: good and evil; pride and shame; hope and despair; virtue and sin; conflict and harmony; and promise and pitfalls. America is, as he sees her, a mecca of freedom, and yet she is also a home of inequality, segregation, and injustice. Americans are, implies Steinbeck, the kindest and the friendliest people on earth, but they can be as mean, cruel, and rude to their own brothers as some savages in the jungle. They love their president, and yet they crucify him, laments the patriotic writer. In "Paradox and Dream" Steinbeck states, in a positive tone, one of the self-contradictory dichotomies of the United States. "We are complacent in our possessions, in our homes, in our education; but it is hard to find a man or woman who does not want something better for the next generation." Throughout the book he points out this kind of dichotomy again and again, hoping that a better America and greater country may someday be created out of such complex characters. The reader will not always agree with Steinbeck, but he will certainly respect the author's passionate love and grave concern for his country and her future, because his love and concern are directed not merely toward America and Americans but also toward all nations and all mankind.

The truths of America and Americans he discovers and discusses in this book is [*sic*] by and large the truths of all nations and peoples on earth. It is truly due to this universal identity that the reader will find Steinbeck's message appealing. In this respect this is a book of prophecy written by a man of mission and vision, a man who loves his country and people so much that he cannot help worrying about their problems, faults, and dilemmas, a man who cannot help telling his people what is wrong with them. After Adlai Stevenson is gone, . . . America's conscience is now represented by Steinbeck who denies a fairy tale of the United States but sees through chaos and confusion a really truthful picture of his country and people.

The author maintains in the concluding chapter that America's hope lies in her insatiable desire, a desire to be rebellious, angry, searching, and dissatisfied with the status quo, for the desire and dissatisfaction are an energy to be greater. In the darkness and despair John Steinbeck finds shining light for America and her people. It is not only America's hope but a hope for all mankind.

Eric Moon.
"New Books Appraised."
Library Journal, 91
(1 December 1966), 5962.

... Don't be misled. It has the look and feel of a coffee-table special. The pictures, the work of 55 of today's best photographers, loom twice as large as the text, and it's a fine, handsome, heavy, impressive book. But what really makes it very much more than just a coffee-table book is the 70-page essay by Steinbeck. In this short space he manages to capture more of the essentials and the paradoxes of America—and Americans—than all the photographers together. He writes, clearly, out of a love for his country and his people, but he is less maudlin and sentimental in this book than he has sometimes been in the past when on the subject of his homeland. This time he has drawn a "warts and all" picture, with the warts exposed full-size and in detail. It is an honest, sincere, powerful piece of writing, better perhaps than most things he has done since the thirties. Not everyone will like everything Steinbeck says in this book, but very few will be able to resist reading it. . . .

David E. Scherman.
"Things and People."
New York Times Book Review, 116
(4 December 1966), 3, 46.

... The most ambitious of the five [pictorial books] is John Steinbeck's *America and Americans*. . . . Pictorially, it is merely an attempt to search out and boil down the entire photographic output of America—all the picture magazines and all copies of *U.S. Camera*, it would seem—into one big, smashing book that spells Yankeeland. A preposterous goal, and in spite of lots of keen snaps of Industry, Sports, Sex, Rich Businessman, Confused Negro, Mom, Baby, College Fun, Serious History, Religion and Monument National Park, Ariz. (our heritage) it is hardly attained. Verbally, it is perhaps not within my competence to comment upon, except to state that Steinbeck's prose is only occasionally relevant to the pictures, at best the intelligent ramblings of a first-rate reporter, at worst the opinionated musings of a liberal Westbrook Pegler. We're a great people, warts and all, and what else is new? . . .

"America and Americans."
Choice, 4 (May 1967), 279.

Steinbeck essays, through a sparing use of words and lavish use of photographs, to present as an American the sort of description-cum-analysis which Europeans have been turning out for centuries. In this respect his work compares well with Brogan's *American Character* (1944). It is avowedly "a book of opinions, unashamed and individual." Some of these are certainly open to challenge, but all are unpretentiously stated and all have the characteristic ring of American thought. The photographs, all full-page or better, some in color, make up three-fifths of the book. They represent the work of Eisenstadt, Adams, Cartier-Bresson, Tom Hollyman, Bruce Roberts, and 50 others. And they are, collectively, beautiful and moving in a measure rarely seen since *The Family of Man* and *The Europeans*. Those who want a beautiful and very American book will be delighted. One would hope to find it in every U.S.I.A. reading room.

Geraldine LaRocque.
"Book Marks:
Potpourri."
English Journal, 57
(May 1968), 751–53.

... Because of the recent television program based on it and because of John Steinbeck's appeal to young adults, *America and Americans* ... might interest many students in the ninth through twelfth grades. Because Steinbeck is openly subjective, the text takes on the added spirit which comes from his conviction. In the Foreword the author states, "In text and pictures, this is a book of opinions, unashamed and individual. . . . I believe that out of the whole body of our past, out of our differences, our quarrels, our many

interests and directions, something has emerged that is itself unique in the world: America—complicated, paradoxical, bullheaded, shy, cruel, boisterous, unspeakable, dear, and very beautiful."

Photography buffs will love the book for its beautiful pictures, which make the volume relatively expensive, and slower readers will find the photographs an added incentive. It is possible for an interested poor reader to read only one or two of the short sections which are complete in themselves.

Steinbeck, as usual, records provocative insights and will enable some readers to view old concepts in a new light. The advanced student will enjoy these flashes while at the same time recognizing that the expression of personal opinion sometimes leads to generalization and oversimplification. At any rate, Steinbeck's view of the paradox of America is lively reading and was obviously written from great devotion to his country. He is concerned about the future of America but sees hope in its vitality. . . .

Ted Atkinson.
"*America and
Americans.*"
Steinbeck Quarterly, 2
(Fall 1969), 66–8.

For the literary scholar I must assume that the text is more important than the pictures of *America and Americans*. If one is granted this assumption, then it follows that the Bantam edition of *America and Americans* (1968) is as valuable to the scholar as the Viking Press edition of 1966. The text for both editions is the same; it is only the size and placement of pictures that differ. If, however, one considers the pictures to be of great significance, then the Viking edition (due to its larger size and clearer reproduction of the pictures) is certainly the superior volume.

America and Americans is a highly subjective work; the author does not claim to be objective. Since the volume is admittedly subjective (Steinbeck states in the "Foreword" that such is the case), we have what amounts to the author's casual reflections on American culture. One of the major strengths of such a work is that the author reveals as much about himself as he does about the American tradition. It becomes quite apparent then that such a volume is valuable to the student or scholar searching for a compendium of Steinbeck's political, social, and economic views.

One of the most striking features about this volume is that its casual style is at once interesting and informative. Personal anecdotes, such as the Tallac hatchery encounter with Jim, heighten the reader's interest and clearly illustrate points of discussion. Steinbeck's personal experience at the hatchery illustrates well "the way the tribesmen can slip back and forth between their two realities and between one culture and another." Other personal observations—the old lady at Third Avenue with her city life and trappings of a rural dream and Mr. Kirk with his haunted house and intriguing characters—also serve to entertain and instruct the reader.

Aside from the power of Steinbeck's style and apart from the value of the subjective revelations, *America and Americans* is interesting because of the tension developed by honestly expressed ideas. "E Pluribus Unum," the first section of the text, is a discussion concerning the complex fusion of geography, climate, and ethnic anarchy that fashioned America and "made us Americans." In "Para-

dox and Dream," Steinbeck continues his analysis of the American identity by discussing the uniquely American dichotomies that most Americans accept as commonplace. The author states that "we are able to believe that our government is weak, stupid, overbearing, dishonest, and inefficient, and at the same time we are deeply convinced that it is the best government in the world, and we like to impose it upon everyone else." The many paradoxes of American life are further explored as Steinbeck indicates that Americans live in cities and dream of the country, earn money only to give it away, and restlessly long for security, only to be deprived of it by restlessness. The many paradoxes of American culture are again developed in "Government of the People." Here the author discusses the American attitudes toward the President and the many "inviolable, deepseated" political customs like the nominating conventions.

In the next two sections of America and Americans, "Created Equal" and "Genus Americanus," Steinbeck's main concern is with race and class prejudice. In the first of these sections the author labors long and well to trace the origins of racial prejudice in America. In the process he attempts to dispel illusions and establish facts. The process is continued in "Genus Americanus" as Steinbeck considers how "members of a classless society . . . work out changes in status levels without violating their belief that there are no such levels." This consideration touches upon the old notions of aristocracy, the new notions of capitalism, the strange structures of the corporation, and the curious need for "orders, lodges, and encampments." The cultural paradoxes explored in the preceding two chapters are further exploited in "The Pursuit of Happiness." In this section problems that occur from childhood to old age are considered within the bewildering American culture that was revealed in the earlier chapters. "Americans and the Land" is a rather tiresome discussion of the American's treatment of their landscape. From the early wanton destruction of forests to the present inadvertent pollution of water and air, the author reveals the means by which the landscape has been victimized by innumerable abuses. The slight value of this section is, however, well offset by "Americans and the World." Here the focus changes from Americans looking at Europeans and Europeans looking at Americans, to Americans looking at themselves and finally creating an American literature. After discussing the American journalist and literary artist, Steinbeck pays a tribute to the historical value of *Huckleberry Finn*, *An American Tragedy*, *Winesburg, Ohio*, *Main Street*, *The Great Gatsby*, and *As I Lay Dying*.

In "Americans and the Future," Steinbeck seems to clearly indicate that the tensions present in American culture will always provide the energy necessary for survival. This idea figures strongly throughout *America and Americans*, but it is particularly clear in this last section. The paradoxes and ironies of American life are successfully resolved in Steinbeck's concluding affirmation of faith in America's future: "I believe that our history, our experiences in America, has endowed us for the change that is coming."

Checklist of Additional Reviews

Walter Havighurst. "The Face of America." Chicago *Tribune*, 16 October 1966, Section 9, p. 12.
Beatrice Washburn. "Steinbeck Takes America Apart." Miami [Fla.] *Herald*, 15 January 1967, Section J, p. 7.
T[etsumaro] Hayashi. "*America and Americans*" (Japanese edition), *Steinbeck Newsletter*, 1 (August 1968), 4.

JOURNAL OF A NOVEL: THE *EAST OF EDEN* LETTERS

JOURNAL OF A NOVEL

The *East of Eden* Letters

JOHN STEINBECK

The *Viking Press*   NEW YORK

William Hogan.
"World of Books."
San Francisco *Chronicle*,
16 December 1969, p. 41.

We enter a low-keyed neurotic wonderland in John Steinbeck's *Journal of a Novel: The East of Eden Letters*. This is a literary document, reminiscent of . . . Thomas Wolfe's self-revealing background notes on the writing of *Look Homeward, Angel* (1935). But the Steinbeck material is a far more personal and revealing emotional catharsis. It is a series of letters to his editor at Viking Press, the late Pascal Covici (who died some four years before Steinbeck did), and who was Steinbeck's mentor, psychiatrist and father-confessor.

The letters were written between January and November, 1951, when Steinbeck was writing *East of Eden*, the long, realistically detailed saga of a Salinas valley family played as a reconstruction of the Cain and Abel story. As it turned out, *East of Eden* was a rather pretentious novel which stirred a mixed critical reception, but it added to the bulk of Steinbeck's work for which, in 1962, he received the Nobel Prize for Literature.

Daily, during the composition of this book, Steinbeck "unblocked" himself by writing a letter to Covici. Most of the letters appeared on left hand pages of a large notebook; the text of his story was on the right hand pages, all written in longhand. They tell much about the writer's creative process, and about this particular author-editor relationship.

It is intimate stuff, never designed for publication. It is chatter about his characters, about his drinking habits, about news events of the day, his wife, sons and his title. Should it be "Salinas Valley," or "My Valley"? "I have never been a title-man," he confided.

This curiosity piece becomes an "arguing ground" for his story, a sharpening of pencils in public (Steinbeck found that long beautiful pencils charged him with energy and invention). His sexual drive grows "stronger than ever, but that may be because it is all in one direction now and not scattered."

The weeks roll on, and the author rides their backs. Suddenly the first draft of what he hoped would be a finer work than *The Grapes of Wrath* is finished. "It is a kind of death," he wrote; "this is the requiem."

The letters become a disturbing fragment of an autobiography, a private notebook that often seems to be just too personal for a stranger to be browsing in. As an admirer of Steinbeck's work, especially the early work, I find it a fascinating set of literary-clinical notes, and only wish after all this posturing and heart-bleeding anguish he had produced a better book. It remains a set of echoes from the confessional, even such asides to Covici as:

"You must be getting damn sick of this endless soapbox and there is not a thing you can do about it . . . the one thing you can do is not to read it and I think you are too curious for that so I have you and I can be as dull as I wish. Ho, ho!"

Clarence Brown.
"The Callus behind the
Fiction."
New Republic, 161
(20 December 1969), 26,
30, 32.

Steinbeck thought that every man had one book in him and that *East of Eden* was his. This naturally made him nervous. It made him, when he finally brought himself to try the book, turn to a kind of athlete's compulsive checking and record-keeping and not a little voodoo to ward off the demons that impede creation: telephones, depression, doorbells, children, advice, and bad pencils. In a large ledger that his editor, Pascal Covici, had given him he wrote letters to Covici on the left-hand page at the start of each working day and the novel on the right. He began at the end of January 1951 and wrote straight through the year deep into the fall. Then the novel, except for some revision, was finished. Just before starting, Steinbeck had emerged from the writer's peculiar hell of a long dry spell and the general hell of a divorce that had deprived him of two sons. But he had remarried, this time to a woman who gave him a buoyant serenity that is evident throughout his journal, and the novel started to come.

East of Eden, as it chances, is the story of two sons who turn up in several guises but always with indelible traces of their models, Cain and Abel. It is also explicitly the story of Steinbeck's own family narrated by himself in his own name and person. Little wonder that he saw it as his one book, for it is his own primal story and the primal story of Man. He read the latter with all the emotional intensity that informs his best pages, the result being that he gradually identified it with the former. When he had settled into his new room and his new chair, before his new drafting table and his new ledger, one part of Steinbeck's mind was anxiously prodding, taunting and encouraging the other. It proposed paradoxes. In the journal the paradox is that a man might arrange himself ever so comfortably, his bowels and soul in some celestial harmony, and still be unable to write. But the paradox of the novel is the supreme, the biblical, paradox of good and evil, of the murderer's *freedom* to triumph over his sin. For passionate analysis, whatever it may lack in scholarship, there must be nothing in all the annals of hermeneutics to match Steinbeck's pages on the single Hebrew verb *timshel.* So the novel is infinitely the greater book, but its greatness confers a remarkable distinction upon the journal.

The journal, never meant for publication, is repetitious and contradictory, but these qualities are not faults, for they provide precious insights into a writer's hesitant awareness of what he was doing. The faults of the book belong chiefly to Steinbeck's anonymous editors, or perhaps just to circumstance. The journal is meaningless without a fresh reading of the novel from which, in a strictly physical sense, it was excised; but even with such reading you are not always sure just which passage is being referred to, and the editors' help on this point is haphazard. But incomparably the greatest lack of all is that of Pascal Covici.

Covici was clearly the kind of editor that every writer longs for, or ought to. His relationship is not that of Maxwell Perkins to Thomas Wolfe, whose ungovernable creativity Perkins brought under some kind of control. If Covici took a hand in Steinbeck's novel, he did it simply by being the one perfect reader of it. In the first draft, parts of the novel had the form of letters to Steinbeck's two boys. But this was abandoned, and I think the reason is clear: the novel itself was never really addressed to anyone but Covici. From 1934, when his editor discovered him—three novels had done poorly and a fourth, *Tortilla Flat*, was being rejected by all publishers — until 1964, when Covici died, he was the writer's confidant, goad, quartermaster and—in Steinbeck's consciousness, I think—his single auditor. Eliot said that writing comes from talking—to oneself, to one other, or to God. For Steinbeck, Covici was the "one other." *East of Eden* was dedicated to him. So, incidentally, was Saul Bellow's *Herzog*. And so was Charles A. Madison's *Book Publishing in America* (McGraw-Hill 1966), which I had to unearth from the British Museum for such information on Covici as one might reasonably expect to find in a preface to Steinbeck's journal. Madison quotes something that Steinbeck said after Covici's death: "Pat Covici was much more than my friend. He was my editor. . . . He demanded of me more than I had and thereby caused me to be more than I should have been without him." And from Covici, in 1941: "In my little life, which is about three-quarters done, you are my rarest experience . . . ." It was that sense of being at least one man's rarest experience that banished from Steinbeck's mind the clouds of depression, the sick fear of rejection and failure, certain frightening impulses in his own soul (all plentifully attested to) and enabled him to write.

The question how Steinbeck or any artist can fuse the dark night of the soul with the radiance of love for wife, sons, and friend into the alchemical product of art is beyond my competence, but I am convinced that this journal will provide material for part of the answer. He was obsessive about the daily production quota. One day, early on in the journal, he perversely declines to work (though he wrote the letter). He will have his hair cut. He might "go farther and get a little sweet-smelling tonic rubbed on. This is a real festive day for me with garlands. And you, old word-Scrooge, will curse and mutter because I am wasting time. Well, I defy you." That is an extraordinary tone of voice, as extraordinary as his non-feasance, and it is uncomfortably somewhere between flirt and bitch. Where does it come from? The answer is elsewhere in the passage, for Steinbeck is preparing to introduce Cathy, whose warped malignancy runs through the novel like the stain of Man's first disobedience. I think he was discovering her in himself, though it was much later in the journal that he explicitly realized his greater kinship with her than with any other character in the book.

I treasure his testimony concerning the physical side of writing. The writing callus on his middle finger grew to bothersome proportions. When he cut his thumb carving something out of wood, the writing suffered. Earlier the slant of his table had seemed wrong, and when he changed it, improving his posture, the work went easier. There was a glare on the light wood of the table, so he painted it black, which was a bad idea, so he put down a restful, green blotter. But all this is mere frippery when compared to the question of pencils. I should like to propose that Steinbeck's numerous comments on the basic instruments of authorship be made into a syllabus for the first course in "creative writing." I am not in the employ of Eberhard Faber, but I regard it as a duty to set down his devotion to the Blackwing ("Half the Pressure Twice the Speed") and, for other moods and stages of inspiration, the Mongol 480 No. 2⅜ F round.

Writers alone will understand that they can use no other information in the book. His comments on character, pace, construction, and so on, are professionally worthless, since if Steinbeck has any message at all, it is that practically nothing can be learned from predecessors, and the little that can must be painfully disremembered. A novel is oneself or it is nothing. He wrote a novel of two families against a background of history with an explicitly moral purpose and an explicitly present author. His method was sharp juxtaposition. But he was not building on Tolstoy: he was reinventing him. That his reinvention lagged behind the original is not so bad when you recall that mere imitation would have been unreadable.

Lawrence William Jones. "Personal History." *Saturday Review*, 52 (20 December 1969), 25–6.

"One should be a reviewer," says John Steinbeck in one of the letters in this posthumous collection, "or better still a critic, these curious sucker fish who live with joyous vicariousness on other men's work and discipline with dreary words the thing that feeds them." Elsewhere in his writings he calls criticism "a bunch of crap" and "an ill-tempered parlor game in which nobody gets kissed," remarks that, although relatively infrequent, seemed to become increasingly venomous in the late stages of his career.

The venom was well deserved, for

Steinbeck's post-war reception was one of nearly unrelieved and often misdirected hostility. Of the eight fictional works published during this period, only *The Pearl* was even fleetingly praised, and it has inevitably suffered from constant comparison with Hemingway's *The Old Man and the Sea*. What distressed Steinbeck most were the "expecters"—those critics who constantly awaited an updated *Grapes of Wrath*, who refused to "go along with the story" in each subsequent work if it did not meet the criteria of his most famous novel. When, for example, Peter Lisca (*The Wide World of John Steinbeck*) wrote a postscript on Steinbeck's "decline as a writer," chiding him for abandoning "his earlier viewpoint," it was clear that balanced opinion had been pre-empted by stylistic prejudice. Other critics, such as Lionel Trilling, Walter Allen, and Mark Schorer, still influenced by Edmund Wilson's knell-like statements of 1940, found the post-war work wanting for much the same reason. Still others somehow saw evidence in the journalism of the Sixties... that the author had lost his creative spark with his first step outside the Salinas Valley.

Whether these letters, written to Steinbeck's editor, Pascal Covici, during the ten-month composition of *East of Eden* in 1951, will have much effect on future criticism is a difficult thing to predict. Written as a warming-up exercise for the actual novel, though, they contain a great deal more than indictment; they reveal much about Steinbeck the man, about his relationship with those closest to him, about his art in general and *East of Eden* in particular. I believe they will be indispensable to future studies of his work.

The autobiographical details are of course invaluable in the absence of any biography. ("Feel free to make up your own facts about me," he told would-be biographers; "biography by its very nature must be half-fiction.") Steinbeck comes across in these letters as an extremely introspective person, often lonely, given to periods of deep depression as well as exquisite joy (during the creative process), possessed of strong personal beliefs often bordering on the arrogant, as enamored of mechanical inventions as of experimental ideas. His self-descriptions often remind one of many characters in his fiction, as do the brief portraits of his relatives—mother and father, sons Thom and John, and wife Elaine.

Most illuminating is the obvious understanding and accepting relationship between the author and his editor, a relationship which Charles Madison (*Book Publishing in America*) has called "the happiest in publishing history." The mutual respect, the sharing of ideas, the attempt to comprehend each other's role—all are evident here, so that one can appreciate Steinbeck's tribute to Covici after his death in 1964: "For thirty years Pat was my collaborator and my conscience. He demanded of me more than I had and thereby caused me to be more than I should have been without him."

Many of the personal details (preference for certain types of pencils, theories about the popular desire for long books) and incidental comments (on Communism, on man's life-patterns) tend to become boring by mere repetition, as is perhaps to be expected of a publication of this nature. By far the greatest worth of *Journal of a Novel* is to be found in its commentary on the nature of writing and on the technical problems involved in a massive creation like *East of Eden*.

Lately, I have been seeking to maintain that Steinbeck's direction in his postwar fiction is fabular rather than novelistic (a view that has always been an undercurrent in criticism, and which I was happy to find I shared with that energetic Steinbeck aficionado Warren French). For it has seemed to me there is ample evidence that in these later works Steinbeck was attempting not to depict real-life situations (as in, say, *In Dubious Battle*) but rather to give us fictional examples of the truth of a formulable moral statement—in other words, to construct fables, parables, apologues. Now the proof of the validity of this perspective is at hand; in a letter of October 10 Steinbeck declares: "I have noticed so many of the reviews of my work show a fear and a hatred of ideas and speculations. It seems to be true that people can only take parables fully clothed with flesh. Any attempt to correlate in terms of thought is frightening."

Furthermore, throughout the letters he speaks of his vital concerns, which are surely those of a fabulist: clothing the thematic skeleton with the "trappings of experience," creating "symbol people" who will merely translate his ethical ideas for the reader, catching the reader in a "trap" of involvement with these ideas, managing the various levels of meaning a parable may evoke, utilizing some pervasive pattern or motif ("the great covered thing") to which everything else in the narrative bears a relation. The writing of parables, it appears, requires attention to such fine points of technique; but the catch is this: a reader must be willing, as Kafka puts it, to "go over" into the special world of parable, to read his own life into that world—and this responsibility the "expecters" have always eschewed.

In *East of Eden*, Steinbeck maintains, he is working with the "microcosm," with a story which is symbolically that of mankind. Thus he sees the moral theme of his Cain-Abel framework as the most vital aspect of his book, something every man must inculcate as he reads. "My wish is that when my reader has finished with this book, he will have a sense of belonging in it," he declares; and again, "I don't want a treatise. I want the par-

513

ticipation of my reader. I want him to be so involved that it will be HIS story." The various ways in which Steinbeck tries to achieve this reader participation are fascinating to watch: manipulation of the book's pace ("much more like Fielding than like Hemingway") to give the reader time for contemplation, the fashioning of symbolic characters like Samuel Hamilton (the "wide open man" who recurs in other parables) and Cathy-Kate (the personification of an inherent human malignancy), the refining of the "universal quality" any parable must have into some manageable objective correlative.

Since it does not take much to upset the delicate sense of proportion in parable form, reasons for the ineffectiveness of *East of Eden* are also found here. At least two are easily detectable. One is Steinbeck's indecision over the nature of Cathy-Kate: at times he seems to believe that the evil she represents is "unearthly," not human at all, whereas at others (as in the letter of May 31) he comes closer to the doctrine of original sin: ". . . while she is a monster, she is a little piece of the monster in all of us. It won't be because she is foreign that people will be interested but because she is not. That is not cynicism either."

There is a hint here of what is glaringly obvious in the books from *Cannery Row* to *The Winter of Our Discontent*: Steinbeck's compelling vision of good (found in unity with the "Whole"—with nature and one's fellows) remains unopposed by an equally compelling vision of evil, and the unresolved tension dissipates the moral thrust.

A second reason for the failure of *East of Eden* to make a serious impact on American literature is that it tackles too much. Repeatedly, Steinbeck insists that the book must be about "everything," that it must be a "key to living" containing "all in the world I know." William

Golding, it may be remembered, had to cope with much the same tendency toward all inclusiveness in the writing of *Lord of the Flies*, and he concluded (in his essay "Fable") that "if one takes the whole of the human condition as background of a fable it becomes hopelessly complex. . . . The fable is most successful *qua* fable if it works within strict limits." Unfortunately, although Steinbeck mentions this problem at least once (July 24) he was unable to overcome it.

Other correlations of these letters to the published novel (Steinbeck does not think of it as a novel but as a pseudo-history or a romance) must await, as the publisher's note indicates, "future scholarship." Read carefully, I think the letters in *Journal of a Novel* might well lead many "expecters" to re-examine Steinbeck's later work and re-evaluate it on his own terms. For the general reader (and popular following remains strong) the *Journal* provides not the wide-angle view of James's prefaces nor the microscopic conciseness of Faulkner's interviews, but a telephoto close-up of a fabulist seriously engaged in the "silly business" of writing. The most eloquent passages in the letters come when Steinbeck discusses this business at length (Jan. 29, Sept. 3):

The craft or art of writing is the clumsy attempt to find symbols for the wordlessness. In utter loneliness a writer tries to explain the inexplicable. And sometimes if he is very fortunate and if the time is right, a very little of what he is trying to do trickles through—not over much. . . . Having gone through all this nonsense, what emerges may well be the palest of reflections. Oh! it's a real horse's ass business. The mountain labors and groans and strains and the tiniest of rodents comes out. And the greatest foolishness of all lies in the fact that to do it at all, the writer must believe that what he is doing is the most important thing in the world. And he must hold to this illusion even when he knows it is not true. If he does not, the work is not worth even what it might otherwise have been. As it says in *The King and I*—"Is a mystery!"

Richard J. Cattani. "Novelist Half in Hiding." *Christian Science Monitor*, 2 January 1970, p. 11.

Men can suffer from their subterfuges—a John Steinbeck no less than others. Writing men defend themselves from these subterfuges or turn them to advantage, or they cease to be writing men and become something else. This something else is usually in part defined by frustration, unrealization—being not half the man one's mental standard would have him be.

Steinbeck had such a bout with self-subterfuge and self-realization with each of his novels. But if he is to be taken at his word, *East of Eden* (with *The Grapes of Wrath* and the short novels behind him, and *The Winter of Our Discontent* still to go) was his big book. It was to be the measure of his powers. It was to be his echo of the big theme of good and evil. It was to reflect the history of the American conscience, his own family chronicle, and a summing up of what wisdom he had as a legacy for his two then young sons.

This very ambition was one of the threats to his big book. He had to keep his intentions from crabbing it. Partly to stay loose, he kept a journal between

January 29 and November 1, 1951, while he set down the first draft of *East of Eden*. He wrote the journal in the form of daily letters to his friend and editor at the Viking Press, Pascal Covici. For those interested in the literature of the creative process, it's worth reading.

Within certain bounds, Steinbeck seems to have been open in his observations to Covici. He describes the separate corridors of his life in the *Eden* period. There was his wife of a recent marriage and their outfitting of a house in New York. Then his paternal eye out for his two sons, living apart from him. And his world of gadgetry—rebuilding electric pencil sharpeners, restoring chairs, wood carving. In all of these, Steinbeck seems remarkably human, and knowingly idiosyncratic.

He seemed to have learned to use what others might call diversions as tuning screws for his writing machine. Steinbeck knew himself well, how to keep up the rhythm of his work. He could often forestall or work out of ugly moods with his hobbies or family attentions. He seldom shorted his daily goal of two pages of handwritten copy.

Steinbeck was a pencil man. He would buy five or six dozen at a time, sharpen the lot of them each morning before he started, then discard them when the metal eraser-band touched his skin. A small matter perhaps, which he discussed endlessly. He insisted they be round and not hexagonal, and of a certain make. Like the several finishes he tried on his drafting table top before finding one that suited him, these humorings were part of the way he kept himself in his writing room. As was the Covici letter-journal ruse.

Reading the journal is like being with a professional athlete in the locker room before and after every game of a season. You learn a lot about how he feels toward the sport, whether he's all courage or scared, whether he's abstracted or vulgar.

But you still don't know what's going on in his head when he's playing the game. That's in the novel itself, in a way. And that's why, as Steinbeck says in *Journal of a Novel*, the reading of a book or the rating of it (and *East of Eden* wasn't rated high by all who read it, not by a long shot) isn't anything like the thrill and gamble of the writing of it.

John R. Willingham. "*Journal of a Novel: The* East of Eden *Letters*." *Library Journal*, 95 (1 March 1970), 899–900.

While writing the first draft of *East of Eden* in 1951, Steinbeck composed almost daily letters in a notebook for his editor, Pascal Covici. In them, he alternately fretted and exulted over the novel's progress. His commentary on his art is neither profound nor frequent (he writes more often of his love for soft new pencils, his wife Elaine, his sons, his aches and pains), but every page reveals his earnestness with each detail of his "big book." *East of Eden* was admittedly, grandiosely autobiographical; it drew upon his country—the Salinas Valley—as well as his family background. Often he apologizes for his pace or his moodiness; but generally he projects a fine detachment proceeding from his awareness that the letters would not be read for at least a year from their beginning. This is not a scholarly edition: comments that might have hurt the living are omitted; minute textual details of the manuscript were not checked. But admirers of Steinbeck or of contemporary fiction generally will be moved and instructed by this intimate record of an important novel's evolution and the surrounding texture of its author's life. . . .

"Notes on Current Books." *Virginia Quarterly Review*, 46 (Spring 1970), lxvi.

This posthumous work, a day-by-day account of the writing of *East of Eden* in the form of a series of letters from John Steinbeck to the late Pascal Covici, editor of The Viking Press, will be of little interest to the general reader, but for the teacher and student of fiction and for those who wish to know the mind and heart, the working habits and daily problems of one creative writer, who after publishing many novels, short stories, and plays was awarded the Nobel Prize (1962), this journal will provide invaluable information and some fascinating, unexpected insights. Of course these same qualified readers will also recognize the irony and pathos of this account, for although John Steinbeck would seem to have regarded *East of Eden* as potentially his most important and profound work critics have generally considered it one of his least successful novels.

Derek Stanford.
"Mother McCarthy's
Chickens."
Books and Bookmen
[England], 15 (August
1970), 14–15.

The book referred to in John Steinbeck's *Journal of a Novel* is *East of Eden*, his longest and most ambitious, though not most famous fiction. Published in 1952, *East of Eden* came 13 years after *The Grapes of Wrath*. When Steinbeck began it in 1951, he was 49 and had another 17 years to live. The product of his mature middle-age, the journal he kept while writing his novel is probably, in one sense, a more noteworthy document than the tale itself. Into it went all sorts of matter: thoughts on the story he was writing, thoughts on the man writing that story. Indeed, in its excavations of the self and its drive towards inner honesty, it makes us think of a very different work: Henri-Frédéric Amiel's *Intimate Diary*, first published in 1883. But whereas Amiel's two great interests are the self and philosophy, those of Steinbeck are the self and psychology—the latter understood in a very homely, concrete yet inquiring fashion.

Steinbeck's journal in question was actually a large exercise book measuring 10 ¾" × 14" which Pascal Covici, his close friend and editor, had given him. Every-day on the left-hand page, Steinbeck prepared for his stint of novel-writing by indicating an entry or "letter" for his friend. This unblocking warming-up work completed, he would then set to on the novel itself, setting down his regular 1,000 words or so on the right hand pages of the journal.

He himself declared that "the best justification of these notes" was that they got "all or most of the kinks out" before he actually started on the book. What is so remarkable about the journal is the way in which it establishes the relevance of fine-spun threads of association to the author's central act of composition. Everything becomes, in one sense simplified, in terms of the role it performs as a hang-up or a stimulus.

Richard Astro.
"*Journal of a Novel.*"
Steinbeck Quarterly, 3
(Fall 1970), 107–10.

It is difficult to know how to assess properly the Viking Press's recent publication of John Steinbeck's *Journal of a Novel*, the series of "letters" Steinbeck wrote to his close friend and editor, Pascal Covici, during the composition of *East of Eden*. At first glance, these "letters," written every working day between January 29 and November 1, 1951, in a large note-book across from the text of Steinbeck's grandly conceived but largely unsuccessful novel, seem to display the last remains of a defeated novelist whose deteriorating literary talents had finally struck bottom. And even upon closer inspection, part of this initial reaction remains.

Put simply, much of *Journal of a Novel* is trivial, and despite the fact that these dispatches were not written to be published, their very existence suggests something rather pathetic about the general quality of Steinbeck's thinking in 1951. It is, in short, rather discouraging to find the author of *In Dubious Battle* and *The Grapes of Wrath* absorbed with such matters as the size of writing pencils, the operation of an electric pencil sharpener, eye doctors, the weather on Nantucket Island, and General MacArthur. And even the uncritical Steinbeck reader can find it difficult not to become annoyed at the forced sense of method and control which the novelist states he imposed on the actual writing of *East of Eden.*

Besides being repetitive, full of irrelevancies, and often just plain dull, *Journal of a Novel* shatters the myth that has often surrounded the novelist as a person. For the Steinbeck of these "letters" appears as a detached, somewhat self-indulgent, comfort-loving member of the New York literati who hardly resembles the Steinbeck that we, in our delusive simplicity, like to imagine fighting the battles of the dispossessed Joads or envision stealing vegetables for the communal stews on Cannery Row.

To the reader genuinely concerned with Steinbeck and his work, however, *Journal of a Novel* is an interesting and highly valuable book for a number of reasons. First, it is a sincere testament of Steinbeck's affection for and trust in Pat Covici who, after the death of Ed Ricketts in 1948, became Steinbeck's closest friend and professional confidant.

Further, the "letters" are highly valuable to the Steinbeck scholar in that they enlarge the critical understanding of *East of Eden* since they contain explicit statements of Steinbeck's intentions in the novel. For example, one learns that Steinbeck regarded *East of Eden* as his "big novel" into which he attempted to pour "every bit of technique I have learned consciously." From the standpoint of Steinbeck's thematic concerns in *East of Eden*, the "letters" to Covici are highly important in that they contain the novelist's insistence that his main concern in *East of Eden* is with people and that he willingly subordinated his usual interest in descrip-

tion and setting to achieve that end. And in talking about people who are to appear in his novel, it becomes apparent that Steinbeck is more concerned with the character of Cathy Ames (Trask) than with any other single figure in the book. Calling her a monster born "with a malformed soul," Steinbeck states his desire to show that Cathy "is a little piece of the monster in all of us."

Also of importance in *Journal of a Novel* are Steinbeck's remarks about the Hamilton stories in *East of Eden.* These "letters" show, for instance, Steinbeck's fondness for the memory of his maternal grandfather, Samuel Hamilton, whom the novelist remembers "surrounded with all manner of birds and beasts and qualities of light" and whom he wants to portray in his novel "in a kind of golden light, the way such a man should be remembered." In addition, Steinbeck explains why he included the strange and very personal episode of Tom and Dessie Hamilton, why he describes the character of Abra as "the strong female principle of good as opposed to Cathy," and accounts for the character of Lee Trask's philosopher-cook, who is in the book "because I need him."

Most importantly, the "letters" to Covici, when taken as a whole, suggest that while Steinbeck consistently maintained that *East of Eden* was "not a story about the Trasks but about the whole Valley," the book was gradually transformed into a sprawling study of good and evil in the world through a symbolic representation of the Cain-Abel story (Steinbeck states that his characters are "symbol people") and an affirmation of free will (the Timshel symbol) by which each individual can maintain his integrity and purposefully assert his creative impulse. In short, *Journal of a Novel* clearly shows that in the process of writing *East of Eden*, Steinbeck's increasing absorption with the theme of good versus evil led to his preoccupation with the story of the Trask family, and the result is less a series of "contrasts and balances" as Steinbeck hoped, but rather a long, incohesive and highly episodic work which reflects the novelist's inability to weave several diverse threads into a coherent fabric.

In addition to the importance of *Journal of a Novel* in illuminating Steinbeck's intentions in *East of Eden* and indirectly accounting for the novel's failures, the "letters" are even more significant in that they clearly demonstrate a shifting balance in Steinbeck's overall world view. In short, the Steinbeck who appears in *Journal of a Novel* is not the writer who, in his best books, extolled the natural beauty of the Salinas Valley, who celebrated the ecological unity of all life, and who could champion the plight of homeless migrants or write with loving acceptance about the antics of the *paisanos* on Tortilla Flat. Rather the Covici dispatches show him as a novelist driven to affirm, at the expense of everything else, the basic humanity of the human animal which, in his earlier fiction, he had accepted *a priori*; his desperate struggle to prove that "although *East of Eden* is not Eden, it is not insuperably far away."

Viewed in retrospect, however, Steinbeck's real contribution as a thinker in his writing is his ecological world view by which he maintains that all living things are important not only in themselves, but also as they relate to the totality of their environment. "Man," says the novelist in *The Log from the Sea of Cortez*, "is related to the whole thing, related inextricably to all reality, known and unknowable." And in his greatest essays, short stories and novels, Steinbeck presents this ecological, balanced view of man and his natural environment. In *Journal of a Novel* (and by stated intention in *East of Eden*), however, Steinbeck

discards or at least minimizes his interest in the natural environment, telling Covici he only wants to give "an impression of the valley" since "this book is not about geography but about people." Under most circumstances, such a one-directional and selective approach in a novel written on an epic scale would be hazardous, but to a writer like Steinbeck it is disastrous.

In one of the last letters to Covici, Steinbeck notes that most reviewers, fearing and hating ideas and speculations unclothed with flesh, will misread *East of Eden* which "is full of such things." And while this critic's objection is not that Steinbeck introduces ideas and speculations into his fiction, but simply that in *East of Eden* he does it to the exclusion of everything else, what we are ultimately left with is Steinbeck's final remark in the original dedication to Covici which appears at the end of the journal: "God damn it. This is my book.... My book is about good and evil. Maybe the theme got into the execution. Do you want to publish it or not?"

In no way can Steinbeck's collection of "letters" to Covici be called a significant literary landmark. Nevertheless, it presents an important portrait of John Steinbeck attempting the impossible task of "putting down the Salinas Valley from a country man's viewpoint" in a New York apartment while a MacArthur Day parade goes on below his window. It shows an already famous writer, with his greatest work behind him, trying methodically and unsuccessfully to do it all over again. No, *Journal of a Novel* is not a good book and to most readers is probably not worth the purchase price, but to the Steinbeck critic interested in what Ed Ricketts once called "the toto-picture," it is indispensable in that it clearly illuminates a highly important chapter in Steinbeck's life and career as a writer.

519

Peter Lisca.
"Journal of a Novel: The East of Eden Letters." *Modern Fiction Studies*, 16 (Winter 1970–1), 571–2.

When Pascal Covici, Steinbeck's editor at the Viking Press, died in 1964, Steinbeck wrote, "For thirty years Pat was my collaborator and my conscience. He demanded of me more than I had and thereby caused me to be more than I should have been without him." Although it is clear in the present volume and elsewhere that Steinbeck resisted strongly any "collaboration," his use of that term in this tribute is a measure of his love and friendship. Their closeness was no secret, and Charles Madison (*Book Publishing in America*) calls their relationship "the happiest in publishing history." *Journal of a Novel* consists of a series of unmailed letters to Covici written every working day that Steinbeck spent on the first draft of *East of Eden*. So absorbed was he in the writing of that novel that between January 29 and November 1, 1951, start and finish, there is a letter for every weekday except perhaps half a dozen, and there are some Saturday and Sunday letters to make up for them when he could not stay away from his book. These letters were used as warm-up exercises—"like a pitcher warming up to pitch"—for the actual writing stint of a carefully controlled, almost invariable quota of about 1500 words. Several letters themselves run to that length, although they vary down to just a few lines, their variation reflecting the difficulty or ease with which Steinbeck was

able to pick up the novel from where he had left off.

The content of these letters is varied, from personal problems or ecstasies to general philosophical speculation; and from complex problems of structuring the novel's action to the shape, size, hardness, color, sharpness, and number of pencils on hand—at least some dozen passages on pencils and almost as many on the physical properties of desk and paper.

What emerges of Steinbeck's personal life is not particularly valuable to the scholar. But it is interesting to note how much pleasure he got from working with his hands at the practical tasks of homemaking—building shelves and doors, painting walls, and at woodcarving and little practical inventions of the moment. Like a good craftsman, he loved good tools. Although the editor of this journal (an unnamed member of the Viking staff) found it necessary to delete a few lines relating to persons still living, those remaining passages show a rich personal life, full of love for his wife Elaine and her daughter, his own two sons by his previous marriage, and a variety of friends.

Although his health was excellent during this period, he seemed often concerned that he be allowed to live long enough to finish his novel, which he thought of as the high point of his career—"everything else I have written has been, in a sense, practice for this." Yet, paradoxically, he so identified his daily life with the writing of the novel that he hated to see the approaching last chapters, and these are the cause of his longest delays.

Despite the much-quoted excerpt about it being "the duty of a writer to lift up, to extend, to encourage . . ." there were other days when he thought his craft a "silly business" and even a "horse's ass business," particularly when he was reminded of critics and reviewers, whom he had once called "lice" and now "curious sucker fish who live with joyous vicariousness on other men's work and discipline with dreary words the thing that feeds them." He anticipated that the great themes, moral earnestness, and technical accomplishments of *East of Eden* would not be appreciated. In fact, his original four-page "Dedication" for the book consisted of an imaginary free-for-all on the book among himself, editor, proofreader, sales department, and reader.

Whatever the justification for Steinbeck's harshness toward the critics in 1951, and it was ample, certainly the five books and a bibliography on his work in the last eleven years, innumerable articles, three conferences of scholars in the last three years (and several books now in preparation) have done much to change that situation. In fact, his frequent insistence in these letters that the current novel's themes and symbols might remain forever inaccessible to the critics seems incredibly naive in the face of that novel's obviousness.

Except for rare passages, these letters have little critical value. As the working notes are about the book's first draft, they are sometimes not clear in terms of the published version, and this edition's scope did not allow the editor to make the kind of extended correlation that might have been interesting. Surely, with a more scholarly and complete re-editing of the journal and access to this first draft of the novel, some valuable observations might be made; but in its present form the journal has little more than a gossip interest.

Walter R. McDonald. "Transfiguring the Word." *North American Review*, 255 (Winter 1970), 74–6.

... The *Journal* is an intriguing thing. In the form of letters to his editor, it was Steinbeck's way of warming up for writing *East of Eden*, "getting my mental arm in shape to pitch a good game." The letters, on the left-hand pages of a notebook, were sometimes used as "a kind of arguing ground for the story" but more often they were random thoughts which open to us the author's mind and show the nature of the creative process. After warming up with a letter, he would fill the right-hand pages of the notebook with the story of *East of Eden*. The *Journal* makes us hungry to see the pages, side by side. As it is published, it is a teasing, enticing part, and we must wait on scholarship to give us the rest of the story. For instance, Steinbeck writes, "There, Pat [his editor], that part is done. And do you think it is good?" Or again, he muses that since the scene he is about to write is "very strange," he will put most of it in dialogue, the best way to make it convincing. Now and then in this edition there is a footnote, but usually we are left to wonder what part of the novel he means. We lose much, therefore, not knowing what his judgment was at such times, and with no way to match ours with his.

But there are fascinating, available parts: his excitement in discovering other translations of the Hebrew word "timshel" ("do thou," "thou shalt," and "thou mayest"), a pivotal discussion in the book. There is his month to month search for a title (he says he was always a poor title man), from *Salinas Valley*, to *My Valley*, to *Valley to the Sea*. Dissatisfied with their provincial ring, he puzzles about for a symbolic title, one that would tie his story in with its root, the Cain and Abel story. *Cain Mark* struck him, until finally three weeks later, after writing in his own hand the sixteen verses of Cain and Abel, he knew he had the one, *East of Eden*.

Perhaps the most revealing part is the way characters come to being, live, become a part of the author. The best example is Cathy. "Cathy Ames is a monster," he introduces her in the *Journal*. Days later he writes, "Cathy is going to start emerging pretty soon now. I hope I can make her believable." After she is in the story, after "warming up" again, he concludes a letter by saying now "I will go back to my dear Cathy." In *The Writer's World* [Joseph] Heller and others discuss what Flaubert meant when he said, "*Madame Bovary, c'est moi.*" Seeing Steinbeck creating his madam, with asides about his own personality ("To that extent I am a monster like Cathy"), we know. And even when Cathy the girl-monster becomes the mature whore, Kate, without a conscience, Steinbeck says, "I think you will find that Cathy as Kate fascinates people though.... While she is a monster, she is a little piece of the monster in all of us. It won't be because she is foreign that people will be interested but because she is not." The writer's world, then, becomes our world, lived once more with meaning....

Checklist of Additional Reviews

Henry Raymont. "Steinbeck's Letters Will Be a Book." New York *Times*, 2 June 1969, p. 52.

"Newsmakers." *Newsweek,* 73 (16 June 1969), 52.

"Forecasts." *Publishers' Weekly*, 196 (6 October 1969), 49.

"*Journal of a Novel.*" *Kirkus Reviews,* 37 (15 October 1969), 1142.

Henry Raymont. "Viking Press Publishes 200 Letters by John Steinbeck on First Anniversary of His Death." New York *Times*, 21 December 1969, p. 49.

Frederick Madeo. "Book Forum." *Saturday Review*, 53 (10 January 1970), 35.

Dorothy H. Vera. "The Chuck Wagon." Salinas *Californian, Western Ranch and Home Magazine,* 28 February 1970, p. 2A.

"*Journal of a Novel.*" *Choice,* 7 (October 1970), 1044.

"Paperbacks." *Publishers' Weekly*, 198 (9 November 1970), 62.

"Brief Mention." *American Literature*, 43 (November 1971), 505.

THE ACTS OF KING ARTHUR AND HIS NOBLE KNIGHTS

JOHN STEINBECK · · the

acts of king arthur and

his noble knights · · · ·

FROM THE WINCHESTER

MSS. OF THOMAS MALORY

AND OTHER SOURCES · ·

· · · · EDITED BY CHASE

HORTON · FARRAR, STRAUS

AND GIROUX · NEW YORK

"Fiction."
Publishers' Weekly, 210
(30 August 1976), 332–3.

When John Steinbeck was a boy, he discovered the Caxton *Morte d'Arthur*. The fascination of the stories, the language, the old words never diminished for him. Eventually he began to work on his own version of some of the 15th century tales. His research took him to the Winchester Mss. (more authentic than Caxton's edited printed edition) and to noted Malory scholar Eugène Vinaver, who helped him with his Arthurian research. The seven tales here were completed in 1959. Steinbeck's aim was "to set them down in plain present day speech . . . (to) keep the wonder and the magic." He does just that for old and young alike. Delightful too is the bonus: correspondence with his literary agent. It reveals the extent of Steinbeck's interest in Malory, his own artistic concerns and his problems with the Arthur project. A wonderful, wise, posthumous gift to us from the prize-winning Steinbeck. . . .

"Non-fiction."
Kirkus Reviews, 44
(1 September 1976),
1025.

"Jehan Stynebec" maintained a lifelong devotion to the 15th-century minor hoodlum and "knyght presoner, sir Thomas Malleorre," and long cherished the idea of retelling the Matter of Arthur for our time. Dating mostly from 1958–59, Steinbeck's fragmentary attempt represents both an earnest effort at scholarly perspective and a broad contemporary reinterpretation. He did not try to "translate," but simplified and condensed Malory's language while tidying up some narrative loose ends. There are five brief, fairly straightforward versions of episodes from the first book (following Eugène Vinaver's edition of the Winchester MS) and two lengthy narratives based on the Tale of Sir Launcelot du Lake and the Gawain, Ywain, and Marhalt episode. The brief pieces are usually best when closest to Malory; the fog-over-the-moors flourishes and frequent sententious interpolations rarely come off. And Malory's blunt, clear prose rhythms find little counterpart in Steinbeck: "And only then did the knights look about them. On a smooth dark water they saw a little ship covered with silken cloth . . ." for "Than the kynge loked aboute the worlde and sawe before hym in a grete water a lytyll shippe all apparayled with sylke downe to the watir." The two long pieces are freewheeling, often playful reworkings of Malory, in which Steinbeck tries to sum up his complex love of all that knighthood and the Arthurian fellowship have meant to him. Here the dominant mode is the arch and whimsical fable, much in the vein of *Pippin IV*, bound to enthrall and exasperate equal numbers of people. The book must be evaluated more as Steinbeckiana than as Arthuriana, not so much for its narrative foibles as because the project remained so fragmentary—including neither the Grail quest, the book of Launcelot and Guinevere, nor the *Morte Arthur*. A complete Arthurian cycle from Steinbeck would have been good to have. The present version remains an erratically charming curiosity.

G. A. Masterton.
"The Acts of King Arthur and His Noble Knights." Library Journal, 101 (15 October 1976), 2178.

The Arthurian legends fascinated Steinbeck. Not only were their themes and symbols in his work but they suffused his life. When he decided to retell Malory, Steinbeck or his agents visited every likely site and purchased or microfilmed every available document and study. This occupied him from at least 1956 to 1965, and he thought of it as the most important work he had ever undertaken. It was to be the "Steinbeck version" of the tales, interlarded with interpretative essays, and, perhaps, both the capstone to his career and the key to his beliefs. However, he never achieved a distinctive voice for his tales, and they remained enmired somewhere between Malory and *The Once and Future King*. Those included here offer evidence for his efforts, but it is the more than 70 exuberant or crestfallen letters excerpted here that offer strong evidence to the argument that Steinbeck's best writing was in his letters.

John Gardner.
"The Essential King Arthur, according to John Steinbeck." New York Times Book Review, 126 (24 October 1976), 31–2, 34, 36.

When John Steinbeck was at work on his *The Acts of King Arthur and His Noble Knights* in the middle and late 1950's, he hoped it would be "the best work of my life and the most satisfying." Even in its original form, the project was enormous—translation of the complete *Morte d'Arthur* of Sir Thomas Malory; and the project soon became still more difficult, not translation but a complete retelling—rethinking—of the myth. Steinbeck finished only some 293 uncorrected, unedited pages, perhaps one-tenth of the original. Even so, the book Steinbeck's friend and editor Chase Horton has put together is large and important. It is in fact two books, Steinbeck's mythic fiction on King Arthur's court, and a fat, rich collection of letters exchanged between Steinbeck, Horton and Elizabeth Otis, Steinbeck's agent. The first is an incomplete but impressive work of art; the second, the complete story of a literary tragedy—how Steinbeck found his way, step by step, from the idea of doing a "translation" for boys to the idea of writing fabulist fiction, in the mid-1950's, when realism was still king. . . .

Steinbeck's Arthurian fiction is, indeed, "strange and different," as he put it. The fact that he lacked the heart to finish the book, or even put what he did complete into one style and tone, is exactly the kind of petty modern tragedy he hated. The idea was magnificent—so is much of the writing—though we see both the idea and the writing changing as they go. In the early pages he follows Malory fairly closely, merely simplifying and here and there adding explanation for the modern young reader.

As he warms to his work, Steinbeck uses Malory more freely, cutting deeply, expanding generously. In the passage on Merlin's defeat by Nyneve he writes like a man retelling a story from his childhood, interpreting as he pleases and echoing hardly a line. Merlin tells King Arthur what he must guard against and says he, Merlin, must go to his doom. Arthur is astonished that the wizard would go to his doom willingly, but Merlin does so nonetheless, because, as he says, "in the combat between wisdom and feeling, wisdom never wins" (Steinbeck's addition). He travels off with the young woman he loves, fated and knowing it. With only an occasional glance at his source—sixteen cool lines (in tight modern English they could be written in three)—but keeping the formal old sound, for the most part, Steinbeck writes:

"Nyneve was bored and restless and she left Ban's court with Merlin panting after her, begging her to lie with him and stanch his yearning, but she was weary of him, and impatient with an old man as a damsel must be, and also she was afraid of him because he was said to be the Devil's son, but she could not be rid of him, for he followed her, pleading and whimpering."

"Then Nyneve, with the inborn craft of maidens, began to question Merlin about his magic arts, half promising to trade her favors for his knowledge. And Merlin, with the inborn helplessness of men, even though he foresaw her purpose, could not forbear to teach her. And as they crossed back to England and rode slowly from the coast of Cornwall, Merlin showed her many wonders, and when at last he found that he interested her, he showed her how the magic was accomplished and put in her hands the tools of enchantment, gave her the antidotes of magic, and finally, in his aged folly, taught her those spells which cannot be broken by any means. And when she clapped her hands in maidenly joy, the old man, to please her, created a room of unbelievable wonders under a great rock cliff, and with his crafts he furnished it with comfort and richness and beauty to be the glorious apartment for the consummation of their love. And they two went through a passage in the rock to the room of wonders, hung with gold and lighted with many candles. Merlin stepped in to show it to her, but Nyneve leaped back and cast the awful spell that cannot be broken by any means, and the passage closed and Merlin was trapped inside for all time to come."

Here there are still Malorian elements—sentences beginning with "Then" and "And," formulaic repetitions, archaic diction—but all the rest is modern. For instance, it is novelistic, not mythic, to speak of Merlin's "panting," "pleading and whimpering," or of "the inborn craft of maidens" and "the inborn helplessness of men," novelistic to speak of riding *slowly* from the coast of Cornwall (a quick touch of verisimilitude), novelistic to show Nyneve clapping her hands with pleasure, or later, leaping back. By the time Steinbeck reached "The Noble Tale of Sir Lancelot of the Lake," he had his method in full control. He makes authorial comments of a sort only a novelist would risk, cuts pages by the fistful, and at the same time embellishes Malory's spare legend with a richness of detail that transforms the vision, makes it no one but Steinbeck's. Here is a passage

527

with no real source in the original:

"A man like Lancelot, tempered in soldiery, seasoned and tanned by perils, lays up supplies of sleep as he does food or water, knowing its lack will reduce his strength and dull his mind. And although he had slept away part of the day, the knight retired from cold and darkness and the unknown morrow and entered a dreamless rest and remained in it until a soft light began to grow in his cell of naked stone. Then he awakened and wrung his muscles free of cold cramp and again embraced his knees for warmth. He could see no source of light. It came equally from everywhere as dawn does before the rise of the sun. He saw the mortared stones of his cell stenciled with patches of dark slime. And as he looked, designs formed on the walls: formal rounded trees covered with golden fruit and curling vines with flowers as frankly invented as are those of an illuminated book, a benign sheltering tree, and under it a unicorn glowing white, with horn and neck lowered in salute to a maiden of bright needlework who embraced the unicorn, thus proving her maidenhood. Then a broad soft bed shivered and grew substantial in the corner of the cell. . . ."

There is nothing at all like this in Malory. What we have here is myth newly imagined, revitalized, charged with contemporary meaning, the kind of thing we expect of the best so-called post-modernists, writers like John Barth. Steinbeck creates a lifelike Lancelot, a veteran soldier who knows his business (how to grab sleep when you can and so on); shows, in quick realistic strokes, how the soldier wakes up, wrings his muscles against cold and cramp; and how magic starts to happen to this cool, middle-aged realist. The falsity of the magic is emphatic—"as frankly invented as [the designs] in an illuminated book."

The paragraph encapsulates Steinbeck's whole purpose at this stage—a purpose close to Malory's yet utterly transformed—to show in the manner of a fabulator how plain reality is transformed by magic, by the lure of visions that ennoble though they ultimately betray. It's a theme we've encountered before in Steinbeck, but a theme that has here the simplicity and power of myth.

The Acts of King Arthur and His Noble Knights is unfortunately not Steinbeck's greatest book, but as Steinbeck knew, until doubt overcame him, it was getting there.

Phoebe-Lou Adams. "The Acts of King Arthur and His Noble Knights." Atlantic Monthly, 238 (November 1976), 118.

The late John Steinbeck learned to read on a cut version of the Caxton Morte d'Arthur, and loved it. Discovering, in due course, that such love is far from general, he embarked on a freely modernized version for readers allergic to archaic language. The result may outrage devotees of Malory, but it makes some fine tales readily accessible. . . .

Edmund Fuller.
"A Splendid Version of
King Arthur's Tales."
Wall Street Journal,
18 November 1976,
p. 22.

Winston Churchill, in his *History of the English Speaking Peoples*, wrote of the legends of King Arthur: "True or false, they have gained an immortal hold upon the thoughts of men.... It is all true, or it ought to be; and more and better besides."

Now we have a fresh treatment of some of those stories in a posthumous volume of John Steinbeck's, *The Acts of King Arthur and His Noble Knights, from the Winchester Mss. of Thomas Malory and Other Sources*. It is splendid in several ways. We may lament that it represents only part of a large design he had conceived but be grateful, anyway, that we have this much, plus collateral material, all ably and lovingly edited by Chase Horton who worked with him from the start.

The novelist's deep interest in the Arthurian canon was seen in last year's massive volume, *Steinbeck: A Life in Letters*, edited by Elaine Steinbeck and Robert Wallsten.... What we have of the work includes seven substantial chapters: "Merlin," "The Knight With the Two Swords" (the story of Balin and Balan), "The Death of Merlin," "Morgan Le Fay" (precipitating the tragedy of Arthur), "Gawain, Ewain, and Marhalt," and "The Noble Tale of Sir Lancelot of the Lake."

Steinbeck says of these tales: "I wanted to set them down in plain present-day speech for my own young sons, and for other sons not so young—to set the stories down in meaning as they were written, leaving out nothing and adding nothing." Further: "If I can do this and keep the wonder and the magic, I shall be pleased and gratified. In no sense do I wish to rewrite Malory, or reduce him, or change him, or soften or sentimentalize him."

He describes movingly how in childhood learning to read had been an agony for him, as it appears to be for many children today: "Perhaps the greatest single effort that the human undertakes, and he must do it as a child ... the reduction of experience to a set of symbols. ... The Bible I absorbed through my skin. My uncles exuded Shakespeare, and *Pilgrim's Progress* was mixed with my mother's milk. But these things came into my ears." Reading tormented him until "one day, an aunt gave me a book and fatuously ignored my resentment." It was selections from the Caxton edition of *Morte d'Arthur*, and young Steinbeck's heart was enthralled by Malory.

The very thing that might seem an obstacle charmed him. "I loved the old spelling of the words—and the words no longer used. Perhaps a passionate love for the English language opened to me from this one book." He was a rare child. Though that could happen also with a rare child today, he is right in feeling that most of today's readers would want to begin with something less exotic, closer to their current tongue.

An important, enriching aspect of the book—the spirit of which increases admiration and liking for Steinbeck—is the 67-page Appendix: letters written by Steinbeck, while at work in England and parts of Europe, between 1956 and 1959. Some, but not all, overlap with the *Life in Letters*.

They are addressed to Mr. Horton and to Elizabeth Otis, Steinbeck's literary agent who was always his trusted friend and counsellor. To her, he said at the start: "When I have some of it done, I shall with an opening essay tell of my own interest in the cycle.... I shall also try to put down what I think has been the impact of this book on our language, with attitudes, and morals, and our ethics." That full essay was never written but the substance of it is in these wonderful letters.

He writes: "So many scholars have spent so much time trying to establish whether Arthur existed at all that they have lost track of the single truth that he exists over and over." Again: "My looking is not for a dead Arthur but for one sleeping. And if sleeping, he is sleeping everywhere, not alone in a cave in Cornwall."

He discerns that "the Arthurian cycle and practically all lasting and deep-seated folklore is a mixture of profundity and childish nonsense. If you keep the profundity and throw out the nonsense, some essence is lost. These are dream stories, fixed and universal dreams, and they have the inconsistency of dreams."

In the brief introduction he observes that these stories contain "courage and sadness and frustration, but particularly gallantry—perhaps the only single quality of man that the West has invented." He remembers, "Children are violent and cruel—and good—and I was all of these—and all of these were in the ... book. If I could not choose my way at the crossroads in love and loyalty, neither could Lancelot. I could understand the darkness of Mordred because he was in me too; and there was some Galahad in me, but perhaps not enough. The Grail feeling was there, however, deep-planted and perhaps always will be."

King Arthur, perplexed when Merlin foretells that his, the magician's, own death will result from his own doting upon a woman, protests: "You are the wisest man alive. You know what is preparing. Why do you not make a plan to save yourself?" Merlin answers: "Because I am wise. In the combat between wisdom and feeling, wisdom never wins."

Some of Merlin's wiser words, quite apt for the aftermath of an election: "Somewhere in the world there is defeat for everyone. Some are destroyed by defeat, and some made small and mean by victory. Greatness lives in one who triumphs equally over defeat and victory."

As if prescient that he would never finish the project Steinbeck concludes his brief introduction: "I can only ask that my readers include me in the request of Sir Thomas Malory when he says: 'And I pray you all that redyth this tale to pray for him that this wrote that God sende hym good delyverance and sone and hastely—Amen.'"

Diana Rowan. "Malory's Tales for Twentieth Century." *Christian Science Monitor*, 12 January 1977, p. 23.

It is a robust and curious work, very much Steinbeck's own, since he changed and added to Malory's tales. His goal was nothing less than to make the Arthurian legends and era come alive for the 20th-century reader; to rescue the tales from the obscurity of Middle English and, he felt, from Malory's faulty narrative construction and one-dimensional characterizations. Malory seemed to have had the disconcerting habit of getting his knights and damsels into trouble, and then forgetting where he left them, as he began new adventures. Worse, in novelist

Steinbeck's eyes, Malory always gave away the climax two or three times before the end of every tale.

Steinbeck denied he wanted to rewrite or change Malory; he particularly refused to soften or sentimentalize him, dealing bluntly with Arthur's sinful dalliances and his Herod-like slaughter of the innocents. He also refused to erase the lusty elements as Tennyson did in the Victorian era (reducing Malory's "muscular prose to watery poetry"); he presents the attempted seduction of Lancelot by the four lascivious witch-queens with graphic drama, and evokes a sensuous tenderness between Guinevere and her chaste knight.

Yet why did he end the tales with the moment of anguished bliss between these two—as if reluctant to follow the legend from that perfect, fatal moment down to its chaotic conclusion? Even his editor, Chase Horton, refers with apparent bafflement to Steinbeck's "block" that might have kept him from finishing the tales. Did he become overwhelmed (as he often worried he would) by the vast undergrowth of Arthurian scholarship, which stretches back across cultures from Islamic to Italian? Was it the sense of the impending close of his own life? (He died in 1968, three years after the last published correspondence on this work.) Or might it have been, in part, the shock he felt at the dubious reaction his agent, Elizabeth Otis, and his friend Horton gave him upon their reading of the first portion in 1959? For that matter, what keeps any writer from completing a work he or she knows (at least at moments) is good? Evidently, something kept even this literary giant from carrying the work through to completion.

In his correspondence on the subject with Otis and Horton (included in this book as a fascinating backdrop for the tales) Steinbeck talked incessantly of his apprehension that the subject would overwhelm and/or escape him. But these spells were broken by long periods when the joyous "fury of writing," as he termed it would sweep him forward—until May, 1959, that is, when Otis's comments and Horton's "almost lack of comment" on the first portion he gave them seemed to stun him past recovering that certain momentum. He struggled to rally his energies ("I hope I am too professional to be shocked into paralysis") but there are no more periods of joyful fury. He stopped writing several weeks later, and correspondence on the subject ceased between 1959 and 1965.

He continues to voice an interest in Horton's new lists of Arthurian "ms., artifacts, and illuminations," but his last published comment on the subject in July, 1965, is significant: "I am struggling along with the matter of Arthur. I think I have something and am pretty excited about it. But I am going to protect myself by not showing it to anybody so that after I get a stretch of it done, if it seems bad, I can simply destroy it. But right now I don't think it is bad. Strange and different, but not bad."

One suspects Steinbeck completed and left behind just about as much of King Arthur as he wanted to give to us.

Mary C. Williams. "Books Considered." *New Republic*, 176 (5 February 1977), 34–5.

... In a sense Steinbeck had always been reading and re-doing Malory, for there are Arthurian themes and echoes throughout his work. The Caxton *Morte D'Arthur*, given him when he was nine, inspired him to act out its adventures. In his introduction to *The Acts* Steinbeck traces his love of language, his moral ideas, and his sympathy for the oppressed to this enchanting book. He structured two early novels around Arthurian themes, the quest of *The Cup of Gold* and the *paisano* Round Table of *Tortilla Flat*; however, each time his hero started out in Camelot and ended up in a spiritual wasteland.

It is probable that what sent Steinbeck back to Malory in 1956 was a despairing mistrust of his creative powers: "I want to forget how to write and learn all over again with the writing growing out of the material," he said. Also, he had a helpless feeling that he did not understand his own age. In this he identified with Malory, and his letters reflect the intensity of the identification. He saw the author of the *Morte* caught up like him in shifting and perilous times and trying to order them through his work. In a flash of insight he saw that Malory's "self-character," the one into which every author puts himself as he is and as he would be, is Lancelot, the man who could not win the Grail because he was stained with sin and imperfection, but who nevertheless could father Galahad. And so, "Malory-Lancelot has in a sense won the Quest." And Steinbeck-Lancelot, one assumes, can achieve it too—and like Malory transmit a moral heritage. In his introduction Steinbeck says that the book is designed "for my own young sons and for other sons not so young." (Daughters, presumably, can read it if they want to.) Using the Winchester manuscript of the *Morte D'Arthur*, he intended to put the stories into simple language without changing them. His desire was to re-create a living story with significance for the present.

Steinbeck began to write in loneliness and uncertainty. But then pleasure and confidence came. As he worked he found it necessary to cut, to explain, to provide continuity—and so he began to feel the work was his own.

Then he received a shock. After reading the Merlin story, Elizabeth Otis was "confused . . . and disappointed." Steinbeck was even more so. He did not, however, wish to change his style and method in order to write an adaptation like T. H. White's *The Once and Future King*. He was sick of his old ways and old tricks, he wrote. But he assured Otis that the work would be rewritten later and that meanwhile he was feeling freer about changing Malory's stories. His letters show him proceeding for a time with renewed confidence. But then he began to express dissatisfaction with Malory's work and finally with his own—it was just "a repetition of things I have written before." And so he suspended work on *The Acts*, though he returned to it for a time in 1965.

Steinbeck died without finishing, correcting, or editing his manuscript. The original plan was to translate all of the *Morte D'Arthur*; this was amended to omit certain parts and concentrate on the Lancelot episodes. The translation, along with commentaries between the tales, was to appear in two volumes. What is published here corresponds to only about one-fourth of Malory's work, through the tale of Sir Lancelot. There is a short introduction, but the commentaries were never written. Chase Horton reports that Steinbeck did not edit his typescript but does not report what editing he himself has done. According to a note about the manuscript by Roy Simmonds, Steinbeck left 154 pages of manuscript of the tale of Sir Gareth; if so, this portion has been omitted without a word from the editor.

Something less than one-half of *The Acts* comes close to straight translation of the stories of the coming of Arthur to the throne, Balin, the marriage of

Arthur and the enchantment of Merlin. Steinbeck has added some explanations, some comments, some scene-painting, and some human interest details—but not too many. Some of the supernatural has been subtracted. The work compares favorably with Keith Baines' translation, which appeared in 1962. Both versions suffer from flatness, but Steinbeck's style is better. He was trying for "a timeless English," which is very successful.

A change begins with the "Morgan Le Fay" episode and accelerates in the final tales of Gawain, Ewain, and Marhalt and Lancelot, written after the shock of Otis' disapproval and the concurrent new feeling of freedom to revise Malory. Incidents, characterizations, backgrounds, themes are invented, changed and developed. Malory's distancing of characters is replaced by carefully established motivation and humanizing detail. But cuteness, sentimentality, sententiousness, contemporary idioms, and some monstrous overwriting creep in and vulgarize the material; Malory's world becomes Disney's world, sexed up—and also T. H. White's world. It is unfortunate that the author never carefully edited the work because his ideas about shaping characters and connecting Malory's incidents are highly intelligent. With his usual interest in men in groups, Steinbeck develops the social importance of Arthur's court in dealing with the difficulties of peace through establishing the King's Justice. Steinbeck is also focusing on Lancelot, inventing a series of Malorian temptations by witch queens to express latent conflicts in the knight and developing the relationship with Guinevere much earlier and more fully. And Steinbeck expands women's roles—but unhappily turns all women, Morgan and Guinevere alike, into manipulators of men.

The opening sentences of the first and last paragraphs of *The Acts* illustrate the contrast between the two parts. The first paragraph begins: "When Uther Pendragon was King of England his vassal, the Duke of Cornwall, was reputed to have committed acts of war against the land." The final paragraph begins: "Their bodies locked together as though a trap had sprung." Quite a difference. This last was not written for sons, nor for admirers of the *Morte* who recall that Malory did not know what Sir Lancelot and Queen Guinevere did together, since love was different in those days.

Steinbeck wanted too much to make Malory's work his own and to make Lancelot a version of himself. He couldn't make the book turn out right: "I don't know what to do with it and I am too old to kid myself about it," he wrote. *The Acts* is not a unified and complete work. Yet, as a revelation of its author and his way of working, it is of much interest.

Derek Mahon. "Round Tables." *New Statesman* [England], 93 (11 February 1977), 195.

John Steinbeck was a curious writer and a curious man. Some, like myself, have not been offered the Nobel Prize; others, like Sartre, have refused it. But Steinbeck is the only one, to my knowledge, who accepted it while making it clear that he didn't deserve it. This estimate of his own work was engagingly candid, and indeed quite true, although *The Grapes of Wrath* has some claim to the status of a minor classic. Steinbeck was first and foremost a pro: he wrote books. His last book, based on Malory, was written in plain present-day speech for my young sons, perhaps to compete with the movies and comic-strip travesties which are the only available source for those impatient with Malory's spelling and archaic words.

Not a work of scholarship, but a competent and useful piece of bookmaking, and as such highly recommended.

Robert E. Morsberger. "The Acts of King Arthur and His Noble Knights." Western American Literature, 12 (August 1977), 163–5.

Sir Thomas Malory's *Le Morte d'Arthur*, published in 1485, is a watershed in the literature of the Western world. It is the culmination of the Arthurian romances, the Matter of Britain, from Gildas through Layamon, Geoffrey of Monmouth, Chrétien de Troyes, and other "Frensshe" books, anonymous alliterative poets, Gottfried von Strassburg; in turn, it profoundly influenced subsequent literature. Milton contemplated writing an Arthurian epic, and Tennyson tried to do so. Matthew Arnold, Swinburne, E. A. Robinson and T. H. White wrote Arthurian material, Mark Twain burlesqued it, *Prince Valiant* borrowed it for the comics, and Hollywood adapted it for the movies.

John Steinbeck had a lifelong love affair with Malory's tales of the Round Table and claimed that the fellowship of *paisanos* in *Tortilla Flat* was a version of them. Finally, in November, 1956, he decided to work with the original and render Malory into English for modern readers, so that they could share his enthusiasm. He was also fascinated by the problem of dictation and style: "I intend to translate into a modern English, keeping, or rather trying to recreate, a rhythm and tone which to the modern ear will have the same effect as the Middle English did on the fifteenth-century ear."

But first, he put in a year and a half of formidable research—a case of overkill so far as translation is concerned, but a labor of love and in some ways a putting off of the actual chore of writing. To obtain background, he made three trips to England and one to Italy, visited Armando Sapori and Bernard Berenson and became good friends with Eugène Vinaver, the world's leading Malory expert, who was impressed with a sample of rough translation and offered any help possible. Steinbeck decided to work with the Winchester manuscript discovered in 1936 rather than with Caxton, and he made microfilm copies of each. Though he read hundreds of books on the Middle Ages, he continued to feel that there were gaps in his reading, scholarship, and the "feel and look" of locations. He felt that the work required him to "know the countryside in which Malory lived and operated. . . . I had to go from one end of England to the other to get a sense of topography, color of soil, marsh, moor, forest, and particularly relationships of one place to another. . . . This is destined to be the largest and I hope the most important work I have ever undertaken." With his wife making a photographic record, Steinbeck roamed all over Somerset, Cornwall, Wiltshire, and Wales. "Building a background for this book has been a long and arduous job," and an expensive one, he added, "but highly rewarding." He began by predicting that the work would go very fast but later thought it might take 10 years. "Why has it been necessary to read so much—most of which will probably not be used? I think it necessary for me to know everything I can about what Malory knew and how he might have felt, but it is also necessary for me to be aware of what he did not know, could not have known, and could not feel," in order to avoid the error of thinking Malory was like a modern man.

Finally, he began writing, working mainly in Somerset, from July, 1958, to October, 1959. He tried for "a close-reined, taut, economical English, unaccented and unlocalized." He succeeded rather well; the prose is vigorous and clear but necessarily a hybrid that is modern in diction but retains an archaic formality. As he got into the material, he took increasing liberties with the text, not only making cuts but additions and elaborations. "I have eliminated a number of the more obscure adventures in Malory, but others I have greatly expanded in a way that might deeply shock the master." The book of Balin, The Knight with Two Swords, is a faithful rendering, extremely well done. On the other hand, Steinbeck expands three and a half pages of the adventures of Sir Ywain to 30 pages of his own, with such interpolations as a lengthy discussion of how the longbow, by destroying knighthood, would revolutionize institutions and lead to government by commoners. Thus long passages are not Malory at all but original Steinbeck in the manner of Malory.

This may explain why the project was aborted. After three years of enthusiasm, he confessed, "The work doesn't jell," and put it aside for The Winter of Our Discontent. In 1965, he briefly returned to Malory, but completed only seven of the adventures. These are self-contained and among the best, so that readers will find the volume satisfying and perhaps wish for more.

In addition, there are 68 pages of letters from Steinbeck to his agent Elizabeth Otis and his friend Chase Horton. Some of these are in Steinbeck: A Life in Letters, but many are printed for the first time. (There are additional letters on Malory to Vinaver, Pascal Covici and others in the Life in Letters.) But since both collections of letters are edited and excerpted, we sometimes have different parts of the same letter in the same two books. The letters deal not only with Steinbeck's research on Malory and his problems with translation and adaptation but with reflections on art and the artist, on language and style, on medieval life and thought, and on the heroic vs. modern anti-heroes. As such, they are revealing both to students of Steinbeck and of Malory and the Middle Ages.

Robert Black. "The Acts of King Arthur and His Noble Knights." Denver Quarterly, 11 (Winter 1977), 206–9.

John Steinbeck's The Acts of King Arthur and His Noble Knights is edited by Chase Horton and published posthumously. The Introduction and Appendix together give Steinbeck's reader both an insight into his craft as novelist and a critical direction one ought to take in reading the novel. In The Acts Steinbeck is neither translator nor redactor but is rather a Nobel Prize-winning novelist who with moral and artistic consciousness is working in one of the West's most traditional narrative forms, the Arthurian romance. His sense of morality comes from Caxton's Morte d'Arthur of Thomas Malory. "I think my sense of right and wrong," he writes in the Introduction, "my feeling of noblesse oblige, and any thought I may have against the oppressor and for the oppressed, came from this secret book." His sense of style also begins with Caxton's Malory, which more than any other book enchanted him as a child and taught him how to read.

In the Appendix, which is made up almost entirely of some seventy letters written between 1956 and 1965 to his agent Elizabeth Otis and his acknowledged collaborator Chase Horton, Steinbeck is intensely conscious of his craft. Enthusiastically he writes, "This is destined to be the largest and I hope most important work I have ever undertaken." In his letters he abandons Caxton's Malory in favor of the Winchester manuscript, discovered in 1936, as the basic text for his novel and declares that he will write in a language which is as out of time and place as the Arthurian legend itself—"a close-reined, taut, economical English, unaccented and unlocalized." His Malory will not be like that of Tennyson or Southey or even T.H. White, all of whom to some extent clean up the tales for young boys. "Let boys beware," Steinbeck writes, for he will be true to the fifteenth-century text for the sake of his "own young sons" as well as for adults, "for other sons not so young."

Although an unfinished work—one of its medieval attractions—*The Acts* presents seven stories, the last two of which are especially successful as "moral parables" without time and place, written in a style which never makes what William Golding calls the "deadliest of literary vices in writing for children, the hideous sidelong twinkle in the direction of other adults." A famous novelist who became intimately familiar with his subject by spending over ten years traveling throughout England, Wales, and Italy and by

reading hundreds of books on the Middle Ages and by visiting and corresponding with Malory scholars like Eugène Vinaver, Steinbeck is finally successful in *The Acts* because for him there was so much good fun in just trying to do it. In a letter to Chase Horton, Elaine Steinbeck tells of her husband carving out wooden spoons for their kitchen in Somerset and speaking of Arthur and Merlin. Vinaver quotes Steinbeck as saying, "I tell these old stories, but they are not what I want to tell. I only know how I want people to feel when I tell them." *The Acts of King Arthur and His Noble Knights* is a modern novelist's *Philobiblon,* his modern *Love of Books.*

In the last two tales, "Gawain, Ewain, and Marhalt" and "The Noble Tale of Sir Lancelot of the Lake (and a noble tale it is. J.S.)," Steinbeck is at his best as a raconteur for the modern age. "If Malory could rewrite Chrétien for his time, I can rewrite Malory for mine," he tells Elizabeth Otis. The tales are expanded into stories which are unified, tough-minded, chatty, and sophisticated. Steinbeck expands Malory's episode of Gawain, Ewain, and Marhalt to present an arrogant Gawain and a delightful Lady Lyne who serves as Ewain's first manager and turns the medieval Pygmalion story upside down. But above all, Steinbeck is more ironical than Malory.

Malory's thirteenth-century "Frensshe books" create a sense of irony through the use of abstract ideals such as honor, courage, and love, as each is understood for better or for worse by the knights and ladies in the romances. For example, love is often presented in Chrétien de Troyes as referring finally to a predictable ideal in a Christian culture, the love of men and women for God. A departure from that ideal is often understood to be unreasonable, comic, and ironical. Malory's *Morte d'Arthur* is different.

Even when the adultery of Guinevere and Lancelot is seen to be central to the dissipation of Arthur's kingdom, Malory's sense of morality is in part superficial—and even sentimental. Steinbeck writes without implicit references to Christian ideals, but he achieves an ironical effect by filling in gaps in Malory, making persistent references to political or economic conditions.

In Malory, for example, Sir Marhalt and his lady are simply turned away when they ask to stay overnight with a poor cotter—who nonetheless directs them to further adventure down the road. In Steinbeck, however, the Ugly Householder is a tough character with his own story. "A knight venturing," he observes of Marhalt; "I know your kind, a childish dream world resting on the shoulders of less fortunate men." And when Marhalt asks to be guided to another place to spend the night, the Ugly Householder demands to be paid first. "I will," says Marhalt, "but if you do not lead us truly I will return and burn your treasured house." "I know you would," he says, "gentlemen always do." The Ugly Householder is significantly not a medieval churl or a deformed or supernatural figure. He is one of many modern men in *The Acts*. His kinsmen are Lady Lyne's bowmen who ironically are more powerful than Arthur's knights and who cannot speak English; his chief protestor is ultimately Arthur himself who at the end of the novel ironically wonders "how long we can leave justice in the hands of men who are themselves unstable."

What Steinbeck sometimes shares with Malory, on the other hand, is a tendency to be somewhat superficial in trying to create a moral effect. At the end of a year spent riding together seeking adventure, Marhalt and his lady finally leave each other as just good friends with no commitments. A mellow heroine, she remains nameless. "I never thought to ask," says Marhalt.

One of the most attractive qualities about Steinbeck's novel is the dialogue between men and women. The women in Steinbeck are real "dames," as he calls them in his letters. Damsels eat a lot of feasts and ladies in distress drive hard bargains when they make knights keep their oaths. Almost all of the queens, maidens, servant girls, nuns, and witches are personalities in the tales. Their conversations with knights establish the links between episodes as much as their actions determine the plots. Everywhere they create enchantment and comedy. Steinbeck is determined to correct what he thought to be a dislike of women in Malory. In his letters he describes Guinevere as "a doodle." In his dedication he even goes so far as to raise his sister Mary to knighthood. His great success with the characterization of women in romance makes one wish for more stories, and one can only regret not having Steinbeck's version of some of the stories in Malory's last two books, particularly a version of the delicate "The Fair Maid of Astolat."

One thing more may be said about Steinbeck's sense of morality and of his art. In *The Acts* Steinbeck "picks up" incidents forgotten by Malory in order to "give reasons for the whole thing." More than Malory, Steinbeck uses morality as an imperative element of the plot. In "The Noble Tale of Sir Lancelot of the Lake" Steinbeck's Sir Lyonel chooses to fight Sir Tarquin alone because of a new-found virtue, achieved through what reads like a Socratic dialogue with Lancelot the previous day. Malory offers no reason at all for Lyonel's decision. Steinbeck's Sir Lancelot, whom Steinbeck in his letters calls "my boy," rides out disguised in Sir Kay's armor because he is reacting morally to the Seneschal's defense of his own loss of powers, brought on by the bureaucratic mess of running the business end of a kingdom.

Ultimately, of course, Lancelot himself fails, but his adulterous love for Guinevere is in Steinbeck a modern virtue rather than a medieval vice. For the Middle Ages that vice betrays the central cause of decadence in Arthur's kingdom. In an earlier confrontation between an incredulous Lancelot and a young enchantress who cannot quite cast a perfect spell, Steinbeck gives his reader a hint of the final catastrophe which will come to Lancelot and Guinevere. But only in the final paragraphs does he continue that theme:

> "Their bodies locked together as though a trap had sprung. Their mouths met and each devoured the other. Each frantic heartbeat at the walls of ribs trying to get to the other until their breaths burst out and Lancelot, dizzied, found the door and blundered down the stairs. And he was weeping bitterly."

"That's why I love Lancelot I guess," Steinbeck writes in one of his last letters. "He is tested, he fails the test and still remains noble."

Barbara McDaniel.
"*The Acts of King Arthur and His Noble Knights.*" *West Coast Review*, 12 (January 1978), 57–9.

Certain letters found in *A Life in Letters*, as well as others, again cut without notation, form the lengthy appendix of *The Acts of King Arthur and His Noble Knights*. Selected for their relation to the work, these letters Steinbeck addressed to his agent and his editor form a moving tale—if an incomplete one. Although editor Horton collaborated closely with Steinbeck during the years 1956–65 when Steinbeck's redaction was alternately pursued and abandoned, Horton's only comment is a very brief note preceding the appendix.

Steinbeck's appropriate title comes from words on the title page of Caxton's manuscript and eliminates the usual misleading *Morte*. The text is the incomplete draft of the first volume of a projected two-volume work based [on] Malory. Far more difficult for him than he anticipated, this goal required considerable reevaluation as he proceeded, but after his painstaking scholarly preparation of many months, he could defend decisions from a sound position, which was very important to him. "Nothing," he wrote, with typical humility and informality, "is so dangerous as the theories of a half-assed or half-informed scholar."

Working with microfilm copies of both the Caxton and Winchester manuscripts, reading and consulting "hundreds of books bought [and] rented," conducting "endless correspondence with scholars in the field," and making trips to England and Italy to turn up new sources of information and to become acquainted with the actual scenes he thought to have influenced Malory, he immersed himself in *The Acts*. When inspiration flagged, he even went to live in Somerset half a year for the sake of his muse. Once he began the actual writing, he remarks that in Malory the straggling sentences, the confused characters and events of the early parts become smooth, showing that "Malory learned to write as he went along"; then with delight Steinbeck found this happening to himself. Only a short way into the material, he evolved hypotheses and methods that prepared him to rewrite what was done, but he resisted the impulse, saying he knew he must proceed and revise later. By this time he knew that, despite all the scholarship published on Malory, he would have to rely on intuition some of the time. Such freedom led to vacillation between exuberance and despair.

One idea governing Steinbeck was the conviction that Malory was at heart a novelist, and the *Morte* therefore Malory's own story, having Launcelot as his "self-character," the symbolic spokesman Steinbeck believed every novel to have. Where he states this his letters acquire considerable value for Steinbeck studies, for the writer declares his view of himself as a novelist: "I suppose my own symbol character has my dream wish of wisdom and acceptance." That Steinbeck conceived of the *Morte* as a novel is a significant fact to bear in mind in reading his version, for it must affect numerous passages, probably including the following one from "Merlin":

Arthur looked upward and he said, "It's a black day, a troubled day." "It is a day, simply a day. You have a black and troubled mind, my lord."

Nothing like these sentences occurs in Vinaver; the addition creates more modern characterization and unity.

Other scholars, C.S. Lewis, for example (in *Essays on Malory*, ed. J. W. W. Bennett, Clarendon Press, Oxford, 1963), do not believe that any Middle English author could have conceived a work of fiction following our principles of unity, much less have undertaken to write one. But Lewis's principles leave room for Steinbeck's art: "The choice we try to force upon Malory, is really a choice for us. It is our imagination, not his, that

makes the work one or eight or fifty. We can read it now one way, now another. We partly make what we read." Alterations in the interest of unity are consonant with Steinbeck's sense that his "tampering . . . at best will make the history available to more readers, and at worst can't hurt Malory very much."

Having begun the writing in July 1958 with "freezing humility," "an uneasiness approaching fright," Steinbeck soon lost his inhibitions. "Almost by enchantment the words began to flow, a close-reined, taut, economical English, unaccented and unlocalized. I put down no word that has not been judged for general understanding. Where my time cannot fill in, I build up, and where my time would be impatient with repetition, I cut. So did Malory for his time." But Steinbeck's new faith in "intuition, my own judgment and the receptivity of our times" was dashed by the reception Chase Horton and Elizabeth Otis, Steinbeck's agent, gave the first section of the manuscript, the Merlin story, which Steinbeck had found particularly difficult. Ironically, the end of four months of his reporting to them with gusto is a paragraph on May 11, 1959, saying, "I resent anything that interrupts the slow, steady flow of this translation." Two days later he was trying to rebound from the criticism he has just received from them, or rather from her remarks and "Chase's almost lack of comment."

A quality in Steinbeck that attracts many readers is never more apparent than in this long letter to them, and several other letters, in which he humbly struggles to understand the objections. One can only infer the nature of the criticism: perhaps what Horton and Otis expected was "form the present-day ear accepts without listening," the ear "trained by Madison Avenue and radio and television and Mickey Spillane." Solemnly expressing his sadness, Steinbeck nevertheless states, "I know I'll have to go along with my impulse." He intends to continue in the same vein until "I've worked the summer away and the fall—if it still seems dull, then I will stop it all, but I've dreamed too many years—too many nights to change direction." Although this letter won him supportive replies from both, Steinbeck never regains his enthusiasm. In September he is "completely dissatisfied"; in October he "might have an answer"; in an undated letter he won't "write a single word on it until after January 1."

A respite longer than that by more than six years appears over in the next letter, dated May 15, 1965, and addressed to Horton. Businesslike in discussing their plans, it lacks Steinbeck's customary warmth toward his editors but indicates that a serious reassessment of the project has taken place; Horton is going to Italy for some new research, and Steinbeck is studying the character of Arthur.

The letters—and apparently the work—stop two months later.

About this, Horton says only, "John did not finish *King Arthur*, and did not say why or how he felt blocked, if indeed he was, when he stopped writing." One is left curious to know Horton's views of Steinbeck. Perhaps this was not the proper place for them, but his insights from his experience with the author, at the very least his letters to Steinbeck, are sorely needed to answer questions he has raised by releasing this book. Incomplete, the work is of more interest to American studies than medieval; hence it seems that Horton's impressions of Steinbeck would make a further contribution to the field.

John F. Kiteley. "Magnificent Obsession." *Books and Bookmen* [England], 23 (March 1978), 55–6.

I have had many problems in considering the Steinbeck Malory. What right had I to pass public judgments on the work of such a distinguished writer as John Steinbeck, author of *Cannery Row, The Grapes of Wrath, Of Mice and Men*, and *East of Eden*, to name but a few of his magnificent novels? Fortunately, this book has been published posthumously, and it is this fact that has made me feel able to express my honest views. It seems pretty clear that Steinbeck himself was far from happy about this book, and the editor, Chase Horton, clearly acknowledges that it was not completed, edited or corrected by the author. . . .

. . . Steinbeck died in New York in 1968. We are left with the first draft. *This* is not strange in itself (although strange in its achievement or lack of it) but frankly it is not good. . . .

Checklist of Additional Reviews

Alice McKenzie. "Steinbeck Tells King Arthur's Tale." Clearwater [Fla.] *Sun,* 26 December 1976, p. 6F.

"*The Acts of King Arthur and His Noble Knights.*" *Choice,* 14 (March 1977), 64.

Roy S. Simmonds. "*The Acts of King Arthur and His Noble Knights.*"

Steinbeck Quarterly, 10 (Spring 1977), 52–7.

Cynthia Johnson. "*The Acts of King Arthur and His Noble Knights.*" *School Library Journal*, 23 (April 1977), 84.

T. A. Shippey. "East of Camelot." *Times Literary Supplement* [London], 29 April 1977, p. 236.

"*The Acts of King Arthur and His Noble Knights.*" *Horn Book*, 53 (October 1977), 561–2.

"Paperbacks New and Noteworthy." *New York Times Book Review*, 129 (11 December 1979), 49.

WORKING DAYS:
THE JOURNALS OF *THE GRAPES OF WRATH* 1938–1941

John Steinbeck

WORKING DAYS
The Journals of
The Grapes of Wrath
1938–1941

Edited by Robert DeMott
Ohio University

VIKING

Brian St. Pierre.
"Steinbeck's Timeless Tale of Migrant Suffering."
San Francisco *Chronicle*, 26 March 1989, Section 4, pp. 3–4.

... From *Working Days*, the journals Steinbeck kept while writing *The Grapes of Wrath*, comes the astonishing fact that he wrote this dense and complex novel in 100 days, by hand, under a fair amount of duress: His publisher was going bankrupt, a noisy housing project was being built next door, he and his wife Carol were ill at times, and he was plagued to the point of depression by doubts about his talent. No wonder he wrote, "I am ready to go to work and I am glad to get into other lives and escape from mine for a while."

Steinbeck undertook this journal to make himself accountable ("If a day is skipped it will show glaringly on this record"), and as editor Robert DeMott notes, it is a "hermetic—even claustrophobic" diary of the making of a book as well as its attendant terrors and distractions.

Many of the entries are rambling and banal, as many of anyone's days would be, but the earnest, die hard effort of writing and the importance of the task have great cumulative power: "I grew again to love and admire the people who are so much stronger and purer and braver than I am," he wrote of the migrants.

DeMott has surrounded the journal entries with a biographical introduction, commentary and illuminating notes, building a good book onto a narrow foundation. While not intended for general readers, the book will be important to anyone seeking a deeper understanding of Steinbeck and his work....

Frederick Turner.
"The Wrath, the Discontent and the Grapes."
New York *Post*, 16 April 1989, p. 10.

Almost half a century ago at the apex of his popularity John Steinbeck saw himself dismissed by Edmund Wilson as a crude artificer unable to breathe life into his fictional characters. When Alfred Kazin repeated and amplified this attack in his path-breaking *On Native Grounds* (1942) the charge stuck. There Kazin wrote of the apprenticelike quality of Steinbeck's work, of his primitiveness, his "slow curiosity," "simplicity of spirit" and "simple indignation" at the suffering of migrant workers in California. The Joad family of *The Grapes of Wrath,* Kazin said, could hardly fail to interest American readers since there was so much of the national experience represented in these characters. But the Joads were, after all, only "symbolic marionettes."

Through the ensuing 20 years Steinbeck's stature with readers remained high as did the sales of his books, and in 1962 he was anointed by the international literary establishment with the Nobel Prize. If readers applauded the award as much-deserved and long overdue, Steinbeck's American critics remained unconvinced and were as baffled by this Nobel as by that earlier given Pearl Buck. When Steinbeck died in 1968 his critical reputation was low and rested on a single novel that many critics refused to consider a novel at all, choosing to regard *The Grapes of Wrath* instead as a sociological phenomenon that had summed up the bygone decade of the '30s. Now, precisely a half-century since its publication, here is *The Grapes of Wrath* again in a handsome anniversary edition and accompanied by the journal Steinbeck kept while working on the novel. The occasion tells us that whether novel, tract or sociological phenomenon, *The Grapes of Wrath* remains a part of our image of ourselves as a people.

Robert DeMott, who has so carefully edited the journal now called *Working Days*, uses his introduction to chart the stages of Steinbeck's thinking during the two years of work on what DeMott calls the "matter of the migrants." First there were Steinbeck's research trips into the fields and camps beginning in 1936, during which he made contact with Tom Collins, the Farm Security Administration manager who provided him with so much crucial material. Also in 1936 there was Steinbeck's seven-part newspaper report on migrant conditions, "The Harvest Gypsies." He followed this with a fictional treatment he was calling "The Oklahomans," but abandoned it early in 1938. Immediately afterward he tried again, this time with a venomous satire, "L'Affaire Lettuceberg," which he also abandoned. But what he had experienced in the fields and camps had so impressed itself on him that it would give him no rest, and so within 10 days of the abandonment of the satire he was back at his desk and at work on the "big book" he felt the subject demanded. Here is where the journal begins.

As with his other "big book," *East of Eden* (1952), Steinbeck used the journal as a warm-up exercise, beginning each day with a few lines in which he confided his hopes and his characteristic self-doubts. And as with the later journal *Working Days* is an oddly vacant-seeming volume. It contains few insights into the author's actual method of composition. Yet in a way that is tellingly replicated in the novel itself, there is something noble here. Paralleling the Joad family's flight along Route 66 through Oklahoma, New Mexico, Arizona and into California is the writer's struggle through the summer and early fall of 1938 to be equal to the tragedy of the story he was evoking. And once he has the Joads in California his struggle is theirs, too, for he has to fight against his own destructive rage at the violence and greed of the local agricultural organizations and their goons. June 18th's entry is typical: "This is a huge job. . . . If only I could do this book properly it would be one of the really fine books and a truly American book. But I am assailed with my own ignorance and inability. If I can keep my honesty it is all I can expect of my poor brain. . . . If I can do that it will be all my lack of genius can produce. . . ."

By early September he thought he saw himself finishing about the middle of the next month. "Europe," he noted, "still tense. Hitler waiting for heaven to speak. Maybe war but I don't think so." By Oct. 14, he was in fact so close his hand was shaking. He finished Oct. 26 and felt it was not "the great book I had hoped it would be."

Maybe not. Steinbeck habitually wrecked perfectly good characters and plots by forcing them to carry monstrous allegorical burdens. This is what ruins *East of Eden* and it is what undermines the aesthetic quality of *The Grapes of Wrath*—but not its force, its enduring claim on us.

"Bookends."
Time, 132
(24 April 1989), 86.

Published 50 years ago, *The Grapes of Wrath* has taken its place among the handful of American novels (*Uncle Tom's Cabin, The Jungle*) that changed public attitudes and policy. To mark its golden anniversary, the book's original publisher has issued a new edition . . . and also the journals Steinbeck kept during the five months (*five months!*) it took him to complete the 200,000-word manuscript.

The author, then 36, used these private notes as warm-up exercises for the day's work. He gave himself pep talks: "This must be a good book. It simply must. I haven't any choice." To readers today, the fascination of this document rests in its portrait of an artist at the peak of his skills. Steinbeck's outrage at the mistreatment of Dust Bowl migrants in California, which he had witnessed first-hand, fused with his storytelling abilities to produce the most powerful book he would ever write. It won him the Pulitzer Prize and contributed mightily to his Nobel Prize in 1962. Both exhilarated and exhausted after finishing the book, Steinbeck wondered whether he would ever write so well again. "That part of my life that made the *Grapes* is over."

Pascal Covici, Jr.
"Struggling to a Classic."
Dallas *Morning News*,
14 May 1989,
pp. 10–11C.

"My laziness is overwhelming," lamented John Steinbeck as he approached the final chapters of his American epic. "I only hope it is some good. I have very grave doubts sometimes."

"My mind doesn't want to work—hates to work in fact, but I'll make it."

If nothing else—and there's a great deal else—Robert DeMott has given us an opportunity to know directly and poignantly, and sometimes painfully, the struggles of will buried behind the seemingly pre-determined procession of words that make great literary art.

How could John Steinbeck have done it? With house problems and money problems, health problems and marriage problems, with problems political, social and even of friendship plaguing the writer, how could *The Grapes of Wrath* ever have been written? Here is the revelation of just how searing that experience of authorship turned out to be.

Mr. DeMott's introduction, uncovering with sure and sensitive knowledge what John Steinbeck did, how he worked and thought, and even how he felt, sets the scene for *Working Days*. This day-by-day account of the book's progress, and of the writer's frustrations, will fascinate a variety of readers.

First of all, those interested in social issues will recognize the tensions in the kind of involvement necessary for a writer to commit himself to what Mr. DeMott calls the "Matter of the Migrants." For over three years, Mr. Steinbeck worked for the dispossessed and oppressed working migrants from Oklahoma in their struggle simply to live despite the Associated Farmers of California and their banking allies.

But then he had to distance himself from demands and invasions that would have made writing the book impossible. Because he had acquired notoriety as author of *In Dubious Battle* (1936) and *Of Mice and Men* (1937), he received countless appeals. Down-and-outers—the people whose stories he had told in articles and whose lives he would transform into art in *The Grapes of Wrath*—wanted money from him because they thought that he had both money and luck. The money had not yet arrived. As for his "luck," his "success," Mr. Steinbeck considered it more a matter of his "destruction." "The Greeks," he wrote in *The Journals*, thinking especially of Homer and of Sophocles, "seem to have known about this dark relationship between luck and destruction." Mr. Steinbeck felt it strongly.

So there is nourishment here for the reader who wonders about writing and for the reader who wonders about success in America. Throughout his life, John Steinbeck could never see himself as the accomplished writer that he was. Success meant mostly that he felt obliged to do more and better than he saw himself as able to do.

The Grapes of Wrath did indeed make him rich, but it also made him a target for the California that he had so greatly offended. He told the truth about the banks, the Associated Farmers, the utilities and their treatment of the dust-bowl victims. Lured west by fraudulent advertising and then exploited, the lucky ones found themselves compelled to work for any wage at all, or else watch their children starve. The less fortunate died.

After the telling, Mr. Steinbeck found himself alienated from his own neighbors. Not only the FBI, but the local folks of Salinas, too, were out to get him. "Don't stay in a hotel room alone," a friendly undersheriff of Santa Clara County told him. "The boys got a rape case set for you. You get alone in a hotel and a dame will come in, tear off her clothes, scratch her face and scream and you try to talk your way out of that one. They won't touch your book, but there's easier ways."

In an earlier *Journals* entry, he had written: "All the growth of the fascist tendency is heart breaking. Nothing seems to work against its stupidity and one gets very tired. . . . I'll probably be framed before very long."

One wonders how he kept his faith in America and in democracy. This edition of *The Journals*, with Mr. DeMott's superb—and superbly documented—notes, demonstrates heart-liftingly that he did. And when a writer's life is as filled with incident as John Steinbeck's, the documentation, the gossip, and the record become, at a distance, an odyssey of delight. The agony of the writer here becomes a reader's informed pleasure.

James D. Houston. "Steinbeck's Obsession." *San Francisco Review of Books*, 4 (Spring 1989), 25–6.

[In 1938], Steinbeck was sitting down to write an as-yet-untitled novel. At the same time he also began the daily journal that Viking brings out on April 14 of this year, as a companion to the fiftieth anniversary edition. Called *Working Days:*

The Journal of The Grapes of Wrath, it covers the period of actual composition, from May to October, 1938, followed by a few post-production entries from the period October 1939 to January 1941. These have been edited, with an admirable commentary—thorough, readable, and generous-spirited—by Robert DeMott, formerly a director of San Jose State University's Steinbeck Research Center.

As DeMott points out in his Introduction, the trip to Visalia and Nipomo was the turning point in the history of [the information on migrant workers he had gathered]: the need to report, as he had done for the [San Francisco] *News*, gave way to something larger and much more urgent.

Steinbeck's leap from right-minded competency to inspired vision was the result of one linked experience that hit him so hard it called forth every ounce of his moral indignation, social anger and pity.

Judging by the detail in *Working Days*, this was a novel born in pain and sustained by pain. Part of the legend of the making of *The Grapes of Wrath* is the feverish obsession of the writing, at the end of which Steinbeck collapsed from nervous exhaustion. His journal bears this out in sometimes excruciatingly intimate detail. As journals go, this is not the kind of literary speculation we find in *The East of Eden Letters*. It is as if a closed-circuit video camera had been mounted above his desk in the eight-by-eight foot workroom on Greenwood Lane in the foothills outside Los Gatos. These are daily, confessional glimpses of a man who, while giving voice to an American legend, is sweating, brooding, counting words and pages, blacking out, fighting nausea....

During these same five hectic months he is also nursing his wife through a tonsillectomy; buying a ranch; entertaining Charlie Chaplin, Broderick Crawford, and film director Pare Lorentz; worrying over reviews of *The Long Valley*, which came out that summer; and trying to ignore reports that his New York publisher, Pat Covici, was going bankrupt.

What emerges from these rushed entries is the picture of a man whose life is filled to overflowing, whose body is falling apart, while his mind and heart are possessed with a story that will not go untold.

The published novel is over six hundred pages long. He wrote it in one hundred working days. Pacing himself relentlessly, he averaged two thousand words a day, commencing on May 31, when his journal begins, "Here is the diary of a book, and it will be interesting to see how it works out." On October 26, the day he completed the final scene, his entry conveys both misery and relief:

I am so dizzy I can hardly see the page. I wonder if this flu could be simple and complete exhaustion. I don't know.... I finished this day, and I hope to God it's good.

Steinbeck didn't get his wish. You never hear the word good used to describe *The Grapes of Wrath*. From day one this has been a novel with devoted friends and powerful enemies. Readers have loved it, and they have hated it. There are still people in Bakersfield who cannot discuss it in a calm voice. They have not yet forgiven Steinbeck for the way he described working conditions there and for the damage they believe this did to Kern County's reputation....

Kenneth S. Lynn.
"Book Reviews."
American Spectator, 41
(August 1989), 41–2.

John Steinbeck's first lengthy examination of the Dust Bowl migrants—a series of investigative reports that were published, alongside photos of the migrants by the Farm Security Administration's Dorothea Lange, in the pro-labor *San Francisco News* in the fall of 1936—made only passing allusions to their trek westward from Oklahoma and concentrated instead on the gypsy-like existence they were reduced to in agriculturally feudal California. Subsequently, he tried and failed to write a novel called *The Oklahomans*, in which, apparently, he zeroed in once again on the California scene. His third attempt to deal with the migrants was inspired by a bloody clash between workers and growers in a lettuce strike in Salinas, California, his birthplace. But *L'Affaire Lettuceberg*, as he dubbed the manuscript he produced, was nothing more, he eventually realized, than a "vulgar" tract, and in mid-May 1938, he destroyed it. With that dark act he might have lapsed into despair—except that it was immediately followed by the mightiest outburst of imaginative energy he would ever experience.

Across a span of no more than ten days, between May 15 and 25, the entire scheme of *The Grapes of Wrath* was envisioned by Steinbeck, beginning with the grand outlines of the Joad family's journey across the country, but also including the symphonic structure of the story, with its alternating modes of exposition and narrative, and the dramatic events of individual scenes, all the way down to Rose of Sharon's gesture at the close of offering her milky breast to a starving man. He also established a writing schedule of 2,000 words a day that would enable him—that did enable him—to complete the novel by the following October. Finally, he decided that he would make a map of his literary progress by keeping a journal. Thanks to Robert DeMott, a professor of English at Ohio University and a recognized authority on Steinbeck, that journal has now been published, with useful notes by Professor DeMott, under the title *Working Days*.

It is a harrowing document. For while *Working Days* testifies to Steinbeck's continuing grasp of his organizational plan for *The Grapes of Wrath*, as well as to his dogged determination to meet his per diem quota of words, it is also a record of doubts of his literary adequacy, of anger at being interrupted by friends and strangers, of disgust with himself about his drinking, cigarette smoking, and general lack of self-discipline, and of fears of nervous collapse and insanity. Here are some representative comments:

"Irritated today. People want to come to see me next Monday. Can't be. Just want to sit. Day not propitious. Have a loose feeling that makes me nervous . . . I get nuts if not protected from all the outside stuff" (June 3). "My whole nervous system is battered. Don't know why. I hope I am not headed for a nervous breakdown" (June 6). "Last night . . . drank a great deal of champagne [and] . . . am not in the dead sober state I could wish . . . I must not be weak. . . . The failure of will even for one day has a devastating effect" (June 13). ". . . once this book is done I won't care how soon I die, because my major work will be over" (July 11). "Drank lots of whiskey . . . and now home with a little stomach ache that doesn't come from the stomach. Terrible feeling of lostness and loneliness" (July

18). "Demoralization complete and seemingly unbeatable" (August 16). "My nerves are going fast. Getting into confusion of many particles—each one beatable, but in company pretty formidable. And I get a little crazy with all of them" (August 24). "This place has become an absolute madhouse . . . I don't know what to do. I wish—Jesus!" (August 26). "Have to cut down smoking or something. I'm afraid this book is going to pieces. If it does, I do too" (September 7). "This book has become a misery to me because of my inadequacy" (September 26). "The disintegration lately has been terrible" (October 4).

Gradually, the struggling novelist became aware that keeping the diary had a therapeutic effect upon him. "Now at last I am getting calm," he wrote on August 2. "This diary is a marvelous method of calming me down every day." And on September 26 he noted that his stomach and nerves were "screaming hell in protest," but that he had written an exceptionally long entry in order "to calm myself." His self-understanding, however, never grew beyond this point. Thus in 1952 he declared that when he wrote *The Grapes of Wrath*, "I was filled . . . with certain angers . . . at people who were doing injustices to other people." No doubt he was—but as the diary demonstrates, he also brought to his writing desk each day a variety of violent emotions that had nothing to do with objective social circumstances and everything to do with the personal life and psychic nature of John Steinbeck. What the diary forces us to reconsider is the relationship of the novelist to his fictive materials.

One of the odd things about the hero of the novel, Tom Joad, is his lack of interest in sex. From the time we meet him in Chapter Two, hitchhiking home to his parents' place after being released from prison in McAlester, Oklahoma, until his disappearance into the darkness of a California night near the end of the story, he is never shown in pursuit of a woman, in contrast to his younger brother, Al, who is constantly scratching a sexual itch. The explanation of Tom's conduct lies not in the novel but in the diary. By 1938, Steinbeck's relations with his wife, Carol, were frequently strained, even hostile, and the tension between them was heightened during the period when he was writing *The Grapes of Wrath* by his abstinence from sexual intercourse with her. Not until October 7, as he was nearing the end of his creative labors, did he feel "a change . . . coming over me—a goatish sexuality. The summer has just been the opposite—very low." So intense was Steinbeck's identification with his fictional hero that, whether consciously or unconsciously, he reduced Tom's sex drive to the same level as his own.

An even greater oddity about the good-guy hero of *The Grapes of Wrath* is defined by his homicidal outbursts. Tom not only has done time at McAlester for killing a man in a social quarrel, but before the novel is over he will kill another in a labor dispute. His sidekick, Jim Casy, the ex-preacher who has the same initials as Christ, is politically radicalized in the course of the novel, and after Casy's symbolic crucifixion Tom consecrates his own life to the cause of social justice. In a secular world, he will be Jim Casy's self-sacrificing disciple. But the question that Steinbeck fails to examine is whether Tom's intentions, as outlined in a farewell speech to his mother, are not an ambiguous mixture of altruism and intoxication with violence for its own sake. "I'll be all aroun' in the dark," he assures Ma Joad. "I'll be ever'where— wherever you look. Wherever they's a fight so hungry people can eat, I'll be

551

there. Wherever they's a cop beatin' up a guy, I'll be there.... I'll be in the way guys yell when they're mad an'—I'll be in the way kids laugh when they're hungry an' they know supper's ready. An' when our folks eat the stuff they raise an' live in the houses they build— why, I'll be there. See?" The diarist who but slenderly understood his own raw emotions ("My whole nervous system is battered. Don't know why.") was correspondingly incapable of plumbing the mysteries of his alter ego's.

The emergence of Ma Joad as a far stronger person than her husband and the other older men in the Joad family is another notable aspect of the novel on which the diary bears. "Carol does so much," Steinbeck said of his wife in the entry of August 2. Indeed she did. Although Carol Henning was a fairly talented poet, prose writer, and painter, as well as being more deeply involved in radical politics than Steinbeck ever was, she gave up her career when she got married. In addition to assuming all the domestic duties of the household, the strong-willed, tough-minded Carol did her best to shield her shy and easily stampeded husband from intrusions on his privacy: oversaw his business relations with his agents; typed and edited his manuscripts; and, in the case of *The Grapes of Wrath*, made critical comments on the manuscript and found the perfect title for it in Julia Ward Howe's "The Battle Hymn of the Republic." On the dedication page of the novel Steinbeck wrote, "To Carol, who willed this book." Just as weakness of the senior male Joads can be linked to Steinbeck's sense of his own weakness and to memories of his weak father, whose mismanagement of a store ended in bankruptcy (the diarist wrote on June 16: "I dreamed a confused mess made up of Dad and his failures and me and my failures"), so Ma Joad's indomitability was a reincarnation of Carol's.

Working Days also contains a section called "Aftermath," which is composed of the diary entries that Steinbeck continued to make in the two years following the publication of *The Grapes of Wrath*. As Professor DeMott aptly observes, the motif of self-doubt is still prominent in these entries, but is compounded by guilt and tempered by foreshadowing, as though Steinbeck felt himself to be hovering on the brink of some enormous catastrophe. If the intimations of dark fatality are not fully articulated, it is because Steinbeck was fearful that the watchful Carol would discover the secret of his love affair with a 20-year-old showgirl named Gwyndolyn Conger, whom he began seeing in the summer of 1939 and whom he would marry in 1943. Was he already dreaming of betraying Carol while he was still writing *The Grapes of Wrath*—and did that dream, too, get into the novel? Quite conceivably. For the weakest link in the Joad family chain is Rose of Sharon's youthful husband, the androgynously named Connie, who, when the Joads finally reach California, deserts his drastically pregnant wife and disappears. An author given to sexual guilt and paranoia might well have created such a character as Connie, out of a terrible premonition of how he intended to reward the woman who had done so much to bring his greatest book into being.

Working Days serves, in sum, to make *The Grapes of Wrath* and its author more complex and more interesting. Studs Terkel's introduction to the fiftieth anniversary edition of the novel accomplishes the reverse. Essentially, it seeks to show that *The Grapes of Wrath* is the fictional equivalent of Terkel's alleged transcripts of the voices of downtrodden little people and that that is a wonderful thing.

Brad Leithauser.
"Books."
New Yorker, 69
(21 August 1989), 90–3.

. . . As is generally the case when diaries or drafts surrounding a famous literary work come to light, *Working Days: The Journals of "The Grapes of Wrath"* provides more confirmation than revelation. Most of what is here could be intuited from the novel itself. That the book was written rapidly, in a fiercely concentrated five-month outpouring, comes as no surprise: the writing feels all of a piece. Nor is one surprised to discover that Steinbeck did little revising. If the achievement of his prose is that he everywhere manages to avoid clutter—no small feat—he pulls off few of those bravura touches that arise when, over time, one stylistic refinement unlocks another. His prose is a bit like a cleared, swept, polished ballroom floor on which nobody dances. What *is* surprising about *Working Days* is just how scanty are its collateral pleasures. Precious few nuggets of humor, intelligence, or curiosity glint within it. What one primarily absorbs is Steinbeck's guilt-inspired drive, and one leaves the book hoping forlornly that he learned to like himself better as the years went by. He criticizes himself on page after page for not working hard or fast enough. He fusses interminably over self-fixed schedules, word counts, and page counts. Rarely have I entered so claustrophobic a journal, and I'm not sure I've ever come across anything so psychologically straitened in connection with an enduring work of art—which, for all its shortcomings, *The Grapes of Wrath* appears to be.

Perhaps the chief wonder of the novel is that it's as good as it is. Steinbeck was a writer of such variable strengths and such uncertain instincts that any attempt at an epic novel would seem destined for failure. What probably saved *The Grapes of Wrath* was his reservoir of rage. He saw his fellow-Californians responding with fear rather than charity to "the flare of want" in the eyes of the newcomers, and this inhumanity liberated him: it justified his characteristic eagerness to lecture his readers, lent a dignity to his indiscriminate savagings of the affluent (into whose ranks the book would irreversibly propel him), and excused his woolly theorizing about the collective "Manself." The book is a call to arms, and it manages, in the enormity of the iniquity it exposes, to render irrelevant many of the aesthetic qualifications it raises along the way. . . .

Checklist of Additional Reviews

Christopher Lehmann-Haupt. "Steinbeck's *Grapes*, with His Diary of Writing It." New York *Times*, 30 March 1989, Section B, p. 2.

William Kennedy. "'My Work Is No Good.'" *New York Times Book Review*, 139 (9 April 1989), 1, 44–5.

Jonathan Yardley. "A New Pressing of *The Grapes of Wrath*." Washington *Post*, 16 April 1989, "Book World" section, p. 2.

Alan Ryan. "50 Years Later, Steinbeck's Works Reflect Agony, Beauty of Writing." Salinas *Californian*, 29 April 1989, p. 2C.

"Brief Mention." *American Literature*, 61 (October 1989), 519.

Index